Management Information Systems in the Digital Era

This book uncovers the latest techniques of information systems analysis, design and development used for managerial decision-making. It cogently deals with a variety of topics such as decision support systems, executive information systems, artificial intelligence (AI) and expert systems, data mining and warehousing.

The book throws light on big data analytics adopting Hadoop and its ecosystems with illustrative practical examples. NoSQL databases have been elaborately described with real-life examples, as well as cloud computing and the internet of things, and generative AI. The illustrative examples and case studies presented in the book will appeal to readers from different backgrounds.

This book would be useful to students, researchers and teachers in the disciplines of Management and Engineering. It would also serve as an invaluable resource for practising business executives to enrich their knowledge and experience with the latest developments in the field of management information system (MIS), particularly in e-Business areas, helping them implement MIS for effective decision-making.

Jaytilak Biswas received his bachelor's and master's degrees in Mechanical Engineering from Jadavpur University, Kolkata, India, and PhD from the Industrial Management Department of the Indian Institute of Science, Bengaluru. He worked for about three-and-a-half decades in senior executive positions of various public sector enterprises and the Government of India. He has published several papers in specialised national and international journals of repute. He is a guest faculty member of many leading management institutions and a member of the Institute of Cost and Management Accountants of India. His areas of academic interest are Management Information Systems, Operations Management, Supply Chain Management and Project Management. He has successfully conducted management development programmes for senior managers of private and public sector enterprises.

Management Information Systems in the Digital Era

Jaytilak Biswas

Routledge
Taylor & Francis Group
LONDON AND NEW YORK

Designed cover image: Getty Images

First published 2026
by Routledge
4 Park Square, Milton Park, Abingdon, Oxon OX14 4RN

and by Routledge
605 Third Avenue, New York, NY 10158

Routledge is an imprint of the Taylor & Francis Group, an informa business

British Library Cataloguing-in-Publication Data
A catalogue record for this book is available from the British Library

ISBN: 978-1-032-83521-1 (hbk)
ISBN: 978-1-032-83522-8 (pbk)
ISBN: 978-1-003-50971-4 (ebk)

DOI: 10.4324/9781003509714

Typeset in Sabon
by Deanta Global Publishing Services, Chennai, India

To my parents, the late Dr Khagendra Nath Biswas and the late Bakul Rani Biswas, with deep regards.

Contents

Figures

Tables

Foreword

Rapid development in information and communications technology has led to significant changes in the use of information systems in managerial decision-making over the years. The first- and second-generation computer systems of the 1960s and 1970s were massive in size and used to occupy big rooms. The computational speed was of the order of milliseconds, and data used to be stored in large magnetic tapes and disks. Today, multiple times faster computers with processing time of the order of nanoseconds and with data storage capacity of gigabytes (10^{12} bytes) or even more are available in laptops, palmtops and even smartphones!

In order to cope with the development in hardware, new software and communication systems have also evolved in the course of time. On the other hand, growing complexities in the business environment have further necessitated the advent of newer types of management information systems (MIS) using the new generation hardware, software and communication technology to facilitate effective and efficient managerial decision-making.

In the above context, this book titled *Management Information Systems in the Digital Era* by Professor Jaytilak Biswas has got a special significance. It traces the evolution and transformation that have taken place over the years in this field of study, and the readers will greatly enhance their knowledge by going through the pages of the book. The coverage in it is wide and very comprehensive across the chronological developments in information systems. It will also help the readers to understand the concepts, organise their thoughts and get a first-hand idea about the phenomenal growth of information and communications technology and their application in business environments.

The language of the book is simple and student-friendly; the concepts have been discussed in a jargon-free manner, to enable students from various backgrounds to have an easy understanding of the basics of the subject. It will serve the purpose of a textbook on MIS well for students pursuing both undergraduate and postgraduate degree courses in various B-schools including the Indian Institutes of Management. The examples cited in the book will be extremely helpful for the students.

The case studies at the end of each chapter will make the readers understand the practical applications of modern developments in the decision-making process such as artificial intelligence, machine learning, artificial neural networks, deep learning, NoSQL databases, big data analytics using Hadoop and its ecosystems.

The material in the book spanning 16 chapters has been organised brilliantly. Chapters contain self-review questions at the end, which will enable the students to test their knowledge gained by reading the corresponding chapters. The chapter-end bibliography will enable the readers to supplement the knowledge on MIS. The computer-based solutions of the problems and examples with screenshots, where relevant, have made the book very informative and engaging for the young readers.

My best wishes for the readers of this book; hope they find the journey into MIS thrilling and inspiring.

J. K. Das
Professor (Statistics), Department of Commerce and Director, Internal Quality Assurance Cell (IQAC) University of Calcutta

Preface

Of late, there has been a spurt in the activities relating to design and development of information systems for managerial decisions. Chief executives of Indian companies, who earlier used to consider their information technology departments as data processing centres generating voluminous clerical reports, have started realising the importance of information systems in achieving organisational success and growth. Information and knowledge management has evolved as a distinct management function. Further, there has been a phenomenal growth in information and communications technology all over the globe during the last two decades. Several institutes of information science and technology have been established in our country, besides separate computer science courses being offered by Indian universities and institutes of higher learning. For more than three decades, I worked with the information technology and management information system (MIS) departments of large engineering industries belonging to public sector enterprises and the government. Later, I have been teaching MIS and allied courses over the past ten years for MBA programmes conducted by the Institute of Business Management of the National Council of Education (NCE), Bengal, affiliated to Jadavpur University, Kolkata, India. Although I have covered the entire syllabus of MIS at the MBA level in the present textbook, it covers the topics included in the syllabus of MIS taught to the students pursuing various other programmes such as BE, BTech, BCA and MCA of Indian universities as well as professional courses run by the Institutes of Chartered/Cost and Management Accountants of India. The present book cogently deals with a variety of topics such as decision support, multi-criteria decision analysis using AHP and TOPSIS, expert systems, database management systems, systems analysis and design, data mining and warehousing, computer-based information systems, big data analytics, cloud computing, internet of things and many allied topics. Latest developments on big data analytics adopting Hadoop, its ecosystems, NoSQL databases and generative AI of various types have been elaborately explained with real-life examples.

Management students, particularly at the MBA level, have different backgrounds: humanities, science, commerce, engineering, management and working executives as well as fresh graduates. The present book has been written comprehensively, considering the diverse groups of management students as mentioned earlier. The illustrative examples and the case studies presented in the book are simple and relevant to Indian organisations. A list of carefully designed self-review questions has been provided at the end of nearly all chapters. This will enable the students to test their level of knowledge after reading the corresponding chapters.

During my long association with Indian industries as a practising manager, I observed a chasm between world-class information technology and the practices prevailing in

Indian industries, particularly in the manufacturing sector. I, therefore, felt the need to bridge this gap. The present book is an attempt in this direction. The book though primarily meant to be a textbook in MIS, nevertheless, targets practising managers also.

The topics covered in this book have been selected based on Indian and foreign books and papers published in various management journals. The book, thus, attempts to present all relevant and current topics in one place.

I am indebted to NCE, Bengal, for the encouragement and support extended to me while writing this book. My thanks are also due to the authorities of the Institute of Business Management of NCE, Bengal, for the facilities provided to me for writing the book.

I would like to thank the authorities of various industrial organisations in India for the necessary permission granted to me for the collection and use of their organisational data.

I would also like to acknowledge the cooperation I received from my colleague faculty members and staff members of the Institute of Business Management of NCE, Bengal.

Credit also goes to my wife Rita, son Tamal and daughter Smita, for their continued patience, support and interest in the progress of my work. I would like to thank Shri Maloy Das and Shri Raja Debnath for typesetting and proofreading the entire book.

Finally, I would also like to thank my publisher for the publishing effort extended to me.

1 Concept and Role of Management Information System

1.1 Introduction

Growing complexities of modern organisations demand fast and complex managerial decision-making. Managers need appropriate information for effective and efficient decision-making. Development of an effective management information system (MIS) is thus one of the primary tasks for efficient management today. Researchers and designers of MIS have put forth many definitions of MIS. To mention a few, the following statements have been quoted:

> A communication process in which information [input] is recorded, stored and retrieved [processed] for decisions [output] on planning, operating and controlling.
>
> Murdick and Ross (1977)

> An organized method of providing past, present and projection information related to internal operations and external intelligence.
>
> Kennevan (1974)

> Produced for all levels of management, the information required to make decisions in two areas:
>
> (i) predicting what will happen by using historical data and simulation to give alternatives and
> (ii) outlining or making change to a present procedure or decision to make predictions.
>
> Martino (1970)

> Facilitates the management functions of planning, organizing, integrating, measuring and controlling.
>
> Breen et al. (1969)

> An operational function whose parts corresponding to functional units are information subsystems of other operational functions.
>
> Blumenthal (1969)

The definition of MIS put forth by the MIS committee of the Financial Executives Institutes, UK, makes clear the relationship between management and information

DOI: 10.4324/9781003509714-1

system (IS): 'MIS is a system designed to provide selected decision-oriented information needed by management to plan, control and evaluate the activities of the corporation'.

In spite of certain variability in the above statements, there is a common and core component of MIS that an appropriate quantum of information be readily available to the management for taking effective and appropriate decisions towards the best interest of the organisations. The definitions also highlight certain essential features of MIS, such as its linkage to an organisational subsystem and its flexible and futuristic nature.

1.2 Schools of Management Analysis

Urwick has defined management as the responsibility for others' work. Bocchino has given a more appropriate explanation of the term management as the responsibility of optimum utilisation of resources to attain the objectives of the organisation. There is no doubt that the ultimate objective of management is to attain the organisational goals through effective and efficient utilisation of available resources, such as men, materials and machines, but the question arises: How do they achieve it? In other words, what are the management processes? Management processes are broad in scope and dimension. Hence, it is difficult to arrive at an all-comprehensive definition of management processes.

However, for the sake of convenience, the different management schools of thought may be organised as follows: behavioural, empirical, decision theory, quantitative and management process.

The behavioural school of management is one of the earliest theories of management. The proponents of this school can be divided between the human behaviour groups, such as Elton Mayo, Roethlisberger and Dickson and the social science groups, such as Maslow, Herzberg and Likert. The proponents of the first group believed that since management is a responsibility of getting work done through others, a manager must have knowledge of human relations and behavioural sciences.

The social science group went a step further and pointed out that an organisation is a social system group where individuals with different ideas, attitudes and aspirations get together for a common purpose. Hence, the manager should study the group as a whole and not just individual behaviour.

The empirical school of management analysis belongs to many practising managers who believe that experience is the single factor that determines managerial success. They attempt to analyse management through practical case studies.

The next school of management analysis is the decision theory school proposed by Simon and others. According to this school, management is mainly decision-making processes. A manager at any level of the organisation has to take fast and complex decisions. The more correct the decisions are, the more successful he/she is as a manager.

The quantitative school of management, also known as the mathematical school, describes management in terms of mathematical symbols, equations and models. Techniques such as operations research, linear programming and simulation were developed by this school for the solution of the mathematical models. Development of high-speed computers facilitated the solution of the problems because of their capability of handling mathematical equations at a very high speed.

The last but most popular analysis of management is the so-called management process school propounded by Henri Fayol, Koontz, O'Donnell and others. The basic and universal functions of management as defined by the management process school are planning, organising, staffing, directing and controlling.

The various schools of management analysis enumerated above are not mutually exclusive, but they form parts of the total management system.

1.3 Management Process as Viewed for MIS

Management, for the purpose of MIS, consists of the activities carried out by managers. Planning, organising, staffing, directing and controlling are five executive functions of management.

While each of the above functions needs relevant information, three particular areas, namely planning, organising and control, need decision-making. MIS becomes a facilitating system for making decisions in planning, organising and controlling in the best interest of the organisations.

According to Burch and Strater, planning, decision-making and controlling are the functions of management for the MIS design purpose. Bocchino has considered planning, analysing and controlling as the basic functions of management for the MIS design purpose.

1.4 Data and Information

Data and information are two separate entities. Data are nothing but isolated events or facts. Data, when processed and presented in a systematic mode to a manager for making specific decisions, become information. The process that converts data into information is known as data processing.

It should be noted that the difference between data and information lies in the mode of presentation, and that information must facilitate decision-making. Information which does not help a manager in his/her role of decision-making is not considered as information in MIS. For example, annual sales figures (salesman-wise) when presented to the sales manager for deciding on a reward scheme, the same figures become information, whereas if the same figures are presented to a production manager, they are of no use and hence not considered as information in MIS.

1.5 Information and Decision-Making

Information is vital for decision-making. It helps a manager in decision-making in two ways.

First, it reduces uncertainty in the decision-making process to a great extent, if not eliminated totally. Most of the managers' decisions, particularly at the top level, are future oriented. He/she is often ignorant of future contingencies and takes decisions under uncertainty. The greater the uncertainty, the greater the difficulty. Information helps a manager under such uncertain situations. For example, a sales manager, while forecasting future sales, looks back to past sales figures to arrive at a reasonably accurate forecast.

Second, information provides feedback to a manager to ensure that his/her decisions are in the right direction, and if not, he/she can amend the decisions at any time for corrective action without any adverse implications. Feedback is also vital for the operational control level of the management where the decisions are very clear and decision rules can be automated or programmed.

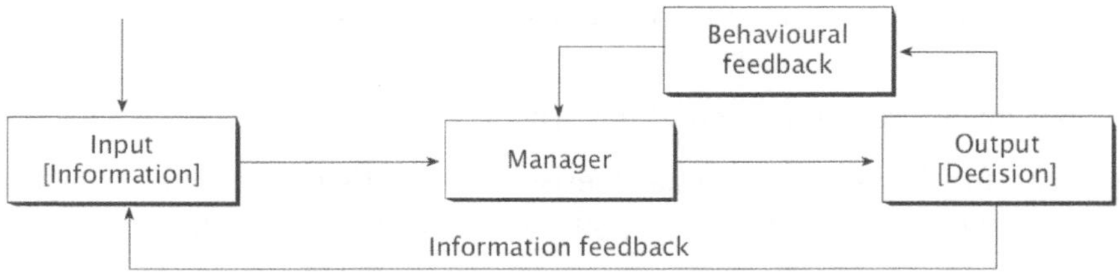

Figure 1.1 Miller-Starr Model of Information-Decision

Feedback information may be formal information such as periodic reports on actual production, sales and profit against targets or informal like behavioural feedback.

Every manager in an organisation can be viewed as a point to which information flows and gives rise to decisions, which in turn produces further information in a closed loop. Miller and Starr developed this concept of information-decision into a model as shown in Figure 1.1.

1.6 The System Approach

The term system has been extensively used in literature on business management, for example, business system, organisation system and human system.

What is a system? More specifically, what makes a system?

Hopkins (1961) defined a system as a set of elements forming an activity or a processing procedure/scheme seeking a common goal or goals by operating on data and/or energy and/or matter in a time reference to yield information and/or energy and/or matter.

The following features characterise a system: (1) plurality of the parts (elements), (2) interdependency of the parts, (3) interaction of the parts with each other and with the environment, (4) common goal(s) and (5) synergy.

A business organisation, for example, consists of a group of people, capital and machines as its elements which interact with each other for seeking a common goal, say, profit. The human body is another example of a system, consisting of many complex organs, which interact simultaneously to maintain homoeostasis.

The synergistic effect of a system is that which enables the parts or elements acting together simultaneously to achieve a combined effect which is greater than the sum of the individual effects of the parts if allowed to function in isolation. For example, sales, production and finance are three departments in a business organisation, but they function in close liaison with each other for optimum profit. If, however, sales, production and finance try to optimise their activities in isolation, it may so happen that more than what can be sold might be produced and finance might face a shortage of cash. The ultimate result is sub-optimised profit.

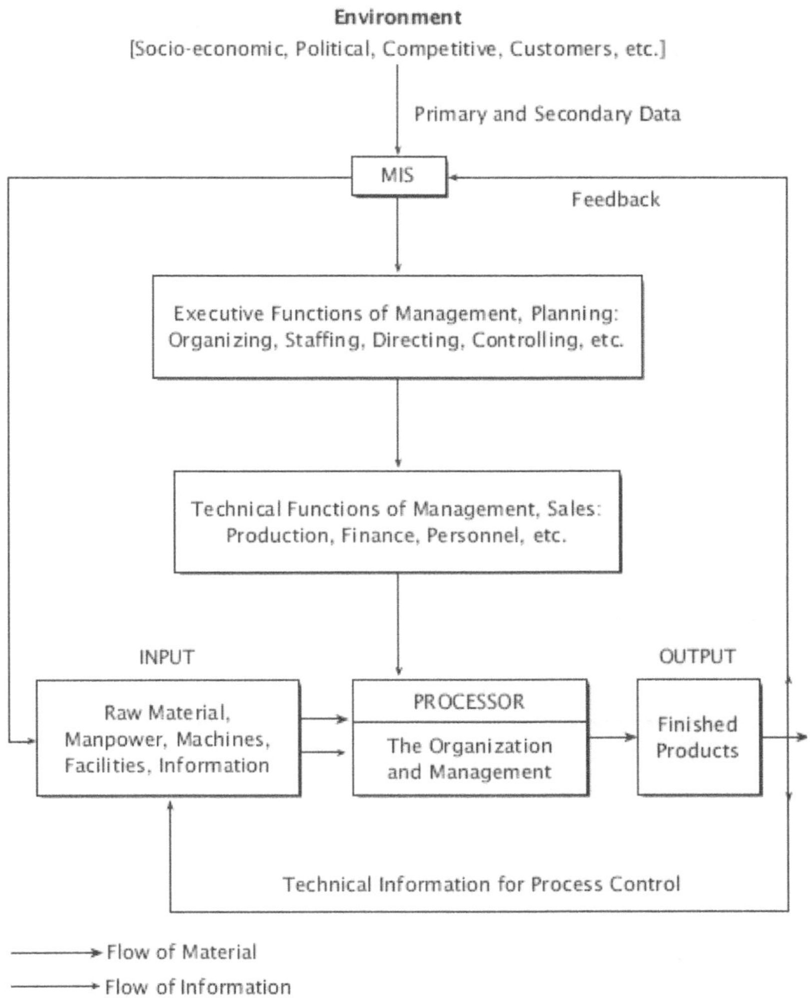

Figure 1.2 MIS in a Manufacturing Organisation

1.7 System Approach to MIS Design

MIS has got as its elements a group of people comprising functional managers, information technologists and programmers, a set of manuals and data-processing equipment, computers, communication networks, files and databases, which select, store, process and retrieve data and yield relevant information to managers at various levels in an organisation when needed to facilitate management functions of planning, decision-making and controlling by reducing uncertainty in decision-making and providing feedback (common goal) to optimise the overall performance of the organisation (synergy).

The position of MIS within an organisation and its environment for three different types of organisations, namely a manufacturing unit, a service organisation such as an institution of higher learning and a public-utility organisation such as an electricity supply corporation, are shown in Figures 1.2–1.4 respectively.

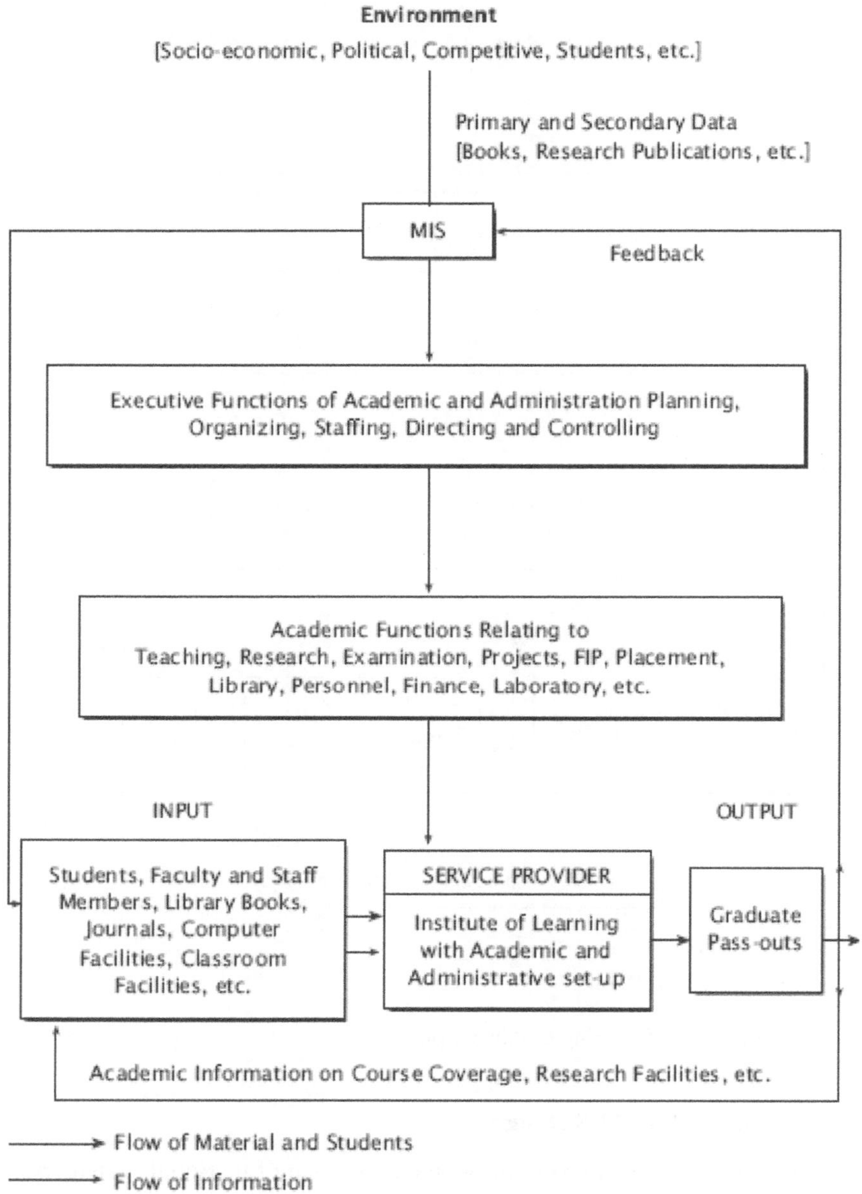

Figure 1.3 MIS in an Institution of Higher Learning

1.8 Organisation and Management Control Systems

Anthony (1965) mentioned about three levels of management in an organisation. These are the strategic planning level comprising the top management, the management control or the middle one and the operational control levels. Anthony's viewpoint was supported by Burch and Strater (1973) who named the three levels of management as the strategic,

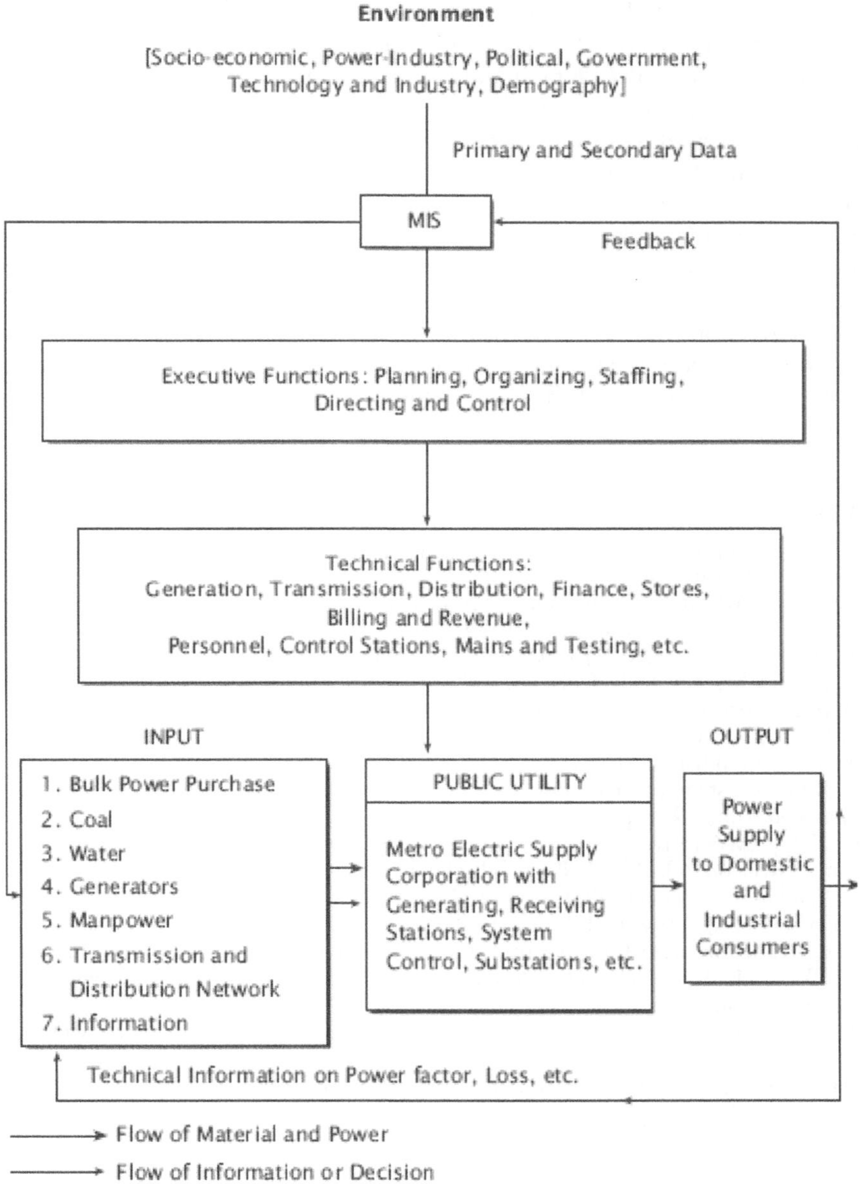

Figure 1.4 MIS in a Public-Utility Organisation (Metro Electric Supply Corporation)

tactical and technical levels. Strategic planning is the management process of deciding on the long-term configuration that the organisation will take in future in terms of inputs and outputs for survival and growth. For example, a strategic plan for a manufacturing industrial organisation may include the volume of production and sales to be achieved after ten years, customer profile, manpower inputs, financing pattern and so on; the management control level receives the strategic plan as an input from the top level and decides the tactical plan to achieve the strategy.

The tactical plans usually are the annual operating plans relating to the technical functional areas of sales, production, personnel, finance, R&D and so on and deployment of organisational resources effectively and efficiently to meet the operating plans. For example, an annual production plan and budget are tactical plans.

The operational control level is the bottom level in the management hierarchy and is concerned with the day-to-day operations to ensure that specific tasks are completed as per programme. Daily job shop scheduling, inventory ordering and purchase are all operational control activities. Although the executive functions of management, mainly planning and control, are being exercised in varying degrees by the three levels of management, planning is the essence of the strategic planning level and control is less as compared with the operational control level, which is heavily dependent on frequent feedback control, both formal and informal. Management control involves both planning and control. Operational control includes both technical control and administrative control. It may be emphasised that the various levels of management are not mutually exclusive.

Bibliography

Anthony, R. N. *Planning and Control Systems: A Framework for Analysis*. Boston, MA: Division of Research, Harvard Business School, 1965.

Blumenthal, S. C. *Management Information Systems: A Framework for Planning and Development* Englewood Cliffs, NJ: Prentice Hall, 1969.

Bocchino, W. A. *Management Information Systems: Tools and Techniques*. Englewood Cliffs,

Breen, R. E., H. Chestnut, R. R. Duersch, and R. S. Jones. *Management Information Systems*, Subcommittee report on definitions, New York, NY: General Electric Co. 1969.

Burch, J. G., Jr., and F. R. Strater Jr. *Information Systems: Theory and Practice*. Santa Barbara, CL: Hamilton Publishing, 1973.

Hopkins, R.C. 'A systematic procedure for system development'. *IRE Transactions on Engineering Management*, June 1961, p85.

Kennevan, W. J. 'MIS Universe'. In *Management of Information Handling Systems*, edited by Paul William Howerton, 63. Roselle Park, NJ: Hayden Book Company, 1974.

Koontz, H., and C. O'Donnell. *Principles of Management: An Analysis of Management Functions*. New York, NY: McGraw-Hill Book, 1972.

Martino, R. L. *Management Information Systems*. New York, NY: McGraw-Hill, 1970.

Miller, D. W., and M. K. Starr. *The Structure of Human Decisions*, 179. Englewood Cliffs, NJ: Prentice Hall, 1968.

Murdick, R. G., and J. E. Ross. *Information Systems for Modern Management*. New Delhi: Prentice Hall, 1977.

Simon, H. A. *The New Science of Management Decisions*. New York, NY: Harper and Row Publishers, 1960.

2 Information Needs and Structure of MIS

2.1 The Information Needs

The information needs of a manager depend on his/her level in the organisation. The type of information needed by a manager at the strategic planning level is different from the same required by managers at the tactical or operational control level of management in terms of important characteristics of the information. The characteristics of information needs are also known as the dimensions of information needs. The important dimensions are source, data volume, consolidation, frequency, accuracy, currency, scope, predictability, user dependence, and real time or delayed. These dimensions of information needs for the decisions taken by various management levels are shown in Table 2.1. A few examples of information needs in terms of the dimensions for typical organisational decisions are shown in Table 2.2.

2.2 Structure of MIS

Since any MIS is mainly to facilitate effective and efficient managerial decision-making related to the executive functions of management at various levels, the structure of MIS in any organisation should be consistent with such decision-making as also with the various levels of management. The basic functions of management, namely planning, organising, staffing, directing and controlling, require appropriate decisions and information. Since the proportion of these functions varies from level to level, the information needs and hence the MIS designs have to be necessarily different for those levels.

The IS for strategic planning needs to be designed mainly for supporting planning activities and hence has to cater to future-oriented decisions. The MIS for this level of management has to provide for exception reports and simulated or 'what-if' type of information apart from future projections. Such an MIS is also called an executive information system (EIS), which also provides intelligent information—market intelligence, capital market intelligence and technology intelligence.

The MIS design for management control has to cater to the tactical needs and mainly includes prediction and optimisation information. The management control level also needs information on actual performance as against the standards with variance analysis. The decision support system (DSS) for this level of management is semi-structured in nature and essentially comprises a database, model base and a processor of the problems. DSSs have been elaborated in the subsequent chapters of this book.

The decisions at the operational control level are structured and programmable decisions. The IS pertaining to this level of management is mainly an automated

DOI: 10.4324/9781003509714-2

Table 2.1 Dimensions of Information Needs

Dimensions of Information Needs	*Strategic Planning*	*Management Control*	*Operational Control*
Source	Mostly external	Mostly internal	Mostly internal
Scope	Wide (organisational)	Wide (functional)	Narrow (departmental)
Volume of data	High	High	Low
Consolidation	More	Less	Less
Frequency	Less	More	More
Accuracy	Low	High	High
Currency	Low	High	High
Predictability	Low	High	High
User dependence	Heavy	Low	Low
Real time/delayed	Delayed	Delayed	Real time

decision-maker in nature as the decision rules are well defined. The management is so confident in the assumptions incorporated in this system that the optimum decisions are left to the IS itself. For example, the IS can monitor the stock level and initiate purchase order printing when the level reaches the reorder point. Similarly, the work order for preventive maintenance due for a particular plant or machinery, when the same becomes due, can be initiated by the maintenance IS. Office automation systems such as payroll, issue of meeting notices and also automatic process control systems belong to the operational control level of management.

The structure of MIS as explained above is shown in Figure 2.1.

2.3 MIS for Functional Management Areas

The structure of MIS as described in the previous paragraphs is applicable for the various functional areas of management which vary from organisation to organisation. For example, the typical management functions in organisations are operations including logistics, marketing, finance, personnel and support services. The MIS to cater to the information support for the various levels of management within the same structure will vary in terms of the actual types of information. The specific applications within these functional areas are broadly listed as follows:

2.3.1 Operations, Production and Logistics

In general, the operations/production functions consist of the following:

- Operations/production planning and control
- Product/service design
- Delivery/facilities planning
- Quality management of goods/services
- Logistics both inbound and outbound.

Table 2.2 Dimensions of Information Needs for Various Organisational Decisions

Decisions	*Source*	*Scope*	*Volume of Data*	*Consolidation*	*Frequency*	*Accuracy*	*Currency*	*Predictability*	*User Dependence*	*Real Time /Delayed*
Manufacturing										
1. Decision: Product diversification in next ten years	Mostly external	Wide	High	Modrate	Less	Low	Moderate	Moderate	Heavy	Delayed
2. Decision : Working Capital Requirement for a year	Mostely Internal	Wide	High	Less	Moderate	High	High	High	Less	Delayed
3. Decision: Daily scheduling of machines for various jobs	Internal	Narrow	Low	Less	More	High	High	High	Less	Real-time
Public Utility (State Road Transport Corporation)										
1. Decision: New routes for passengers in next five years	External	Wide	High	High	Less	Low	Moderate	Moderate	High	Delayed
2. Decision: Public buses requirement for a particular year	Mostly Internal	Wide	High	Less	Moderate	Moderate	High	Moderate	Less	Delayed
3. Decision: Bus and crew scheduling for a particular day	Mostly Internal	Narrow	Moderate	Less	More	High	High	High	Less	Real-time

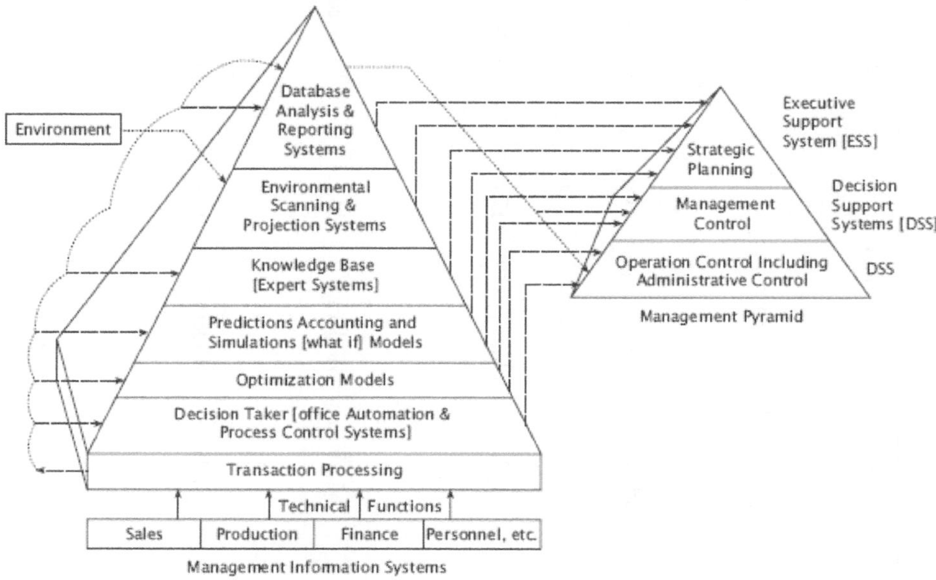

Figure 2.1 Structure of MIS

2.3.2 *Sales/Marketing/Revenue*

In general, sales and marketing functions include the following:

- Sales
- Marketing
- Distribution
- Revenue collection for services
- Customers/consumers' feedback and after-sales services.

2.3.3 *Finance*

In general, the finance function consists of the following:

- General ledger
- Final accounts
- Accounts payable and receivable
- Cash book
- Reconciliation
- Working capital
- Budgetary control
- Taxation
- Annual report
- Employee payroll

- Employee statutory benefits such as provident fund, bonus, gratuity, pension and group insurance
- Leave record
- Cost accounting and control.

2.3.4 *Personnel*

In general, the personnel function consists of the following modules:

- Induction
- Training/skill development
- Placement/posting
- Career progression/promotion
- Wage/salary administration
- Transfers
- Attendance recording, leave sanction, leave rules
- Employee counselling, grievance handling
- Competency mapping
- Incentive scheme
- Performance appraisal
- Disciplinary proceedings
- Personnel data bank
- Administration of terminal benefits
- Safety and security aspects
- Negotiations with trade unions and so on.

2.3.5 *Support Services*

The support services may include the following:

- Welfare activities—school, housing, recreation, healthcare and so on
- Utilities—electricity, petrol, diesel, fuel, water, steam and air conditioning/refrigeration
- Environmental management plan including pollution control, afforestation
- Material handling and transportation
- Telecommunication—including telephone, fax and email.

2.4 Important Factors for MIS Design

2.4.1 *Nature of the Organisation*

The nature of the organisation and its business activities play an important role in the design and complexity of its ISs. A non-profit social organisation will need many ISs to cater for diverse socio-economic applications rather than a very formal and precise IS suitable for a profit-making manufacturing unit producing consumer goods.

2.4.2 *Critical Success Factors*

The critical success factors (CSFs) for the industry type to which an organisation belongs are also crucial in IS design. In most industries, there are usually three to six factors that determine success. These key factor jobs must be done exceedingly well for a company to be successful. As a result, CSFs are areas of activities that receive constant and careful attention from management, and the MIS must cater for information on these factors. The CSFs are mainly as follows:

1. Structure of the particular industry—the nature, competitive strategy, industry position, geographical location, size of the organisation and its dispersion, forward, backward and vertical integration and so on.
2. Environmental factors—such as government rules and control over industries.
3. Political factors.
4. Temporal factors such as local inflation and the effect of the economic cycle.

2.4.3 *Scale of Operation*

The scale of operation and the volume of customers are important considerations for IS design. An Internet broadband service provider company, for example, has a massive customer base compared to its employee strength, and hence the IS design has to be necessarily different from that for a city club having a limited number of members only.

2.4.4 *Level of Information and Communications Technology*

Another important factor that determines the nature of an information system is the level of information and communications technology in the organisation. For example, the IS for fully computerised and networked branches of any bank will be different from the banks that are not fully computerised. The other examples are supermarkets providing barcodes on the items, smart cards to customers for electronic purchase and payment, and smart cards provided by a health insurance company to the insured for admission and treatment at hospitals and nursing homes without cash payment.

2.4.5 *Organisational Culture and Leadership Styles*

The behavioural aspects of an organisation also have a significant role in MIS design. The styles of management, including the individual characteristics of the managers, are also important in this regard. The important variables of organisational behaviour for the sake of IS design may be formal versus informal, rigid versus flexible, participative versus dictatorial and centralised versus decentralised. The number and nature of the legacy systems also affect the design of an integrated MIS. Another important behavioural aspect which the IS designer has to face is people's resistance to change, which is a basic and universal human attribute.

2.4.6 *Number and Nature of User Interaction*

The size of users and their nature of interaction with the IS also determine the nature of the same. For example, an airline seat reservation system has to be accessed by a large number of passengers all over the globe through the internet and hence needs to be designed web-enabled, online and real time. On the other hand, a typical back-office automation system like payroll processing, having an entirely different number and nature of user interaction, can be designed as a batch-processing system, since the idea is to improve processing efficiency and not customer service in terms of response time.

2.5 Some Guidelines for Successful Design of MIS

2.5.1 Business Process Re-engineering

The most important prerequisite to a successful design of MIS is business process re-engineering (BPR). The analysis and design of workflows and processes within an organisation need to be carried out systematically, analysed and redesigned before the MIS is designed and implemented to have maximum benefit. A business process is a set of logically related tasks performed to achieve a defined business outcome. MIS development aims to integrate a large number of business functions. Enterprise resource planning (ERP), supply chain management (SCM), knowledge management system, groupware and collaborative system, human resource management system, customer relationship management (CRM) system and many such systems require a prior re-engineering of the business processes.

2.5.2 Top-Down Approach Rather Than Bottom-Up Approach

In the bottom-up approach, the subsystems are designed and developed in piecemeal or as and when required without any overall initial planning. This approach is also known as the inductive approach, where the focus is on the parts rather than the whole. The subsystems are synthesised at a later stage to have an integrated system. In the process, incompatibility often arises and if the subsystems are not properly redesigned, the integrated system may run sub-optimally. The top-down approach first decides on the total MIS and the overall objectives, and then requirements for the subsystems are framed before the design and implementation of the subsystems. The bottom-up approach is the approach frequently adopted by many organisations particularly in the Indian context, where the design and development of the initial systems, such as payroll, personnel information and stock ledger, are completed in an unplanned way. Later on, at the time of development of an integrated system, the organisations face enormous difficulties.

2.5.3 Top Management Support and Involvement

In many cases, the failures of the MIS have been found to be due to lack of support from the top management. Apart from the financial sanctions, top management awareness and active support at every stage of MIS design and implementation are essentially needed for the success of the MIS designed and developed. The top management should hold periodic progress review meetings with the MIS team consisting of the users, the information technology (IT) specialists and the designers.

2.5.4 Users' Training

Users' training on the new MIS after implementation is vital for the success of the MIS. The users must be aware of the various aspects such as the capabilities of the ISs, various reports, source data preparation, data feeding and benefits of the new MIS.

2.5.5 *Employee Involvement*

The active involvement of the employees is another key factor leading to the success of the MIS. Employees, particularly the managers of the organisation, must realise that the ISs are for promoting productivity, efficiency, welfare and overall organisational development. On the contrary, if they treat the MIS as a threat to their authority, power and career prospects, the proposed information system is bound to be a failure. It is through employee training and awareness programmes that this type of misapprehension can be eliminated.

2.5.6 *Phased Implementation*

A successful MIS developer would undertake implementation in phases. Usually, a careful MIS developer would select the systems which are likely to yield significant benefits in a short time to the organisation for the first phase of implementation. Often, the cost or investment consideration determines the systems to be implemented in the first phase. The above phased implementation strategy gives rise to adequate support within the organisation for the integrated MIS.

2.6 Stages of Growth of MIS

Nolan (1979) mentioned about six stages of growth of electronic data processing and computerised applications. These stages are also applicable to the growth of MIS in organisations.

The first stage *initiation* starts with cost reduction applications in individual functional departments such as accounts, stores and purchasing. The second stage of *contagion* begins with the proliferation of applications in all functional areas such as production, sales, finance and personnel. The third stage *control* shifts emphasis from application proliferation to management control like budgetary control. In order to facilitate the same, the upgrading of documentation and restructuring of existing applications often becomes a necessity. In this stage, there is a transition from the management of the computer to the management of data resources in an organisation. The fourth stage *integration* involves the use of database technology and increased user involvement in the control of data and information processing activities. The fifth stage *data administration* features organisational integration of information subsystems. A formal MIS department becomes functional at this stage. The sixth and final stage of *maturity* is the ideal stage but never really attainable in the dynamic environment in which organisations have to survive. However, at this stage, the emphasis shifts from the computer as a resource to information as a resource.

In the Indian context, the initiation stage in general is identified with the computerisation of financial accounting and other clerical labour-saving applications like payroll. The contagion stage has witnessed the development of ISs in other functional areas such as stores accounting and personnel IS, all in an unplanned way, and many a time, the growth is marked with IS relating to operational control.

In the control stage, the emphasis shifts towards the management control role of MIS such as variance analysis and reporting systems for the middle and top levels of management.

The integration phase is marked by considerable investment in hardware and software and includes database creation in diverse functional areas. The use of communication technology in networking of remote locations through client-server technology is facilitated in this stage. The trading of the National Stock Exchange and network banking operations are typical examples of integration.

Date administration envisaged corporate database creation, and the Indian business organisations recognised information as a valuable organisational resource. The elaborate MIS planning and control for the passengers and goods traffic management by Indian Railways is a typical illustration of data administration. ERP implementation in various organisations is another example of data administration.

In the maturity stage, the ISs facilitated organisational growth and many Indian companies started forming subsidiary companies for information services such as Reliance, Siemens and Canara Bank. At this stage, the top management, along with the MIS team, also determines MIS strategy and implementation priorities.

2.7 Case Study: A System Approach

2.7.1 Background

M/s ABC Company Limited (actual name is suppressed due to obvious reasons) manufactures electric motors, generators and heavy transformers for supply to various state electricity boards, metro-city electricity supply corporations and various manufacturing industries. The company also sells electric motors of lesser horsepower (HP) ratings to domestic users through its distribution channels.

The organisation chart of the company is shown in Figure 2.2.

2.7.2 Planning and Reporting System of ABC Company Limited

The GM (Planning and Material Management), in consultation with the other GMs, prepares five-yearly perspective roll-on plans which are then approved by the CEO following the company's policy, vision and mission. Besides, annual operating plans for all functions such as sales, production and finance are formulated in January each year, for the next financial year in the annual target fixation meeting chaired by the CEO, where all the GMs, along with their supporting managers, remain present. In the same meeting, the GM (Finance) furnishes the previous financial year's figures of actual total sales

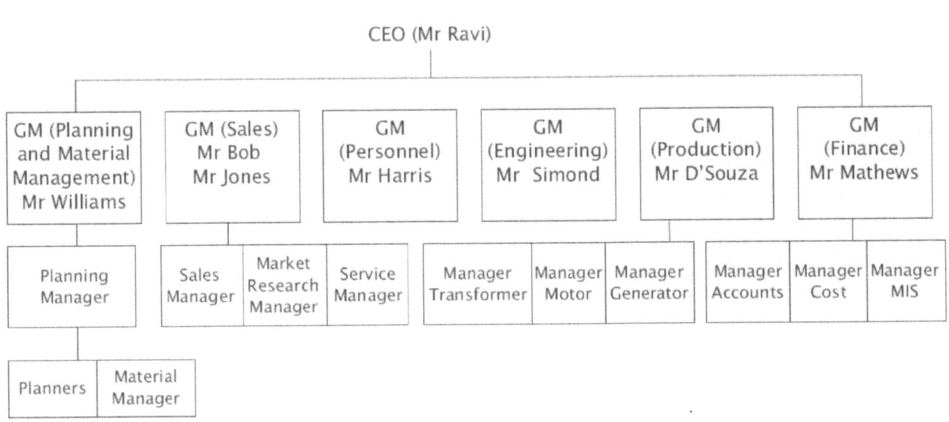

Figure 2.2 The Organisation Chart of the Company

revenue, production in quantity and cost item-wise, profit before and after taxes and cost of capital. He also provides his estimation of anticipated price escalation for the various finished products of the company.

Thereafter, the CEO sets the sales (revenue) target product-wise, considering the likely inflation of price of raw materials and bought-out components, an increase in wages and salaries, support services such as electricity, other miscellaneous overhead costs and a growth rate in real terms consistent with the perspective plan.

The CEO also seeks the opinion of Mr Bob, GM (Sales), who used to invariably accept the sales target set by the CEO, without bothering about the sales forecast report forwarded to him by his managers. Mr Bob used to believe in achieving the sales target set by the CEO with an aggressive push strategy for sales promotion.

Mr D'Souza, GM (Production), used to come prepared with his capacity plan for catering to the sales target. He used to overcome bottlenecks through outsourcing.

The GM (Planning and Material Management), GM (Engineering) and GM (Personnel) had only advisory roles in the annual target fixation meeting.

In the target fixation meeting for the financial years 2008–2009 and 2009–2010, Mr Bob, the then GM (Sales), and Mr D'Souza, GM (Production), received high appreciation from the CEO for meeting the sales and production targets for the years 2007–2008 and 2008–2009. ABC Company Limited made profits for both the above years.

Mr Bob retired from service on attaining the retirement age on 31 May 2009. Thereafter, Mr Jones was directly recruited as the GM (Sales). The year 2009–2010 was, however, dismal for ABC company as the company, for the first time, incurred a loss of ₹100 million in the same year.

Actual sales in crores of rupees for the above three years were 10, 12 and 8 as against the targets of 10, 11 and 12, respectively. Some figures from the balance sheet of the above-mentioned three years for ABC Company Limited are reproduced and shown in Table 2.3.

Mr Ravi was highly dissatisfied with the performance of Mr Jones, the new GM (Sales), for not achieving the sales target for the year 2009–2010. Mr Jones, however, pointed out that he could not achieve the target of ₹120 million as Mr D'Souza could not produce and supply the required number of transformers (a high-value and high-demand product of the company) in time, which led to lost sales. Mr D'Souza, however, put the blame on Mr Williams for not arranging the silicon sheets from M/s Rourkela Steel Plant and M/s GKW in the time needed for the manufacture of transformers. Mr Williams, on the other hand, told Mr Ravi that the purchase requisition for silicon sheets was placed quite late by the production department in the month of June 2009. As a result, the purchase order for silicon sheets was placed on the above-named two established sources in July 2009.

Mr Ravi, however, independently contacted the CEOs of M/s Rourkela Steel Plant and M/s GKW, but both of them told him that there had been no delay on their part in supplying the silicon sheets to M/s ABC Company Limited. However, they told Mr Ravi that some of their old bills were pending with the accounts department of M/s ABC Company Limited and requested Mr Ravi to look into the matter.

Mr Ravi was at a loss to understand why M/s ABC Company Limited, which had been making profits all along up to 2008–2009, suddenly ran into a loss in the year 2009–2010. He was thinking of engaging a consultant to find out where the system failed.

Note: The above case study is an exercise for the students to go through and find out what was lacking in the system, which led to its failure. The students should also suggest remedial measures for ABC Company Limited.

Table 2.3 Figures Extracted from the Balance Sheets of ABC Co. Ltd (Figures: ₹ in Crores)

As on March 2008				*As on March 2009*				*As on March 2010*			
Liability		*Asset*		*Liability*		*Asset*		*Liability*		*Asset*	
Capital	21	Land and building	5	Capital	22	Land and building	5	Capital	24	Land and building	5
Unpaid wages	40	P & M depreciation net	10 −1 9	Unpaid wages	25	P & M depreciation net	9 −0.9 8.1	Unpaid wages	30	P & M depreciation net	8.1 −0.81 7.29
Sundry creditors	2	WIP	1.5	Sundry creditors	2	WIP	1.5	Sundry creditors	2.5	WIP	0.50
Profit (+) loss (−)	3.15	Finished goods	0	Profit (+) Loss (−)	4.09	Finished goods	0	Profit (+) loss (−)	−0.10	Finished goods	0
		Sundry debtors	2.5			Sundry debtors	4			Sundry debtors	3
		Cash at bank	1.5			Cash at bank	0.05			Cash at bank	0.05

Review Questions

1. Give three examples of MIS that you may like to install for a state bus transport corporation.
2. The information needs for a vice-president of the marketing department of a mobile telecom company are different from those for the after-sales service manager of the same company in terms of important dimensions. Illustrate with three examples.
3. Classify the following as office automation, executive support, decision support and transaction processing systems:
   (i) Word processing
   (ii) Airline reservation system
   (iii) Traffic simulation package
   (iv) Mathematical programming software
   (v) Reporting system models
   (vi) Remote sensing and control
   (vii) Environmental scanning and projection
4. Trace the evolution of three well-known MIS applications and identify the stages outlined by Richard Nolan with them in the Indian context.
5. A courier company has got branches all over India. The top management of the company decided to monitor the various functions of the company on a monthly basis. What will be the source data, and in what format and frequency the same should be collected by the branches and forwarded to the head office? How will the data be processed by the head office and furnished to the top management?
6. What are formal and informal sources of information?
7. How areis data converted into relevant information?
8. What is BPR? How is it important in developing MIS?
9. What are the sources of information for environmental data for an organisation?
10. Can the same data generate a variety of information? Explain.

Bibliography

Anthony, R. N., J. Dearden, and F. W. Vancil. *Management Control Systems: Text Cases and Readings*. Homewood, IL: Richard D. Irwin, 1965.

Drucker, Peter. 'The Effective Decisions'. *Harvard Business Review* 45, no. 1 (1965): 92–98.

McFarlan, W. F. 'Problems in Planning the Information System'. *Harvard Business Review* 49, no. 2 (1971): 75–89.

Nolan, R. L. 'Managing the Crisis in Data Processing'. *Harvard Business Review* 57, no. 2 (1979): 115–126.

O'Brien, J. J. *Management Information Systems, Concepts, Techniques, and Applications*. New York, NY: Van Nostrand Reinhold Co., 1970.

Patel, N. R. 'Locating Rural Social Service Centres in India'. *Management Science* 25, no. 1 (1979): 22–30.

Prince, T. R. *Information Systems for Management, Planning and Control*. Homewood, IL: Richard D. Irwin, 1966.

Rockart, J. F. 'Chief Executives Define Their Own Data Needs'. *Harvard Business Review* 57, no. 2 (1979): 81–93.

Zani, W. M. 'Blueprint for MIS'. *Harvard Business Review* 48, no. 6 (1970): 95–100.

3 Decision-Making

3.1 Decision-Making Process

All of us have to make decisions every day. It is an integral part of the management process involving all levels and functions of management. Some decisions are relatively simple, such as whether to place a purchase order for a particular inventory item at a particular time, depending upon the stock and the reorder level of the same. However, some decisions that managers have to take are quite complex in nature, such as which employee should be selected for a particular job and how much quantity of consumer goods is to be produced in the next year for sale. Simple decisions need a simple decision-making process, which can be programmed by a suitable algorithm. However, difficult decisions arise due to the decision-making process involving complexity (in terms of many interrelated factors and multiple decision criteria), uncertainty, high risk, many options or choices available, and unpredictable behavioural issues such as how other employees or groups will react to the decisions.

With the above difficulties, the best way to make a complex organisational decision is to design an effective decision-making process and decision rules. Such clear decision-making processes result in effective and efficient decisions in the best interest of the organisations.

3.2 Programmed and Non-programmed Decisions

Herbert A. Simon classified decisions into two categories, namely programmed and non-programmed decisions.

Programmed decisions are repetitive and routine in nature, and set procedures or decision rules can be defined for such decisions. These can be automated through algorithms describing the decision rule. These are also known as structured decisions and usually involve 'things' rather than people and are fit for delegation to the operational control level of management. Examples of programmed decisions are inventory control, job shop scheduling, discount to customers and accounting decisions.

Non-programmed decisions are novel, non-routine and unstructured in nature, which involve a high degree of uncertainty of the outcomes, and as such no clear decision rule can be defined. Non-programmed decisions cannot be automated and always involve people. Examples of non-programmed decisions are future sales/production planning, capacity augmentation, launching of new products, recruitment of personnel, mergers and acquisitions.

DOI: 10.4324/9781003509714-3

Programmed and non-programmed decisions are two extremes of the range of managerial and organisational decision-making. Many decisions which involve characteristics of both the above extremes are semi-structured in nature. An example of a semi-structured decision is a new incentive scheme for piece workers in a factory where the incentive payment for different levels of output and productivity can be precisely determined, but the actual effect of the scheme in motivating the employees and the extent of productivity increase remain uncertain. Pay Commission decisions for increases in pay and allowances of central government employees are also unstructured in nature because of many interrelated factors involved in the process.

3.3 ISs for Different Types of Decisions

The MIS for an organisation provides information to support semi-structured and unstructured decision-making and also may take structured or programmed decisions. At the operational control level of management hierarchy, the majority of the decisions are structured with known decision rules and objectives. Semi-structured and unstructured decisions are mostly taken at the management control and strategic planning levels. However, certain structured decisions, particularly those that have organisation wide impact, are taken at a high level. For example, a very costly renovation decision in a manufacturing industrial unit which is likely to affect the operations of the entire unit and for which decision rules are available might be taken at the strategic level.

A broad overview of decision-making at the three levels of management and the related ISs are shown in Figure 3.1.

The boundaries between structured and semi-structured or unstructured decisions are constantly changing with the development of decision tools and techniques.

3.4 A Systematic Approach to Decision-Making

Herbert A. Simon, in his decision theory, mentioned three phases of decision-making, namely intelligence, design and choice. The intelligence phase relates to environmental scanning and finding conditions calling for decisions. The design phase is for setting goals, developing possible courses of action and analysing the alternative courses of action. This involves processes to understand the problem, to generate solutions and

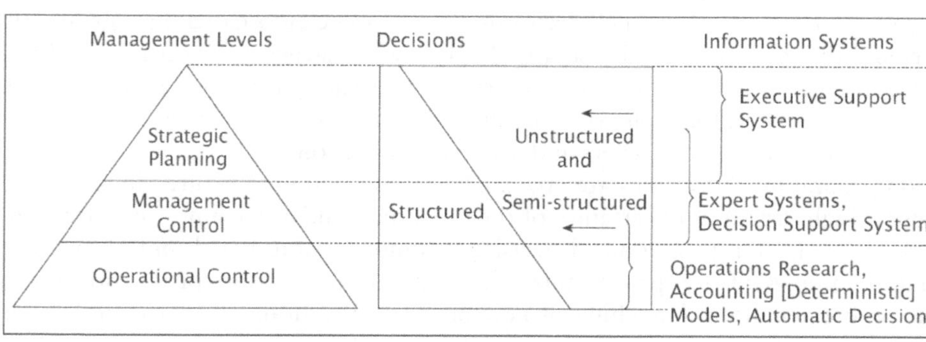

Figure 3.1 Decision-Making and Information Systems

the testing of solutions for feasibility. The choice phase is for selecting one among the feasible alternatives available depending on set goals or objectives. A choice is made and then implemented. The implementation part is sometimes considered as a fourth phase of decision-making.

Let us illustrate the above phases of the decision-making process by a simple example. A licensed sporting rifle manufacturing unit in India, through environmental scanning, got the market intelligence that out of ₹5,000 million of sporting rifles purchased by the Shooters Association in India per annum on average, its share was only 10% (₹500 million) approximately. Through further survey and intelligence, the unit observed that about 70% of sporting rifles of various bore sizes are imported from European manufacturers of small arms because the heavier metal components of rifles were replaced by fibre-reinforced plastics, making the rifles lighter in weight and also cost-effective, and these features attracted Indian shooters. The top management of the Indian unit realised that there was a strong case in favour of developing fibre-reinforced plastic (FRP) components for the rifles to increase the customer base and thereby market share. This market condition called for a decision for action for the development of plastic sporting rifles. This can be treated as Simon's first phase of decision-making, namely the 'intelligence' phase.

The second phase is the design phase when the corporate management sets goals of replacing the metal components of their products with FRP components at a competitive price within a time schedule and an estimated investment cost. The alternative courses of action to achieve the above goals were also chalked out as follows:

1. To import the FRP technology through transfer of the technology route;
2. To indigenously develop the FRP technology through in-house R&D efforts;
3. To enter into a foreign collaboration agreement on a long-term basis with foreign manufacturers to import the FRP components and assemble them in India;
4. To enter into a joint venture with a foreign manufacturer for co-production of rifles in India with profit sharing.

The feasibility of the four above alternatives has to be worked out with reference to the existing technology, input material availability in India, time and cost-effectiveness and customer preferences. This phase can be called Simon's second phase, namely the 'design' phase.

In the next phase, one of the four alternative courses of action available as mentioned in the design phase needs to be selected based on the pre-set criteria for choice, judgement, intuition and 'bounded rationality'. The term bounded rationality has been explained elaborately in the subsequent paragraphs in this chapter. In this example, the manufacturing unit decided to go for the second alternative which was to indigenously develop the FRP technology through in-house R&D. This phase constitutes the third phase of the decision-making process, known as the 'choice' phase.

The implementation phase starts with the process of developing the FRP components with their own R&D efforts or by getting assistance from R&D institutes in India on FRP technology, and the implementation phase ends when the regular production of FRP components commences.

It is pertinent to mention here that although there is a general flow from intelligence to design, choice and implementation of decisions at every phase, there has to be feedback and a review, and the whole decision-making process is an iterative process. In other words, it may so happen that the decision-maker may not find any suitable choice in the choice phase and may return to the design phase to explore more alternatives.

3.5 The Steps of Decision-Making

The phases of decision-making as explained earlier can be organised into the following steps for an effective decision:

Step 1: Define what you want to achieve.
Step 2: Organise a team for involving the right people for environmental scanning for problem identification.
Step 3: Encourage team members to be participative and assertive during discussion for problem identification. The problems calling for decisions should be arrived at by a consensus opinion of experts and not by any compromise.
Step 4: Set objectives and goals.
Step 5: Generate ideas through brainstorming considering different perspectives.
Step 6: Organise the ideas into common themes and groups as various alternatives.
Step 7: Explore the alternatives considering feasibility, risks and implications of each of the alternatives.
Step 8: Choose the best alternative using various decision tools such as decision trees (described in subsequent paragraphs) and factor comparison analysis to determine the relative importance of various factors. The selection of the best alternative has to be necessarily with reference to the goals or objectives set.
Step 9: Review of the decision is essentially needed at every step mentioned above to ensure that the process is thorough and without any discrepancies at any stage.
Step 10: Communicate the decision to all affected by the same and also explain the same to those involved in the implementation of the decision. This may also need a change management to facilitate a smooth implementation.

3.6 Decision-Making under Various Conditions

Decisions can be categorised into five broad categories depending upon the prior knowledge of the outcome of the various alternative decisions. The categories are as follows:

1. **Decisions under Certainty**: When there is only one definite outcome for each alternative, there is a finite number of alternatives and exact knowledge about the outcomes; such decisions are deterministic in nature. Many managerial decisions mainly at the operational control level and to some extent at the management control level are taken under certainty.
2. **Decisions under Risk**: When there are multiple possible outcomes for each alternative and a value and probability of occurrence of each outcome can be assessed, the decision under risk is taken based on the value of each outcome and the probability of occurrence of that particular outcome with respect to the objective. The decisions under risk are therefore prone to certain risks since the outcome for a particular alternative is probabilistic in nature and the risk can only be assessed. Many decisions at the strategic and tactical levels are taken under risk. Sensitivity analysis is a method to insulate a decision-making process or model from risk. It is

also referred to as 'what-if' or simulation analysis which in a way predicts the outcome of a decision given a certain range of variables. By creating a given set of variables, the analyst can determine how changes in one variable impact the outcome. Vendors of perishable commodities such as fruits have to take decisions regarding the quantities of commodities which they have to purchase from wholesale markets based on their past experience. However, such decisions are associated with some risk.

3. **Decisions under Uncertainty**: In the case of decision-making under uncertainty, the probabilities of outcomes associated with the alternatives are not known to the decision-maker. In a real business environment, managers are often required to take decisions under varying degrees of uncertainty and in such situations the managers or decision-makers, particularly at the strategic level, exercise their experience and judgement based on available information to assess the uncertainties as probable risks. An example of a decision under uncertainty is to select the venue (indoor or outdoor) for holding a party by a clubhouse on a future date. The outcome of the decision is the level of enjoyment which obviously depends on the venue and the weather conditions such as sunny, cloudy, rainy, cold or hot. The weather conditions on a future date are not known to the decision-maker at the time of selection of the venue. Managerial decision-making under uncertainties and risks is a sequential process wherein the decision-maker has to consider possible alternative actions in a logical sequence of the actions and the corresponding outcomes.
4. **Decision-Making under Conflicting Environment**: Ranking and selection of an alternative among many feasible ones, based on a set of conflicting criteria, are important in the case of multicriteria decision-making problems as explained in the subsequent chapter.
5. **Decision-Making in a Fuzzy Environment**: In a fuzzy environment, the goals and the constraints of the decision-making problem are fuzzy in nature, which means that those constitute classes of alternatives whose boundaries are not well defined. An example of a fuzzy goal is: 'return on investment (ROI) should be *close* to 20%'. Similarly, an example of a fuzzy constraint is: 'the price of an alternate item should not be *much higher* than the main item'. The italicised words in the above examples create the fuzziness. Fuzzy situations often make use of linguistic variables which consist of one or more words to represent some facts. For example, 'rich people', 'hot climate' are linguistic variables.

Let us illustrate a few categories of the decisions as mentioned above with typical business decisions. A manufacturing unit requires component X as one of the components for its finished product Y. The component in machined and annealed condition can be bought from the market at a price of ₹110 per piece. The same component can be made in-house by purchasing raw material for the component at a cost of ₹60 per piece, the cost of machining and annealing being ₹40 and ₹20 per piece respectively. The production manager has to decide whether to buy or make the finished component. The objective is cost minimisation. This is a case of decision under certainty, since there are only two alternatives either to buy or to make and the outcome in terms of cost is known with certainty. If bought, the cost would be ₹110, and if made, the cost would be ₹(60 + 40 + 20) = ₹120. Hence, the choice is to buy the component since the cost will be less in the case of buying.

An example of decision-making under risk is when a retail fruit seller has to decide how many crates of a particular fruit he has to purchase from wholesale market every day for selling the same in the next two days.

The particular fruit is a perishable item and he earns a profit of ₹75 per crate in case the fruit seller can sell within two days, but incurs a loss of ₹50 per crate if he fails to do so. He has to decide how many crates he should purchase for two days' sales of fruits in order to earn maximum profit. The fruit seller is uncertain about the demand for the fruit in the next two days. However, with his experience of past sales and judgement, he could convert the uncertainty into likely sales quantities with probabilities associated with such quantities and then can assess purchase quantity from the wholesale market to have maximum profit. However, there is a risk in his assessment.

He has estimated the sales for the next two days as follows:

Sales in Crates	*Probability (%)*
0	5
1	30
2	45
3	20

Now the various alternatives available to him are purchasing 0, 1, 2 or 3 crates of fruits. Let us evaluate the outcome for each of these purchase quantities in terms of net expected profit/loss as follows:

Expected Profit (₹)				*Expected Loss (₹)*			*Net Expected Profit/ Loss (₹)*
Purchase (Crates)	Profit	Probability	Expected Profit	Loss	Probability	Expected Loss	
0	—	—	—	—	—	—	—
1	75	0.95	71.25	50	0.05	2.50	68.75
2	150	0.65	97.5	100 +	0.05		
				50	0.30	20	77.50
3	225	0.20	45	150	0.05		
				100	0.30	60	-15
				50	0.45		

From the outcomes, it can be seen that if his choice is 2 crates, he earns an expected maximum profit. However, the risk involved is a 5% loss in his decision.

3.6.1 *Models of Decision-Making*

There are two models of decision-making, namely the prescriptive or normative model and the descriptive model.

A prescriptive model is one which selects the optimum (best) alternative. Such models are generally mathematical models developed by operation researchers and economists. Linear programming, integer programming, dynamic programming and models

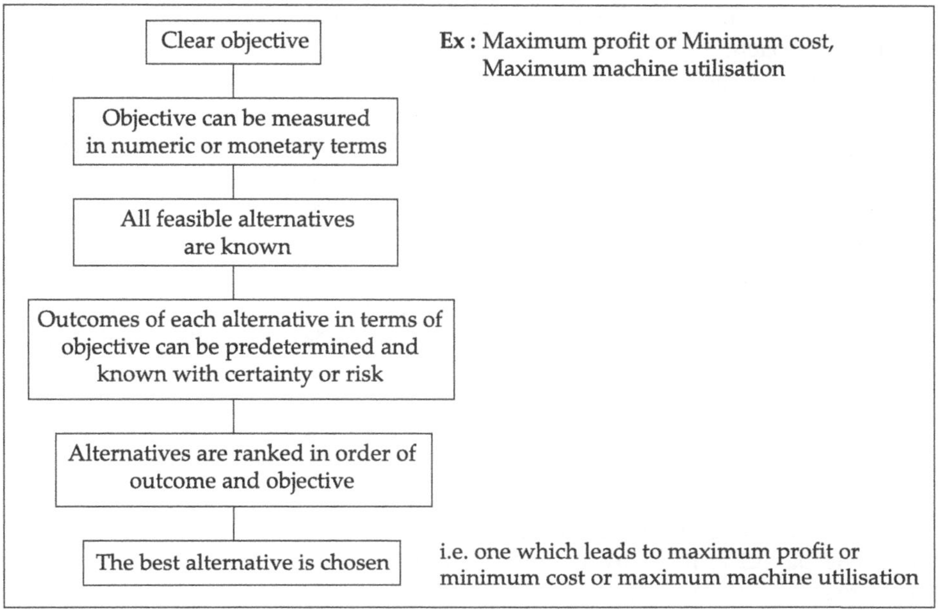

Figure 3.2 Rational Decision-Making Process

to automate decisions on process control, machine replacement and so on are examples of the prescriptive model. Basically, these models are optimising techniques under conditions of certainty and also risk. The prescriptive model is also known as 'rational decision-making'. The model assumes perfect knowledge and information about all the factors relevant to the decision and adopts a rational and structured approach to arrive at the decision. Rational or prescriptive models of decision-making are more common with operational control and management control decisions like optimum allocation of funds. Figure 3.2 shows the features of the rational decision-making process.

The descriptive model of decision-making, also known as the 'behavioural model', which was developed by behavioural scientists like Simon Herbert, J. Von Neumann, O. Morgenstern, A. Tversky and many others, seeks to describe the actual behaviour of the decision-maker while making a decision. This approach vindicates a concept proposed by Simon known as 'Satisficing' to describe the behaviour of decision-makers in a complex and partially unknown situation. Decision-makers in the actual business environment are neither fully aware of all the alternatives available, nor is there always a single clear-cut objective. They often make only a limited search to discover a few satisfactory alternatives and finally make decisions that satisfy their aspiration level. The decision-making is heuristic in nature, which generally yields a near-optimal satisfactory decision as per their aspiration but not necessarily the optimum decision.

In the descriptive model, there is not complete rationality as in the case of the prescriptive model, but there is bounded rationality due to imperfection in the information available to the decision-maker, his/her cognitive limitations to perceive alternatives and outcomes and also the time available for decision-making. An important characteristic of this type of decision behaviour is the application of intuition, judgement and rules of thumb in making decisions rather than the use of explicit decision rules. Many of the decisions at the strategic and also tactical levels of management follow the bounded rationality approach.

Let me illustrate this approach with the example of a housewife. While deciding on the investment for her savings in a particular period, the investment options available to her may be many, such as small savings deposits with post offices, term deposits with banks, mutual funds, shares and debentures. She often considers a few satisfactory options and then decides to select one or more ways of investing her savings to get a satisfactory return on the same according to her aspiration level. Although her decision may not yield the maximum (optimum) return due to her limitation of time and effort to work out the return on all possible investment options and her inability to get the details of all investment schemes available, she has to adopt a bounded rationality while arriving at her choice or decision.

3.6.2 Decision Criteria

Managers or decision-makers, while taking decisions under uncertainty without any knowledge of the probabilities of outcomes of various alternatives, adopt various payoff criteria. The payoff criteria are mainly the following: (1) maximax, (2) maximin, (3) minimax regret (savage), (4) Hurwicz and (5) Laplace.

The payoff related to the alternative decisions varies depending upon the state of nature, which remains unknown at the time of decision-making, and the same is also beyond the control of the manager or decision-maker. The payoff can be profit, time, distance, cost or regret. Regret is the opportunity loss for any particular alternative under a particular state of nature.

Let me explain the above payoff criteria with the example of a particular investor who wants to invest for profit. There are three alternatives of investment available to the investor, namely gold, stocks and real estate. The state of nature is the economic condition such as boom, recovery or recession. The payoff table in this case is assumed as follows:

State of Nature (Economic Condition)

Alternatives	*Boom*	*Recovery*	*Recession*
Gold	3000	1100	300
Stocks	2000	1800	100
Real estate	1100	1000	1000

Criterion 1: Maximax (optimistic) criterion. The alternative having the maximum among the maximum payoffs of all the alternatives needs to be selected.

Alternatives	*Maximum Payoffs*	*Maximax*
Gold	3000	3000
Stocks	2000	
Real estate	1100	

Decision is to invest in gold if maximax is the criterion.

In case of cost, however, the optimistic criterion will be minimin which is the minimum of the minimum costs (loss) for the alternatives.

Criterion 2: Maximin (pessimistic) criterion. The alternative having the maximum among the minimum payoffs of all the alternatives needs to be selected.

Alternatives	*Minimum Payoffs*	*Maximin*
Gold	300	
Stocks	100	
Real estate	**1000**	**1000**

Decision is to invest in real estate if maximin is the criterion.

Criterion 3: Hurwicz, α = 0.8 (weighted average) criterion. The alternative having the highest weighted average payoff is to be selected. The weighted average for an alternative = α (maximum payoff) + (1 – α) (minimum payoff).

Since we have taken α as 0.8, the weighted averages for the alternatives are as follows:

Gold: 0.8 × 3,000 + (1 – 0.8) × 300 = *2,460* (maximum weighted average)

Stocks: 0.8 × 2,000 + (1 – 0.8) × 100 = 1,620

Real estate: 0.8 × 1,100 + (1 – 0.8) × 1,000 = 1,080

Decision is to invest in gold if Hurwicz is the criterion with α = 0.8.

Criterion 4: Laplace (equally likely) criterion. The alternative having the highest average payoff is to be selected. In this case, the average payoff for each alternative is calculated as follows:

Gold: (3,000 + 1,100 + 300)/3 = *1,467* (maximum average payoff)

Stocks: (2,000 + 1,800 + 100)/3 = 1,300

Real estate: (1,100 + 1,000 + 1,000)/3 = 1,033

Decision is to invest in gold if Laplace is the criterion.

Criteria based on regret (opportunity loss). Regret (also known as opportunity loss) for any alternative for a particular state of nature is the difference between the highest payoff for that state of nature and the actual payoff of the particular alternative. Referring to our example, in the case of stocks as the alternative, the actual payoff for the economic boom is 2,000. However, the highest payoff under the same condition of boom is 3,000 for the alternative gold. So, the regret or opportunity loss for the alternative stocks under boom is (3,000 – 2,000) which is 1,000. Proceeding this way, we can calculate the regret values for all the alternatives under the various economic conditions and construct a regret table corresponding to our payoff table.

The regret table is as follows:

State of Nature (Economic condition)

Alternatives	*Boom*	*Recovery*	*Recession*
Gold	0 = (3000–3000)	700 = (1800–1100)	700 = (1000–300)
Stocks	1000 = (3000–2000)	0 = (1800–1800)	900 = (1000–100)
Real estate	1900 = (3000–1100)	800 = (1800–1000)	0 = (1000–1000)

Criterion 5: Minimax regret (savage) criterion. The alternative with the minimum of the maximum regrets of all the alternatives needs to be selected. The maximum regret for each of the alternatives is as follows:

Alternatives	*Maximum Regrets*	*Minimax Regret*
Gold	*700*	*700*
Stocks	1000	
Real estate	1900	

So, the decision is to invest in gold following the minimax criterion.

3.6.2.1 *Decision Criteria under Risk*

In this case, the probabilities for the various states of nature are known. The criteria of decision-making under risk are: (1) expected value (EV) or EMV and (2) expected value of perfect information (EVPI).

Let us now find out the above criteria based on our previous example, assuming the probability values for boom, recovery and recession as 0.2, 0.5 and 0.3 respectively. The same payoff table along with the above probability values is as follows:

State of Nature (Economic Condition)

Alternatives	*Boom*	*Recovery*	*Recession*
Gold	3000	1100	300
Stocks	2000	1800	100
Real estate	1100	1000	1000
Probability	0.2	0.5	0.3

1. *EMV* is calculated for each alternative as follows:
   (i) EMV (Gold) = (3,000 × 0.2) + (1,100 × 0.5) + (300 × 0.3) = 1,240
   (ii) EMV (Stocks) = (2,000 × 0.2) + (1,800 × 0.5) + (100 × 0.3) = 1330 (maximum)
   (iii) EMV (Real estate) = (1,100 × 0.2) + (1,000 × 0.5) + (1,000 × 0.3) = 1,020

Hence, decision is to invest in stocks.

2. *EVPI* is the additional payoff for perfect information, which is expressed as follows:
   (i) EVPI = EV (with perfect information) – EV (without perfect information) = EV (with perfect information) – maximum EMV; maximum EMV = 1330.
   (ii) Perfect information would reveal to the decision-maker the fact that gold, stocks and real estate would fetch the highest payoffs under economic conditions of boom, recovery and recession respectively.

Hence, EV (with perfect information) will be:

(0.2 × 3,000) + (0.5 × 1,800) + (0.3 × 1,000) = 1,600; and
EVPI = 1,600 – 1,330 = 270.

3.7 Decision-Making Tools

3.7.1 Decision Tree

A decision tree is a diagram which can organise a decision-making problem's alternatives, risks and uncertainty in the forms of activity forks and event forks associated with each activity.

This analysis consists of the following steps:

1. Identify all possible alternatives (activities) and the risks associated with each situation (event).
2. Calculate the consequences of each of the alternatives in EMV.
3. Determine the uncertainty (risk) associated with each alternative.
4. Combine 1, 2 and 3 into a tree diagram.
5. Determine the best alternative considering the EMV. A decision tree consists of three types of nodes: decision nodes commonly represented by squares, chance nodes represented by circles and end nodes represented by triangles.

3.7.1.1 Examples of Decision Tree

Example 1: A company is considering whether to launch a new product or improve an existing product as per customer preferences. If it launches the new product, it has to hire a new plant exclusively for the new product which will cost ₹20 lakhs or work overtime with additional expenses on labour to the extent of ₹8 lakhs. If it decides to improve upon the existing product, it will incur an additional cost of ₹12 lakhs in modernising its existing plants. A market survey has revealed the following data regarding the magnitude of sales of the new product and also the same for the improved product.

	Probability		*Resulting Profit in (₹ in Lakhs)*	
Magnitude of Sales	*New*	*Improved*	*New*	*Improved*
High	0.50	0.40	40	30
Medium	0.30	0.35	18	12
Low	0.15	0.20	8	6
Nil	0.05	0.05	−10	-4

However, high sales cannot be fulfilled by working overtime or by improving upon existing products. Further, the cost of a new plant, additional costs for modernising the existing plant and the additional expenses for working overtime have not been considered in the resulting profit calculations. The decision tree in this case is shown in Figure 3.3. So, the EMV is maximum for a new product by working overtime (₹7.10 lakhs), hence the decision is to develop a new product with overtime working.

Example 2: A student after higher secondary examination is to decide whether to study engineering or medicine for a graduation course of four years' duration. The probability that the demand for engineering graduates will boom in the next four years is 0.40 (40%). Similarly, there is a probability of 0.50 (50%) boom in demand for medical graduates. If there is a boom in the demand for engineering graduates, the average annual cost to company (CTC) for a fresher is assessed to be ₹9 lakhs, otherwise the same is

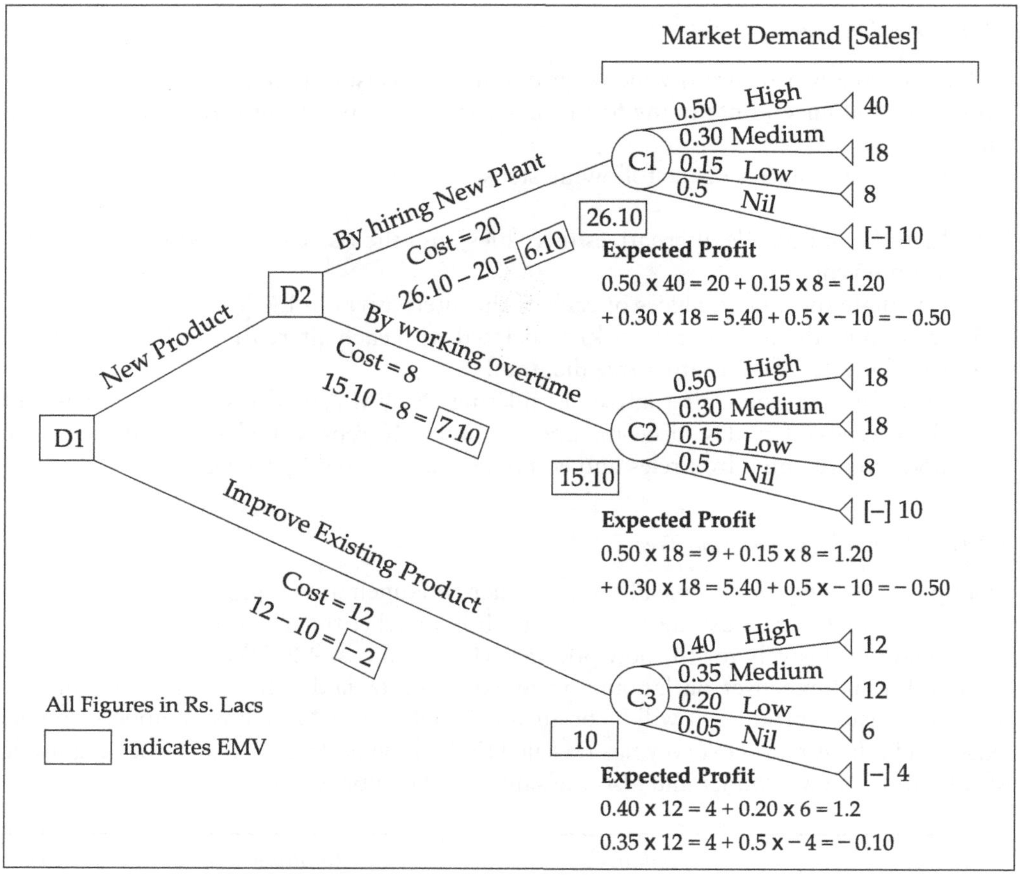

Figure 3.3 Decision Tree for Example 1

expected to be ₹5 lakhs. In the case of fresh medical graduates, the corresponding figures are ₹8 lakhs and ₹7 lakhs respectively. Let us draw a simple decision tree in this case to find out which stream the student should select, without considering the cost of studies as a parameter for the decision. The decision tree is shown in Figure 3.4. From the decision tree, it can be seen that expected CTC is ₹7.50 lakhs for a fresh medical graduate after four years which is more than the same (6.60) for engineering streams. Hence, the choice is to select the medical stream.

Example 3: A multi-storey building owner is considering drilling a deep borewell to augment municipal water supply. In the past, only 70% of wells drilled in the area were successful at 250 feet depth. Moreover, on finding no water at 250 feet, some owners drilled further up to 300 feet, but only 40% struck water. The cost of drilling is ₹30 per foot. The owner has estimated that the other alternative is to buy additional water from the municipal corporation at a cost of ₹3,000 per annum over the next 10 years. Let us draw an appropriate decision tree and determine the owner's strategy for minimum cost. The decision tree is as shown in Figure 3.5.

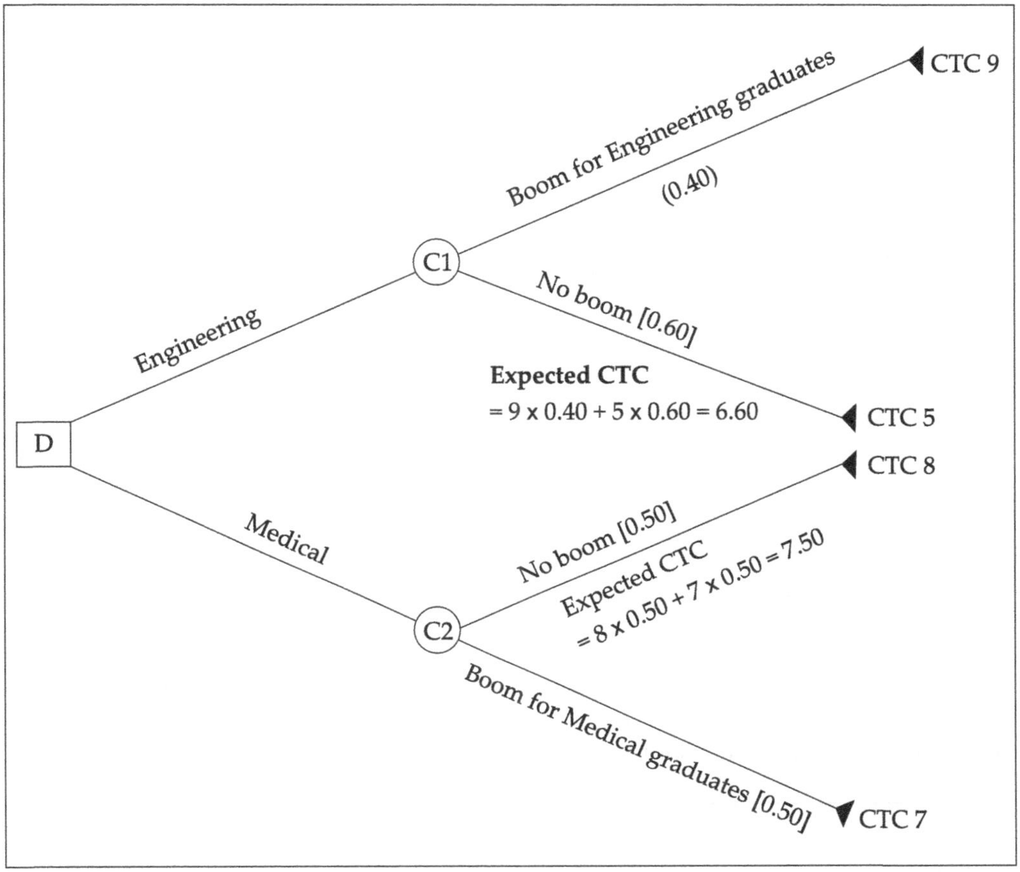

Figure 3.4 Decision Tree for Example 2

Decision Point D2:

1. Expected cash outflow for drilling up to 300 ft = (0.60 × 39,000) + (0.40 × 9,000) = 23,400 + 3,600 = 27,000
2. Cash outflow for not drilling up to 300 ft = 37,500

Decision Point D1:

1. Do not drill, cash outflow = 30,000
2. Drill up to 250 ft

Expected cash flow = (27,000 × 0.30) + (7,500 × 0.70) = 8,100 + 5,250 = 13,350

Hence, decision is to drill with a minimum cash outflow of 13,350.

Example 4: A private inter-state bus transport company is considering operating on a new route. It has got two alternatives, Route 1 and Route 2, as the traffic is more compared to the available state bus service operating in either of these two routes. The company is also contemplating introducing four new buses, either deluxe or ordinary, and the cost of a new deluxe bus would be ₹20 lakhs and that for an ordinary bus would be ₹15 lakhs. The

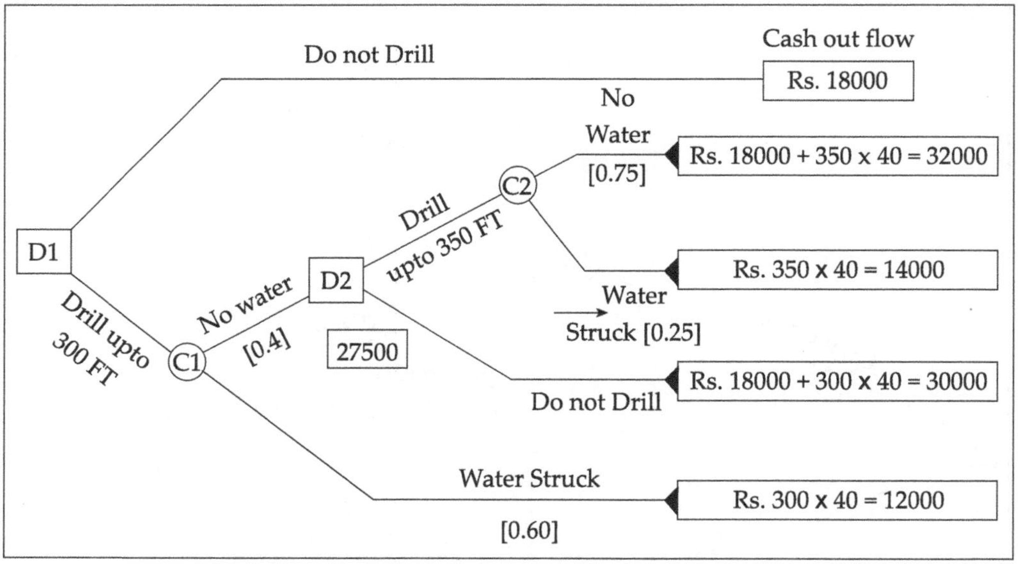

Figure 3.5 Decision Tree for Example 3

company assessed passenger volume and likely resultant operating profit without considering depreciation of the buses over their total life span for both deluxe and ordinary bus service for the two routes separately. The assessed figures are shown in the following table.

Route 1					*Route 2*				
Resultant Profit					*Resultant Profit*				
Volume of Passengers	*Probability*		*(₹ in Lakhs)*		*Volume of Passengers*	*Probability*		*(₹ in Lakhs)*	
	Ordinary	**Deluxe**	**Ordinary**	**Deluxe**		**Ordinary**	**Deluxe**	**Ordinary**	**Deluxe**
High	0.45	0.25	400	600	High	0.50	0.20	500	700
Medium	0.30	0.35	300	500	Medium	0.35	0.30	400	600
Low	0.25	0.40	200	300	Low	0.15	0.50	300	500

The company also feels that there is a 60% chance of getting state government approval for operating in Route 1 and a 70% chance for the same in case of Route 2.

Due to the minimum cooling-off period required between two consecutive trips for the buses running in Route 2, it is not possible to cope with the high passenger volume in Route 2, and four buses running in Route 2 (being a long-distance route) can handle only medium and low passenger traffic. The decision tree in this case is shown in Figure 3.6.

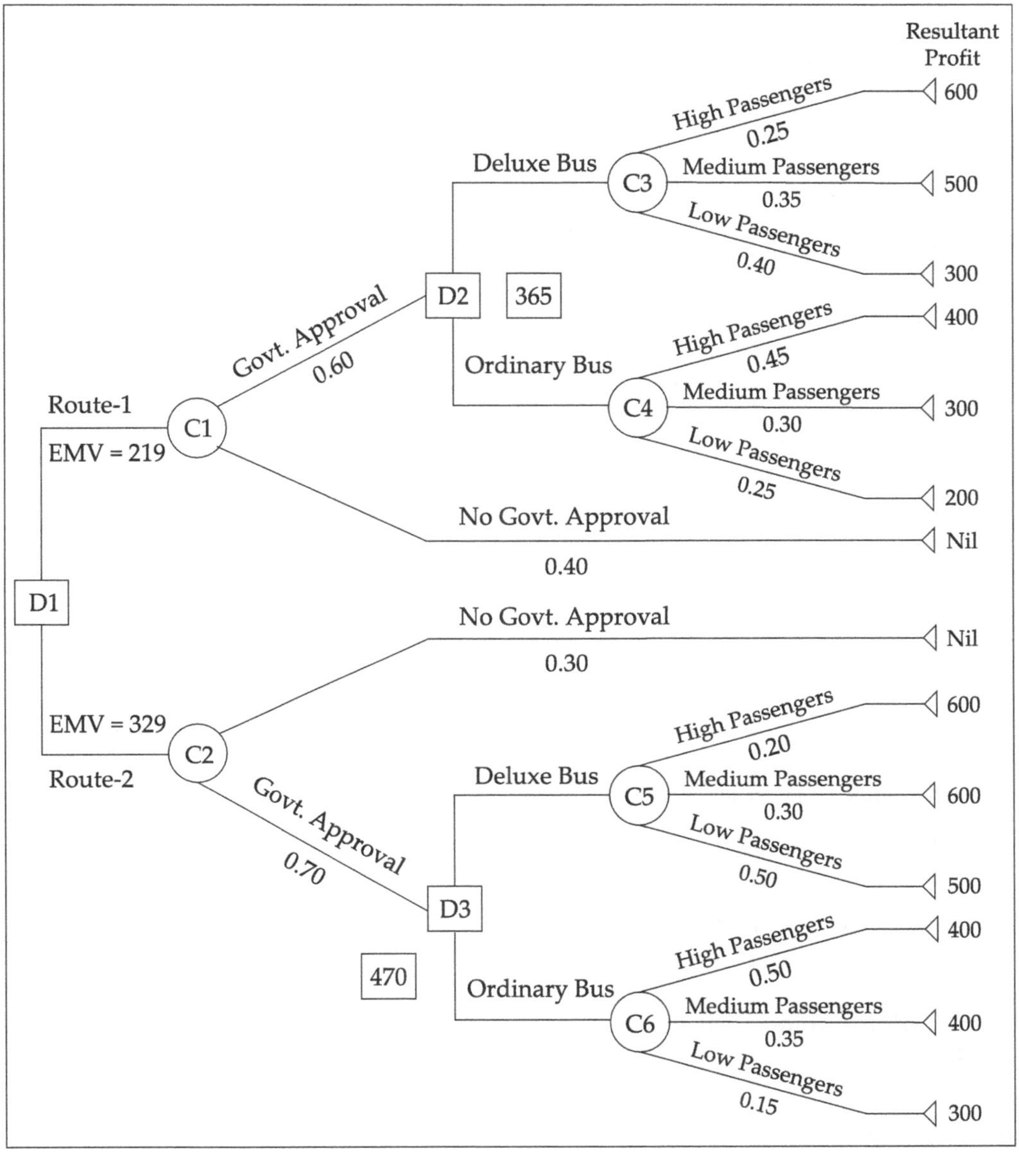

Figure 3.6 Decision Tree for Example 4

Decision Point D2:

Deluxe bus: Expected resultant profit

= (600 × 0.25) + (0.35 × 500) + (0.40 × 300)

= 150 + 175 + 120 = 445

Cost of deluxe buses = 80

EMV = 445 – 80 = 365

Ordinary bus: Expected resultant profit
= (400 × 0.45) + (300 × 0.30) + (200 × 0.25)
= 180 + 90 + 50 = 320

Cost of ordinary buses = 60
EMV = 320 – 60 = 260

Net EMV at D2 = 365 for deluxe buses.

Decision Point D3:

Deluxe bus: Expected resultant profit
= (600 × 0.20) + (600 × 0.30) + (500 × 0.50)
= 120 + 180 + 250 = 550

Cost of deluxe buses = 80
EMV = 550 – 80 = 470

Ordinary bus: Expected resultant profit
= (400 × 0.50) + (400 × 0.35) + (300 × 0.15)
= 200 + 140 + 45 = 385

Cost of ordinary buses = 60
EMV = 385 – 60 = 325

Therefore, net EMV at D3 = 470 for deluxe buses.

EMV for Route 1 = (0.60 × 365) + (0.40 × 0)
= 219 + 0 = 219

EMV for Route 2 = (0.70 × 470) + (0.30 × 0)
= 329 + 0 = 329

Since EMV for Route 2 is higher than that for Route 1, the decision is to run deluxe buses on Route 2.

3.7.2 Decision Table

Decision tables are used to list out in tabular form all possible situations (set of conditions) which a business decision may encounter and to specify which action to take in each of those situations. A decision table is a tabular form that represents a set of conditions and their corresponding actions.

A decision table essentially consists of: (1) condition stubs, (2) action stubs, (3) rules consisting of the condition alternatives and combinations thereof and (4) the action entries. *Condition stubs* describe the conditions or factors in different rows that will affect the decision or policy. They are listed in the upper part of a decision table.

Action stubs which form the lower part of the decision table describe in the form of statements the possible action entries or decisions in different rows. Rules describe unique combinations of conditions and the actions associated with each such combination.

II. Rules (R1 … to R8)								
I. Condition Stub	R1	R2	R3	R4	R5	R6	R7	R8
Condition C1	Y	Y	Y	Y	N	N	N	N
Condition C2	Y	N	N	Y	N	Y	N	N
Condition C3	Y	Y	N	N	Y	N	Y	N
III. Action Stub								
Action A1	X		X				X	
Action A2		X		X	X			
Action A3			X		X			
Action A4	X				X	X		
IV. Action Entries								

Action entries contain the list of actions associated with each rule specified by putting a cross (X) in the appropriate columns of the action entries section of the decision table. The above sections can be represented in the form of four quadrants of a decision table as shown above. For example, Rule R2 is to take action A2 when conditions C1 and C3 exist but condition C2 does not exist.

A decision table can, in a precise and compact way, model complicated logic and decision rules. It can associate many independent conditions and their various combinations and the corresponding multiple actions in an elegant way like a checklist.

Apart from the basic four-quadrant structure, decision tables vary widely in the way the condition alternatives or rules and action entries are represented. Some decision tables adopt only true/false values (Y/N) to represent the presence or absence of a condition, whereas other tables may use different data attribute values for the conditions, such as the gender of an employee (male or female) and age group (young, middle, senior). Some decision tables even use fuzzy logic or probabilistic representation for the conditions in a rule.

Action entries in a similar way can simply represent whether an action is to be performed (check the actions to perform as a checklist) or in more advanced decision tables the sequencing of actions to perform (numbering the actions as 1, 2, 3 and so on.)

3.7.2.1 Methodology of Preparing a Decision Table

The whole methodology of framing a decision table can be divided into the following steps in sequence:

Step 1: *Identify conditions and the values.* Identify all the conditions relevant to the situation and the possible values associated with the data attribute of each condition. For example, the possible values of the attribute states of a traffic signal can be 'red', 'green' or 'yellow' only. Similarly, the possible values of a condition that a machine is idle can be two, namely 'Yes' or 'no'. 'Yes' if the machine is idle and 'no' if the machine is running.

Step 2: *Compute the maximum number of rules.* Multiply the number of values for each condition data attribute by each other. For example, if there are three conditions and each condition can have two values for attributes such as 'true' or 'false', the maximum number of rules will be $2 \times 2 \times 2 = 8$.

Step 3: *Identify possible actions.* Determine each independent action to be taken for the decision rule.

Step 4: *Enter all possible rules in the decision table.* Fill in the values of the condition data attributes in each rule column.

Step 5: *Define actions for each rule.* For each rule, mark the appropriate actions with an X in the decision table.

Step 6: *Verify the decision rules or policies.* Review completed decision table with end users.

Step 7: *Simplify the table.* By eliminating and/or consolidating rules which are unfeasible or repetitions, reduce the number of columns.

Step 8: For very complex business problems involving many rules, make multiple decision tables and arrange the tables in a hierarchy of rules in the logical sequence of their application in the problem-solving scenario.

Example 5: A marketing company wishes to construct a decision table to decide the different discount rates to different categories of customers. The categories of customers are retailers and distributors, each having a status of either registered with the company or not and the average volume of business per year: A (below ₹10 lakhs), B (between 10 and 20 lakhs) and C (over 20 lakhs). The company offers four discount rates, namely 5%, 8%, 10% and 12.5%. A discount of 5% is allowed to retailers who have average business below 10 lakhs, an 8% discount is allowed to all retailers having a volume of business between 10 and 20 lakhs, and an 8% discount is allowed to all registered distributors having annual business volume less than 10 lakhs. All registered distributors having annual business between 10 and 20 lakhs are allowed a 10% discount, and a 12.5% discount is allowed to all retailers and distributors having annual business volume over 20 lakhs. All distributors who want to make an annual business of ₹1 lakh and above have to register themselves.

No discount is allowed to any unregistered retailer. However, a discount of 5% is allowed to all unregistered distributors having a volume of business in a year less than ₹10 lakhs.

Step 1: *Identify conditions and values.* The three data attributes tested by the conditions in this problem are categories, with values retailers (R) and distributors (D); registration status with values Y (registered) and N (not registered), and average annual business volume with values A, B and C as stated in the problem.

Step 2: *Compute maximum number of rules.* The maximum number of rules is $2 \times 2 \times 3 = 12$. However, all of them are not feasible.

Step 3: *Identify possible actions.* The four actions are: offer discount rates of 5%, 8%, 10% and 12.5%.

Step 4: *Enter all feasible rules.* The upper portion of the table would be as follows: It may be noted that all combinations of values are present.

Rules												
Conditions	1	2	3	4	5	6	7	8	9	10	11	12
Category	R	D	R	D	R	D	R	D	R	D	R	D
Status of registration	Y	Y	N	N	Y	Y	N	N	Y	Y	N	N
Average annual business	A	A	A	A	B	B	B	B	C	C	C	C

Rules 3, 7, 8, 11 and 12 are not possible since unregistered retailers and also unregistered distributors having annual business of B and C are not allowed. Hence, the feasible rules are only seven as follows:

Rules							
Conditions	1	2	3	4	5	6	7
Category	R	D	D	R	D	R	D
Status of registration	Y	Y	N	Y	Y	Y	Y
Average annual business Lakhs	A	A	A	B	B	C	C

Step 5: *Define actions for each rule*. The bottom of the table would look as follows:

Rules							
Offer Discount	1	2	3	4	5	6	7
5%	X		X				
8%		X		X			
10%					X		
12.5%						X	X

Step 6: *Verify the policy*. Let us assume that the client agreed with the above discount policy.

Step 7: *Simplify the table*. There appears to be no infeasible rule. Note that rules 6 and 7 have a similar action pattern (12.5% discount) and have two of the three condition values (status of registration and average annual business) as identical and all the two values of non-identical value (category) are covered, so they can be condensed into a single column 6. The revised table is as shown in Table 3.1.

Table 3.1 Decision Table for Example 5

Actions: Offer Discount	*1*	*2*	*3*	*4*	*5*	*6*
5%	X		X			
8%		X		X		
10%					X	
12.5%						X

Rules						
Conditions	1	2	3	4	5	6
Category	R	D	D	R	D	—
Status of registration	Y	Y	N	Y	Y	Y
Average annual business	A	A	A	B	B	C

Example 6: A Central Government Health Scheme (CGHS) beneficiary can avail themselves of the following medical facilities. He/she can consult the CGHS doctor and with his/her reference get the treatment performed in a CGHS recognised hospital or nursing home with full reimbursement of all costs including medicine costs. However, in case of emergency he/she can get directly admitted to the nearest hospital/nursing home without any reference. In that case, if the hospital/nursing home is not a CGHS recognised one, he/she can get reimbursement for treatment at the rates charged by the All India Institute of Medical Sciences for the same. However, if the hospital or nursing home happens to be a CGHS recognised one, he/she will get reimbursement at CGHS package rates only irrespective of the actual costs incurred. In either case of emergency admission and treatment, the cost of medicines consumed is reimbursable in full. However, in case of non-emergency, if anyone avails themselves of any treatment without CGHS reference, he/she is not entitled to any reimbursement including the cost of medicines. The decision table in this case can be formed as shown below.

	Rules							
Conditions	1	2	3	4	5	6	7	8
1. CGHS reference	Y	Y	Y	Y	N	N	N	N
2. CGHS recognised	Y	N	Y	N	Y	Y	N	N
3. Emergency case	Y	Y	N	N	Y	N	Y	N
	Actions							
1. Full reimbursement	X		X					
2. Reimbursement at CGHS package rates					X			
3. Reimbursement at AIIMS rates							X	
4. No reimbursement						X		X
5. Reimbursement of actual cost of medicines	X		X		X		X	

The simplified decision table is as shown in Table 3.2.

	Rules					
Conditions	1	2	3	4	5	6
1. CGHS reference	Y	Y	N	N	N	N
2. CGHS recognised	Y	Y	Y	Y	N	N
3. Emergency case	Y	N	Y	N	Y	N

Table 3.2 Decision Table for Example 6

Actions						
1. Full reimbursement	X	X				
2. Reimbursement at CGHS package rates			X			
3. Reimbursement at AIIMS rates					X	
4. No reimbursement				X		X
5. Reimbursement of actual cost of medicines	X	X	X		X	

Example 7: A technical support company writes a decision table to sort out computer printer troubleshooting as shown in Table 3.3.

Rules								
Conditions	1	2	3	4	5	6	7	8
1. Printer does not print	Y	Y	Y	Y	N	N	N	N
2. A red light is flashing	Y	Y	N	N	Y	Y	N	N
3. Printer is unrecognised	Y	N	Y	N	Y	N	Y	N

Table 3.3 Decision Table for Example 7

Actions								
1. Check the power cable			X					
2. Check the printer-computer cable	X		X					
3. Ensure printer software is installed	X		X		X		X	
4. Check/replace ink	X	X			X	X		
5. Check for paper jam		X		X				

The above decision table is a simple one, but even so, it demonstrates how decision tables can scale to several conditions, many possibilities and a checklist of actions associated with each decision rule.

Example 8: A preliminary decision table for the driver of a car in case of engine troubleshooting may be as shown in Table 3.4.

Rules								
Conditions	1	2	3	4	5	6	7	8
Car does not start	Y	Y	Y	Y	N	N	N	N
Charge indicator is red	Y	Y	N	N	Y	Y	N	N
Fuel indicator is red	Y	N	Y	N	Y	N	Y	N

Table 3.4 Decision Table for Example 8

Actions								
1. Check/Fill fuel	X		X		X		X	
2. Check battery/recharge	X	X						
3. Check the dynamo belt/replace	X	X			X	X		
4. Employ choke				X				
5. Check/clean oil filter				X				

3.7.2.2 Hierarchy of Multiple Decision Tables in Case of Complex Problems

In many practical and complex decision-making situations, there may be many decision rules and the rules applicable may depend upon the actions taken and the outcome pursuant to an earlier decision rule. In other words, there may be levels of decision tables, with an overall decision table at the first level, and depending upon the outcome of the actions taken, there may be a greater number of decision rules at the second, third levels and so on. The following example of a medical diagnosis of a patient having a fever will illustrate such a hierarchy of decision tables.

Diagnosis of a patient having fever (body temperature above 98.4° F)

Level-1 Decision Table

Rules								
Condition of Patient	**1**	**2**	**3**	**4**	**5**	**6**	**7**	**8**
Body temperature above 100° F	Y	Y	Y	Y	N	N	N	N
Fever persists more than 72 hours	Y	N	Y	N	Y	N	Y	N
Having cough and cold	Y	Y	N	N	N	Y	Y	N

Actions								
Paracetamol tablets	X	X	X	X				
General antibiotec	X	X	X	X	X	X	X	X
Cough syrup	X	X				X	X	
Pathological tests	X		X		X		X	
	Level 2		Level 2		Level 2		Level 2	

Level-2 Decision Table

Rules								
Condition of Patient	**1**	**2**	**3**	**4**	**5**	**6**	**7**	**8**
Urine Report OK	Y	Y	Y	Y	N	N	N	N
Sr Bilirubin OK	Y	N	Y	N	Y	N	Y	N
Malaria parasite present	Y	Y	N	N	N	Y	Y	N

Actions								
Consult General Physician			X					
Consult Malaria Clinic	X	X				X	X	
Consult Urologist					X		X	X
Consult Liver specialist/Gastroenterologist		X		X				X

The above two decision tables are only illustrative examples for showing the hierarchy of decision tables at various levels and not an exhaustive case of actual diagnosis. Decision tables are often good methods of documentation of decision rules and actions relating to operational control and management control levels of decisions.

3.8 Case Study: Credit Risk Assessment Is Carried Out by Bank of America for Making Credit Lending Decisions

3.8.1 Methodology Adopted by Bank of America

Bank of America uses credit risk scoring in making its credit-lending decisions. Credit scoring is not only applied to assess lending decisions, but also used for ongoing credit-risk management and collection strategies. A spectrum of scorecard development methodologies, such as logistic regression, decision trees, mathematical programming, survival analysis and modelling, is used by different lines of business. Among all these techniques, logistic regression is the most commonly used method for scorecard building at Bank of America. Logistic regression has been an optimal choice for developing credit-scoring models as it is designed to handle binary outcomes and it provides probability values which cannot lie beyond the range of 0–1. Logistic regression uses maximum likelihood estimation processes, which transform the dependent variable into a log function and estimate the regression coefficients in a way that maximises the log-likelihood.

For front-end approval/rejection decision-making, application scorecard (A-score) is used, while for back-end customer-risk management, behaviour scorecard (B-score) is used. Both these measure the likelihood of a customer becoming a defaulter over a certain period of time (known as the performance window). The performance window for both A-score and B-score was chosen to be 12 months. Bank of America portfolio mostly consists of retail consumers, and the data set was extracted from external sources (bureau data) and internal data warehouses, which contained the following information:

- Customer information (e.g., customer ID, age, years in job)
- Product information (e.g., number of credit cards, credit limit of the cards)
- Internal behavioural information (e.g., number of past dues and delinquency records)
- External information (e.g., credit bureau score)
- Macroeconomic indicators (GDP and unemployment rate by geographical areas).

As for the default, a definition of 'bad' behaviour is when a payment is 90 days or more overdue. The status of a customer is monitored over 12 months after the date of issuance of the card to predict any 'bad' behaviour.

The data set contained more than 200 predictor variables and a binary flag variable for default instances. The data set was partitioned into simple random samples of 70% observations for the training set and 30% observations for the validation set. The initial stage of the model development process involved analysing distributions of predictor variables and checking for outliers and missing values. Data treatments were conducted to account for anomalies in the data.

The model is built using statistical analysis system (SAS). SAS is a commercial statistical software. 'Proc logistic' was leveraged to estimate the model parameters. Information value (IV) statistics were used for selecting predictor variables for the binary logistic regression. Based on the average predictive performance of the independent individual variables, the variable selection cut-off point was set at IV of 0.1. Out of more than 200 predictor variables in the data set, 52 variables were selected for the final model. Once the short list of 52 variables was selected, further assessment was done to check for multicollinearity among the variables for the final model. Highly correlated variables with a correlation coefficient of more than 0.5 were dropped. Stepwise regression was carried out by an iterative process using forward selection of variables, which starts with no variable in the model, adding a single variable at each step using a chosen model comparison criterion. Predictor variables are added in their order of relative improvements to the model and the process is repeated until none of the remaining variables improve the model. Akaike information criterion (AIC) and Bayesian information criterion (BIC) were used for the final variable selection of the model based on stepwise forward logistic regression.

The final model had 14 independent variables. Once the logistic regression model was built, the model performance on the testing sample for validation was done. Widely used statistics such as Kolmogorov-Smirnov (KS) chart and Gini coefficients were computed for the purpose of evaluating the improved odds to differentiate the good credit applicants from bad credit applicants.

3.9 Summary and Conclusions

Credit risk scorecard development is an iterative process, and the resultant scorecard must satisfy a number of performance standards, including stability and interpretability. However, there is no unique quantitative framework that all organisations must follow, and the decision-making process varies for each organisation, depending on a range of factors such as the available data and resources and the risk appetite of the organisation. The industry standard for credit-lending risk is less than 2%, which implies that out of 100 cases of credit-lending decisions taken by a bank, only in 2 cases may there be a default. The banks and other financial institutions may design innovative and improved credit risk assessment methods to even reduce the chance of default to less than 2%.

Review Questions

1. What are programmed and non-programmed decisions? Illustrate with suitable examples.
2. What are the phases of decision-making as per Simon? Is the decision-making process iterative in nature? Explain.
3. What are the various ISs for the typical decisions taken by the different levels of management in an organisation?
4. What is Simon's 'Satisficing principle'? Explain with suitable illustrations relating to organisational decisions.
5. A manager has a choice between: (1) a risky contract promising ₹8 lakhs with a probability of 0.7 and ₹5 lakhs with a probability of 0.3 and (2) a diversified portfolio consisting of two contracts with independent outcomes and each promising ₹4.5 lakhs with a probability of 0.55 and ₹2.5 lakhs with a probability of 0.45. Construct a decision tree using EMV criteria. Can you arrive at the decision?
6. ABC Co. is considering the manufacture of a new product. If manufacturing is started without research, it is estimated that there is a 60% probability of good sales, giving a net profit of ₹35,000 and a 40% probability of poor sales with a resultant net loss of ₹25,000. If research is undertaken (at a cost of ₹7,000), it is estimated that there is a 90% chance it will indicate that sales will be high and a 10% probability that it will forecast low sales. It is possible, however, for research of this type when it gives a good indication, to be correct 70% of the time (when the net profit is calculated to be ₹45,000) and incorrect 30% of the time (when a net loss of ₹6,000 is incurred). If research forecasts poor sales, there is an 80% chance it is correct (with a net loss of ₹11,000) and a 20% chance it is wrong (when profit is ₹9,000 net). Prepare a decision tree showing the various alternative lines of action open to the company and indicate the optimum strategy.
7. A doctor has to decide whether or not to perform a serious surgical operation on a patient suspected of a malignant tumour in the upper abdomen. If the patient has a tumour and the doctor operates, the chance of recovery is 65%; without an operation, the chance of recovery is only 15%. On the other hand, if the patient does not have a tumour and an operation is performed, there is a 70% chance of survival of the patient whereas there is no chance of death without the surgical operation. Use the decision tree approach to determine whether to perform the operation or not. Assume only two possibilities—either recovery or death.
8. A car air-conditioning manufacturing unit is considering whether to release a new model in the market or to continue further testing to make it problem-free in operation. Releasing it immediately will ensure good sales, since no other competitor

is there for this type of model. However, this would involve an estimated risk of 12% because of serious operational problems which may tarnish the image of the unit and result in decreasing the revenue from ₹150 lakhs to ₹75 lakhs. However, another four months of testing would reduce the chance of problems to 6%, but there will be an estimated 8% risk of a competitor developing a similar model and, in that case, a loss of revenue to the extent of 20% will result. However, even after testing for four months, if there is any problem, the revenue will become half. Use a decision tree to calculate the EMV of the options to decide what the unit should do.

9. Draw a decision table for the following discount policy of a distributor of mobile cell phones. If the order is more than 5,000 units, allow a 3% discount. If delivery is within 45 km, allow a 2% discount; if not already given the 3% quantity discount as above, otherwise only a 1% discount is to be allowed. A further discount of 2% will be allowed to a retailer if the total purchase made during the last 12 months is 2 lakh units or more.
10. An employee payroll system computes the salary of the employees as follows: The employees can be workers, supervisors or managers. If the employees work more than 160 hours in a month, they are given fixed salary plus extra amount per hour at the rate of ₹200, 100 and 50 for a manager, a supervisor and a worker respectively. In case any of them works more than 200 hours per month, he/she is given an additional allowance of ₹600 per month irrespective of the category of the employee. Prepare a decision table to show the above decision rules and the associated extra payments for each category of the employees.

Bibliography

Bellman, R. E., and L. A. Zadeh. 'Decision-making in a Fuzzy Environment'. *Management Science* 17, no. 4 (1970): 141–164.

Quinlan, J. R. 'Simplifying Decision Trees'. *International Journal of Man-Machine Studies* 27, no. 3 (1987): 221–234.

Ross, R. G. 'Decision Tables, Part 1~The Route to Consolidated Business Logic'. *Business Rules Journal* 6, no. 7 (2005). Available at: http://www.brcommunity.com/a2005/b240.html (accessed on 26 March 2020).

Ross, R. G. 'Decision Tables, Part 2~The Route to Completeness'. *Business Rules Journal* 6, no. 8 (2005). Available at: http://www.brcommunity.com/a2005/b243.html (accessed on 26 March 2020).

Ross, R. G. 'Designing Decision Tables Part 1: Basics'. *Business Rules Journal* 15, no. 4 (April 2014). Available at: http://www.brcommunity.com/a2014/b754.html (accessed on 26 March 2020).

Ross, R. G. 'Designing Decision Tables Part 2: Fundamental Styles'. *Business Rules Journal* 15, no. 5 (2014). Available at: http://www.brcommunity.com/a2014/b759.html (accessed on 26 March 2020).

Ross, R. G. 'Designing Decision Tables Part 3: Representing Meaning (Semantics)'. *Business Rules Journal* 15, no. 6 (2014). Available at: http://www.brcommunity.com/a2014/b764.html (accessed on 26 March 2020).

Simon, H. A. 'A Behavioural Model of Rational Choice'. *The Quarterly Journal of Economics* 69, no. 1 (1955): 99–118.

Simon, H. A. 'Bounded Rationality and Organizational Learning'. *Organization Science* 2, no. 1 (1991): 125–134.

Wagner, H. M. *Principles of Operations Research with Application to Managerial Decisions*, 2nd ed. Englewood Cliffs, NJ: Prentice Hall, 1975.

4 Decision Support Systems

4.1 Introduction

Information system (IS) designers, researchers and technology experts had been developing and investigating decision support systems (DSSs) for nearly four decades. This development in DSS started with building model-driven DSS in the early 1970s, theory development in the late 1970s and the implementation of financial planning systems, spreadsheet DSS and group DSS in the early and mid-1980s. DSSs represent systems to support decision-making. In the context of business organisations, decision-making includes all types of decisions taken by managers at all levels in the hierarchy. In fact, DSSs are models which analyse business data into information to facilitate quality decisions. DSS applications are systems and subsystems that help managers to make decisions based on data from a wide range of sources.

4.2 Taxonomies

As with the definition, there is no universally accepted taxonomy of DSS. Different authors propose different classifications. Hatten Schwiler differentiates passive, active and cooperative DSS. A passive DSS is a system that aids the process of decision-making, but cannot bring about explicit decisions, suggestions or solutions. An active DSS can bring about such decisions, suggestions or solutions. A cooperative DSS allows the decision-maker (or its advisor) to modify, complete or refine the decision suggestions provided by the system, before sending them back to the system for validation. The system again improves, completes and refines the suggestions of the decision-makers and sends them back to them for validation. The whole process then starts again, until a consolidated solution is generated.

Alter classified DSSs into six types. His classification was based on what the user does with them. The first and the simplest type of DSS is the one that retrieves isolated data items. A common example of this type of DSS is a shop floor IS, wherein the shop supervisor juggles this information to obtain productivity data by operation, machine or operator-wise. The second type of DSS is the one that both retrieves and analyses the data, such as a portfolio analysis system in a bank. The third type of DSS is the one that uses multiple databases and obtains prespecified aggregation of data in the form of reports. An example of this type of DSS is the sales IS. The fourth type of DSS is the one that evaluates decisions using an accounting or simulation model. The purpose is to find the consequences of alternative decisions. Examples of this type of DSS are accounting models for source and application of funds, marketing decision systems such

DOI: 10.4324/9781003509714-4

as levels of advertisement, pricing and many others. The fifth type of DSS proposes decisions by mathematical modelling and optimisation techniques known as programming. An example of this type of DSS includes optimisation of resource allocation and usage. Operational research (OR) techniques come under the purview of this category. The sixth and the latest type of DSS is one that makes decisions. This type of system is applicable in cases where the decisions are highly structured and programmable. The sixth type of DSS is usually online and real time in nature such as process control, airline seat reservations and many such applications.

Another taxonomy for DSS has been created by Daniel Power, according to the mode of assistance as the criterion, namely communication-driven DSS, data-driven DSS, document-driven DSS, knowledge-driven DSS and model-driven DSS. A communication-driven DSS supports more than one person working on a shared task such as Microsoft's 'NetMeeting' and 'Groove' for a peer-to-peer solution. A data-driven DSS or data-oriented DSS emphasises access to and manipulation of a time series of organisational data and external data to yield decision-assisting information. A document-driven DSS manages, retrieves and manipulates unstructured information in a variety of electronic formats. A knowledge-driven DSS provides specialised problem-solving expertise stored as facts, rules, procedures in similar or in other forms. Certain expert systems are knowledge-driven DSSs.

A model-driven DSS emphasises according to manipulation of a statistical, financial, optimisation or simulation model. Model-driven DSS uses data and parameters provided by users to assist decision-makers in analysing a situation; they are not necessarily data intensive. General Purpose Simulation System (GPSS) and Arena 5.0 are examples of computer-driven simulation models.

Power mentioned two different types of DSS, namely enterprise-wide DSS and desktop DSS. An enterprise-wide DSS is linked to large data warehouses and serves many managers at all levels in the organisation. A desktop with single-user DSS is a small system that runs on an individual manager's PC, such as a spreadsheet model developed by a manager on his computer. In fact, there can be a third type known as group decision support system (GDSS), which facilitates decisions taken by a group of managers collectively.

A study and analysis of the DSSs for managerial decision-making reveal that not every DSS fits into one category or architecture exactly, but the DSSs often are a mixture of more than one architecture.

Holsapple and Whinston classified DSS into six frameworks. Those are text-oriented DSS, database-oriented DSS, spreadsheet-oriented DSS, solver-oriented DSS, rule-oriented DSS and compound DSS. A compound DSS is the most popular classification of a DSS. It is a hybrid system that includes more than one of the first five frameworks as mentioned above.

4.3 Components of a DSS

The main components or subsystems of a DSS are the following (Figure 4.1):

1. User interface subsystem
2. Database management subsystem
3. Model base management subsystem
4. The users (decision-makers) themselves.

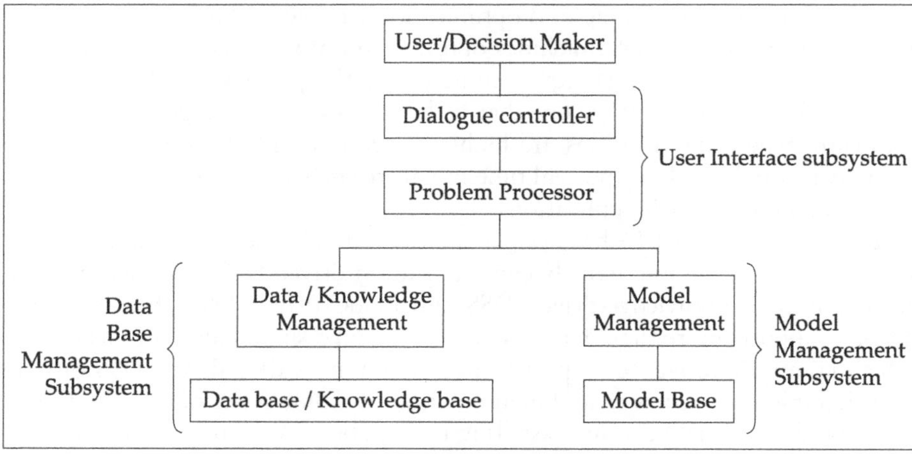

Figure 4.1 Components of a DSS

Generally, a DSS has three major components:

1. The data and knowledge management subsystem, which is a body of knowledge and data, selects the particular model that fits into the specific problem and also the data that must be fed into the model by manipulating the database.
2. The language system, which is the total medium of communication between the decision-maker and the DSS for decision-making based on the data and models made available to him/her, also provides help facilities to the user/decision-maker.
3. The problem processor is the interface between the language system (dialogue controller) and the knowledge and data subsystems. The problem processor contains algorithms for tools and techniques such as discrete simulation, statistical techniques for regression analysis, trend analysis and projection, linear programming, integer programming and dynamic programming.

4.4 Model Management System: Arena 5.0

As an illustration of a model management system, let us highlight the features of Arena 5.0. Arena 5.0 was developed by Rockwell Software, California, USA, for the purpose of computer simulation to mimic the behaviour of real systems on computer to enable decision-makers to have forward visibility of the systems on computer and to further enable decision-makers to test the outcome of what-if type of decisions relating to those systems. Unlike special purpose simulation languages such as GPSS, SIMSCRIPT and SLAM, Arena 5.0 combines the ease of use found in high-level simulators with the flexibility of simulation languages and even all the way down to general purpose programming languages such as the Microsoft Visual Basic programming system or 'C'. Arena 5.0 does this by providing alternative and interchangeable templates of graphical simulation modelling and analysis modules that one can combine to build a fairly wide variety of simulation models. For the ease of display, organisational modules are typically grouped into panels to compose a template. By switching panels, one can gain access to a whole different set of simulation modelling constructs and capabilities.

Arena 5.0 is flexible in modelling because of its hierarchical structure with a single graphical user interface consistent at any level of modelling. At the lower end of the hierarchy are user-written codes in Visual Basic, C/C++, and at the higher end are user-created templates which are constructs on company-specific processes. The intermediate levels of modelling may include elementary blocks of SIMAN simulation language, advanced process and transfer panels, basic process panels and application solution templates such as assembly and testing lines. Arena 5.0 enables a manager/decision-maker to do the following tasks:

1. Model processes to define, document and communicate.
2. Simulate the future performance of the business, to understand complex relationships among various parameters and to identify areas for improvement.
3. Visualise the operations and flow processes with dynamic animation graphics.
4. Plan for facilities for delivery of goods and services.
5. Analyse how the business system will perform in its current configuration and under a set of feasible 'to-be' alternatives so that one can confidently choose the best way or 'satisficing' way to run the business. Modelling and simulation enable the decision-makers to take decisions leading to business process improvement. The purpose of simulation models is to compare the current business processes with the unlimited realm of 'would be' processes in the best interest of the business. All these experiments are performed without disrupting the day-to-day operations.

Since the 1980s, business process improvement and simulation have become leading methodologies to allow corporations to deliver high-quality products and services through business process modelling (BPM). Businesses are seeking not only to automate existing operations, but to re-engineer business processes to achieve customer satisfaction through the delivery of products and services on time at a competitive price. Simulation models have a wide scope and application for decision-making relating to BPR in diverse industries such as manufacturing, petrochemical, food processing, transport, power transmission and distribution and also the service sector.

4.4.1 Salient Features of Arena

The main features of Arena are as follows:

1. **Basic Process Panel**: The basic process panel consists of flow-chart modules and data modules. Flow-chart modules comprise create, process (resource), decide, assign, batch, separate, record and dispose. The data modules consist of entity, queue, resource, schedule, set and variable. Figure 4.2 shows the pictorial representation of these modules of the basic process panel in Arena 5.0.
2. **Statistical Distributions**: Arena 5.0 contains a set of built-in functions for generating random numbers involving the commonly used probability distributions, such as beta, continuous, discrete, Erlang, exponential, gamma, Johnson, log-normal, normal, Poisson, triangular, uniform and Weibull.
3. **Picture Libraries**: The picture libraries in Arena 5.0 consist of pictures of basic processes, buildings, equipment, faces, factories, machines, medical objects, offices and office equipment, people, symbols, vehicles and workers.

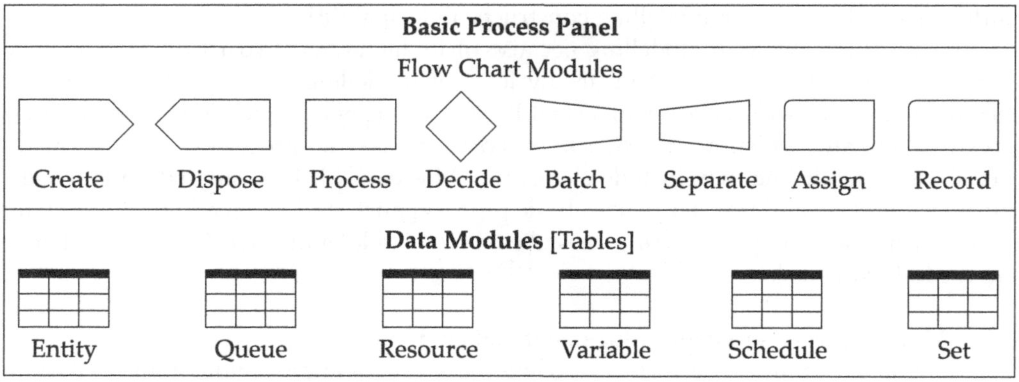

Figure 4.2 Basic Process Panel (Arena 5.0)

Illustrative Example 1: To illustrate the decision support capability of the Arena 5.0 system, let us consider the following facilities planning example for delivering public service by the regional transport authority of a state for delivering road permits to owners of light vehicles. The owners are divided into three types based on their car registration numbers. The owners arrive and enter one of the three queues before the three counters. The three independent arrival streams follow exponential inter-arrival time distribution with a mean of 10 minutes for each stream. Each counter is manned by a single clerk who processes the application forms and accepts payment for the road permit. The service time is uniform (8, 10) minutes for all the three counters. After completing the formalities at the counters, all owners are sent to a second clerk who checks the payment receipts and issues the permits for all types of owners. The service time for this activity is uniform (2.66, 3.33) minutes for all types of owners. Let us develop a model of this system and run the simulation for 10 days of 6 hours of work each day and obtain the results. Also, let us consider a BPR by making a single counter with three clerks to cater to the checking of application forms and receive payment, where all types of owners can arrive with the same statistics of inter-arrival time and let us find the results for a similar time period. Finally, in order to decide on the service strategy of having either three separate reporting counters with one clerk for each counter or having a single counter with three clerks, let us compare the results to decide the better strategy for service quality in terms of average waiting time.

The created simulation model is as shown in Figure 4.3 where the three types of owners (1, 2 and 3) arrive in three different streams and line up before the application processing and payment (cash) receipt counters 1, 2 and 3 respectively. The create 1, 2 and 3 are the basic process modules for creating entities (owners of the three types) with inter-arrival time exponentially distributed with a mean of 10 minutes.

The entities created by the create modules 1, 2, 3 are assigned attributes of arrival time ('TNOW' the parametric representation of the same by Arena 5.0) by the modules assigned 1, 2 and 3 respectively. The entities seize the resources (counter 1, 2 and 3 respectively) depending upon their types (owner 1, 2 and 3) for the processing of applications and obtaining cash receipts for payments made by them, and the process involves delay (processing time). Finally, the entities release (leave) the resource (respective counter) for the next entity (owner for that counter). The waiting time for an entity consists

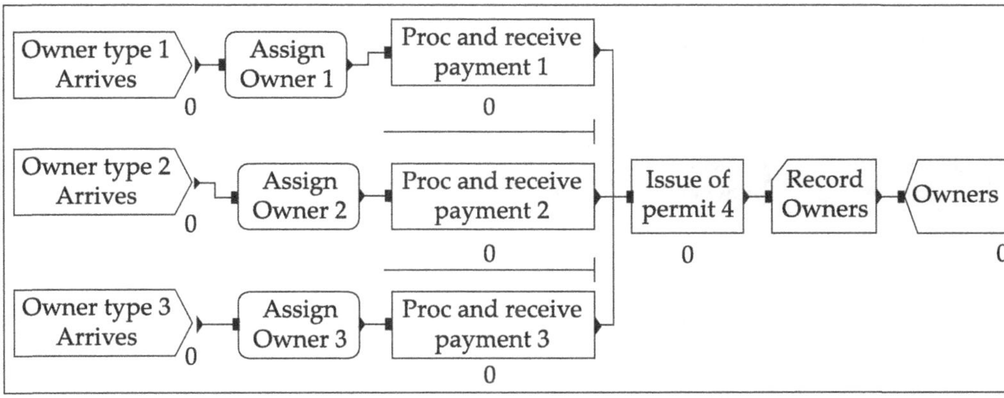

Figure 4.3 Simulation Model with Three Processing Counters in Parallel

of the processing time (time taken by the clerk at the counter) plus waiting time, if any, in the queue before the counter. The processing time of an application including the payment receipt time has been assumed to have a uniform distribution within 8 and 10 minutes. The entities (all types of owners) next arrive at counter 4 for the issue of their permits, and the process of issue of permits has also been assumed to have a uniform distribution within 2.66 and 3.33 minutes. The waiting time for each entity in this counter similarly consists of the waiting time, if any, in the queue plus the time for the issue of the permit by the clerk. Finally, from counter 4, the entities are disposed of, depicted by the disposal module, which records the statistical results of the simulation run. Before the disposal module, there is a record module also to record certain attribute statistics of the entities, for example, the time interval between arrival time and disposal time.

The model has been run for 10 days consisting of 6 hours working by the clerks per day, and the number of replications was 1. The picture on completion of the run is as shown in Figure 4.4. It can be seen that 1,056 numbers of entities were created (328 + 377 + 351) and finally 1,040 numbers were disposed of, and 16 numbers (2 + 9 + 3 + 2) are in queue and under processing in counters 1, 2, 3 and 4 respectively.

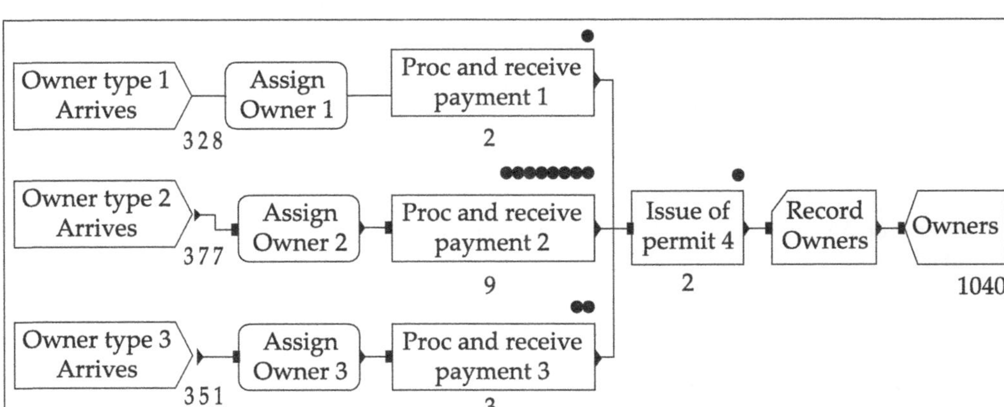

Figure 4.4 Status after Completion of the Simulation Run for the First Model

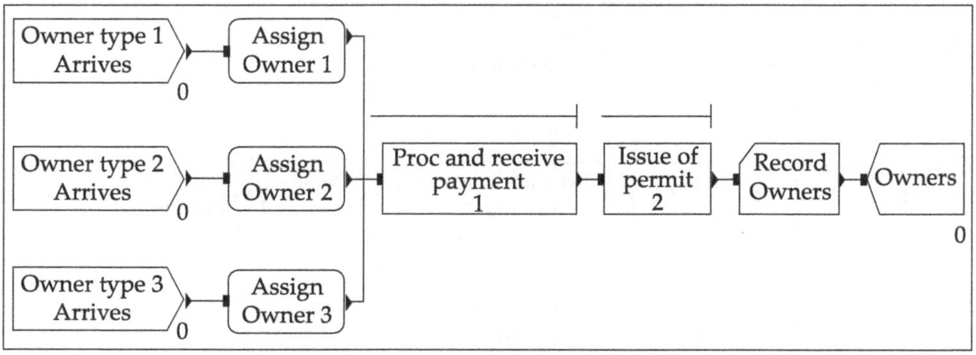

Figure 4.5 Simulation Model with One Processing and Payment Receipt Counter

Next, the arrangement is changed by making only one processing of application and payment receipt counter having three clerks who can process any of the applications, and the owners of all types have to line up before the counter. The inter-arrival time for the three types of owners and the processing time have been assumed to be the same as in the previous model. The capacity of the counter has been made three in each six-hour day working. The second model is shown in Figure 4.5 and the picture on completion of the simulation run is shown in Figure 4.6. The second model is also run for 10 days of 6 hours working each day. The statistical result relating to queues and resource utilisation for Model 1 and Model 2 is shown in Figures 4.7–4.10 respectively. It can be seen from the same figures that Model 2 has shown better performance results compared to those for Model 1 in terms of both waiting time and resource utilisation.

4.5 DSS Generators

DSS generators are computer software that facilitate developing DSSs by the decision-makers to enable them to take effective and efficient decisions. Spreadsheets such as Microsoft Excel are one of the DSS generators. Extensive use of spreadsheet software is made by managers or decision-makers for financial planning systems such as the interactive financial planning system (IFPS) developed by Wagner. The earlier spreadsheet

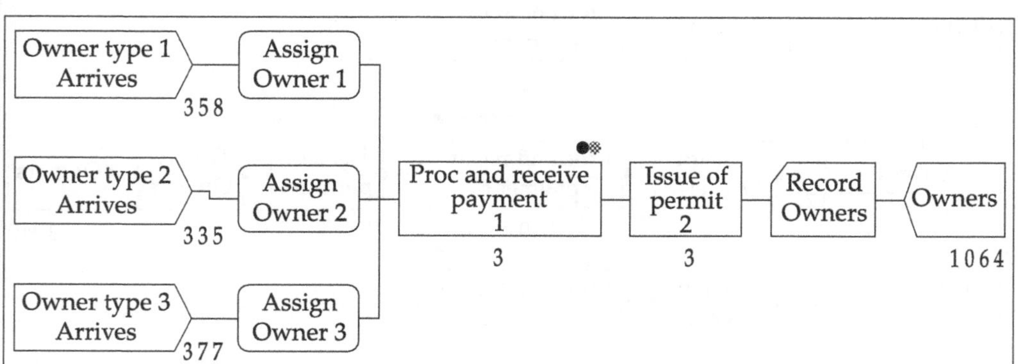

Figure 4.6 Status after Completion of the Simulation Run for the Second Model

Queues			
			Replications: 1
Replications: 1 Start Time: 0.00 Stop Time: 3,600.00 Time Units: **Minutes**			
Queue Detail Summary			
Time		**Other**	
	Waiting Time		Number Waiting
Issue of permit Queue	2.00	Issue of permit Queue	0.58
Proc and receive payment 1. Queue	18.00	Proc and receive payment 1. Queue	1.64
Proc and receive payment 2. Queue	46.87	Proc and receive payment 2. Queue	4.91
Proc and receive payment 3. Queue	28.42	Proc and receive payment 3. Queue	2.76
Total	95.29	**Total**	9.89

Figure 4.7 Queues Statistical Results for Model 1

Resources						
						Replications: 1
Replications: 1 Start Time: 0.00 Stop Time: 3,600.00 Time Units: **Minutes**						
Resource Detail Summary						
Usage				**Other**		
	Number Busy	Number Scheduled	Utilization		Number Times Used	Schedule Utilization
Counter 4	0.86	1.00	0.86	Counter 4	1041.00	0.86
Counter 1	0.81	1.00	0.81	Counter 1	327.00	0.81
Counter 2	0.92	1.00	0.92	Counter 2	369.00	0.92
Counter 3	0.87	1.00	0.87	Counter 3	349.00	0.87

Figure 4.8 Resource Utilisation Statistical Results for Model 1

software was further developed into the programmable spreadsheets for ease of generating DSSs. Let us consider a simple example of a five-year plan for manufacturing and sales of an industry unit using a spreadsheet as a DSS, as shown in Tables 4.1 and 4.2 and the graphical output of the model in Figure 4.11 respectively. The plan is for the period from the financial year 2022–2023 to 2026–2027, considering the base year as 2022–2023.

The important characteristics of the spreadsheet DSS models are:

1. Capabilities to support mathematical and statistical functions and operations which enable it as a good DSS model generator particularly involving financial decision-making.
2. Multiple what-if type of scenario analysis.

Queues					
					Replications: 1
Replications: 1	Start Time:	0.00 Stop Time:	3,600.00	Time Units: **Minutes**	
Queue Detail Summary					
Time			**Other**		
	Waiting Time			Number Waiting	
Issue of permit Queue	2.29		Issue of permit Queue	0.68	
Proc and receive payment Queue	12.31		Proc and receive payment Queue	3.66	
Total	14.60		**Total**	4.34	

Figure 4.9 Queues Statistical Results for Model 2

Resources						
						Replications: 1
Replications: 1	Start Time:	0.00 Stop Time:	3,600.00	Time Units: **Minutes**		
Resource Detail Summary						
Usage				**Other**		
	Number Busy	Number Scheduled	Utilization		Number Times Used	Schedule Utilization
Counter 1	2.66	3.00	0.89	Counter 1	1070.00	0.89
Counter 2	0.88	1.00	0.88	Counter 2	1065.00	0.88

Figure 4.10 Resource Utilisation Statistical Results for Model 2

Table 4.1 Spreadsheet Sample Model for Manufacturing Planning

Profit = Sales – Total cost (TC)
Sales = Units × Price
TC = Fixed cost (FC) + Variable cost (VC)
Units (Nos.) = 10,000, previous × growth
Fixed cost (₹) = 600,000, previous × escalation-1 (ESC-1)
Variable cost = Units × Unit variable cost (UVC)
Unit variable cost (₹) (UVC) = 240, previous × escalation-2 (ESC-2)
Price = Total unit cost (TUC) + Margin
TUC = (FC + VC) / Units
Margin (%) = 25; growth (%) = 10; ESC-1 (%) = 4; ESC-2 (%) = 3

Table 4.2 Results of Spreadsheet Sample Model

Years					
Variables	2022–23	2023–24	2024–25	2025–26	2026–27
Growth		0.10	0.10	0.10	0.10
Units (Nos.)	10,000	11,000	12,100	13,310	14,641
ESC-1		0.04	0.04	0.04	0.04
FC (₹)	600,000	624,000	648,960	674,918	701,915
ESC-2		0.03	0.03	0.03	0.03
UVC (₹)	240	247	255	262	270
VC (₹)	2,400,000	2,717,000	3,085,500	3,487,220	3,953,070
Margin	0.25	0.25	0.25	0.25	0.25
TUC = (FC + VC) / Units	300	304	309	313	318
Price (TUC + 0.25 × TUC)	375	380	386	391	398
Sales (₹)	3,750,000	4,180,000	4,670,600	5,204,210	5,827,118
Total cost (₹)	3,000,000	3,341,000	3,734,460	4,162,138	4,654,985
Profit (₹)	750,000	839,000	936,140	1,042,072	1,172,133

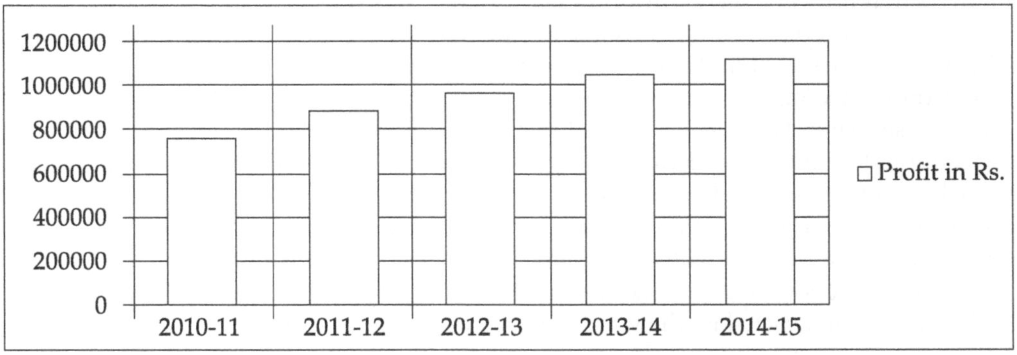

Figure 4.11 Graphical Representation of the Spreadsheet Sample Model on Profit Plan

3. Programming features as in Microsoft Excel.
4. Goal-seeking capabilities.
5. Sensitivity analysis leading to optimum solution of a problem.
6. Built-in capability to support corporate database and scanning the same.
7. Powerful report generation and graphical user interface (GUI).

4.5.1 Analytica Software as a DSS Generator

Lumina Decision Systems, Inc., California, USA, has developed a software Analytica (4.2) beyond the spreadsheet, which uses the Influence diagram concept to model the essential qualitative nature of the decision problem to arrive at either the optimum or near-optimum solution of the problem. Using a visual point-and-click approach, one can draw nodes and arrows to depict the relationship among the model components which can be variables, modules, decision variables, objectives, chance variables and so on. Another important feature of Analytica is the use of intelligent arrays which allow anyone to add or remove dimensions such as time periods, locations, various conditions and the associated parameters.

The added features of Analytica over the spreadsheets are:

1. Analytica separates the dimensions from relationships so that one need not repeat formulae when new dimensions are added, or existing dimensions are deleted.
2. It is faster in speed of computation.
3. Each node or object in an Analytica model has a window that displays the inputs and outputs of the node, definitions, descriptions and units of measure whose features make Analytica easier and more user-friendly. Further, Analytica also has a built-in capability of integrated risk and sensitivity analysis for analysing models with uncertain inputs. It has also got powerful facilities for time-dependent dynamic situations, powerful GUI and more than 200 financial, statistical and scientific functions inbuilt with the software.

4.5.1.1 Influence Diagram

An Influence diagram is a graphical representation of a model, showing the relationships and interactions among the different variables (factors) in a model. A typical influence diagram consists of a number of nodes connected by arrows. The nodes may include modules to represent a hierarchy of Influence diagrams to depict a complex model, where the lower-level modules are represented as modular nodes in the higher-level diagrams. The typical nodes used in Analytica are shown in Figure 4.12.

Illustrative Example 2: Let me illustrate the influence diagram with a simple car-cost model as shown in Figure 4.13. Annual fuel cost in rupees for a car over a period of years depends on the annual kilometres run by the car (assumed 12,000 km), kilometres per litre of fuel (petrol or diesel) defined as 15 for a new car and 11 for a hired second-hand car and fuel price per litre is ₹45 for the current year, with the expected rate of inflation of fuel price per year assumed to be normally distributed with a mean of 3.5% and a standard deviation 1.5% and the period (in this model assumed from 5 to 10 years in steps of 1 year).

This has been depicted by the way of connecting the nodes for annual kilometres, km/l, inflation (a chance variable), fuel price and period with arrows terminating at the fuel cost node. The total cost of buying (if the decision is to buy a new car) is dependent on the fuel cost for a new car (at 15 km/l) and the buying cost of a new car (assumed ₹3 lakhs, that is, three hundred thousand). This is represented in the Influence diagram by connecting the

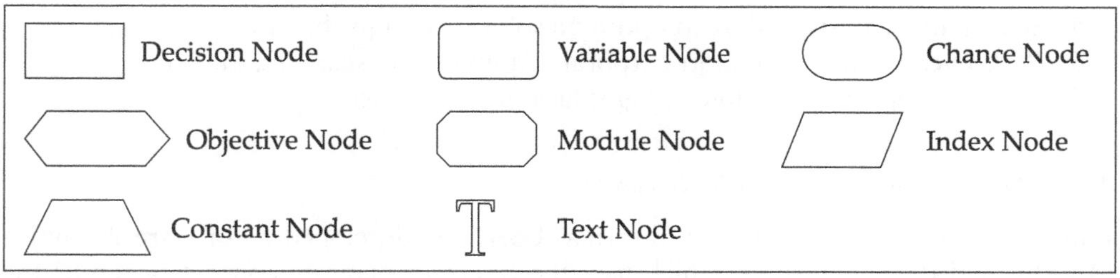

Figure 4.12 Nodes in Analytica

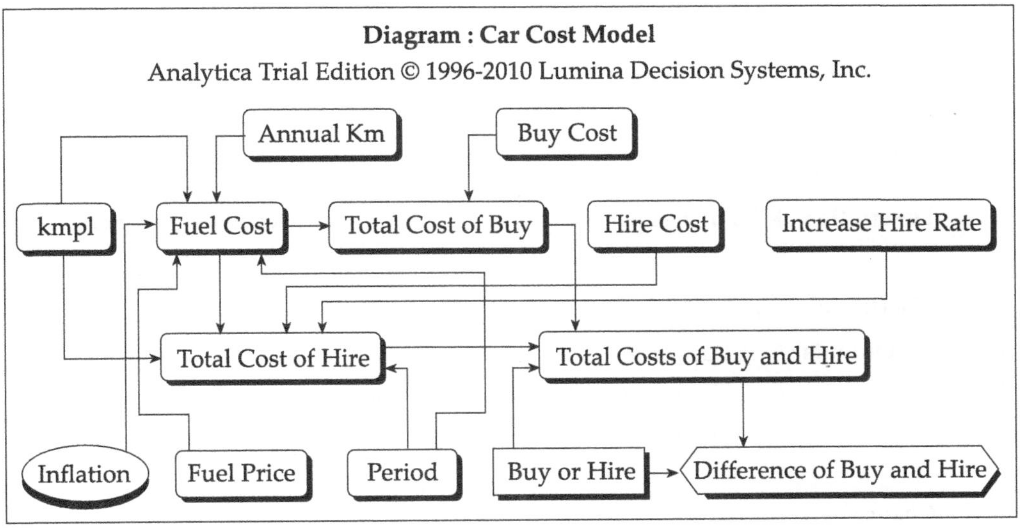

Figure 4.13 Influence Diagram for Car Cost Model

nodes for buying cost and fuel cost to the total cost of buying with arrows. Similarly, the total cost of hiring a car (if the decision is to hire a second-hand car) is dependent on the hire cost (assumed in this case ₹10,000 per month), the contractual rate of increase in hire rate every year (assumed 5% on the previous year rate) over the period under consideration by the decision-maker (to decide whether to buy or to hire) and the fuel cost for hiring a second-hand car (at 11 km/l). This has been represented by connecting the nodes accordingly with the node for total cost of hire. Next, the decision whether to buy or hire is dependent on the total cost of buying vis-à-vis hire. This is represented by the variable node of the total costs of buying and hire indexed by buy or hire which is a decision variable as represented by the 'buy or hire' node which is a decision node. Therefore, the variable nodes representing the total cost of buy, total cost of hire and the decision variable buy or hire (which is a list of 'buy' and 'hire') are connected with arrows with the total cost of buy and hire node. Finally, the objective has been represented as the difference between the total cost of buy and total cost of hire over the period of time which decides the choice of the decision-maker.

The definitions of some of the variable nodes, decision node, chance node and the objective node as explained earlier are shown in Figures 4.14–4.17 respectively, which show the windows of the nodes separately as obtained by double clicking on the node icons. Any of the nodes can be deleted or new nodes can be added or connected without repeating the definition and modifying the formulae of the affected nodes which are automatically modified by Analytica. The results associated with any module of the car-cost model can be obtained by clicking only once on the module and then clicking on the result button on the tool menu bar. The result as obtained with the values of the model for the module of total costs of buying and hire is shown in Figure 4.18 for the period varying from 5 years to 10 years. The result shows that for a period up to 7.5 years, it is economical to hire a car but beyond that it is economical to buy a car. The same result is shown in Figure 4.19 in the graphical form. Analytica has also got options for showing the results in various statistical forms such as probability bands and cumulative probability distribution of probable values.

Object : kmpl

Analytica Trial Edition c 1996-2010 Lumina Decision Systems, Inc.

Variable kmpl **Units :** Killometers/Litre

Title : kmpl

Description : Killo-meters per litre

Definition : Edit Table indexed by kmpl

Outputs : Fuel_cost — Fuel cost

Total_cost_of_buy — Total cost of buy

Total_cost_of_hire — Total cost of hire

kmpl [Killometers/Litre]

Buy	15
Hire	11

Chance I **Units :** %

Title : Inflation

Description : Rate of Inflation per year

Definition : Normal [3.5, 1.5]

Outputs : Fuel_cost — Fuel cost

Variable Period **Units :** Year

Title : Period

Description : Time Period of Analysis

List

Definition :

5
6
7
8
9
10

Outputs : Fuel_cost — Fuel cost

Total_cost_of_hire — Total cost of hire

Figure 4.14 Variable and Chance Nodes

The decision-maker who decides whether to buy a new car or hire a second-hand car can vary the range of variables such as their usage in terms of annual kilometres, fuel price for petrol or diesel cars and also the hiring period and rate, and buying cost of various models of cars to find out the best decision for the objective of minimising total cost.

Illustrative Example 3: Let us consider a two-branch decision tree for deciding a location for arranging a party. The decision tree is shown in the upper portion of Figure 4.20. The equivalent Analytica model (influence diagram) is shown in the lower portion of the

Object : Fuel Cost

Analytica Trial Edition c 1996-2010 Lumina Decision Systems, Inc.

Variable	Fuel_cost	**Units :** Rs
Title :	Fuel cost	
Description :		
	expr	
Definition :	Annual_kms*Fuel_price*period*[1 + I/100]^Period/kmpl	
Inputs :	Annual_kms	Annual Kms
	Fuel_price	Fuel Price
	I	Inflation
	Kmpl	kmpl
	Period	Period
Outputs :	Total_cost_of_buy	Total cost of buy
	Total_cost_of_hire	Total cost of hire

Figure 4.15 Variable Node Fuel Cost

same figure. The decision-maker's problem is to select a clubhouse location for a party which will provide the optimum value to the decision-maker. The value depends on the weather, temperature and the location. Three locations have been considered, namely outdoor, porch and indoor. The weather condition is a chance variable and can be either sunny or rainy and is defined as a probabilistic table indexed by weather table (list of two labels, i.e., sunny or rainy) as shown in Figure 4.21. The input to the weather is the probability of sunshine (p), which is the probability that the sun will be shining on the day of the party. This is the range of probabilities from 0 to 1, and the decision-maker has to select one value or all, using the pop-up menu. In this example, p has been assigned the value 0.4.

The temperature is also a probability table indexed by temperature (which can be cold, warm or hot) as shown in the domain of list of labels in Figure 4.21. The discrete probabilities associated with these labels are cold: 0.2, warm: 0.5 and hot: 0.3 respectively. The value to the decision-maker is the objective node that computes the value to the decision-maker for each possible outcome of location—weather—temperature, by assigning a rupee value to each combination. The decision-maker selects the prospect (party location) which has the highest EV. The EV (mean value) for a given location is the average of the values of the outcomes for that location, weighted by their probabilities.

The value to the decision-maker is defined as a multidimensional deterministic table indexed by temperature, weather and party location. The deterministic values are as shown in Figure 4.22. The results of the model (mean value to the decision-maker) are as shown in Figure 4.23. Also shown in Figure 4.23 are the cumulative probabilities for possible values to the decision-maker associated with each of the three locations. It may be noted that Analytica simulates all probability distributions and calculates the expected (mean) value of a distribution by computing the average of the samples.

Object : Total cost of buy

Analytica Trial Edition c 1996-2010 Lumina Decision Systems, Inc.

Variable	Total_cost_of_buy	**Units :** Rs.	
Title :	Total cost of buy		
Description :	Total Cost of buying a car		
	expr		
Definition :	Buy_cost + Fuel_cost [Kmpl = "Buy"]		
Inputs :	Buy_cost	BUY COST	
	Fuel_cost	Fuel Cost	
	Kmpl	kmpl	
Outputs :	Total_costs_of_buy_a	Total costs of buy and hire	
Variable	Total_cost_of_hire	**Units :** Rs.	
Title :	Total cost of hire		
Description :	Total Cost of hiring a second hand car		
	expr		
Definition :	Fuel_cost [Kmpl = 'Hire'] + Hire_cost*12*[1 + Increase_hire_rate/100]^ Period		
Inputs :	Fuel_cost	Fuel Cost	
	Hire_cost	Hire cost	
	Increase_hire_rate	Increase hire rate	
	Kmpl	kmpl	
	Period	Period	
Outputs :	Total_costs_of_buy_a	Total costs of buy and hire	

Figure 4.16 Variable Nodes

For a discrete distribution (like the party location model), the computed mean converges, with increasing sample size towards the value obtained by multiplying the probabilities with the discrete outcome values. According to the result shown in Figure 4.23, the location 'indoors' for the party returns the highest EV to the decision-maker of ₹2,300 and hence the same has to be chosen. The idea behind showing the above illustrative examples of applications of Analytica is only to demonstrate how to generate DSS models using Analytica. However, those readers who are interested in knowing the details including advanced features of Analytica may refer to Analytica Tutorial Release 4.2.

4.6 Multiple-Criteria Decision Analysis (MCDA)

Decision-making in a real-life situation is typically a complex and confusing analysis, characterised by trade-offs between multiple criteria such as cost, quality, sociopolitical and economic factors such as growth, employment and pollution. Cost–benefit analysis is

Object : Buy or hire

Analytica Trial Edition c 1996-2010 Lumina Decision Systems, Inc.

Decision Buy_or_hire **Units :**

Title : Buy or hire

Description : Buy or hire

Definition : Buy
Hire

Outputs : Diff_of_buy_and_hir Diff. of Buy and hire
Total_cost_of_buy_a Total costs of buy and hire

Variable Total_cost_of_buy_a **Units :** Rs.

Title : Total costs of buy and hire

Description : Total costs of buy and hire

1, 2

Definition : Edit Table indexed by Buy or hire

Inputs : Buy_or_hire Buy or hire
Total_cost_of_buy Total cost of buy
Total_cost_of_hire Total cost of hire

Outputs : Diff_of_buy_and_hir Diff. of Buy and hire

Objective Diff_of_buy_and_hir **Units :** Rs.

Title : Diff. of Buy and hire

Description : Difference of buy and hire

expr

Definition : Total_costs_of_buy_a [Buy_or_hire= 'Buy']-Total_costs_of_buy_a [Buy _or_hire = 'Hire']

Inputs : Buy_or_hire Buy or hire
Total_cost_of_buy_a Total costs of buy and hire

Figure 4.17 Decision Variable and Objective Nodes

often used for such projects as building a new railway station or a new technology-based oil refinery. Sensitivity and risk analysis are also often carried out among the competing factors. However, unlike a single criterion optimisation decision problem, MCDA calls for consideration of the competing multiple objectives. Further, some of the criteria cannot be easily condensed into a monetary value, which complicates the integration problem inherent in making comparisons and trade-offs. Even if it is possible to convert multiple criteria into a common unit, this approach is based on subjective assessment and may not always include all stakeholders' preferences, which may be lost in the process.

Print Preview

Analytica Trial Edition c 1996-2010 Lumina Decision Systems, Inc.

Fuel Price [Rs.] ⇨ **45**

Buy or hire

▼ **Period [Year]** ▶

	5	6	7	8	9	10
Buy	513.8K	565.5K	620.6K	679.2K	741.6K	807.8K
Hire	444.7K	522.9K	606.1K	694.4K	788.3K	887.9K

Figure 4.18 Total Costs of Buy and Hire

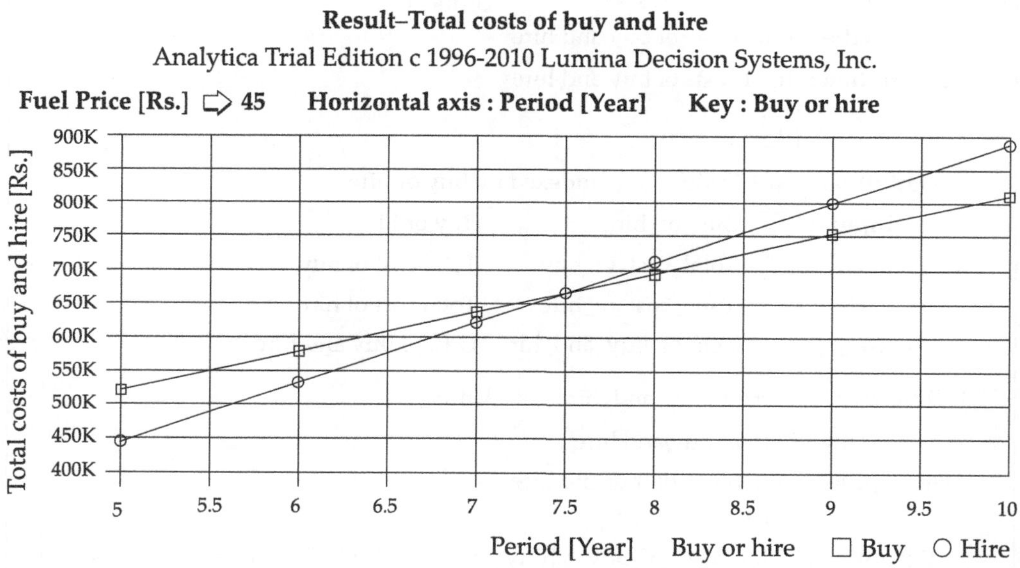

Figure 4.19 Results—Total Cost of Buy and Hire (Graphical)

Considerable research in the areas of MCDA has developed practical methods for applying scientific decision approaches to multiple-criteria problems.

4.6.1 MCDA Methods

There are many MCDA methods that have evolved over the years. They are based on different theoretical foundations and behavioural sciences such as optimisation, goal aspiration or outranking or a combination of them. However, the following are the five popular approaches to MCDA that are discussed.

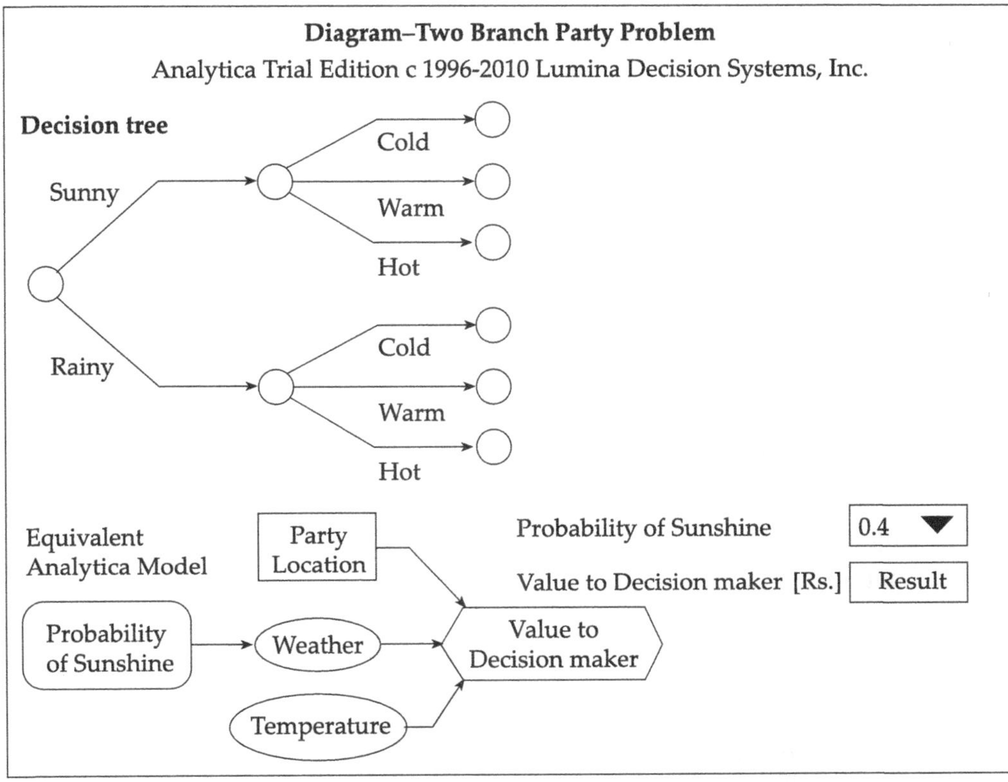

Figure 4.20 Decision Tree and Influence Diagram for Two-Branch Party Location Problem

4.6.1.1 *Elementary Methods*

These methods intended to convert complex problems to a singular basis for the selection of a preferred alternative. For example, an elementary method may rank alternatives in terms of number of performance or criteria thresholds met or exceeded, and the one achieving the maximum number may be chosen. Some of the elementary methods are pros and cons analysis, such as strengths, weaknesses, opportunities and threats (SWOT) analysis, decision-tree analysis, and influence diagrams. However, the elementary methods, though simple and capable of being executed even without the help of computer software, are best suited for single decision-maker problems involving a few alternatives and criteria and, as such, are not suited to real-life situations involving MCDA.

4.6.1.2*Multi-attribute Utility/Value Theory (MAUT/MAVT)*

MAUT/MAVT is a technique for formally drawing multiple perspectives and evaluations into the decision-making process. The goal of this approach is to find a simple expression for the decision-makers' preferences. Through the use of utility/value functions, this approach transforms diverse criteria (often conflicting in nature) such as price, safety, reliability and comfort into one common dimensional scale of utility/value. The main considerations used in MAUT/MVAT are: (1) how great the score is and (2) the relative

Object –Weather

Analytica Trial Edition c 1996-2010 Lumina Decision Systems, Inc.

Chance Weather **Units :**

Title : Weather

Description : Weather has two possible values : sunny or rainy. It is defined as a discrete distribution, using the Probability of Sunshine

1, 2

Definition : Prob Table indexed by Weather

Domain : List of Labels

sunny
rainy

Inputs : P Probability of Sunshine

Outputs : Value_to_me Value to Decision maker

Chance Temperature **Units :**

Title : Temperature

Description : Temperature is modeled as being cold, warm, or hot. It is defined as a discrete probability distribution

1, 2

Definition : Prob Table indexed by Temperature

Domain : List of Labels

Cold
Warm
Hot

Outputs : Value_to_me Value to Decision maker

Figure 4.21 Chance Variables: Weather and Temperature

importance (weighting) of the criteria being measured compared to all the other criteria. MAUT/MVAT follows a systematic approach of identifying the key attributes of a problem and then the top-level attributes are split into finer attributes in a top-down fashion. The steps in the MAUT/MVAT analysis are as follows:

- **Step 1**: Identify the key attributes (criteria).
- **Step 2**: Define weightage for the attributes based on decision maker's preferences.
- **Step 3**: Define the attribute levels and the scoring scale.
- **Step 4**: For each alternative, we have to define the level (rating) for the qualitative attributes based on subjective assessment and considering all the other alternatives.

Temperature **Cold**

Party Location

Weather

	Sunny	Rainy
Outdoors	3000	0
Perch	2500	1000
Indoors	2000	2500

Temperature **Warm**

Sunny	Rainy
5000	0
4500	1000
2000	2500

Hot

Sunny	Rainy
3500	0
3000	1500
2000	2500

Figure 4.22 Value to Decision-Maker in Rupees Regarding Party Location

Party Location	Expected values [Rs.]
Outdoors	1687.50
Porch	2180.00
Indoors	2300.00

Party Location

Possible values to Author [Rs.]

	0	1000	1500	2000	2500	3000	3500	4500	5000
Outdoors	0.6	0.6	0.6	0.6	0.6	0.67	0.785	0.785	1
Porch	0	0.415	0.6	0.6	0.67	0.785	0.785	1	1
Indoors	0	0	0	0.4	1	1	1	1	1

Figure 4.23 Results of the Model for Example 2

For the non-qualitative attributes, the actual quantitative values are to be assigned for each alternative.

- **Step 5**: Convert the levels for qualitative attributes into scores as per the scale (Step 3). For non-qualitative attributes, actual quantitative values need to remain.
- **Step 6**: For non-qualitative attributes, the best and worst levels are assessed and defined.
- **Step 7**: Normalisation of the scores for all attributes is done.
- **Step 8**: For all alternatives, the weighted average normalised scores (utility) are calculated and the alternative achieving the highest such score is considered.

The goal of the MAUT/MVAT approach is to maximise the utility/value, which is a compensatory optimisation approach. Nevertheless, MAUT/MVAT leads to a complete ranking of all the alternatives based on the decision-maker's preferences. The goal is not only to reach a forced 'consensus' through averaging different decision-makers/stakeholders weightages, but also to clarify the position and to test the feasibility of the objectives.

MAUT/MVAT relies on the assumption that the decision-maker is rational, that is, he/she prefers more to less, his/her preferences do not change, he/she has perfect knowledge and the preferences are transitive.

Implementation of considerations for MAUT/MVAT led to the development of the simple multi-attribute rating technique (SMART), which comprises simple utility relationships. SMART allows for the use of a shorter range of utility scales if the data do not discriminate widely. For example, in the case of SMART alternatives that are not significantly different with respect to a particular criterion, they can be assigned equal scores.

Illustrative Example 4—MAUT: A buyer of a car has to decide which car out of three choices, namely Alto, Swift Dzire and Santro Xing to select based on the criteria of price, fuel efficiency, performance, comfort, safety and reliability. This is a good case of MAUT application for the decision-maker. Let us proceed step by step as explained earlier.

Step 1: Identify the key attributes (criteria) which are price, fuel efficiency, performance, comfort, safety and reliability.

Step 2: Define weightages for the criteria based on the decision-maker's (buyer) preference. Let us assume the following weightage:

Attributes	*Weightage*
Price	100
Fuel efficiency	20
Performance	30
Comfort	30
Safety	20
Reliability	20

Step 3: Decide the attribute levels and the scoring scale. Let us assume the same as follows:

Attribute Level and Score

Attributes	Worst	Poor	Average	Good	Best
Price	0	25	50	75	100
Fuel efficiency	0	25	50	75	100
Performance	0	25	50	75	100
Comfort	0	25	50	75	100
Safety	0	25	50	75	100
Reliability	0	25	50	75	100

Step 4: For each alternative, the decision-maker has to assign a level for the qualitative attributes based on his subjective assessment and for the non-qualitative attributes, the actual values are to be assigned for each of the alternatives assumed as follows (figures are illustrative):

Attribute Levels

Attributes	*Alto*	*Santro Xing*	*Swift Dzire*
Price (₹.)	200,000	300,000	400,000
Fuel efficiency	20	15	18
Performance	Poor	Average	Average
Comfort	Good	Poor	Best
Safety	Good	Average	Best
Reliability	Best	Average	Good

Step 5: Convert the levels for the qualitative attributes into corresponding scores as per the scale decided in Step 3. For non-qualitative attributes, the actual values will remain.

Attribute Scores			
Attributes	*Alto*	*Santro Xing*	*Swift Dzire*
Price	200,000	300,000	400,000
Fuel efficiency	20	15	18
Performance	25	50	50
Comfort	75	25	100
Safety	75	50	100
Reliability	100	50	75

Step 6: For non-qualitative attributes, the best and worst levels are assessed by the decision-maker. Let us assume the best price is 100,000 and the worst price is 600,000. Similarly, the best fuel efficiency is 30 and the worst fuel efficiency is 5.

Step 7: Normalisation of the scores using the formula:

$$Normalised\ score = 100 \times (Actual\ score - Worst) / (Best - Worst)$$

The normalised scores for the attributes are accordingly computed and are as follows:

Normalised **Scores**			
Attributes	*Alto*	*Santro Xing*	*Swift Dzire*
Price	80	60	40
Fuel efficiency	60	40	52
Performance	25	50	50
Comfort	75	25	100
Safety	75	50	100
Reliability	100	50	75

Step 8: For each alternative, apply the weightage as shown in Step 2 for the attributes to the normalised scores to arrive at the weighted average scores for utility for the same alternative and finally, the choice is the one that gets the highest utility score.

For Alto = [(80 × 100) + (60 × 20) + (25 × 30) + (75 × 30) + (75 × 20) + (100 × 20)] / (100 + 20 + 30 + 30 + 20 + 20) = 71.36

Santro Xing = [(60 × 100) + (40 × 20) + (50 × 30) + (25 × 30) + (50 × 20) + (50 × 20)] / (100 + 20 + 30 + 30 + 20 + 20) = 67.27

Swift Dzire = [(40 × 100) + (52 × 20) + (50 × 30) + (100 × 30) + (100 × 20) + (75 × 20)] / (100 + 20 + 30 + 30 + 20 + 20) = 59.27

Alto, having the highest multi-attribute utility of 71.36 is to be considered by the buyer.

4.6.1.3 *Analytical Hierarchy Process (AHP)*

The AHP is a MCDA process developed by Saaty in 1980. Like MAUT, AHP also completely aggregates various aspects of the multiple-criteria decision problem into a single objective function. AHP also selects the alternative that results in the greatest value of the objective function. However, AHP adopts a quantitative comparison method based on a pairwise comparison by the decision-maker. Behavioural scientists believe that a human being can better compare two criteria at a time on their relative importance to them rather than comparing a number of criteria at a time and assigning weightage in order of relative importance. In other words, the AHP method relies on the supposition that human beings are more capable of making relative judgements than absolute judgements. In the case of AHP, evaluators express the intensity of a preference for one criterion versus another (pairwise comparison) using a nine-point scale as follows:

- 1—If the two criteria are equally important.
- 3—If one criterion is weekly/moderately more important than the other.
- 5—If one criterion is strongly more important than the other.
- 7—If one criterion is very strongly more important than the other.
- 9—If one criterion is absolutely/extremely more important than the other.

In AHP, all individual criteria or attributes are compared against all others and results are compiled in a matrix form. It may be stated that if a criterion i is compared with a criterion *j* and a value of importance of *i* with respect to *j* is a_{ji}, then the reciprocal score is awarded to the opposite relationship, that is, say if $a_{ij} = 5$ then, $a_{ji} = 1/5$. Obviously, $a_{ii} = 1$. The normalised weight is calculated for each criterion by dividing each element in a column of the matrix by the sum of all the elements in the same column. For a perfectly consistent decision-maker, each column should be identical. However, in case of small inconsistencies in the decision-making process, the same is corrected by averaging across each row, and the average figure will then represent the relative weight on the criterion as shown against that row. The normalised weights (after averaging) for all the criteria (all rows) should add up to 1 but may vary slightly because of half rounding or truncation of figures during computation. Let me illustrate the AHP by bringing the same example (as in the case of MAUT) of deciding by a buyer which car to purchase out of three choices, namely Alto, Santro and Swift, considering the preferences based on criteria of price, fuel efficiency, performance, comfort, safety and reliability.

Step 1: To determine the preferences for the criteria mentioned above by pairwise comparison on the nine-point scale and after getting all preferences, the following matrix is formed.

j						
i	*Price*	*Fuel Efficiency*	*Performance*	*Comfort*	*Safety*	*Reliability*
Price	1	5	3	3	5	5
Fuel efficiency	1/5	1	1/3	1/3	1	1
Performance	1/3	3	1	1	3	3
Comfort	1/3	3	1	1	3	3
Safety	1/5	1	1/3	1/3	1	1
Reliability	1/5	1	1/3	1/3	1	1

Step 2: Normalise the figures (elements) in each column of the matrix as obtained in Step 1 by the sum of all the elements in that column. For example, (price-safety) entry would end up as $(5/[5+1+3+3+1+1]) = 0.35$. The matrix finally obtained will be as shown below.

	Price	*Fuel Efficiency*	*Performance*	*Comfort*	*Safety*	*Reliability*	*Average*
Price	0.44	0.35	0.5	0.5	0.35	0.35	0.42
Fuel efficiency	0.09	0.07	0.06	0.06	0.07	0.07	0.07
Performance	0.15	0.12	0.17	0.17	0.21	0.21	0.18
Comfort	0.15	0.12	0.17	0.17	0.21	0.21	0.18
Safety	0.09	0.07	0.06	0.06	0.07	0.07	0.07
Reliability	0.09	0.07	0.06	0.06	0.07	0.07	0.07
							$\sum = 0.99$

All the columns should be identical, but we find small inconsistencies and hence we correct by averaging the figures in a row, and the same have been shown in the average column. The average figures added up to 0.99 (should be 1 if no truncation, half rounding).

Step 3: Next, we evaluate all three cars on each criterion separately. For instance, if we consider price, the importance of Alto will be more than either Santro or Swift because of the lowest price and we might get a matrix as follows:

Criterion: Price

	Alto	*Santro*	*Swift*
Alto	1	3	5
Santro	1/3	1	3
Swift	1/5	1/3	1

By normalising and averaging, we get the following matrix:

Criterion: Price

	Alto	*Santro*	*Swift*	*Average*
Alto	0.652	0.690	0.550	0.630
Santro	0.217	0.230	0.330	0.250
Swift	0.130	0.100	0.110	0.110
				$\sum = 0.99$

In a similar way, we can obtain for Alto, Santro and Swift, the relative weights for preferences with respect to fuel efficiency, performance, comfort, safety and reliability. We get the matrices for relative scores for all the criteria as shown below.

Criterion: Fuel Efficiency

	Alto	*Santro*	*Swift*	*Average*
Alto	0.60	0.60	0.60	0.60
Santro	0.20	0.20	0.20	0.20
Swift	0.20	0.20	0.20	0.20
$\sum = 1$				

Criterion: Performance

	Alto	*Santro*	*Swift*	*Average*
Alto	0.14	0.14	0.14	0.14
Santro	0.43	0.43	0.43	0.43
Swift	0.43	0.43	0.43	0.43
$\sum = 1$				

Criterion: Comfort

	Alto	*Santro*	*Swift*	*Average*
Alto	0.25	0.40	0.24	0.29
Santro	0.05	0.08	0.10	0.07
Swift	0.75	0.56	0.70	0.67
$\sum = 1.03$				

Criterion: Safety

	Alto	*Santro*	*Swift*	*Average*
Alto	0.24	0.33	0.22	0.26
Santro	0.08	0.11	0.13	0.11
Swift	0.72	0.55	0.65	0.64
$\sum = 1.01$				

Criterion: Reliability

	Alto	*Santro*	*Swift*	*Average*
Alto	0.65	0.60	0.67	0.64
Santro	0.13	0.11	0.11	0.11
Swift	0.22	0.29	0.27	0.26
$\sum = 1.01$				

Then, the relative values for the criteria for all three types of cars can be combined into one matrix as follows:

	Alto	**Santro**	**Swift**
Price	0.63	0.25	0.11
Fuel efficiency	0.6	0.2	0.2
Performance	0.14	0.43	0.43
Comfort	0.29	0.07	0.67
Safety	0.26	0.11	0.64
Reliability	0.64	0.11	0.26

Step 4: Now, with the weights of the criteria as determined in Step 2 and the relative score for the criteria for all the three cars as determined in Step 3, we get a score for each car as follows:

Alto: $(0.63 \times 0.42) + (0.60 \times 0.07) + (0.14 \times 0.18) + (0.29 \times 0.18) + (0.26 \times 0.07) + (0.64 \times 0.07) = 0.447$

Santro: $(0.25 \times 0.42) + (0.20 \times 0.07) + (0.43 \times 0.18) + (0.07 \times 0.18) + (0.11 \times 0.07) + (0.11 \times 0.07) = 0.224$

Swift: $(0.11 \times 0.42) + (0.20 \times 0.07) + (0.43 \times 0.18) + (0.67 \times 0.18) + (0.64 \times 0.07) + (0.26 \times 0.07) = 0.321$

Therefore, Alto getting the highest value can be considered as the choice of the decision-maker (buyer).

4.6.1.4 Outranking

The concept was first defined by B. Roy in 1970. Unlike MAUT and AHP, outranking is based on the principle that one alternative or choice may have a degree of dominance over the other rather than a single-best choice or alternative. The alternatives are compared in pairs, on each criterion, an alternative a_1 is said to outrank the other alternative a_2, if a_1 performs better than a_2 in some criteria and at least equally well in all the other criteria. In this case, a_1 is said to be the dominant alternative and a_2 is the dominated one. Under no circumstance or no combination of weightage will a_2 (dominated alternative) be preferred by the decision-maker. In the outranking method, preferences between the paired alternatives (say, X and Y) are expressed for each criterion as one of the following four types:

1. XPY strict preference of X over Y
2. XQY weak preference of X over Y
3. XIY indifference between X and Y
4. XJY inability to compare the actions.

In the outranking method, preference and indifference thresholds are introduced for each criterion to avoid exaggerating the importance of small differences in performance. The indifference threshold is the difference level below which the decision-maker considers no preference as the distinction is too small. Likewise, the preference threshold is the difference level above which the decision-maker prefers one alternative to another. In other words, the preference threshold is the smallest value that is a deciding factor when comparing two alternatives, while the largest value of no preference represents the indifference threshold. In the case of outranking, the preference function can take different forms for different criteria and decision-makers, but certain forms may be suggested generally to assess the performance of the criteria, depending upon the nature of the criteria. For quantitative criteria such as cost and price, the preference function may be a linear function; for semi-quantitative criteria such as prestige value (high, medium or low), the function may be a stepped one; and for non-quantitative criteria such as colour and appearance, the function may be a set of choices/preferences. For example, colour red and yellow are preferred, and violet and blue are not in the list of choices.

Outranking is a partial compensatory method and does not rely upon optimisation. The emphasis is on understanding trade-offs and a structured comparison of strengths and weaknesses of the alternatives. Also, the outranking method is flexible in allowing the decision-makers to change their preferences by adjusting inter-criteria weightings, introducing new criteria and alternatives during the analysis phase.

4.6.1.5 TOPSIS (Technique for Order of Preference by Similarity to Ideal Solution)

TOPSIS is another method of multi-criteria decision analysis which was invented by Hwang and Yoon in 1981 with further improvements to the method by Yoon, Hwang, Lai and Liu in 1993.

TOPSIS is based on the proposition that the best choice among the multi-criteria decision alternatives is the one having the shortest distance from the positive ideal solution and the longest distance from the negative ideal solution. The alternative choices are ranked with an overall index calculated based on the distances from ideal solutions. The steps involved in the method are explained with the same example of selecting a car, out of three options, namely, Alto, Santro and Swift. The attributes with their levels are reproduced as follows for the three cars.

Attributes

Cars	*Price (₹)*	*Fuel Efficiency km/litre*	*Performance*	*Comfort*	*Safety*	*Reliability*
Alto	200,000	20	Poor	Good	Good	Best
Santro	300,000	15	Average	Poor	Average	Average
Swift	400,000	18	Average	Best	Best	Good

Step 1: Convert the qualitative levels into numeric values on a scale of 1 to 5 as follows:

Worst	*Poor*	*Average*	*Good*	*Best*
1	2	3	4	5

Step 2: Normalisation—Vector normalisation (Euclidean) is used for all criteria (attributes) irrespective of benefit or cost. The formula used is as follows:

$$r_{ij} = \frac{x_{ij}}{\sqrt{\sum_{i=1}^{m}(x_{ij})^2}}$$

where i is the number of choices (alternatives) which in this example is 3 cars; with i = 1 for Alto, i = 2 for Santro and i = 3 for Swift, and j is the number of criteria which in this case is 6; j = 1 for Price ... and j = 6 for Reliability. x_{ij} is the value of each cell before normalisation and r_{ij} is the corresponding normalised value.

Attribute	*Price (Lakh)*	*Fuel Efficiency*	*Performance*	*Comfort*	*Safety*	*Reliability*
Alto	2	20	2	4	4	5
Santro	3	15	3	2	3	3
Swift	4	18	3	5	5	4
$\sqrt{\sum_{i=1}^{m}(X_{ij})^2}$	5.39	30.80	4.69	6.71	7.07	7.07

(m = 3) $2^2 + 3^2 + 4^2 = 29$

$\sqrt{29} = 5.39$ (approx.)

Step 3: The normalised decision matrix is obtained as follows:

Attribute	*Price (Lakh)*	*Fuel Efficiency*	*Performance*	*Comfort*	*Safety*	*Reliability*
Alto	2/5.39 = 0.37	20/30.80 = 0.65	2/4.69 = 0.43	4/6.71 = 0.60	4/7.07 = 0.57	5/7.07 = 0.71
Santro	3/5.39 = 0.56	15/30.80 = 0.49	3/4.69 = 0.64	2/6.71 = 0.30	3/7.07 = 0.42	3/7.07 = 0.42
Swift	4/5.39 = 0.74	18/30.80 = 0.58	3/4.69 = 0.64	5/6.71 = 0.75	5/7.07 = 0.71	4/7.07 = 0.57

Step 4: Calculation of weights of the attributes:

The weights of the attributes (criteria) are calculated by using an appropriate method and for this example let us adopt the weights as calculated by the AHP method (refer to Step 2 of AHP).

	Price	*Fuel Efficiency*	*Performance*	*Comfort*	*Safety*	*Reliability*
Weights	0.42	0.07	0.18	0.18	0.70	0.07

In this context, it may be mentioned that the weight assigned to each criterion is subject to the judgement of the individual decision-maker (the buyer of a car in this example).

Step 5: Calculate the weighted normalised decision matrix by multiplying the normalised values as obtained in Step 3 with the appropriate attribute weights as obtained in Step 4. Let the value in each cell be represented as Z_{ij}.

Attributes	*Price*	*Fuel Efficiency*	*Performance*	*Comfort*	*Safety*	*Reliability*
Weight	0.42	0.07	0.18	0.18	0.07	0.07
Alto	0.37 × 0.42 = 0.155	0.65 × 0.07 = 0.045	0.43 × 0.18 = 0.077	0.60 × 0.18 = 0.108	0.57 × 0.07 = 0.040	0.71 × 0.07 = 0.050
Santro	0.56 × 0.42 = 0.235	0.49 × 0.07 = 0.034	0.64 × 0.18 = 0.115	0.30 × 0.18 = 0.054	0.42 × 0.07 = 0.030	0.42 × 0.07 = 0.030
Swift	0.74 × 0.42 = 0.311	0.58 × 0.07 = 0.040	0.64 × 0.18 = 0.115	0.75 × 0.18 = 0.135	0.71 × 0.07 = 0.050	0.57 × 0.07 = 0.040

Step 6: Identification of Ideal best and Ideal worst:

In case of cost attributes like price, the ideal best is the lowest value, and the ideal worst is the highest value. In the case of benefit attributes like fuel efficiency, the ideal best is the highest value, and the ideal worst is the lowest value. The ideal best and ideal worst for each attribute are as follows:

Attributes	*Price*	*Fuel Efficiency*	*Performance*	*Comfort*	*Safety*	*Reliability*
Type	Cost	Benefit	Benefit	Benefit	Benefit	Benefit
Alto	0.155	0.045	0.077	0.108	0.040	0.050
Santro	0.235	0.034	0.115	0.054	0.030	0.030
Swift	0.311	0.040	0.115	0.135	0.050	0.040
Ideal best (Z_i^+)	0.155	0.045	0.115	0.135	0.050	0.050
Ideal worst (Z_i^-)	0.311	0.034	0.077	0.054	0.030	0.030

Step 7: Calculate the separation measure (Euclidean distance) for each car type. The formulae are as follows:

Ideal best separation $D_i^+ = \sqrt{\sum_{j=1}^{n}\left(Z_{ij} - Z_j^+\right)^2}$

Ideal worst separation $D_i^- = \sqrt{\sum_{j=1}^{n}\left(Z_{ij} - Z_j^-\right)^2}$

The calculated values of D_i^+ and D_i^- are as follows:

Attributes	*Price*	*Fuel Efficiency*	*Performance*	*Comfort*	*Safety*	*Reliability*	*Di+*	*Di–*
Type	Cost	Benefit	Benefit	Benefit	Benefit	Benefit		
Alto	0.155	0.045	0.077	0.108	0.040	0.050	0.047	0.167
Santro	0.235	0.034	0.115	0.054	0.030	0.030	0.117	0.085
Swift	0.311	0.040	0.115	0.135	0.050	0.040	0.156	0.092
Ideal best zj^+	0.155	0.045	0.115	0.135	0.050	0.050		
Ideal worst zj^-	0.311	0.034	0.077	0.054	0.030	0.030		

For example, D_1^+ and D_1^- are calculated as follows:

$$D_1^+ = \sqrt{(0.155-0.155)^2 + (0.045-0.045)^2 + (0.077-0.115)^2 + (0.108-0.135)^2 + (0.04-0.05)^2 + (0.05-0.05)^2}$$

$$D_1^- = \sqrt{(0.155-0.155)^2 + (0.045-0.045)^2 + (0.077-0.077)^2 + (0.108-0.054)^2 + (0.04-0.03)^2 + (0.05-0.03)^2}$$

$D_1^+ = 0.047$ and $D_1^- = 0.167$

Step 9: Calculate the relative closeness of each alternative to the ideal solution. The formula is as follows.

$$C_i = D_i^- / \left(D_i^+ + D_i^-\right)$$

The higher the value, the better the choice of the alternative. Based on the values of C_i, the alternatives are ranked as follows:

	D_i^+	*D_i^-*	*$D_i^+ + D_i^-$*	*C_i*	*Rank*
Alto	0.047	0.167	0.214	0.78	1
Santro	0.117	0.85	0.202	0.42	2
Swift	0.156	0.092	0.248	0.37	3

Modified TOPSIS Method:

Modified TOPSIS method is very similar to the TOPSIS method except that the Modified method applies the attribute weights to the normalised performance ratings in a different way as compared to the TOPSIS method. Similar to the TOPSIS method, the overall performance score is obtained from the distances (Euclidean) from ideal positive and ideal negative solutions. However, the distance is related to the attribute weights in the case of the Modified TOPSIS method unlike the TOPSIS method which assumes equal weights for the Euclidean distances. The previous example is again worked out using the Modified TOPSIS method as follows:

Steps 1 to 4 remain the same and let us proceed with the normalised decision matrix as obtained in Step 3 and the attribute weights as shown in Step 4 of the TOPSIS method.

Step 5:

Attribute	*Price*	*Fuel Efficiency*	*Performance*	*Comfort*	*Safety*	*Reliability*
Alto	0.37	0.65	0.43	0.60	0.57	0.71
Santro	0.56	0.49	0.64	0.30	0.42	0.42
Swift	0.74	0.58	0.64	0.75	0.71	0.57
Ideal best (z_j^+)	0.37	0.65	0.64	0.75	0.71	0.71
Ideal worst (z_j^-)	0.74	0.49	0.43	0.30	0.42	0.42

Step 6: Calculation of the weighted Euclidean distances:

The weighted Euclidean distances from the positive ideal and negative ideal solutions for each alternative are obtained from the following formulae:

$$D_i^+ = \sqrt{\sum_{j=1}^{n} W_j \left(Z_{ij} - Z_j^+\right)^2} \text{ and } D_i^- = \sqrt{\sum_{j=1}^{n} W_j \left(Z_{ij} - Z_j^-\right)^2}$$

where W_j ($j = 1, 2, \ldots, n$) are weights for attributes ($1, 2, \ldots, n$).

Attributes	*Price*	*Fuel Effciency*	*Performance*	*Comfort*	*Safety*	*Reliability*	D_i^+	D_i^-
Weight	0.42	0.07	0.18	0.18	0.07	0.07		
Alto	0.37	0.65	0.43	0.60	0.57	0.71	0.116	0.288
Santro	0.54	0.49	0.64	0.30	0.42	0.42	0.255	0.147
Swift	0.74	0.58	0.64	0.75	0.71	0.57	0.243	0.229
Ideal best z_j^+	0.37	0.65	0.64	0.75	0.71	0.71		
Ideal worst z_j^-	0.74	0.49	0.43	0.30	0.42	0.42		

Step 7: Calculate the relative closeness of each alternative to the ideal solution. The formula is as follows:

$$C_i = D_i^- / \left(D_i^+ + D_i^-\right)$$

The higher the value, the better the choice of the alternative. Based on the values of C_i, the alternatives are ranked as follows:

	D_i^+	D_i^-	$D_i^+ + D_i^-$	C_i	*Rank*
Alto	0.116	0.288	0.404	0.713	1
Santro	0.255	0.147	0.402	0.366	3
Swift	0.243	0.229	0.472	0.485	2

4.7 Group Decision Support Systems

A GDSS is a class of electronic meeting system which is a collaboration technology designed to support meetings and group work leading to group decisions. A GDSS contains most of the elements of DSS plus software to provide effective support in group decision-making.

4.7.1 Components of a GDSS

The important components of a GDSS are:

- Database
- Model base
- Communication capability
- GDSS processor
- Groupware, which is a special software that facilitates people located all over the globe to work on the same project, the same document and files efficiently and at the same time.

Examples of groupware supporting group decision-making are IBM Lotus Notes, Promino 8.0 and commercial software products such as SmartSpeed Connect, Facilitate Pro and ThinkTank, which work over the Internet in both synchronous and asynchronous settings.

- Dialogue manager
- External databases including other corporate databases
- Users and hosts.

4.7.2 Characteristics of a GDSS

The characteristics of a GDSS are as follows:

- Special design
- Ease of use
- Flexibility
- Decision-making support
- Delphi approach—a consensus decision-making approach where decision-makers (experts in various fields) are geographically dispersed
- Brainstorming
- Electronic mail system
- Group consensus
- Nominal group technique
- Anonymous input
- Reduction of negative group behaviour
- Parallel communication
- Automated record keeping
- Cost, control, complexity factors
- Flash plug-in of the browser.

GDSSs can be categorised into various types depending on the location and decision frequency: decision room, local area GDSS network, wide area GDSS network or teleconferences and so on.

Decision room and local area GDSS network are meant for low decision frequency and close location of group members, whereas wide area GDSS network and teleconferences are for groups of decision makers located around the world and working on common problems also known as virtual work groups.

4.7.3 Online Electronic Meeting Systems

Online electronic meeting systems usually have the following tools for:

1. Automatic meeting minutes and reports generation
2. Meeting set-up
3. Building an agenda either from scratch or from a template
4. Online meeting tools:
   (i) Brainstorming with electronic flip charts
   (ii) Voting and analysis
   (iii) Discussion
   (iv) Notebook
   (v) Presentation
   (vi) Action tracking

4.7.4 Group Decisions

Many business decisions are collectively taken by a group of managers/individual decision-makers, and therefore, a need arises for a consensus decision for a group consistent with individual choices or preferences. In actual practice, inconsistencies often arise in group decisions which have been pointed out by various authors from time to time. For example, the Pareto optimality condition attempts to eliminate such inconsistencies by restricting the list of alternative group decisions to a few important ones which can be considered for final choice based upon one or more criteria.

Likewise, voting, although considered a method for group decision-making with the majority principle to decide the best, often suffers inconsistencies due to possible bias in the selection process.

Finally, the famous Arrow's 'impossibility theorem', also known as 'Arrow's paradox', rules out any consistent or fair group decision in view of the incompatibility of the conditions of unanimity, non-dictatorship and independence of irrelevant alternatives.

In spite of the complexities involved in group decision-making for arriving at consistent and rational decisions, GDSSs, as described earlier, attempt to eliminate some of the limitations by way of software and adopting tools such as 'Delphi', brainstorming, analysis and nominal group techniques. For details of these features, interested readers may refer to popular GDSS software like SmartSpeed Connect.

4.8 Case Study: Application of Analytic Hierarchy Process (AHP) in Supplier Selection

4.8.1 Background

In today's competitive environment, the selection of the right suppliers for input items and various components is crucial for the success of any manufacturing organisation.

Supplier selection is a complex process involving multi-criteria decision-making. A trade-off between the qualitative and quantitative criteria is essential for the selection of the optimum supplier. The present case study relates to a manufacturing factory located in India and producing a variety of specialised opto-electronics equipment such as binoculars, telescopes, cameras and night vision devices. Of late, the factory has been exporting finished equipment to Nepal, Sri Lanka, Nigeria and Thailand. Although the factory produced many components in-house, the present study is related to a particular component which was outsourced. There were three potential suppliers 'A', 'B' and 'C' (actual names not mentioned due to obvious reasons) and the application of AHP was for the selection of the best out of the three suppliers.

4.8.2 AHP Model

The criteria considered for the supplier selection in this study were price, service, quality and logistics. The AHP model with its three levels has been shown as follows:

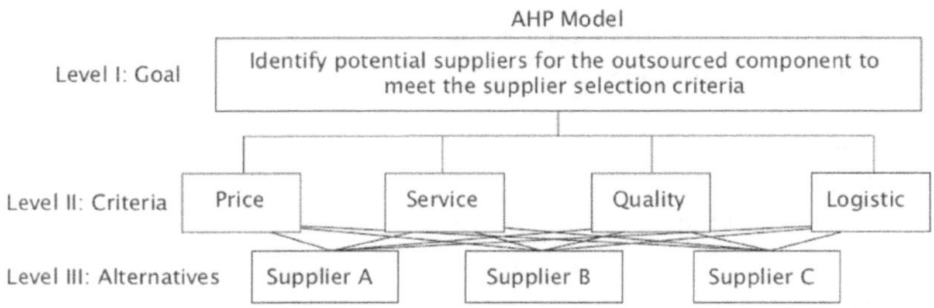

At the top level is the goal of the model, followed by the four criteria at level II, and the three suppliers at level III are the alternatives. They are to be evaluated in order to select the best supplier.

Methodology and Data Collection: All the primary data relating to pairwise comparison of the suppliers were collected based on interviews of the employees concerned with the process of selection of the suppliers. These data were analysed using Microsoft Excel in order to interpret the data in a simple and comprehensible way. Two managers looking after purchasing and engineering were interviewed to get their pairwise judgements for assessing the weights of the four criteria.

4.8.3 Result and Discussion

A five-point rating scale (1, 2, 3, 4 and 5) was designed and the priority weights of the criteria as well as the weights of the suppliers for each criterion were determined. The pairwise comparison matrix for the criteria formed with the pairwise judgement has been shown as follows:

Criterion	*Price*	*Service*	*Quality*	*Logistic*
Price	1	1/5	1/4	1/3
Service	5	1	1/3	1
Quality	4	3	1	1
Logistic	3	1	1	1

After normalisation of each column with a sum of 1.0 or 100% and averaging the values of the elements in each row, the priority vector denoting the approximate weights for the criteria of price, service, quality and logistics was obtained as follows:

$$\begin{bmatrix} Price \\ Service \\ Quality \\ Logistic \end{bmatrix} = \begin{bmatrix} 0.08 \\ 0.25 \\ 0.39 \\ 0.28 \end{bmatrix}$$

Evaluating the alternative suppliers with respect to the criteria was the next step. The pairwise comparison matrix for the three suppliers with respect to price formed with the primary data was as follows:

Criterion: Price

Supplier	A	B	C
A	1	1/4	1
B	4	1	5
C	1	1/5	1

Following the normalisation and averaging of the row elements, the priority vector, showing the weights for the three suppliers for the criterion of price, was obtained and shown as follows:

$$\begin{matrix} \text{Supplier} & & \text{Price} \\ \begin{bmatrix} A \\ B \\ C \end{bmatrix} & = & \begin{bmatrix} 0.161 \\ 0.690 \\ 0.149 \end{bmatrix} \end{matrix}$$

Proceeding in the same way as for price, pairwise comparison matrices and the priority vectors for service, quality and logistics were obtained. The pairwise comparison matrices are shown as follows:

Criterion: Service

Supplier	*A*	*B*	*C*
A	1	3	1/3
B	1/3	1	1/4
C	3	4	1

Criterion: Quality

Supplier	*A*	*B*	*C*
A	1	4	3
B	1/4	1	1/3
C	1/3	3	1

Criterion: Logistic

Supplier	*A*	*B*	*C*
A	1	1	1/5
B	1	1	1/3
C	5	3	1

The priority weights of the three suppliers for the four criteria obtained following the normalisation and averaging of the values of the row elements have been shown as follows:

Supplier	*Price*	*Service*	*Quality*	*Logistic*
A	0.161	0.272	0.608	0.158
B	0.690	0.120	0.120	0.187
C	0.149	0.608	0.272	0.655
Sum	1.00	1.00	1.00	1.00

Based on the priority weights of the criteria as shown earlier and the priority weights of each supplier with respect to the criteria as shown in the table above, the overall rankings of the suppliers were calculated as follows:

Supplier A = (0.161 × 0.08) + (0.272 × 0.25) + (0.608× 0.39) + (0.158 × 0.28) = 0.3622

Supplier B = (0.690× 0.08) + (0.120 × 0.25) + (0.120 × 0.39) + (0.187 × 0.28) = 0.1844

Supplier C = (0.149 × 0.08) + (0.608 × 0.25) + (0.272 × 0.39) + (0.655 × 0.28) = 0.4534

Supplier C with the highest score of 0.4534 was selected.

4.9 Conclusion

The case study shows the application of AHP for identifying the potential suppliers for input materials and outsourced components required by manufacturing organisations based on set criteria of performance on the part of the suppliers.

Review Questions

1. What are DSSs? Illustrate with suitable examples.
2. What are the main components of a DSS? Explain their roles.
3. What constitutes the knowledge system in a DSS environment?
4. What are DSS generators? Is Arena 5.0 a DSS generator? Explain.
5. In what ways is Analytica different from spreadsheet software such as Microsoft Excel? What are the advantages of Analytica as a DSS generator?
6. What is an influence diagram? Explain with a suitable example.
7. What are the distinguishing features of MAUT and AHP?

8. What is the outranking method? How is it different from AHP? Explain.
9. What is the implication of Arrow's paradox for group decisions?
10. What are GDSSs? How do they facilitate group decision-making?

Bibliography

Alter, S. 'How Effective Managers Use Information Systems'. *Harvard Business Review* 64, no. 6 (1976): 97–104.

Arrow, K. J. 'A Difficulty in the Concept of Social Welfare'. *The Journal of Political Economy* 58, no. 4 (1950): 328–346.

Bose, U., A. M. Dave, and D. L. Olson. 'Multi-Attribute Utility Methods in Group Decision Making: Past Applications and Potential for Inclusion in GDSS'. *Omega, International Journal of Management Sciences* 25, no. 6 (1977): 691–706.

Holsapple, C. W., and A. B. Whinston. *Decision Support Systems: A Knowledge Based Approach*. Saint Paul, MN: West Publishing, 1996.

Janakiraman, V. S., and K. Sarukesi. *Decision Support Systems*. New Delhi: PHI, 2008.

Keeny, L., and H. Raiffla. *Decisions with Multiple Objectives: Preference and Value trade-offs*, Cambridge: Cambridge University Press, 1976.

Linkov, I., A. Varghese, S. Jamail, T. P. Seager, G. Kiker, and T. Bridges. 'Multi-Criteria Decision Analysis: A Framework for Structuring Remedial Decisions at Contaminated Sites'. Proceedings of the Comparative Risk Assessment and Environmental Decision -Making Conference, Nato Science Series: IV: Earth and Environmental Sciences, 38, pp. 15–54, 2004.

Power, D. J. *Decision Support Systems: Concepts and Resources for Managers*. Westport, CT: Greenhood Publishing Group, 2002.

Saaty, T. L. 'Decision Making with the Analytic Hierarchy Process'. *International Journal of Services Sciences* 1, no. 1 (2008): 83–98.

Velasquerz, M., and P. T. Hesrter. 'An Analysis of Multi-Criteria Decision- Making Methods'. *International Journal of Operations Research* 10, no. 2 (2013): 56–66.

5 Executive Information Systems

5.1 Introduction

Executive information systems (EISs) are of paramount importance for senior executives such as functional heads and CEOs of organisations. The evolution of EISs was necessary in view of the very nature of information requirements for the decisions taken by senior managers of any organisation. The traditional MISs fail to provide such information. This development was further facilitated because of a gradual shift from a batch to an interactive environment and also an increase in information focus and integration. Each of these transitions results in technological and organisational changes. The information and decision-making needs of senior executives can be provided by easy access to both internal and external information relevant in meeting the strategic goal of an organisation. It is commonly considered a specialised form of a DSS.

5.2 Definition of EIS

An EIS is a set of tools supporting the information and decision-making needs of senior managers through timely, summarised and relevant information available within the organisation and also external information in an analytical framework.

The purpose of an EIS is to provide senior executives or managers, at the strategic and tactical levels in an organisation, access to the relevant data/information either directly online or through periodic reports. The idea is that the managers can identify trends, measure performance and raise queries to facilitate managerial learning and thus decide on the future course of action.

5.3 Characteristics of an EIS

The important characteristics of an EIS can be listed as follows:

1. Tailored to senior executives' information needs.
2. Reports are of executive summary or exception type.
3. 'Drill-down' process associated with each summary information/data item.
4. Online and interactive type.
5. User-friendly with GUI.
6. Performance indicators and factors are highlighted (a recent concept is the performance dashboards explained in the succeeding paragraphs in this chapter).

DOI: 10.4324/9781003509714-5

7. Provides access to both organisational databases and external business intelligence (BI).
8. New concepts of BI, performance dashboards and so on.
9. Provision for information of both hard and soft nature.

5.4 History of Evolution of EIS

The term 'executive information systems' was introduced in 1982 by Rockart and Treacy to describe the kind of systems which a few senior corporate officers were using on a regular basis to retrieve information needed by them for decision-making. In 1988, Rockart and Delong defined the term executive support system (ESS) to refer to systems similar to EIS but with a broader set of capabilities than EISs. These, apart from providing information, also might include communication support, such as emails and teleconferencing, data analysis facilities such as spreadsheets, influence diagrams, query languages, DSSs to evaluate decisions of simulated or 'what-if' types, artificial intelligence (AI) and expert systems and organising tools such as electronic calendars and electronic flip charts. Rockart (1979) mentioned about four major approaches of defining top executive information needs, namely by-product approach, null approach, key indicator approach and the total study method. In the 'by-product' method, little attention is paid to any formal study of information needs of the top executives. More attention is focused on data processing such as payroll, accounts receivable and payable and billing customers, and the information by-products of these data-processing systems are made available to the interested executives, and at most, some aggregation of data, such as total sales over a period of time, is passed to the top executives. In the 'null approach', the proponents such as Mintzberg (1976) point to the uselessness of any formal MIS for top executives. According to them, top executive activities are dynamic and ever changing, so one cannot predetermine exactly what information will be needed at any point in time. A great deal of top executive information needs is met by informal sources such as words, hearsay and gossip. Hard data such as written reports are of little use for this purpose. The 'key indicator' system is based on three concepts. The first concept is that for every organisation, irrespective of the type, there is a set of key indicators of the health of the organisation and data are collected on the basis of each of these indicators. The second concept is the principle of exception reporting. It means that managers should be provided with only those indicators where performance is significantly different from expected results. Senior executives, therefore, need to focus their attention on areas where actual performance is different from the planned targets. The third concept underlying the key indicator system is the expanding use of visual displays such as computer consoles, digital displays and other video displays. In the fourth approach in the study of information needs of top executives, known as the total study process, a large sample of managers are interviewed about their information needs and the results are compared with the existing IS. The gap is bridged by designing subsystems to provide information currently not available. IBM's business system planning (BSP) is the most widely used total study process. It is aimed at a top–down analysis of the information needs of an organisation. There are two phases in it. In the first phase, executives starting from the top are interviewed to determine their environment, objectives, key decisions and information needs. This helps the analyst to form an overall understanding of the business and the existing IS. The second phase consists of designing new information subsystems and implementing them to provide necessary information currently unavailable.

Each of the above-mentioned approaches to the study of the senior executive's information needs has its advantages and limitations. The by-product method is aimed at paperwork processing inexpensively, rather than fulfilling real management information needs. The null approach, with its emphasis on soft, diverse and ever-changing information needs of a top executive, has saved many organisations from building useless ISs and expenses. It, however, places too much stress on the executives' strategic and interpersonal roles and overlooks the management control role of the executives. The key indicator system provides a significant amount of useful information. It, however, tends to be all inclusive rather than on target to a particular executive's specific information needs. The total system process is expensive in terms of manpower and all-inclusive in terms of scope.

One of the important current approaches to the study of executives' information needs is the CSFs method developed by a research team of the Sloan School of Management Information Systems at the Massachusetts Institute of Technology (MIT). The CSF approach is actively researched and applied at the MIT centre too. The CSF approach is based on the identification of CSFs that help in attaining organisational goals. In most industries, there are usually three to six factors that determine success. These key jobs must be done exceedingly well for an organisation to be successful. As a result, CSFs are areas of activity that receive constant and careful attention from management. The four prime factors that determine critical success for any industry are: (1) structure of the particular industry, that is, the nature of the industry, competitive strategy, industry position and geographical locations, (2) environmental factors such as the socio-economic environment, (3) political factors and (4) temporal factors such as inflation, Sensex fluctuations and oil price.

Four frameworks for EIS development, namely (1) Evaluation, Survey, Prototype, Review, Implement and Transfer (ESPIRIT); (2) Structural; (3) Path and (4) Structuration framework have been described in the following sections.

5.5 ESPRIT Framework

The first framework ESPRIT is a sequential framework in the form of a six-phase development project. It is essentially an evolutionary prototyping method and starts with a feasibility study and follows on to other stages of development until installation of the final system and training of users. The second phase is the survey of business needs, followed by the third phase of prototyping the current requirement. The fourth phase is the review of the benefits. The fifth phase is the implementation phase, and the sixth and final phase is the transfer of the skills in-house. This last phase involves the design and implementation of training courses for the users of the system.

5.6 Structural EISs Framework

The structural framework stems from practical experience in developing EIS, a large number of literatures on EIS and discussions with EIS vendors, consultants and EIS staff members. There are three components which comprise the structural framework. The first component is a structural perspective of the development of EIS and describes the key elements such as internal and external environment and data, executive sponsor, operating sponsor, executive users, functional areas, organisational database, the information science and technology group, vendors, consultants and builders and their interactions with each other and the EIS. The second component of the framework relates to issues relevant to the development process such as development time, methodology and the spread of the system among the other members of the organisation. The third component is the user-system dialogue. The user-system dialogue is concerned with issues such as user knowledge to operate the EIS, response time, the user-system interface and mode of presentation of the information.

5.7 Path Framework for EIS

The path framework draws attention to the importance of timing and coordinating EIS development so that it is appropriately matched with the organisation's level of decision-making maturity and technical capabilities. It also describes how EIS evolves from MIS foundation to cater to the senior executives' integrated, focused and easily accessible information needs for decision-making. The evolution of an EIS from traditional MIS requires changes in stages, mainly in two areas. First, there has to be a shift from a batch to an interactive environment, and second, an increased focus and integration of information organisation-wide. Each of these transitions results in technological and organisational changes. Table 5.1 summarises the evolution stages of the path framework of EIS. The 'focus and integration' dimension is concerned with the system's ability to provide and integrate information about specific performance measures relevant to various functional areas in the organisation. The 'mode of operation' differentiates between batch systems (designed for periodic reporting) and online systems (allowing interactive retrieval of information). The two dimensions result in four types of systems, as shown in Table 5.1. Typically, the starting point is the operation of a traditional MIS and the 'online EIS' stage representing the most advanced stage in this framework.

There can be various paths of evolution of ISs from the MIS to an online EIS in an organisation.

Table 5.1 A Path Framework for EIS

		3. Batch EIS	**4. Online EIS**
Focus and Integration	High	• Key performance indicators • Critical success factors • Integrated information • Periodic paper reports	• Selective, ad-hoc monitoring • Key indicators and back up detail
		1. MIS	**2. Query**
	Low	• By-product • Bottom–up approach • Isolated, scattered high volume reports	• Selective, ad-hoc access for query and analysis used by staff
		Batch	online

Source: Kaniclides and Kimble (1994).

Table 5.2 Orlikowski and Robey's Framework

Realm of social structure	System developers are informed by systems development methodologies and knowledge about their organisations to build information systems.	System developers work within the constraints of time, budget, hardware software and authority to build information systems.	System developers draw on the values and conventions of their organisation occupation and training to build information systems.
Modalities	Interpretive schemes	Resources	Norms
Realm of human action	System developers create meaning by programming assumptions and knowledge into information systems.	System developers create IS through the organisational power capabilities they wield in their organisational roles.	System developers create sanctions by designing and programming legitimate options and conventions into information systems.

5.8 Structuration Framework

The structuration framework of EIS development is based on a systematic study and investigation of the interaction between human actors and the social structure during the development of the EISs.

The structuration framework was brought out by Orlikowski and Robey in 1991. Orlikowski and Robey's framework is described in Table 5.2. The utility of this framework is in the fact that it provides a means of integrating the elements in a coherent manner and linking them explicitly to human action.

Each of the four frameworks mentioned in Table 5.1 has a considerably different perspective of EIS development. This is mainly due to differences in purpose, nature, emphasis and focus of each framework. Nevertheless, they together describe the various aspects of successful EIS development.

Kaniclides and Kimble (1994) put forward a new framework of EIS development, namely, the 'PAS' framework, where 'PAS' stands for the People, Activities and Systems of the framework. The 'PAS' framework can be described using Set theory. Each of the three main components can be considered to be sets containing elements present in an organisation during system development. The set of people {P} in an organisation comprises subsets or elements such as people who are neither involved in the development of EIS nor using the resulting EIS, the people who are involved in the development process but are not users of the system, the people who are actively involved in the development process and are also users of the EIS, and the people who are not involved in the development process but are users of the system.

Similarly, the activities {A} set comprises subsets of organisational activities not directly related to EIS but can influence the development or use of EIS, activities directly connected with EIS developmental efforts, and the subset of activities representing post-implementation efforts.

The set of systems {S} comprises other organisational systems operational in the organisation, the subset of the systems in the organisation representing the EISs applications operational in the organisation and the subset of systems including enhancements or expansion to the initial implementation.

Besides, an integral part of the framework of EIS development is the environment in which the organisation operates and the time dimension for each activity. The detailed interactions of the above components and elements employing set theory in EIS development can be studied from the paper of Kaniclides and Kimble (1994).

5.9 EIS and BI

In recent years, the term EIS has become less popular, while BI techniques (with the sub-areas of reporting, analytics, digital dashboards and so on) have become more popular for the sake of information and decision-making, particularly at senior management echelons.

The BI refers to computer-based techniques used in locating, digging out and analysing business data, such as sales revenue by products and/or departments. The BI technologies provide historical, current and predictive views of business operations. Common functions of BI technologies are reporting, online analytical processing (OLAP), analytics, data mining, business performance management and control through digital dashboards, benchmarking and predictive analytics. The BI can be applied to the following business purposes in order to derive business value:

1. Measurement of progress against business goals through a hierarchy of performance metrics and benchmarking. The idea is to manage the business processes accordingly.
2. Analytics through program that builds quantitative processes for a business to arrive at optimal decisions and to perform business knowledge discovery. This frequently involves data mining, statistical analysis (such as risk and sensitivity analysis), predictive modelling and BPM. The concept of data mining has been discussed in subsequent chapters of this book.
3. Enterprise reporting through a program that builds infrastructure for strategic reporting to serve the strategic management of a business such as customer service, sales promotion, market analysis of new products, trend analysis, inventory control, sales decisions and similar ones. Enterprise reporting frequently involves data visualisation, EIS and OLAP, as described in a subsequent paragraph of this chapter.
4. Collaboration platform through a program that gets different areas (both internal and external to the business organisation) to work together through data sharing and electronic data interchange (EDI).
5. Knowledge management through a program to make the company data driven through strategies and practices to identify, create, represent, distribute and enable the adoption of insights and experiences which are true business knowledge. Knowledge management leads to learning management and regulatory compliance.

5.10 BI and Data Warehousing

Often, BI applications use data gathered from a data warehouse or a data mart. However, not all data warehouses are used for BI, nor do all BI applications require a data warehouse. Data warehouses have been characterised by the following features:

1. **Subject-oriented:** Data are organised according to major subjects or processes of an organisation, such as products, customers, materials, machines, vendors and employees. The subjects are common to various application-oriented operational systems.
2. **Integrated:** The data from various subject areas should be rationalised with one another. The integration is achieved through the data model and physical tables or databases in the warehouse.
3. **Non-volatile:** Data in a data warehouse, unlike data from online operational databases, are not updated. Once a data record is properly stored in the warehouse, it is not subjected to change. For example, a particular customer record will be retained with the period of tenure even if the customer ceases to be a customer subsequently. The data records in a data warehouse are snapshots and time-stamped, and updates are not allowed.
4. **Time Variant:** A data record is accurate only as of some moment in time. In some cases, the moment in time is a single moment. In other cases, it is a span of time. However, in any case, the values of data found in a data warehouse are accurate with reference to the particular time moment or time span.
5. **Facilitator of Managerial Decisions:** Data warehouses are created for the purpose of managerial decisions. The operational systems provide operational information for facilitating day-to-day operations of a company, whereas data warehouses are basically ISs to facilitate managerial decisions for deriving value to the business.

Apart from the above characteristics, which define the data warehouse, the additional features are:

(i) Detailed or granular data
(ii) Historical data
(iii) Faster Navigation through related data and information
(iv) Heterogeneous data set transformed into a common format.

A data warehouse is a physically distinct place from online operational applications.

5.11 Architecture of a Data Warehouse

The typical architecture of a data warehouse is shown in Figure 5.1. The architecture is a top-down one where the departmental data marts (explained in subsequent sections) have been shown as subordinate to the main data warehouse and created from the same.

The important components are:

1. *Operational data sources*, which consist of the following:
   (i) External systems such as the Internet, commercially available database or database associated with the suppliers or customers of the organisations and the databases of the statutory or regulatory authorities such as the government.
   (ii) Corporate applications, including ERP, legacy systems such as payroll, store ledger and similar ones.
2. *Operational data stores/files* which are *stores of current and integrated operational data*. The operational data store is often structured and supplies data in the same form as to be stored in the warehouse but may often act as a staging area for the data to be loaded into the data warehouse.

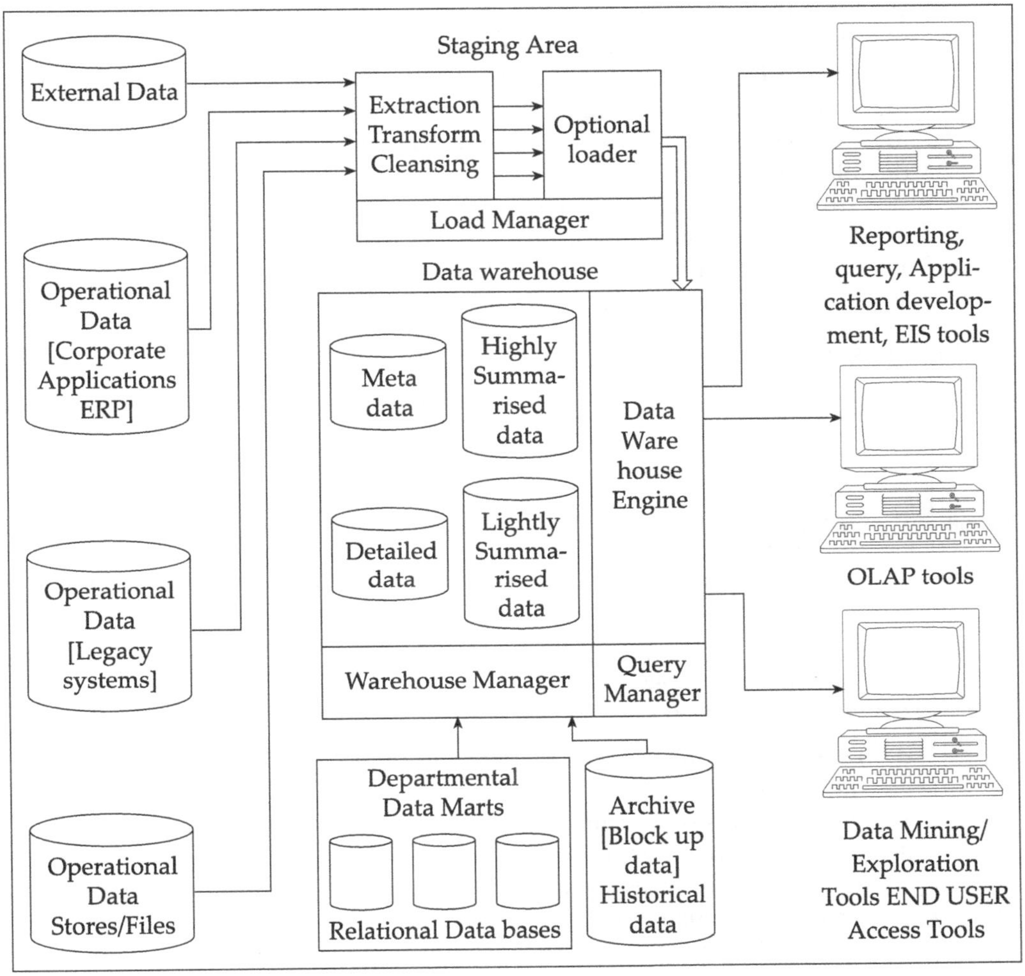

Figure 5.1 Typical Architecture of a Data Warehouse

3. *The load manager,* also known as the front-end component of the data warehouse architecture, performs all operations such as the extraction of data from the operational systems, the transformation of data into internal format and the structuring of the data warehouse, cleansing to improve the quality of data, and the loading of the data into the warehouse. The four processes from extraction through loading are often called collectively 'data staging'. Let us elaborate on the four processes as follows:
   (i) *Extract:* It is necessary to extract only the relevant and useful data for decision-making processes from the operational databases before including it in the warehouse. The extract process specifies:
      a. Which data files and tables are to be accessed in the source databases?
      b. Which fields of the data records are to be extracted from (a) above? For example, in case of a Goods Receipt Note record, the delivery truck or lorry number field may not be relevant for decision purposes, whereas the supplier field is very relevant and needs to be extracted.

c. What are the extracts to be incorporated in the resulting database?
d. What is the target and database format of the output?
e. The schedule of the extraction process.

(ii) *Transform:* The transform process deals with rectifying any inconsistency among the data from different sources. The idea is to transform the data into a common form for storing in the data warehouse. The inconsistencies are mainly due to the following:

a. Attribute naming inconsistency, for example, customer name may be cust_name, custname and so on.
b. Mixed text containing upper and lower cases.
c. Numerical data in different formats in different databases.

Examples of data transform process

					Warehouse	
Source	*Employee Name*	*Date of Birth*	*Salary*	*Target*	*DOB*	*Salary*
Payroll system	BANERJEE SOUREN	30.11.1949	60000.00	SOUREN BANERJEE	11301949	60000.00
Personnel Information System	SOUREN BANERJEE	NOV 30 1949	60000.00	SOUREN BANERJEE	11301949	60000.00
ERP HR Module	Souren Banerjee	NOV 30 1949	60000.00	SOUREN BANERJEE	11301949	60000.00

d. Date formats are different, for example, mmddyy, ddmmyy or 30NOV1949 and so on.
e. Different units of measure, for example, ₹/$, number/dozen and so on.
f. Coded data in different formats, for example, male/female, M/F.

All the above inconsistencies need to be eliminated by transforming and converting to a common format, for example: (a) all characters can be converted into ASCII, (b) texts may be converted into uppercase, (c) common format for numeric and date fields, (d) one unit of measurement for similar physical quantities and (e) coded data must be in uniform format.

(iii) *Cleansing:* The quality of information is one of the key considerations that determine the value of information to a manager. The process of data cleansing is to eliminate errors in the data as far as possible to make it error-free before entry into the data warehouse. The possible errors that need elimination are missing data, abnormal values of data, invalid data, inconsistent data and conflicting data arising out of more than one source. Examples of such errors are numbers in the name field, alphanumeric characters in the value field, two different dates of birth for the same employee, missing serial numbers in vouchers and date of birth and age as on a particular date not tallying; for example, if the date of birth is 30 November 1949 and the age as on 1 January 2017 is 70 years.

iv. *Loading:* Loading implies physical movement of the data from the computers storing the source database to the data warehouse database, assuming the two are different. Loading takes place after extraction, transformation and data cleansing. The most common channel for data transfer/loading is a high-speed communication link. Loading puts raw/detailed data in the form of fact tables and also generates a report of the data loaded into the warehouse.

4. A *warehouse manager* performs all the operations associated with the management of the data in the warehouse. The operations performed by the warehouse manager within the data warehouse include analysis of data to ensure consistency, time stamping, creation of indexes and views such as bitmap indexes and join indexes which considerably reduce data scanning, partitioning of data to create multidimensional views of the same, de-normalisation and aggregations, creation of data marts, archiving and backing up of historical and other data. The storage of data in various forms is explained in subsequent sections in detail.
5. *Detailed/granular data*, lightly and highly summarised data, in the form of various schemas and data models, achieve backup data in a warehouse (explained subsequently).
6. A *query manager* is also called a back-end component as he/she performs the task of managing user queries for data/information. He/she is the interface between the warehouse and end-user access tools and directs the queries to the appropriate tables (fact tables and dimensional tables explained in the next section of this chapter) and also schedules the execution of queries.
7. *Metadata* is an essential feature of the warehouse. Metadata is data/information about the data in the warehouse. It contains information about the components of the corporate information factory (CIF) as named by Bill Inmon, known as the father of data warehouses. Metadata has two major functions: to describe the data found in the architectural component of a data warehouse and to exchange metadata with other components. Besides, metadata in the data warehouse plays several roles, such as describing the location of various data in the warehouse for usage, coordinating between different operations starting with extract, transform, load (ETL) to information access for facilitating various queries and other end-user access modes.
8. There can be different *types of metadata,* such as technical metadata, which describe the structure and content of different types of data; operating metadata, which are generated as metrics (measures) of day-to-day operations of the data warehouse, such as the number of records accessed or transferred from one component to another, the total number of records in a table or a database; and business metadata, which consist of business definitions, formulae, rules and conditions, glossaries and dictionaries of business that people understand.
9. *End-user access tools* can be categorised into five main groups: data reporting and query tools, application development tools, EIS tools, OLAP tools for analysis such as aggregation (total sales, percentage of sales of a particular product to total sales), comparison (budget versus actual), ranking (top 10, quartile, percentile analysis), access to detailed data (drill) and aggregate data (roll-up), complex criteria specification, visualisation and data mining developed from research into statistical analysis and AI, which is the process of extracting previously unknown information patterns and linkages from large databases to facilitate proactive information delivery leading to knowledge for the decision-makers such as senior managers/executives. Data mining helps build predictive models for future values of target variables. The process has been successfully used for credit analysis, fraud detection, target marketing, banking and insurance, healthcare and many other areas of application.

For example, Electronic Point of Sale (EPOS) data analysis of the shopping baskets in a shopping mall is often applied by mall managers to find relationships among the product mix of choice of the buyers in order to refine purchasing, display and promotional decisions by the shopping mall.

5.12 Some Important Physical Aspects of a Data Warehouse

5.12.1 Data Model

The design of a data warehouse begins with a data model. At the highest level, a data model represents an entity relationship diagram (ERD). Each entity represents a subject such as customer, product, vendor, machine and employee. Each entity is further defined at a lower level of data modelling called the data item set (DIS). The DIS specifies a lower level of detail than the entity does, such as keys and attributes as well as the structure of the keys and attributes. The DIS is further broken down into a lower level of physical design, creating the physical characteristics of the data such as alpha and numeric. Figure 5.2 shows a nursing home data model as an illustration.

5.12.2 Physical Tables

The data warehouse is made up of interrelated tables or physical databases. Within the data warehouse, there are different physical areas. Each subject area may comprise one fact table and a number of dimension tables related to each other by means of a shared key or foreign key relationship. Collectively, the different tables along with their relationships form a data warehouse. The dimension tables arise because of the multidimensional data in a warehouse.

The dimensions may be product, region, time and so on. For example, a sales revenue of ₹100 million of a consumer goods company in a year may comprise products sold such as soap, toothpaste, milk, fruit juice and cosmetics. The total sales may consist of sales of all products region-wise, such as North India, South India, East India and West India. Similarly, the total sales of ₹100 million may be split up into quarterly, monthly, weekly

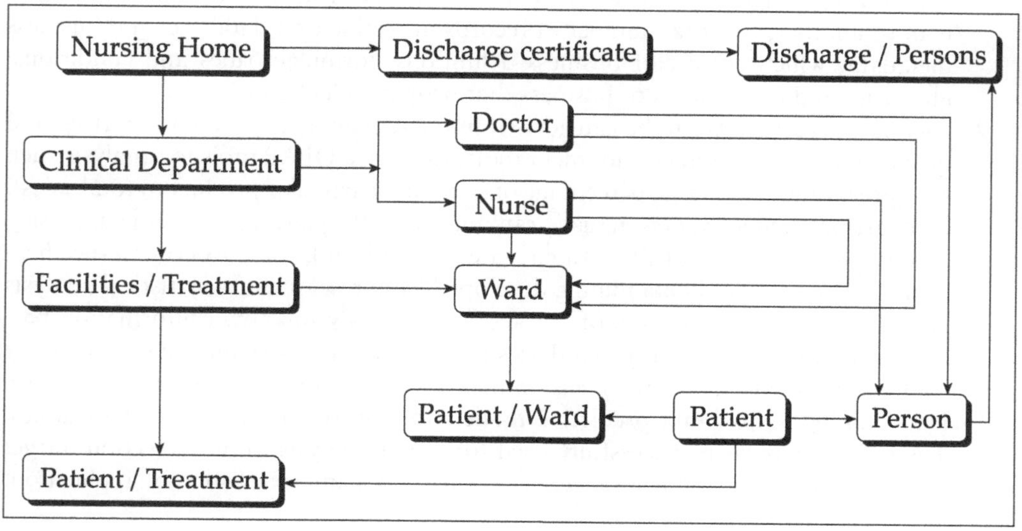

Figure 5.2 A Nursing Home Data Model

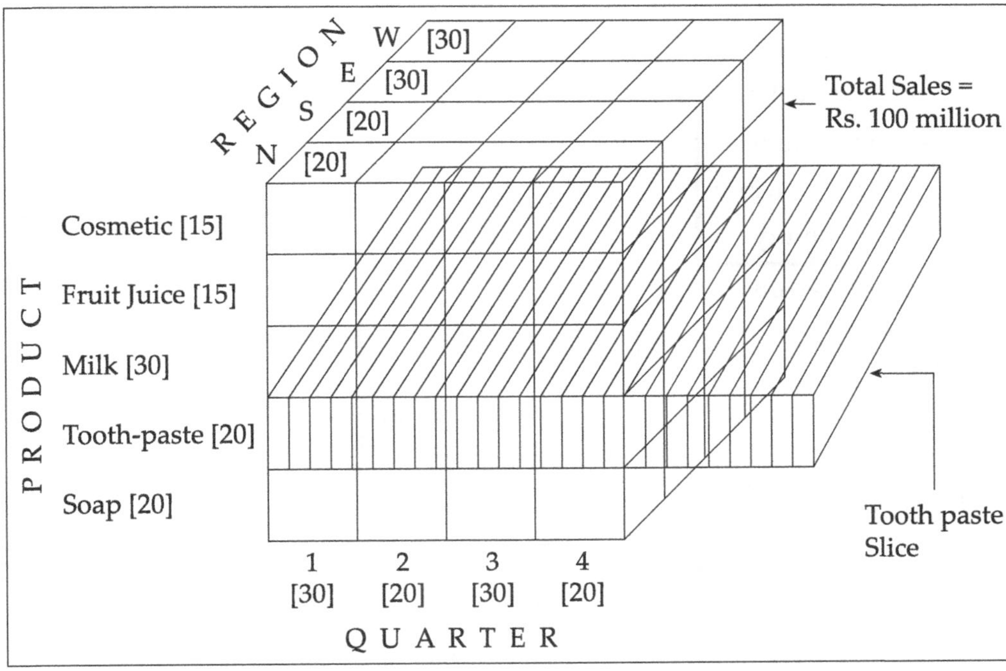

Figure 5.3 Multidimensional Data

and daily sales for 4 quarters, 12 months, 52 weeks and 365 days. The multidimensional sales data, as mentioned above, can be represented as shown in Figure 5.3.

The multidimensional data leads to 'slicing and dicing' for data analysis and query response. For example, the total sales of ₹100 million, as shown in Figure 5.3 comprises slices such as the toothpaste slice. The slices constitute the cube (dice) of total sales of ₹100 million.

5.12.3 Corporate Data Model Architecture

The corporate data model is the intellectual road map for the development of the data warehouse. The architecture of the data model in a data warehouse comprises: (a) Third normal form (3NF), (b) star, fact constellation and snowflake schema and (c) data vault.

The above architecture is based on the data tables collectively along with their relationships.

1. **3NF**: The 3NF is a normal form used in database normalisation and the concept has been described elaborately in a subsequent chapter on database management systems (DBMSs) of this book.
2. **Star Schema**: The star schema has been described in Figure 5.4. It comprises of a fact table which contains all the records of aggregate transactions of a subject (in the example daily sales) and the dimension tables which, in the example shown in Figure 5.4 are store location, time (period of sales), product and customer tables containing different numbers of records.
3. **Snowflake Schema**: The snowflake schema is similar to the star schema. However, the difference is that in the snowflake schema, dimensions are normalised into

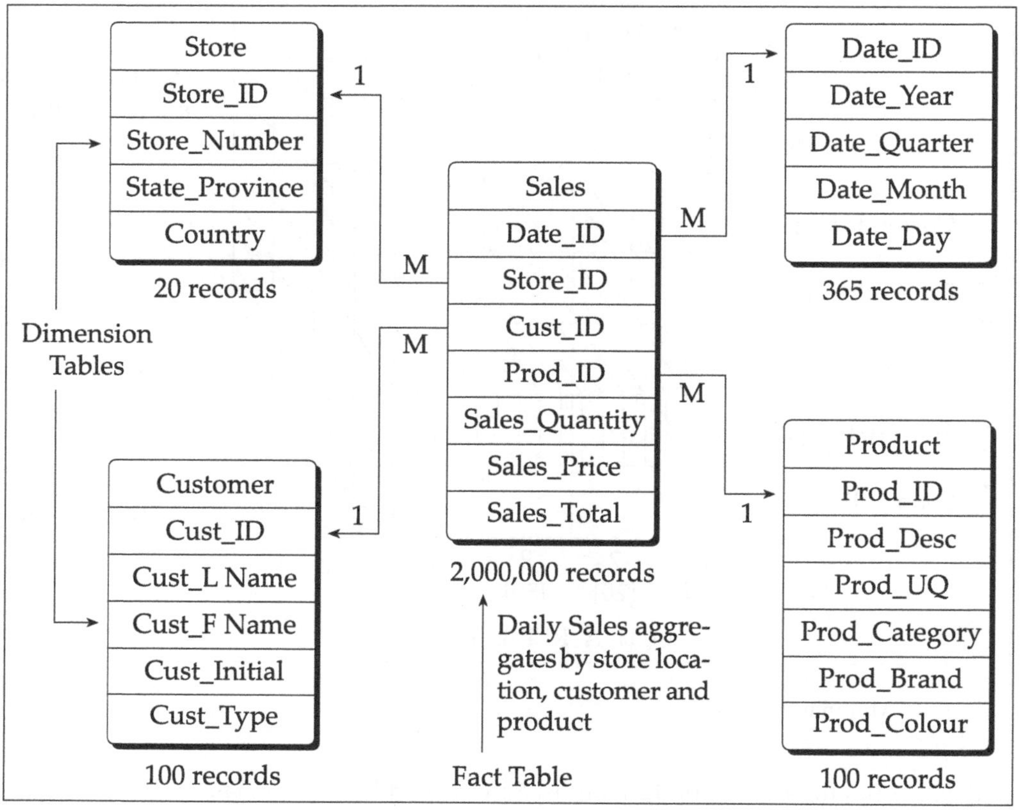

Figure 5.4 Star Schema for Sales

multiple related tables, whereas in the star schema dimensions are denormalised with each dimension represented by a single table.

The example shown in Figure 5.4 is normalised and shown as a snowflake schema as shown in Figure 5.5.

4. **Fact Constellation Schema**: For each star schema, it is possible to construct fact constellation schemas (e.g., by splitting the original star schema into more star schemas, each of which describes facts on another level of dimension hierarchy). The fact constellation architecture contains multiple fact tables that share many dimension tables. This schema is used mainly for the aggregate fact tables or where we want to split a fact table for better comprehension. The split of fact tables is done when we want to focus on aggregation over few facts and dimensions. The main shortcoming of the fact constellation schema is a more complicated design because many variants for particular kinds of aggregation must be considered and selected. Moreover, dimension tables are still large. Figure 5.6 is an example of fact constellation schema.
5. **Data Vault**: Data vault concept of data modelling in warehouse was first developed in the late 1990s and released in 2000 onwards. The proponent was Dan E. Linstedt, USA. The data vault is a detail-oriented, historical tracking and uniquely linked set of 3NF tables that support one or many functional areas of business. It

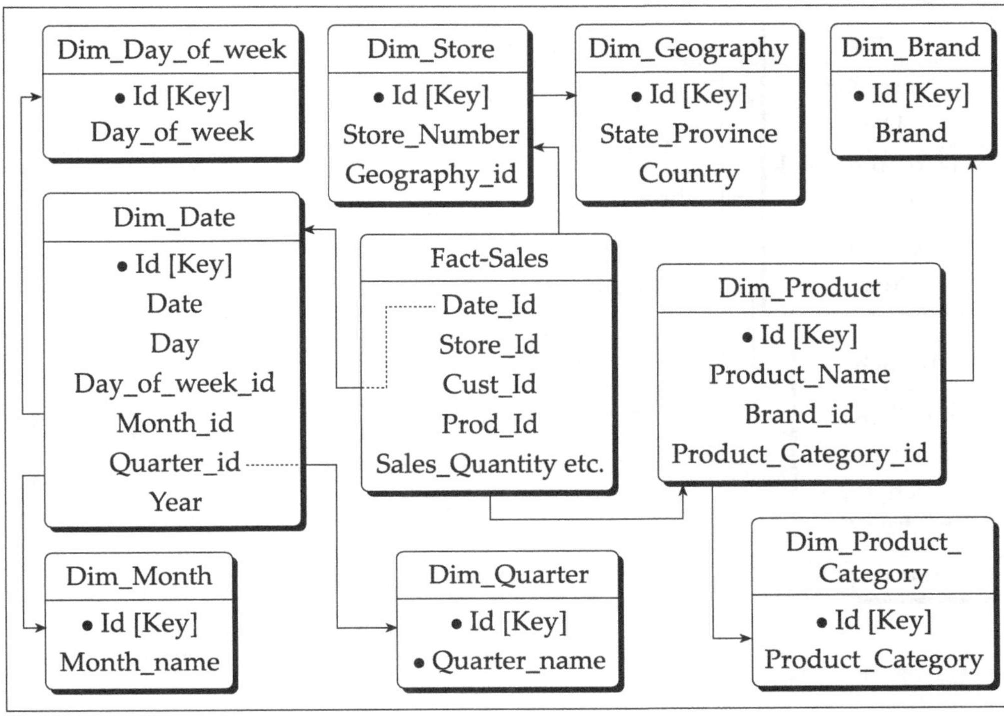

Figure 5.5 Snowflake Schema for Sales

is a hybrid approach with the best features of 3NF and star schema as explained in earlier sections. It is the latest concept of data model and is the architect to meet the needs of enterprise data warehouse. A data vault can act as an operational data store (ODS) and at the same time can handle large sets of granular data in the range of terabytes in a smaller, more normalised physical space in comparison to both 3NF and star schema. Inside the data vault are familiar structures that match traditional definitions of star schema and 3NF that include dimensions, many-to-many linkages and standard table structures. The distinctive features are the relationship representations, field structuring and granular time-stamped data storage. The data vault consists of the following minimum and essential components:

(i) Hub entities or hubs are a single table carrying a minimum unique list of primary business keys, for example, employee number, customer number, supplier number, item number, machine number and so on. These keys are those utilised by businesses for day-to-day operations. Other attributes in the hub are surrogate keys, that is, optional components, such as sequence number, load date-time stamp recording from the first instance of time of the arrival of the key and record source for traceability of the source system of the key.

(ii) The second component of the data vault is the link entities, which are a physical representation of a many-to-many 3NF relationship. The link represents the relationship or transaction between two or more business components (two or more keys). The link also contains the entities of surrogate key, hub 1 key to hub N key, load date-time stamp and the record source for traceability.

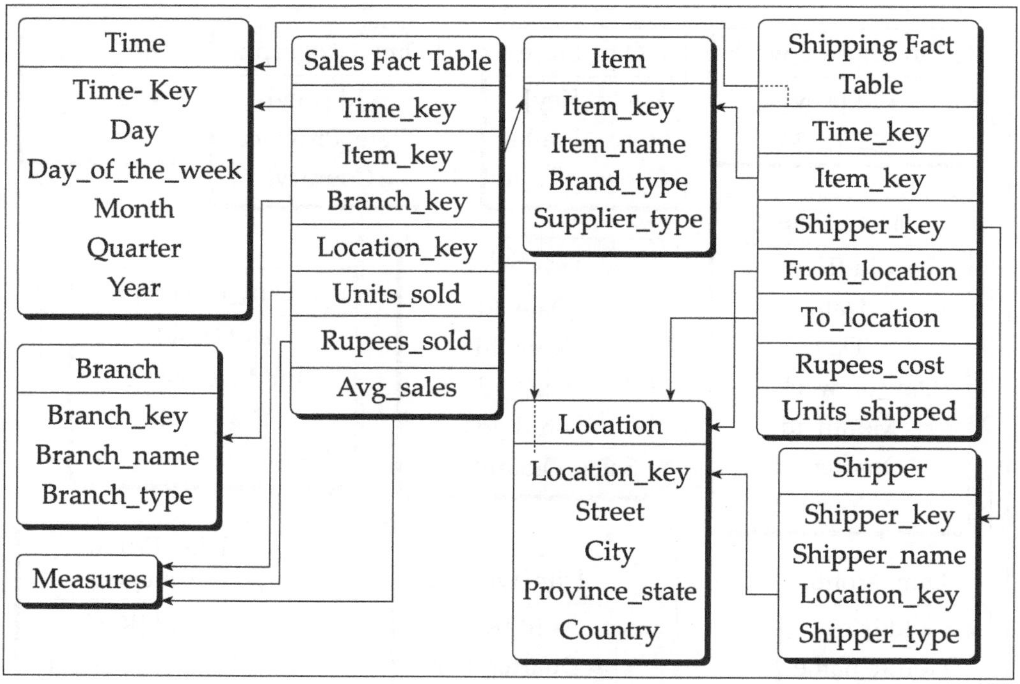

Figure 5.6 Fact Constellation Schema

(iii) The third component is satellite entities or satellites which are hub-key context information to describe the hub key. The satellite information is subject to change over time, and the structure of the satellite is capable of storing new or altered data at the granular level. For example, a particular milling machine may be retrofitted with an add-on component (feature) to make it not a milling machine but a special purpose gear-cutting machine. The attributes of the satellite are—the satellite's primary key, that is, the hub or link primary key migrated from hub or link into the satellite, load date-time stamp which records the time of the context information that first came to exist in the warehouse, satellite's optional primary key and sequence surrogate number utilised for satellites that have multiple values and record source for data traceability. Building a data vault involves modelling the hubs, links, satellites and point-in-time tables which is a satellite derivative.

Other aspects of a data warehouse are as follows:

1. **Granular Data**: The data found in a data warehouse are very granular in nature. This implies that the data in a warehouse is placed in a very detailed form. The data may then be shaped by an application so that it can be viewed in a distinct manner. The granular data at the core of the data warehouse provide many benefits. A primary benefit is that the same data can be viewed in different ways but there is a single source of reconciliation. Figure 5.7 shows how the same granular data can

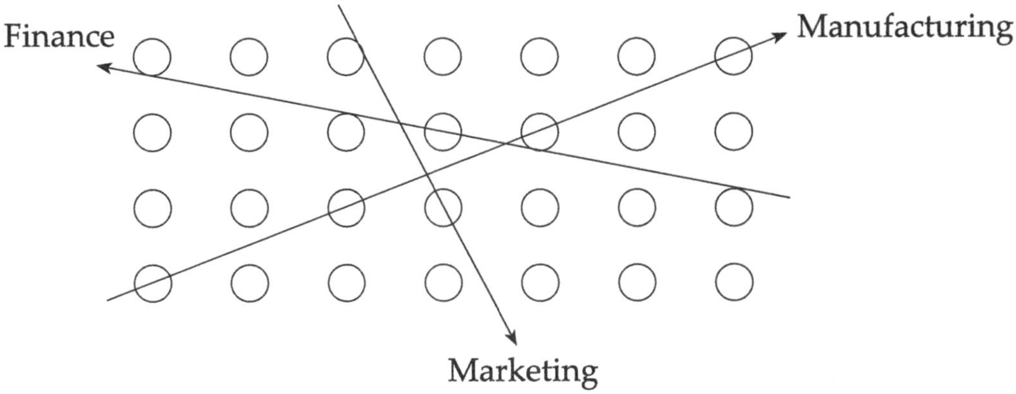

Figure 5.7 Granular Data Allows the Source Data Viewed in Different Ways

be examined in different ways by three departments in an organisation. Usually, each grain of information in the data warehouse represents some finite unit of business activity for the company such as an order, a sale, manufacture of an item, a payment and a telephone call. All the above grains of information may be uniquely specified by the date, the item, the amount, length of call, the customer, the person making the payment or the call and the person receiving the payment or the call as the case may be.

Each grain of information can be combined with other grains to provide a different perspective of data. For example, a sale can be combined with the corresponding order (another grain) to find whether the order was executed in time.

In addition to allowing data to be viewed differently by different parties, another benefit is that granular data may lie in the data warehouse for unknown future requirements. So, we can say the data warehouse keeps the senior executives in a proactive position rather than a reactive one for new needs of information.

2. **Historical Data**: A data warehouse contains a robust amount of historical data. Many companies keep year-wise history of data in the data warehouse for the past 5–10 years.

   A data warehouse can benefit many organisations such as metro city municipal corporations, universities, offices of the registrar of assurances and courts by replacing huge record rooms associated with the problem of space and preservation of the old records. The retrieval of old data/information also becomes faster and easier. Although historical data have many applications, perhaps the most potent is the ability to step backward in time and extrapolate the future trend or perform a 'what-if' analysis.
3. **Time Stamping and Data Relationships**: The units of data stored in a data warehouse are time stamped so that each unit of data record in the data warehouse has some element of time associated with the same. Time stamping of records in a data warehouse is either continuous or discrete as shown in Figure 5.8. In case of a discrete record, there is one instant in time for which the record is accurate, and this is true in the case of fast changing variables such as gold price and share value.

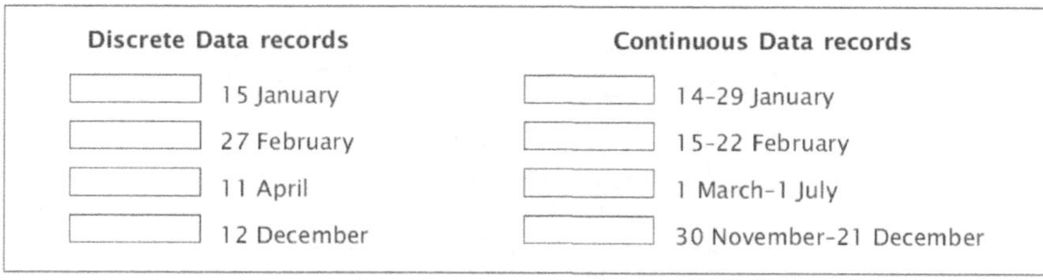

Figure 5.8 Time Stamping of Either Continuous or Discrete Records

In the case of continuous records, there is a span of time for which the record is accurate such as variables that change slowly and for which there is an advantage in knowing information over time. The records in the data warehouse have a distinctive structure including (a) a time stamp, (b) a key, (c) a primary data and (d) a secondary data. For example, in case of an order record, there will be a time stamp corresponding to the order date, order number, product or products ordered, quantity, amount and delivery date and so on which are primary data and the secondary data are package type, mode of delivery and so on. The different types of data found in a data warehouse relate to each other by means of foreign keys pointing to actual keys. For example, an end product EP1 requires a component COMP1. There would be an end product record for end product EP1, as well as a separate component record for the component COMP1. The component record COMP1 in its body would have a foreign key reference to end product EP1.

It may be noted that the data relationships found in the data warehouse are delimited by time. This implies that when a relationship is indicated in the data warehouse, the relationship is only valid for the moment in time indicated by the time stamps found on the participating records. This interpretation of data relationship in the case of a data warehouse is quite different from that of referential integrity found in the case of an online database environment.

4. **Data Volume in a Data Warehouse**: Today the usual volume of data in a data warehouse is of the order of terabyte (10^{12} bytes) or petabyte (10^{15} bytes)! As the volume of data increases in a data warehouse, the ratio of inactive to active data increases at a very high rate and in the case of a terabyte warehouse, it may be as high as 90%. This makes the cost of the warehouse very high and at the same time, data access very slow. It is therefore the practice to periodically remove inactive (dormant) data from main storage and place the same in alternate storage. This results in a significant reduction in the cost of active data storage and increases the speed of access to the active data in the data warehouse. However, in order to make the active data and inactive (dormant) data in separate storage work well, a cross-media storage manager (CMSM) technology is utilised. The CMSM acts as a link between main storage and alternate storage and manages the traffic between the two so that the end users are presented with a seamless view of the data residing in the data warehouse.
5. **Data Marts**: Data marts are simple forms of data warehousing, and in the case of top-down architecture, they are supposed to be created out of and subordinate

to the data warehouse. However, data marts can also be created independently for various functions and then, they may collectively represent a corporate data warehouse as a bottom-up approach. In other words, data marts are scaled-down versions of the data warehouse and created with specific objectives or functions of the company. The functions specific to data marts are related to functions such as marketing, manufacturing, personnel and logistics.

The advantages of the creation of data marts are low cost and less time requirement. Data marts are also often created with specific focus. For example, data marts may be created for the purchase department of a company with supplier's information only to develop better sources of supplies. This kind of approach is useful so far as a relevant information base to cater to managerial decisions is concerned. Instead of creating a full-scale data warehouse, data marts sometimes provide tremendous service to meet immediate and specific information need.

The data warehouse gave birth to different forms of environment that accomplished very different types of information processing. At the centre of all the different architectural structures such as operational data stores, alternative forms of storage, data marts, data mining and so forth is the data warehouse. The data warehouse provided the granular data that was reshaped into many different forms in order to feed many different forms of decision support processes. The architectural framework that emerged is called the 'corporate information factory' as shown with a simple illustration in Figure 5.9.

5.13 Some Popular Data Warehouse Software

Some of the popular software products and tools relating to data warehouse ETL and data mining are listed below:

1. Warehouse Products:
   (i) 'CA—Ingress'—Computer Associates
   (ii) 'All Base/SQL'—HP
   (iii) SQL Server—Microsoft
   (iv) 'Informix XPS'—Informix
   (v) Oracle 8, 'Oracle Parallel Server'—Oracle
   (vi) SQL Server 11.0—Sybase
2. Data-mining Products:
   (i) 'Mine Set'—on silicon graphics platform
   (ii) 'Intelligent Miner'—IBM
   (iii) 'Knowledge Seeker'—Angloss
   (iv) 'Neuro agent'—Data Mind
   (v) 'IDIS3'—Information Discovery
   (vi) 'SAS/Neuro nets'—SAS Institute
3. ETL Tools:
   (i) 'Passport'—Carleton Corporation
   (ii) 'Data Junction' ETL Tool—Data Junction Corporation
   (iii) 'Data Mapper' for transform—Applied Database Technology
   (iv) 'Prism Warehouse Manager'—Prism Solutions
4. OLAP and EIS:
   (i) 'Pablo'—Andyne computing
   (ii) 'Plato'—Microsoft

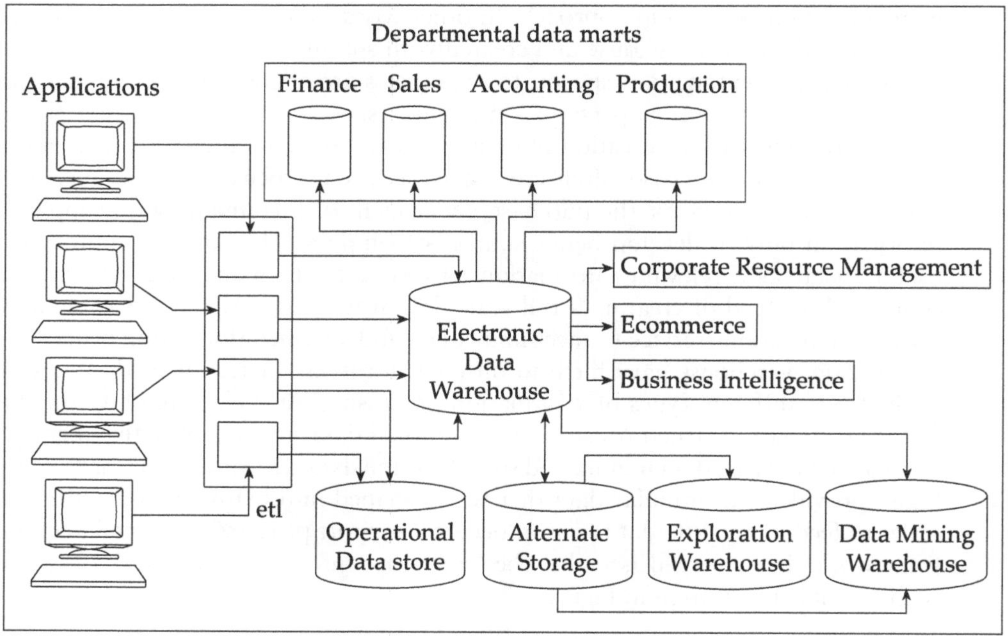

Figure 5.9 Corporate Information Factory

   (iii) 'Express'—Oracle
   (iv) 'Meta cube'—Informix
   (v) 'SAS/EIS', 'OLAP + +'—SAS Institute

5. Reporting Tools:
   (i) 'Discoverer 2000'—Oracle
   (ii) 'Info maker'—Power software
   (iii) 'Vision'—Sterling Software.

5.14 Business Dashboards

A dashboard is a user interface that somewhat resembles an automobile's dashboard organises and presents information in a way (usually in the form of charts, graphs and dials and so on) that is easy to read and interpret. However, a business dashboard, usually in the form of a computer dashboard, is an interactive one through which the users, usually the senior business executives, can visualise the data or information relating to the key performance indicators (KPIs) of the business they are interested in, and also in a fashion of their choice so as to pay their attention where needed.

A dashboard more or less resembles a GUI. However, some product developers consciously employ this metaphor (and sometimes the term) so that the user instantly recognises the similarity.

Dashboards usually integrate information from multiple components into a unified display. For example, a dashboard may obtain information from the local operational database of a computer, from one or more applications running concurrently and also from a remote location on web servers and present them on the same display board (dashboard). A project monitoring and control centre dashboard can monitor the progress of projects located in various distant locations. Hewlett Packard (HP) developed the first dashboard for customising windows desktops.

The HP dashboard was subsequently acquired by Borland, and then a company called Star Fish was established. Microsoft's digital dashboard tool incorporates web-based elements such as news and stock quotes, together with corporate elements (such as email and applications) into Outlook. Dashboards may be customised in a multitude of ways and named accordingly, for example, enterprise dashboard, CEO dashboard and executive dashboard.

5.14.1 Examples of Dashboards

Example 1: Let us illustrate a simple dashboard for monitoring and control of inventory level for a manufacturing unit by the senior materials manager. The dashboard is for showing raw material and work-in-process (WIP) inventory both in value and in days of average consumption for raw materials and days of production for WIP. The dashboard shows only quarterly figures for each quarter completed, which are compiled with the figures for the three consecutive months of the quarter. The dashboard consists of bar charts, pie charts and dials as shown in Figure 5.10.

Example 2: A sales analysis dashboard to facilitate sales promotion drives is shown in Figure 5.11. There are many dashboard software options available in the market, and the available software invariably has the open database connectivity (ODBC) feature to get the source data from various types of files such as Microsoft Excel, dBase, Oracle, MySQL, DB2 and Access. The dashboard software also has excellent interactive features, by dint of which the users can select the type of visual display such as chart, pie or dial and score speedometer. The users of the dashboard also have the options to select data ranges, define regions on the displays as 'bad', 'warning' or 'good' to attract attention when the performance measure is not satisfactory. In the case of Excel files, the data rows/columns can be suitably defined to indicate values associated with the KPIs and also the date hierarchy (day/month/quarter/year and so on) corresponding to the performance indicators.

The dashboard software through ODBC accesses the Excel data files and converts the data in the form of display as defined by the user relating to fiscal quarter, fiscal month and so on.

5.14.2 Some Important Features in a Dashboard Design

Some very important aspects that make a good dashboard application and which decide the choice of the dashboard software are

1. Customisable reports, charts and graphs
2. Options to adjust the measures of performance
3. Sharing of the dashboards with other team members of the company
4. Option to present an automatic report generation date and time

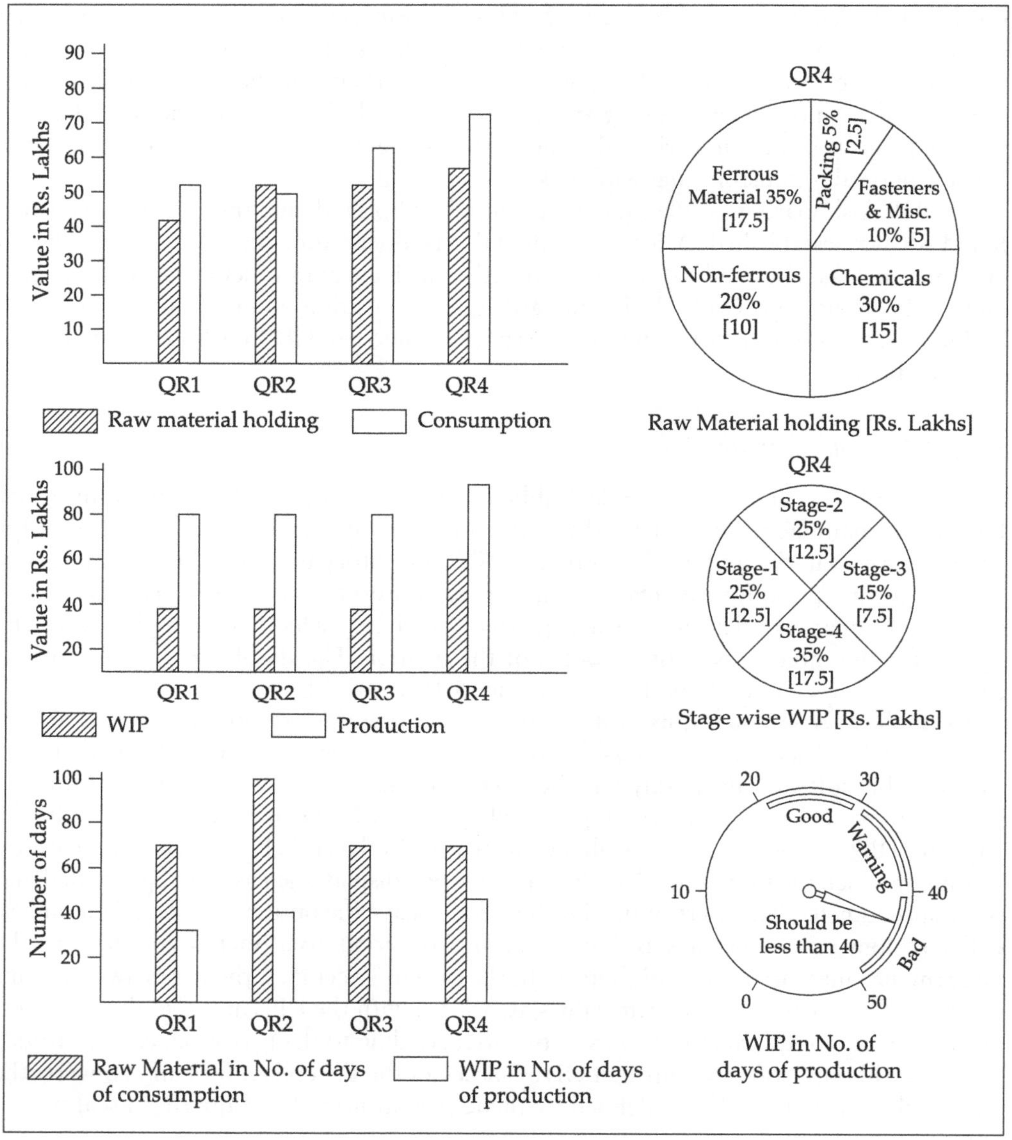

Figure 5.10 Dashboard for Inventory Control

5. Collection and analysis of data according to a preselected set of rules as opposed to merely recording
6. ODBC to various types of files and web-enabling features
7. User-friendly with no need for coding; easy to use and easy to learn.

5.14.3 Practices to Design Good Dashboards

The points that should be kept in mind while designing a dashboard are as follows:

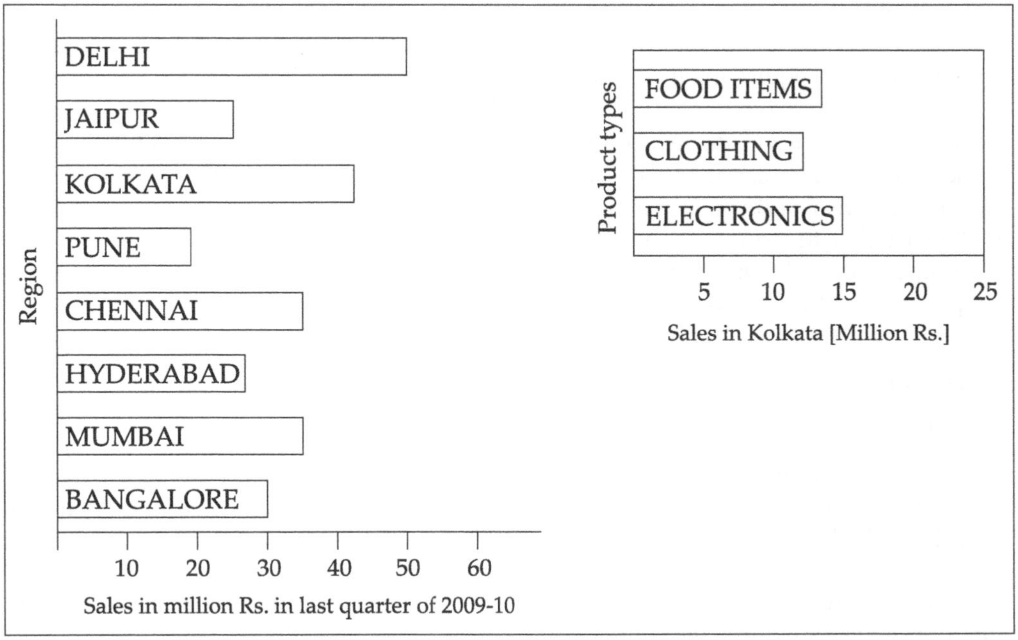

Figure 5.11 A Dashboard for Sales Analysis

1. The dashboard should be designed to have a diagnostic approach to business problems.
2. Before designing the dashboard, the designer should choose wisely and decide the most important data points for the management team. In other words, the designer needs to know the KPIs and the CSFs for the organisation for which the dashboard is designed.
3. The dashboard should be simple and must not be cluttered with too many unnecessary graphs, charts and so on, which may distract attention so that important things may be overlooked.
4. The dashboard screen design should be such that no horizontal scrolling is necessary. It is best if the dashboard is a single-page design without any scrolling at all.
5. In order to get concise results, the period of time over which reports are generated should be kept to a certain minimum. If the need arises to compare data over a longer period of time, it is better to generate two dashboard graphs for comparison.
6. The design should be such that there is adequate interactivity, such as the selection of a certain region, drilling down, which adds to perceived usability.

5.15 Artificial Intelligence

There can be more than one definition of AI such as:

1. AI is the study of how to make machines (rather than computers) do certain things which human beings can also do using their intelligence.

2. AI is a branch of computer science, which deals with the automation of intelligent behaviour.
3. AI is the study of computational processes and techniques for performing tasks that apparently require intelligence, performed by humans.

All the above definitions have a commonality, which is that AI is similar to human intelligence which when ascribed to computers or machines makes them perform tasks as humans can also perform using their intelligence. Hence, AI is machine or computer intelligence that functions like human intelligence.

Comparison and contrast of machine intelligence versus human intelligence from the perspective of AI are shown in Table 5.3.

5.15.1 Areas of AI

5.15.1.1 Natural Language Processing (NLP)

This involves the understanding of natural human languages such as English, speech understanding, machine translation and language generation. Making computers understand English allows non-programmers to use them with little training. Natural language understanding in specific application areas such as access to a database is easy.

Natural language generation is easier than natural language understanding and can be accomplished through inexpensive output devices.

Machine translation is a usable translation of text and is important for organisations having global operations.

5.15.1.2 Perception

It facilitates recognising shapes, features and so on by machines automatically and to initiate automatic action. Perception involves machine vision, speech understanding, tactile sensation and so on. Machine vision can be developed by interfacing a camera to a computer, which gets an image into the computer memory. The problem is with matching the image with patterns already stored in the computer system and understanding what the image represents.

Speech understanding systems are available now, and some systems need to be trained for individual users and require parsing between words. However, understanding continuous speech with a large vocabulary may be difficult for machines to perceive. Tactile sensation is common with computer touch screens, robotic tasks and so on. Perception leads to actions (tasks) by intelligent robots.

5.15.1.3 Machine Learning

It is a method of programming a computer which learns from experience with reference to some specific type of tasks, and the performance for the tasks of the same type also improves with the experience. In other words, it is the ability of a machine to improve its own performance through the use of algorithms that employ techniques to mimic the ways by which humans seem to learn, such as repetition and experience.

Learning techniques are broadly classified as learning from examples, advice of experts, and analogy. Learning from examples and analogy gives rise to knowledge induction

Table 5.3 Comparison and Contrast of Human and Machine Intelligence

Human Intelligence	*Machine Intelligence*
1. Human intelligence is derived out of knowledge stored in human brain.	1. Machine intelligence is derived out of knowledge stored in the machine.
2. Knowledge is acquired through the process of learning (formal or informal education).	2. Knowledge is acquired out of learning (instructions).
3. Knowledge is gained out of experience (expertise).	3. Knowledge is gained through perception (machine vision).
4. New knowledge is created out of existing knowledge and expertise (derived knowledge).	4. New knowledge is created out of existing knowledge (derived knowledge).
5. Human intelligence is derived out of knowledge possessed by human beings by dint of memory/ comprehension, logic, mental arithmetic, perception and program/reasoning, recognition and so on.	5. Machine intelligence is derived by processing of knowledge through searching of knowledge base, language understanding, symbolic representation through logic and frames, rules, program, pattern matching, reasoning, resolution and so on.
6. Human beings also derive intelligence out-of-computer programs that are able to exhibit expert-like performance in a specific domain of application by way of consultation with domain knowledge experts.	6. Intelligence is also derived out of computer programs that are able to exhibit expert-like performance in a specific domain of application.
7. Intelligence (actions) arises because of stimulus (perception), understanding of languages and foresight.	7. Intelligence (actions) arises because of natural language processing, machine (computer) vision and environmental scanning and projections.
8. Knowledge is stored in human memory (brain).	8. Knowledge is stored in machine (computer) by way of knowledge representation methods.
9. Complex problems are solved by intuition to arrive at optimal or near optimal solution.	9. Complex problems are solved by heuristic problem-solving methods.
Contrast	**Contrast**
10. Human intelligence and behaviour are subject to emotions and sentiments.	10. Machine intelligence and behaviour are not subject to emotions and sentiments.
11. Human intelligence deteriorates with ageing.	11. Machine intelligence does not deteriorate with ageing.

in the form of an induction algorithm. Input to the induction algorithm is classified examples, and output from the same algorithm is a decision tree with features labelling interior nodes and the classifications labelling the leaves of the tree. Depending upon the combination of various features as observed in the learnt examples, there can be multiple classifications, as illustrated in Figure 5.12.

In the example shown in Figure 5.12, the classifications, features and the domains are as follows:

Classifications: (Scooter, bicycle, auto-rickshaw, cycle rickshaw, trailer, car, bus)

Features: (Number of wheels, engine, weight)

Domains:

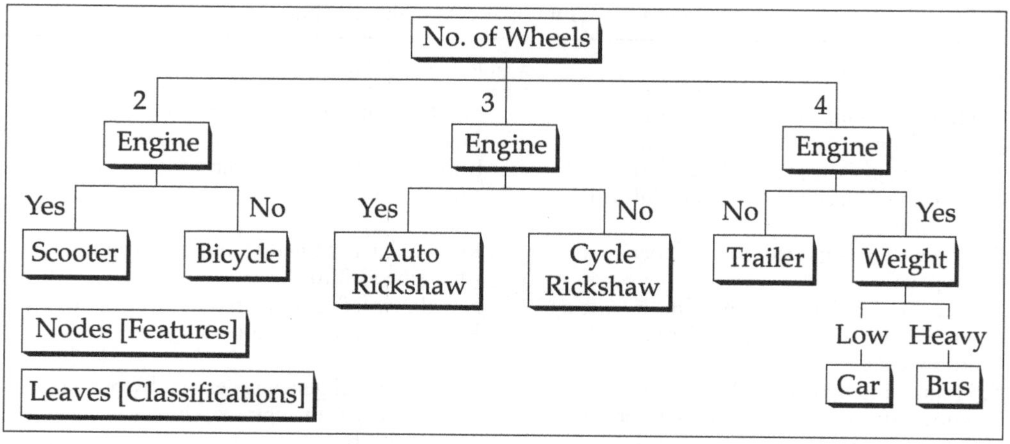

Figure 5.12 Classification of Transport Vehicles According to Features

Number of wheels = (2, 3, 4)
Engine = (Yes, No)
Weight = (Low, Heavy)

New objects can be classified using the decision tree.

The algorithms for rule of knowledge induction have inputs of instances, a set of training examples, known as the training set and the associated features known as the feature vector ($f_1, f_2, \ldots, f_n$).

The algorithms employ various selection strategies for features such as (a) random selection to make a decision tree consistent with the training set and with no guarantee of optimality, (b) information theoretic selection to select features which maximally divides the training set and (c) minimum cost selection which considers evaluation of features. For example, the feature of blood group may be costly to determine in a group of mammals.

Learning from the advice of experts is based on the assumption that it is easier for experts to demonstrate his/her expertise in respect of the learning than to record all of his/her knowledge. Interactions with experts often reveal new knowledge and rules. For example, for a young male patient of 19 years of age, the symptoms of persistent knee and ankle joint pains, swelling of joints and muscular inflammation necessitate the correct diagnosis consistent with the symptoms which is osteoarthritis. However, experts opined that osteoarthritis could never be expected in a male patient at this young age. This results in a new rule added to the existing knowledge to rule out osteoarthritis in young male patients.

Conceptual Islands:

Conceptual islands are tools for collecting knowledge from experts about a domain. These concepts reduce the number of rules required for the knowledge and also facilitate introducing new rules to become effective along with the rest of the system knowledge.

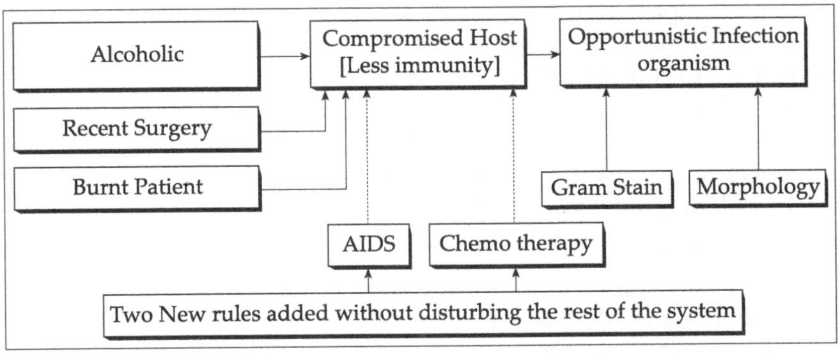

Figure 5.13 A Conceptual Island

A classic example of a conceptual island is the expert system 'MYCIN', that diagnosed blood diseases with a compromised host as shown in Figure 5.13.

However, there are many tasks for which it is impossible or rather difficult to design and implement machine learning software with expert advice. A few of such cases are as follows:

1. There are problems where human experts are unable to demonstrate their expertise, for example, handwriting experts. In such cases, machines are provided with examples of inputs and correct outputs to those inputs for future knowledge extraction.
2. There are totally new problems for which no human expertise exists; for example, launching spacecraft towards Mars with human beings for the first time.
3. There are problems where significant events are rapidly changing, such as foreign currency exchange rates, behaviour of the stock market and so on. In these cases, a continuous learning program on a real-time system constantly modifies and fine-tunes the learnt prediction rules.
4. Customised applications for each user separately, for example, a program to eliminate unwanted email messages.

Learning Tasks:

Learning tasks can be classified according to many different dimensions, and one such dimension is the distinction between empirical and analytical learning. Empirical learning is learning that relies on some form of external experience, while analytical learning needs no external inputs. The various types of empirical learning tasks are supervised learning, unsupervised learning, reinforcement or Q-learning and so on, while speed-up learning is a form of analytical learning. Let us explain in brief the above types of empirical and analytical learning.

Supervised Learning:

The task of supervised learning is to construct a classifier given a set of classified training examples such as photographs of sports personalities with the games they play. A pair consisting of an object along with the associated class is called a labelled example and the set of such labelled examples is known as the training set. The training set facilitates the development of the learning algorithm. Apart from learning classifiers, supervised training also includes learning functions to predict numerical values. The task is called regression. For example, given the three-dimensional view of a building, a civil engineer might like to predict the construction cost, years elapsed since its construction and so on. A major challenge to supervised learning is the problem of generalisation. The generalisation accuracy depends upon the (1) sise and complexity of the classifiers and also (2) upon the volume of training data (examples). The accuracy improves with the increased sise of classifiers up to a certain maximum and then decreases with further increase. However, the accuracy increases with the increase of training data volume.

Unsupervised Learning:
Unsupervised learning is to describe a wide range of different learning tasks which analyse a given set of objects that do not belong to defined class labels. The unsupervised learning tasks are generally of the following types:

1. **Object Completion:** The object completion task involves predicting missing parts of an object or a situation and then constructing the full object or completely describing the situation, given a partial description of the object or situation. For example, if it is said, 'Ram went to the fruit shop and paid money to the shopkeeper for some fruits and then left', we may as well find out the missing situation 'Ram picked up some fruits from the shop and put the same into his bag' before he left. Another example that can be cited for object completion is if one sees the front side of a car visible around the corner of a building, he/she can predict what the rest of the car looks like and then complete the picture of the car.
2. **Understanding and Visualisation:** The idea of understanding and visualisation is basically to study the relationships existing among a large collection of objects in order to arrange them into a hierarchy of classes known as clusters based on the relationships. The relationship among the objects in a hierarchical cluster is based on one or more attributes such as length, height, width, colour, density and chemical composition. For example, income taxpayers can be arranged into hierarchical clusters as shown in Figure 5.14.
3. **Density Estimation and Anomaly Detection:** This type of unsupervised learning task is based on the probability distribution of the attribute values of a random sample of objects. The objects that do not belong to the underlying probability distribution are considered anomalous. The statistical quality control procedure adopted in manufacturing falls under the purview of unsupervised learning to identify anomalous products produced by a defective machine or process.
4. **Data Compression:** This involves identifying and returning the essential aspects of data. Data compression is a method of storing frequently occurring substrings or sub-images of objects into a dictionary. Then each occurrence of such substrings and sub-images can be replaced by a much more precise reference to the corresponding dictionary entry for those substrings or sub-images. Data compression in the case of unsupervised learning is associated with modelling and coding. Coding is much easier for machines as compared with humans since it requires computation based on history. For example, if an algorithm is used to compute the probability of occurrence of a string S, P(S) in a natural language, the same algorithm can be duplicated while decompressing. Further, there are efficient algorithms for mapping strings to codes given any distribution P(S) of such arithmetic coding.

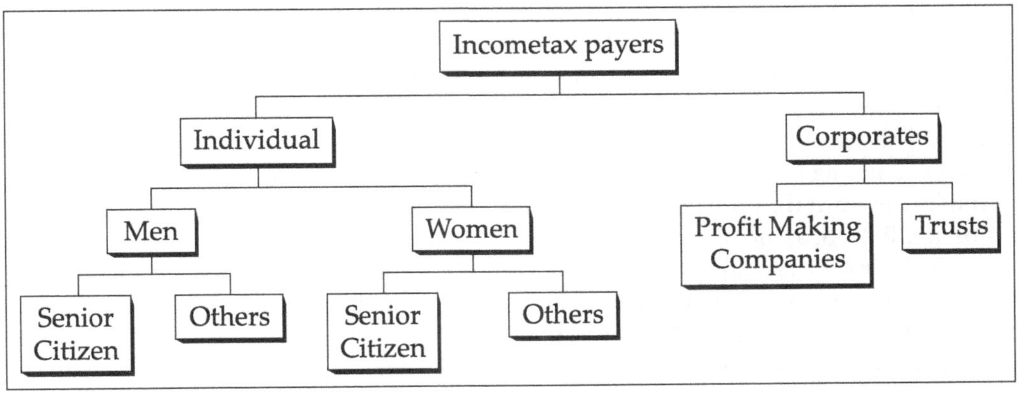

Figure 5.14 Hierarchical Clusters

Example 1: A numeric figure such as 51.55555 can be expressed as 51.(5)5 meaning after the decimal there are five numbers of '5'. The decompressor will use the same algorithm exactly to decompress 51.(5)5 into 51.55555. However, humans may decompress it as 51.56. Modelling is, however, easy for humans compared to machines since humans, with their real-world knowledge and good ability to apply the same, are in a better position to distinguish between high-probability strings and low-probability strings.

Example 2: Let us consider two strings, the 'sky is blue' and the 'sky blue is'. Human beings are able to identify the former as the high-probability string and the latter as the low-probability string. This is precisely the hard problem that a text compressor must solve so that it can assign shorter codes to more probable strings. However, the fact remains that no two humans are going to agree exactly on P(S) for all S. Moreover, P(S) to a person changes over time as he/she learns and forgets.

5. **Information Retrieval**: Another type of unsupervised learning task is to retrieve objects (documents, images, fingerprints) from a large collection of objects. Clustering methods can be applied to this type of unsupervised learning task.

Reinforcement Learning:

Also known as Q-learning, it is a type of learning facilitating sequential decision-making. In the case of supervised and unsupervised learning tasks, the decisions made by the machine or computer system after learning are non-sequential in nature; that is, if the machine or computer system commits a mistake on one decision, the same will have no effect on the subsequent decisions. For example, if the barcode reader misreads a barcode for the price of a particular item in a shopping mall, the billed amount for that item will be reflected wrongly, but that will have no effect on the next item. Contrary to the above, if a pilot of an aircraft makes a mistake at one decision point during the flight, this will affect the situation that the pilot has to take care of in the next decision point. In other words, in the case of sequential decision-making, the decision-makers' decisions at any point have to consider the consequences of their previous decisions also. Sequential decision-making tasks arise in the case of many control systems such as control of spacecraft, oil refineries and nuclear plants.

Reinforcement learning is the task of learning a control policy by interacting with an unknown environment. It can be either model-based or without the same. In the case of model-based reinforcement learning, the learner performs an action (a) in the state of the control system (S) and observes the next state (S′) and the rewards (r) associated with the change from S to S′ and records his/her observation in the form of a quadruple tuple (S, a, r, S′). For example, for a driver controlling the movement of a car, the state of the car can be a vector expressed as (velocity, position, acceleration) and also notes the result (reward [r]) as to whether the car is moving in the proper position on the road or displaced from the proper track and then controls the car by the next action. After performing a large number of actions and noting the change of states with each action, the learner (the driver in the above example) can learn the probability of transition from one state (S) to another state (S′) by an action (a), P (S′, S, a) and the result (reward [r]) associated with S, a, and S′ as a function R (S′, a, S). Once the transition probability and the reward function are known, a dynamic programming algorithm can be formulated to find the optimum control policy. This is known as model-based reinforcement learning. However, reinforcement learning algorithms can be developed as Q-learning where the control policy is learnt by directly interacting with the environment without learning the transition probability and reward functions.

Analytic Learning:
As already stated earlier, analytic learning does not require any external input. Instead, the emphasis is on speed and the reliable inferences and decisions performed by the machine or computer. This type of learning is therefore known as speed-up learning. For example, a mason can mix cement, sand and stone chips in various proportions, check the strength, then find the proportion which maximises the concrete strength, and note down the same in his handbook. After that, when another mason wants to make concrete, the same handbook can be referred to find the proper proportion of mixing the ingredients of concrete. A form of speed-up learning is explanation-based learning. For example, the mason might have discovered that it is important to add cement, sand and stone chips slowly while mixing it with water. The generalised explanation of this is that when adding fine particle ingredients to a liquid, adding them slowly facilitates homogeneous mixing.

Deep Learning:
One of the big challenges with traditional machine learning is that it is not suitable for high dimensionality of data where managers or decision-makers have to deal with a very large number of inputs and outputs.

Moreover, machine-learning models are not able to solve complex and crucial AI problems involving natural language processing, voice and image recognition. The above-mentioned limitation of machine learning arises due to a lack of a process called feature extraction during the learning phase of complex problems such as object or handwriting recognition. A machine-learning model cannot on its own detect all the right features for a complex problem. Deep-learning models are, however, capable of focusing on the right features by themselves, requiring little guidance from the programmers.

Deep-learning models learn through actual examples during the training phase and do not perform any specific task programmed by a programmer. These models can also solve the data dimensionality problem as mentioned earlier. Deep learning emerged as a subset of machine learning. Though the concept of deep learning was developed much earlier in 1985, it could not be exploited fully because of the limitation of the computing power of the computers that existed during that time. However, the next significant evolutionary step for deep learning took place in 1999 when computational speed increased 1,000 times. Deep learning, as a subset of machine learning, gained wide popularity from 2006 onwards. Deep-learning models were developed and applied for commercial use from 2010 onwards.

Neural Networks and Deep Learning: Deep learning makes use of neural networks to simulate human thinking and decision-making. The motivation behind neural networks is the biological neuron as shown below:

The biological neuron consists of the cell nucleus, the dendrite which receives input, a tail-like structure known as the axon, and at the end of the axon a synapse, which transmits the output of the neuron to the dendrite of the next neuron as input. The neurons are connected with one another, and each one receives signals as inputs from other neurons or body parts and then gets activated or not based upon the inputs, such as a binary gate.

The human brain consists of innumerable neurons through which it functions. Similarly, the artificial neural network (ANN) is based on the principle of the human brain, and its smallest component is an artificial neuron also known as a perceptron. Figure 5.15 shows an artificial neuron. It has a central unit that receives inputs which, for example, may be pixels for image processing. The inputs $x_1, x_2, \ldots, x_n$ multiplied by corresponding weights $w_1, w_2, \ldots, w_n$, are added up in the central unit, and to the sum is added a bias multiplied by its weight. The bias value (offset) is always +1 for all neurons, and bias weights only vary to change the offset. The weights can be positive, negative or very near to zero depending on the influence of the inputs. Initially, random values are assigned as input weights.

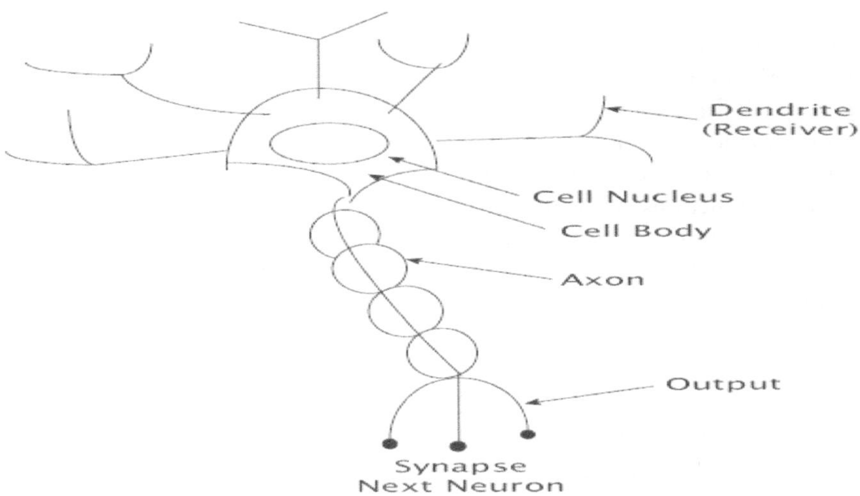

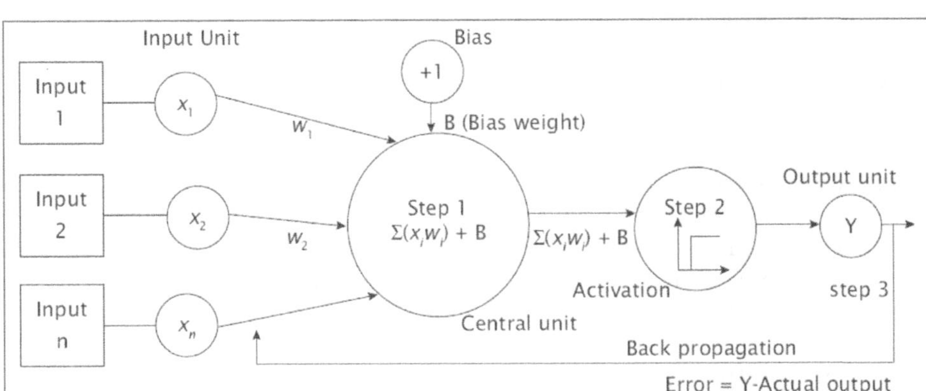

Figure 5.15 Artificial Neuron

The output of Step 1 as obtained above is fed as input to an activation function in Step 2. The purpose of the activation function is to convert the input into an output Y depending upon the type of activation function. Some types of activation functions convert the input into binary output (0 or 1), which decides whether the neuron should fire (1) or not (0). However, there are other types of activation functions also which do not generate binary output and in that case depending upon some threshold value, the neuron will either fire or not fire. The output Y of the neuron is compared with the actual or expected value also known as the labelled information, and the difference is the error which is fed to the neuron for updating the weights of inputs and the bias such that the output Y conforms to the actual or expected value either exactly or as closely as possible. The process of feeding the error as feedback to the neuron or neural network is called back propagation. The process of updating the weights through back propagation is an iterative one, and the iteration continues till the error becomes either zero or close to zero. The whole purpose of training a neural network is to update the weights of the inputs and the bias to achieve the minimum error in the output of the network. The rate at which the ANN is trained to adjust the weights for its inputs and bias in order to attain convergence of its output with expected or labelled values is known as the learning rate of the ANN.

1. **Activation Functions**: An activation function takes the 'weighted sum of inputs plus bias' as the input to the function and returns an output which decides whether the neuron will fire or not depending upon the threshold. The main purpose of an activation function is to induce non-linearity in the output. There are different types of activation functions and the output is different for the different types. The common activation functions are as follows:
   (i) *Sigmoid function*: In the case of the sigmoid function, the output is always between 0 and 1 as shown in the figure below. It is used for situations where the output is required to be expressed as a probability. The function is expressed as:

$$Y(X) = 1/(1 + e^{x})$$

where X is the input and Y is the output of the function.

   (ii) *Step function:* The step function is also a threshold-based activation function, but unlike the sigmoid function, the output for the step function is only 0 or 1 and not any value between 0 and 1 as shown in the figure below. The function is expressed as:

$$Y(X) = 1, \text{ if } X > 0 \text{ else}$$
$$= 0, \text{ if } X < 0$$

   (iii) *ReLU function:* ReLU, also known as the Rectified Linear Unit, is the most widely used activation function. The function returns an output value equal to zero if the input value is zero or less than zero, and an output value equal to the input value if the input value is greater than zero, as shown in the figure below.

Mathematically, the ReLU function is expressed as:

$$Y(X) = \max(X, 0)$$

(iv) *Hyperbolic tangent function:* This function is similar to the sigmoid function except that it returns an output which is bounded between –1 and +1 for all values of input, as shown in the figure below. The function can be expressed as:

$$Y(X) = (e^{x} - e^{-x}) / (e^{x} + e^{-x})$$`

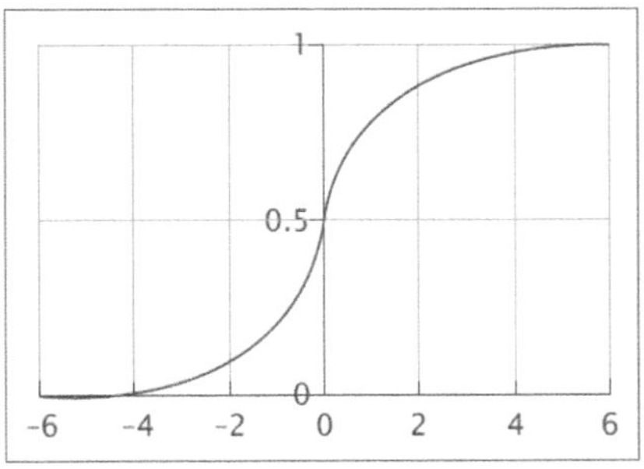

Sigmoid Function

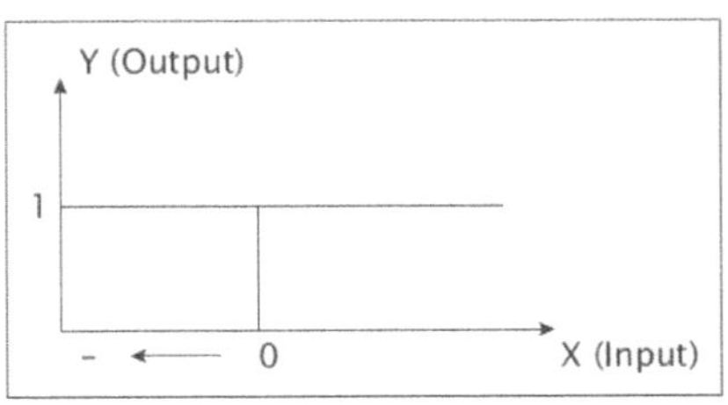

Step Function

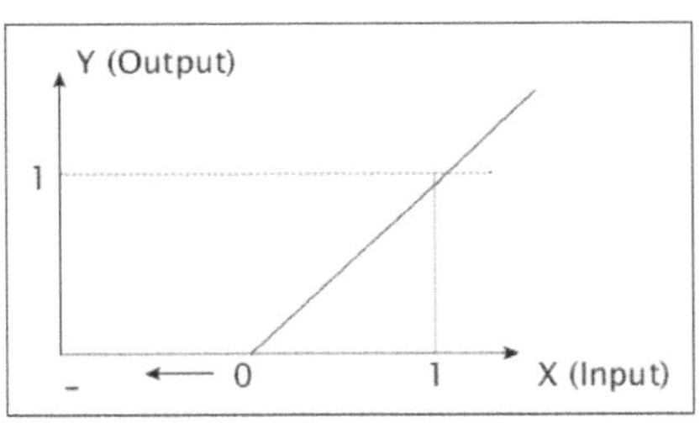

ReLU Function

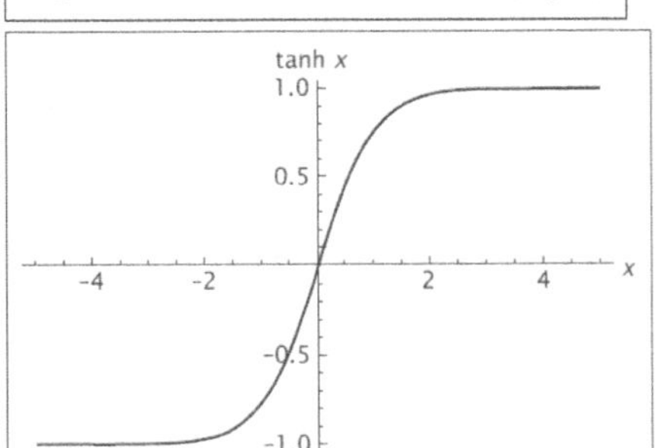

Hyperbolic Tangent Function

The choice of the particular activation function depends upon the type of neural network model and the application for which the model is used.

Deep learning is performed with deep networks, which are neural networks with multiple hidden layers in between the input and the output layers. All the nodes of hidden layers are activation nodes, and the outputs of any particular hidden layer will become inputs for the next layer with corresponding weight.

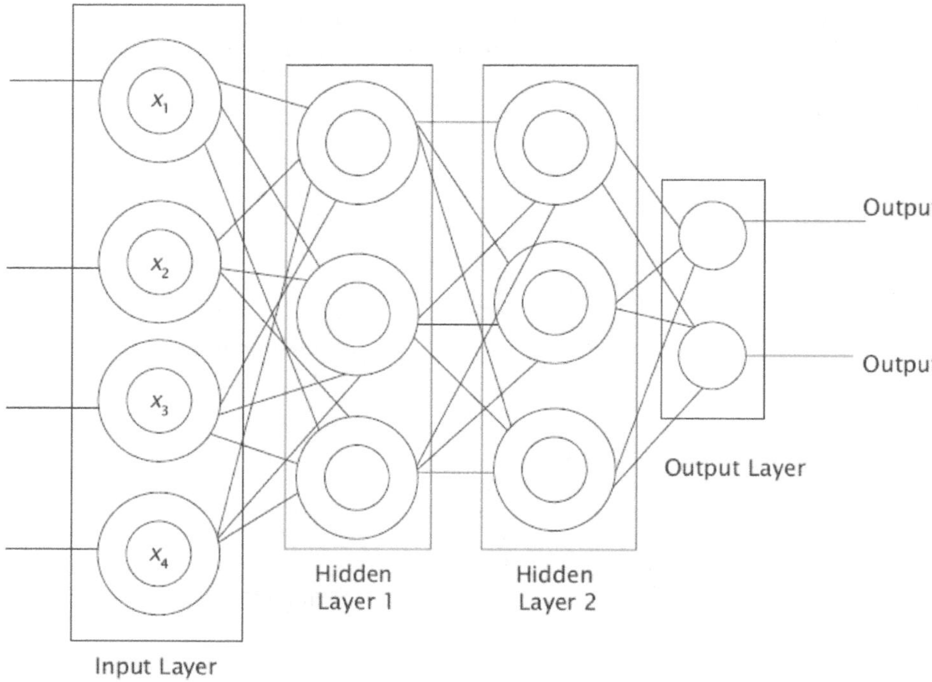

Figure 5.16 Deep Neural Network with Two Hidden Layers

However, the output of any node of any layer may also be the input to a node of the previous layer, and in that case, the neural network is termed a recurrent neural network (RNN), which has been explained in a subsequent paragraph. The hidden layers may be fully connected, in which case the nodes of the same layer may also be connected with each other or partially connected. Figure 5.16 shows a deep neural network with two hidden layers.

Example: Let us illustrate deep learning with a simple example. Suppose students, after passing their higher secondary examination, appear in an entrance examination for admission to state medical colleges. The subjects of the examination are three, namely physics, chemistry and biology. The students who pass the entrance examination are called for an interview for the final selection. The criteria for passing the entrance examination are either a pass in all three subjects or a pass in physics or chemistry with distinction (80% or more marks) in biology. A deep neural network for this example, which can be trained for adjusting the weights for output ('0' for fail and '1' for pass) conforming to the above criteria, can be as follows (Figure 5.17):

Let us initially assign the weights as follows:

$$w_{11} = 1, w_{12} = 1, w_{13} = 1, Bw_{11} = 1, Bw_{12} = 1, w_{21} = 1, w_{22} = 1 \text{ and } Bw_{21} = 1$$

However, in this case for a student who has passed in physics and biology only but has not got a distinction in biology, the output of the deep neural network is 1 (selected for interview), which is not the correct output since the student with passing marks in

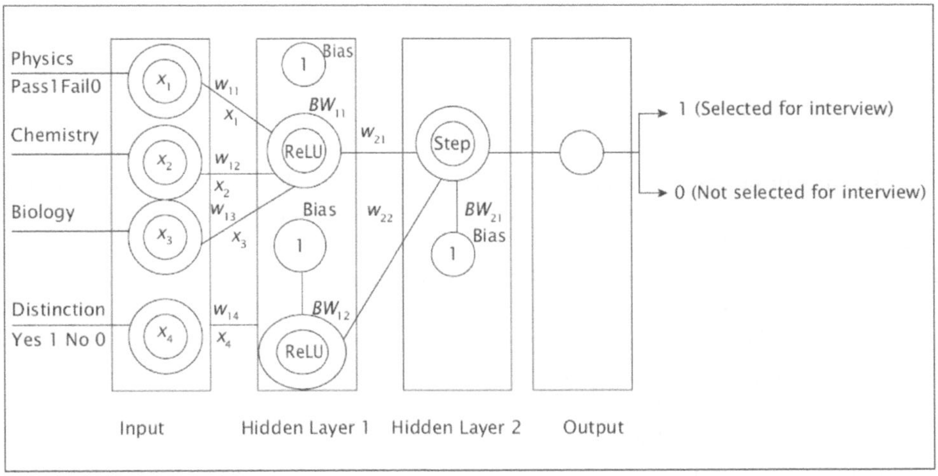

Figure 5.17 Deep Neural Network for the Example

physics and biology cannot be selected for interview unless he/she secures a distinction in biology.

Hence, the back-propagation process will update the weights through iterative trials. It can be seen that for the following weights, the network will be fully accurate conforming to the correct output for all valid input.

$$w_{11} = 2, w_{12} = 2, w_{13} = 2, Bw_{11} = -5, Bw_{12} = 1, w_{21} = 1, w_{22} = 1 \text{ and } Bw_{21} = 1.$$

Types of Neural Networks: There are various types of neural networks with different features, and the selection of the proper type mainly depends upon the particular application. Some of the popular types of networks and their distinctive features are as follows:

1. **Feedforward Neural Network:** It is a very simple form of ANN where the data or input travels in one direction from the input nodes to the output nodes. Feedforward neural networks may have or may not have hidden layers. Such networks have front propagation only and no back propagation. Generally, they work on classifying activation functions. Feedforward neural networks find use in computer image and voice recognition where due to the very nature of the computer images and voice, classifying the target classes is very difficult and complicated. This type of neural network finds wide application in X-ray image fusion, which is the process of superimposing one image over the other based on the edges. MRI and CT images can be overlaid into a fused image.
2. **Recurrent Neural Network:** RNN works on the principle of saving the output of a layer and feeding the same back to the input to help in predicting the outcome of the layer. This implies that each neuron will remember the information it had in a previous time step ($t - 1$) which can be compared with the current information at time. In order to achieve the same feature, each neuron or node acts like a memory cell in the case of making a computation.

   Example of RNN:

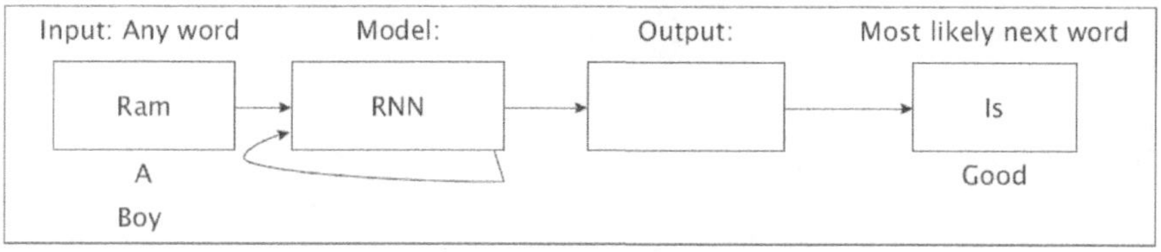

Recurrent neural networks are perhaps the most widely used ANNs, and they are used in text processing, text-to-speech conversion (TTS), stock price prediction and many other applications.

3. **Long Short-Term Memory (LSTM)**: This artificial recurrent neural network is used in deep learning. Unlike feedforward neural networks, LSTM possesses feedback connections. It can process sequential data such as speech, video or time series data. A usual LSTM has an 'input' gate, an 'output' gate and a 'forget' gate. The gates enable an LSTM to remember values over arbitrary time intervals and also to control the flow of information from its input to output. LSTM networks are well suited for making predictions based on time series data.
4. **Convolutional Neural Network (CNN)**: CNN is perhaps the most important deep learning neural network for computer vision, which facilitates image classification with a high degree of accuracy. For example, a computer can recognise an image of an animal and classify it as a dog, a cat or a horse. However, CNN can be applied in other areas of deep learning also such as trend analysis using time series data.

The computer is able to perform image classification by looking for low-level features such as edges and curves and then building up more abstract concepts through a series of convolutional layers. The basis of the functioning of a CNN is the biological visual cortex, which has small regions of cells that are sensitive to specific regions of the visual field.

The first convolutional layer is basically a filter which slides or convolves around the input such as an image. As it convolves, it multiplies the values of the filter with the original pixel values of the image for each location on the image, and the values of the multiplications for all the locations on the image are summed up to have a single value. The purpose is to detect low-level features on the image such as curves or edges. The output of the first convolution layer is fed as input to the second convolutional layer. The input to the second layer is the activation maps that result from the first layer. The output of the second and subsequent convolutional layers are the activations that represent higher levels of features such as semi-circles or squares which are only combinations of several curves or straight edges. As we go through deeper convolutional layers, we get activation maps representing more and more complex higher-level features.

The last convolutional layer is connected to a fully connected network (FCN) at the end of the network. FCN basically takes the output of the convolutional or ReLU or pool layer preceding it and generates outputs which are the probability values for the input image to match with the different classes such as dog, cat or horse. This is, in short, the function of a CNN. A classic CNN architecture is as follows:

Input → Convolution → ReLU → Convolution → ReLU → Pool → FCN

Important Applications of Deep Learning: The deep learning method is adopted in a variety of applications such as:

- Cancer detection by early identification of cancerous tumours in the human body
- Robot navigation for manufacturing operations
- Oil exploration
- Surveillance and security
- Self-driving cars
- Music composition
- Colourisation of images
- Machine translation of languages such as Spanish, French or German

5.15.1.4 Knowledge Representation

Since AI is created through a computer's knowledge of the world, it is necessary to represent the computer's knowledge by some kind of data structures in the memory of the computer. Apart from traditional computer databases which deal with large amounts of structured data, AI programs need to deal with complex entities having complex relationships on a conceptual level. In the case of AI, several kinds of knowledge need to be represented—factual knowledge which are known facts such as 'the Sun rises in the east', universal rules or principles such as 'every cow is a mammal', hypothetical data which the computer has to consider in order to reason about the effects of actions which are contemplated. There are also several ways of knowledge representation as described in the following paragraphs. There are also several issues in knowledge representation such as knowledge storage, knowledge retrieval applicable to a problem and reasoning (logic) to derive implied knowledge.

Rule-based Knowledge:
Knowledge-based systems often represent knowledge by if-then type rules. The expert systems, which will be discussed in a subsequent section, are built on if-then rules. For example, a medical specialist with years of clinical experience can create knowledge based on rules as follows:

Rule 1: IF (Body temperature above 100°F AND no cough) THEN prescribe 'Calpol' and antibiotic tablets.
Rule 2: IF (Body temperature below 100°F AND fever persists for more than 2 days) THEN advise blood test and prescribe antibiotics.
Rule 3: IF (Fever accompanies tremor) THEN advise tests for malaria parasites.
Rule 4: IF (Mild fever persists AND pale-yellow eyes) THEN advise treatment for 'jaundice'.

Ontology Tools:
Ontology describes the relationships among entities on a conceptual level. It also describes the hierarchy of classes and subclasses for an object entity together with the relationships, contrasts, constraints and other information about objects.

Example: Ontology for the Judiciary of India.

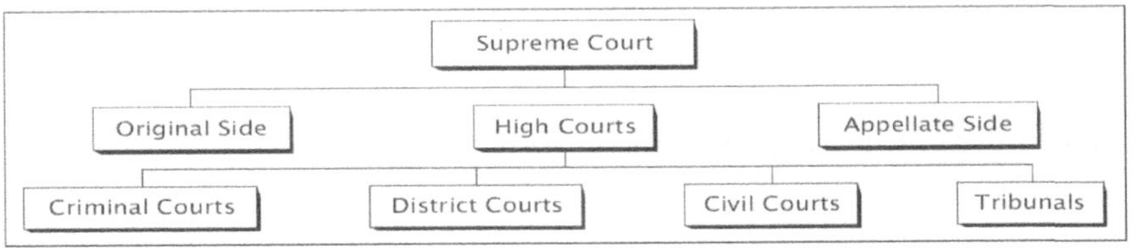

Ontology tools such as Protégé (frames and editors), knowledge acquisition systems and Gene Ontology tools facilitate knowledge acquisition, representation and also generation of new knowledge out of existing knowledge.

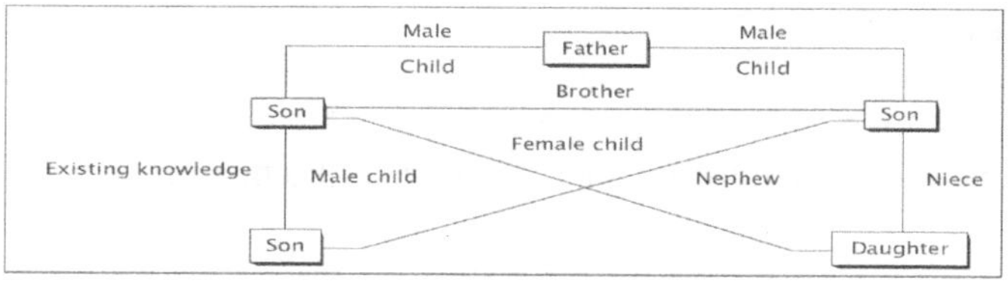

Leads to new knowledge as follows:

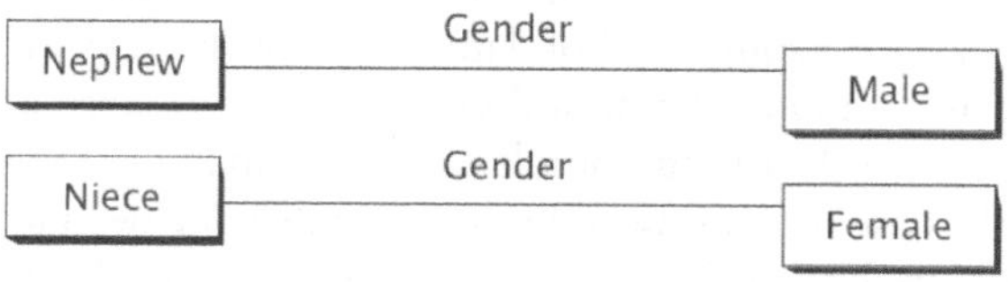

Ontology provides vital information to search agents, intelligent agents and databases. Agents use ontology and perform powerful reasoning to represent knowledge. Ontology is modelled using the web ontology language (OWL) and gives rise to a web encyclopaedia of knowledge.

Logic:

Knowledge representation methods based on mathematical logic retrieve intelligence by the use of first-order predicate logic. A predicate resembles a function that returns either true or false for a proposition. While propositional logic deals with simple declarative propositions, first-order logic incorporates predicates and quantifies additionally. For example, 'Kalidas is a poet' and 'Tagore is a poet' are two unrelated propositions. However, in predicate logic, these two propositions can be expressed with a syntactic entity 'Poet' as Poet (x), which asserts that the object represented by x is a poet. If x is Kalidas, then Poet (x) represents the first proposition, whereas if x is Tagore, Poet (x) represents the second proposition. An assignment of semantic meaning, as explained above, is called an interpretation. First-order logic allows reasoning about properties that are shared by many objects. For example, if Poet (x) asserts that x is a poet and if Linguist (x) asserts that x is also a linguist, then the formula

$$\text{Poet}(x) \rightarrow \text{Linguist}(x)$$

asserts that if x is a poet, then x is also a linguist. The symbol → is used to denote a condition. The hypothesis lies to the left of the arrow and the conclusion to the right. Now, if we assume that for every x, if x is a poet, then x is also a linguist, the first order sentence will be expressed as follows using the universal quantifier ∀

$$\forall x\, (\text{Poet}(x) \rightarrow \text{Linguist}(x))$$

The universal quantifier ∀ expresses the idea that the above claim holds for all choices of x.

If the universal claim that 'if a poet then a linguist' is false, then there has to be some poet who is not a linguist. This counterclaim against universality can be expressed in first-order logic with existential as quantifier ∃

$$\exists x \, (Poet\ (x) \wedge \neg\ Linguist\ (x)),$$

where ¬ is the negation operator and means that ¬ linguist (x) is true if and only if linguist (x) is false or, in other words, if x is not a linguist. Λ is the conjunction operator which asserts that x is a poet and also not a linguist.

In the above example, predicates Poet (x) and Linguist (x) take only one parameter each. First order can express predicates with multiple parameters. For example, 'there is some employee x, who can be relied upon for every work y', can be expressed as:

$$\exists x \, (Employee\ (x) \wedge \forall w \, (work(y)\ can\ Rely\ (x, y)))$$

The range of the quantifiers is the set of objects that can be used to satisfy them and is known as the domain of discourse or universe for the quantifiers.

Through logic and reasoning, information is derived that is implied by existing knowledge but not stored directly.

Knowledge representation through predicate calculus has definite strengths of logical power and a mathematical foundation. However, it has inherent weaknesses of low speed and rigidity.

Knowledge representation and retrieval in predicate calculus is through the storing of facts in a propositional database, and facts can be retrieved in response to patterns as illustrated below:

Fact:

RAM
(PRAISES)
SITA

Retrieval of Facts:	Does Ram praise Sita?	(PRAISES RAM SITA)
	Whom does Ram praise?	(PRAISES RAM? X)
	Who praises Sita?	(PRAISES? X SITA)
	All pairs of appraisers and appraisees	(PRAISES?X?Y)

Knowledge is stored as logical axioms which can be used for deductions. For example, the rule that 'all dogs bark' can be represented as:

(ALL X (IF (DOG X) (BARK X)))
OR
(IF (DOG? X) (BARK? X))

Deduction, Induction and Abduction: These are various methods of application of principles to infer or explain facts logically. Deduction applies a general principle to infer a fact.

Example: Deduction

Given: Every dog barks. Sweety is a dog.
Inference: Sweety barks
Induction: It assumes a general principle that subsumes many facts.

Example: Induction

Given: Rose, jasmine and lotus are flowers. Rose, jasmine and lotus are fragrant. Bakul is a flower. Bakul is fragrant.
Assume: Every flower is fragrant.
Abduction guesses a new hypothesis that explains some facts.

Example: Abduction

Given: Every dog barks. Sweety barks.
Guess: Sweety is a dog.

Deduction is sound, whereas induction and abduction are not, but essential for intelligence. However, logic is a preferred method of representation and reasoning in cases where the data are discrete and there is absolute truth. Such applications include (a) mathematical theorem proving, (b) proofs of correctness of computer programs and (c) proofs of correctness of logic designs.

5.15.1.5 Semantic Networks and Frames for Knowledge Representation

An alternative to logic for knowledge representation formalism is semantic networks and frames. The term frame was first introduced by Malvin Minsky of the Massachusetts Institute of Technology, USA. Frame-based knowledge representation captures a set of related facts about an object, image or a situation in the form of a frame. Frames are important because they allow deep understanding of new situations about which only minimal information is directly available. They represent our understanding of regularities in the universe that allows intelligent action based on minimal clues. A frame can represent an individual object or a class of similar objects. Instead of properties, a frame has slots. A slot is like a property but can contain more kinds of information (sometimes called facets of the slot).

According to Minsky, 'We can think of a frame as a network of nodes and relations. The top level of a frame is fixed and represent things that are always true in the supposed situation. The low levels have many slots that must be filled with specific instances or data'.

Example of knowledge frame:

Slot Name	*Data*
Mammal	True
Legs	4
Gender	
Food habit	

The above frame captures information about all mammals having four legs in the world. However, the same frame, as shown below, will capture information regarding all mammals having four legs, male and who eat flesh, such as dog.

Slot Name	*Data*
Mammal	True
Legs	4
Gender	Male
Food habit	Carnivorous

Frames can thus capture both the concepts of generalisation and specialisation which facilitate representation of knowledge. A semantic network is a collection of related frames which link together into a frame system. The different frames of a semantic network have the same terminals, which feature makes it possible to coordinate information gathered from different points of view of objects. The semantic networks are linked in turn by an appropriate information retrieval network. A semantic network is a directed graph consisting of vertices, which represent concepts and edges that connect pairs of vertices as shown in Figure 5.18.

There can be various types of semantic networks. A few examples are as follows:

Word Net:
It is an example of a semantic network which is a lexical database of English vocabulary. It groups English words into sets of synonyms called *synsets* and provides the various relations between the synsets. If A and B represent two synsets, then the relationships between A and B can be: synonym (A and B denote the same thing), antonym (A denotes the reverse of B), meronym (A is a part of B, expressed as B has A as a part of itself), holonym (B is a part of A expressed as A has B as a part of itself) and so on.

Winston in 1971 proposed a 'similarity network' wherein pointers from each description of an object/concept point to other descriptions of similar objects/concepts, with each pointer labelled by a difference marker. Complaints about mismatch are matched with the difference pointers leaving the frame and thus may propose a better candidate

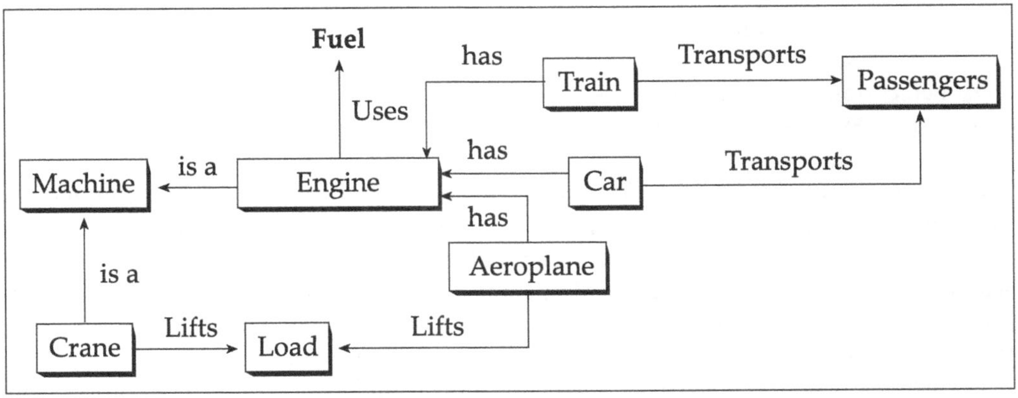

Figure 5.18 A Semantic Network

frame. For example, a furniture network with chair, couch, table, stool, desk and so on and their similarities and differences can be represented as follows:

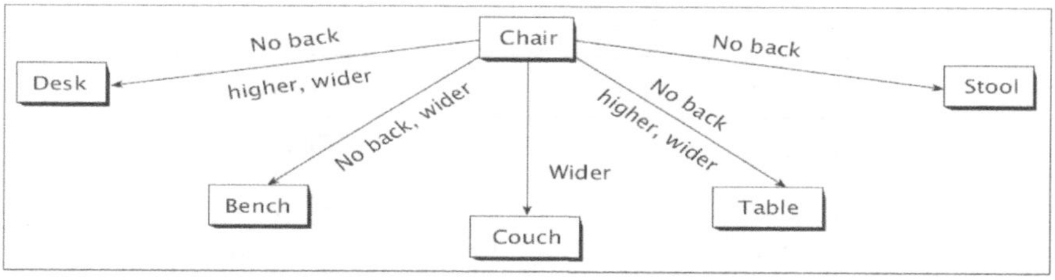

It can be observed from the above examples that semantic networks capture a far deeper knowledge representation through multiple relationships, implication, set and subset association, generalisation, specialisation, instantiation and so on.

Search:
Search programs find a solution for a problem by trying different sequences of actions (operators) until a solution is found. For example, a program can be written to play chess using search; if one knows the rules of chess, it is not necessary to know how to play good chess. However, there is an inherent disadvantage of search if the search space is very large, as is the case with many problems (such as game playing). For example, chess has been estimated to have 10,120 possible games, and a search in such a case requires huge memory space and computer time also. However, with the application of 'combinatorial explosion' facilitating combinations of possible moves, the problem can be simplified. Search is necessary as there are practical problems which cannot be modelled precisely for exact computation. Moreover, any intelligent system must encounter surprises. Such problems need to be solved dynamically, starting with observed data. Search arises in almost all areas of AI such as:

1. **Theorem Proving**: Searches for a sequence of proof steps that will prove a desired conclusion.
2. **Natural Language Processing**: A writer or composer searches the vocabulary to find words and structure to assign meaning to ambiguous sentences.
3. **Planning**: A planner searches for action plans to achieve goals in the best possible way.
4. **Learning**: A learning program searches for a compact description of a set of training instances.
5. **Perception**: Searches for a consistent interpretation of input signals or feedback.
6. **Expert Systems**: Adopt rules applicable to the current problem.

Broad categories of search include state space search, problem reduction search including game tree search, simulated annealing and Waltz filtering. The various strategies for search include depth-first, breadth-first, hill climbing, heuristic search, uniform cost search, bidirectional search, iterative deepening and so on. Let us briefly explain the concept of state space search and heuristic search strategy with suitable illustrations since these are of considerable significance in problem solving using AI.

State Space Search A state space represents a problem in terms of states and operators that change states. It consists of:

1. A representation of all possible states of a system. Each state is an abstract representation of the system configuration. For example, in a board game, the board represents the current state of the game.
2. Initial state: The description of the starting configuration of the system.
3. An action/operator that takes the system from one state to another state. For example, in a board game, the operators have the legal moves from any given state. The actions/operators are also known as the production rules or programs that change a state representation to represent a new state. A state can have a number of successor states.
4. A plan is a sequence of actions or production rules.
5. A set of final states: some of these may be desirable (goals), others undesirable. Goal states are often specified by a goal test, and a program implicitly detects the goal states.
6. Path cost is the sum of the costs of all steps leading from the initial state to the terminal states.

Example of State Space Search: Using two empty water jugs of 4 litres and 5 litres capacity. It is required to fill 3 litres of water from a tap into either of the jugs.

Here, the state can be represented as a set of ordered pairs of integers as:

(X, Y) where X = 0, 1, 2, 3 or 4 (Quantity in 4-litre jug)
Y = 0, 1, 2, 3, 4 or 5 (Quantity in 5-litre jug)

Start state is (0, 0).
Goal states are (3, n) or (n, 3).

The operations or production rules are as follows:

Production Rules (PR)	*Initial State*	*Final State*	*Operations*
1.	(X, Y) if X < 4	→ [(4 – (4, Y)]	Fill 4-litre jug.
2.	(X, Y) if Y < 5	→ (X, 5)	Fill 5-litre jug.
3.	(4, Y)	→ (0, Y)	Empty 4-litre jug.
4.	(X, 5)	→ (X, 0)	Empty 5-litre jug.
5.	(X, Y)	→ [(X – (5 – Y), 5]	if X + Y ≥ 5 and X > 0, Pour water from 4-litre jug into 5-litre jug until 5-litre jug is full.
6.	(X, Y) if X + Y ≥ 4 and Y > 0	→ [4, Y – (4 – X)]	Pour water from 5-litre jug into 4-litre until it is full.
7.	(X, Y) if X + Y ≤ 4 and Y > 0	→ (X + Y, 0)	Pour all water from 5-litre jug into 4-litre jug.
8.	(X, Y) if X + Y ≤ 5 and X > 0	→ (0, Y + X)	Pour all water from 4-litre jug into 5-litre jug.

The production rules applied in sequence and the state space for the state changes and paths leading to goal states are shown in Figure 5.19.

The paths from the start state (both jugs empty) to one of the goal states (any jug having 3 litres of water) as shown in Figure 5.19 are having the actions denoted by production rules as:

1. PR1—PR5—PR1—PR5 (4 actions) and
2. PR2—PR6—PR3—PR8—PR2—PR6—PR3—PR7—PR2—PR7 (10 actions)

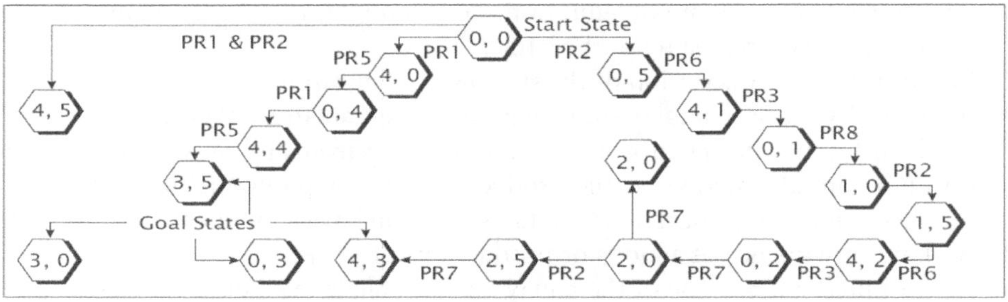

Figure 5.19 State Space and Paths for Production Rules and Change of States Leading to Goal States for the Two Water Jugs Problem

Since Path 1 has a smaller number of actions, it is preferable to Path 2.

Heuristic Search: There are practical state space search problems where the state space becomes enormously large and involves considerable search time as well as computer storage space to reach the goal state. In such situations, the magnitude of the search can be significantly reduced by resorting to heuristic search.

Heuristics use domain-specific knowledge to estimate the quality of intermediate states or potential of partial solutions. The domain-specific knowledge may be established knowledge such as science or intuition acquired through experience. In order to explain how heuristics facilitate state space search, let us cite the example of the famous game of eight numbered tiles as follows:

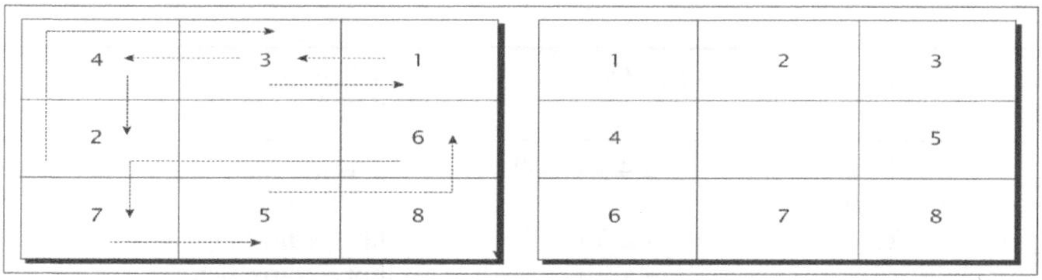

Consider the arrangement of the eight tiles on the left-hand side to a pattern on the right by moving one square at a time into the empty slot. Let us introduce a term called 'distance' in terms of units of one tile moving either horizontally or vertically on slot. For example, in the case of the pattern on the left, if the tile number 3 is shifted down into the empty slot below, the distance moved is 1 unit. Similarly, if either tile 2 is moved to the right or tile 6 is moved to the left into the empty slot, the distance moved is 1 unit only. Now the heuristics in this case is that in order to arrange the tiles into the pattern on the right, the total distance (in units) moved by all the tiles from their initial position (left-hand side arrangement) by whatever state space search path will obviously always be equal to or greater than the individual distance in units measured for each tile from their initial position and the same totalled for all the eight tiles. Let me list below such distances for each tile (the distances are shown through dotted arrows in the pattern shown above.

Tile Number	*Distance (Units)*
1	2
2	2
3	1
4	1
5	2
6	3
7	1
8	0
Total	12

The above total of 12 units is the lower bound of the number of shifts of the tiles by state space search for arranging the tiles from the state on the left to the pattern on the right. Hence, the heuristic in this state space search problem suggests that at each state, the action for the next state (until the goal state is reached) is to move one of the tiles one slot at a time and the tiles to be considered for this move are those involving minimum distances from the present position to the goal state position.

Simple Language Processing: Earlier generation AI program, ELIZA, developed by Joseph Weizenbaum, simulated a psychotherapist and achieved very good performance simply by matching the patient's input to patterns.

Pattern: (I AM FEELING *)
Response: (WHY ARE YOU FEELING *)
The * above matches anything; and the same is repeated in the response.

Patient: I am feeling nervous.
Doctor: Why are you feeling nervous?

However, ELIZA and a general natural language grammar represent two extremes of language processing. ELIZA is too restricted and requires a huge number of patterns; otherwise, there can be a lack of real understanding, as illustrated below:

Patient: I feel like jumping in the river.
Doctor: Tell me more about the river.

The response of the doctor lacks real understanding. General natural language grammar, on the other extreme, contains hundreds of interpretations of ordinary sentences and is full of ambiguity.

5.16 Expert Systems

Expert systems are knowledge-based systems that provide specific knowledge about narrow problem domains through the use of knowledge stored in the knowledge base and an inference (reasoning) procedure to solve problems that would otherwise require human competence or expertise. Features of expert systems are as follows:

1. They are usually computer systems that try to mimic human expertise.
2. Produce decisions that do not require judgement.
3. They assist decision-makers but do not substitute for them.

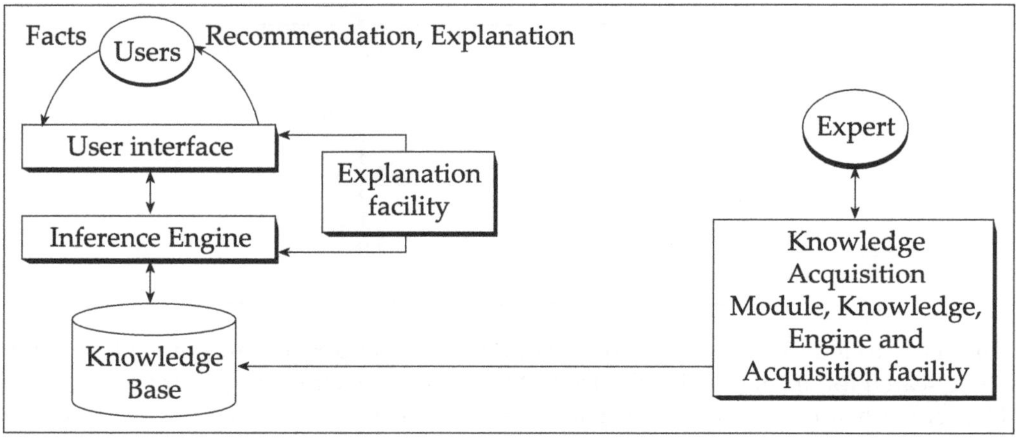

Figure 5.20 Components of an Expert System

Expert systems are a sub-area of AI. While AI is a group of technologies that attempt to emulate certain aspects of human behaviour such as reasoning and communicating with the primary objective of evolving strategies of general problem-solving using intelligence, expert systems concentrate on problem-solving in specific problem domains. Examples of expert systems are oil exploration, medical diagnosis, crime investigation and so on.

5.16.1 Components of Expert Systems

A typical expert system consists of a knowledge base, inference engine, knowledge acquisition module and an explanatory interface as shown in Figure 5.20. The knowledge base is a representation of both book knowledge about a problem domain and the accumulated wisdom of an expert acquired through years of study and experience. The expert knowledge is stored in the knowledge base as rules of thumb used by the human experts in the domain. The knowledge base is built up through a knowledge acquisition module used by experts to enter rules or facts with the help of a knowledge engine. The inference engine controls the order in which the production rules (described elaborately in subsequent paragraphs of this chapter) are applied to solve the problem and resolve conflicts if more than one rule applies. The inference engine functions on a 'reasoning' process. The explanatory interface is the user interface wherein users input the facts of the case and query with the expert system and obtain recommendations/query explanations. The explanatory interface subsystem of an expert system also shows the trail of reasoning it used to reach a decision, that is, (a) explains the facts used, (b) the rules applied and (c) the order in which the rules were applied.

5.16.2 Knowledge Representation in an Expert System

As already stated, earlier knowledge representation in expert systems is in a variety of ways including (a) rules and (b) case-based reasoning. Let us explain these in detail:

Rules: Rules are heuristics obtained from experts and consist of an IF part and a THEN part.

IF <condition> THEN <action>.

Example: Heuristic rule

IF good customer and
credit requested < `10,000
and loan term < 2 years
then grant credit

Case-Based Reasoning: In case of case-based reasoning, the expert system draws inferences by comparing a current problem or case with hundreds of similar past cases. It is best suited when the situation involves too many nuances and all the delicate differences need to be generalised into rules.

Example: The chance of survival of a critically ill patient admitted in the intensive care unit of a hospital can be predicted by entering the vital statistics of the patient including the medical history and so on into the expert system which draws records of thousands of previous intensive care patients with similar illnesses to predict the chance of survival of the patient.

5.16.3 How Does an Expert System Work?

User presents a set of facts describing a situation to the expert system. The inference engine compares facts of the case with the knowledge base. The system then either gives a recommendation or asks for more information.

The inference strategy for a rule-based system can be either to prove that a conclusion (goal) is true or to verify the conjecture that a particular premise is true. The former strategy of inference is called forward chaining, whereas the latter strategy is known as backward chaining. Forward chaining is data driven where inference moves from facts to a goal. In case of backward chaining, inference moves from a possible goal state to premises that will satisfy it.

Example: A general physician with considerable experience has expressed his expertise for the treatment of a patient with fever particularly in the form of simplified rules as follows:

Rule 1: IF (Body temperature 98.4°F or above AND body ache) THEN prescribe antibiotics.
Rule 2: IF (Fever more than 3 days AND body ache) THEN prescribe Cifran tablets.
Rule 3: IF (Viral infection AND prescribe antibiotic) THEN prescribe Cifran tablets.
Rule 4: IF (Viral infection) THEN body ache.
Rule 5: IF (Prescribe Cifran tablets) THEN prescribe dose 500 mg.

Fact: Assume a patient Mr X has a temperature of 101°F and viral infection; Query is what should be the prescription for Mr X?

The rules can be written down then as follows:

R1: IF (A & C) THEN E
R2: IF (D & C) THEN F
R3: IF (B & E) THEN F
R4: IF (B) THEN C
R5: IF (F) THEN G

With these simplified rules, and input facts being A and B, if our objective is to prove G is true or not, we can proceed either by forward chaining or backward chaining as shown below.

1. Forward Chaining:

Rules Applicable							
Iteration	*Facts/Updated Facts*	*R1*	*R2*	*R3*	*R4*	*R5*	*New Fact*
1.	A, B	N	N	N	Y	N	C
2.	A, B, C	Y	N	N	—	N	E
3.	A, B, C, E	—	N	Y	—	N	F
4.	A, B, C, E, F	—	N	—	—	Y	G

So, we have reached our claim that G is true by firing R5 at iteration 4.

Notes: 1. Firing a rule at any iteration leads to a new fact.

2. After a rule is fired at any iteration, subsequently the question of firing the same rule will not lead to any new fact.

   The above iterative forward chaining process can be described by an inference diagram as shown in Figure 5.21.

2. **Backward Chaining:** As stated earlier, the backward chaining process attempts to solve the problem by moving backward from the goal and trying to locate only the rules whose consequences are the goal and sub-goals and to verify whether the antecedents can be established from the facts available.

   For the example stated above, let us start from goal G and scan the rules which have G as their consequence. We find only R5 has G as a consequence. However, we cannot fire R5 at this stage since we do not know whether F is true. Hence, our sub-goal is now to prove whether F is true by applying the backward chaining process. Again, scanning through the rules, it can be seen that R2 and R3 have F as their consequence. Next, we look at rule R2 and find that it can be fired only if both D and C are true. However, there is no rule to prove whether D is true. Hence, R2 cannot be fired. Next, we look at R3. Since B is true, we have to establish that E is true to prove that F is true. Now E is the consequence of R1, if only both A and C are true. A is true; hence our sub-goal is to establish C is true. C is the consequence of R4 and R4 can be fired since B is true. Hence, all the sub-goals stand established

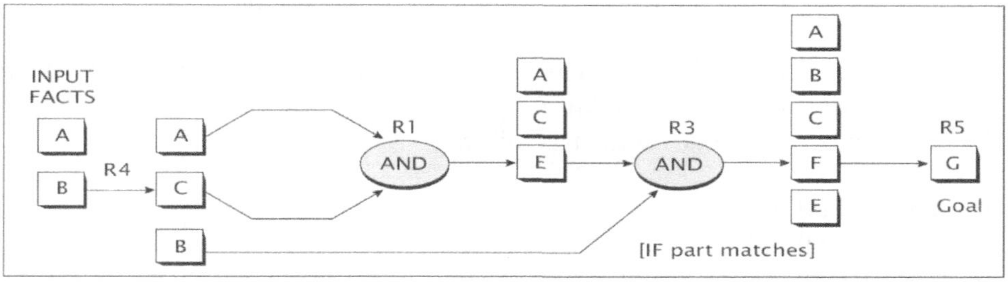

Figure 5.21 Inference Diagram Showing Forward Chaining Process

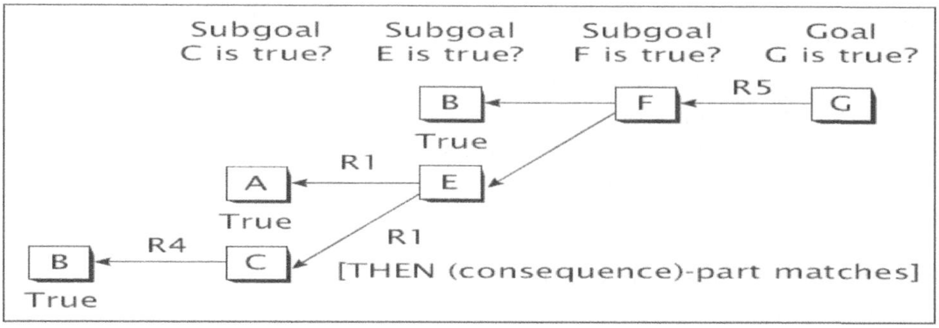

Figure 5.22 Backward Chaining Process

and obviously the goal that G is true gets established. The backtracking process has been described in the Figure 5.22. The backward chaining process is sometimes cumbersome but nevertheless has been found to be faster.

Computer-based expert systems adopt a backward chaining process for inference. In the process of backward chaining, problems are often faced when more than one rule is applicable for the same consequence. In such situations, the strategies for deciding the order of firing of the rules include: (1) Natural order, (2) Fact order (recently updated), (3) Priority order for the rules.

5.16.4 Application Domain for Expert Systems

Expert systems have applications involving technical disciplines with large bodies of complex information such as diagnosis, analysis, interpretation, consultation and design. They further facilitate situations requiring decisions and also articulate decision rules that a decision-maker uses. Typical applications of expert systems include the 'MYCIN' project.

5.16.5 Rule-Based Expert Systems

Rule-based expert systems were highly developed and published in the case of typical medical applications. A very notable among them is the 'MYCIN' project at Stanford University, California. 'MYCIN' diagnosed infectious blood diseases using a backward chained (exhaustive) control strategy.

There are other applications also such as XCON, a project of Digital Equipment Corporation to configure equipment related to VAX minicomputers, PROSPECTOR for mineral prospecting through observations obtained in exploratory drilling, and DENDRAL developed at Stanford University for chemical applications for possible structure of molecules.

5.16.6 Expert System Shells

Expert system shells are inference engines (described earlier in this chapter) consisting of computer programs that derive answers from a knowledge base. Similar to DBMS software for the creation and management of databases and also retrieval of data from the database, expert system shells provide all tools, including the inference engine, for the creation and management of a knowledge base for an expert system. EMYCIN (which stands for empty MYCIN) was the first widely used expert system shell. EMYCIN as a shell was the outcome of efforts made to build expert systems similar to MYCIN using the structure, interface and control mechanism of MYCIN redefined with the new system. This facilitates much faster development of expert systems. EMYCIN was also found to have the following features:

1. Good for learning expert systems
2. Limited in applicability to 'finite classification' problems such as medical diagnosis and identification
3. Good explanatory capabilities
4. Inbuilt certainty factors

Today, several derivative versions of EMYCIN exist.

Other popular expert system shells include OPS5, VP-expert, which runs on PCs, EXSYS and so on.

5.16.7 Advantages of Expert Systems

The main advantage of expert systems is that on the demise of an expert, his/her knowledge and expertise will not be lost if the same has been captured by an expert system. Further, the knowledge of experts can be made available to one and all at a reasonable and affordable cost by the expert systems. Through the expert systems, others who are less experienced may be trained with the distilled expertise of many human experts. Finally, expert systems facilitate documenting the expertise for future generations.

5.17 PROLOG and LISP

The programming languages PROLOG and LISP are associated with AI, expert systems and computational linguistics. PROLOG (programming logic) has its roots in first-order logic and, unlike many other procedural programming languages, PROLOG is declarative. A declarative programming language is a programming paradigm that expresses the logic of a computation without describing its control flow by way of an explicitly provided algorithm. While PROLOG was initially adopted for natural language processing, the language has, in the course of time, stretched far into other areas such as theorem proving, expert systems, games, ontology and other sophisticated control systems.

In PROLOG, programming logic is expressed in terms of relations, and a computation is initiated by running a query over these relations. Relations are represented by clauses. The label of the clauses is known as a predicate, and the objects of the clause are called arguments.

5.17.1 Data Types

PROLOG's single data type is the term. Terms are either atoms, numbers, variables or compound terms. An atom is a general-purpose term with no inherent meaning such as X, Y and green. A number can be a float or an integer. Variables are denoted by a string

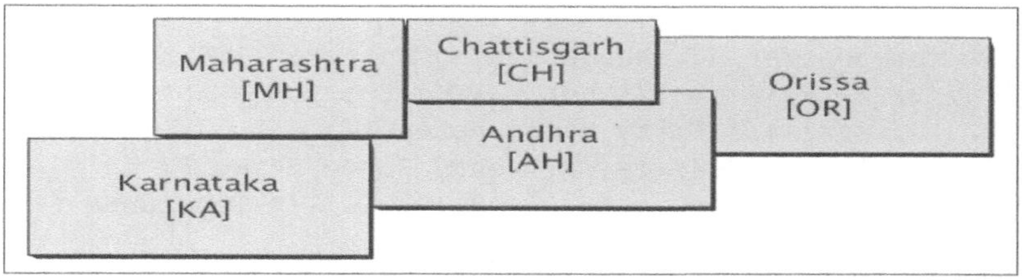

Figure 5.23 Five Adjacent Indian States

Note: For simplicity, we have assumed regular shapes and boundaries.

consisting of letters, numbers and underscore characters and beginning with an uppercase letter or underscore. A compound term is composed of an atom called a 'functor' and a number of 'arguments' which are again terms. Examples of compound terms are:

Car-model ('Maruti', 800) and manager-subordinates (Johan, [Jones, Smith, Marie]).

5.17.2 Rules and Facts in PROLOG

An unconditional clause is a fact, while a conditional clause is a rule.

A rule is of the form:

Head: Body and is read as 'Head is true if Body is true'. Clauses with empty bodies are called facts; for example, cat (Micky).

The adjacency information for neighbouring Indian states in Figure 5.23 is represented in PROLOG through the following unit clauses or facts.

adjacent (MH, CH) adjacent (CH, MH)
adjacent (MH, KA) adjacent (KA, MH)
adjacent (MH, AH) adjacent (AH, MH)
adjacent (CH, OR) adjacent (OR, CH)
adjacent (CH, AH) adjacent (AH, CH)
adjacent (OR, AH) adjacent (AH, OR)
adjacent (KA, AH) adjacent (AH, KA)

If the above clauses are loaded into PROLOG, we can observe the following behaviour of some goals:

? — adjacent (MH, KA)
yes
? — adjacent (OR, KA)
no
? — adjacent (AH, X)
X = 1;
X = 2;
X = 3;
X = 4;
No

Example 1: Program for change for a hundred-rupee note.

```
/* Program for generating change adding up to a `100 note*/
Change {{H, S, T, F, R}}: —/* not taking two-rupee note */
member {H, {0, 1, 2}}/* Fifty Rupee notes */
member {S, {0, 1, 2, 3, 4, 5}}/* Twenty Rupee notes */
member {T, {0, 1, 2, 3, 4, 5, 6, 7, 8, 9, 10}}/* Ten-rupee
notes */
member {F, {0, 1, 2, 3, 4, 5, 6, 7, 8, 9, 10,/* Five-rupee
notes */
11, 12, 13, 14, 15, 16, 17, 18, 19, 20}}
A is 50 * H + 20 * S + 10 * T + 5 * F,
A = < 100
R is 100 - A
```

Several kinds of goals are possible, for example:

```
? —change {{H, S, T, F, R}}
```

will list all possible ways of giving change for a 100-rupee note, and

```
? —change {{0, 2, 3, 4, 6}}
no
```

Since two 20-rupee notes, three 10-rupee notes, four 5-rupee notes and 6 rupees do not make

```
100-rupees and
? —change {{1, 2, 1, 0, 0}}
T
Also? —change {{0, 2, 3, 4, P}}
P = 10
```

The most important feature of this example is to show how a member can be used to generate choices for values of some variable in order to satisfy some constraints! PROLOG's backtracking mechanism then automatically pursues each of the alternatives.

Example 2: Towers of Hanoi puzzle.

The object of this famous puzzle is to move N disks from the left peg to the right peg using the centre peg as an auxiliary holding peg as shown in Figure 5.24 for a set-up for N = 3 disks. At no time can a larger disk be placed upon a smaller disk. The puzzle can be solved using a recursive PROLOG program. The recursive program solves the problem by breaking the problem into a collection of smaller problems and further breaking these smaller problems into even smaller problems till a solution is reached. The steps for this recursive approach are:

Step 1: Label the pegs X, Y, Z, … . These labels may move at different steps to follow.
Step 2: Number the discs from 1 (smallest topmost) to N (largest, bottom most)
Step 3: Move (N – 1) discs from X to Y. This leaves N alone on peg X.

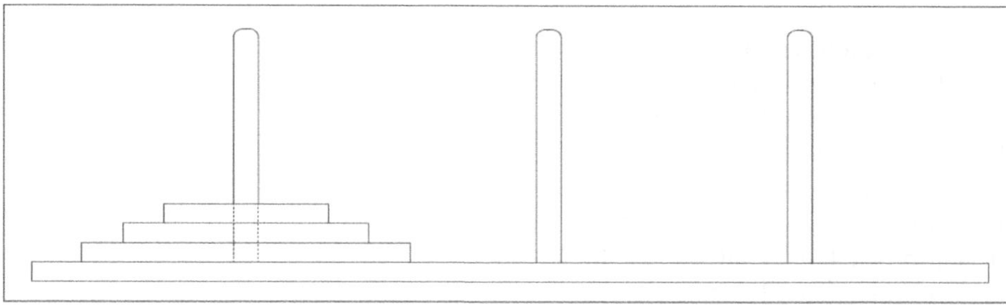

Figure 5.24 Tower of Hanoi Puzzle

Step 4: Move disc N from X to Z.
Step 5: Move (N – 1) discs from Y to Z so that they sit on disc N.

The above (step 3 to step 5) is a recursive algorithm (recursion is the process of repeating items in a self-similar way) since to carry out steps 3 and 5, the same algorithm is to be applied for (N – 1) discs again. After a finite number of recursions, the number of discs remaining on peg X will be 1, which is a trivial process to move a single disc from X to Z.

The recursive PROLOG program consists of two classes as shown below:

```
move (1, X, Y, _): —
Write ('move top disk from'),
Write (X),
Write ('to'),
Write (Y)
n1.
move (N, X, Y, Z): —
N > 1,
M is N – 1
move (M, X, Z, Y)
move (1, X, Y, _),
move (M, Z, Y, X)
```

The variable filled in by '_' (underscore) is a 'do not care' variable, which PROLOG allows to freely match with any structure, but no variable binding results from this gratuitous matching.

The first clause in the above program describes the move of a single disk. The second clause declares how a solution could be obtained recursively. For example, for N = 3, X = left, Y = right and Z = centre, the clause is

```
move (3, left, right, centre) if
move (2, left, centre, right) and
move (1, left, right, centre) and
move (2, centre, right, left).
```

The output of the program is:

```
? —move (3, left, right, centre)
Move top disc from left to right
Move top disc from left to centre
Move top disc from right to centre
Move top disc from left to right
Move top disc from centre to left
Move top disc from centre to right
Move top disc from left to right true.
```

5.17.3 LISP

LISP was invented by John McCarthy in 1958 at the Massachusetts Institute of Technology, USA. From the very inception, it was associated with the AI research workers. Since its first implementation, LISP had various versions such as Stanford LISP, standard LISP and common LISP available for wide-ranging platforms. LISP was originally developed as a practical mathematical notation and symbol for computer programs. Soon it became a favoured programming language for AI. LISP stands for 'list processing'. Major data structures and LISP source code are made up of linked lists and other lists. A function is written as a list with the function or operator's name first, and the arguments following, such as function f with two arguments will be invoked using (f arg1 arg2). Common LISP reads an expression entered by the user and the LISP prompt evaluates the expression and then prints the result.
Example:

```
USER (1): (*2(Cos 0) (*2 3)
12.0
```

It may be noted that LISP represents a function f(x) as (f x) such as Cos (0) as (Cos 0); LISP expressions are case-insensitive. LISP evaluates function calls in applicative order, that is, all the argument forms (except conditionals) are first evaluated before invoking the function containing the arguments. LISP has got built-in usual numeric functions such as '+', '–', '*', '/', 'abs', 'max' and 'min'.
Example:

```
USER (2): (max 7 11 13)
13
USER (3): (/28 2)
14
```

Introductory comments are preceded by ';; '. LISP allows user-defined functions (UDF) also.

```
; triple the value of a number
defun triple (x)
'Compute three times X.'; inline comments can
```

```
(*3 X); be written here
USER (4): (triple 4)
12
```

5.17.3.1 Recursions and Conditionals in LISP

LISP includes relational operators and expressions such as (= xy) x is equal to y; (/ = xy) x not equal to y; (< x y) x less than y; (> x y) x is greater than y; (≤ x y) x is less than or equal to y and (≥ x y) x is greater than or equal to y. 'If' form checks the condition of the relational expression and returns values either 'T' if true or NIL if false. LISP allows recursions also. In other words, the definition of a function may involve invocation of itself. Recursion facilitates looping behaviour in programming.

Example: Let us write down a recursive definition of XY (X raised to the power Y), assuming both X and Y are non-negative and non-zero integers.

```
(defun power (X Y)
'Compute the value of X raised to the power Y'
(if (= Y 1)
X
(*X (power (X (–Y 1))))))
```

The 'if' form is not a strict function (as strict functions evaluate their arguments in applicative order). Instead, the 'if' form evaluates the condition (= Y 1) before further evaluating the other two arguments. If the condition evaluates to true (Y is equal to 1), then only the second argument is evaluated, and its value is returned as the value of the 'if' form; otherwise, the third argument is evaluated and its value is returned. In order to facilitate the recursion, we can make use of the debugging facility 'trace' as follows:

```
USER (5): (trace power)
(Power)
USER (6): (power (2 6))
0: (POWER (2 6))
1: (POWER (2 5))
2: (POWER (2 4))
3: (POWER (2 3))
4: (POWER (2 2))
5: (POWER (2 1))
5: returned 2
4: returned 4
3: returned 8
2: returned 16
1: returned 32
0: returned 64
```

Multiple recursions are also possible.

Example: Sum of N Fibonacci numbers. By definition, the first two Fibonacci numbers are 1, 1 and each subsequent number is the sum of the preceding two, for example, 1, 2, 3, 5, 8, 13, … . The Nth number is

Fib(N) = Fib(N – 1) + Fib(N – 2) for N > 1. The above definition can be directly translated to the following LISP code:

```
(defun fibonacci(N)
'Compute the Nth Fibonacci number'.
(if ( = N1) or (zerop N))
1; for N equal to 0 or 1 the
; value is 1
(+ (fibonacci (–N1)) (fibonacci(–N2))))
```

The function (zerop N) tests if N is zero. Like 'or', LISP allows other logical operators such as 'and' and 'not' also.

The above function definition for Fibonacci number involves two recursions:

First recursive evaluation for (fibonacci [–N1]) and second recursive evaluation (fibonacci [–N 2]) and finally return their sums.

5.17.3.2 Lists

LISP supports symbolic computing in addition to numeric computing. The fundamental LISP data structure for supporting symbolic manipulation is lists. Lists are containers that support sequential traversal. A list is also a recursive data structure. In order to better appreciate a recursive abstract data type and develop recursive operations on the same, the data types need to be presented in terms of their constructors, selectors and recognisers. Let me explain these three terms as follows:

Constructors are forms that create new instances of a data type (possibly out of some simpler components):

Example 1. Nil: Evaluating nil creates an empty list
2. Cons (AB): Creates a list containing A followed by the elements in B

Instead of typing 'Cons' if we already know the elements in a list, we could as well enter the list as list literals by way of 'quote' or '''

USER (7): quote (A B C D E F)
(A B C D E F)
USER (8): '(A B C D E F)
(A B C D E F)

The second ingredient of an abstract data type is its 'selectors'. A 'selector' form returns one of the components out of a composite object made up of several components.

Examples:

```
USER (9): (first '(7 8 9))
7
USER (10): (rest '(7 8 9))
(8 9)
USER (11): (rest (rest '(7 8 9)))
(9)
USER (12): (rest (rest (rest '(8 9)))
NIL
```

The last ingredient mentioned earlier is 'recognisers', which tests how an object is constructed. Corresponding to each 'constructor' of a data type is a 'recogniser'. For example, it is 'null' for 'nil'.

Constructors, selectors and recognisers of lists enable one to develop recursive functions that traverse a list. This requires the use of a function for determining list length recursively; we can define such a function as follows:

```
(defun recursive-list-length (L)
'A recursive implementation of list-length'. (if (null L)
0
(1 + (recursive-list-length (rest L)))))
```

The recogniser null is to differentiate how list L was constructed. In case L is nil, 0 will be returned as its length. Else L was a list created by the constructor cons and in that case 1 plus the length of rest (L) is returned recursively. For example:

```
USER (13): (trace recursive-list-length)
(RECURSIVE-LIST-LENGTH)
USER (14): (recursive-list-length '(1 2 3 4)
0: (RECURSIVE-LIST-LENGTH (1 2 3 4)
1: (RECURSIVE-LIST-LENGTH (2 3 4)
2: (RECURSIVE-LIST-LENGTH (3 4)
3: (RECURSIVE-LIST-LENGTH (4))
4: (RECURSIVE-LIST-LENGTH NIL)
4: returned 0
3: returned 1
2: returned 2
1: returned 3
0: returned 4
4
```

5.17.3.3 Symbols

LISP allows lists with symbols, alphanumeric and special characters such as '—'. LISP is also case insensitive.

Example:

```
USER (15): '(What is your name?); A list of symbols
(WHAT IS YOUR NAME?)
USER (16): '(1 + 3 * A * B); A list of symbols and numbers
(1 + 3 * A * B)
USER (17): '(Jaytilak (Biswas M)); A list containing 'Jaytilak and
'(Biswas M)
(Jaytilak (Biswas M))
```

Note that the list as above only has a length of 2.

Example:

USER (18): (nth 0 '(c a t))
C
USER (19) :(nth 2 '(c a t))
T

nth is a function in LISP as (nth N L) which returns the Nth member of the list L, assuming members are numbered from zero onwards.

Like first L, LISP has a built-in function (last L) that returns the last cons structure in a given list L.

Example:
USER (20): (last '(Ram Shyam Jadu))
(Jadu)

Append: LISP defines a function append that appends one list to another.
USER (23): (append '(R A M) '(C H A N D R A))
(R A M C H A N D R A)

Using Lists as Sets: Lists are ordered sequences, whereas sets are not. Further, sets do not have multiple occurrences of the same element, whereas lists do have multiple occurrences. For example, (x y z) and (y x z) are two different lists although the elements of both the lists are the same. Similarly, (x x y z) and (x y z) are two different lists. LISP defines functions such as (intersection L1 L2), (union L1 L2) and (difference L1 L2) for Boolean operations on sets.

Example of Intersection:

USER (24): (trace list-intersection) (LIST-INTERSECTION)
USER (25): (list-intersection '(A C E G) '(A B C D))
0: (LIST-INTERSECTION (A C E G) (A B C D))
1: (LIST-INTERSECTION (C E G) (A B C D))
2: (LIST-INTERSECTION (E G) (A B C D))
3: (LIST-INTERSECTION (G) (A B C D))
4: (LIST-INTERSECTION NIL (A B C D))
4: returned NIL
3: returned NIL
2: returned NIL
1: returned (C)
0: returned (A C)
(A C)

The above examples are only to illustrate certain features of LISP. It may be mentioned that with the features of linear recursions, member, append and Boolean operations such as intersection, union and difference, LISP enables pattern matching and retrieval of knowledge, thus making it a powerful language along with PROLOG for artificial intelligence as well as expert systems.

5.18 Case Study: Deep Learning—Crypto Currency Exchange Price Prediction Using Limit Order Book

5.18.1 Background

High-frequency trading or algorithmic trading is popular in stock exchanges. In current stock markets over the globe, a sizeable portion of the daily trading volume is carried on by specialised companies adopting those techniques. In the elaborated stock market, it is not possible for individuals to get fast access to data to gain any advantage from stock trading without heavy computing machines and technology because margins and arbitrages are closed in a fraction of a second.

The case pertains to the development of a deep machine learning model using an RNN for predicting future prices of digital assets such as cryptocurrencies like bitcoin based on input data obtained from the limit order book. It may be mentioned that the limit order book captures all pending order data for 'bids' and 'asks' with the reserved price limit. A snapshot of the limit order book represents the demand and supply position of any asset at a certain point in time in the exchange market.

Cryptocurrency is a type of digital currency that uses cryptography for security and anti-counterfeiting measures. It usually uses 'blockchain' technology. Although a digital asset was chosen in the present model development, the principles and methods are applicable to any asset or stock that is tradable on an exchange. The RNN-based model was developed based on real-time data such as limit order book snapshots, price history and data from an exchange to predict the future price of the cryptocurrency.

Identification of the right feature set from the data, selection of the correct model architecture, and configuration of the hyperparameters and choice of the cost function were the challenges faced by the development team.

5.18.2 Data Acquisition

Data were obtained by sampling the Bittrex exchange every minute using the API provided and storing the data. About 3,000 samples representing 3 weeks of trading data were collected. The data were not 100% consecutive because of networking disturbances and related disruptions. Since every order in the limit order book has two parameters (quantity and price), the data could not be used as it was. A small modification was applied to the data to extract training sets. Bins of 10 USD were defined and the quantities relating to each bin were added together. Hundred bins were created for 500 bid orders representing the last price and up to the last price minus 1000 USD. Models of Neural Networks adopted and the results Five different models were applied in order to improve the accuracy of prediction of future price of the bitcoin.

1. The initial model was a fully connected network (FCN) architecture as shown below:

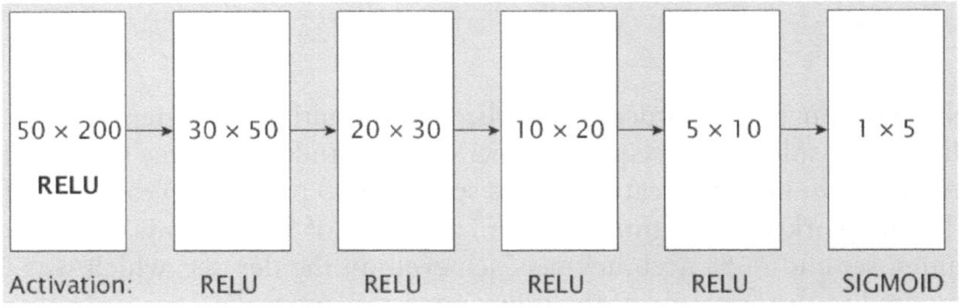

The key objective of this model was to find correlation and validate the data from the order book as a valid predictor. Twenty-one thousand training samples with training/dev sets as an 80%/20% split were fed to the model, and the model compared bitcoin prices 1, 2, 3, 5, and 10 minutes into the future with the current price. The fully connected network architecture achieved approximately 95% accuracy on the training set and 64% accuracy on the dev set at around 31,000 epochs.

2. RNN architecture with the same inputs and outputs of the fully connected network:

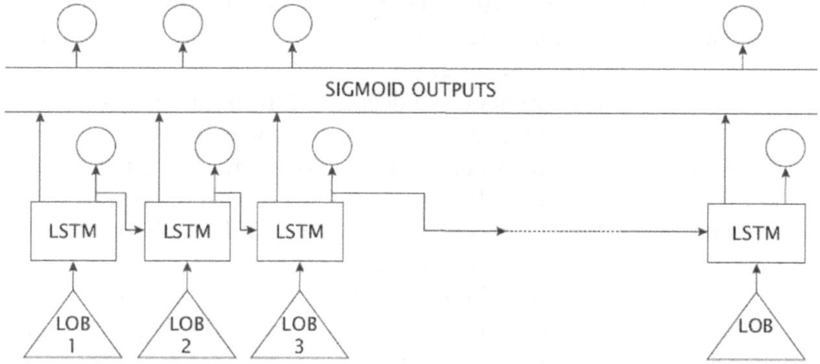

Limit order book (LOB) provides input to an LSTM network followed by a sigmoid output prediction of an increase or decrease like the fully connected network. By adding L2 regularisation (L2 regularisation is a technique to reduce overfitting of the model to improve its performance with highly variable input data), a 10% increase in dev accuracy was achieved while the training accuracy was reduced close to dev accuracy.

3. RNN with fully connected network acting as encoder to provide RNN input:

In this model limit order book, data were encoded using a FCN and the activations from the last but one layer of the FCN were fed into the RNN. Performance was similar to the previous RNN architecture where the order book was directly fed as input.

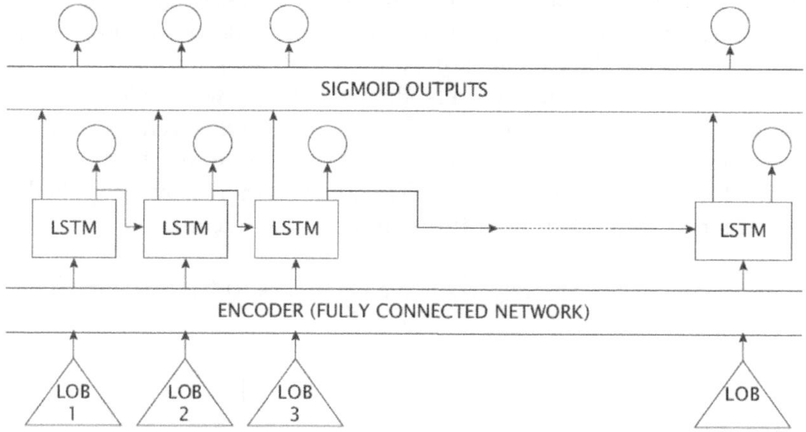

4. RNN with single limit order book spliced into multiple time steps:

Input was split into an equal number of parts and fed to time steps in the LSTM network. Two hundred feature inputs split into 10 parts of 20 each were fed to the LSTM network with 20 time steps. An accuracy of 95% plus was achieved on the training set and 66% accuracy was achieved on the dev set, which was 3% more compared to the accuracy of the fully connected network.

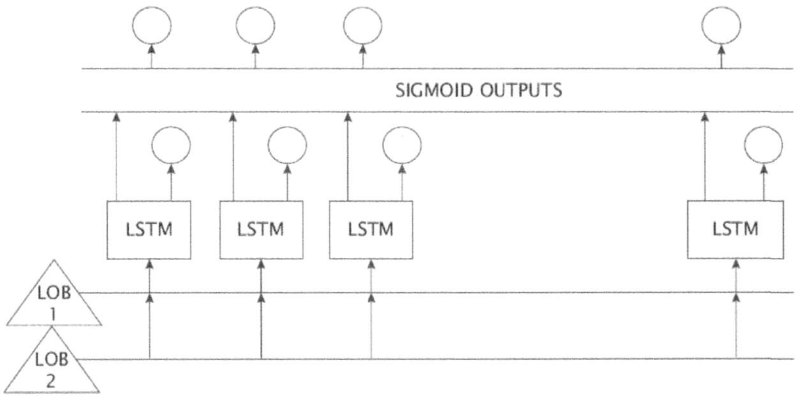

5. In the categorical model, the output labels were grouped under three categories as follows:
   (i) Category with output more than a threshold percentage
   (ii) Category with output less than the threshold percentage
   (iii) Category with output equal to threshold percentage.

   The signal in the categorical model was created with four dimensions—the first one being the threshold (0.1%, 0.2%, 0.3%, 0.4% and 0.5%), and second dimension being the future prediction look ahead (1, 2, 3, 5 and 10 minutes). The other two dimensions were the RNN time step or window size and the batch. The best result was achieved with a two-minute look-ahead prediction and 0.2% threshold change.

   Categorical model architecture had three convolutional layers of one dimension each connected to two layers of LSTM RNN with 256 hidden nodes each and one softmax layer with three categories for the output. The architecture for the categorical model is as follows:

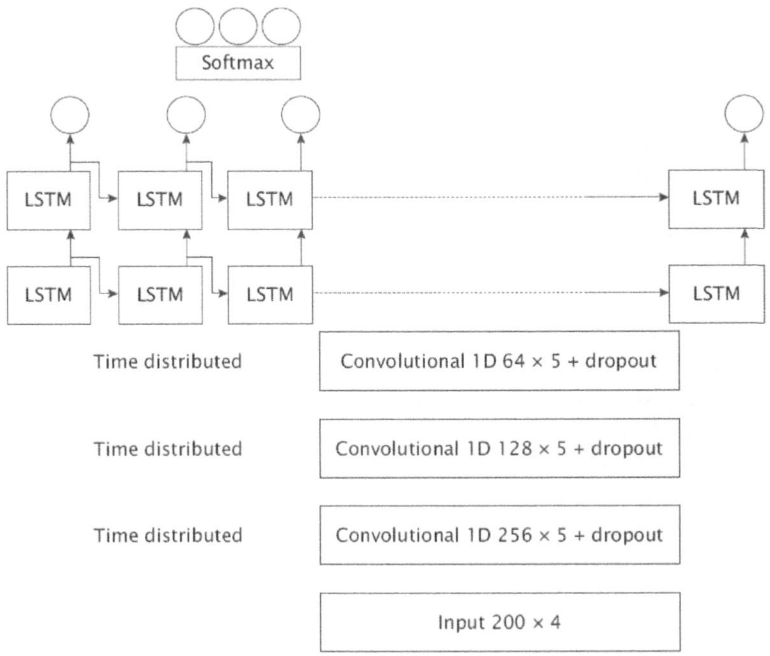

Sample label distribution and result obtained: 25,000 sample labels distribution was as follows:

	Increase	No Change	Decrease
Training set	3,126	16,310	3,060
Dev set	278	1,928	290

With the sample distribution as shown earlier, the following results were obtained for the categorical model:

	Increase	No Change	Decrease
Ground truth (dev set)	278	1928	290
Predicted increase	87	247	17
Predicted no change	181	1505	196
Predicted decrease	10	176	77

Using the categorical model and the network described above, 70% accuracy for the training set and 67% accuracy for the dev set were obtained.

5.19 Conclusion

The case study shows a clear correlation between LOB and future price. Further, it was found that RNN performs better than a fully connected network for the price prediction problem of this kind. However, by using a categorical model with a threshold, modifying the loss function and adding convolutional layers, the best result was obtained.

Source: Padmanabhan, Gilboa and Biswas (2018).

Review Questions

1. What is an EIS? Mention the broad types of EIS.
2. What is BI? Explain.
3. What capabilities must a machine or computer have in order to pass the Turing test?
4. Mention a few tasks which you feel computers or machines are not able to do now and also in the near future.
5. Design a few questions which you would like to ask a man and a machine for the sake of the Turing test.
6. What is machine learning? What is supervised learning? Is reinforcement learning a type of supervised learning? Explain your answer.
7. What are the different methods of knowledge representation for AI?
8. Distinguish between forward chaining and backward chaining with a suitable example. Why do computer-based expert systems use backward chaining for inference?
9. What is 'heuristic'? How do heuristics facilitate state space search?
10. What are expert system shells? Mention any expert system shell you are familiar with.
11. Mention two possible applications of expert systems.

12. What is declarative programming? How is it different from procedural programming? Is PROLOG a declarative programming?

Bibliography

Gordon, S. Novak Jr. *Lecture Notes on Artificial Intelligence (CS343)*. Austin, TX: University of Texas at Austin, 2007.

Inmon, W. H. Claudia Imhoff, and Ryan Sousa. *Corporate Information Factory*, 2nd ed. New York, NY: Wiley, 2002.

Kaniclides, T., and C. Kimble. *Executive Information Systems: A Framework for Their Development and Use*. YCS247, Department of Computer Science, University of York, UK, 1994.

Koutsoukis, N. S., and G. Mitra. *Decision Modelling and Information Systems: The Information Value Chain*. Boston, MA: Springer Science, Business Media, 2003.

Linstedt, D. E. 'Data Vault Series 1 to 5'. *The Data Administration Newsletter*, September 2012.

McCarthy, J. 'Recursive Functions of Symbolic Expressions and Their Computation by Machine, Part I'. *Communication of the ACM* 3, no. 4 (1960): 184–195.

Minsky, Marvin. 'A Framework for Representing Knowledge'. *MIT-AI Laboratory Memo* 306, 1974. Available at: https://courses.media.mit.edu/2004spring/mas966/Minsky%201974%20Framework%20for%20 knowledge. pdf (accessed on 24 January 2020).

Mintzberg, H. 'Planning on the Left Side and Managing on the Right'. *Harvard Business Review* 54, no. 4 (1976): 49–58.

Orlikowski, W. J., and D. Robey. 'Information Technology and Structuring of Organizations'. *Information Systems Research* 2, no. 2 (1991): 143–169.

Padmanabhan, A. S., Ben Gilboa, and Tamal Biswas. 'Crypto Exchange Price Prediction Using Limit Order Book Project'. Report No. CS230, University of California, Los Angeles, CA, 2018. Available at: https://cs230. stanford.edu/projects_spring_2018/reports/8289864.pdf (accessed on 24 February 2020).

Rockart, J. F. 'Chief Executives Define Their Own Data Needs'. *Harvard Business Review* 57, no. 2 (1979): 81–93.

Rockart, J. F., and M. Treacy. 'The CEO Goes On-Line'. *Harvard Business Review* 60, no. 1 (1982): 82–88.

Weizenbaum, J. 'Eliza: A Computer Program for the Study of Natural Language Communication Between Man and Machine'. *Communication of the ACM* 9, no. 1 (1966): 36–45.

Winston, P. H. 'Learning Structural Descriptions from Examples'. In Marvin Minsky: *AI Technical Reports of Computer Science and AI Lab*. Cambridge, MA: MIT, 1970.

6 Information System for Planning

6.1 Introduction

Planning is the managerial process of deciding in advance what has to be done, how it has to be done, who has to do it, when it has to be done and what resources are to be provided for doing it. It bridges the gap from where the organisation is to where it has to go in a defined time span. It may be noted that planning is an activity of managers which is very much integrated with decision-making and control. It provides the guidelines necessary for decision-making and resulting action throughout the organisation.

6.2 Need for Planning

Planning is essentially needed for an organisation to decide its course of action or strategy to cope up with the changes in the environment of the organisation for its very survival and growth. An organisation has to function within an industry where its competitors also act, and the industry as a whole is to operate within the broader socio-economic and political environment. The competitive forces within the industry determine the position of the organisation in the industry, and with those external environmental forces, the organisation has to plan the strategy considering its inherent strengths and weaknesses. Planning, together with industry analysis, competitor analysis and strategic positioning, is therefore an essential practice of management, particularly at the strategic level. Michael E. Porter (2008) in his famous 'five forces model', mentioned five competitive forces which jointly determine the intensity of industry competition and thereby the profitability of the industry. The Porter model is shown in Figure 6.1.

Further analysis of industry environmental factors reveals that statutory regulations and technological changes also play vital roles for organisations to plan their strategy. Broader social expectations and corporate social responsibility are also important factors external to an organisation that affect the planning of a strategy. Porter's five forces and the other factors external to an organisation as mentioned above, force an organisation to plan its course of action for the future or the strategy. However, there are factors internal to the organisation such as its inherent strengths and weaknesses, personal values of the top management including prominent

shareholders, the value system and ethics prevalent in the organisation, which collectively determine the internal limits (to the organisation) for the formulation of plans that the organisation can successfully adopt. All these factors, external and internal, to the organisation necessitate the formulation of a corporate strategy and plan for an organisation as shown in Figure 6.2. It may be observed from Figure 6.2 that the corporate

DOI: 10.4324/9781003509714-6

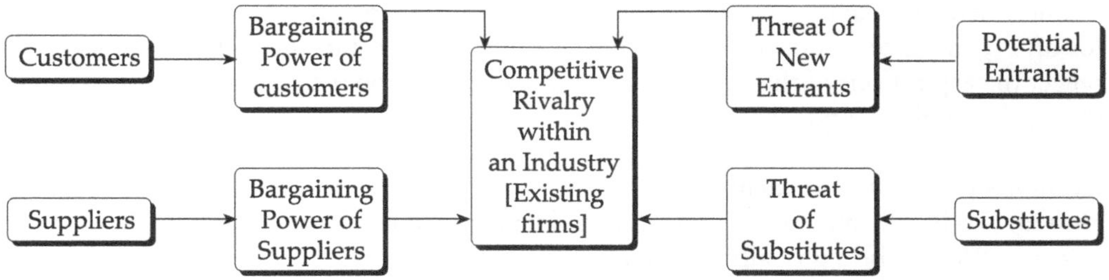

Figure 6.1 Porter Five Forces Model

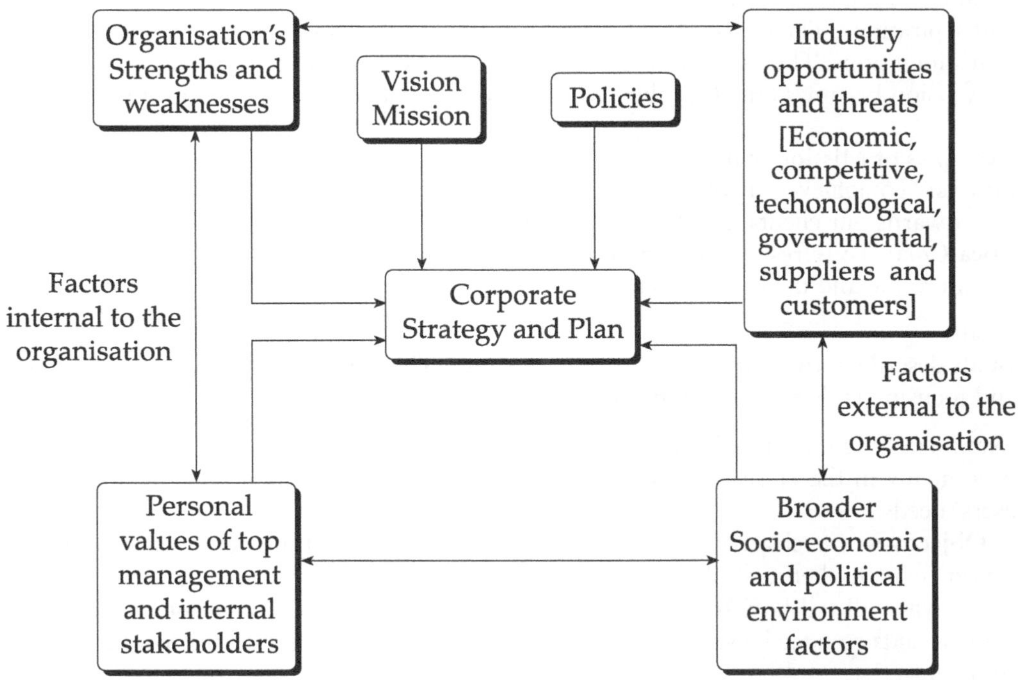

Figure 6.2 Context in Which Corporate Strategy and Plan Are Formulated

strategy and plan, also called the strategic plan (described in detail subsequently in this chapter), is guided by the other planning parameters such as vision and mission and also influenced by the policies of the organisation. The terms vision, mission and policies have been described in the subsequent paragraph.

6.3 Planning Terms and Their Inter-relationship

Strategic intent is a term coined by Hamel and Prahlad (1989) and is the ambition of an organisation. For example, a B-school might have a strategic intent that one day in the future it will be reckoned as one of the top five B-schools in India.

Vision can be said to be the future aspiration that leads to an inspiration to be the best in one's field of activity. It may be mentioned that the strength of the vision statement for an organisation is not in the wording of the statement, but the statement must truly reflect the aspirations of the stakeholders of the organisation (employees, customers, suppliers, shareholders and so on).

Examples of Vision Statements:
Honda: 'To be a company that our shareholders, customers and society want'.
Infosys: 'We will be a globally respected corporation'.

Mission of an organisation is the description of the purpose of the organisation as a whole and relates it to society. A mission statement ensures that all employees are working towards a common purpose, enables employees to identify themselves better with the organisation and serves to state explicitly or implicitly the organisation's beliefs, values and aspirations. The vision of an organisation is only a broad indication of the organisation's intentions. The aspiration level embodied in the vision is often too lofty.

A vision becomes tangible when it is expressed in the form of a mission statement.

Examples of Mission Statements:
Infosys: 'To achieve our objectives in an environment of fairness, honesty and courtesy towards our clients, employees, vendors and society at large'.
Coca-Cola: 'To refresh the world, to inspire moments of optimism and happiness, to create value and make a difference'.

Goals:
Goals describe future expected outcomes or states. They provide programmatic direction and focus on ends rather than means.

Example of organisational goals:
A company in the IT sector—'To provide high-quality information services that satisfy users' needs'.

Objectives are clear, realistic, specific, measurable and time-bound statements of action, which when completed will move the organisation towards goal achievement. Objectives will tell how to meet a goal. They can be either outcome objectives, which address ends to be achieved, or process objectives, which specify means to achieve outcome objectives.

Examples of Objectives:
For a company in IT:

1. **Outcome Objectives:**
   (i) 'By the end of financial year 2026–2027, 50% of all employees will be aware of three library services'.
   (ii) 'By 31 March 2027, achieve an objective of 75% customer satisfaction rating on the basis of requests entertained'.
2. **Process Objectives:** 'To provide online database search training to all users of the service'.

It may be noted that whereas goals are general and broad in nature, objectives are specific, quantifiable and time-bound in nature.

Plans are statements of specific activities to achieve the objectives of an organisation. Plans are the means and objectives are ends. For example, the capacity augmentation plan of a manufacturing industrial unit may be to increase the current level of output to 100% in the next 10 years.

The values and ethics are the beliefs that define a company's culture and help managers to set priorities and guide the day-to-day operations.

For example, the top management may give the highest importance to transparency and integrity on the part of employees. Likewise, fairness and impartial treatment of all customers may be practised in an organisation.

Policies are statements that attempt to inform and guide employees so that the totality of actions by individuals is consistent with the sense of direction of the company. Policies are of two types: (1) they provide limits for discretionary action by specified individuals and (2) they specify a procedure or action under specific circumstances. Thus, policies are representations of both the methods of implementing plans and methods of controlling such implementation.

Examples of Policies:

Function	*Policy*	*Examples*
1. Production	Make or buy	Make if price difference exceeds cost of capital.
	Inventory holding	Do not hold raw materials more than 60 days of consumption.
2. Sales and marketing	Price discount	10% discount on lots of 1000 pieces or more.
	Credit sales	Credit sales not more than 20% of total sales.
3. Finance	Working capital	Maintain [2:1] acid test ratio.
	Capital procurement	Through retained profit only.
4. Personnel	Promotion	Based on last 3 years' appraisal report on performance.
	Training	All executives have to attend one week training with an external institute in India.
5. General	Competitive actions	No collusion in any way with the competitors to increase prices of products.

Corporate plans may be of various types depending on the different dimensions of the plans as illustrated below.

Dimensions	*Illustration of Plans*		
Time	Long-term	Medium-term	Short-term
Level	Corporate	Managerial	Operational
Function	General management	Marketing	Production
Purpose	Strategy	Tactical	Task-oriented
Scope	Company-wide	Functional	Departmental

The types of corporate plans will be described further in detail in subsequent paragraphs of this chapter as the information requirements are different for the different types of planning.

The relationship among the planning parameters defined and explained in the previous paragraphs is shown in Figure 6.3.

6.4 Types of Plans

All levels of management plan, but obviously the type of planning done at each level varies in scope and time frame, as already explained earlier. The planning commences with the strategic planning at the top level of the management hierarchy, and all other plans are for a shorter time frame and consistent with the strategic plan. The strategic plan is long-term in nature and consists of the (1) strategy and (2) steps, the time and costs associated with the steps. Strategy, in the context of strategic planning, is the desired configuration of a company at a future specified date. The configuration may be expressed in terms of the following:

1. **Scope of Business**: Scope of the business of the company in future in terms of products or services, customer profile, markets, suppliers, price and quality and other characteristics of the products and services.
2. **Competitive Edge**: Special market segment, niche market, product distinction, financial strength, unique technical and managerial skills and so on.

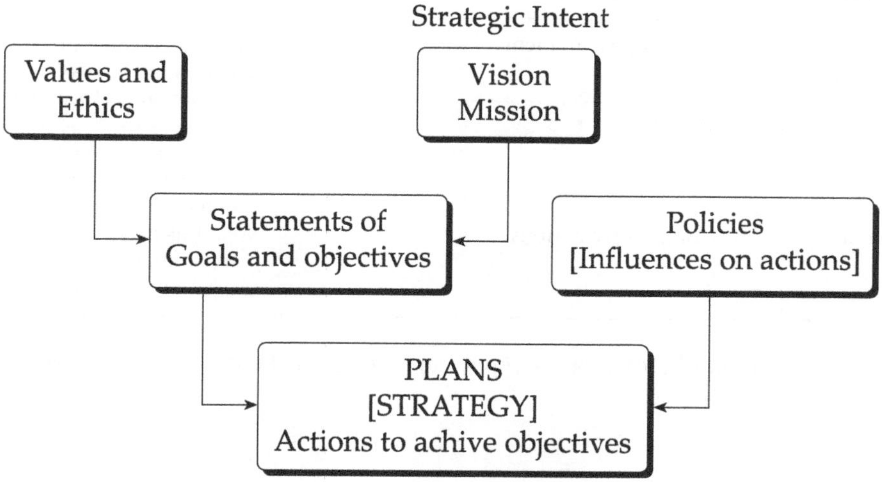

Figure 6.3 Relationship among Planning Parameters

3. **Future Inputs**: Specification of future inputs in terms of financing, manpower, plant and machines, facilities and so on.
4. **Future Targets**: Specifications of targets both financial and non-financial such as quantitative statements of size of the company, turnover, profitability, ROI, market share, assets and trade-off between risk and reward.
5. **Allocation of Resources**: Allocation of long-term capital, investment and divestment, deployment of manpower, emphasis on functional areas such as marketing, production and operations, management development and market segments.

6.4.1 *Strategic Planning Process*

The strategic planning process consists of the following steps shown schematically in Figure 6.4.

Step 1: Environmental scanning. The scanning of the socio-economic, governmental, technological, market and competitive environment, both existing and future conditions will enable the strategic planners to identify the environmental threats and opportunities for the organisation on the one hand and to make projections for the future in terms of technological forecasts, economic growth and so on, on the other hand.

Step 2: A systematic study and analysis of the environmental threats and opportunities together with future projections will also lead to the determination of the CSFs for the particular type of industry to which the organisation belongs. For example, in the food processing industry, the nutritional value of the products is one of the factors leading to success.

Step 3: Identification of strengths and weaknesses. A systematic review of products, markets, facilities, value addition processes, R&D, management skills and financial conditions will enable the strategic planners to identify the strengths and weaknesses within the organisation and in turn the competitive advantages.

Step 4: Opportunities and risks. Steps 1 to 3 described above will reveal the opportunities and risks for the organisation.

Step 5: Establish overall corporate objectives. Based on the opportunities and risks as revealed in Step 4 and considering the personal values of top management and major shareholders relating to economic, social responsibility, ethical, political, religious and so on, the overall corporate objectives are set in terms of product or service, market, scope and so on.

Step 6: Revise objectives and performance measures. In this step, the strategic planners revise the overall corporate objectives according to corporate policies and also formulate, if possible, alternative objectives together with performance measures associated with each alternative objective. Quantitative targets may be established for parameters such as annual growth rate for sales, profit, ROI and market share.

Step 7: The alternative objectives, if any, as determined in Step 6 are evaluated based on predetermined evaluation criteria and compared with each other.

Step 8: Strategic plan. Finally, in this step, the best alternative objective is selected as the strategic plan, which covers the pattern of deployment of resources such as men, machines and facilities in the long term. The process is also known as SWOT analysis.

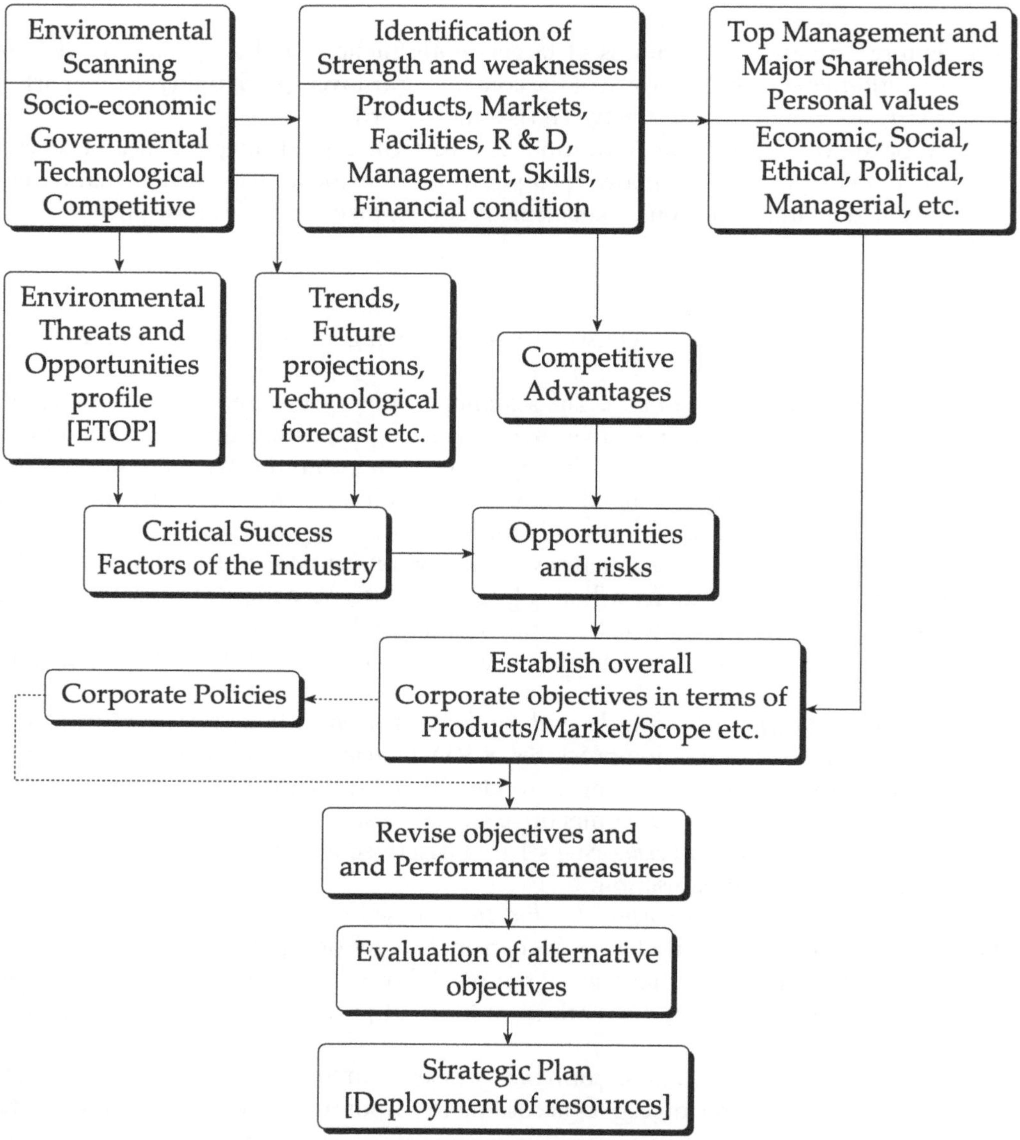

Figure 6.4 The Strategic Planning Process

6.4.2 *Development Plan*

The strategic plan described earlier is specific but not detailed because, although the strategic plan establishes long-term configuration or goals to be achieved by an organisation, the same must be backed by detailed short-term plans known as development plans in line with the current environmental and competitive conditions. The long-term goals of the strategic plan set the constraints for the intermediate and short-term goals in the form of development plans and the operations plan, usually the annual operating plan.

The development plans focus mainly on capacity augmentation, acquisitions and diversifications, modernisation, R&D, market, product and so on. The time horizon of the development plans depends upon the time horizon of the strategic plan and various other factors, both internal and external to the organisation.

6.4.3 *Operating Plan*

Operating plan, also known as the annual operating plan, is mostly financial in nature such as the annual performance budget which sets the objectives and standards of performance in financial terms. The basic idea is to decentralise the profit responsibility to profit centres and cost control to cost centres. The determinants for such decentralisation of profit and cost are sales turnover, cost of sales and further split into elements such as investments in fixed assets, inventory, cash, accounts receivables, direct material, direct labour and overheads. The advantage of the annual operating plan lies in the identification of determinants of profit for separate organisational entities and also in providing measurable performance yardsticks for those entities. However, the plan being short-term operational in nature, its contributions to the long-term objectives are not generally assessed. The overview of corporate plans described earlier is shown in Figure 6.5.

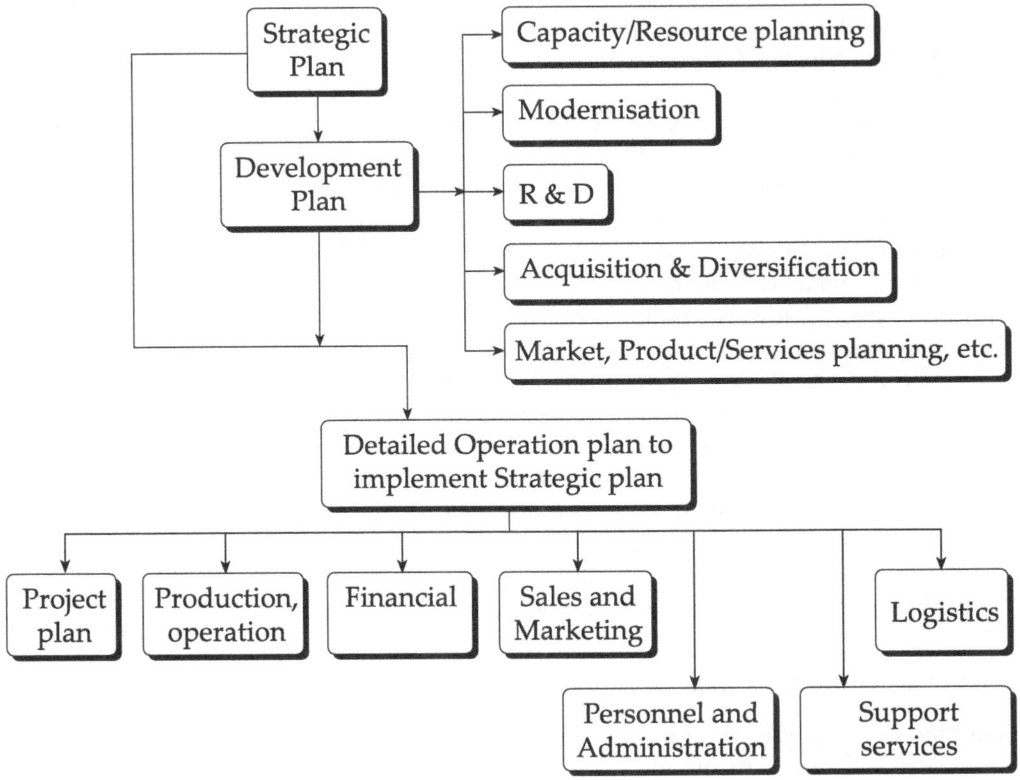

Figure 6.5 Overview of Corporate Planning

6.5 Information for Planning

The first, second and third steps in the planning process of developing an environmental threats and opportunities profile, future projections and identifying internal strengths and weaknesses depend heavily upon the availability and utilisation of vital information. The planning information needs of an organisation can be classified into the following broad categories:

1. Environmental information;
2. Competitive and industry-related information;
3. Internal information.

Each of the above categories needs detailed elaboration.

6.5.1 Environmental Information

Environmental information needs can be classified and described as follows:

1. **Demographic and Socio-economic Trends**: The products, services or outputs of most firms and organisations are affected by the population strength and its dispersion. Social trends and consumer buying behaviour are important inputs for planning. Similarly, the economic trends such as GNP level and consumer disposable income, price, wage level and cost of living index are vital for planning at the corporate level in almost all organisations. Other economic indicators such as employment, productivity and capital investment provide valuable planning information.
2. **Technological**: Because of rapid technological innovation resulting in technological obsolescence of existing products and processes, it becomes necessary for many organisations to forecast the technological changes in their industry in general and the individual organisation in particular. Companies such as Lockheed Martin and Intel forecast key technological advances in all fields for a period of 20 years.
3. **Political and Governmental Factors**: Information relating to the political stability of the state as well as the federal government is very relevant for forecasting long-term plans. Different political parties forming a government may have different priorities relating to agriculture, industry and so on, which have vital repercussions on the strategic plans of organisations. Further, statutory government regulations, controls and fiscal policies are to be taken into account by strategic planners as such factors have a significant impact on the planning decisions, particularly the long-term ones.
4. **Factors of Production and Services**: Information pertaining to the factors of production are source, cost, availability, accessibility, quality and productivity of major factors (inputs) of production and services such as raw materials and components, labour, capital, power, water and other utilities.

6.5.2 Competitive and Industry-related Information

A competitive analysis of an industry and its competitors requires a great deal of data, some of which are difficult to obtain. There are three specific types of information concerning factors which affect the operations of a company within an industry. The three types are:

1. **Industry Demand**: Because the sales/level of operations for any single unit within an industry largely depends upon the level of demand for the given industry, firms or units in the industry must have information on industry demand to facilitate strategic planning.
2. **Firm Demand**: The demand for products and services of the individual unit or firm, which is a function of the total industry demand and the resources, capabilities and actions of the individual firm as compared to those of the other competing firms in the industry.
3. **Data of Competitors**: Data of competitors are very vital for long-term forecasting of individual demand, which in turn facilitates a strategic plan to achieve the forecast. This information can generally be divided into three types:
   - (i) Past performance of competitors on profitability, market share, ROI, growth in market share and so on often provides a yardstick for setting performance objectives for individual units or firms.
   - (ii) Present activities relating to competition, such as price strategy, advertising campaigns and changes in distribution channels.
   - (iii) Plans concerning new products, acquisitions, modernisation, R&D efforts and other plans that affect the individual firm's future.

6.5.3 Internal Information

Internal information influences the planning decisions of almost all levels in the organisation. The information pertaining to the business environment and premises surrounding the competitive industry mainly facilitates planning decision-making by relatively few managers in a firm, mainly top managers and marketing managers. However, internal information such as a budget or production plan, once framed, becomes essential planning data for a number of connected plans such as the material plan, capacity utilisation plan and manpower deployment plan. The internal information for planning is of the following types:

1. Marketing and sales information on performance, revenue, market shares, channels of distribution, retail outlets and franchise stores, customer feedback and so on. Sales forecast is another vital planning information in an organisation and all other plans for allocation of company resources are derived from the sales forecast.
2. Financial information on profits, costs, cash flows, investments, ROIs and so on. The budget is the financial plan of an organisation and involves the entire organisation and links all activities of the organisation in monetary terms.
3. Production and operational information on assets, rated and available capacities, product mix, capacity utilisation, lead time, quality standards, support facilities and so on.
4. Personnel information on skills availability, industrial relations, training and development facilities and so on.
5. Source, availability and limitations of supply factors like manpower, capital, plant and machinery and others.

6. Research and development activities on new products, intellectual property rights, knowledge base and so on.
7. Basic policies are relatively fixed for long-run purposes and cannot readily be changed to permit flexibility in developing alternative courses of action in the short run.

6.6 Sources of Data for Industry Analysis

A systematic and organised approach is necessary for conducting an industry survey for collecting data—both primary data from the field and secondary data from published sources.

1. **Primary Data from Field:** In collecting primary data from the field, it is important to develop a framework for possible source identification. The major sources of primary data for industry analysis are the firms or competitor units in the industry, suppliers, distributors, customers, service organisations such as banks and trade associations, industry observers such as the financial community and the regulators including the government. Out of all the above sources, industry competitors may not always be eager to furnish data about their units because of apprehension on their part that if they furnish data, it may harm them. The service organisations such as bankers, auditors, experts and trade associations also often maintain confidentiality of data relating to their clients. The most perceptive sources of primary industry data are the suppliers, customers, retailers and wholesalers, who take a keen interest in the entire range of industry participants over a long time period. Figure 6.6 shows the important sources of field data for industry-related information to facilitate corporate planning.

The initial contact for collection of field data can be with any of the sources shown in Figure 6.6. In order to get the background for the collection of industry data, it is appropriate to make contact with some person who is knowledgeable about the industry but at the same time who does not have any competitive or direct economic stake in the industry.

2. **Secondary Data for Industry Analysis from Published Sources:** The published sources of data are mainly as follows:
   a. **Journals and Bulletins:** Trade journals in customer, distributor or supplier industries are often useful sources of industry-related data.
   b. **Study Reports for Industries:** Industry study reports often provide important data for industry analysis.
   c. **Annual Reports of Various Companies:** A quick review of the annual reports of a number of companies over a 10- or 15-year period facilitates understanding of the industry. Industry analysts as well as strategic planners should look for the reasons given for good as well as bad financial results, which, in turn, will expose the CSFs for the type of industry under analysis.
   d. **Business Press Publications:** Business standards, business periodicals and index, RBI bulletins, *Dalal Street Journal* and so on.

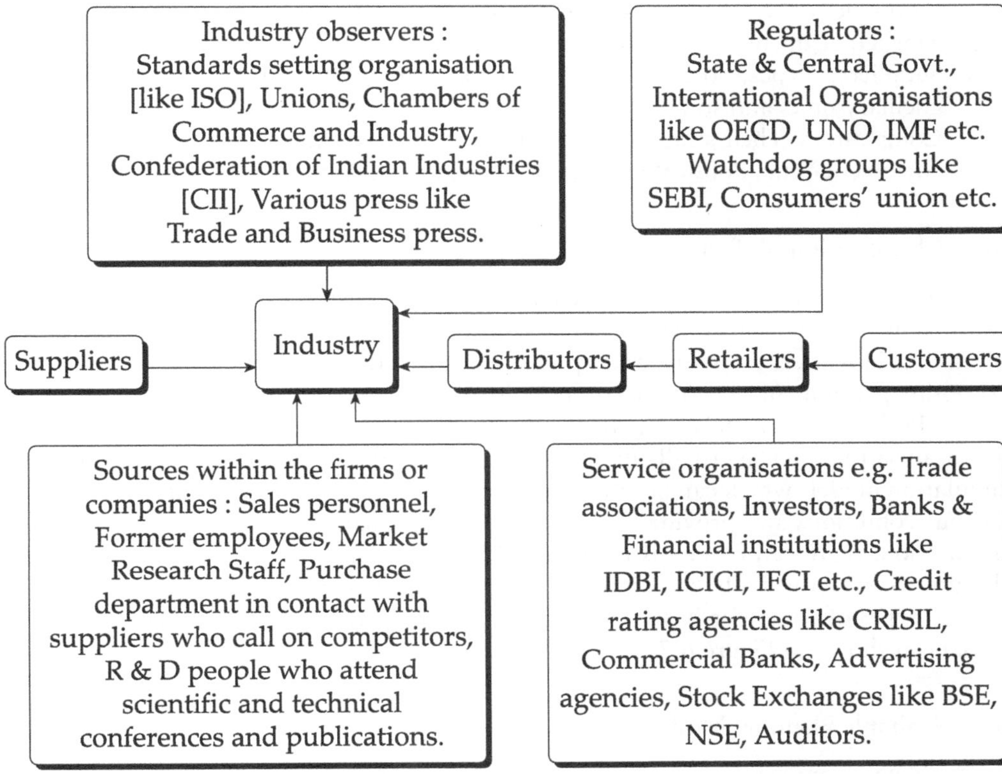

Figure 6.6 Important Sources of Field Data for Industry Analysis

e. **Company Directories**: Statistical data can be obtained from company directories like the Million Dollar Directory, CRISIL ratings, Dun and Brad Street business information report and similar global publications.
f. **Government Publications**: Such publications furnish statistics on manufacturers, retail traders, mineral industries, etc.
g. **Publications of Trade Associations: Many industries** have trade associations, which serve as clearing houses for industry data and sometimes publish detailed industry statistics.

The broad categories of data for the purpose of planning information are:

a. **Industry Participants**: A list of major industry participants, especially the leading companies.
b. **Product Lines**: Company and year wise.
c. **Major Customers**: Customer preferences.
d. **Complementary and Substitute Products**: Specifications of those products.
e. **Industry Growth**: Rate, pattern (seasonal, cyclical and so on) and determinants of growth.

f. **Production and Distribution**: Technology, life cycle, cost structure, value addition, economics of scale, logistics, labour and other factors of production/operation.
g. **Market**: Segmentation, marketing practices and so on.
h. **Suppliers**: Types, sources of innovations, supply channels, (indigenous/import), ancillary units and so on.
i. **Competitors**: Their strategy, goals, strengths and weaknesses and so on.
j. **Socio-economic, Political and Legal Environment**: At macro-level.

6.7 Classification of Planning Models

The typical planning models are mathematical models consisting of mathematical expressions including financial statements. The models are either deterministic or probabilistic in nature. However, the scope and applicability of deterministic models are limited for corporate planning in view of uncertainties involved in external and competitive environments. Probabilistic models are better in this regard. The planning models being adopted by organisations can be broadly divided as optimisation models (deterministic in nature), simulation models which can be either deterministic or probabilistic in nature to simulate various conditions and provide 'what-if' type of information to the corporate planners. In addition, there can be heuristic models. Models are mostly computer-based and use the processing power of the computer to enhance a manager's analytical ability. The various types of computer-based planning models and their typical business applications have been shown in Figure 6.7.

6.8 A Simple Planning Model

A simplified example of a deterministic simulation model involving profit planning based on the output of a particular product manufactured by a manufacturing unit is as follows:

Output = Input variable
Sales = Price × Output
Price = ₹450 (price is fixed, the item being covered under rate contract)
Cost of sales = Direct cost + Overhead cost
Direct cost = Direct material cost + Direct labour cost
Direct material cost = Output × 200
Direct labour cost = Output × 50
Overhead cost = Variable overhead + Fixed overhead
Variable overhead = Output × 50
Fixed overhead = 40,000
Profit before tax = Sales – Cost of sales
Taxes = 0.50 × Profit before tax
Net profit = Profit before tax – Tax
Assuming, output = 1,000 units
The profit plan for a particular year, say 2026–2027, is as follows:
Output = 1,000
Sales = 450 × 1,000 = 450,000
Less: Cost of sales = 1,000 × 200 + 1,000 × 50 + 50 × 1,000 + 40,000 = 340,000
Profit before tax = 1,10,000
Less: Taxes = 55,000
Net profit = 55,000

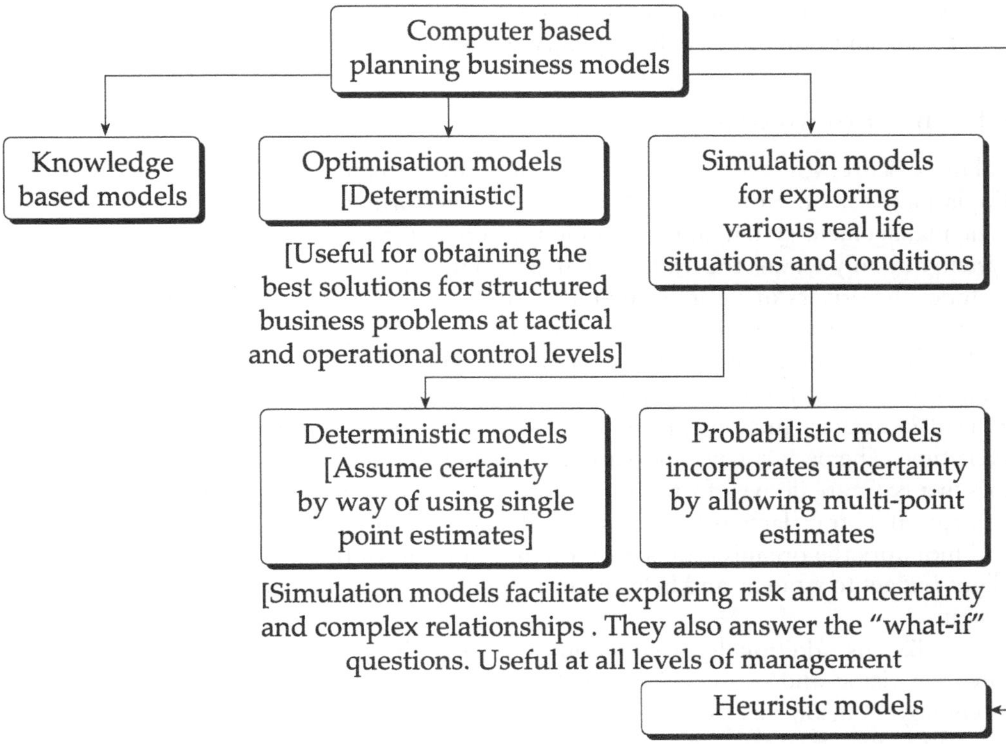

Figure 6.7 Classification of Planning Models

The above planning model is a very simple example illustrating the form of a planning model. However, more complicated and yet comprehensive business planning models can be developed in a similar fashion for planning sales, production, capacity utilisation, level of advertising, level of outsourcing, pricing at micro- (unit level) and at macro-level, estimation of gross national income (GNP), disposable consumer income, planning of manufacturing and service sector industries and so on. However, the planning models irrespective of the complexities involved must include the following:

1. A set of input data to the model;
2. The processing formulae, logic, equations, flow charts and so on to operate on the input data;
3. A format for presenting the results obtained after processing by the model.

6.9 Risk and Sensitivity Analysis of Planning Models

With most planning models, it is possible to assess risk by way of sensitivity analysis. The process of sensitivity analysis is to study the effect of any variable at a time on the result or outcome of the model. The objective of the analysis is to identify the 'critical' or 'sensitive' variables, which are variables having more than a proportionate effect on the result. For example, a simulation model involving financial investment might include variables such as unit cost, unit price, volume of sales and amount to be invested. Sensitivity analysis in such a case might show that the resulting profit arising out of the investment is little affected by unit cost or price, but significantly affected by the volume of sales.

6.10 Balanced Scorecard

Balanced scorecard (BSC) is a new tool for strategic management developed by Robert Kaplan and David Norton, which comprises a performance measurement system, strategic management system and a communication system. The performance measurement system not only retains the traditional financial measures such as ROI and profit but also includes the drivers of future economic performance and value creation through investment in customers, suppliers, employees, technology and process innovation.

The financial measures are mainly indicators of past performance and hence called lag indicators, but the future drivers of economic performance and value creation are known as lead indicators such as customer satisfaction, employee skills and reduced process cycle time. The performance measures as mentioned above, both the lag and lead indicators in a BSC, are derived from the organisations' mission statement and overall business strategy. BSC translates the organisational strategy into specific, quantifiable objectives and monitors the organisation's performance in terms of those objectives. The BSC also aligns budget to strategy and helps in developing an enterprise performance management system.

The BSC is additionally a communication tool in an organisation as it communicates the vision and strategy translated in terms of performance measures to all levels of employees insofar as they are individually or jointly concerned. The communication role of the BSC facilitates strategy execution by removing the barriers of vision, people, management and resources as shown in Figure 6.8.

6.11 Four Perspectives of a BSC

While the scorecard retains the traditional financial measures, it takes a total view of an organisation by complementing the financial perspective with three other distinct perspectives: the customer perspective, internal business process perspective and learning and growth perspective. The BSC developed objectives, metrics (measures), targets and initiatives to collect data and analyse the same related to each of these perspectives.

Figure 6.9 shows the framework of the BSC with vision and strategy at the centre of the scorecard and with the four perspectives as mentioned above around it. Let me explain the four perspectives along with the performance measures for each of them.

6.11.1 Customer Perspective

Organisations have, in recent times, realised the paramount importance of customer focus and customer delight in any business. If customers are not satisfied, they will eventually find alternative suppliers who will meet their needs. Poor performance from this perspective will lead to future decline in growth even though the current financial scenario may appear satisfactory. In developing objectives and measures for this perspective, two important factors must be considered—the target customers (focus) and the value proposition for the products or services provided to them. The value propositions may include:

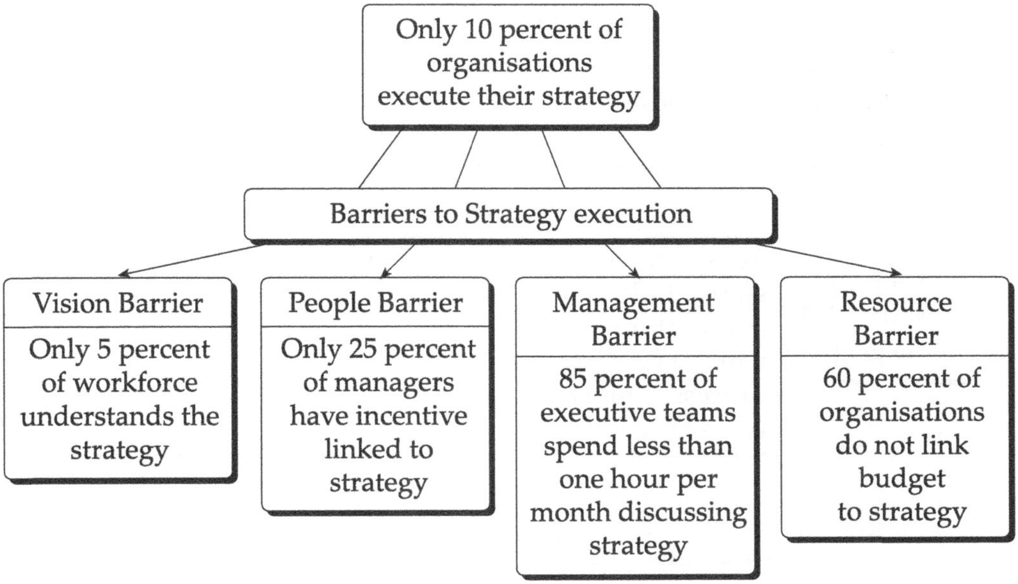

Figure 6.8 Barriers to Implementing Strategy

Source: Adapted from material developed by Robert S. Kaplan and David P. Norton.

1. Operational excellence leading to cost leadership as in the case of Walmart.
2. Product leadership through constant product innovation, as is the case with Nike, a product leader in the field of athletic footwear.
3. Customer intimacy by way of developing long-term relationships through a deep understanding of customer needs and providing solutions. For example, Dr Fixit of Pidilite Industries Limited providing long-term waterproofing and allied solutions epitomises the customer-intimate organisation.

6.11.2 Internal Business Process Perspective

In the internal process perspective of the scorecard, the key processes at which the organisation must excel in order to continue adding value to customers are identified. This requires that business organisations identify entirely new internal processes through re-engineering rather than concentrating on incremental improvement of existing processes and activities.

6.11.3 Learning and Growth Perspective

The learning and growth perspective includes employee skills, satisfaction, availability of information, corporate cultural attitude, employee training, learning and development. In a knowledge worker organisation, employee—the repository of knowledge—is the main resource. The measures in the learning and growth perspective of the BSC are really the enablers for the other three perspectives. Like the other perspectives of the scorecard,

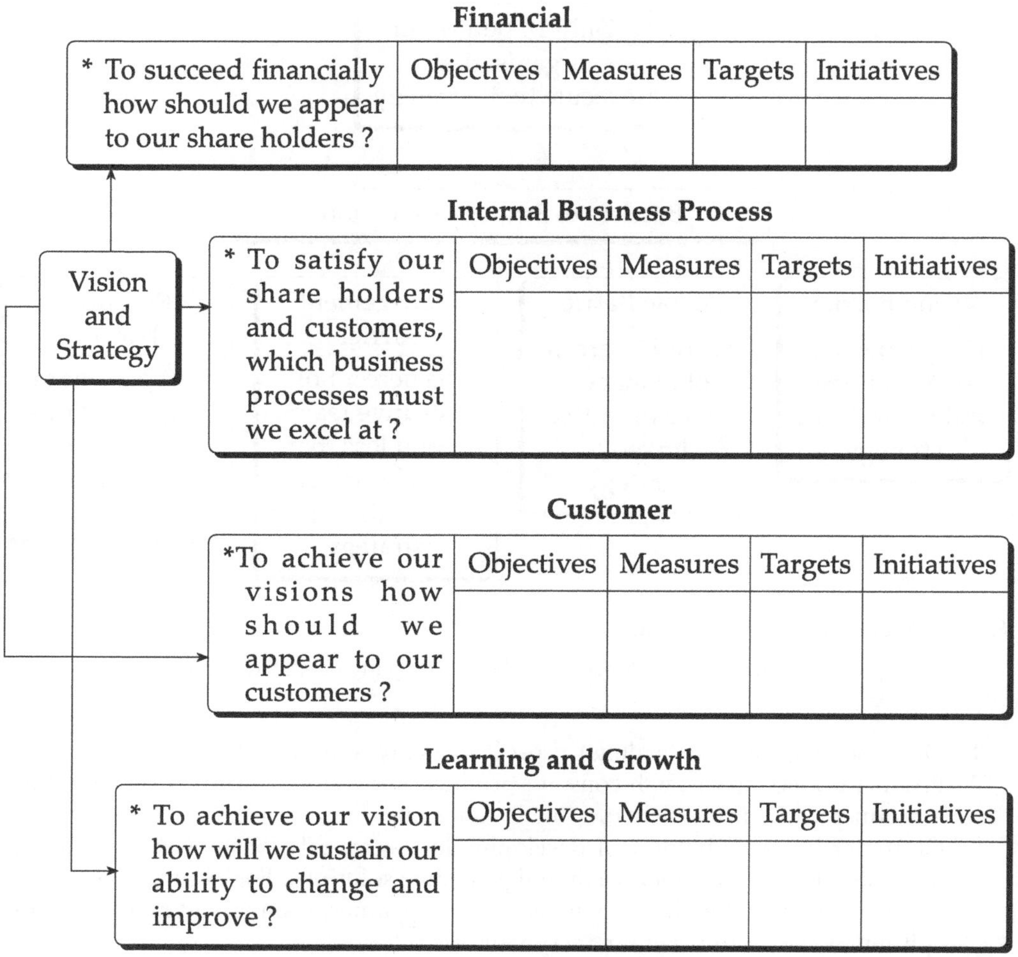

Figure 6.9 The Balanced Scorecard

Source: Kaplan and Norton (1996).

there will be a mix of core outcome (lag) measures and performance (lead) measures to represent the learning and growth perspective.

6.11.4 Financial Perspective

Traditional financial measures are important components of the BSC. In the case of profit organisations, the classic financial lag indicators include: revenue, profitability and budget variances. In the case of non-profit and public sector organisations, financial measures ensure that the organisations are achieving results in an efficient manner that minimises cost.

6.12 Application of BSC in Private Sector in India

BSC has been very successfully applied in the private sector in India. Tata Motors was the first company in India to win the BSC Hall of Fame award. In the corporate private sector in India, the adoption rate of BSC is about 45%.

BSC Example in Private Sector:

The application of BSC in the case of Air Deccan is as shown below:

Vision: 'To be the preferred airline of air travellers in India'.

Mission: 'To demystify air travel in India by providing reliable, low-cost air travel to the common man by constantly driving down the air fares as an ongoing mission'.

Air Deccan started its operations in civil aviation as a low-cost airline and had been able to compete with full-service airlines such as Indian Airlines by adopting cost-saving measures as follows:

1. **Food Cost:** Food is not provided on board since domestic flights are of short duration.
2. **Extra Seats:** Since no food is provided, no space is required for food and the space could be utilised for providing extra seats. It was possible to provide 40 seats more than the number of seats provided by the other full-service airlines.
3. **Sale of Tickets Is Done Online** through the Internet, and with the booking, the passengers get the boarding pass at the airport. This change in the ticket sales saved the cost of engaging travel agents, the stationery and printing charges of tickets.
4. **Turnaround Time Management:** Turnaround time is reduced to 20 minutes only, nearly 50% reduction as compared to the same for other airlines. This was possible since the time for loading and unloading of meals is saved along with the cleaning time, thereby resulting in increased flying time.
5. **Repair and Maintenance Cost:** Air Deccan had only one type of aircraft in its fleet, and hence it held a smaller number of maintenance spares as compared with the same for other airlines. Further, the repair and maintenance function is outsourced partially to economise cost of repair and maintenance.
6. **Pricing Strategy:** Apart from low fares, Air Deccan offered various incentives to passengers like the 'Frequent flyer' scheme. From the above data obtained from an article published by Dr Mukesh Chauhan, a strategy map for Air Deccan can be developed which will facilitate drawing the BSC for Air Deccan as shown in Figure 6.10.

6.13 Application of BSC in Public Sector Not-for-Profit Enterprises

The scope and applicability of BSC in public sector non-profit enterprises and government are enormous. The public sector enterprises, unlike the private sector where profit is the prime objective, have to cater to the needs of all stakeholders such as customers, the community, the physical environment and the people at large.

The performance measurement system for non-profit organisations has to essentially address the following areas:

Vision and Strategy

"To be the preferred air line of air travellers in India" thru lowest cost tickets

Financial			
Objectives	**Measures**	**Targets**	**Initiatives**
1. Higher revenue	Passenger/kilo meters	15% increase in passenger/kilo meters per year	Traffic study, route optimization etc.
2. Lower cost	Fleet lease cost	5% reduction in fleet cost per year	Fewer aircrafts and increased utilization by optimum scheduling

Internal Business Process			
Objectives	**Measures**	**Targets**	**Initiatives**
1. Maximise air time	Ground turnaround time	Not more than 25 minutes	Cycle time optimisation program
2. Optimised inventory of spares	No. of spares and total value thereof	5% reduction in value of spares per year	VED analysis and outsourcing

Customer			
Objectives	**Measures**	**Targets**	**Initiatives**
1. Lowest ticket price	Benchmarked price	Number 1 in price in market	Special fares and customer loyalty programs
2. On-time flights	On-time arrival routing	95% on-time arrivals	Rewards to employees for on-time performance

Learning and growth			
Objectives	**Measures**	**Targets**	**Initiatives**
Employee development and skill enrichment	Ground crew training and development in multi-skill	200 employees to be trained every year thru in-house and outside training programs	Outsource training to external expert agencies etc.

Figure 6.10 Balanced Scorecard for Air Deccan

1. **Financial Accountability**: The performance measurement system includes standards of financial accounting, documentation and reporting relating to proper utilisation of funds for the purpose for which the same are provided by the funding agencies.
2. **Products and Services Delivered:** This category represents the classical measurement efforts for counting the number of products and services delivered and the number of people served.

3. **Adherence to the Quality Standards of Service Delivery**: The quality of service delivery is of paramount importance in the case of public sector enterprises and the government.
4. **Customer-need-based Measures**: These measures are taken to ensure in-service delivery.

5. **KPIs**: KPIs can serve as a repository for all areas of measurement such as the cost of service provided and response time for customer complaints.
6. **Client Satisfaction**: Among the indicators of satisfaction that are measurable, important ones are: overall satisfaction, accessibility and so on.
7. **Corporate Social Responsibility (CSR)**: CSR is becoming more and more important for the public sector and government sector since the aspects of environmental, social and cultural impacts and related issues are also related to good governance of the organisations.

Figure 6.11 displays the BSC model applicable to public sector non-profit enterprises. The salient differences between the private and public sector use of the scorecard are as follows:

1. Mission is at the top of the BSC in the case of the public sector, unlike the private sector, where improving value to the shareholders is of prime importance and the management is accountable to their financial stakeholders. In the case of public sector enterprises, apart from efficient allocation and utilisation of funds, the

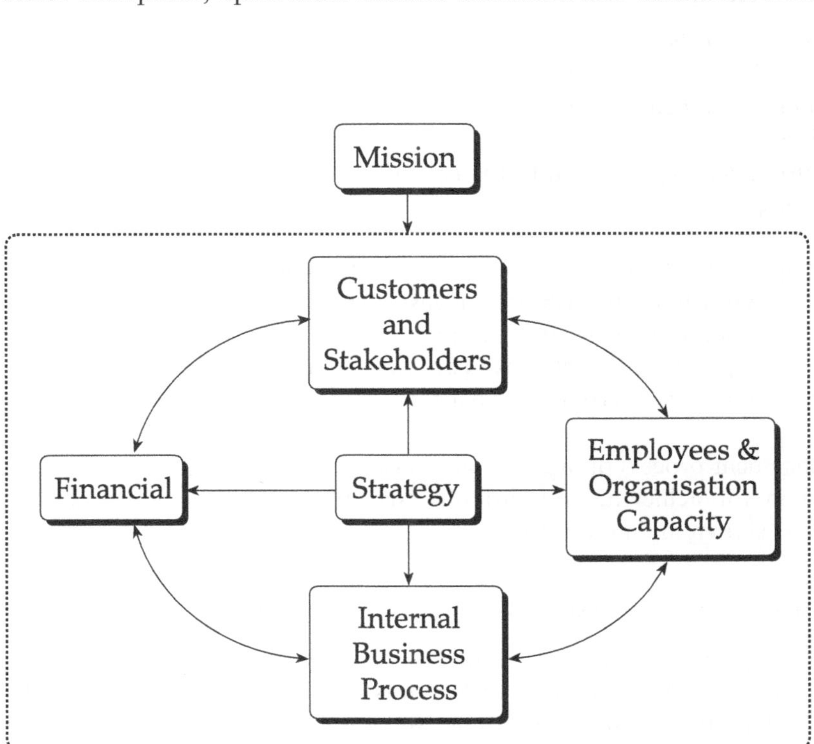

Figure 6.11 Public Sector Balanced Scorecard

enterprises function to serve higher social purposes such as 'public safety', 'green environment' and 'eradication of poverty'.
2. Strategy remains at the core of the BSC. In the case of public sector and non-profit enterprises, it is very difficult to define a clear and concise strategy as in the case of private enterprises with a profit motive.
3. Customer perspective is elevated, and customer here includes not only financial stakeholders but also all those whom the organisation aims to serve. The important issue involved is who the customers are for public sector and non-profit enterprises and how the enterprises create value for the customers. Establishing the real customers in many ways depends on the perspective of the designers of the BSC. For example, in the case of a metro city municipal corporation, the unauthorised hawkers who sit on the pedestrian footpath and are periodically evicted are also treated as customers or stakeholders, as the municipal corporation has to deal with them to keep the footpath free from any encroachment.

6.14 BSC for a State Government

The strategy map relating to the top level of a state government administration is shown in Figure 6.12. The four perspectives are customer, financial, internal administration processes and the state government's capacity for learning and improvement. The BSC has been shown in Figure 6.13.

6.15 Information and Organising Function

According to Murdick and Ross, 'organizing is required of managers because it is the method by which effective group action is obtained. A structure of roles must be designed and maintained in order for people to work together in carrying out plans and accomplish objectives'.

Organising is a key function of management, and the process of organising involves the following:

1. Grouping of activities and tasks necessary to achieve the plans.
2. The assignment of the tasks to various departments by allocation of responsibilities and commensurate delegation of authority.
3. To make provision for effective coordination of the tasks, activities and responsibilities of the work groups and departments.

The management process of organising, as described above, addresses itself to the structural system for achieving responsibility allocation, coordination and delegation of authority as shown in Figure 6.14.

6.16 Classical Vis-à-Vis Systems Approach to Organising

The classical, also known as the pyramidal organisation, structure is hierarchical and at one time was most widely accepted by business organisations and is the foundation upon which all adaptations and modifications are constructed. The keywords of the hierarchical organisation structure are: *structure* and *formal*. The basic ideas of the classical

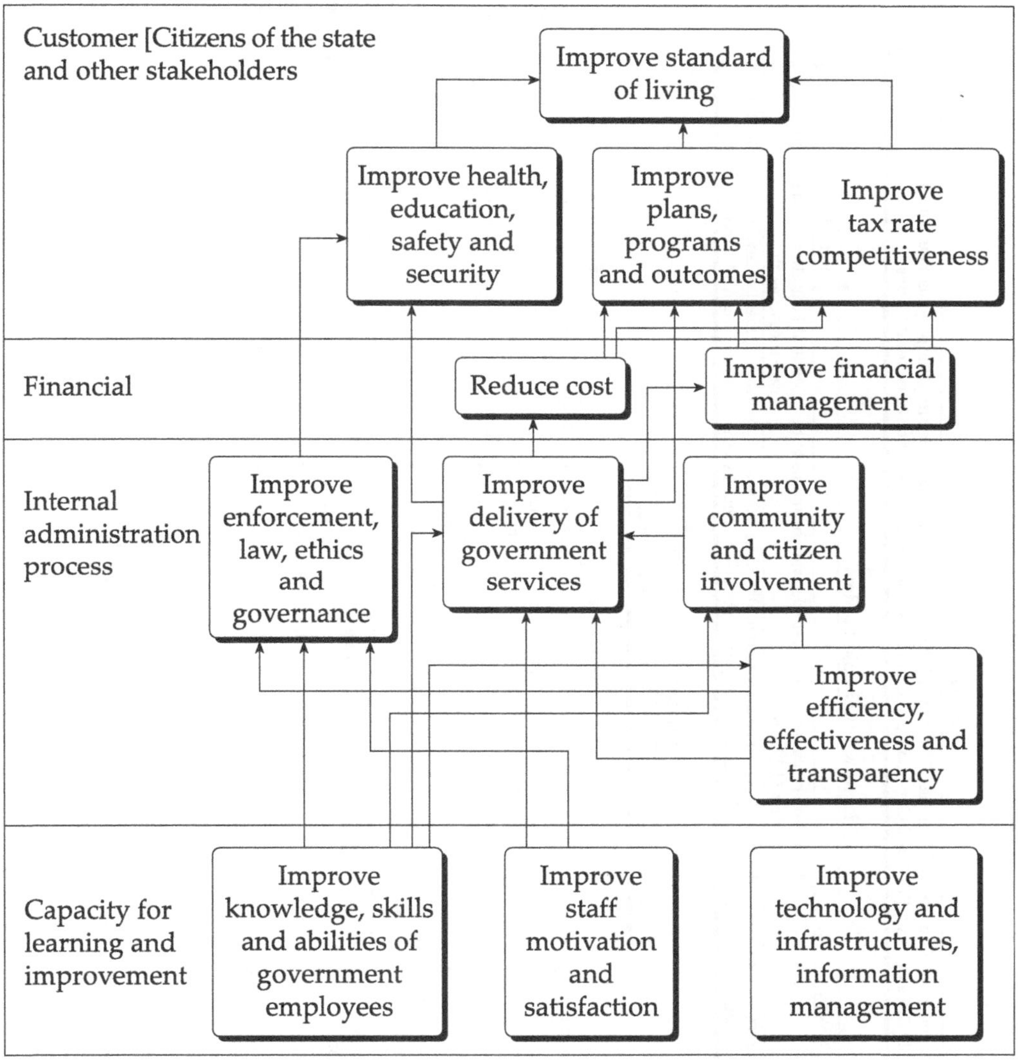

Figure 6.12 Strategy Map for State Government Administration

organisation structure are: specialisation of work (departmentalisation), span of control (supervision of a limited number of subordinates), chain of command (authority delegation) and the unity of command (no subordinate has more than one superior).

Although the classical organisation structure is easily understood and was widely applied in business organisations, but due to its inherent limitations, such as being too structured to adapt to change, inhibiting innovation, being too mechanistic and job-centric, and not human-centric, the classical approach has become outdated with the current needs of business; hence, the systems approach to organising has developed. The systems approach to organising is based on the following concepts:

MISSION

Improve Standard of Living and "Gross State Happiness" through [i] Health, education, Safety, Security, Employment measures, [ii] Sustainable Development, [iii] Good Governance and [iv] Preservation and promotion of cultural Values.

↓

Citizens & other stakeholders

Objectives	Measures	Targets	Initiatives
1. Improve health of people	Health care	100 health centers and 10 super speciality hospitals to be opened by 31.12.2019	Medical Education, modernised health care measures etc.
2. Improved Education	1. Adult literacy programmes 2. Higher Educational facilities	Literacy Level to be increased to 70% in next 3 years. seats for higher education to be doubled in next 4 years	Recruitment of teachers, upgradation of teaching & research facilities

↑

Strategy

Efficient Governance with full involvement of public

Internal Administration Process

Objectives	Measures	Targets	Initiatives
Law and order, safety enforcement	Crime, Accident Rates	No. of crimes and accidents to reduce by 30% in current year	Modernisation of Police department etc.
Speedy delivery of Govt. services, Maximise benefit/cost to public	Time, cost and No. of outlets for delivery of services	Delivery of essential service time not more than 3 days	Improved service delivery mechanism
Improve Productivity through technology innovation	Publication of pilot technology strategy document	By October 2022	Facilitate strategic technology plan for the state

Learning & Improvement

Objectives	Measures	Targets	Initiatives
Close skill gaps	No. of Employees trained in a year	100 employees of all categories to undergo 2 weeks training in a year	Outsourcing of training activities to reputed institutions
Achieve positive employee climate	Employee Productivity, satisfaction index	Satisfaction index to be 6 out of 10 in a 4-point scale	Reward Incentive schemes for good performance
Improved technology, Infrastructure & information management	Development of common data base for technology and infrastructure development plan for the state	By 31.3.2021	Strategically focused guides to facilitate progress towards smart growth initiatives

Financial

Objectives	Measures	Targets	Initiatives
Reduce Expenditure	Government expenditure under various heads	5% reduction in non-plan expenditure in next two years	Austerity measures
Financial Management	Self-Sufficient in Financing the state Plan and Programs	GDP growth rate not less than 8%, Tax revenue to increase by 5% every year	Rapid industrialisation, Tax collection drive, etc.

Note : Employee satisfaction
Index : 0 for no satisfaction, 3.5 for somewhat satisfied, 6 for satisfaction and 10 for highly satisfied

Figure 6.13 An Illustration of BSC for State Government Administration

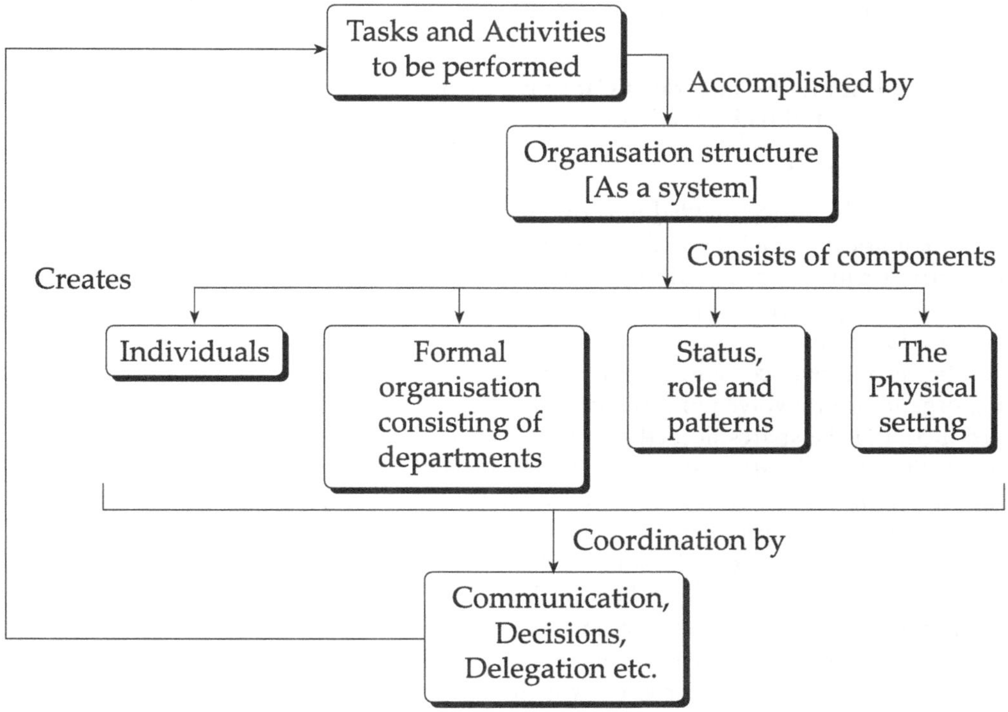

Figure 6.14 Integration of the Organisational System through the Management Process of Organising

1. Integration of subsystems to make up the whole organisation;
2. Decentralisation leading to improved morale and motivation of managers;
3. Centralised control with decentralised operations through information flows;
4. Process orientation rather than structure;
5. The systems approach to organising lays emphasis on the system as opposed to organisational functions such as sales, finance and personnel.

The systems approach to organising is very much dependent on the integration of the subsystems through information flows. Each organisational entity, such as the subsystem, the responsibility centre or the manager, can be viewed as an IS having input (information), processor (for example, the manager) and the output, which is the decision or else input information for the other entities. Each organisational entity becomes a decision point. It may be emphasised here that organisations consisting of the entities must be designed around information flow, and the information must facilitate the planning and control of performance. However, frequently organisational structures and performance reporting do not match with each other. In such cases, ISs cannot facilitate proper planning and performance reporting.

Organisations have to change with the changes in the environment and other internal changes in structure, management and so on. It is therefore essentially needed that with the above changes the ISs also change. In case the ISs are not changed to match a change in organisational responsibilities and the needs of managers, the result will be 'information lag' as mentioned by Murdick and Ross.

6.17 Case Study: An Integrated Capacity Expansion Plan for Manufacture of a Product and Its Future Requirement of Spares

6.17.1 Background

The case study can be divided into two parts. The first part relates to the development of an empirical model for realistic assessment of future requirements of spares for an end product in service based on the initiation of the end product into service and past consumption patterns of spares depending upon the age profile of the population of the end product in use.

The second part considers the integrated capacity expansion plan of a manufacturing organisation involved in producing the end product, which is a complex engineering product, and the spares needed to meet the replacement demand for worn-out components. Precisely, the study shows how to earmark the net requirement of capacity at any machine centre during any future period in the planning horizon, both for meeting the demand for the end product and also for its spares.

An interesting aspect of the study is that the demand for spares increases as more and more quantities of the end product are inducted into service and so with the ageing of the population of the end product in service. However, the demand for the end product is dependent on the user requirement for the same for immediate need and also for the replacement of the old end products which may be beyond economic repair.

Often the requirement of capacity for manufacture of spares is significantly less than that for regular manufacture. Nevertheless, the need for planning for this part of plant capacity cannot be discarded in view of the corporate commitment to supply spares for operating the products in use, particularly for products manufactured for exclusive use by the users. In general, once a customer buys a product of a particular brand, the same customer will be totally dependent on the specific original equipment manufacturer (OEM) for the supply of spares for the product in future. The OEM may also be bound by contractual obligation to meet the spares requirement during the entire life cycle of the product, even if the same product model is phased out due to obsolescence. The above-mentioned situation offers both an opportunity and a challenge for the manufacturer, as the profit margins for the sale of spares are normally higher in a captive market for the sale of spares for the original equipment.

The specific product considered in this study relates to the supply of a particular defence use product and its related spares manufactured by the Indian Ordnance Factories (IOFs). The product has been in use by the Indian army and other paramilitary forces in India for a considerable period. The IOFs are captive production units under the Ministry of Defence, Government of India and the units manufacture a variety of products used by the armed forces as well as the paramilitary forces. As a matter of policy, the Government of India does not allow the manufacture of these products by private manufacturers. IOFs are the sole manufacturers of their products and the related spares.

6.17.2 *Methodology Adopted for Formulation of the Model for Capacity Expansion Plan*

A lag regression model was formulated with past requirements of capacity at machine centres, calculated based on historic data on spares consumption as the dependent variable and the corresponding quantities of the product initiated into service earlier as the independent lag variables. A lag regression model can be expressed as:

$$Y_t = \alpha_0.X_t + \alpha_1.X_{t-1} + ... + \alpha_s.X_{t-s} \qquad 6.1$$

In Equation 6.1, Y_t is the value of the dependent variable Y at time t and is expressed as a function of the current (at time t) and s is the previous values of an independent variable X. In the above equation, X_t, X_{t-1} and like are called lag variables, s is the lag period and α_0, α_1 are called the coefficients of lag regression.

In our present study, the dependent variable is the total capacity requirement for spares for any time period and the lag variables are the number of end-products inducted into service during the particular time period and the previous lag period.

Almon's methodology for transformation of lag variables and principal component analysis had been adopted in the development of the lag regression model to find out the coefficients of the lag regression equation. Almon's method is an approach to overcome the difficulty associated with the reduction in degrees of freedom with an increase in the length of the lag period, and principal component analysis was done to overcome the problem of multi-collinearity associated with lag regression models.

Readers may refer to the book titled *Econometric Methods* (2nd ed., 1972) by J. Johnston, and the book titled *Classical and Modern Regression with Applications* (2nd ed., 1990) by H. Myers Reymond.

The lag regression model was used for the estimation of future capacities of different machine centres based on the anticipated entry of quantities of the product into service.

An integer linear programming model was also formulated for modelling the aggregate capacity expansion problem for meeting the future requirement of capacity. The model also takes into consideration the erosion of existing capacity and capacity replacements. General cost functions for capacity expansion were considered besides maintenance and operating costs. The model seeks to minimise the total present worth of all costs associated with future capacity expansion plans.

Statistical tests were conducted to prove the validity of the capacity estimation model for spare parts manufacture. The model was also externally validated using independent observations. The model is applicable in situations where the manufacturer of a product is also the exclusive supplier of the spares for the product. The product for the study was an assembly of 120 different components, out of which 40 were plastic components, fasteners and other simple components and those were procured from the market in 'ready to use' condition. The remaining 80 components were manufactured in-house by the manufacturing unit (ordnance factory in this case). In all, 15 different types of machining processes were involved in the in-house manufacture of these components by four machining centres.

As manufacture of this product was established many years ago and there had been many capacity expansions, an exact estimate of the capacity of the different machine centres for manufacture of these components during the past is not readily available. However, the supply of these components towards spares requirement had generally not been adequate in the past. The actual annual spares converted to aggregate requirement of manufacturing capacity required at the four machining centres during 15 years from 1975–1976 to 1989–1990 are shown in the following table:

Actual Requirement of Capacities for Spares Manufacture (Machine Hours Per Year):

Year	*Machine Centre 1*	*Machine Centre 2*	*Machine Centre 3*	*Machine Centre 4*
1975–76	4780.64	2648.94	2554.58	4294.61
1976–77	7309.11	6588.67	4765.24	2744.23
1977–78	9181.50	11732.06	5149.56	3401.87
1978–79	16868.28	10992.18	11081.38	5923.80
1979–80	11075.26	9702.87	6283.64	21154.12
1980–81	22487.61	15769.39	13263.88	10404.85
1981–82	21183.29	10707.14	10800.92	9505.81
1982–83	25113.82	17792.20	18920.99	10881.01
1983–84	32603.62	25669.34	25129.64	16622.98
1984–85	41261.62	31703.71	33762.21	17627.67
1985–86	26845.25	15262.85	15649.96	11339.55
1986–87	28829.26	20552.03	15729.91	13141.00
1987–88	30939.94	20963.34	16428.76	15874.59
1988–89	23220.06	19082.44	14397.26	13417.02
1989–90	29167.92	22674.13	18678.37	11001.12

The annual production figures of the end product from 1963 to 1993–1994 are as follows:

Year	*Production (Numbers)*	*Year*	*Production (Numbers)*	*Year*	*Production (Numbers)*	*Year*	*Production (Numbers)*
1963–64	13,882	1971–72	51,612	1979–80	20,000	1987–88	20,300
1964–65	37,500	1972–73	68,336	1980–81	20,005	1988–89	20,000
1965–66	48,800	1973–74	52,225	1981–82	20,000	1989–90	18,570
1966–67	41,500	1974–75	52,415	1982–83	20,005	1990–91	20,3000
1967–68	36,000	1975–76	53,004	1983–84	17,000	1991–92	25,760
1968–69	38,260	1976–77	45,005	1984–85	12,000	1992–93	30,425
1969–70	44,541	1977–78	35,010	1985–86	12,002	1993–94	26,000
1970–71	29,545	1978–79	22,920	1986–87	18,300	1994–95	Not Available

Validation of the Model:

The lag regression model was validated internally using the significance tests for the t-statistic associated with the regression coefficients, the overall F-statistic of the regression model and the R-squared statistic. Additionally, the model was also externally validated. This was done by splitting the data collected for the selected model into two portions. The first portion (data corresponding to 1975–1976 and 1986–1987) was used to develop a lag regression model and internally validate it. The second portion (data corresponding to 1987–1988 and 1989–1990), which was independent from the first, was then used to compare with predicted results from the model.

Results of the Study:

Results of the regression analysis for a particular machine centre have been shown in the following table as an illustrative sample. Similar results were also obtained for the other three machine centres.

Results of Lag Regression Analysis for Machine Centre 1:
The table below shows the variation of the F-statistic, mean squared error S of regression, mean of observed values of the dependent variable (capacity required at the machine centres during the years), observations omitted from the analysis based on R-student statistic and the ratio C_v, the coefficient of variation corresponding to lag periods varying from 10 to 25 years. For each lag period, the combination that gave the best value of the F-statistic was chosen. The final choice of the lag regression model was based on the highest F value. The details of the chosen lag regression model for estimation of capacity for machine centre 1 are given in the following table.

Length of Lag (Year)	*Order of Polynomial*	*Regression Variance (S)*	*Coefficient of Regression (F)*	*Mean of Observed Dependant Variables*	*Coefficient of Variance (CV)*	*Corresponding to Data Not Included in the Analysis*
10	4	9612.00	32.51	22,056	0.4358	—
12	2	8259.80	58.12	22,056	0.3745	—
15	3	3829.00	158.07	20,685	0.1851	1983–84
16	4	3765.00	122.95	19,768	0.1905	1983–84, 1984–85
17	2	3514.00	239.55	20,685	0.1699	1983–84, 1984–85
18	3	3113.50	612.30	19,768	0.1575	1983–84, 1984–85
19	2	3104.00	725.33	20,685	0.1501	1984–85
20	2	2971.00	793.00	20,685	0.1436	1984–85
21	4	3236.00	333.65	20,685	0.1564	1984–85
22	4	3304.50	319.77	20,685	0.1598	1984–85
23	4	3240.00	222.25	20,685	0.1566	1984–85
24	4	3247.00	331.39	20,685	0.1570	1984–85
25	4	3281.00	324.46	20,685	0.1586	1984–85

Details of the Lag Regression Model for Estimation of Capacity at Machine Centre 1 for Manufacture of Spares:

Parameters and Their Combination for the Best Value: F-Statistic: 793; coefficient of variance: 0.1436; lag period: 20 years; S: 2971.00

Total number of observations: 15; number of observations deleted: 1; number of observations used: 14.

Result of Residual Analysis:

Year	*Actual Capacity Required as Observed (Hours/Year)*	*Capacity Required as Computed from Equation 6.1 (Hours/Year)*	*Residues (Absolute)*	*Residues (R-student)*
1975–76	4780.64	3292.97	-1467.87	-0.48055
1976–77	7309.11	6625.98	-683.13	-0.22238
1977–78	9181.50	8289.18	-892.32	-0.29170
1978–79	16868.28	21241.72	4375.45	1.57043
1979–80	11075.26	6879.84	-4195.42	-1.50438
1980–81	22487.61	26562.32	4074.72	1.46690

Year	*Actual Capacity Required as Observed (Hours/Year)*	*Capacity Required as Computed from Equation 6.1 (Hours/Year)*	*Residues (Absolute)*	*Residues (R-student)*
1981–82	21183.29	20434.38	−748.91	−0.25162
1982–83	25113.82	24388.28	−725.54	−0.24731
1983–84	32603.62	36559.44	3955.82	1.48068
1985–86	26845.25	25234.43	−1610.82	−0.56114
1986–87	28829.26	29266.68	437.42	0.15052
1987–88	30939.94	33040.16	2100.22	0.73982
1988–89	23220.06	17428.59	−5791.47	−2.44345
1989–90	29167.92	29895.81	727.88	0.25094

The requirement of capacity as shown in the above table was computed from Equation 6.1 based on the actual number of products inducted in service for the lag period of 20 years and the coefficients of lag regression as shown in the following table for machine centre 1. The lag regression coefficients were obtained following Almon's methodology and the principal component analysis as mentioned earlier.

Lag Year	**1**	**2**	**3**	**4**	**5**
Coefficient of lag regression	0	0.000283	0.001105	0.002464	0.004361
Lag Year	**6**	**7**	**8**	**9**	**10**
Coefficient of lag regression	0.006795	0.009768	0.013279	0.017327	0.021913
Lag Year	**11**	**12**	**13**	**14**	**15**
Coefficient of lag regression	0.027038	0.03270	0.038900	0.045637	0.052913
Lag Year	**16**	**17**	**18**	**19**	**20**
Coefficient of lag regression	0.060727	0.069078	0.077968	0.087395	0.097360

The F-statistic, which is a measure of the association of the dependent variable with the independent variable, increases with an increase in the length of the lag period up to a maximum value. Significant improvement in the performance of the above model was noticed when the lag length reaches 15 years. Thereafter, the result continued to improve, but beyond a definite lag length, the strength of the association started declining, and the F-value too declined. In the case of machine centre 1, a lag period of 20 years resulted in the highest F-value.

From the results of external validation, it was observed that in the majority of the cases the observed values were within the 95% confidence interval of prediction and in all cases within the 95% confidence interval for individual observation thereby proving the validity of the lag regression model.

6.18 Conclusion

The above analysis proves the suitability of the lag regression model for estimation of capacity for manufacture of spares. Source: Mohanan (1995).

Review Questions

1. Define the terms: (a) vision, (b) mission, (c) strategic intent, (d) strategy, (e) goals, (f) objectives and (g) policy.
2. What is corporate strategy? How is it formulated?
3. What are the five forces mentioned by Michael E. Porter? How do they facilitate industry analysis?
4. What are the different types of corporate plans? Illustrate.
5. What is environmental scanning? How does it facilitate strategic planning in an organisation?
6. What are the main sources of planning information?
7. What is a planning model? Describe briefly any planning model that you know.
8. What is a BSC? What are its major perspectives? Illustrate with a suitable example.
9. How do BSCs for public sector not-for-profit enterprises differ from those for profit-making private enterprises?
10. What is the systems approach to planning and organising?

Bibliography

Hamel, G., and C. K. Prahalad. 'Strategic Intent'. *Harvard Business Review* 67, no. 3 (1989): 63–76.

Kaplan, R. 'Strategic Performance Measurement and Management in Non-profit Organizations'. *Non-profit Management and Leadership* 11, no. 3 (2001): 353–370.

Kaplan, R., and D. P. Norton. 'The Balanced Scorecard–Measures That Drive Performance'. *Harvard Business Review* 70, no. 1 (1992): 71.

Mohanan, K. T. 'An Integrated Capacity Expansion Plan for Manufacture of a Product and Its Spares'. Doctoral thesis, Department of Industrial Management, IISc, Bengaluru, India, April 1995.

Murdick, R. G., J. E. Ross, and J. R. Clagett. *Information Systems for Modern Management*, 3rd ed. New Delhi: Prentice Hall India, 1985.

Porter, M. E. 'The Five Competitive Forces That Shape Strategy'. *Harvard Business Review* 88, no. 1 (2008): 78–93.

7 Information System for Control

7.1 Control as a Management Function

Control is a primary function of management and also the management process which ensures that (a) operations or performance proceed according to plans and (b) the plans themselves result in attaining the objectives or goals of the organisation.

Basically, the control process consists of three steps, namely (a) setting the standards of performance or plans, (b) measuring actual performance against the standards or plans and (c) correcting deviations, if any, from standards or plans.

Any organisation, whether it is a manufacturing unit, a public utility such as a metropolitan electricity supply corporation or a non-profit social organisation such as a school or a club, has to produce goods, services or other facilities to fulfil its objectives—profit, quality service at reasonable cost and so on. In order to facilitate the same, planning must be undertaken as a first step, and once the plans have been formulated, control needs to be exercised to ensure conformity to the plans and relevancy of the plans in the future.

The first step in control in an organisation is setting the standards of performance, which involves defining for employees at all levels what is expected of them in terms of job performance or individual targets. The standards, which are criteria against which results are measured and compared, can be either quantitative or qualitative. For example, the quantitative target for the works manager of a factory can be a 5% increase in labour productivity in a particular year as compared to the previous year. The qualitative standard may be maintaining satisfactory industrial relations. Besides employee performance standards, as mentioned above, many organisations have identified key result areas relating to overall performance. Indeed, by evaluating organisational performance in these key areas, the top management monitors progress towards the basic objectives. General Electric Company of the USA mentioned eight such key areas as follows:

1. Productivity
2. Profitability
3. Market position
4. Personnel development
5. Innovation and product leadership
6. Employee attitude
7. Public responsibility
8. Balance between short- and long-term goals.

DOI: 10.4324/9781003509714-7

For each of the above key areas, performance targets are established for the activities. The targets have dimensions of profit, cost, time, quantity and quality. Furthermore, the targets can be tangible or intangible. Tangible targets or standards are physical measures such as colour, hardness, quantitative measures (man-hours, machine hours, kilos of materials and so on), monetary values in terms of cost of operations, revenue such as sales, profits and programmes involving physical performance with respect to time. Intangible targets are performance standards not measurable in quantitative terms such as employee morale and motivation, peace and happiness. Table 7.1 illustrates a few criteria of performance along with the dimensions within the key areas as mentioned above.

7.1.1 Measurement of Actual Performance

Once the standard of performance has been established, it is necessary to measure actual performance against the standard. This needs to be done in an accurate, speedy and unbiased manner using the same relevant units as specified in the standards such as time taken, expenditure in rupees and output in standard man-hours. Measurement of performance may be through personal observations or reporting which may be either oral or written. Personal observation is one of the most prevalent methods of performance measurement, in which case the managers visit the shops, fields, offices and departments to gather first-hand information about the state of affairs and performance. However, this form of measurement is more suitable at the operational control level of management. Oral reporting about performance is in the form of interview, group discussion and meetings such as periodic production review meetings, finance liaison meetings, budget meeting and various unit level management committee meetings.

Both personal observation and oral reporting do not result in any permanent record of performance, except that in the case of meetings, minutes are kept for record purposes. Increasingly, performance reporting is in written form due to the use of computer-based IS for performance reporting. Written reports of performance measures provide permanent records and may take various forms such as narrative reports, statistical reports, graphical reports such as charts, summary and exception reports.

Table 7.1 Criteria of Performance within Key Result Area

Dimensions					
Key Result Area	*Criteria of Performance*	*Cost*	*Time*	*Quantity*	*Quality*
Productivity	Output in standard man-hours per employee per annum		✓	✓	
Profitability	Return on investment	✓	✓	✓	
Market position	Market share			✓	
Personnel development	Ratio of number of employees fit for promotion to total number of employees in a particular trade			✓	
Employee attitude	Positive attitude towards change and innovation				✓

The last but not the least important step in the control process is correcting deviations if the actual performance deviates adversely from the standards. Methods and techniques for correcting deviations take the form of review of the original standards, modification of the same if needed, organising, staffing and directing. All these actions are required to be taken by the control unit of any organisation either to alter performance to adhere to the standards or to modify the standards as mentioned above.

7.2 Control of Physical Systems and Organisational Control

In case of physical systems including mechanical systems, control is in-built and is an integral part of the system design. Control in such cases is based on direct measurement of physical parameters such as temperature, speed and weight through sensors. Examples are the control systems for thermostats, engine governors, overload circuit breakers and so on.

In case of management and operation control systems of organisations, the need to monitor activities is not necessarily so apparent and the control systems are appropriately designed throughout the organisation. Another important difference between the organisational control and mechanical control system is that the former is based on the use of appropriate information flow throughout the organisation, whereas the latter is based on direct measurement of physical parameters. Managers in an organisation mostly exercise control on the basis of information about the activities which take place in the organisation, and hence designing formal ISs is of paramount importance for all levels of management and in particular for the operational and management control levels.

7.3 Types of Control Systems in an Organisation

Control in an organisation can usually be categorised into two groups, namely operating and management control. Operating control systems are simple, deterministic in nature and can be automated with the help of computers. Such systems hardly require management intervention and are based on routine information flows.

Management control systems, on the contrary, are complicated and attempt to control numerous factors including behavioural aspects and hence are mostly based on human control through managerial decisions with the help of various information, formal and informal in nature.

However, before we analyse the details of ISs for the above types of organisational control, let me explain some salient features of control in subsequent paragraphs.

7.4 Closed- and Open-Loop Systems

The system of feedback described in the Miller and Starr model explained in an earlier chapter of this book is a closed-loop feedback system, where control is an integral part of the system and feedback based on output measurement is fed to the controller (manager) to make appropriate decisions to modify the inputs to the organisational system. Closed-loop systems are more appropriate for mechanical systems as well as operational control systems in organisations such as stock-control systems. The stock replenishment orders are dependent on the actual measurement of stock levels and comparing the same with the reordering level.

Open-loop systems, on the other hand, are those where no feedback loop exists, and control is external and not an integral part of the systems. Open-loop control systems are more suitable in organisations where the environmental factors are rather unpredictable and more adaptation is required. In such cases, management intervention is necessary, and open-loop control systems are adopted. For example, unpredicted factors such as the emergence of a new competitor and liberalisation of the import policy of the government need appropriate actions on the part of strategic planners through open-loop control.

Positive and Negative Feedback: Positive feedback causes a system to move in the same direction as the measured deviation. Negative feedback, on the contrary, dampens or reduces deviations from the standard. The corrective action in case of negative feedback is in the opposite direction of the observed deviation. Positive feedback is generally incorporated with open-loop control systems where managerial intervention is required to deal with changing environmental circumstances. Negative feedback, on the other hand, is mostly incorporated with operational and tactical levels of management to ensure that operations and activities conform to plans.

Examples: A company might diversify into four types of new businesses and plan an equal amount of investment in each of the new businesses. However, after one year of investment, it was found that one of the new businesses was more profitable than the others, necessitating positive feedback for managerial intervention for enhanced investment in the profitable business as compared to the others.

Budgetary control involves negative feedback as, if the actual expenditure on any budget head exceeds the budgeted amount, then control is exercised to curtail expenditure.

Information Equivalents: Any control system needs information regarding the tangible inputs to the system and the outputs from the system. Such information, which represents the physical inputs and outputs, is called the information equivalents. These information equivalents, which may take various forms such as printouts, vouchers, fax messages and emails, provide the basic inputs to the ISs that facilitate control.

For example, information equivalents to physical inputs and outputs may be represented in the case of a healthcare system as shown in Figure 7.1.

Single-loop and Multi-loop Feedback: A single-loop feedback is a simple feedback system where the performance standards or plans are more or less fixed and the actual

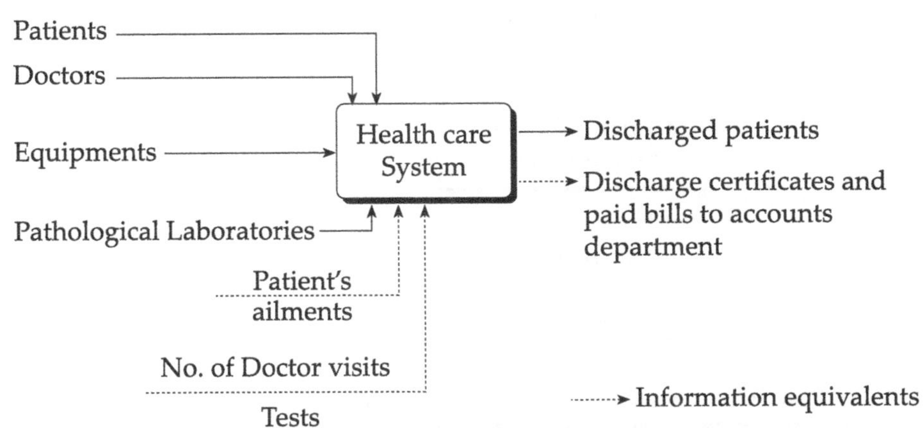

Figure 7.1 Information Equivalents for a Healthcare System

variations are relatively small in magnitude so that corrective actions can be taken without any difficulty to bring the actual output or performance in line with the plan. Typical examples of single-loop feedback include inventory control, cost control, budgetary control and many other operational and tactical control systems.

The single-loop feedback control systems are very much suitable for computerisation and automated decision-making.

The multi-loop feedback is primarily designed to ensure that the plans, performance standards and the operational and management control systems themselves are changed to suit the changes in environmental conditions for the very survival and growth of the organisation. A double-loop feedback control for daily provisioning in a restaurant is shown in Figure 7.2. The multi-loop feedback is also necessary in organisations to synchronise the multiple activities, each of which may be controlled by a single-loop feedback system. This is achieved through nesting of multiple control loops, as shown in Figure 7.3.

The double and higher-order feedback systems are more common at the strategic management level, which has to deal with environmental uncertainties relating to socio-economic and political change, changes in competitors' actions, consumer behaviour and tastes, technological innovation and new legislation.

There are mainly three types of system control, namely feedforward, concurrent and feedback control. Feedforward control, also known as preliminary or preventive control, aims at controlling the inputs to the system by anticipating the environmental disturbances and problems in advance to prevent any deviation in the system output from the standard.

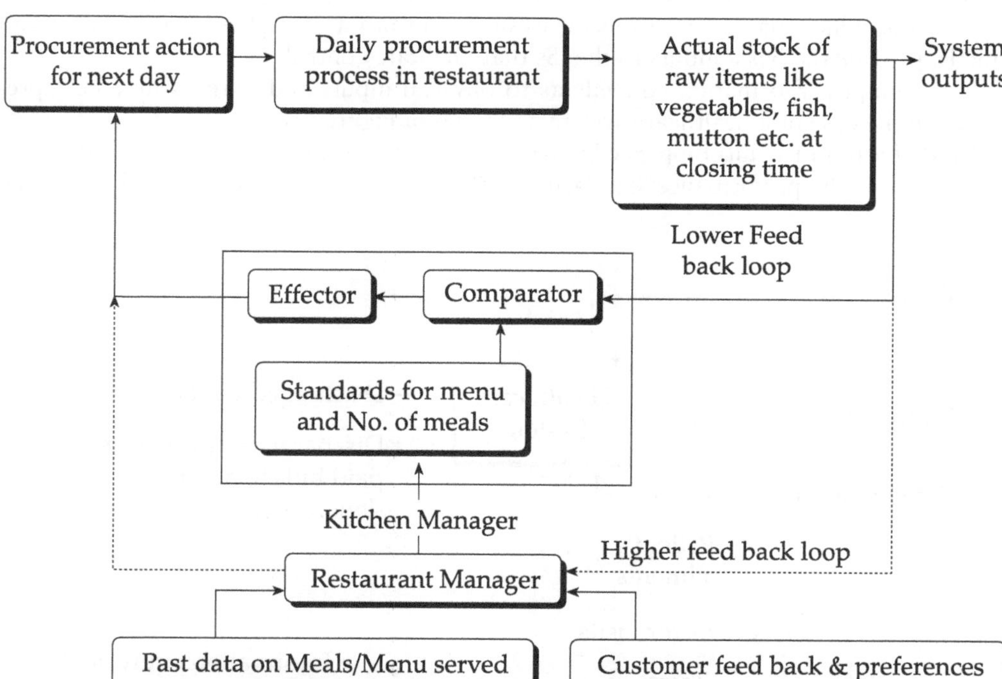

Figure 7.2 A Double Loop Feedback System for Restaurant Procurement

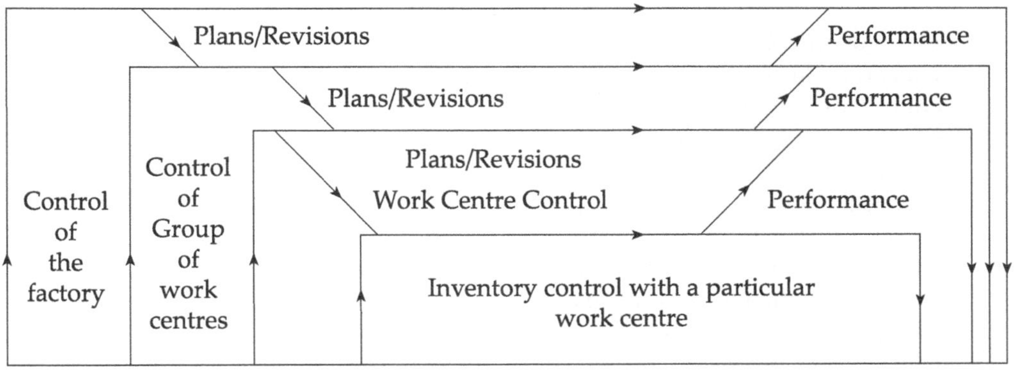

Figure 7.3 Nesting of Control Loops

Feedback control, on the contrary, monitors the output in terms of quantity and quality to detect any deviation from the standard and correct the same to adhere to the standard. Feedback control is therefore also called post-action or output control.

Concurrent control monitors the ongoing activities or processes and thereby ensures that the processes or activities being undertaken are consistent with the standards. Concurrent control concentrates on the ongoing processes to ensure that the same are under control. Statistical quality control and statistical process control are typical examples of concurrent control. The three types of control as described above are diagrammatically represented in Figure 7.4.

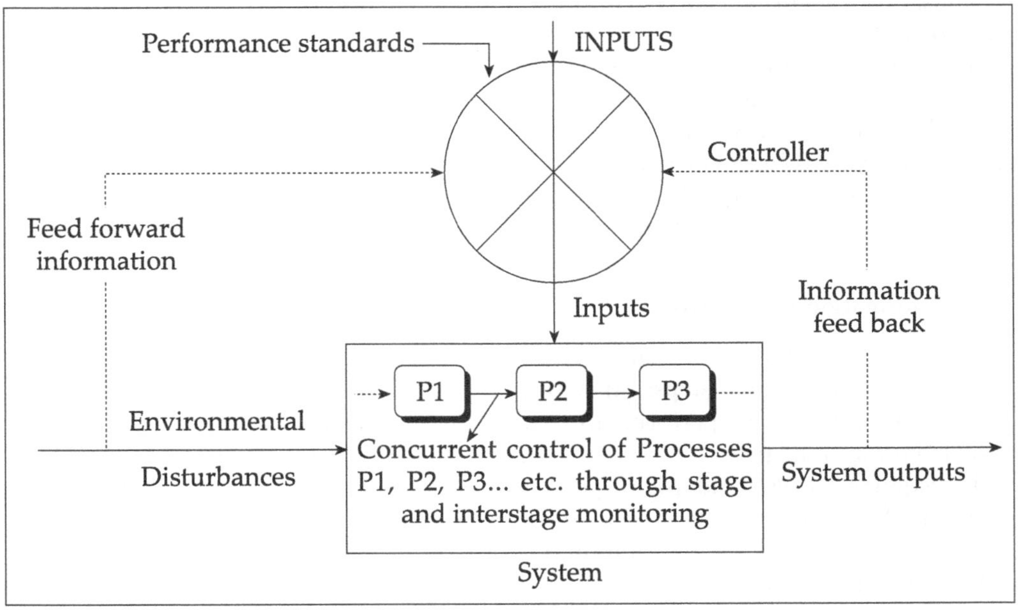

Figure 7.4 Feed Forward, Feedback and Concurrent Control of a System

Examples of the three types of controls:

1. **Feed Forward Control**: (a) Inspection of input materials at the receipt stage to avoid rejections during processing, (b) training and selection of skilled manpower, (c) control of capital investment through financial risk management and (d) socio-economic and political disturbances are anticipated in advance to take corrective actions.
2. **Feedback Control**: (a) Final inspection of an automobile in the assembly shop provides feedback to the production managers about the quality of the automobile components produced, (b) student results and feedback provide feedback control to improve teaching and (c) customer surveys provide feedback to sales managers to control the after-sales service and so on.
3. **Concurrent Control**: (a) Total quality management adopting statistical process control and so on, (b) employees try to control themselves in order to adapt to the culture of the organisation they belong to.

It may be noted that feed forward control requires a thorough knowledge about the behaviour of input variables to the system and their relationships both individually and jointly with the results (output). Only then is it possible to monitor and change the inputs in order to attain the desired output. However, in the case of organisational control with environmental changes, it is not always possible to derive a precise relationship between the input variables and the output. Moreover, such a relationship changes with time and is dynamic in nature.

In any organisation, it is unlikely to have only feed forward control. Control is exercised through both feed forward and feedback. Feed forward control is risky, whereas feedback control has the inherent delay associated with the control action to correct any unfavourable deviation of the output from the standard set. In practical situations, organisational control is exercised through a combination of feed forward, concurrent control and feedback.

Harold Koontz and Robert W. Bradspies (1972) illustrated the feed forward approach to cash budgeting as shown in Figure 7.5. In Figure 7.6, a typical feedback control system relating to operation and maintenance of a city passenger transport system has been shown. In order to cite an example of both feed forward and feedback control simultaneously, the training and development system for industrial employees in a manufacturing type of industry is shown in Figure 7.7.

7.5 Information for Control

In the earlier sections of this chapter, we have seen control as a function of management consisting of three steps: (a) setting the standards of performance or the plans, (b) measuring the actual performance against the plans and (c) correcting deviations, if any, from the standards or plans. It is then obvious that relevant information is essentially required to set standards of performance or plans. Similarly, for controlling the actual performance, the same needs to be communicated to the controllers (managers at various levels in an organisation) in the form of formal reports or informal feedback. The control information to be fed to managers varies depending upon the levels of the organisation to which they belong and the functional areas such as operations, personnel,

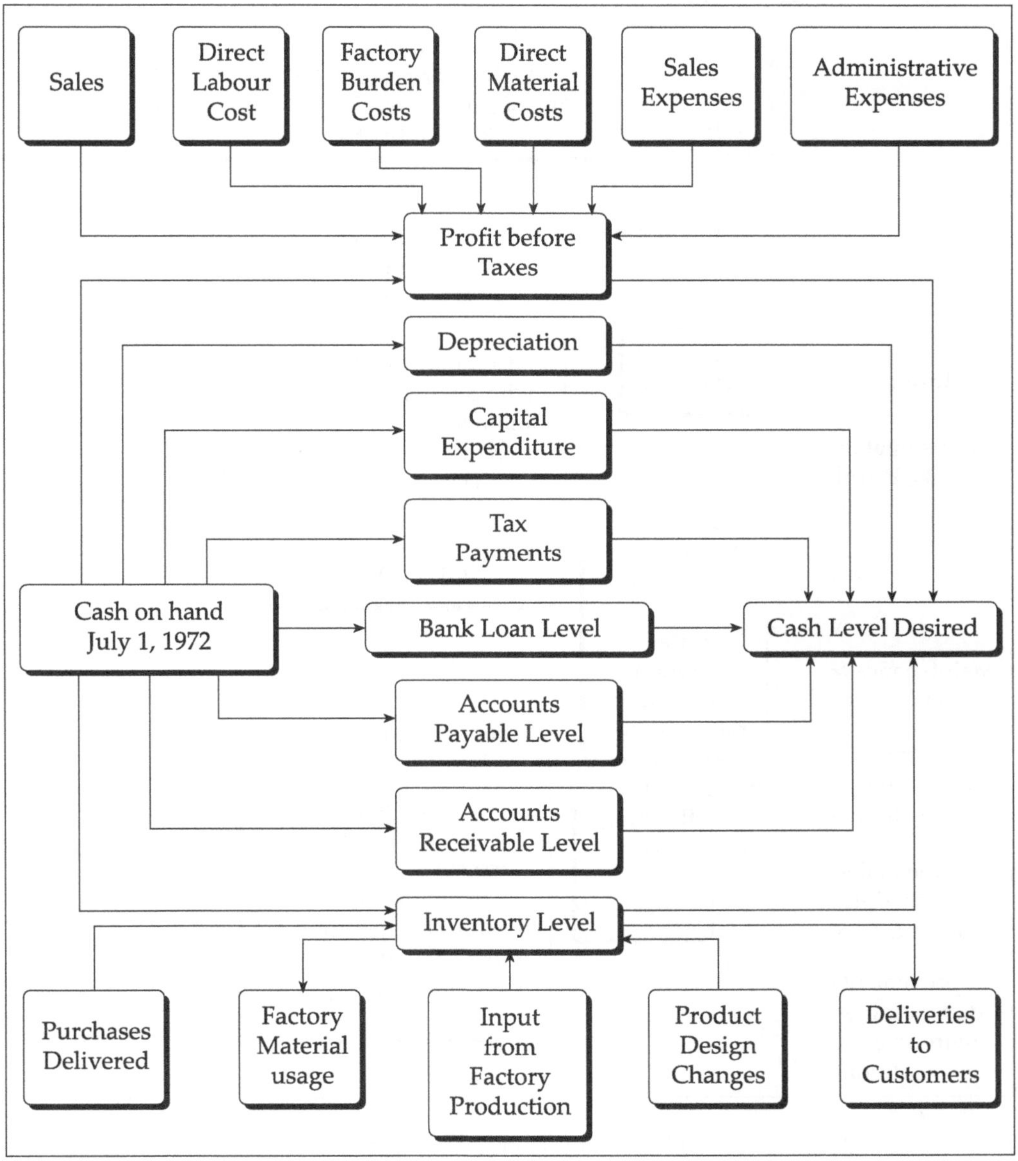

Figure 7.5 The Feed Forward Approach to Cash Budgeting

Source: Koontz and Robert (1972).

finance, logistics and R&D. However, before we describe the IS for organisational control, mainly to facilitate operational control and management control, certain important factors must be considered while designing a control system to make it successful. The factors are listed as follows:

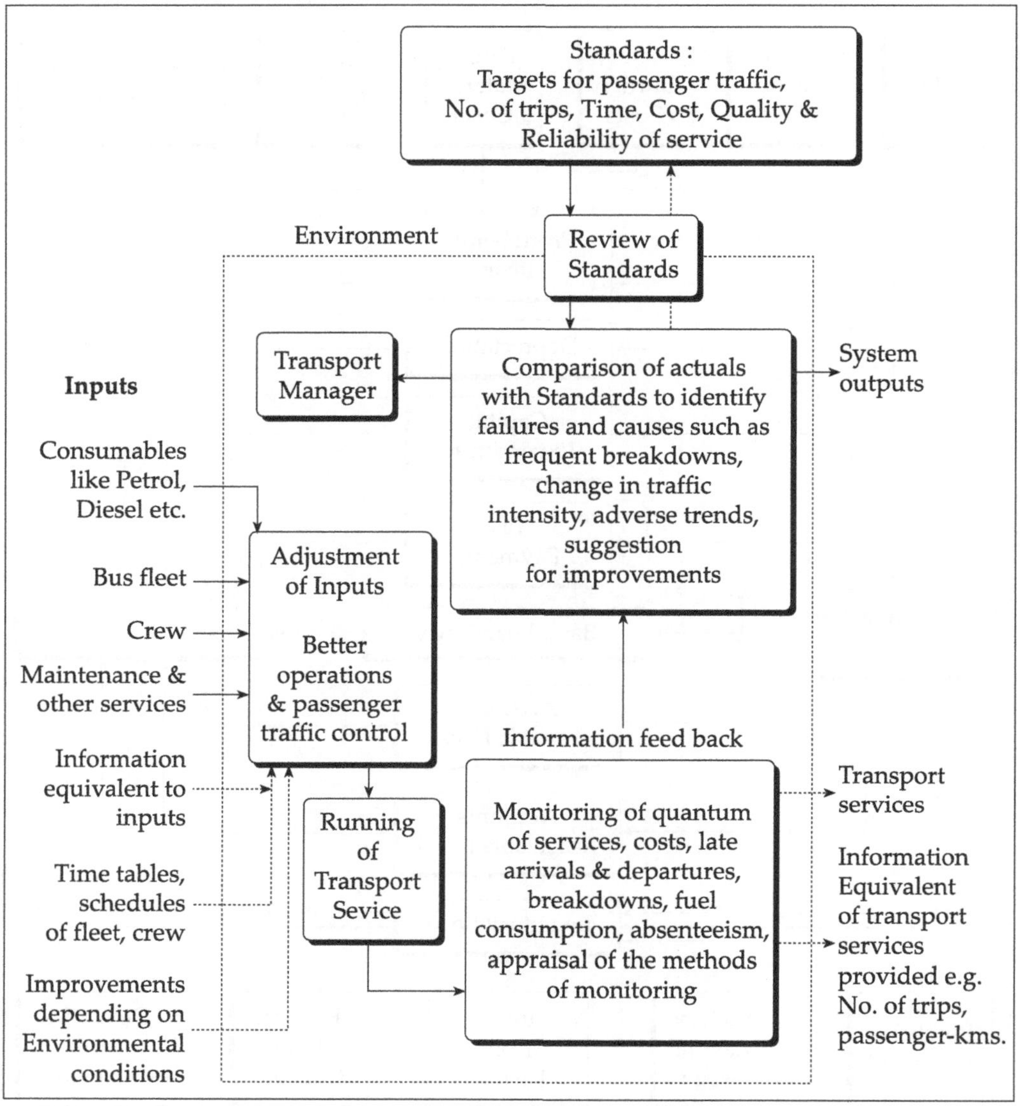

Figure 7.6 Feedback and Control for a City Transport Corporation

1. Setting standards of performance or plans should be related to overall long-term objectives and growth of the organisation.
2. Participation of all connected with the performance at any level in the organisation needs to be ensured while setting the standards or plans.
3. Each level of plans has to provide the standards of performance for the next lower level of operations.
4. The control system should be designed relating to the organisational structure.
5. The control system should facilitate decentralised decision-making to improve organisational efficiency.

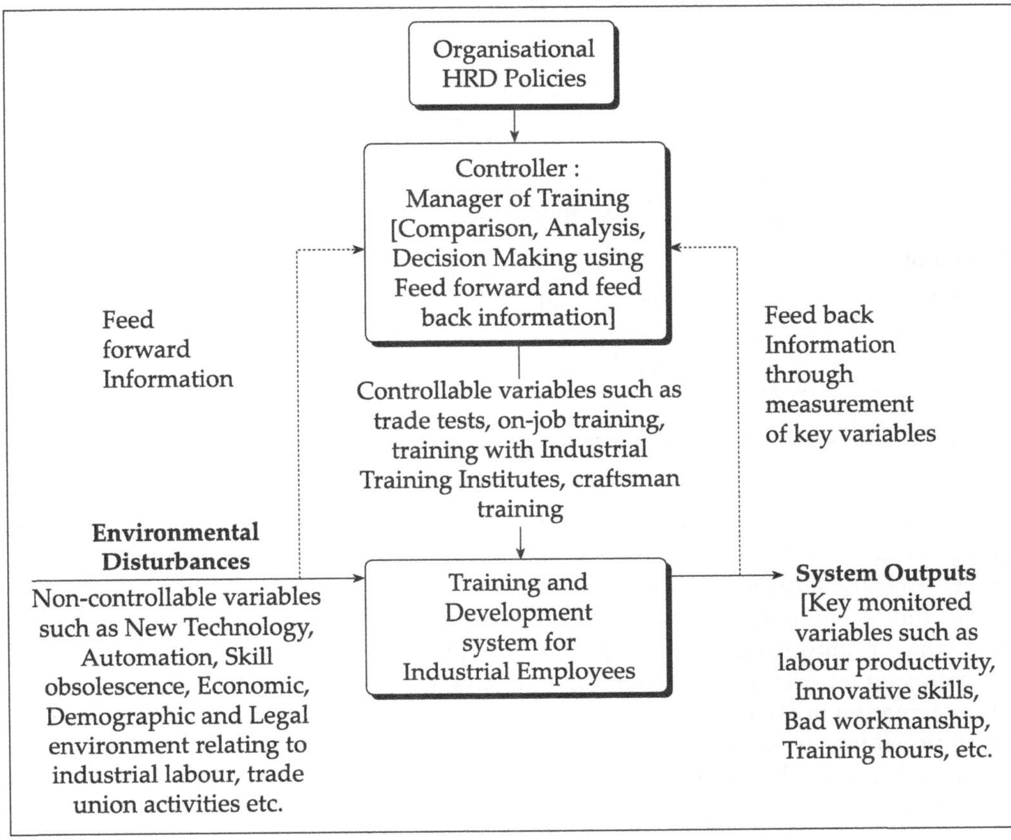

Figure 7.7 Feed Forward and Feedback in Training and Development System for Industrial Employees

6. The control system should consider both the quantitative performance levels and the behavioural factors described in the subsequent paragraphs.
7. The information to facilitate control should be timely, relevant and with proper aggregation to reduce information burden on managers.
8. Informal feedback through meetings, personal contacts and so on should be suitably incorporated in the control system to foster human contacts.
9. The control system should be designed to control performance at each level of the organisation with adequate flexibility for freedom of operations at those levels, to encourage initiative and drive.

7.5.1 Operational Control

Operational control in an organisation takes place at the operational level of the organisation and is exercised to monitor and control the day-to-day operations. Monitoring and control at this level can be broadly divided into operational management, which is basically offline in nature and online monitoring and control. Whereas the former is

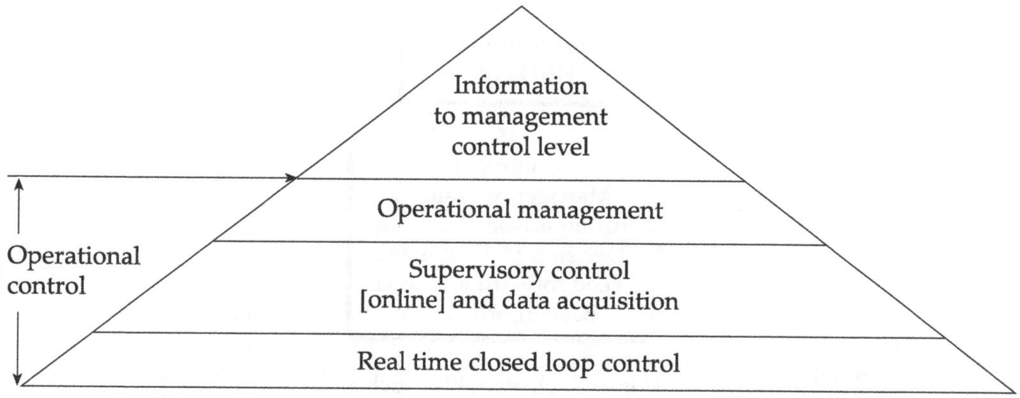

Figure 7.8 Information System Hierarchy for Operational Control in an Organisation

mostly model-based operational planning including optimisation of the activities and processes, the latter is well structured and repetitive in nature with deterministic rules and pre-set standards for control of operations.

The online monitoring and control of operations in an organisation can be either real time which is automatic closed-loop control of plants, machines or processes or may be programmed into a supervisory control and data acquisition system with human operator intervention in alarm or emergency situation only through human–machine interface. Operational management is the function of technical and managerial personnel who are not directly involved with online monitoring and control of the IS hierarchy for operation control in an organisation as shown in Figure 7.8.

A systematic and detailed study and analysis of the characteristics of the above-mentioned discrete functional levels for operational control reveal the traits as shown in Table 7.2.

7.5.2 *Examples of Operational Control Systems*

Typical examples of operational control systems, as mentioned in the preceding paragraph, for business organisations based on functional divisions and further subdivisions of tasks are shown in Table 7.3.

7.6 Management Control Systems

Management control systems are organisational systems which evaluate the performance of the organisational resources through pertinent information and thereby control the behaviour of the organisational resources such as human, physical and financial to ensure that organisational strategies are achieved. Unlike operational control systems that deal with a limited number of factors, management control systems are more complex and deal with multiple control factors such as productivity, human resource development, employee morale and attitude, market share, ROI, innovation, corporate social responsibility and short- and long-term goal congruence.

Table 7.2 Discrete Functional Levels of Operational Control and Associated Traits

Discrete Functional Levels of Operational Control	*Traits*
1. Real-time control (closed loop system)	• Data required is real-time. • Closed loop control achieved through programmable logic controllers (PLCs). • Operations/process parameter are measured through sensors and fed to PLCs. • Data validation through signal processing and noise elimination. • Data for control are mostly technical and internal to process/operations. • Control is stable and usually no human intervention. • Data for control are exact, reliable and consistent. • Suitable for continuous processes, for example, chemical processing, water treatment and so on.
2. Supervisory control and data acquisition	• Data for control are current and online. • Data fed through transaction processing. This includes also recording of transactions, file maintenance, periodic generation of transaction summary and totals. • Data validation through limits, abnormality checks and so on. • Data may be monetary or non-monetary. • There is need for human operator intervention in case of emergency or alarm situation through human–machine interface (HMI). • Data acquisition and archiving is mostly through internal sources. • Predetermined decision rules, procedures and standards. • Scope is precise. • Control is repetitive, stable and prescribed. • Control can be linked to multiple processes, activities and work centres spread over a wide geographical area. • Control is basically reactive in nature. • Provides feedback to workers relating to their performance against targets, generates various control reports such as 'Exception reports', 'scorecards' and so on regularly and also handles numerous enquiries from operational management.
3. Operational management system	• Control is offline and proactive. • Short-term current perspective is pre-dominant. • It is often mathematical-model-based. • Facilitated through decision support systems. Information needs are fulfilled through data archiving, analysis and reporting. • Data validation is also manual and requires audit trails. • Cost data are engineered. • Operational planning and optimisation are the essence of operational management.

The multiple control factors include performance levels in quantitative terms as well as behavioural factors such as leadership, employee involvement and motivation, team spirit, cooperation among employees, employee aspirations and satisfaction. These behavioural factors need to be controlled by the managers at the management control level to ensure that employees work towards achieving the organisational objectives.

Table 7.3 Operational Control Systems for Business Organisations

Operational Control Systems			
Functions	*Real time (Closed loop)*	*Online (SCADA)*	*Offline (OMS)*
Production of goods and services	Job/process control in nuclear reactor, chemical plant, refinery and so on.	Machine loading, predictive management, stock control, power transmission and distribution, traffic monitoring and control in a marshalling yard and so on.	Scheduling, supply chain management, planning of transport and distribution of power and so on.
Sales and marketing		Invoicing, packaging, customer order processing and so on.	CRM, planning after sales services, optimisation of advertising budget and so on.
Human resource management		Electronic attendance recording system, payroll, security and safety.	Optimum deployment of personnel, productivity analysis and reporting, safety and security planning and so on.
Financial management including accounting		Time booking, payroll accounting, computerised journal, ledger keeping, cost data tabulations and so on.	Cost variance reporting, credit control and so on.

Note: The list of functions as shown above is illustrative only and not exhaustive.

Management control has a broader function than merely monitoring performance to adhere to the original plan or target. In many cases, the management control system facilitates the review of plans set for the operational control level through higher-level feedback. Management control systems must consider both long-term and short-term objectives to be an effective control system. For example, human resource development, total productive maintenance, modernisation, research and development are long-term in nature, whereas profitability is a short-term factor. However, if a manager concentrates on profitability only, the long-term factors, as mentioned above, might be ignored.

Robert N. Anthony (2007) defined management control as the process by which managers influence other members of the organisation to implement the organisation's strategies.

According to Horngreen et al. (2005), management control system is an integrated technique for collecting and using information to motivate employee behaviour and to evaluate their performance.

7.6.1 Management Control Systems Are Interdisciplinary

According to Maciariello et al. (1994), management control is concerned with coordination, resource allocation, motivation and performance measurement. It is obvious that

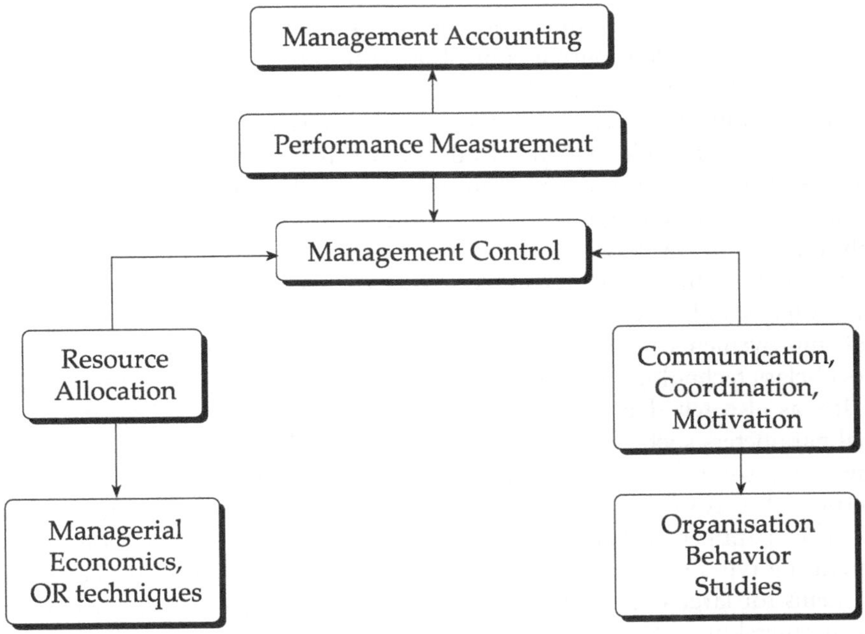

Figure 7.9 Interdisciplinary Approach to Management Control

the practice of management control and design of management control systems are therefore based on disciplines such as management accounting for performance measurement, managerial economics and operations research for resource allocation, organisational behaviour studies for motivation, effective communication and coordination. This interdisciplinary approach to management control system design is shown in Figure 7.9.

7.6.2 *Functional Categorisation of a Management Control System*

Like any other system, a management control system has certain characteristics such as realistic standards or plans, a performance measurement system, a comparison of actual performance with the standards, variance analysis if any, and a reporting system meant for the concerned authorities for appropriate and timely corrective actions, which may necessitate alteration of predetermined standards.

These functional criteria are achieved through organising, planning, budgeting, accounting, variance analysis and revision/adjustments. Organising involves the work breakdown and allocation of responsibilities based thereupon through functional lines. Besides, two other important factors of organising which have significant influence on the effectiveness of the management control system are the structure and culture of the organisation. The organisation structure determines the various positions of managers at decision-making levels and their relationships. The structure depends on the type of work, the process or technology adopted, competitive edge and similar uncontrollable external factors. The organisation's culture which also affects the effective functioning of a management control system is the set of beliefs, values, norms and ethics shared by the people in the organisation such as the belief for many organisations that quality is the most important factor for customer satisfaction.

7.6.3 Performance Measurement Systems

Performance measurement is an essential function of management control. It facilitates a dual role. The first role is output control or results control in which specific outcomes are measured and compared with the expectations, and variations are corrected through administrative controls or actions that involve formal rules, procedures and handbooks. The measurement of results will also lead to rewards for satisfactory performance. The second role of performance management involves behaviour controls, which direct the behaviour of use of physical, financial and human resources in order to achieve the strategic objective of an enterprise.

Various performance measurement systems evolved from time to time starting with the traditional standard costing system of measurement. However, there were chronological improvements in the performance measurement systems to cater to the new and world-class technology and management methods such as just-in-time, lean and six sigma. It was also felt that apart from the measurement of financial parameters, non-financial parameters such as customer delight, market share, internal business processes and innovation were also important to meet the financial and other strategic objectives of an enterprise. It was further observed that the performance measurement system and the measurement parameters thereof need to take care of profit, not-for-profit, service and manufacturing types of organisations. It was also observed that performance measurement systems for large organisations may not suit small organisations such as a proprietary or partnership firm.

Lynch and Cross (1991) first developed a new approach to performance management—the Balanced Scorecard 'BSC'. The emphasis of this BSC was on integrating financial and non-financial measurements. Thereafter, by the early 1990s, Kaplan and Norton (1992) introduced the popular version of BSC. In their approach, Kaplan and Norton linked performance measurements to strategy management in a 'top–down' model of measurement and control. During this time, a need was also felt for a 'bottom-up' methodology by experts such as Lynch, Cross and others, wherein the objective was to measure performance relating to the operational level to reflect the strategy.

Both the 'top-down' or 'bottom-up' approaches to development of performance measurement systems have several drawbacks, as mentioned below:

1. They do not create value in their metrics system. For while the customer perspective is important in BSC, a direct measure of the company's performance in the eye of the customer was not incorporated.
2. Causal interrelations among the classical perspectives of learning and growth, internal processes, customers and finance do not or may not necessarily exist under all circumstances.
3. Environmental, social and other external groups such as competitors are not considered.
4. The models often prove to be a misfit for small and service-type organisations.
5. The models do not show linkages with other key performance measurement concepts, such as CSFs and KPIs.
6. The models did not explicitly tie in performance rewards to the overall measurement model.

A chronology of performance measurement models with a brief description of the models is shown in Table 7.4. It may be noted that in the chronology of the development as shown in the table, there is a change in focus from performance management and control to strategic management. This strategic development of the BSC of Kaplan and Norton in 1992 was made possible by introducing the lead and lag indicators which provided the two directional cause-and-effect chains. The lead indicators are the 'performance drivers'

Table 7.4 A Chronology of Performance Measurement Model

Authors and Models	*Description*
Epstein and Manzoni (1997) Bourguignon et al. (2004) Pezet (2009) *The tableau de bord*	The concept of the *tableau de bord* has been in use, in some way or other, since the late 19th century. However, it was not until the 1950s that it was formalised as a tool in the service of corporate management. The various Tableau de Bord are not limited to financial indicators but are developed in the context of the mission and objectives of each unit. This involves translating the vision and mission of the unit into a set of objectives from which key success factors are identified and then transformed into a series of quantitative key performance indicators.
Keegan et al. (1989) The performance measurement matrix	The performance measurement matrix categorises measurement as being 'cost' or 'non-cost' and 'internal' or 'external'. Key to the model is the use of the key metric approach and the 'determine and decompose' method. This involves decomposing departments into functional equivalents and assessing how the departments support the business.
Lynch and Cross (1991) The strategic measurement and reporting technique (SMART pyramid)	This also supported the need to include internally and externally focused measures of performance and added the notion of cascading measures down the organisation so that measures at department and work centre level reflect the corporate vision as well as internal and external business objectives.
Fitzerald et al. (1991) The results and determinants framework	The model classified measures into two basic types: those relating to results (competitiveness, financial performance) and those that focus on the determinants of those results (quality, flexibility, resource utilisation and innovation). A particular strength of the results-determinants framework is that it reflects the concept of causality.
Kaplan and Norton (1992) The balanced scorecard	The balanced scorecard reflects many of the attributes of other measurement frameworks but links measurement to the organisation's vision. It grew out of the realisation that no single performance indicator can capture the full complexity of an organisation's performance. The balanced scorecard translates the vision of a business into objectives and performance measures in four perspectives: financial, customer, internal business process, learning and growth.
Brown (1996) The input–process–output–outcome framework	This macro process model links the five stages of a business process and the measures of their performances.

which lead to being on track to achieve the strategic goals, whereas the lag indicators are the 'Outcome measures'. Lead indicators without lag indicators may focus on short-term performance of the enterprise but will not be able to confirm that long-term objectives will be achieved. For example, 'on-time delivery' is a lead indicator for the outcome of customer satisfaction which can be measured by the lag indicator of reducing the number of 'customer complaints'. The ultimate purpose of selecting performance metrics is to enable management to track performance towards goals.

7.6.4 *The Performance Wheel*

The different performance measurement models mentioned in Table 7.4 can be reduced to one overarching model known as 'the performance wheel' developed by Watts and McNair (2012). The performance wheel incorporates and addresses the identified weaknesses of previous models such as 'top-down' or 'bottom-up' orientation, linking performance metrics with CSFs, KPIs and value creation. Moreover, the performance wheel can be adapted to large organisations of various types such as service, not-for-profit, profit and manufacturing. The performance wheel laid out straight and as shown in Figure 7.10 adds value to the CSFs and creates a linkage to the external stakeholder performance wheel. The performance wheel is subdivided into three sub-groups: (1) those controlled by top management, (2) those under the purview of middle management and (3) those which only operational managers, supervisors and other operational control levels of employees can alter. These three divisions coincide with strategic objectives, CSFs and KPIs.

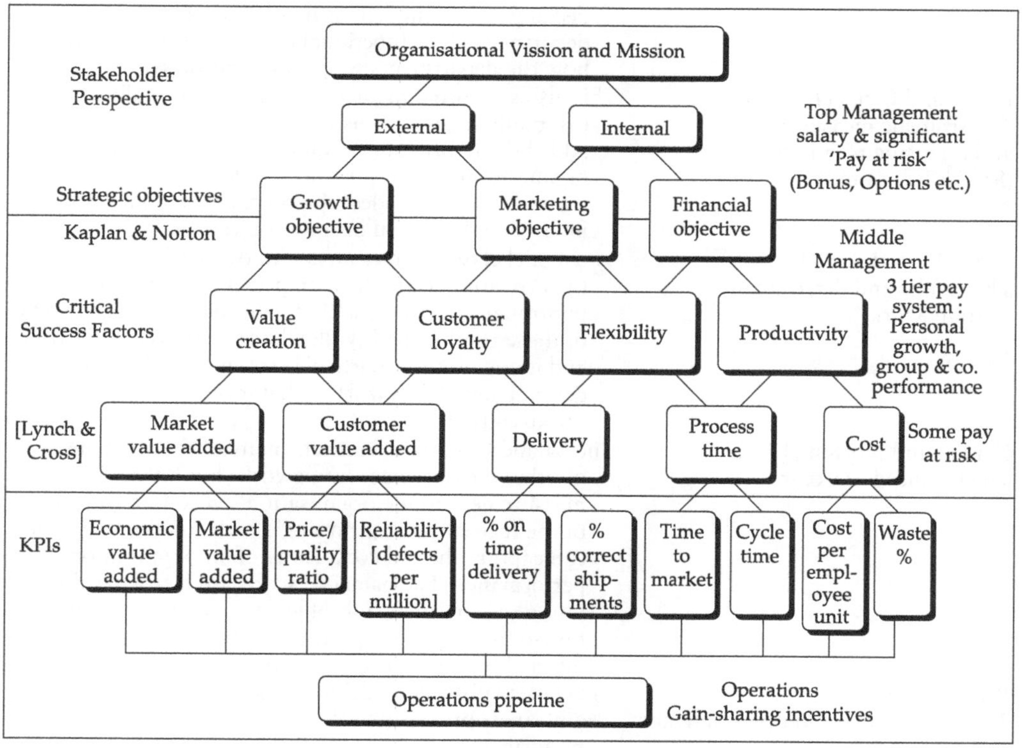

Figure 7.10 The Performance Wheel—Laid Out Straight

7.6.5 The Performance Wheel in Case of Not-for-profit Organisations

The applicability of the performance wheel in the case of a service organisation is shown in Figure 7.11 for the vehicle licence authority of a state government, known as the Regional Transport Authority. It differs clearly in that the work it performs takes place in the public domain and is service-based. Its primary objective is to attain a high level of service delivery and also to control hazards due to vehicle emissions, breakdowns and accidents on roads. Whereas a manufacturing company might focus on productivity and

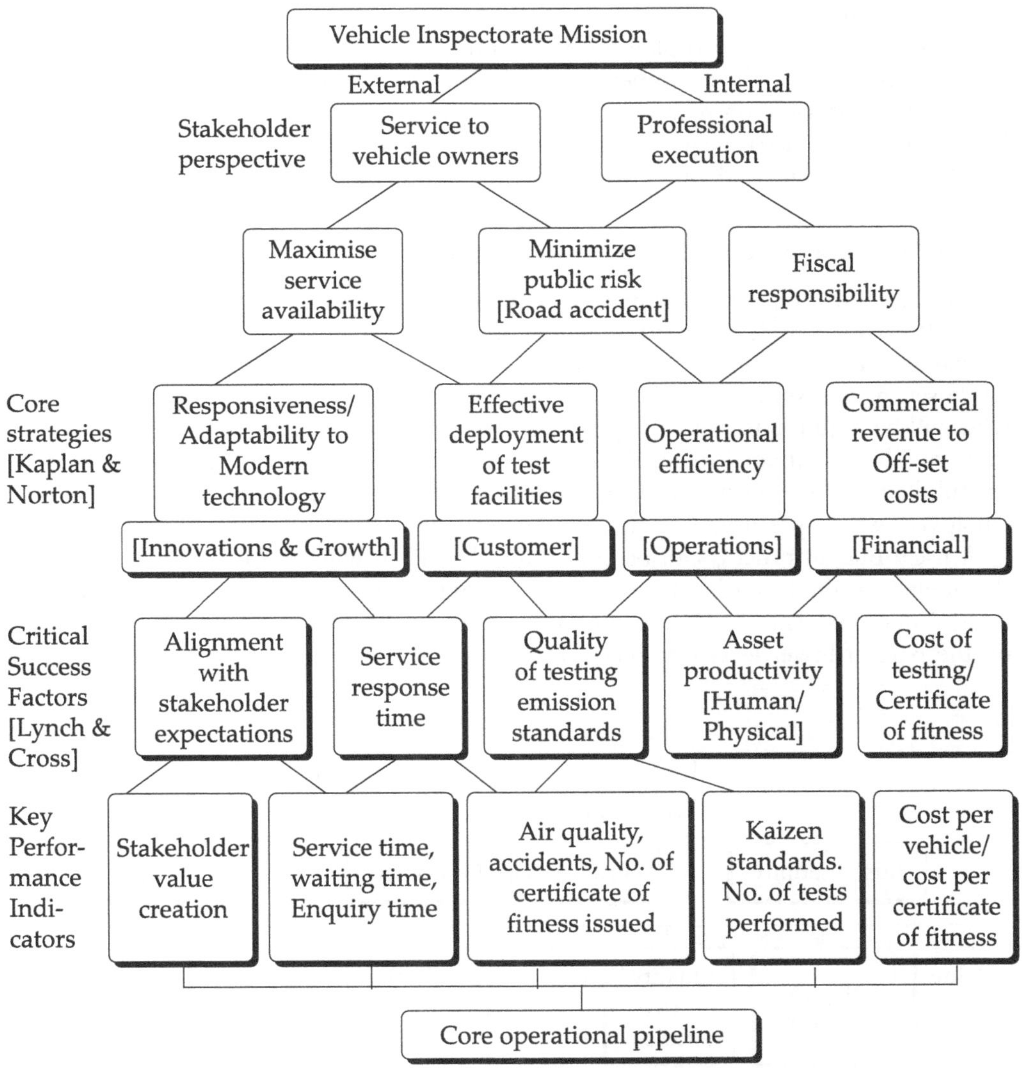

Figure 7.11 Vehicle Inspectorate (Regional Transport Office) Performance Wheel—An Integrated View

efficiency for profit maximisation, the primary goal of the vehicle inspectorate is effective and efficient service to reduce accidents.

7.6.6 The Small Business Performance Pyramid

The small manufacturing and service organisations present different challenges—to simplify the model and to keep the integral nature of the model intact. The performance wheel can be modified for small business organisations to form the small business performance pyramid as shown in Figure 7.12. It can be seen from Figure 7.12 that the middle of the flattened version of the performance wheel (Figure 7.10) has been removed reflecting the fact that middle management is non-existent in small business. The key factors to the survival and growth of a small business are sustainability, productivity and liquidity. These three dimensions are then expanded to a set of operational measures that allow the small business owner to plan for and control the operational pipeline that connects the small business to the customer. It may be observed that the KPIs for small business also capture information relating to customer satisfaction and thereby customer loyalty because the customer is never far away from the operational control level. Therefore, in small business, value is always created for the customer from the bottom-up.

7.7 Behavioural Aspects of Management Control

One of the aims of an effective management control system is to motivate the managers to be effective and efficient in attaining the organisational goals. The behavioural aspects of management control are important factors to motivate the managers. For example, while setting the standards of performance or plans of an organisation, the managers who will be required to meet the plans need to be involved in the process. They will, in that case, be encouraged to see that the standards of performance or plans set by them are fulfilled. Further, performance standards should be set by managers with input from employees whose performances are measured.

A fiscal budget process can be either 'top-down', in which case senior managers set the budget for the lower levels, or 'bottom-up' wherein the lower-level managers set the budget amounts. The top-down approach hardly works because of lack of commitment on the part of lower-level managers. The bottom-up approach of budgeting, although

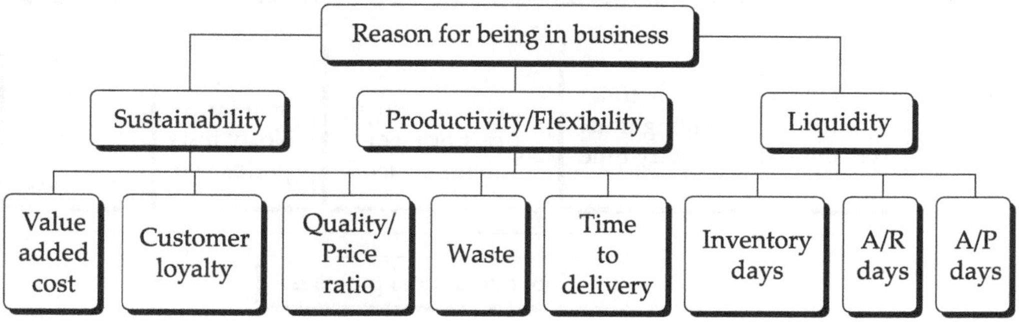

Figure 7.12 The Small Business Performance Pyramid

encourages budgeters to meet the budget in their respective areas of responsibility, may not match the corporate objectives unless carefully controlled. Therefore actually, an effective budget process blends the two approaches as mentioned above.

Management control originates from the individuals, and therefore the successful operation of a management control system requires the study of the social and psychological characteristics of the people involved and their attitude and aspiration.

Every individual employee in an organisation has individual goals as well as his/her contribution towards organisational goals. The behavioural aspect of management control demands that the actual performance results of the employees and rewards for the same should be such as to orient individual expectations/goals towards the organisational goals. According to Horngreen et al. (2005) management control system is an integrated technique for collecting and using information to motivate employee behaviour and to evaluate performance. A formal IS partially represents the management control process. For example, a formal production achievement report would contain nothing about the bargaining, negotiations, conflicts, direct and indirect workers involved with the production on the shop floor. A manager's control behaviour is influenced by numerous factors and interactions as shown in Figure 7.13.

7.7.1 Avoiding Behavioural Problems in Management Control

Managers exercise control for effective and efficient utilisation of organisational resources and need information for the same. The nature of information or reports varies depending on the individual characteristics and styles of control of the managers. There cannot be any uniform standardised system of reporting and control. Control systems which are designed and operated without considering the behavioural factors can produce various adverse effects such as reduction of overall organisational efficiency, lack of goal

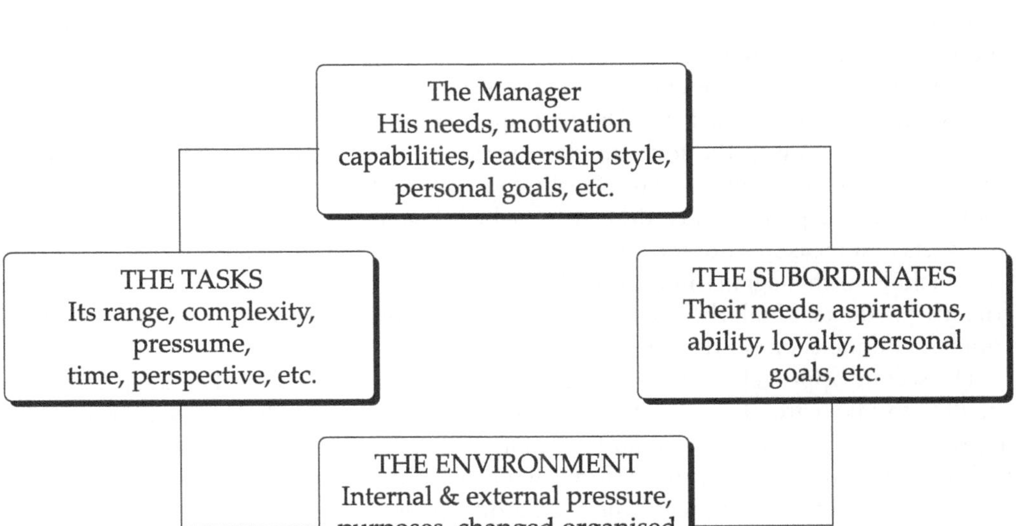

Figure 7.13 Influences on the Manager's Control Behaviour

Source: Lucey (2017).

congruence between short-term and long-term goals and formation of unreliable and informal information and control systems within the organisation.

Some of the measures which can be adopted to avoid such behavioural problems are as follows:

1. Managers should encourage the participation of all concerned employees in the process of designing the control system.
2. Control reports should be designed to suit the individual needs and capabilities of the manager who will use the reports.
3. Reduce the information load on managers by way of proper design of reports, exception reporting and executive summary.
4. Improve the level of contacts and interaction among employees through committee meetings and the like.

7.8 Management Control for Sustainability

The performance measurement systems for management control such as Kaplan and Norton's BSC basically link operational and non-financial corporate activities with the firms' long-term strategy through causal chains. In other words, the BSC takes into account the non-financial strategic perspectives such as customer, internal business process, learning and growth which have a significant effect on the financial prosperity of the business. Since, as of today, organisations have to deal with environmental and social aspects of the business also, it is appropriate to incorporate those aspects into the management control system of the firms or business enterprises. This can be facilitated suitably by integrating the three pillars of sustainability, namely economic, social and environmental performance of firms into a single and overarching performance management system. Conceptually, value-based sustainability management seeks to address the issue of the contribution of firms towards sustainability. Figge et al. (2002) mentioned about 'sustainability BSC' as a tool for value-based sustainability management. They have mentioned three different approaches to integrating the environmental and social aspects into the BSC of a firm. The first approach is to integrate the social and environmental aspects into the four standard perspectives. This means that environmental and social aspects are integrated into the four perspectives through respective strategic core elements or performance drivers for which lagging and leading indicators as well as targets and measures are formulated. For instance, in the customer perspective, a firm may include in the lagging indicator of 'market share' a dimension for environmentally friendly products. Similarly, the leading indicator 'product features' could have an environmental dimension of 'recycling of the waste'.

The second approach is the introduction of an additional non-market perspective into the BSC to take care of the social and environmental aspects. The rationale behind this approach is that environmental and social aspects as social constructs can become strategically relevant for firms through mechanisms other than the market exchange process, such as sociocultural, legal and regulatory spheres. The necessity for an additional non-market perspective arises when environmental or social aspects significantly affect a firm's performance or success in all four perspectives of the conventional BSC and at the same time such aspects cannot be included within the same four standard perspectives due to their strategic relevance.

The third approach to integrating sustainability into the BSC is the deduction of an environmental and/or social scorecard derived as an extension to the two variants of BSC described in the earlier paragraphs.

The possibility of such a derived scorecard is of particular interest to environmental and/or social management departments which are mainly concerned with cross-sectional and coordinative management tasks. The choice of the particular approach for integrating the strategically relevant environmental and social aspects with the core BSC during the process of formulating the sustainability BSC has to be taken during the process itself. Figure 7.14 illustrates the strategy map of a typical chemical plant for a sustainability BSC. It may be seen that while some of the strategic environmental and social aspects such as import content in the end products have been incorporated into the conventional internal process and customer perspectives, aspects such as adult and skilled workers have been shown in the non-market perspective.

7.9 Techniques for Management Control

Management control system uses many techniques for effective and efficient utilisation of organisational resources such as:

1. Activity-based costing (ABC)
2. BSC
3. Budgeting
4. Capital budgeting
5. Just-in-time (JIT)
6. Kaizen
7. Kanban
8. Target costing
9. Programme management techniques
10. Total quality management (TQM)
11. Total productive maintenance (TPM) and many others.

Advanced manufacturing technology (AMT) and JIT systems have TPM in which zero defects, zero accidents, zero breakdowns and zero losses are the acceptable levels of quality, safety, reliability and resource utilisation. These levels of organisational performance can be achieved through the eight pillars of TPM as shown in Figure 7.15.

The eight pillars are built on the foundation of the Japanese concept of 5S. The goal of 5S is to create a clean and organised work environment necessary for implementing TPM through the eight pillars.

The first pillar of TPM is the individual improvement (*kobetsu kaizen* in Japanese) to create an engine for continuous improvement by employees either individually or in small groups for overall equipment efficiency and productivity through the elimination of all types of losses such as failure losses and defect losses. Continuous improvement also leads to the identification of and solution to chronic problems existing in the workplace.

The second pillar of TPM refers to planned maintenance, which includes scheduled maintenance activities such as time-based and condition-based maintenance, control of replacement of parts, failure analysis and preventive measures and lubrication control. The purpose of this pillar is significant reduction of unplanned downtime and control

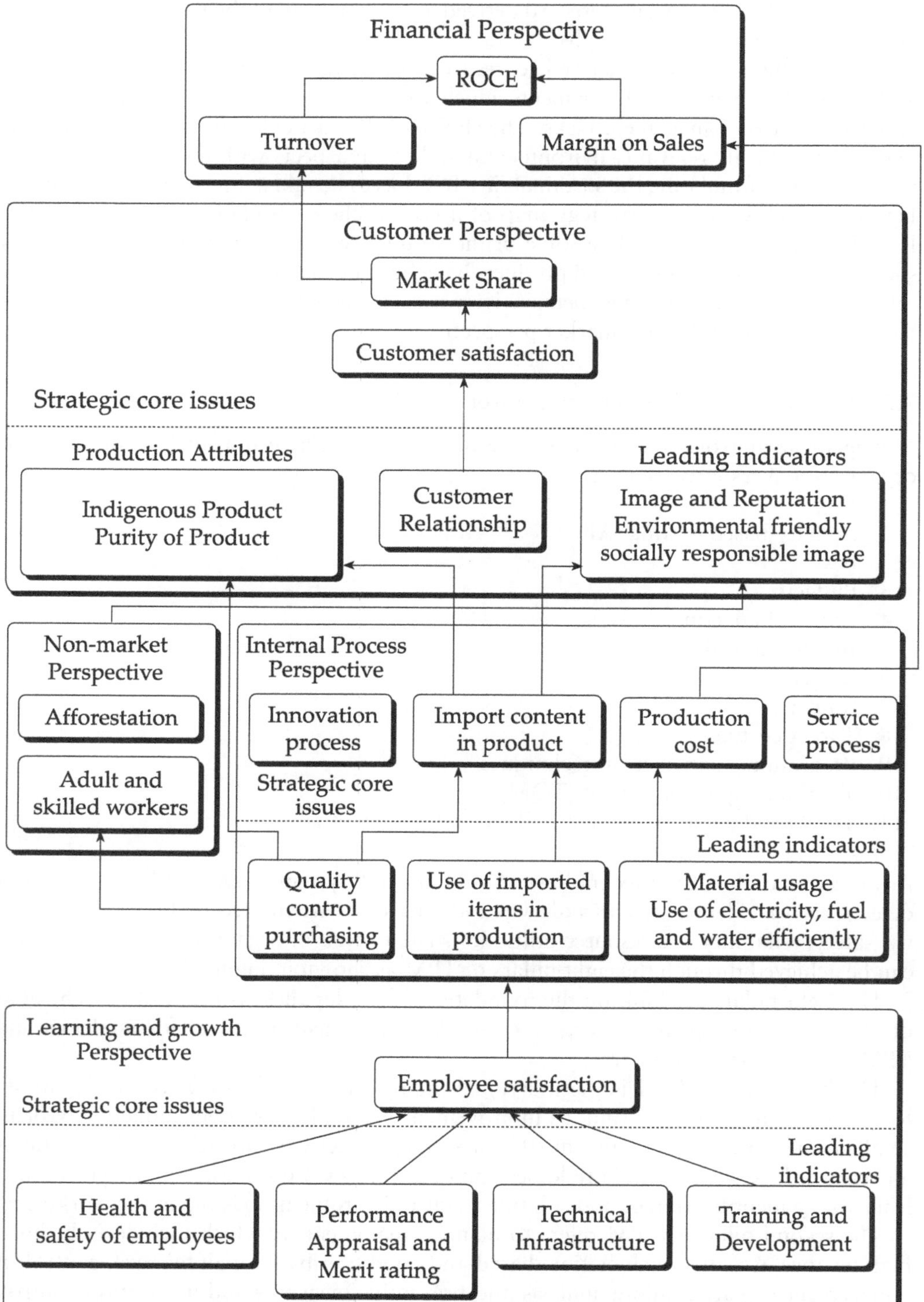

Figure 7.14 Strategy Map of a Chemical Plant for Sustainability Balanced Scorecard

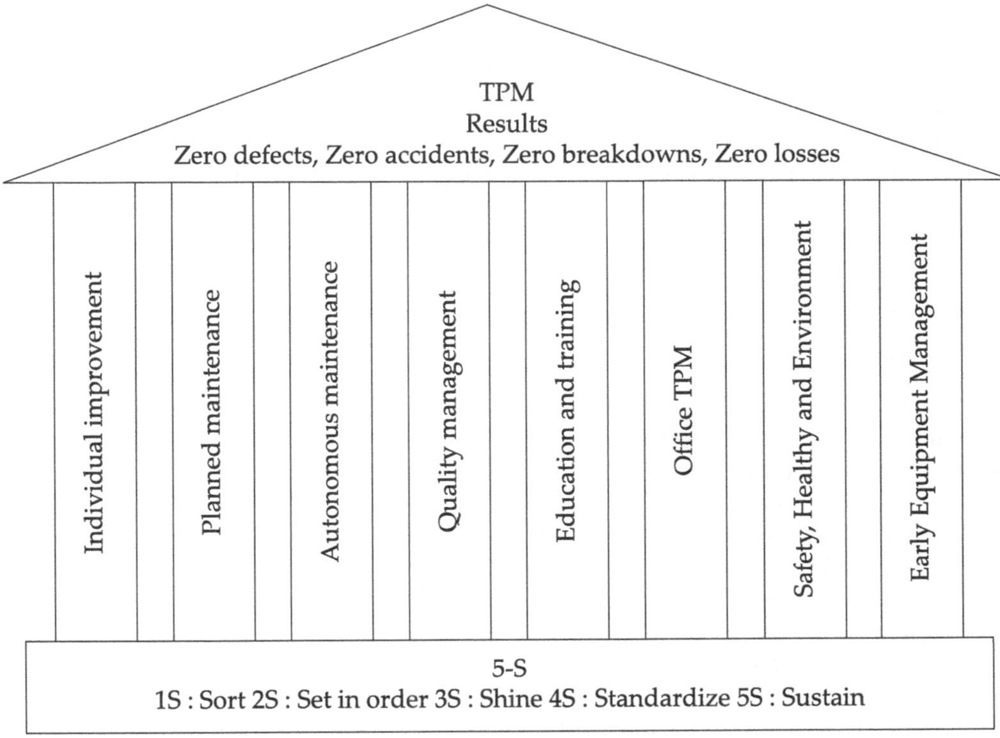

Figure 7.15 The Traditional TPM Model

of spare parts leading to improvement of the overall efficiency of the maintenance department.

The third pillar of TPM is autonomous maintenance (*jishu hozen* in Japanese), which is meant for assigning the responsibility for routine maintenance of equipment such as cleaning, lubricating and inspection by the respective operators themselves. This pillar requires prior training of operators for gaining proficiency in the operation of the equipment. Autonomous maintenance involves seven steps: initial clean up, countermeasures against contamination or ingress of dirt, creation of standards of autonomous maintenance, general inspection, autonomous inspection, standardisation and all-out goals management.

The fourth pillar of TPM is quality management. The main idea behind this pillar is to apply root cause analysis for quality defects and their elimination. The ultimate objective is to achieve zero defects in products.

The fifth pillar of TPM is early equipment management. The purpose of this pillar is to facilitate faster equipment development and to reduce the prototyping time. Because of early equipment management, operators gain practical knowledge and understanding of the operations of the equipment prior to installation, thereby leading to easy maintenance of the equipment.

The sixth pillar of TPM, namely the education and training pillar, deals with introducing technical education for operators, maintenance personnel and managers so that operators can maintain equipment regularly and identify troubleshooting. Maintenance personnel can perform preventive maintenance and managers become acquainted with TPM principles as well as with employee training and development.

The seventh pillar of TPM is office TPM to create efficient offices to provide supporting services to production departments. Office TPM facilitates the elimination of waste in administrative operations such as order processing, procurement and scheduling.

The eighth pillar of TPM is the safety, health and environment pillar, which serves the purpose of creating a healthy, safe and environmentally friendly working environment to achieve an accident-free workplace with healthy and motivated employees.

7.10 Case Study: The City of Charlotte—A BSC Success Story

7.10.1 History and Background

The city of Charlotte, North Carolina, USA, implemented BSC in 1996 and is considered by many people to be the best example of successful implementation of BSC in a public sector and not-for-profit organisation. The BSC has paid substantial returns to the city of Charlotte's efforts towards performance management efforts.

Prior to the implementation of BSC by the then city manager, Mr Pam Syfert, the top management echelon was practising Management by Objectives (MBO). However, the city mayor and Council of Charlotte were very much interested and also looking for a new measurement and reporting system for their strategy which they thought would facilitate improved decision-making.

Initially Mr Pam Syfert and three other key implementers had to make the following changes to the typical Kaplan and Norton model of the BSC for the private sector enterprises to suit the needs of the city of Charlotte, a public sector organisation:

1. The first change was to place the customer perspective at the top of the other perspectives. This change was necessary as the key implementers felt that being a public sector organisation catering to the services for the citizens, who are also taxpayers, it is of utmost importance for the city of Charlotte to meet the needs of citizens who are the customers for them.
2. The perspectives were renamed to be consistent with the terminologies internally used by them. The phrase 'internal processes' was replaced with the phrase 'running the business'. The term 'customer' was changed to 'serve the customer'. Similarly, 'financial perspective' was renamed as 'manage resources'. The term 'employee learning and growth' perspective was changed to a new terminology 'develop employees'.
3. The implementers of the BSC for the city of Charlotte retained the terms objective, measure, target and initiative in consistency with the model of scorecard framed by Kaplan and Norton. However, they expanded measures into four types, namely activity measures, input measures, output measures and outcome measures.

Employee training and development were accorded very high priority all along the implementation phase. For the same purpose, handbooks, newsletters, glossaries of terms and scorecard training sessions were frequently utilised.

A top-level 'corporate scorecard' was constructed for the city first, followed by the development of scorecards for five focus areas of community safety, communities within the city, transportation, economic development and restructuring government. Each of the focus areas has a cross-functional team that meets regularly to identify strategic initiatives and measures achieving the overall vision of the focus areas. The scorecard was cascaded to all key business units (KBUs) throughout the city. Each KBU, with its cascaded scorecard, identifies the resources required to achieve the BSC objectives. A sample of Charlotte's corporate-level scorecard measures has been shown as follows:

Perspective	*Objective*	*Sample Measure*	*Target*
Serve the customer	Strengthen neighbourhoods	Number of stable neighbourhoods as measured by the Quality-of-Life index	102 Stable neighbourhoods
Run the business	Develop collaborative solutions	Percentage of strategic transportation and land use projects utilising integrated land use and transportation planning	100%
Manage resources	Expand tax base and revenue	Percentage change in tax valuation in targeted neighbourhoods	10% increase in tax valuation
Develop employees	Recruit and retain skilled and diverse workforce	Percentage increase in city average turnover rate	5% increase in turnover

7.10.2 Resultant Benefits Achieved by the City of Charlotte

Many benefits accrued to the city of Charlotte consequent upon the implementation of the BSC as mentioned above. Some of the major benefits are as follows:

1. Before the BSC, the city had to monitor more than 900 performance measures, which dropped down to a more manageable 375 measures spread across 14 KBUs after the launching of the BSC.
2. Awareness and understanding of strategy increased significantly among the employees. Almost 70% of the employees reported that they understood the goals of their respective business units.
3. Linkage between budget and strategy was established.
4. Improvement in the process of management decision-making was made.
5. The BSC enabled the city of Charlotte to report outcomes to the communities and citizens of Charlotte, the taxpayers.

Source: Niven (2003)

Review Questions

1. What are the basic steps of a control process?
2. What is the difference between control of a physical system and an organisation?
3. What is feedback with reference to a control system? How is it different from feedforward?
4. Why is information important for management control?
5. What are single and double-loop feedback?
6. What is an open-loop feedback system? How is it different from a closed-loop feedback system? Illustrate both with suitable examples.

7. What is positive feedback? What is negative feedback?
8. What are the basic differences between operational and managerial control?
9. What is real-time control of a system? Illustrate.
10. What is the meaning of control in management control?
11. Why are behavioural aspects important in management control? How can behavioural problems be avoided in management control?
12. What are the roles of a 'performance measurement system' in management control?
13. What are 'top-down' and 'bottom-up' approaches to development of performance measurement systems?
14. What are the important perspectives of a BSC? What do you understand by 'leading' and 'lagging' indicators of a BSC?
15. What is the drawback of a BSC?
16. What is a 'performance wheel'? Illustrate how it overcomes the drawbacks of other performance measurement models.
17. What is a 'performance pyramid'? What is its applicability?
18. What is a 'sustainability BSC'? What are the different approaches to formulating the same?
19. What is TPM? What are its objectives?
20. What are the pillars of TPM? Explain how TPM facilitates management control.

Bibliography

Anthony, R. N., and V. Govindarajan. *Management Control Systems*, 12th ed. Boston, MA: McGraw-Hill Irwin, 2007.

Bourguignon A., Malleret V.C., and Norreklit H., ' The American Balanced Scorecard Versus the French Tableau de bord: The Ideological Dimension' Management Accounting Research, 15(2) , 107–134 June 2004.

Brown M, ' Keeping Score: Using the Right Metrics to Drive World Class Performance', Quality Resources , New York, NY, 1996.

Epstein M. J and Manzoni J. F. 'The balanced scorecard and tableau de bord: translating strategy into action.' Management Accounting, August 1997, 28–36.

Figge, F., T. Hahn, S. Schaltegger, and M. Wagner. 'Development of a Sustainability Balanced Scorecard: Translating Strategy into Value-based Sustainability Management'. *Journal of the Asia Pacific Centre for Environmental Accountability* 8, no. 1 (2002): 269–284.

Fitzerald, L., R. Johnson, and S. Brignall. *Performance Measurement in Service Business*. London: CIMA, 1991.

Horngreen, C. T., A. Bhimani, S. M. Datar, and G. Foster. *Management and Cost Accounting*, 3rd ed. Harlow: Pearson, 2005.

Johnson, I. M. 'Information System Architecture for Operational Management and Control'. *Journal of Computing and Information Technology* 1, no. 4 (1993): 265–272.

Kaplan, R. S., and D. P. Norton. 'The Balanced Scorecard: Measures That Drive Performance'. *Harvard Business Review* 70, no. 1 (1992): 71–79.

Keegan, Eiler and Jones, 'Are your performance measures obsolete?" Management Accounting, 45-50 June 1989.

Koontz, H., and R. W. Bradspies. 'Managing through Feed Forward Control'. *Business Horizons* 15, no. 3 (1972): 25–36.

Lucey, T. *Management Information Systems*, 8th ed., 13. New Delhi: BPB Publication, 2017.

Lynch, R., and K. F. Cross. *Measure up! Yardstick for Continuous Improvement*, 1st ed. Blackwell, 1991.

Maciariello, J. A., and C. J. Kirby. *Management Control Systems*, 2nd ed. Pearson, 1994.

Niven, Paul R. *Balanced Scorecard Step-by-step for Government and Non-profit Agencies*, 271–285. Hoboken, NJ: John Wiley & Sons, 2003.

Pezet, A. 'The history of the French tableau de bord (1885 - 1975): evidence from the archives' Accounting History Review, 19(2): 103-125 July 2009.

Watts, T., and C. J. McNair. 'New Performance Measurement and Management Control Systems'. *Journal of Applied Accounting Research* 13, no. 3 (2012): 226–241.

8 System Analysis

8.1 Characteristics of a System

A system is characterised by plurality of parts, which along with their properties define the structure of a system. Systems in the context of business or ISs have specific inputs, processing and outputs of material, energy and/or information. The parts of a system interact with each other and are interdependent in order to attain the common goal and synergy of the system. A system is also characterised by its boundary which isolates the parts of the system from the surrounding environment.

8.2 Classification of Systems

8.2.1 Physical or Abstract Systems

Physical systems are tangible, whereas abstract systems are conceptual in nature and not physical entities. Computer systems, automobiles, human beings, organisations and so on are examples of physical systems. Abstract systems can be mathematical models representing a real-life system, ethics and value systems and so on.

8.2.2 Open or Closed Systems

Open systems interact with their environment to achieve their goals. Obviously, open systems need to be dynamic in nature to cope with the changing environment. Mostly, all practical systems are open systems and have interfaces with the environment to receive input from the environment and to deliver output to the environment. A business enterprise is an open system. Closed systems are those systems which do not interact with their environment. A closed system does not exist in reality and is only a concept.

8.2.3 Static or Dynamic Systems

The parts of a static system usually do not change their properties with respect to time. A classroom, for example, consists of static parts such as tables, chairs and blackboards. ISs are dynamic in nature since data, information, reports and applications can change according to the users' needs.

DOI: 10.4324/9781003509714-8

8.2.4 *Formal or Informal ISs*

Formal ISs deal with the flow of information within an organisation in the form of written reports, instructions, procedure manuals, electronic mails, text messages and formal minutes of meetings. The channels of information flow are predefined and usually routine in nature. Informal ISs are employee-based and non-routine in nature. Hearsay, gossip, rumours and personal contacts constitute informal channels of informal flow within an organisation.

8.2.5 *Analogue or Digital Systems*

Analogue systems are physical systems which receive inputs from their environment in the form of physical parameters or signals such as pressure, temperature, length, humidity and density. Digital systems are also physical systems which receive inputs through numbers or characters (bits). A digital computer used for business data processing is an example of a digital system.

8.2.6 *Real-Time or Delayed Systems*

Both real-time and delayed systems function on the feedback control principle. However, they differ in the response time of the system to adjust itself to any environmental change before any adverse impact due to such change occurs. Real-time systems are those systems that can react to any environmental disturbance or change and adjust the system functioning before any adverse impact takes place on the system due to such environmental change. For example, an airline reservation system is a real-time system since any particular request for seat booking instantly disables the entire reservation system from taking any further booking requests momentarily in order to avoid double booking of seats. Real-time systems are early warning systems and are usually operational control systems. Delayed systems, on the other hand, take corrective actions only after environmental changes affect the systems.

8.3 System Analysis

System analysis is a method of problem solving that disintegrates a system into its constituent parts for the purpose of studying how well those parts function individually and interact with each other to accomplish the common goal and synergy of the system. The analysis involves critical examination of the existing system and improvements thereof by addition, modification and/or deletion of system parts, if considered necessary to meet the requirements of the system from the users' point of view.

8.3.1 *ISs Analysis*

ISs analysis mainly focuses on business objectives, business problems and requirements of information for managers at all levels in order to implement a solution to the problems. A systematic study and analysis of the information requirements of managers and the resources they handle is essentially needed to find solutions to many business problems. The various methods of identifying information needs of managers have been mentioned in subsequent paragraphs of this chapter.

8.4 Model-Based Approach to Problem Analysis

The approach to problem solving lays emphasis on the drawing of system models in pictorial form to document and validate both the existing and the proposed systems. The proposed system model forms the blueprint of developing an improved system. There are many model-driven approaches to problem analysis. A few important ones out of those have been described in the following paragraphs.

8.4.1 Structured Analysis

The structured analysis method is based on function-based decomposition while modelling a problem. It focuses on the flow of data through the various functions or processes in the problem domain which converts input data into processed output data. The output of a process may again form input to other processes in the domain. The model so developed through structured analysis is called a data flow diagram (DFD) and its associated data dictionary. DFD is effectively used for the study and analysis of a system. It treats a system as a function or process (called a bubble) which transforms input into desired output.

This transformation will not be performed in a single step, but data will undergo transformations through a series of processes (or bubbles) within the system. A DFD shows the flow of data through different transformation processes in a system. The processes are represented by circles with appropriate names within them, and data flows are shown by named arrows entering (inputs) or leaving (outputs) the bubbles. A rectangle in a DFD represents a source (originator) or a sink (consumer) of data. Figure 8.1 shows a

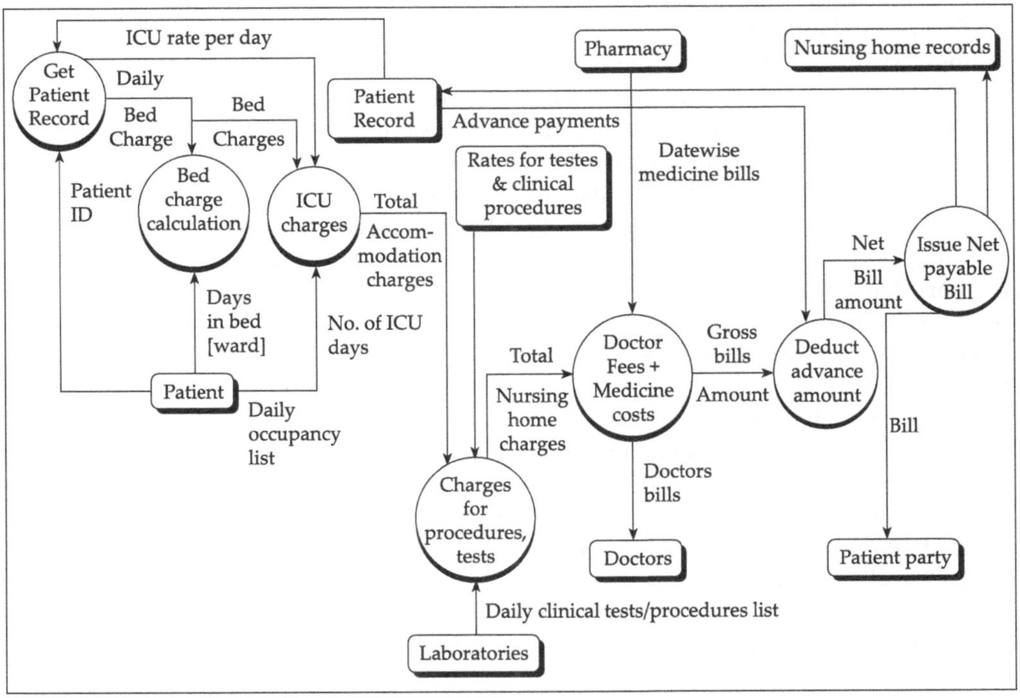

Figure 8.1 Data Flow Diagram for Indoor Patient Billing System

DFD for an indoor patient billing system that produces bills for medical services availed of by indoor patients in a nursing home. In this DFD, there are four basic input data flows: the daily occupancy list originating from the patients, daily test/clinical procedures list emanating from laboratories, daily medicine bills generated from pharmacy and doctors' bills raised by the attending doctors. The basic output is net bill payable, the sink for which is the patient party. In this system, patient records are retrieved using patient ID which links them with the patient occupancy register. The daily rates for beds in wards as well as in intensive care units (ICU) are obtained from the patient record. It may be stated that the daily occupancy rate for a bed in a ward or in an ICU is not the same for all patients and may vary depending upon male, female, child, company-sponsored, senior citizens and patients availing of cashless facilities offered by health insurance companies. These rates together with the days in bed and days in ICU (obtained from the patient occupancy register) are used to compute total nursing home accommodation charges. After the bed/ICU charges are determined, the charges for in-house laboratory tests and clinical procedures are added to the determined charges for in-house laboratory tests and clinical procedures are added with the same to arrive at the total nursing home charges. Next, the visiting doctors' fees for attending to the patient and also the costs of medicines supplied to the patient by the pharmacy are calculated based on bills raised by doctors for visits on different dates and the bills sent by the pharmacy for the patient linked through the patient name and ID number respectively. The charges for these two services are added to the total nursing home charges to arrive at the gross bill amount. Next, any advance amount paid by the patient at the time of admission in the nursing home is deducted from the gross bill amount to arrive at the net amount payable by the patient for indoor treatment in the nursing home and the bill is presented to the patient party for payment. The net amount billed to the patient is also recorded in the records of both the patient and the nursing home.

The DFD shown in Figure 8.1 is an abstract representation of the indoor patient billing system of a nursing home irrespective of whether the system is a manual or a computer-based one. The DFD can also be refined to indicate further details, minor data paths, error checks and report generation. For example, detection of discrepancies, if any, in the patient occupancy register, such as more than one patient shown occupying the same bed and occupancy by a patient even after discharge, have not been shown in the DFD. Similarly, checks can be introduced in the system to avoid over billing.

It may be pointed out that a DFD shows only the flow of input data into a process and the corresponding output of the process. It does not, however, show the procedure or how the input data are converted into the output within the process. A DFD is also different from a flow chart. A flow chart shows the flow of control, whereas a DFD shows the flow of data only.

Data Dictionary: In a DFD, data flows are shown by named arrows. The names are so chosen that they convey some idea about the data and uniquely identify the data flow. However, the precise structure of the data flow is not shown in the DFD. The structure of each data flow in a DFD is shown in the data dictionary, which is a collection of descriptions of all data flows in the DFD. The data dictionary thus helps programmers, system analysts and others who need to refer to those data descriptions. The data dictionary also specifies the components in the structure of data flows and the structures of files shown in the DFD. The data dictionary pertaining to data flows relating to indoor patient billing has been shown as follows:

Daily occupancy list = Patient_ID + Patient_name +
(Ward_Bed_number|ICU_bed_number)
Daily_bed_charge = Patient_ID + ₹_amount
ICU_rate_perday = Patient_ID + ₹_amount
Daily_tests_clinical_procedures = Patient_ID + {(test_code + test_name) |
[procedure_code + procedure name)}*
Doctor_bills = Patient_ID + Patient_name + (Doctor_name + Date + No_of_
visits + Total_ Fees)*
Daily_medicine_bills = Patient_ID + Patient_name + (Medicine_name +
price + quantity) *
Patient_ID = digit + digit + digit
Patient_name = (MR/MS) + Lastname + Firstname + Middlename
test_code = digit + digit + digit
test_name = characters(50)
procedure_code = digit + digit
procedure_name = characters(50)
Date = mm/dd/yyyy
Price = unit +₹_amount
Doctor_name = Lastname + First name + Middle name
Medicine_name = characters(50)

In the above data dictionary, the symbol '+' has been used to denote concatenation; vertical bar '|' has been used to denote one OR the other and '*' has been used to denote multiple occurrences.

Context Diagram: Structured analysis is based on a top–down approach with levels of DFDs. The reason for this is that systems often are too large and complicated for a single DFD to describe the data flows in detail with clarity. Therefore, a level-by-level decomposition and abstraction mechanism is adopted for such large systems. The analysis starts with a top-level DFD, known as the context diagram, wherein the whole system is considered as a single process with all major inputs to the system from its environment and major outputs from the system to the environment are considered as the data flows.

Figure 8.2 shows a context diagram for a nursing home, of which the DFD for the indoor patient billing system has been shown in Figure 8.1.

In the context diagram, doctors, nursing and other staff, and nursing home managers have been considered a part of the total nursing home and not shown separately. Starting with the context diagram, the refinement process starts with the description of the different parts of the system and the data flows among them in a logical sequence. This leads to a levelled set of DFDs till the final level of refinement.

The system analyst, however, has to ensure that consistency is maintained and net input and output are preserved during this level-by-level refinement of the DFDs.

Structured analysis is an important tool to analyse a system and represent information about it. The various processes and the data flow facilitate a good understanding of the existing system, which indirectly helps the system analyst to design a new and improved system.

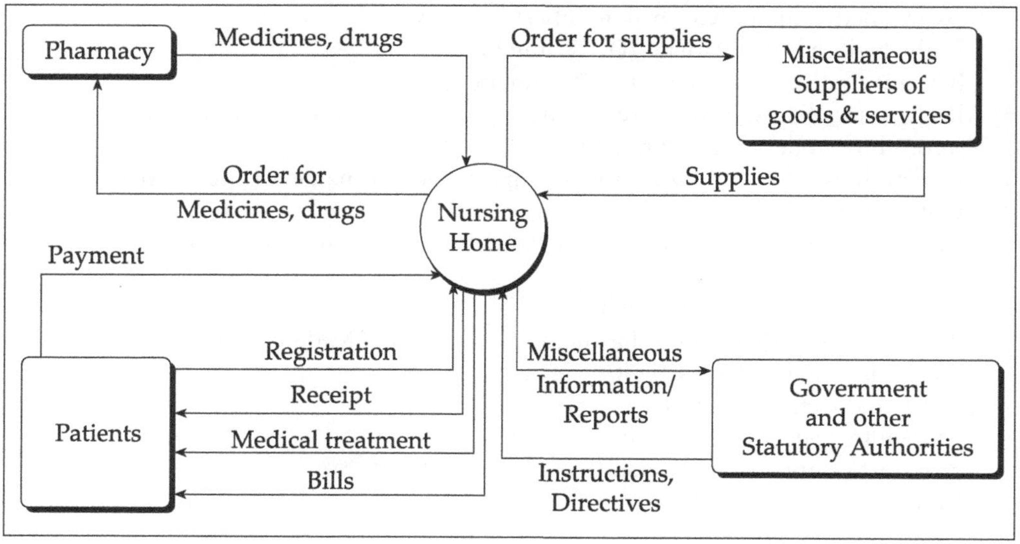

Figure 8.2 Context Diagram for a Nursing Home

8.4.2 *Object-Oriented Analysis*

The study and analysis of a system in the case of object-oriented analysis is based on the partitioning of the system with respect to objects, which are physical entities or concepts. Physical objects are computers, chairs, tables and so on, while concepts are formulas, mathematical models, processes, projects and so on. Object-oriented analysis and modelling techniques view a system as a set of interacting objects through their actions (services they provide) in order to identify the system requirements and develop system specifications in terms of an object model of the system. Some objects also interact with the system users who get the desired services through them. The main difference between object-oriented analysis and structured analysis is that in the case of the former, the analysis is organised around identifying objects, which integrate both encapsulated data and functions. The encapsulated data are the values of attributes which define some properties of the object. The values of the attributes of the object at any time determine its state at that point in time. The functions of the object are the behaviour of the object, which are externally visible activities of the object. Objects interact with each other and the users for their behaviour or action, and after the completion of such activities change their states. For example, a regular stock item is an object with two important attributes as name (static attribute) and quantity (dynamic attribute) in stock. If some quantity of the item is issued by the storekeeper (an activity by the object storekeeper), the value of the attribute of quantity decreases, thereby changing the state of the same item object.

The main tasks involved in object-oriented analysis are the following:

1. Identifying the objects, both physical and conceptual.
2. Arranging the objects in an orderly fashion depending on their relationships into an object model diagram.
3. Defining the attributes of the objects.

4. Defining the object behaviours or actions.
5. Describing the interactions among the objects.

8.4.2.1 Concepts and Notations Used in Object-Oriented Modelling

Class:
A class represents a collection of objects having some common properties and behaviour. An object is a particular instance of a class only. A class can also represent a collection of objects which constitute the parts of the class. Let me cite some examples of a class.

Mammals are a class consisting of humans, dogs, cats, elephants and so on, with some common properties of possessing hair, mammary glands and others. Each of them represents an instance of a mammal. However, the class 'mammal' is different from the class 'birds' since birds do not possess all the common characteristics of mammals.

Another example of a class is a library, which consists of books, journals, librarians and so on, which are separate objects but are parts of the aggregate class 'library' also known as the 'container' class. The usual notations for representing the above classes in object-oriented analysis are shown in Figure 8.3.

In an object diagram, which represents the object model graphically, an object class is represented by a rectangle divided into three parts. The uppermost part contains the name of the class, such as 'mammals' shown in the example in Figure 8.3, the middle part lists the attributes that objects belonging to the particular class possess, such as height, weight and number of legs, and the lower part lists the services or actions provided by objects of the class, such as 'move' and 'hear'.

Inheritance:
Objects and classes are related through inheritance in the real environment. Inheritance is the mechanism that permits specialised classes to be created out of a general class, by adding some special attributes or services to the general class. The structure through which inheritance is derived is known as 'Generalisation–Specialisation', which represents a hierarchy of relationship between the general class (known as super class) and the specialised classes (known as subclasses) which inherit the attributes and services of the

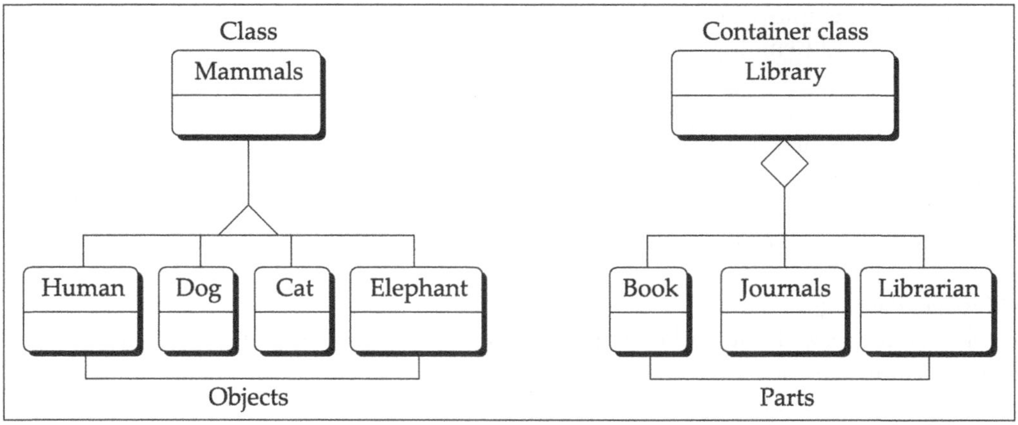

Figure 8.3 Examples of Class

former class. It may be noted that many specialised classes can be created from a general class. For example, 'doctor' is a general class of all who provide medical treatment to patients. The specialised classes arising out of this class are the classes known as 'cardiologist', 'radiologist', 'urologist' and many others. All these specialised classes of doctors inherit the attributes and services of the class 'doctor', like all of them are medical graduates and all offer medical treatment. However, each subclass such as 'cardiologist' has specialised knowledge and skill of a particular organ of human beings, such as the heart.

Aggregation:
The aggregation structure models the whole-part relationship between the container class and the parts comprising the same. This has already been shown in Figure 8.3.

Associations denote the relationships among the objects (instances) pertaining to the various classes in the object model. For example, the class 'employer' of a particular company has multiple associations with all the instances of the class 'employee' since one employer has many employees. An association is shown in an object diagram by a straight line joining the two classes. An association between two classes can be of three types: (a) one-to-one (one instance of one class is related to only one instance of the other class), (b) one-to-many (one instance of one class is related to many instances of the other class) usually represented by a solid dot (.) on the line adjacent to the class representing zero or more instances and (c) optional association (one instance of a class with another class may be optional, i.e., zero or one). Optional association is usually represented by a hollow circle (o) on the line next to the class whose association is optional.

Encapsulation (Data Hiding):
Data encapsulation, also known as data hiding, is a basic property of an object which encapsulates or hides data, information and their implementation details from the users. It only provides a set of services to the users from outside through an interface. The internal operations of the object do not form any part of the interface. Encapsulation has two major advantages. First, the internal data, information and operations thereof cannot be manipulated from outside. Hence, the integrity of the data and information is preserved. Second, as long as the interface between the object and the users is preserved, implementation of an object can be changed without affecting the users of the object, who continue to get the defined services from the object through the interface. For example, the object employee register of a company provides through its interface user operations such as add employee(), change employee data() and find employee(). There are, however, internal operations within the object 'employee register', such as insert() and sort(), which are used to support the user services through the interface but do not form any part of the interface and thus are not accessible to the users. Moreover, the object may alter the arrangement of the employee data for implementation from a stack to a linked list structure while preserving the user interface at the same time, enabling the user to get the earlier defined operations in the object and obtain the desired services out of it.

Message Passing:
Objects interact with each other by passing messages. An object can send or receive messages or information. Through message passing, objects and users can get the desired services from other objects. Message passing involves a message which is a function. The function has to be applied to the object with information associated with it.

8.4.2.2 Object-Oriented Analysis Techniques

Object-oriented analysis uses the following techniques in conjunction with each other. The techniques are:

1. Object modelling;
2. Dynamic modelling;
3. Functional modelling (already described earlier in structured analysis).

The object modelling technique first of all identifies objects in the system and groups them into different classes. The second step is to establish relationships among the classes in the form of structures, which represent either generalisation–specialisation or whole-part hierarchy as already explained earlier. The third step defines the object attributes. For example, for the object 'student', the attributes can be roll numbers, name, sex, courses opted and so on. The fourth step is to define operations or services that can be performed on the objects. A pre-defined service is performed by an object when it receives a message for the same either from any other object or from the user. Objects change their states by providing the desired services, and thus the services are responsible for state change and the dynamism in the object-oriented modelling. Also, a system provides the functional services to the users through the object services. The fifth step in object modelling is to identify the associations among the objects pertaining to various classes in the object model. The associations can be one of the types 1:1, 1:M (many) or M:M and the same are derived from the point of view of the problem domain and the objects in the system.

Finally, after following the five steps, an object model diagram of the system is constructed.

For example, let us consider the case of a paint shop which sells varnishes, paints and primers of various types.

All the products of a typical paint shop have a definite shelf life and accordingly, the manufacturing date as well as the expiry date of a product are embossed by the manufacturer on the product container. The paint shop owner manages all sales through counter salesmen. Each salesman every day sells the products to customers and collects the total amount for the products sold to each customer through cash memos. The cash memo is dated and shows the serial number, salesman identification number, name of customer, the products along with the quantities sold and the total amount of the cash memo. The object model represents the system to be designed for a paint shop to compute the total sales for a particular period of time for all products of the shop through the sales effected by each salesman of the shop during the same period. The system also additionally highlights the products due for placement of supply orders because of nil stock and also because the time-expired products require their removal from the active stock bins. The object model diagram for the system is shown in Figure 8.4.

The system in this case has eight classes of objects, each with a name, attributes and services. For example, the paint shop is an aggregation of the classes: 'product', 'salesman' and 'cash memo', which implies that the paint shop is composed of products, salesmen and cash memos. The products are varnishes, paints and primers. Product is a super class having attributes name, quantity in stock, expiry date and so on and services such as out of stock() (requiring placement of orders for products having nil stock) and expired() (to list products expired and requiring removal from the shop). The classes varnishes, paints and primers are specialised subclasses of the class 'product' and inherit all the

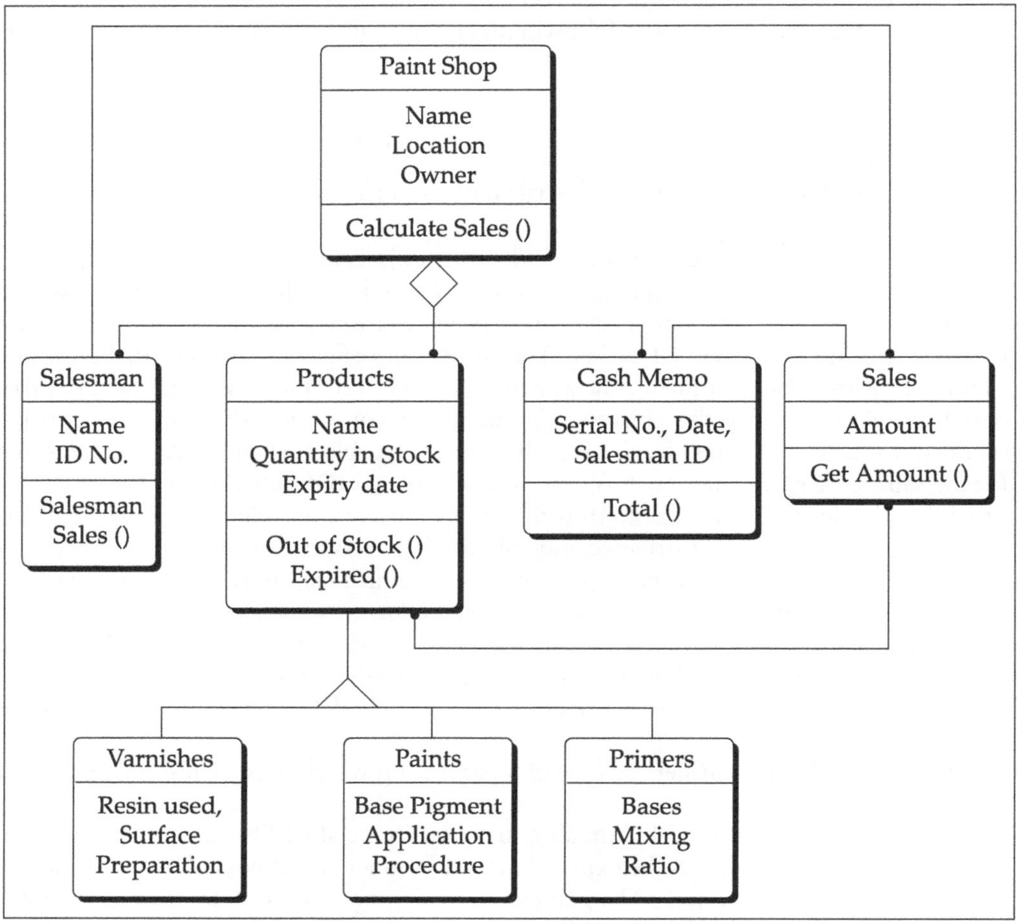

Figure 8.4 Object Model of a Paint Shop

attributes and services of the class 'product'. Additionally, the varnish class has attributes such as resins used and surface preparation. Similarly, the paint class has additional attributes of base pigments, application procedure and so on and primer class has additional attributes such as base and mixing ratio. The various associations in the model are also shown in Figure 8.4. The association between products and sales is many to many since one sale may comprise many products and vice versa. Similarly, the paint shop is associated with product, salesman and cash memo. Salesman and cash memo are individually associated with sales.

8.4.2.3 Dynamic Modelling

Dynamic modelling studies the behaviour of a system with respect to time and events which can be either internal in nature triggered by other objects within the system or external events caused by the outside environment. The steps involved in dynamic modelling are as follows:

1. Identification of the possible states of each object in terms of object attributes;
2. Analysis of the applicable actions and consequent events which lead to change of states;
3. Construction of the dynamic model diagrams comprising the state transition diagrams and interaction diagrams;
4. Validation of the above-mentioned diagrams.

A graphical representation of the state transition diagram is known as a state machine diagram which models the entire transition of a single object, specifying the sequence of states that it undergoes during its entire life period in response to events. The states are represented by rounded rectangles with the name of the state written inside and the transitions by solid directed arrows. A transition consists of five parts, namely source state, event trigger, guard condition, action and destination state. The five parts are illustrated with the example of a ballistic missile operation involving the various steps as shown in Figure 8.5.

The initial and final states are denoted by a filled circle and a hollow circle with a dot inside, respectively, and both states may also be labelled with a name. The action (fire) is executed with the event trigger which is the launch time and the guard condition written within parentheses {} indicates the condition for the transition of the object (missile from stationary to flying state) which in this case is the OK signal by the commander of the missile operation.

In dynamic modelling, the state machine diagrams need to be drawn for all the objects included in the problem domain of the system.

Interaction Diagram:

The interactive behaviour among the different objects in an object-oriented model is represented through interaction diagrams, which capture the snapshot of a dynamic system at any particular point in time. There are basically two types of interaction diagrams, namely the sequence diagram and the collaboration diagram. The sequence diagram represents the message flow among the objects in sequence of time, whereas the collaboration diagram represents the arrangement of objects in the system, which takes part in the above-mentioned message flow. Figures 8.6 and 8.7 are examples of the sequence diagram and the collaboration diagram for an online air ticket purchase system. The sequence diagram as shown in Figure 8.6 has got passenger as the user of the system and four objects, namely home page, flight reservation page, flight numbers with seat

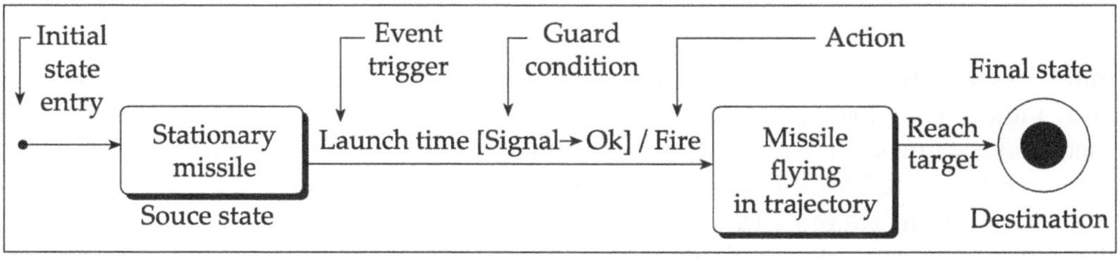

Figure 8.5 State Machine Diagram for a Missile

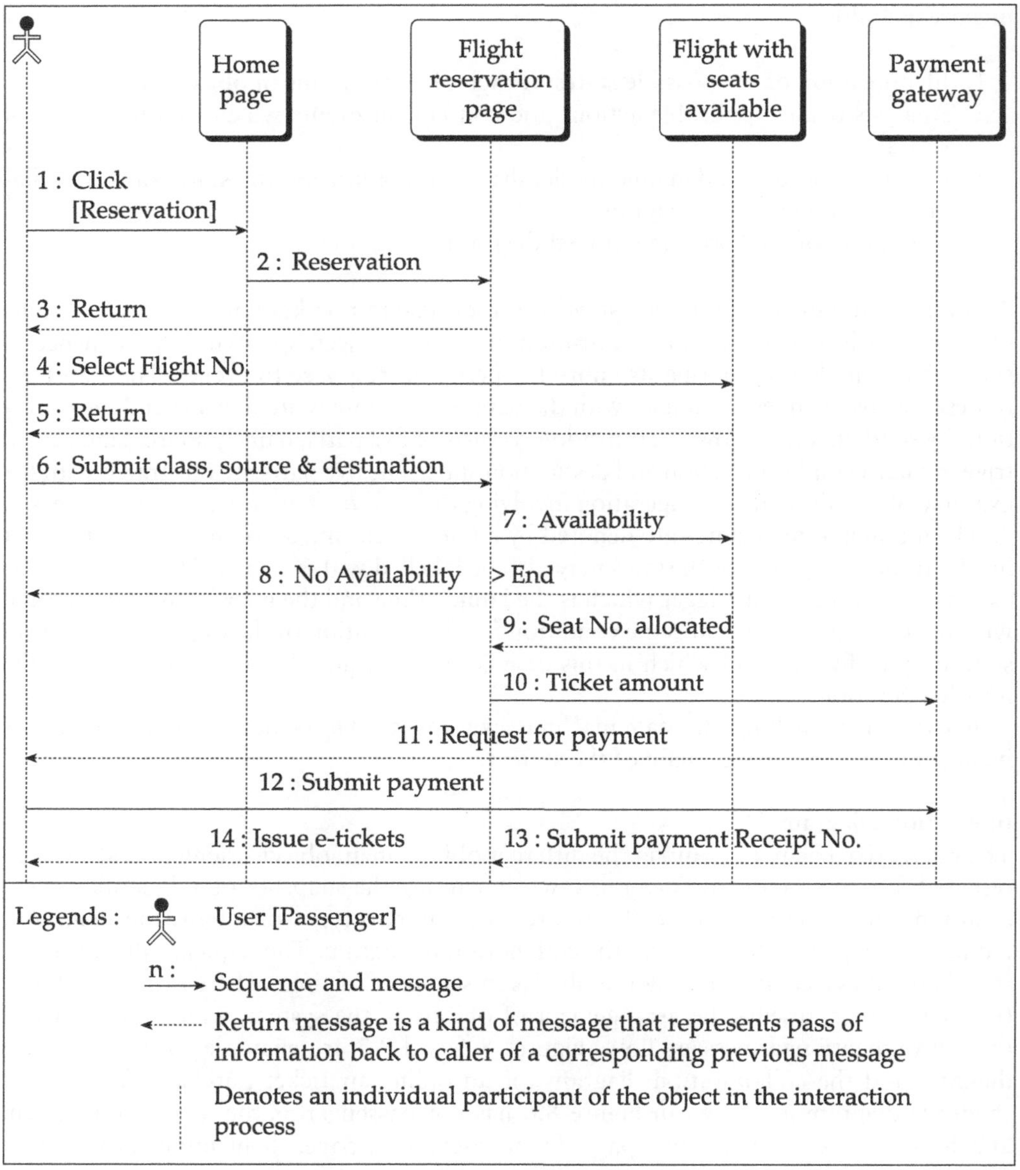

Figure 8.6 Sequence Diagram for Online Air Ticket Purchase System

numbers available and payment gateway. The time sequence of the message flows has been indicated by arranging them vertically from top to bottom. The various legends used in the sequence diagram are shown in Figure 8.6 itself. Collaboration diagram are shown in Figure 8.7 for the same online air ticket purchase system.

Collaboration diagrams can be compared with sequence diagrams. Every sequence diagram has an equivalent collaboration diagram and vice versa. Both show interaction

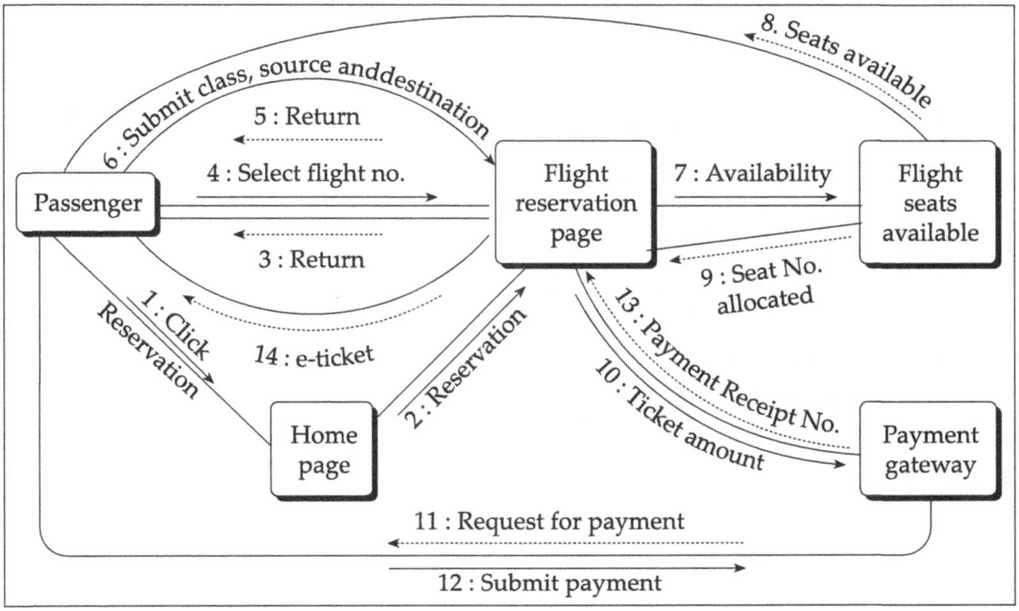

Figure 8.7 Collaboration Diagram for Online Air Ticket Purchase System

among objects. However, collaboration diagrams show interaction without the time dimension but do include object links. Sequence diagrams are helpful because they capture visually the sequence of events over time.

Collaboration diagrams, on the other hand, capture more directly the interactions among actors and objects. Besides the object model, state machine model and the interaction model consisting of the sequence and collaboration diagrams, the system use case model is also quite useful in object-oriented analysis of a system, particularly while systematically studying the user's interaction with the system. The use-case diagram can be used to describe the usage requirements for a system from the user (external to the system) point of view.

Figure 8.8 illustrates a use case diagram for a beauty parlour assumed to be a system where customers get hair dressing and/or facial makeup services. The users of the parlour system are the customers, the beautician, the barber and the cashier.

System use case model leads to the development of the object model, interaction model and the state machine model iteratively and they are all interdependent as shown in Figure 8.9.

Many languages and related tools and techniques have been developed by analysts and researchers for system analysis. Some of them worth mentioning are structured analysis and design technique (SADT) for information processing systems, the problem statement language (PSL) designed to specify requirements of ISs and a language for real-time control systems. Readers who may be interested in the above-mentioned techniques may refer to the references listed at the end of this chapter.

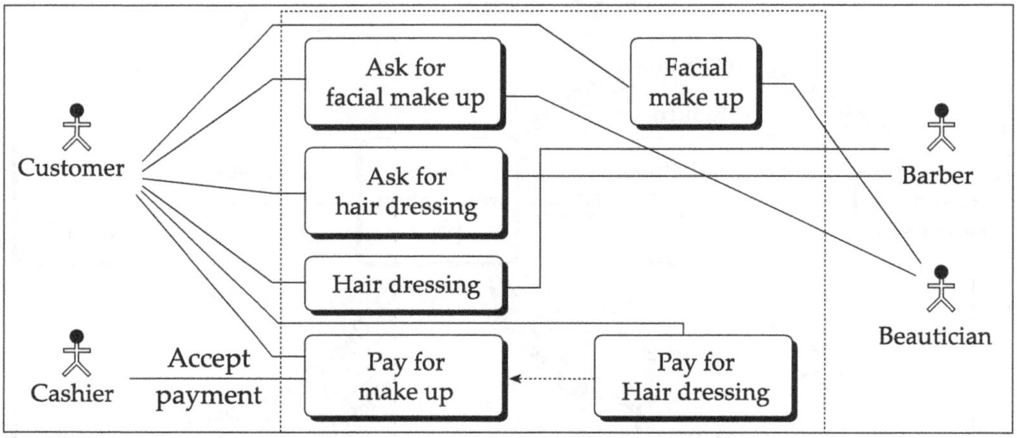

Figure 8.8 Use Case Diagram for a Beauty Parlour

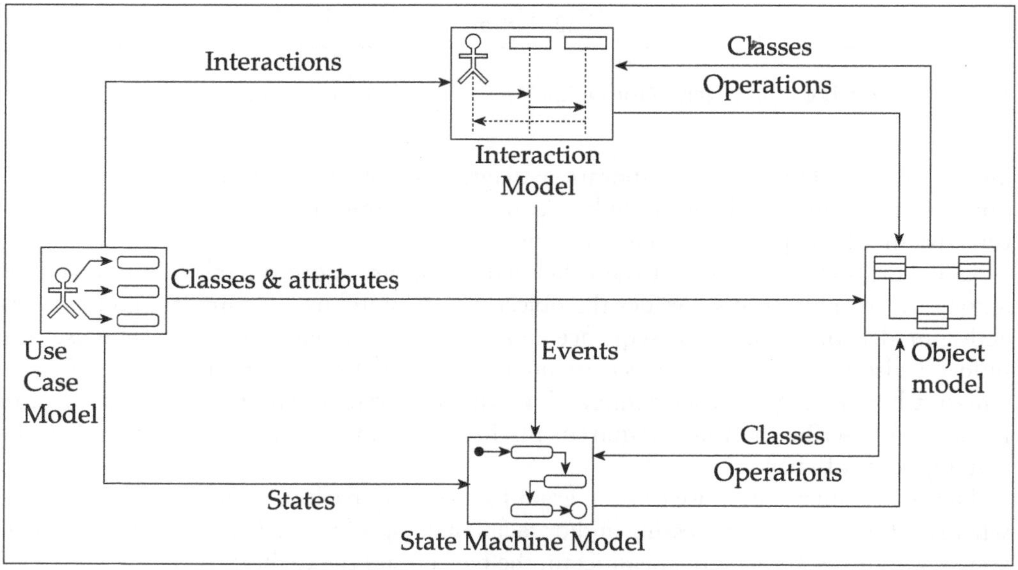

Figure 8.9 Interdependency among Interaction, State Machine and Object Models Derived from Use Case Model

8.4.3 Entity-Relationship (ER) Modelling

ER modelling can be effectively adopted for designing databases relating to ISs. The ER model develops the conceptual schema (the model) for the data items and their relationships from the users' perspective. The ER model is a canonical conceptual data model which represents the true data interrelationships and can be used to design various database models such as relational, network and hierarchical. The ER model consists of entities, entity types and their attributes and the relationship between entity types. Entities are either physical things in the real world such as chairs, tables and persons or concepts, such as professions and courses of study. Entities are similar to objects in object-oriented modelling explained in earlier paragraphs of this chapter.

Entity types are similar to classes in object-oriented modelling and represent the general structures of entities of a particular type such as professors, lawyers and managers. Attributes are the features that describe a particular entity type. For example, the entity type doctor has attributes such as name, specialisation, department and hospital name. An attribute may be a composite attribute consisting of sub-attributes. For example, the attribute name has sub-attributes such as last name, first name and middle name. Entities have associations among themselves and such associations are expressed as relationships in the ER model. For example, the entity type doctor has a relationship with the entity type patient.

Relationship types may also have attributes. Figure 8.10 describes ER model for a nursing-home database with the associated diagrammatic notations.

Entity types are represented by rectangles as shown in Figure 8.10. In this example, there are three entity types, namely employees, patients and departments. The relationships between entities are represented by a single straight line for partial relationships and double lines for total relationships. The relationship in this example is a binary relationship (with degree 2) since the relationships indicate association between entities of any two types. There can be ternary associations with degree 3 also. Relationship types are indicated by diamonds, and these are diagnoses, serves, works for and instructs in this example. A partial relationship indicated by a single line exists when some entities of one type may not be related to any entity of the other type, whereas a total relationship exists when each entity of a type is related to at least one entity or instance of the other type in

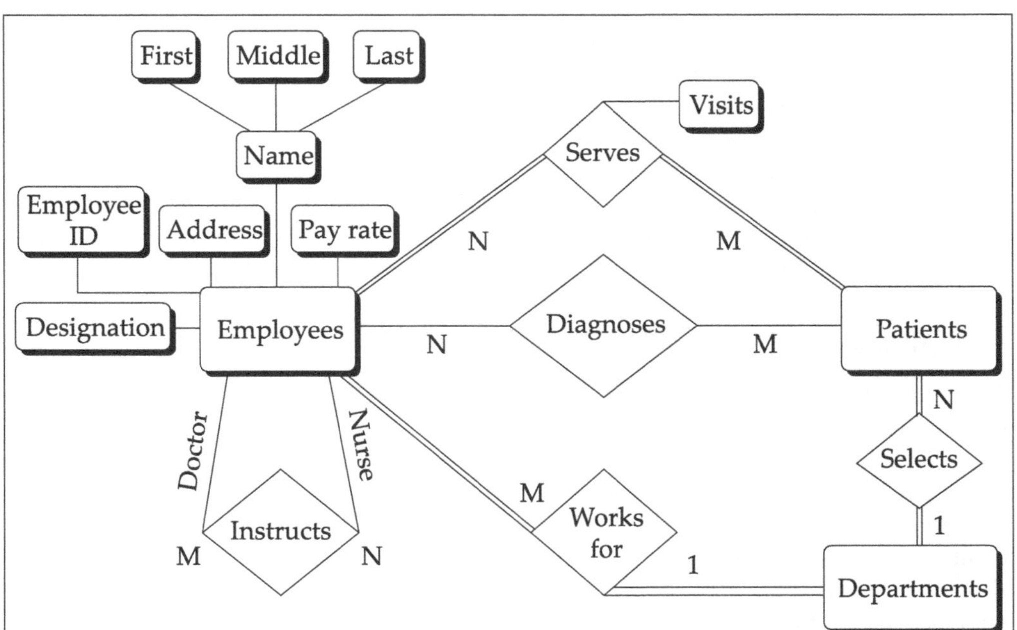

Figure 8.10 ER Diagram for a Nursing Home Database

the relationship. For example, Diagnoses is a relationship between employee and patient, representing that some employees of the nursing home (doctors) diagnose patients. In this case, the relationship is partial for employees since not all employees diagnose, and the same for patients in total since not all patients are diagnosed by employees (doctors).

Cardinality ratio denotes the number of relationships in which one entity instance of a particular entity type can participate with another entity type. The three types of cardinality ratios are one-to-one (1:1), one-to-many (1:M) and many-to-many (M:M). For example, the relationship diagnoses between employee and patients is M:M since one employee (doctor) can diagnose many patients and vice versa. The relationship ratio between employee and departments is M:1, since one department consists of many employees, whereas one employee is attached to only one department. Attributes, as well as composite attributes, are denoted by oval shapes attached to the entity with the attribute names written inside. A relationship can have attributes also. For example, the relationship 'serves' has an attribute 'visits' which indicates the number of visits the employee (doctor or nurse) has made for the patient. It may be noticed that a relationship can exist between entities of the same type. For example, in the case of 'Instructs', the two entities of the same type 'Employee' are 'Doctor' and 'Nurse'.

The ER modelling focuses on data and relationships between data items in the IS, and therefore the model is suitable for database applications.

8.5 Fact Finding and Information Gathering

A systematic study and analysis of an existing system and the organisation, including various modelling approaches as described in the previous paragraphs, need fact-finding and relevant information gathering by the system analysts. The various kinds of information needed for the purpose can be broadly divided into the following categories:

1. Information about the organisation such as its vision, mission, policies, goals, objectives and organisation structure.
2. Information relating to the users of the system such as their functions, authorities and responsibilities, resources handled by them and information needs.
3. Financial reports, system documentation and procedure manuals, forms, memos, business plans, policy statements, other miscellaneous organisational charts, information about the operations and processes of the organisation such as workflow, methods and procedures, work schedules and flow process charts.

8.5.1 Sources of Information

There are mainly internal and external sources of information about the organisation to be studied. Internal sources are the employees, mainly staff, managers, professionals, internal auditors, users of the system and so on and the written documents from within the organisation. The external sources are stakeholders such as customers, vendors, competitors, government, concerned public, including shareholders of the company, government publications, annual reports of the company and various newspapers such as the *Business Standard*, *The Economic Times*, trade and professional journals, which are also vital external sources of information about a company.

8.5.2 Tools and Methods of Information Gathering and Fact Finding

The various tools and methods applied by the system analysts for information gathering and fact finding are mainly:

1. **Review of Various Reports, Forms and Procedures:** Review of reports, forms and procedures involves a critical study of their importance to the users in the context of the objectives of the organisation and its subsystems. The study also leads to addition, deletion, modification, simplification, standardisation and redesigning of the existing forms and reports, if any, required to facilitate understanding of the problems and better decision-making by the users.
2. **On-site Observations:** On-site observations involve the observation and study of the system while it is actually running. They also include the function of identifying the key person involved in running the system in order of their relative importance. If the on-site observation happens to be for a subsystem, its nature and role in comparison with other subsystems and the organisational system as a whole are also observed on site. Observations also lead to important findings such as the chronological developments of the system from inception to its present stage and most importantly whether the system, as it is working, fulfils its desired role towards the attainment of the objectives of the organisational system as a whole. On-site observations can be made either directly or indirectly. In the case of direct on-site observations, the observer or the system analyst actually observes himself/herself the subject or the system at work. In the case of indirect observation, the system analyst uses audio and video recording devices to record all information about the system while it is working and later analyses the recorded matter about the system. Direct observation by the system analyst often becomes obtrusive in nature where the persons involved with the working of the system become aware of the situation that they are being observed. Indirect observation can be made unobtrusive by placing the recording devices in secret positions.
3. **Interviews:** An interview is a face-to-face interpersonal interaction in which the interviewer asks pre-designed questions to another person who may be an employee, user of the system or manager, called the interviewee, to gather information or find facts relating to a problem in the system. Interviewing as a technique of information gathering has many advantages, such as exploring complex areas, validating the gathered information, and people being interviewed enjoying the process and becoming assertive irrespective of the problem area. However, for the successful conduct of an interview, the interviewer needs to be well prepared in advance. The questions to be asked should be properly designed and sequenced in a questionnaire. A well-designed questionnaire facilitates reliable responses from the interviewee and the recording of the same precisely and accurately. There should be a friendly atmosphere during the interview so that the respondents feel at ease. A prior appointment made by the interviewer with the interviewee, including the proper place and time of the interview, is an essential requirement to ensure privacy and minimal interruption during the interview to make it successful. The interviewer should strictly adhere to the appointed time period. The interviewer should ask questions clearly and try to avoid arguments during the interview. The entire proceedings of the interview should be properly recorded for subsequent analysis. Above all, the interviewer should give patient hearing to the interviewee and must not interrupt or influence the responses of the interviewee.

4. **Questionnaires**: Questionnaires contain questions to which individuals (employees, users or managers and so on) respond, and in the process, information and facts about the existing system and problems are gathered. The design of the questions and their proper sequence in the questionnaire are vital for information and/or facts gathering. A questionnaire may be used as a guide for personal interviews or can be distributed to a large number of individuals to collect their responses simultaneously to save the analyst's time and cost of information gathering. There are other advantages of questionnaires, such as uniformity of questions posed to individuals, respondents get more time to think and submit more accurate information and candid responses to the questions. The questions can be either open-ended or closed-ended. In the case of open-ended questions (such as 'what are your views on the present system of training and development'?), the respondents submit their subjective responses freely and spontaneously in their own words. An open-ended question requires no specific or structured response on the part of the respondents. In the case of closed-ended questions, however, the responses have to be presented from among a prescribed set of alternatives of the following types:
   (i) Fill in the blanks
   (ii) 'Yes' or 'No' type questions
   (iii) Multiple choice questions (MCQs)
   (iv) Select the most appropriate type of questions
   (v) Ranking-scale questions such as comparing a list of goods or services in order of their importance to the respondent or ranker. For example, please rank cost, quality, maintainability and durability in order of importance to you as 1–4; 4 being the most important and 1 the least important.
   (vi) Rating-scale questions, for example, how do you rate the quality of food on the scales of 'very poor', 'poor', 'OK', 'good', 'very good'? Closed-ended questions, being structured in nature, facilitate ease of analysis of the collected data and information through responses against such questions.

8.6 Tools Used for Data and Information Analysis

Commonly used tools are DFDs already described in earlier paragraphs, system flow charts, connectivity diagrams, grid charts, decision tables and so on.

System flow charts display an IS, such as a snapshot of the various resources and related business processes. They show clearly the origin of data/information, users/managers who handle the information and how information is summarised for the sake of decision-making and controlling events. The various symbols used in a flow chart are shown in Figure 8.11.

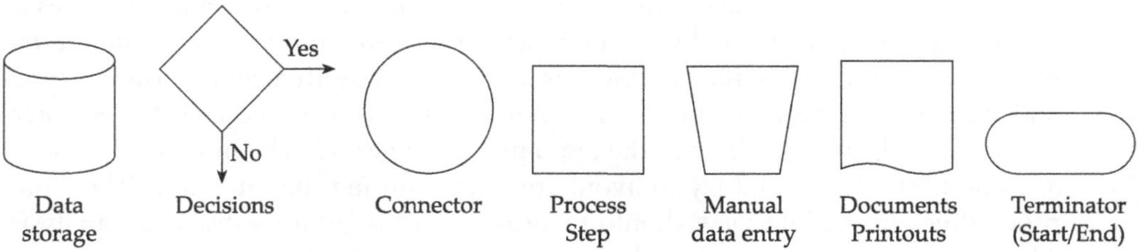

Figure 8.11 Various Symbols of Flow Chart

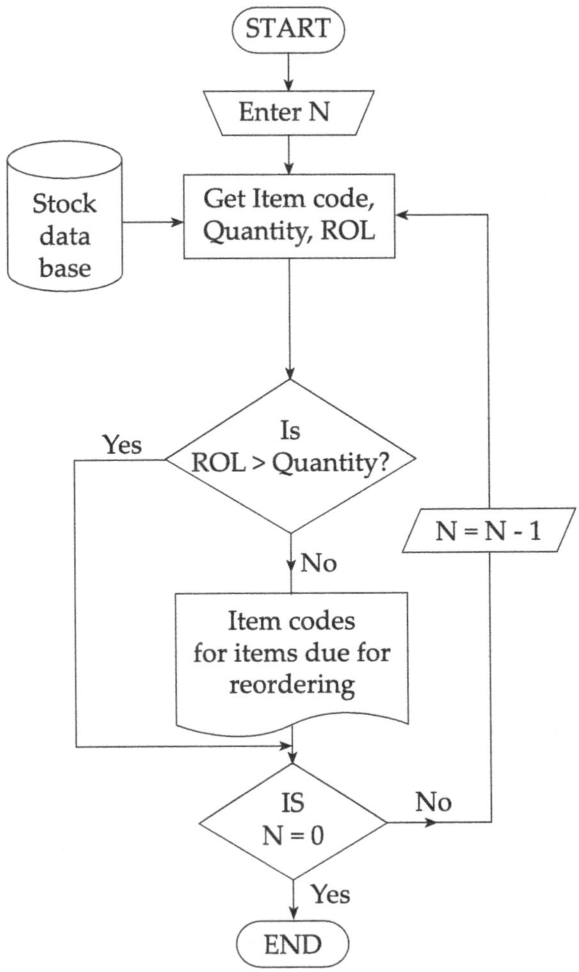

Figure 8.12 Flow Chart to Print Item Codes Due for Reordering

Figure 8.12 shows a flow chart pertaining to an inventory control system to find out the stock items due for reordering. There are a total N number of items.

Connectivity diagrams show how the various system modules (components or subsystems) are logically connected with each other. A connectivity diagram for a local area network (LAN) showing how the users or clients are connected to the communication server through a hub and router is shown in Figure 8.13.

A *grid chart* is a tabular statement which shows the relationship between input data items in forms and the corresponding output reports generated out of one or more of those data items. Grid charts are used to study the duplication of information present in various reports in order to eliminate unnecessary reports and standardise or simplify existing reports. Table 8.1 shows example of a grid chart for a perpetual inventory system.

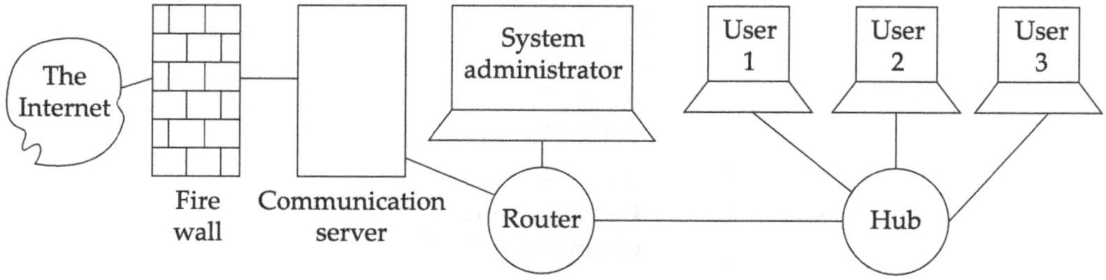

Figure 8.13 Connectivity Diagram for a Local Area Network

Table 8.1 A Grid Chart

	Report (Output)		
(Input) Forms	*Material Receipt Summary*	*Consumption Summary*	*Priced Stores Ledger*
Receipt vouchers	✓		✓
Demand notes		✓	✓
Return notes		✓	✓

8.7 Case Study: Customer Order Processing System for a Manufacturing Organisation Producing Defence Stores

8.7.1 Background of the Case

The case pertains to a manufacturing organisation, which produces defence stores for use by defence forces. The organisation has a corporate head office located in a metro city that controls a number of manufacturing units located in various geographic locations. The units are of two categories: the finishing units which make the complete end-products for issuing to the customers (defence forces in this case) and the feeder units, which manufacture components and sub-assemblies required for the end-products and supply the same to the finishing factories. Both the feeder units and the finishing units also purchase some trade items needed for the manufacturing activities through local as well as foreign suppliers.

The earlier customer order processing system was such that the head office receives the orders directly from the customers and based on the same, it forwards the manufacturing orders for end-products specifying the delivery schedule to one or more appropriate finishing units with proper allocation of quantity based on the capacity of each unit.

The finishing units after receiving the manufacturing orders from head office send manufacturing orders for components and sub-assemblies to one or more appropriate feeder units with proper allocation of quantity based on the capacity of each feeder unit and the bill of components and sub-assemblies. The feeder units thereafter manufacture components and sub-assemblies and issue those to the respective finishing units who then further process the same into end-products for issue to the customers.

The above-mentioned system of customer order processing was found to be unsatisfactory as on many occasions in the past, the finishing units could not supply the end products to the customers and meet the delivery schedules stipulated by the customers. The finishing units, however, ascribed the delay in supplies to customers to the late receipt of components and sub-assemblies from the feeder units.

8.7.2 Methodology Adopted for Analysis of the System

A structured analysis with function-based decomposition was adopted. DFDs were developed for the present system. The context diagram and the level 1 DFD in a simplified form have been shown as follows:

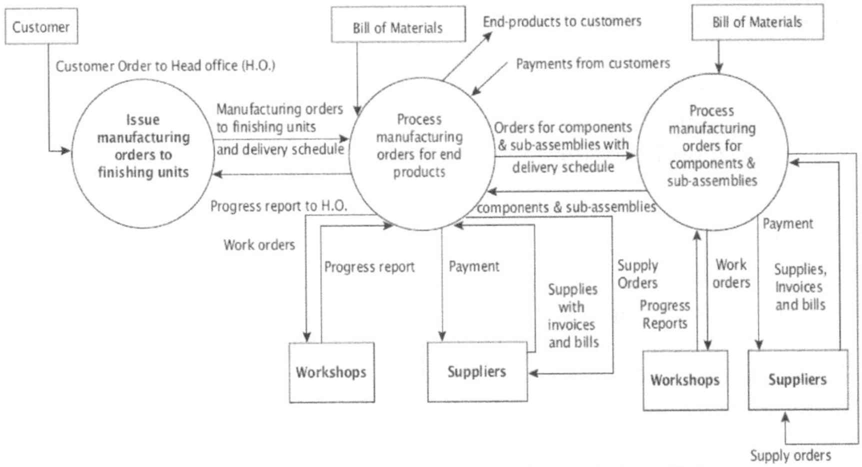

Context Diagram and Simplified Level 1 DFD for Customer Order Processing System (Earlier)

It was observed that the customer order processing system was defective, because the feeder units that had to start their manufacturing activities first received the manufacturing orders from the respective finishing units last in the sequence of information flow. Hence, the system was modified.

8.7.3 Modified Customer Order Processing System

The level 1 DFD for the modified system is as follows:

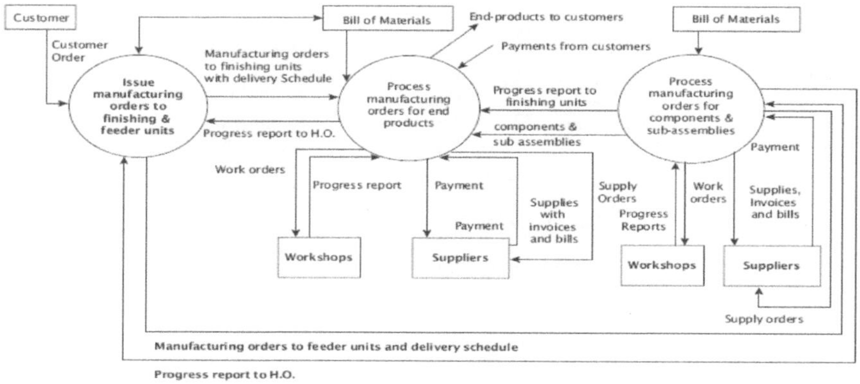

Simplified Level 1 DFD for Customer Order Processing System (Modified)

In the modified system, the head office on receipt of the customer orders converts the same into manufacturing orders for the finishing units and at the same time generates and sends manufacturing orders for components and sub-assemblies to the feeder units based on the end products and the bill of materials of the finished end-products. In order to facilitate the same, the head office has access to the bill of material files of the finishing units also.

8.7.4 Result and Conclusion

The modified customer order processing system considerably reduced the delay in meeting the customer delivery schedules from 30% to nearly 4% in terms of number of orders met with delay. This delay of 4% was also due to delayed receipt of trade supplies from local and foreign suppliers.

The case study shows how the application of system analysis techniques can help diagnose organisational problems for designing better organisational systems and procedures.

Review Questions

1. Define a system. What are the characteristics of a system?
2. What are the important classifications of a system?
3. What is the necessity of system analysis for developing MIS?
4. What is structured analysis? How does it facilitate systems analysis?
5. What is a data-flow diagram? Illustrate.
6. What is a context diagram? Is it a data flow diagram?
7. What is the principle of object-oriented analysis of a system?
8. What are the important concepts underlying object-oriented modelling?
9. What do you understand by the term 'encapsulation and data hiding'?
10. What is dynamic modelling? What are the important diagrams that represent the dynamic model of a system?
11. Describe ER modelling with a suitable example.
12. What are the important methods of fact-finding adopted by a system analyst?
13. What is a connectivity diagram? Illustrate.
14. What is a grid chart? What is its role in system analysis?

Bibliography

Gabbert, P. 'Systems Analysis: The Challenge of Integrating Two Competing Technologies'. *Journal of Computing Sciences in Colleges* 16, no. 2 (2000): 193–200.

Hawryszkiewycz, I. T. *Introduction to Systems Analysis and Design*, 2nd ed. New Delhi: Prentice Hall India, 1991.

Jacobson, I. *Object-oriented Software Engineering: A Use Case Driven Approach*. Boston, MA: Addison-Wesley, 1992.

Jalota, P. *An Integrated Approach to Software Engineering*, 2nd ed. New Delhi: Narosa Publishing House, 1997.

Kenneth, C. L., and P. L. Jane. *Management Information Systems: Managing the Digital Firm*, 9th ed. New Delhi: Prentice Hall India, 2006.

Lynch, R., and K. F. Cross. *Measure UP! Yardsticks for Continuous Improvement*. Oxford: Blackwell Business, 1991.

Maciariello, J. A., and C. J. Kirby. *Management Control Systems*, 2nd ed. Pearson, 1994.

Marca, D., and C. McGowan. *Structured Analysis and Design Technique*. New York, NY: McGraw-Hill, 1987.

Murdick, R. G., J. E. Ross, and J. R. Clagett. *Information Systems for Modern Management*, 2nd ed. New Delhi: Prentice Hall India, 1977.

Ohlhorst, F. *Big Data Analytics: Turning Big Data into Big Money*. Hoboken, NJ: John Wiley & Sons, 2012.

Pressman, R. *Software Engineering: A Practitioner's Approach*, 7th ed. New York, NY: McGraw-Hill, 2009.

Rumbaugh, J. *Object-oriented Modelling and Design*. New Delhi: Pearson Education, 2004.

Preda, P., and T. Watts. 'Contemporary Management Accounting Techniques in Australia: Manufacturing Versus Service Organizations'. *Journal of Applied Management Accounting Research* 2, no. 2 (2004): 17–27.

Watts, T., and C. J. McNair. 'New Performance Measurement and Management Control Systems'. *Journal of Applied Accounting Research* 13, no. 3 (2012): 226–241.

9 System Design and Development

Based on user requirements and the detailed analysis of the existing system as already described in Chapter 8, the new and improved system is designed. The conceptual system design arrived at as a result of system analysis is converted into physical system design. Generally, system design is divided into two stages, namely the preliminary or gross design as the first stage, followed by the second stage called the detailed system design.

9.1 Gross System Design

In the gross design, the features of the new system and the feasibility for meeting the objectives of the IS and user requirements are specified. The output of gross design is a set of documents showing how the system will broadly work. The same documents describing the ISs will enable the technical personnel to begin the detailed system design.

The important activities during gross system design are discussed further.

9.1.1 Setting the System Objective in Detail

System objective should be specific and relate to each functional subsystem of an organisation in terms of information needs to improve managerial effectiveness. Precisely, system objectives should be expressed in terms of what managers can do after the ISs meet their information needs. A statement of system objectives should include what the system is supposed to do to improve managerial effectiveness and by which means the same improvement can be evaluated. Table 9.1 illustrates some important objectives for a few organisational subsystems:

9.1.2 Identifying Information Needs for Users (Managers) and the Sources of Such Information

Burch and Strater (1973) suggested three different approaches to study the information needs of managers. The first approach is the decision-level analysis. The main rationale for this approach is that all managers, irrespective of their positions in the hierarchy, need an IS that provides information about the use of resources handled by them and not a system that provides information only by organisational functions. Once the resources of the organisation (both tangible and intangible) are identified and categorised, the IS analyst breaks each one of the resources into decision points or levels so as to identify information required for each decision level. Once this is done, the next step is to ascertain

DOI: 10.4324/9781003509714-9

Table 9.1 Organisational Subsystems and Objectives

Subsystems	*Few Objectives*
Purchase	To provide information on price negotiations with vendors so that price variance can be controlled within set limits
Training and development	To provide information on effectiveness of industrial training programmes in increasing productivity of industrial workers
Cost control	To identify cost variances within one month to institute stringent cost control
Maintenance	To provide information on breakdowns in a particular time period to assess efficiency of preventive maintenance.

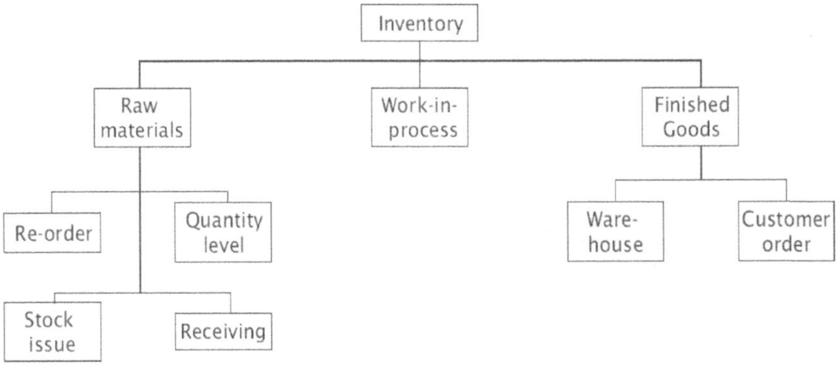

Figure 9.1 Decision Points Based on Inventory Resource Breakdown

the sources of data which generate the required information. For example, one resource is inventory which consists of raw materials, work in progress and finished stores. This resource can be broken down into major decision points concerned with it as shown in Figure 9.1. A distinct advantage of this approach is that it enables the system analyst to know the interaction of the decisions made by one manager on the others. For example, production planning decisions affect stock-level decisions and reorder decisions.

The second approach proposed by Burch and Strater to identify the managers' information needs is the information flow analysis. The analyst is concerned with what information a manager needs from others such as his supervisors, peers and subordinates and what information is required of him from others such as his own boss. This approach is illustrated in Figure 9.2.

The third approach is input/output analysis. When the analyst is investigating the existing system to gain an understanding of what is being done, facts can be collected in terms of inputs and outputs to the system. In this approach, each input and each output are only described. Nothing is said about how the input was converted to the corresponding output, or about decision-making, information requirements and information flows. For example, in the case of the computer-based personnel IS, the inputs can be

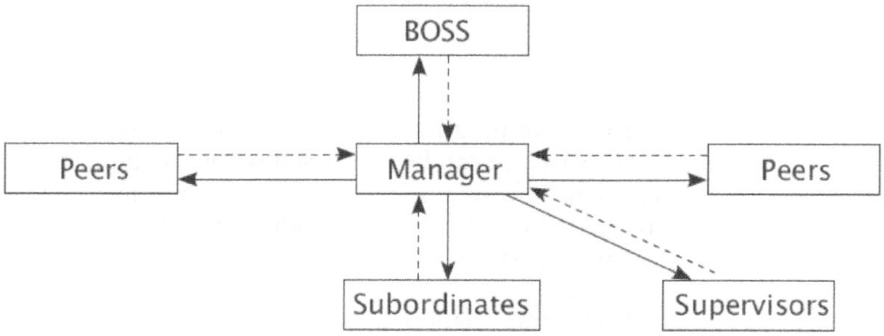

Figure 9.2 Information Flow in an Organisation

the biodata of employees and the outputs are various reports such as seniority lists of employees, retirement analysis, promotion prospect reports.

9.1.2.1 Information Sources

Information needs can hardly be met unless matching information sources are determined. Information sources can be either external or internal to the organisation. External information is obtained from a number of sources such as newspapers, trade journals, government statistics, Reserve Bank of India bulletins on trade and commerce, annual reports of companies and similar publications. Internal sources of information are the records, files, statistical and accounting documents, various reports on sales, production, personnel and so on.

Sources of information may also be categorised as follows:

1. **Internal Sources**: These include internal files, records, various reports, procedure manuals, circulars, office notes, letters, memoranda, existing system documentation and so on, which can be either hard copies or soft copies in digital form on computer storage devices.
2. **External Sources**: External sources include external data and information relating to socioeconomic, political, technological, demographic, competitive environment and government rules and regulations.
3. **Informal Sources**: Informal information obtained through interviewing managers and other employees, committee meetings, group discussions and the like is also an important source of information to satisfy the information needs of users of an IS. However, unlike written reports and records, information gathering through informal sources as mentioned above involves communication problems, which can be eliminated to a large extent by proper planning and gaining the confidence of the concerned persons.
4. **Various Mathematical and Statistical Models**: These models generate information adopting simulation, estimating, forecasting, work sampling and various other techniques. These techniques are adopted to facilitate input/output analysis and multidimensional flows.
5. **Input/Output Analysis**, which has already been mentioned in earlier paragraphs of this chapter, is done on a two-dimensional matrix in which inputs (information

Table 9.2 Information Needs/Information Sources Matrix

Subsystems	*Information Needs*	*Information Sources*
Inventory	Items with stock equal to or less than reorder level	Bin card showing stock quantity and re-order level quantity
Production	Prime cost variance more than 10%	Material, labour abstracts
Accounts receivable	Credit sales, overdue for payment	Sundry debtors' ledger
Project control	Progress against plan for critical path events	Project time sheet

sources) are listed as rows and the corresponding outputs (information needs) are column headings, and the relationships are shown by tick marks (✓) at the points of intersection. The analysis helps eliminate duplicate sources. Table 9.2 shows a matrix to illustrate the matching of information needs with the information sources for a few subsystems.

6. **Multidimensional Flow** is another technique of organising information sources to match the information needs in the existing design of a subsystem.
7. **The Flow of Information** from origin to destination in a chronological sequence through the organisational subsystems is shown as a flow chart. Apart from the identification of information sources, the frequency, volume, time, cost and physical distance of information flow can also be shown in such a flow chart additionally.

9.1.3 Setting the System Constraints

Constraints are the restrictions imposed upon the system design and are the conditions under which the system objectives are to be achieved. By their very nature, constraints can be classified as internal or external to the system. External constraints are related to customers, legal and government regulatory frameworks, suppliers, shareholders, technology and so on. Customer-related constraints demand that customer needs, insofar as the interface of the system being designed with the customer system is concerned, be fulfilled. For example, while designing system outputs such as the format of invoices, bills, cost breakdown and receipts for payments, the needs of the customers, particularly the compatibility with input to their various subsystems, must be considered.

The legal and regulatory framework imposed by the government (central, state or local authorities) covers the security and privacy of data, bookkeeping and financial reporting as per prescribed standards such as companies and other relevant acts.

Suppliers, like customers, are also important for designing subsystems which interface with their subsystems. For example, notice inviting quotations may be sent in electronic form through the e-procurement system. SCM demands total compatibility of the systems of the suppliers and customers with the subsystems of the manufacturers and service providers. Shareholders demand that the performance of the organisation during a specified period be reported in a prescribed format such as the International Financial Reporting System (IFRS). Finally, technological innovations such as ERP, data warehouses, data vaults, the Internet and World Wide Web, social networks and other information and communications technology impose restrictions on gross system design.

Table 9.3 Internal Constraints on System Design

Internal Constraints Arising Out of	*Nature of Constraints*
Cost-benefit	Cost associated with the new system is a major limitation. The cost to achieve the objective of the system should be commensurate with the benefit derived out of the system. Cost consideration demands optimum utilisation of resources allocated for the new system.
Top management involvement	The top management support is essentially needed to make any new system design and development a success. This constraint can be to a great extent overcome by involving top management in the conceptual system design.
User involvement	Like top-management involvement, user involvement is also equally important for ultimate acceptance of the new system.
Technology compatibility	In designing the system to achieve objectives, the designer has to scale down several requirements to make the system fit for existing technology.
Organisation and its policy	Organisational structure including the head of the cost, profit and responsibility centres influences the flow of information and system outputs. Company policies relating to operations, marketing, finance, personnel, information technology and R&D have a vital role to impose restrictions on system design. For example, an in-house R&D policy would have an effect on the system design to build research aptitude among technical personnel. Audit and accounts policy also imposes restrictions on system design.
Employees including managers	Employee knowledge and experience are important considerations in system design. A sophisticated computer-based system may prove futile if computer literacy level is poor among employees. Personal characteristics including the psychological type among managers also plays a vital role in system design.
Resource availability	Computer hardware, software and manpower are important considerations for design of computer-based information systems.
Legacy systems	Any new system design needs to consider the conversion of existing data base and utilisation of technology available with the legacy systems.

Internal constraints on gross system design arise out of organisation and its policy, employees including managers, available resources, legacy systems, cost-benefits, top management involvement in the system design, user involvement and technology compatibility. Illustration of internal constraints imposed on the system design is shown in Table 9.3.

9.1.4 Developing Alternative Gross Designs of the System and Selecting One

Development of a gross IS design is a creative process which involves many alternatives in respect of pattern and channels of information flow across the managers of the organisation. Moreover, the gross design must also include a linkage of the IS with all functional subsystems of the organisation such as personnel, finance and accounts, operations and marketing. Depending upon the nature of such linkage, there can be more than one variation of gross or conceptual IS design. Let us illustrate alternative gross designs with a simple example. A heavy vehicle manufacturing company has four plants located in various distant geographical locations in India. Three of the plants manufacture different components and sub-assemblies and supply the same to the fourth plant which assembles the complete end product (heavy vehicle) for the customers. The headquarters of the company is located very near to the assembly plant. According to the existing system of production planning and control, the marketing division of the headquarters receives customer orders for heavy vehicles and, in turn, furnishes the production target for the end product to the assembly plant of the company. The assembly plant, based on the production target for the complete heavy vehicle, calculates the requirements of components and sub-assemblies and provides manufacturing targets for the three component and sub-assembly manufacturing units in turn.

The above-mentioned system of regulating production and inventory of the manufacturing plants gives rise to frequent delays in delivery to customers because the manufacturing units for components and subassemblies, which have to initiate the manufacture of the required components and sub-assemblies for a customer order, get the information about their manufacturing targets from the assembly plant quite late.

Therefore, a better conceptual or gross design of the IS may be one wherein the headquarter marketing division, which receives customer orders, should set targets not only for the assembly plant but also work out the targets for component and sub-assembly manufacturing units and provide the same to the corresponding units simultaneously in order to avoid any delay in initiating manufacture of components and sub-assemblies by the respective plants. It is obvious that every alternative gross design has its own merits and demerits. The selection of one among the alternative designs will be on the basis of a number of criteria, such as the fulfilment of the system objectives, cost effectiveness of the designs, quality of information and the time lag for information to be made available to managers to facilitate decision-making relating to organisational functions.

9.1.5 Documenting the Gross System Design

The system concept developed during the gross design needs to be documented properly for the next phase of detailed system design. The documentation essentially includes the following:

1. **System Flow Chart**: A system flow chart shows the flow of information through the system reaching the various decision points. Further, the various functional subsystems and their integration through the flow of information are clearly depicted in the chart. The gross design flow chart is similar to the system flow chart described in Figure 8.12. However, additionally, system objectives, system constraints—both internal and external, information needs, information sources, various decision rules connected with the decision points and various inputs and outputs connected with the information flow process are suitably incorporated and designated into the chart.
2. **System Inputs**: System inputs and their formats for capturing data obtained from sources outside the firm such as customer orders, invoices and bills raised by the vendors are also included in the gross design document. The input formats should be designed and documented considering compatibility, conversion and collation of the input data by the subsystems. In case of inputs received from other subsystems within the company, the formats need to be designed for integrating the subsystems through common data items having compatibility. Further, since inputs must be checked for validity, the

Table 9.4 Input Format for Inventory Re-ordering Subsystem

Code '01' or '02'	Item code (5 numeric digits)	Unit of quantity (2 alpha characters)	Quantity NNNNNNNN–NN (N: A numeric digit)

Table 9.5 Input Format for Inventory Valuation Subsystem

Code '01' or '02'	Item code (5 numeric digits)	Unit of quantity (2 alpha characters)	Quantity NNNNNNNN–NN (N: A numeric digit)	Value of receipt or issue (₹NNNN–NN)

editing procedures for accepting valid inputs for the system should be specified in the gross design documentation. The format of input data should also consider the subsystems which will accept the data and process the same to facilitate decisions.

As an example, the input transaction formats for updating store records for decisions regarding the reordering of items are shown in Table 9.4. The essential data elements are the code for the type of input such as, say, '01' for material receipt vouchers through purchase, '02' for material issue vouchers for consumption, item code (say five numeric digits), unit of quantity (say km, kg, kl and so on) comprising two alpha characters and the quantity of material either received in store in case of receipt vouchers or issued out of the available balance in the store warehouse. Quantity is a numeric field of width 11 digits inclusive of 2 digits after the decimal.

The processing logic is such that if the transaction item code and unit of quantity match with the same in the stock file record, the available balance will be increased by the transaction quantity if the transaction code is '01'; otherwise, if the code is '02', the available balance will be decreased to the extent of the transaction quantity. However, before accepting the transaction for updating the stock record as above, the validity of the data fields of code, item code, unit of quantity and quantity will be checked by the subsystem.

If, however, the same type of input transactions are considered for updating priced stores ledger for inventory valuation subsystem, the formats will undergo a change as reflected in Table 9.5.

3. **System Outputs**: System output formats for three illustrative subsystems, namely inventory control, machine capacity utilisation and customer complaints handling, which are required to be designed to satisfy the information needs of managers to facilitate decisions relating to the above subsystems, have been shown in Table 9.6.

Table 9.6 Output Formats Related to Three Subsystems: Inventory Control, Capacity Utilisation and Customer Complaint Handling

Daily Stock Review Report Date: 06.10.2025

Item Code	*Description*	*UQ*	*EOQ*	*ROL*	*Balance*	*Pending Orders*	*PDS**	*Received under Inspection*	*Action*
101	Washer	Doz.	200	100	95	200	06.01.25	-	Expedite supplier.
102	Bearing	Nos.	50	20	18	50	05.27.25	30	Inspect 30 Nos. received.

Note: PDS: Probable date of supply (as per supply order).

Machine Capacity Utilisation Report Date: 06.02.2025

Machine No.	Description	Shop	Unit	Available time	Preventive maintenance time	Loading time	Actual loading time	Utilisation (%)	Action
101	Horizontal milling centre	Machine shop-A	Hrs	16	02	14	Job Time J1 4 J2 6 Total 10	71.40	Analyse idle time
102	Vertical turning centre	Machine shop-A	Hrs	16	04	12	Job Time J3 3 J4 4 J7 5 Total 12	100	Nil

Customer Complaint Report Week Ending 05.31.2025

Customer	Nature of complaint	Complaint received on	Complaint resolved on	Type of fault	Remedial action	Days taken to resolve	Reasons for delay in resolving complaint if beyond 48 hours
M/s Zenith Co.	Machine not getting 'On'	05.26.2025	05.27.2025	Starter switch burnt	Starter switch replaced	1	NA
M/s Machino Techno Industries	Lubricant leakage from machine T001	05.27.2025	05.30.2025	Lubricant seal broken	New seal inserted	3	Seal was not available in local market and had to be brought from outstation

Table 9.7 Activity Sheet for Production Control Subsystem Activity: Production Control

	Key	Name	Volume
Customer order subsystem:			
As received	*10:*	*Customer orders*	*10 per day*
Inputs			
Scheduling subsystem:	11:	Despatch to customers	10 per day
Daily	12:	Defectives returned by customers	
Inputs		**Outputs**	
Production progress reporting:	20:	Pending order status	500 per day
Monthly	21:	Overdue orders for expediting	50 per day
Inputs	22:	Production schedules	5 per day (For 5 shops)
	22:	Work-in-process status (work centre-wise)	200 per day
Files:	23:	Production plan	5 per month (shop-wise)
30: Customer order file 1,000 records			
31: Work-in-process file 1,000 records			
32: Manufacturing estimate file 2,000 records			
33: Capacity master file 1,000 records			
34: Finished products dispatch file 1,500 records			

Note: The volume indicated is only illustrative.

Apart from the output format designed to suit the information needs of managers, the other important factors for output data and information are as follows:

(i) Destination of the output reports in terms of their recipients
(ii) Distribution of output—number of copies to be sent to various recipients and mode of distribution such as online and through courier
(iii) Frequency and timing of output distribution
(iv) Form of output data, such as hard copy, data terminal and soft copy
(v) Detailed or summarised
(vi) Routine, on demand or exception reporting.

4. **Activity Sheet and the System Narrative**: The other frequently used means of documenting the gross system design are the activity sheet and the system narrative. The activity sheet is a description of inputs, outputs and various files associated with a subsystem in terms of transaction volume for the inputs, outputs and the records of the files. Table 9.7 illustrates an activity sheet for the production control subsystem, consisting of customer order, scheduling and production progress reporting. The system narrative is basically a written narrative about the system details such as the functional subsystems, the decision points or managers, the resources handled by them, the flow of materials and other resources including information within the subsystems. The routine operations performed by the various individuals within the functional areas are also mentioned in the system narrative.

5. **Gross Design Report**: The gross design report is a report prepared by the design team leader for forwarding the documentation of the conceptual or gross design and is meant for the top management to accept the same for the detailed system design to follow and also to approve the necessary expenditure of funds and organisational changes needed for the conceptual system designed. In a sense, the gross design report is similar to the detailed project report (DPR) for a project for seeking approval of the competent authority for the same. The gross design report should be concise and summarised mentioning the problems necessitating the system, objectives, reasons why the particular conceptual design was chosen from among the alternatives, the time schedule, manpower and other resources required to design, develop and implement the system and the performance metrics for the system. Along with the above summary, the complete conceptual design documentation described in earlier paragraphs, such as the system flow chart, input and output formats, activity sheet and system narrative, should be enclosed.

9.2 Detailed System Design

Detailed design of the system commences after the conceptual framework has been chalked out. The conceptual or gross design shows the broad concept of the system along with its overall performance specifications. The detailed design, however, yields the construction and operating specifications.

The idea of detailed design is to provide a detailed description of operating subsystems which fulfil the objective of the gross design requirements. The detailed description is represented through different types of flowcharts and activity sheets showing the inputs, outputs and decision rules.

Design of database and master files, specification of computer hardware and software, personnel requirement and the final performance parameters including cost of installation, implementation and operations are also furnished.

9.2.1 Detailed Design Steps

9.2.1.1 Review of the Conceptual Design

Review of the conceptual design is done in order to redefine the subsystems if necessary.

9.2.1.2 Identification of Dominant and Trade-off Criteria of the System

Dominant criteria for a system define an activity as being of utmost importance to dominate all other activities. For example, a dominant criterion might be that the system operates without any delayed supply to the customers. This criterion might override the other criteria such as cost of production and machine utilisation. The zero-delay criterion, as above, usually holds in the case of supply made to the defence forces by the manufacturing units such as ordnance factories and defence public sector undertakings. Any delay in such a case might jeopardise defence preparedness. There can be other examples of dominant criteria such as zero-defect products, zero machine breakdown, no stock-outs and no wastage.

Trade-off criteria are those where one criterion may be improved while deteriorating the other. In other words, they are criteria associated with two activities that are negatively correlated. For example, the criterion of low inventory cost might be traded off against the low stock-out cost.

The identification of dominant and trade-off criteria is a necessity before the subsequent detailed system design steps. The detailed design involves the identification of decision-makers (managers), who have to achieve the dominant criteria and also make trade-offs. The detailed MIS should be designed to provide the necessary information to the above-mentioned decision-makers.

9.2.1.3 Detailed Break-Up of Subsystems

The next step is to break down the major blocks of subsystems of the gross design into functional components, tasks, subtasks and finally the operational elements which activate functional components. For example, Figure 9.3 is a system flow chart which is a simplified representation of gross system concept for a hospital. The flow chart is, however, not exhaustive but is only a simple illustration. The billing and cash collection subsystem needs to be broken down into a hierarchy of functional components, tasks, subtasks and operational elements as shown in Figure 9.4.

The various activities/operations along with the information inputs and outputs relating to the billing activity have been shown in Figure 9.5. It is important to mention that the IS must be based upon the operating system. Once the operating system has been outlined by the general system concept as shown in Figure 9.4, the basic relationships among major activities become generally established, such as the relationship between the billing and cash collection activity and the patient registration activity. However, during the process of breakdown of major activities, considerable flexibility is achieved in establishing

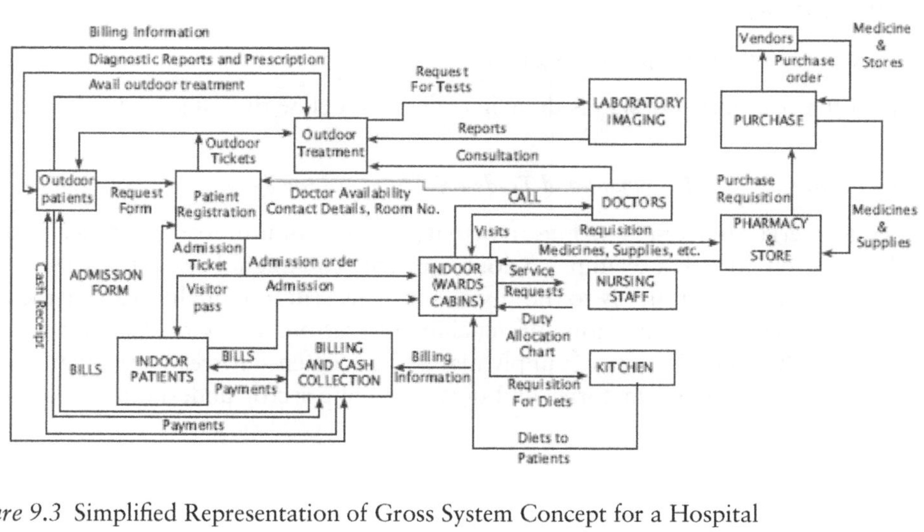

Figure 9.3 Simplified Representation of Gross System Concept for a Hospital

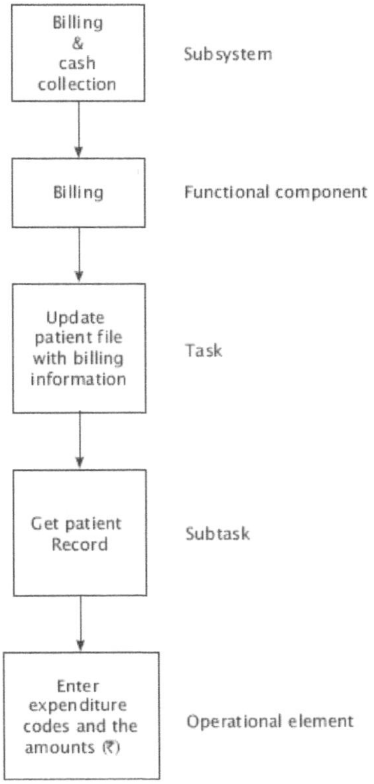

Figure 9.4 Hierarchy of Activity Breakdown Structure

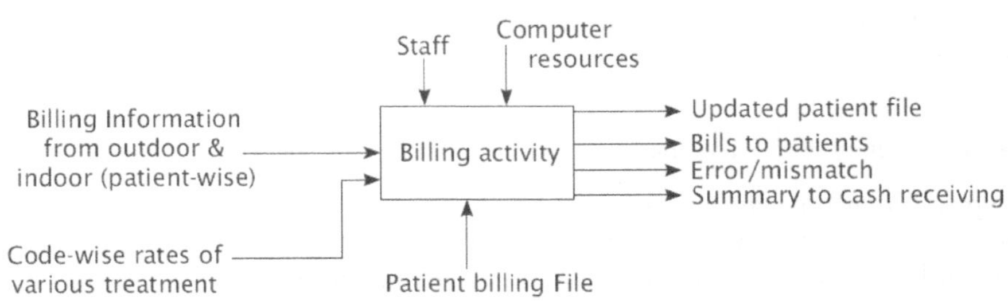

Figure 9.5 Activity Operations and Information Inputs and Outputs

the detailed activities, including the operational elements and inter-relationships. The detailed activities, once identified and defined, may be related among themselves in a flow chart as shown in Figure 9.6 for two detailed activities relating to the billing activity.

The degree of breakdown of the major activities as mentioned above depends upon the nature of the system, including the size and complexity. It should be sufficiently detailed to reveal the operating elements, information, and the decisions, and also to facilitate examination of various options for regrouping the activities. Table 9.8 is a typical form

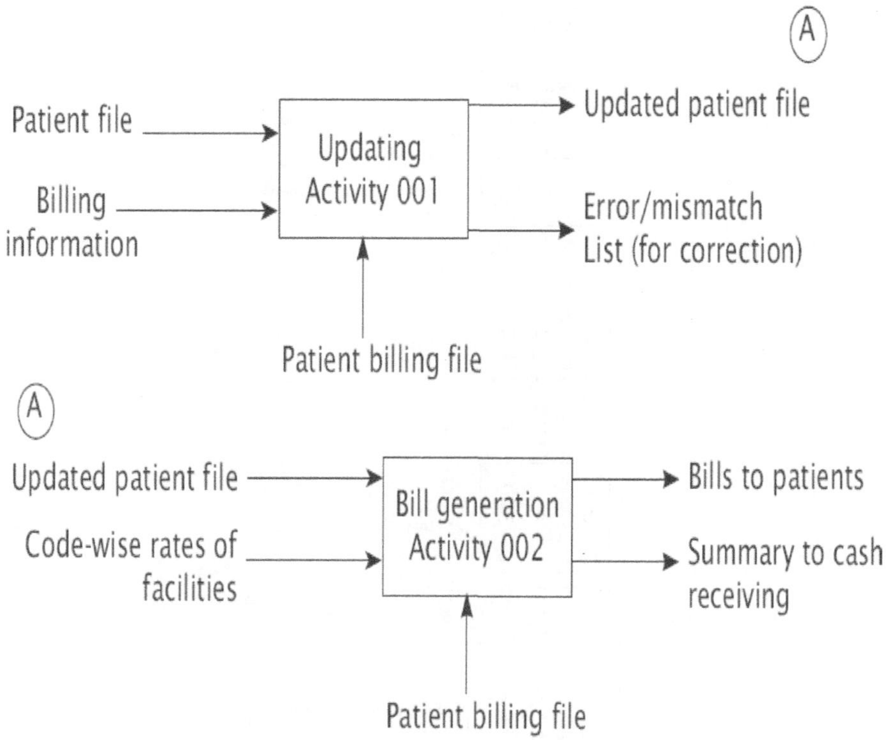

Figure 9.6 Interrelated Activities

of an operation activity sheet for the billing activity of a hospital. Similar operation activity sheets facilitate the development of a description of each activity during detailed system design.

9.2.1.4 Regrouping of the Activities

This step is to regroup the activities starting with the operational elements and synthesising them into subtasks, tasks and finally develop an activity network at the functional component level. Once activity networks are developed to include each major activity of conceptual design, the subsystems can be redefined with the help of various information such as performance specifications obtained from the conceptual design, dominant and trade-off criteria for the operating and ISs combined, available resources, required activities and their inter-relationships, major decision points, control positions, specific input information and output required for all subsystems.

9.2.1.5 Representing Detailed Operating Subsystems through Flow Charts

Operating subsystems and information flows are represented through flow charts. Usually, three types of flow charts are used to sketch the detailed design of the operating

Table 9.8 Operation Activity Sheet

Activity: Billing Activity	Activity Number: 002
Purpose and Description: With the updated patient billing file and the rates for various codes of facilities, individual bills for each category of patient is generated and also a summary statement of total billed amount is printed for the cash office.	
Inputs	Media
1. Updated patient billing file	Off-line magnetic storage
2. Code-wise rates of facilities	Off-line magnetic storage
Outputs	Media
1. Patient bills	Hard copy (printouts)
2. Summary of bills	Hard copy (printouts)
Sequence of element of activity only one activity	Performer: Decision rule billing section in-charge

subsystems, namely task-oriented, forms oriented and program flow charts. Task-oriented flow charts are block diagrams showing the various tasks or activities and their relationships. For example, Figure 9.7 is a task-oriented flow chart for the billing and cash collection module of the hospital IS. Forms-oriented flow charts show the forms used in communicating or reporting relevant information within a system. Additionally, these flow charts also show the number of copies, the colour of the copies meant for different recipients such as managers and the sequence of movement of the forms in chronological order. Figure 9.8 is an example of a form-oriented flow chart for indirect material purchase subsystem from purchase requisition up to the ordering stage.

Program flow charts are block diagrams prepared by computer programmers to pass instructions to the computer. These flow charts basically describe the computer algorithms. Figure 9.9 shows a program flow chart for computing the factorial of a number. The flow charts are sketches describing the detailed system design by the information flows and relationships with the inputs and outputs in gross form.

9.2.1.6 Specification of the Inputs, Outputs and Database

The specifications for the construction of the detailed MIS design also include the format for inputs, outputs and design of database and associated master files.

Each operating subsystem receives information as input and also produces output information which in turn will act as input to other subsystems. In order to achieve compatibility with the different subsystems, it is essentially needed to specify the inputs and outputs and forms for inputs and outputs designed properly during the detailed design process. The best practice is to design the inputs and outputs in consultation with the users who will actually use those forms.

The database is the repository of the total business system data stored for future retrieval for managerial decision-making, including automated decisions. It is therefore of paramount importance that the total management needs for information to facilitate decisions be studied in depth and an integrated approach be adopted to design the database to avoid any redundancy.

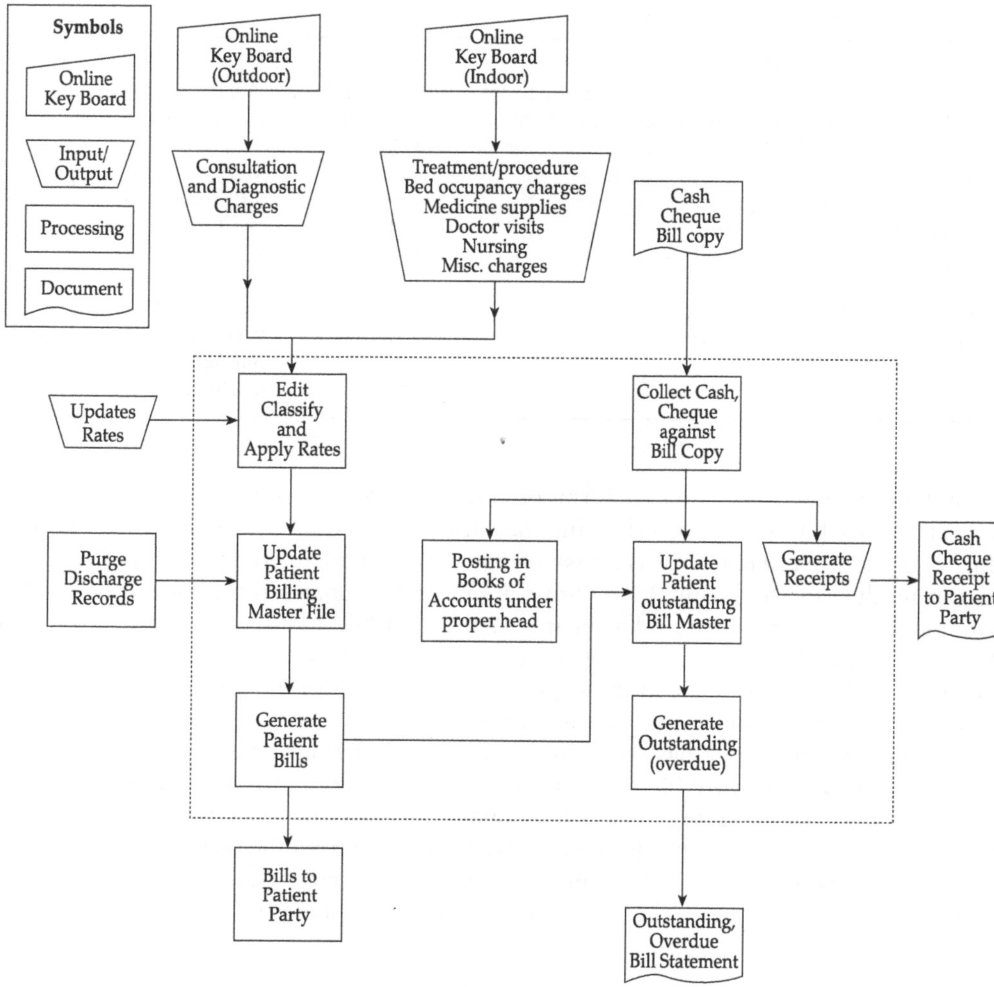

Figure 9.7 Task-oriented Flow Chart for Billing and Cash Collection Module

9.2.1.7 *Inform and Involve People at All Levels of the Organisation*

The awareness of the employees, particularly the top management, about the new system and involvement of all levels of managers, particularly the users during the detailed system design stage itself, are also pre-requirements for acceptance of the new MIS at all levels in the organisation. Top management support is essentially needed to get funds necessary for design, development and implementation of the new system. Last, but by no means least important, is that the final users of the system/subsystems be explained about the system in detail. Acceptance at the level of final users is critical for the success of the new MIS. It is therefore necessary to include as many members in the study and detailed design of the system as possible to involve them and get their support and acceptance. Furthermore, it is equally important to reassure the employees through various awareness programmes that the new system, when implemented, will benefit all of them both financially and otherwise.

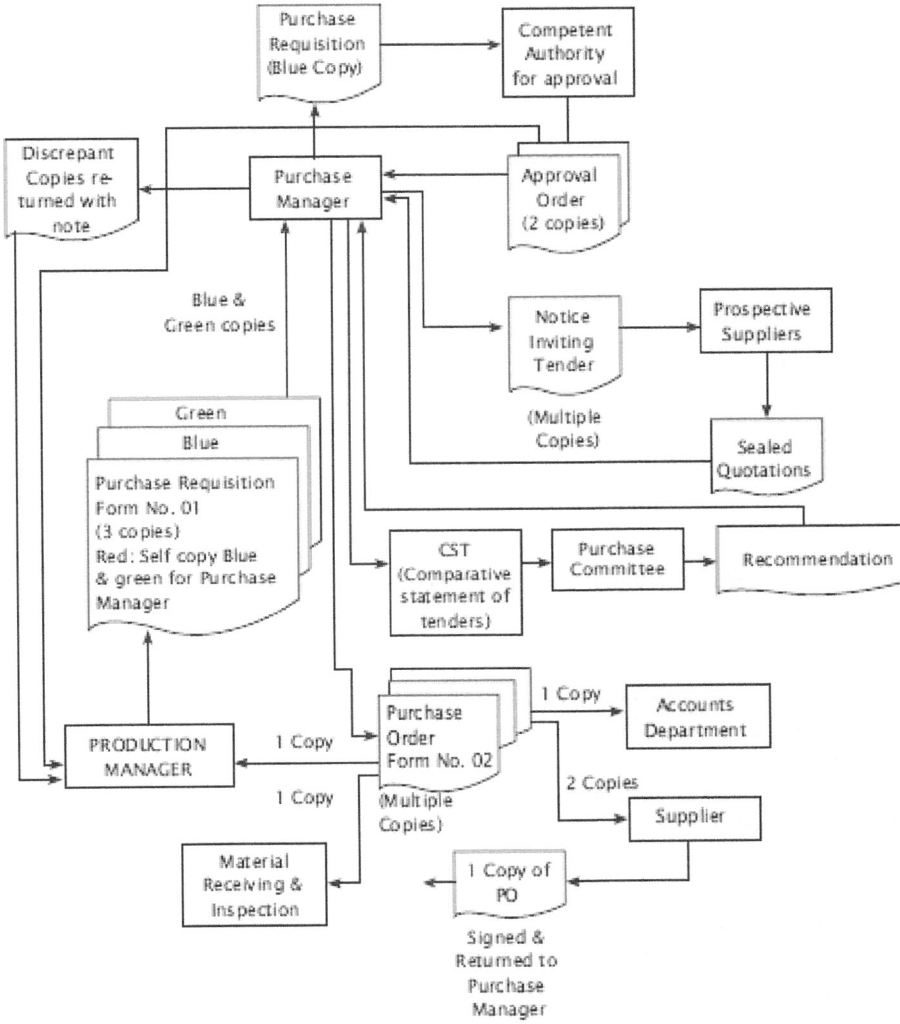

Figure 9.8 Form-oriented Flow Chart for Indirect Material Purchase up to Ordering Stage

9.2.1.8 System Testing

System testing at the detailed design stage is of paramount importance as it is very easy and cheaper to fix any problem or defect relating to the functions of the MIS at the design stage itself rather than at the implementation stage or even the operational stage. Testing during the design of the MIS mainly concentrates on the following aspects of the MIS:

1. Business processes are tested to ensure that they meet their intended functional requirements which the user needs.
2. Risks that may jeopardise the system's functioning are identified.
3. The interfaces of the subsystems (modules) and the cross-module impacts are systematically studied and analysed.

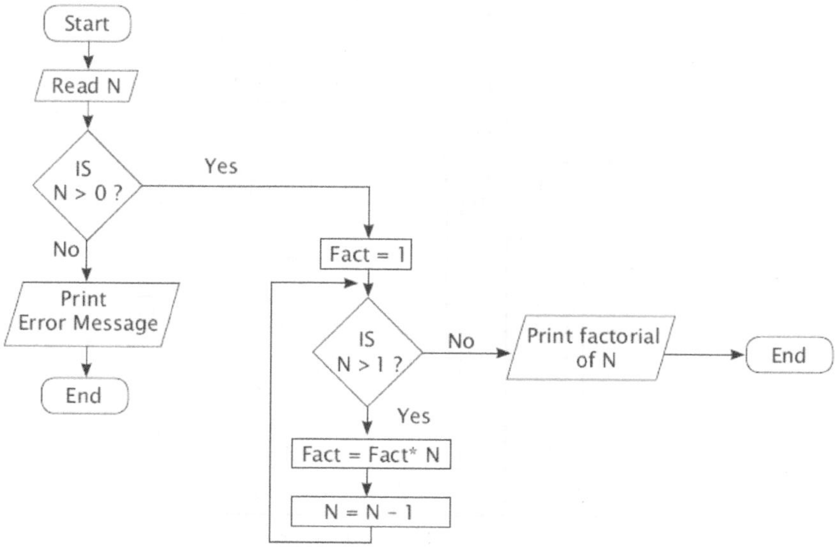

Figure 9.9 Program Flow Chart for Computing Factorial of a Number

4. Compatibility of legacy systems with the new MIS designed is studied to determine the conversion efforts needed during the subsequent implementation stage.
5. Quantitative ranges for valid inputs and outputs and their relationships are determined.
6. Time and reliability responses for the operations involving the system are studied.
7. Security aspects, including security restrictions, are studied during system testing.

Various types of system testing are (1) integration testing to find out the bugs in complete functions and processes within the subsystems and among them. This testing basically ensures correct linking of the subsystems, (2) system testing to validate that the system performs functionally as specified in the design, (3) input-output testing to ensure that the valid ranges of inputs and outputs are accepted by the system and the transfer functions are the same as specified in the design and (4) user testing to provide the opportunity to the users of the system to validate the functionality of the system prior to implementation.

System testing plans should cover the level of detail including the conditions to be tested for each subsystem and the overall system being designed. Inputs, outputs and databases will have separate test plans. Test plans also include appropriate test conditions for valid as well as invalid situations.

There are three methods of system testing. These are as follows:

1. **Modelling** is basically to determine the quantitative ranges for inputs and outputs and establishing relationships between them. It also considers the time response and reliability of the system operations. Decision modelling may take the form of either decision tables or a set of mathematical equations. Decision tables have been elaborately described in a previous chapter of this book.
2. **Simulation Testing** is suitable for large and complex systems for which actual testing, debugging and modifications of the system, subsystems and functional

components during conversion to the new system and changeover may become too expensive and may also be detrimental to the morale of the implementation team. In the case of such systems, simulation may be adopted to test the functional subsystems and the components of the large system. In such cases, simulation further facilitates performance evaluation of the system against the performance specification of parameters such as speed and throughput. Simulation testing of a management IS is carried out in the following steps:

(i) By the Monte Carlo technique, random values of exogenous variables within the ranges of their values as specified in the IS designed are generated. For example, random values may be generated for manufacturing lead time, procurement lead time, demand and supply of raw materials, cost of raw materials, inflation rate and so on for an inventory control system. Non-quantitative input variables such as employee morale are usually selected randomly from among the various alternative attributes of such variables.

(ii) The second step is to simulate the effect of the random values of the exogenous variables as obtained in Step (i).

(iii) The third step is to examine the outputs of various subsystems obtained following the Steps (i) and (ii) described above. The outputs should be checked for consistency and adherence to the specified limits as stipulated in the conceptual design.

(iv) Steps (i) through (iii) are to be repeated many times to test the system by simulation.

3. **Test Planning** pre-defines the strategy to be followed for testing the new MIS, resources to be deployed for testing, the testing environment, test data, test cases, schedule of activities relating to testing and the shortcomings of testing. It also covers the features and the deliverables of the new MIS that need to be tested. Basically, test planning formulates the quality assurance plan for the new MIS.

9.2.1.9 Documenting the Detailed Design

Finally, like any other design, it is necessary that at the end of the detailed design, the same be recorded in the form of suitable documentation for later implementation. The documentation usually consists of the following:

1. A summary flow chart similar to the one shown in Figure 9.9
2. Detailed flow charts showing interrelated activities
3. Operations activity sheets showing inputs, outputs and their relation
4. Specifications of inputs, outputs and the database
5. Requirement of computer hardware and software resources in broad terms
6. Personnel requirements for the new system specifying the type of skills
7. Final performance specifications
8. Estimated cost of installation, implementation and operation of the system
9. Programme for maintenance, modification and termination of the system
10. An executive summary of the detailed system design, particularly meant for the top management in order to enable them to get an essence of the system including the general configuration, estimated cost and benefit of the system for the company as a whole.

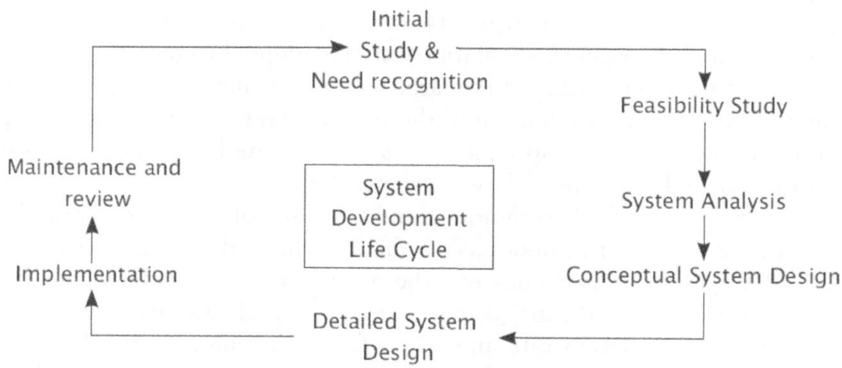

Figure 9.10 Phases of System Development Life Cycle

9.3 System Development Life Cycle

ISs are created to solve problems related to managerial decision-making. The system life cycle is an organisational process of problem investigation, analysis, design, development and maintenance of the system including a review of the same with the changing scenario. IS development involves various activities performed in various phases which constitute the system development life cycle (SDLC). The various phases of the SDLC are as follows:

1. Initial need recognition
2. Feasibility study
3. System analysis
4. Conceptual system design
5. Detailed system design
6. Implementation
7. Post-implementation, maintenance and review of the system.

The different phases of SDLC are shown in Figure 9.10.

9.4 Phases of SDLC

Let us now describe the different phases and related activities of the SDLC.

9.4.1 Initial Study and Need Recognition

This is the first phase of SDLC and mainly covers the following activities:

1. Problem identification and project initiation
2. Background analysis
3. Recognition of needs for a new system
4. Justification for a new system
5. Preparation of a system proposal for obtaining management approval for 'go-ahead' or otherwise.

The initial study must address the scope of the proposed system and the perceived problems, opportunities, constraints and the requests of the stakeholders that triggered the idea of the proposed system. The management may accept the proposal or reject it or even suggest suitable modifications to the proposal.

9.4.2 *Feasibility Study*

In case the system proposal is accepted by the management, the next phase of SDLC is the study of the feasibility of the system. There are basically five types of feasibility related to ISs which are usually addressed in this phase, namely technical feasibility, economic feasibility, schedule feasibility, motivational feasibility and operational feasibility. Technical feasibility assessment is focused on gaining an understanding of the present technical resources of the organisation such as hardware, software, legacy systems and skill of technical personnel to meet the expected needs of the proposed system. Technical feasibility study ensures whether the proposed system can be made feasible with the available technical resources of the company. For example, a computer-based inventory control system can be technically feasible, only if the operational staff are computer literate.

Economic feasibility assessment is to find out the positive economic benefits that the proposed system is likely to bring to the organisation. The assessment includes identification of both expected benefits with as much quantification as possible as well as the costs involved. An economic feasibility study, basically, is a cost-benefit analysis of the proposed system. For example, a proposed computer-based project control system is expected to bring benefits like savings in project time and cost while incurring a little cost in the design and development of the proposed system.

Schedule feasibility is estimating the time needed to develop the system. If the time schedule for development is too long, the proposed system may not be of any use because of technological, organisational and environmental changes in the meantime. Schedule feasibility is further to check the reasonableness of the time frame of design and development of the proposed system against the backdrop of available technical expertise.

Motivational feasibility study is the investigation of the impact of human factors on the proposed IS development. The complexity of the design of the proposed system, the technical challenges and the available development tools have an important bearing on the motivation of the system developers, which in turn affects the development process. In short, motivational feasibility is to study and analyse the motivation of the system developers.

Operational feasibility is a measure of how well the proposed system solves the problems and satisfies the requirements identified during the analysis phase of the system. The important aspects covered under the operational feasibility study are throughput, response time, quality of information, accuracy, operational and managerial control and so on arising out of the proposed system.

In short, the operational feasibility study finds answers to the questions of whether the current organisational practices and procedures will support the proposed system and whether the proposed system, when developed, will become workable?

During the feasibility study phase, the cost and the likely benefits of the proposed system are estimated as accurately as possible to find out the return on investment (ROI) of the proposed system. It is worth mentioning that there may be both tangible and intangible costs and benefits. The intangible costs and benefits cannot be quantified; nevertheless, they need to be identified and assessed as far as practicable. At the end of the feasibility study, as mentioned above, a feasibility report is prepared and submitted to the management for acceptance, rejection or acceptance with modifications. The SDLC can proceed to the next phase only if the feasibility report is accepted by the management.

9.4.3 *System Analysis*

This phase of the SDLC has already been explained elaborately in Chapter 8 of this book.

9.4.4 *Conceptual and Detailed System Design*

This phase has also been explained elaborately in earlier paragraphs of this chapter.

9.4.5 *Implementation*

Implementation is the stage where the system designed and accepted by the users is actually put into practice. Implementation is a very important stage in the entire SDLC and it ensures the success of the new MIS. If not implemented properly, even a well-designed system can fail. Further, it is worth mentioning that the implementation stage involves considerable time and cost as compared to the other stages of the total SDLC.

The major steps involved during implementation are briefly explained as follows:

1. **Acquiring and Installation of the Necessary Hardware, Software and Supporting Services:** The required hardware and the relevant software have to be installed and made fully operational. Prior to the acquisition of hardware and software, vendors for the same need to be selected. Along with hardware and software, support services such as electricity, air conditioning and also computer-related materials such as furniture, stationery items and data storage like compact discs need to be provisioned.
2. **Conversion of Existing Data Files, Creation of New Files and Databases:** The data from the old legacy systems need to be converted to be compatible with the formats of the new system. The database needs to be set up with proper backup, security and recovery procedures. During this step, all the programmes developed for the system are loaded on the computers of the users of the new system.
3. **Training of the Users:** A comprehensive awareness-cum-orientation programme needs to be organised for the management and support personnel to make them aware of the various features of the new system, its nature, objectives and benefits to the organisation derived out of it. The awareness programme may be a seminar or a workshop of short duration of about a week or so. The training of the users of the system should be a comprehensive one, covering all important aspects of the system, particularly the operational details such as:
    (i) What is the new system supposed to do?
    (ii) What are the salient differences in the operation of the new system with the previous one, if any?
    (iii) How to execute the system?
    (iv) How to feed the input data to the system?
    (v) What are the scrutiny and internal checks to be exercised with the system?
    (vi) The processing details of the system to convert data into meaningful information must be understood.

(vii) What are the various reports and their formats? How to make use of the reports?

(viii) What are the measures of performance of the system and the operating personnel?

(ix) What new skills are to be developed by the users as well as their subordinates?

(x) What changes have to be made in the existing system and procedures? Elaborate and formal training programmes should be conducted for the operating personnel of the system who perform daily operations such as computer operators and file maintenance personnel.

4. **Changeover**: Changeover is basically the shifting of working from the existing to the new system. The changeover is usually completed in one of the following ways:

   (i) **Direct Changeover**: This is the complete cut-off of the existing system and installation of the new system. Direct changeover is risky and there is a time gap during changeover during which no system (existing or new) is in operation. This is suitable for very small MIS.

   (ii) **Parallel Run and Cut Off**: In parallel run, both the existing and the new systems are run simultaneously for a predefined period of time depending upon the size, complexity and importance of the system being implemented. This method of changeover, though expensive, is less risky as the new system becomes foolproof. It is suitable for essential systems such as payroll and billing.

   (iii) **Changeover in Segments**: This method of changeover is basically phased replacement of the existing system with the new one. In this case, the subsystems of the existing system are replaced by the same from the new system in a phased manner and in logical sequence. This method is less risky than the direct changeover method.

5. **Documentation**: Documentation is of paramount importance in SDLC. It ensures the continuity of the system with the employees leaving the organisation. Moreover, documentation is essentially needed in case of troubleshooting, modification and upgrading the system to cope with organisational changes. There are usually two types of documentation, namely user or operator documentation and system documentation. User documentation is primarily meant for the users of the new system and contains operational details such as how to operate the system, how to feed data or information to the system, how to generate various management information reports, various types of error messages to be faced by the users and the remedial actions thereof. User documentation takes the form of a user manual. System documentation facilitates understanding of the system. It is also vital for developing an altogether new MIS, if need arises due to organisational changes.

   System documentation contains the details of system design, software development, programmes, coding, description of master files, database, data processing and retrieving of data and information and so on.

6. **Maintenance and Review of the New System**: The maintenance function commences after the system has been implemented fully. Maintenance of the system is needed to reduce or eliminate errors during its working life arising out of design and environmental changes. It is an ongoing monitoring process with an objective of improving the effectiveness and efficiency of the system within the cost constraints. The review of the system is done for understanding the full capabilities of

the system and its performance and for identifying the required changes, which may be needed pursuant to the following changes:

(i) Policy change
(ii) Change of management resulting in a change in reports
(iii) Changes in forms
(iv) Operating system and procedural changes
(v) Changes in hardware and software
(vi) Changes due to internal controls, checks and security needs.

Maintenance and review of the system may also become necessary due to environmental changes related to changes in government rules, regulations and legislation, general economic conditions, industry and market competition and emerging technologies. In short, there is a continual flow of organisational and environmental changes that require constant updating of the MIS in an organisation.

9.5 Case Study: Medallion Theatre—Ticket Sales System

9.5.1 Background

Dr Thomas Waggoner, a professor of ISs with an American university, came to the Will Call window at the Medallion Theatre to pick up two tickets he had reserved for himself and his wife to celebrate their marriage anniversary. However, to his utter surprise, he found that his tickets for the reserved seats had been sold to another patron due to an oversight. Fortunately, the box office manager could arrange for Dr Waggoner and his wife two box seats which had not been claimed by any other patron.

In the course of conversation with the box office manager, Dr Waggoner came to know that a similar type of mistake due to oversight was frequent and he offered to help the Medallion theatre management to analyse, redesign and develop their ticket sales system to avoid this type of problem in future and to improve customer satisfaction.

9.5.2 Objective

The objective of this case study is to provide insight for MIS students to apply their knowledge of data modelling, process modelling and user interface design. Moreover, they can also apply their knowledge and skills to design class diagrams/entity relationship diagrams as well as create a physical database based on IS requirement specifications for this case and similar other cases. This case study presents a small but realistic example of system analysis, design and development.

Specific requirements of the ticket sales system:

The Medallion theatre ticket sales office has to monitor the patrons, productions, performances, seats and tickets. So far as a computerised system is concerned, for each of the above entities, the following information needs to be kept.

Patron: Unique patron number, last name, first name, street address, city, state, pin code, telephone number and email address.

Productions: Production name and production type (such as play or concert).

Performance: Date of the performance and the time of performance (such as matinee, evening or night performance). A production can have multiple performances on

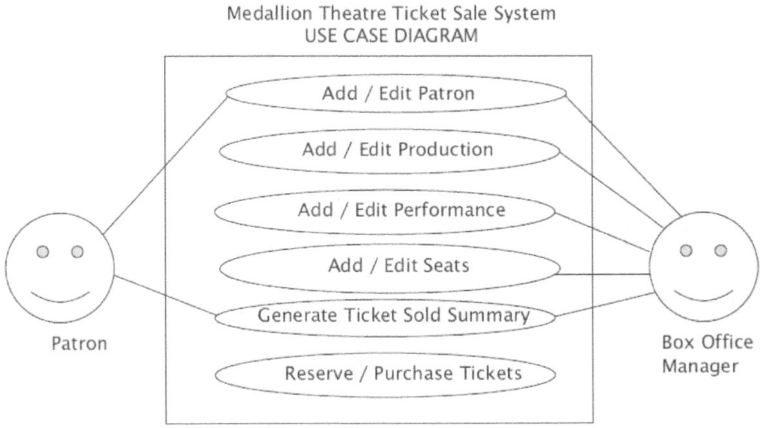

Figure 9.11 Medallion Theatre Ticket Sale System Use Case Diagram

different dates and also, a production can have multiple performances (such as matinee, evening and night) on the same date.

Seats: Unique seat number, seat category (such as orchestra, mezzanine, balcony and box) and the ticket price.

Tickets: Ticket number, seat number and ticket price.

When patrons either call or get down to reserve or purchase tickets, their names, addresses and contact information are recorded, if those are not already there in the computer files. Patrons then select the production, performance date and time and their seats from the available seats as displayed or shown to them. A ticket identifies a particular seat for a specific performance. Appropriate and user-friendly data entry/edit screens need to be designed and created to enter and edit data for patrons, performances as well as ticket sales for various seat types. The ticket sale system should generate and display information on seats sold or seats vacant for a particular performance.

The system should also generate the seats reserved/purchased by patrons (patron number or name wise) for any specific performance.

9.5.3 *Solution*

The proposed solution has been made based on object-oriented analysis and design. The use-case diagram, class diagram and the user interface design in the form of create/edit screens are shown in Figures 9.11–9.18.

9.6 Conclusion

This case study is an application of concepts and techniques of systems analysis and design, database and system development.

Source: Fox (2017).

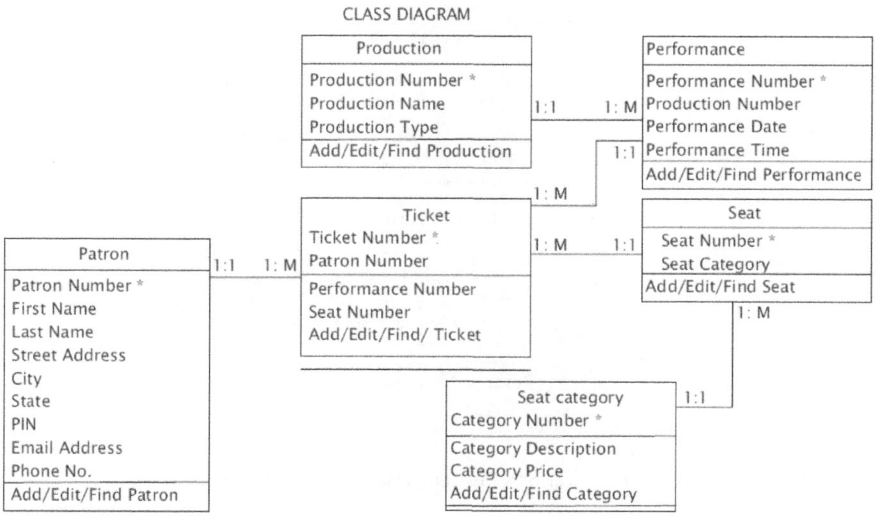

Figure 9.12 Class Diagram

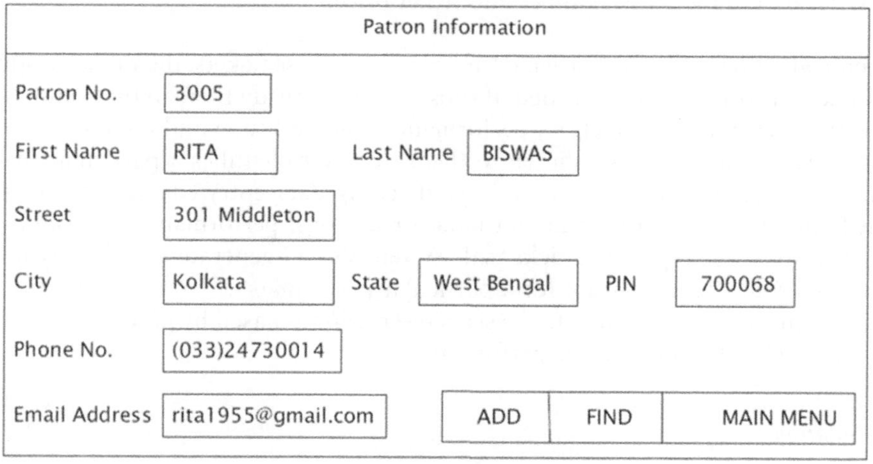

Figure 9.13 User Interface Diagrams: Patron Information Create/Edit Screen

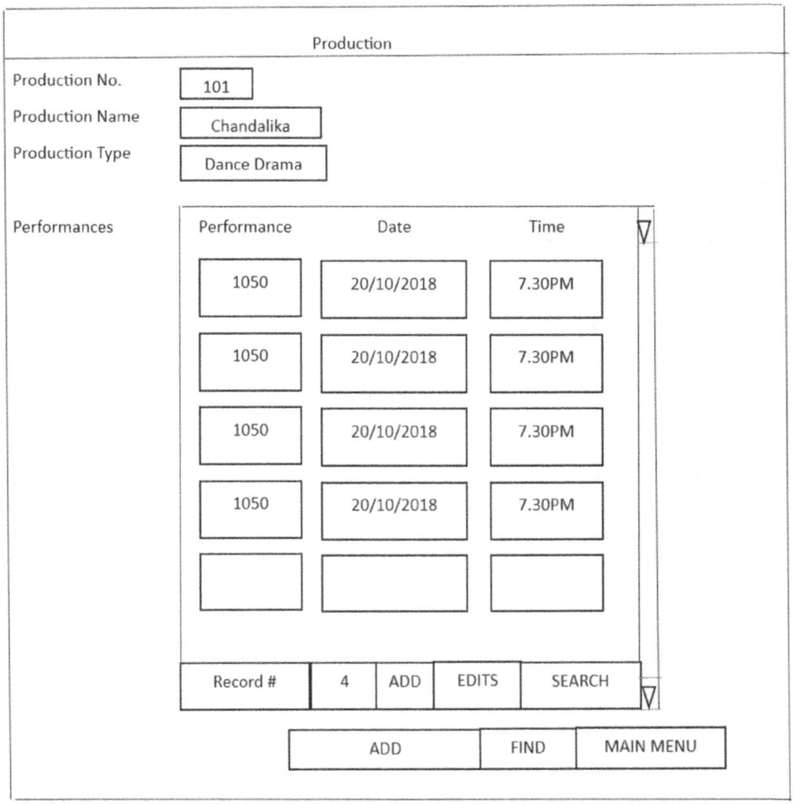

Figure 9.14 Production and Performance Create/Edit Screen

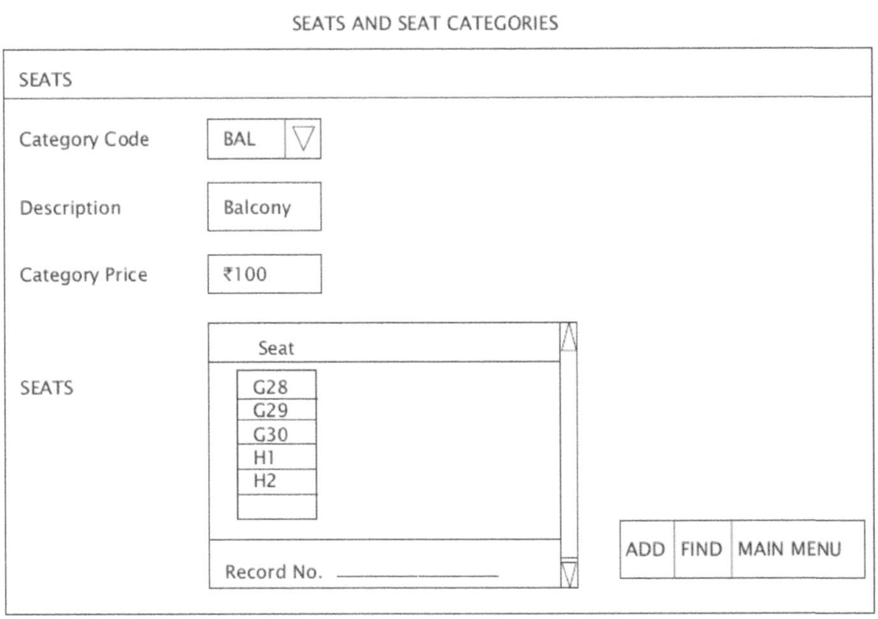

Figure 9.15 Seats and Seat Categories

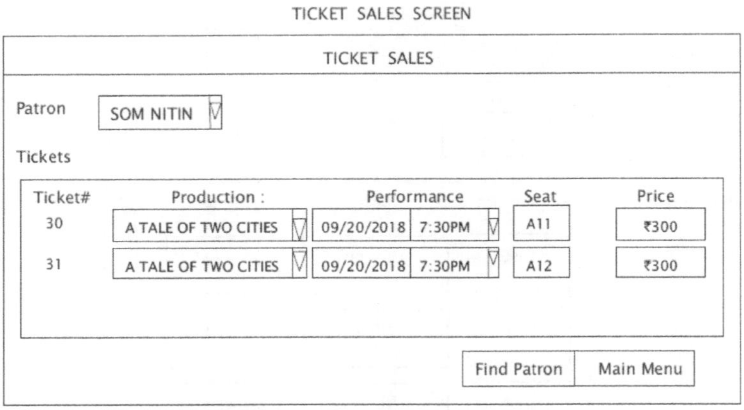

Figure 9.16 Ticket Sales Screen

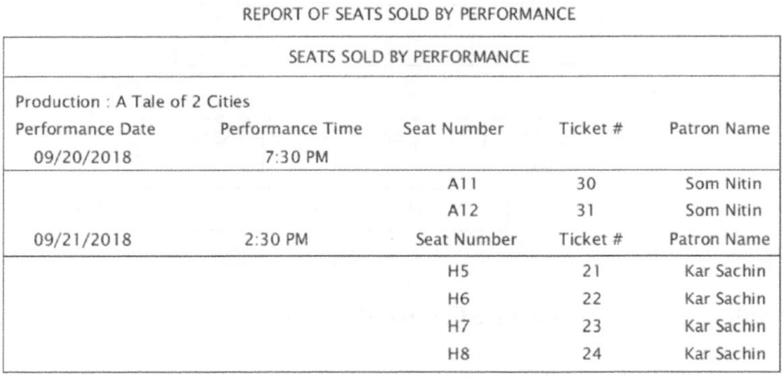

Figure 9.17 Report of Seats Sold by Performance

Figure 9.18 Report of Seats Sold to Patrons

Review Questions

1. What are the popular approaches to study the information needs of managers?
2. What is conceptual design of a system? What are the key tasks associated with it?
3. What are the criteria for comparing alternative conceptual designs?
4. Match the items in column A with those in column B.

Column A	*Column B*
System	Purchase control
Subsystem	Enter supply order details
Functional component	Update supplier file
Task	Find supplier record
Subtask	Vendor rating package
Operational element	Supplier file processing

5. What are the different types of charts used to sketch the detailed system design? Explain the charts.
6. What is SDLC? What are the important phases of SDLC?
7. What is system feasibility study? What are the different types of feasibility studies? Briefly explain.
8. What are the important tasks covered under the implementation phase of SDLC?
9. Briefly explain the two major types of system documentation.
10. What are the major reasons for system maintenance?

Bibliography

Burch, J. G., Jr., and F. R. Strater Jr. *Information Systems: Theory and Practice*. Santa Barbara, CA: Hamilton Publishing, 1973.

Fox, T. L. 'Case Study: Systems Analysis, Design and Development Case Study: Medallion Theatre—Ticket Sales System'. *Journal of the International Academy for Case Studies* 23, no. 1 (2017): 11–17.

Murdick, R. G., and J. E. Ross. *Information Systems for Modern Management*. Englewood Cliffs, NJ: Prentice Hall, 1971.

Senn, J. A. *Analysis and Design of Information Systems*, 2nd ed. New York, NY: McGraw-Hill, 1989.

10 Database and Database Management Systems

10.1 Introduction and Database Definition

The concept of MIS is to convert business data into appropriate management information to facilitate decision-making. Business decisions are supported by information or processed data and the data are stored and emanate from a database. The information obtained from the database is provided to various database users or decision-makers.

According to James Martin, 'A database is a collection of data that is shared and used for multiple purposes'. A company database is a repository or store of all types of company data which are captured, validated and stored into proper physical locations in the database for subsequent retrieval as information to various categories of users. A database caters to the information needs of the managers belonging to the various functions such as sales, manufacturing, purchase, finance and personnel as well as to various levels in the hierarchy of the organisation such as strategic planning, management control and operational control.

10.2 Data Aggregates

The data stored in a database are in the form of files such as customer file, product file and employee file. The files comprise data records which are also known as individual instances or entities in a file. For example, an employee file consists of many employee records. Each record in turn consists of individual fields or elements known as the attributes of a record such as for an employee record, the data fields may be employee identification number, name, date of joining, grade and salary. Figure 10.1 shows the concept of data aggregates in a database. It may be mentioned here that the classic database was based on the above concept. However, with the recent development in big data analysis, the concept of data aggregates has undergone modification, where data records are not only entities with fields of data attributes consisting of text, numeric data and dates but the records may be in the form of documents, images (photographs) in addition to conventional data records as described above. Such types of databases have been described later.

10.3 Data Organisation in a Database

The physical arrangement of data records in a database determines the location of the data records in the database as well as the structure of the arrangement. The organisation of data in the database can take various forms known as database models such as:

DOI: 10.4324/9781003509714-10

Employee File Comprising Employee Records

Employee ID (Numeric)	Employee Name (Text)	Data of Joining (Date)	Grade (Text)	Salary (Currency)
1001	Ashok Bose	04/04/2009	C	30000
1002	Biplab Kundu	03/01/2010	D	15000
1003	Tamal Sen	11/12/2010	A	40000
1004	Parimal Das	15/01/2011	C	28000
1005	Kausik Sharma	16/02/2012	B	35000

Employee Records

Fields in Employee record

Figure 10.1 Date Aggregates in a Database

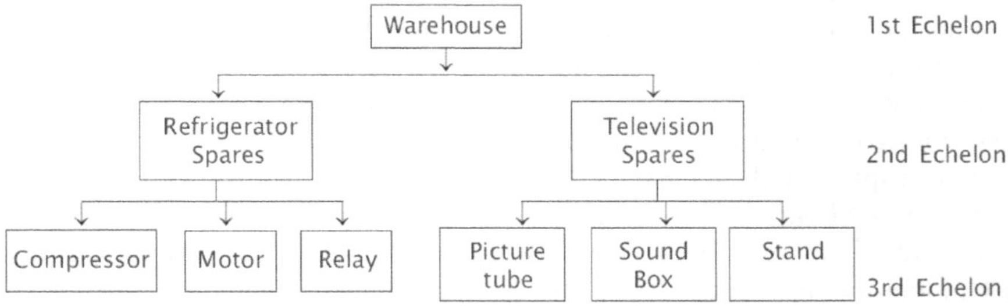

Figure 10.2 Hierarchical Arrangement of Data Records

Hierarchical Model: In case of hierarchical model as shown in Figure 10.2, the data records in a file are arranged into echelons or levels, the records in a higher level are the parent records for the corresponding child records which are placed in the next lower level or echelon. Each parent record can have multiple child records in one-to-many relationship. However, a child record cannot have more than one parent record. The records bearing parent–child relationship are connected through links (fields which indicate the relationship). Hierarchical storage structure of data records is also known as the tree structure.

Referring to Figure 10.2, if we wish to obtain a record pertaining to the third echelon, say, a 'relay' of a particular make and model, we have to first go to the particular warehouse which stores spares of refrigerators and search records for the same until we reach the records of 'relay' and then finally search the particular 'relay'.

Network Model: In a network model, complex associations are organised among data records belonging to related groups. Figure 10.3 shows a network database relating to a maintenance system.

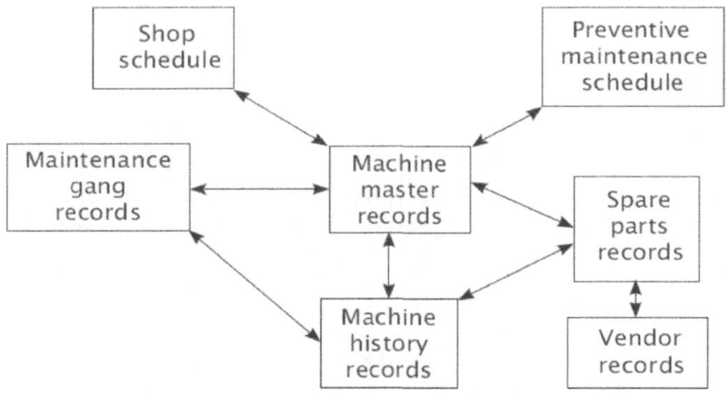

Figure 10.3 Network Arrangement of Data Records

An employee ordering the spare part of a machine will search for the machine to be ordered, then will search for the machine records for the particular machine in the machine master to find the link (pointer), which will locate the frequency of replacement of the spare in the machine history records. It may be mentioned here that the physical representation of the above structure including the linkages is very complex and beyond the scope of the conceptual point of view presented here.

Relational Model: In the case of a relational database, the data are stored in the form of tables (known as relations) consisting of rows and columns. The individual rows known as the tuples are the data records or entities, and the columns constitute the fields or the attributes of the data records as already shown in Figure 10.1. The relational approach to the database model is perhaps the most popular one among various classic database models because of the ease of the procedural tasks related to creation, retrieval, updating and deleting (CRUD) of data records. The features of relational databases and their programming have been elaborated in subsequent paragraphs of this chapter.

Physical and Logical Data Records in a Database: The physical data records in a database are the physical arrangement of the data records in their respective locations. However, logical data records represent the relationship among the records irrespective of their physical locations or arrangements in a database.

Table 10.1 Physical and Logical Arrangement of Data Records

Employee ID (Numeric)	*Employee Name (Text)*	*Date of Joining (Date)*	*Grade (Text)*	*Salary (Currency)*
1001	Ashok Bose	04/04/2009	C	30000
1002	Biplab Kundu	03/01/2010	D	15000
1003	Tamal Sen	11/12/2010	A	40000
1004	Parimal Das	15/01/2011	C	28000
1005	Kausik Sharma	16/02/2012	B	35000

(a) Physical arrangement: 1001 → 1002 → 1003 → 1004 → 1005
(b) Logical relationship (1) In alphabetic order of Name: 1001 → 1002 → 1005 → 1004 → 1003
(c) Logical relationship (2) In alphabetic order of Grade: 1003 → 1005 → 1001 → 1004 → 1002
(d) Logical relationship (3) In ascending order of Salary: 1002 → 1004 → 1001 → 1005 → 1003

Further, for a particular physical organisation of data records, there can be more than one logical relationship among the records. The above views of database records are illustrated in Table 10.1 where the same physical arrangement of employee records in a table as shown in Figure 10.1 has been reproduced. The physical arrangement of the five employee records is as shown in Table 10.1(a). However, relationships among the records can be more than one as shown in Table 10.1(b), (c) and (d) depending on the name in alphabetical order, grade and salary in ascending order of value.

10.4 Data Independence (Schemas and Sub-schemas)

A database integrates the data files pertaining to the various applications of interest to the users of data of an organisation. The purpose is mainly to eliminate redundant data files being maintained by the different applications as also to avoid duplication of efforts in maintaining separate data files for the separate applications. Moreover, such stand-alone and isolated data files may also cause further complications, if such files are used or shared by a number of application programs in an organisation. The above statements are clarified with a simple example as shown in Figures 10.4 and 10.5 respectively.

In Figure 10.4, job allocation and employee pay are two separate tables and are used by the job allocation manager and accounts manager. In this arrangement, the two tables

Job Allocation Table

Job #	Job Description	Employee #	Employee Name
J01	Pin grinding	E001	Arun Gupta
—	—	—	—
—	—	—	—
—	—	—	—

Separate tables

Employee Pay Table

Employee #	Employee Name (₹)	Basic Pay (₹)	Allowance
E001	Arun Gupta	8000	4000
—	—	—	—
—	—	—	—
—	—	—	—

Figure 10.4 Job Allocation and Employee Pay Tables

Job Allocation Table

Job #	Job Description	Employee #
J01	Pin Grinding	E001
—	—	—
—	—	—
—	—	—

Employee Pay Table

Employee #	Basic Pay (₹)	Allowance (₹)
E001	8000	4000
—	—	—
—	—	—
—	—	—

Employee Name Table

Employee #	Employee Name
E001	Arun Gupta
—	—
—	—
—	—

Figure 10.5 Job Allocation, Employee Pay and Employee Name Tables

have both employee names, which is a duplication and therefore needs more data storage space and also duplication of efforts while updating employee names in both the tables. However, the two tables can be integrated as shown in Figure 10.5 where unlike employee names being stored twice in a separate table, an employee ID and name have been created and linked with the job allocation table as well as the employee pay table. Any subsequent updating of employee names (addition of new employee names, deletion of names or amendment of names) can be performed only on the employee-name table. It may be, however, noted that the two tables, namely job allocation and employee pay, use data from the employee-name table. Therefore, changes to the employee-name table structure are likely to call for changes in both the application programs related to job allocation and employee pay. Likewise, any change in one of the two above-mentioned application programs is likely to necessitate changes in the employee name table directly and in the other application program indirectly.

The above difficulty led to the concept of physical data independence as an essential requirement of an integrated database. Precisely, it means that the physical data structure in a database can be changed independent of the application programs. For example, an employee table consisting of employee#, name, date of joining, salary as attributes can be changed with respect to the attributes date of joining and salary in whatever way, without affecting an application program using or viewing the employee# and name only.

This can be achieved by a three-tier architecture of an integrated database. The three tiers are known as internal schema, conceptual schema and external schema (or subschema) in database parlance.

Internal Schema shows the physical storage structure of data in the database. It describes the complete data storage in the database and the paths to access the data. The conceptual schema, also known as the logical organisation of the database, hides the details of physical storage structures and concentrates on describing entities, data attributes and their types, relationships and their operations and constraints.

External Schema also known as the sub-schema, is a subset of the database in which a particular application or user group is interested. Thus, the database software, also known as the Data Base Management System (DBMS) (to be described later), provides different views or sub-schema to different users of the database depending upon individual needs without exposing the entire conceptual or internal schema of the database to the users. The application programmer's view is referred to as the sub-schema or the local view as compared to the global view or conceptual schema. This feature facilitates the concept of data independence as shown in Figure 10.6.

10.4.1 Metadata

Metadata is only data about the data, which actually exists in the database storage. The three schemas, namely internal schema, conceptual schema and external schema are only metadata describing the actual data.

Any user request for specific data (external schema) needs information in metadata in order to accomplish mapping among the conceptual schema and then into the internal schema. The mapping among the levels is accomplished through metadata which precisely describes the location and the type of data in the database.

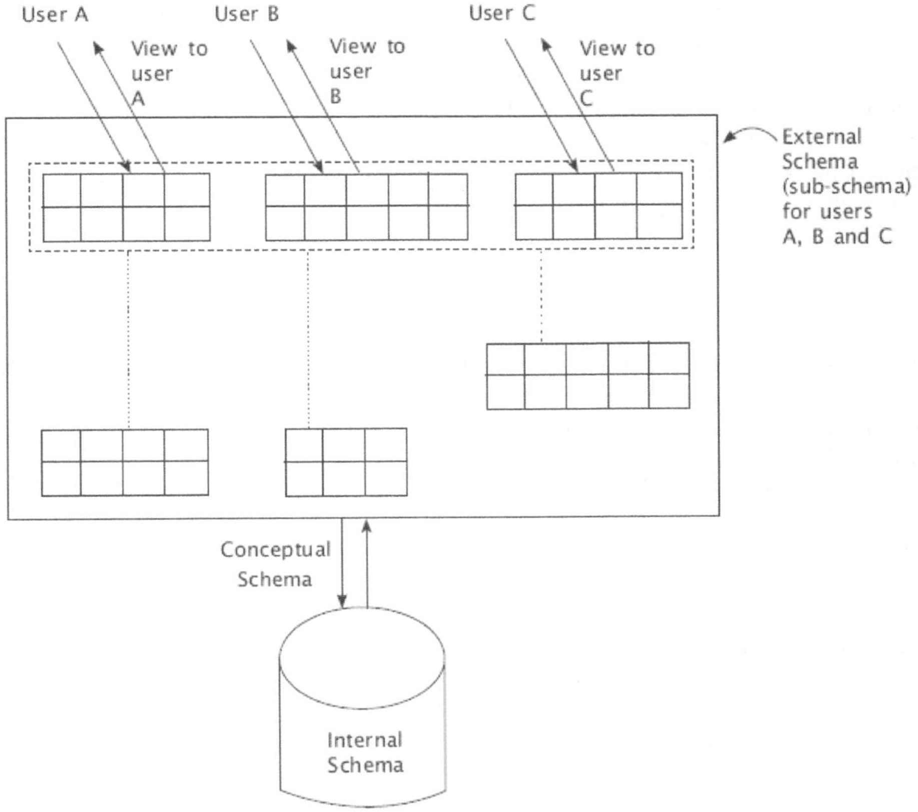

Figure 10.6 Schema, Sub-schema and Data Independence

10.4.2 Database Schema and Database Instances

In any database model, it is important to differentiate between the overall description of the database and the database itself. The former is called the database schema, while the latter is known as database instance.

Database schema shows the overall description of the data in the database including locations through a set of definitions or mappings which are specified during database design and which do not frequently change.

Database instance, on the other hand, is the content or actual data at any particular instant, and the same may change frequently during database operations to be described later in this chapter. It only depicts the database state at any point of time. For example, when a database defined through the schemas remains in empty state and data are subsequently loaded into it, the initial state is obtained.

10.5 Features of a Relational Database

A relational database consists of tables which are the building blocks of the database. As earlier stated, each table consists of rows and columns similar to a spreadsheet. Each row in a table contains data related to the same kind of thing. However, each table contains data related to a particular thing. For example, you may have one table for data related to your customers where each row contains data related to one single customer only. Similarly, we may have different tables in the database for data related to employees, inventory, customer orders and so on. Each repeating row in an employee table contains the same formatted data about one single employee. Each column in a table contains a particular piece of data related to that row. For example, in the employee table, we may have columns representing employee name (text), date of birth (date), grade (numeric) and salary (currency). However, the columns, once defined, become fixed insofar as the types of data are concerned. For example, we cannot store text data in the grade column or the date of birth column. The structure of each table, which depicts the type of data it contains as explained above, is defined initially and also subsequently during day-to-day operation of the database. Data can be modified, retrieved or deleted from the tables, but strictly conforming to the initially defined structures of the tables at any point in time. This concept of data manipulation is known as 'CRUD' which has been explained in Figure 10.7. A table is also known as a relation in which each row is an entity known as 'tuple' and each column is an 'attribute'.

10.5.1 Attributes

Attributes (columns in a relation) are the characteristics which together specify an entity. The attributes can be classified into five different types, namely simple or composite, keys

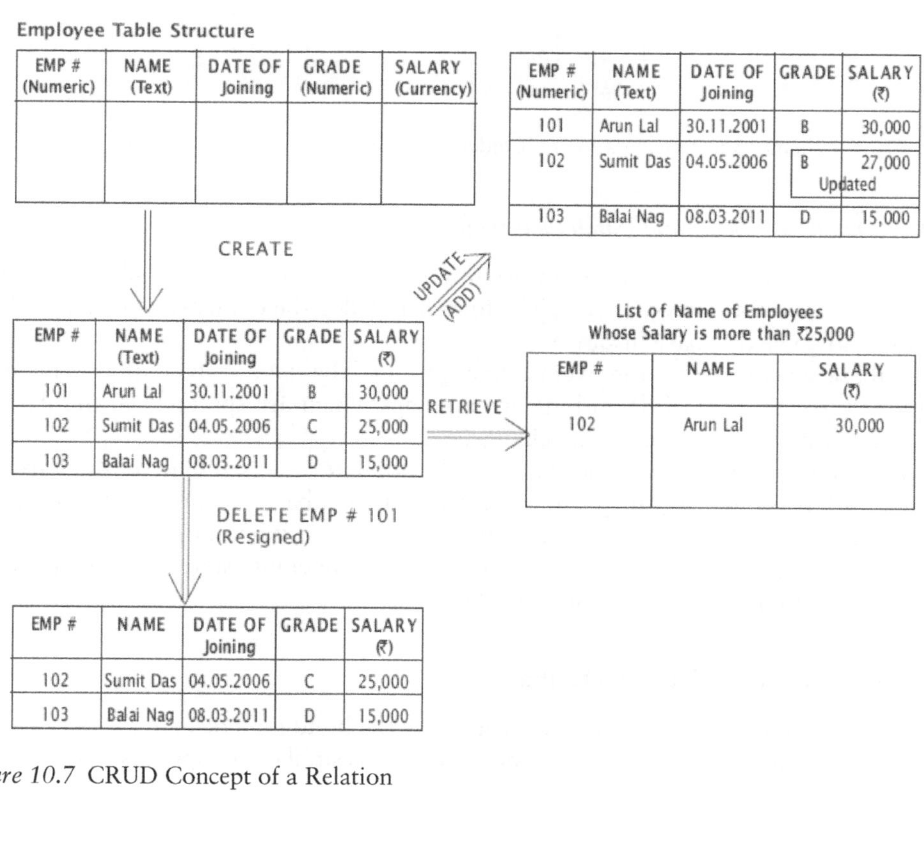

Figure 10.7 CRUD Concept of a Relation

and non-keys, single or multiple value, stored or derived, required or optional attributes. Let the above types of attributes be explained with simple examples.

Simple attributes cannot be split into smaller parts, whereas composite attributes can be divided into sub-parts. Age and date of joining of an employee are simple attributes, whereas the name of an employee is an example of a composite attribute since it consists of last name and first name.

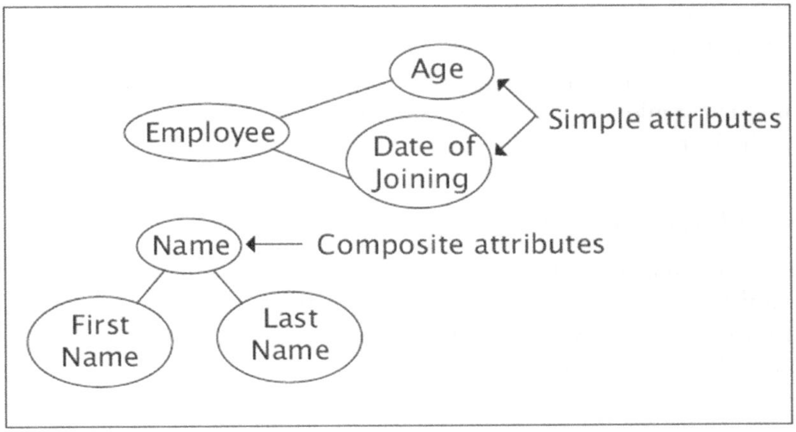

Keys are employee ID, product ID and department ID, which uniquely define an entity in a relation, whereas age, salary, address and so on are non-key entities since two employees (entities) can have the same value for these attributes.

Single-value attributes are those which can have only one single value for any one entity, whereas in the case of multi-valued attributes there can be more than one value for any particular entity. For example, the last name of an employee is a single-valued entity since an employee can have one last name only. However, cell phone number is a multi-valued attribute since one employee can have more than one cell phone.

Derived attributes are those whose values can be derived based on other attributes known as stored attributes. For example, the date of birth of an employee is a stored attribute, while the age of an employee is a derived attribute which can be arrived at from his/her date of birth.

Required attributes are essentially needed to have values such as employee ID and name, whereas optional attributes may or may not have any value such as the spouse of an employee, which a particular employee may or may not have.

In a table, there can be unique and non-unique columns. Unique columns are those where the data corresponding to all rows in that column are unique and no two values are the same at any point of time. For example, name, date of joining, grade and salary can be non-unique columns since there can be instances that name or date of joining or grade or salary for two employees may be the same. However, employee number (employee#), which is generated for each employee record, is unique for each employee.

A column in a table which is a generated unique one is called the primary key of the table. The primary key uniquely identifies any row of a table in a database. Incidentally, it may so happen that a column other than the generated primary key may be unique. For example, if we add a column in the employee table shown earlier to include the permanent account number (PAN) allotted by the income tax department, the column obviously will be a unique one as no two employees can have the same PAN. However, any DBMS always generates the primary key known as the generated primary key or the surrogate primary key irrespective of whether the table already has got one unique column. The primary key, in addition to uniquely identifying any row (entity), also helps in establishing a relationship among tables as explained in the following paragraph.

10.5.2 Tuple

A 'tuple' is a particular row in a table. For example, in an employee table there will be as many tuples (rows) as the number of employees. Each tuple is uniquely identified in the above-mentioned employee table by the employee identification number. Each tuple in a table is one distinct entity.

10.5.3 Establishing Relationships among Tables—Foreign Keys

The tables in a database contain data which are naturally connected, and therefore in a database, tables need to be connected through their relationships. For example, in the case of a college database, we may define a student table, a faculty member table and a department table, each one of which has a primary key for its entities. However, there

Student Table

Student ID	Student Name	Tel. No.	E-mail	Present Class
101	Joyeeta Basak	9830612881	basakj@.....	B.Sc First year
102	Arnab Saha	9435712096	arnab@.....	B.A. Second year
103	Partha Banerjee	9737145111	banerjeep@.....	B.Sc Third year
—	—	—	—	—

↑ Primary Key

Figure 10.8a Student Table

Department Table

Department ID	Department Name	Name of HOD	Tel. No.	E-mail of HOD
11	Physics	Dr. Santanu Roy	9431012095	santanu@.....
12	Chemistry	Dr. Ila Mitra	8411225150	mitra.ila@.....
13	English	Dr. Robin Das	9830132424	rabindas@.....
—	—	—	—	—

↑ Primary Key (Unique) Link 1

Student Table with a Foreign Key

Primary key (Unique) ↓ Non-unique Foreign Key

Student ID	Student Name	Tel. No.	E-mail	Present Class	Department
101	Joyeeta Basak	9830612881	basakj@.....	B.Sc First year	11
102	Arnab Saha	9435712096	arnab@.....	B.A. Second year	13
103	Partha Banerjee	9737145111	banerjeep@.....	B.Sc Third year	11
—	—	—	—	—	—

Link 2

Figure 10.8b Foreign Key Connection Student Table with Department Table

exist relationships among the tables because students are taught by the faculty members and students belong to the departments. Although the data contained by the three tables is different, there exist relationships among them.

The relationships among the tables are established through foreign keys which are primary keys in one table, but non-unique in the other table and which establish relationships between the two tables. For example, Figures 10.8a and 10.8b describe tables for students and departments of a college. The primary keys for the two tables are the student ID and the department ID respectively. Now, any student belongs to a particular department only, but a department has many students. This is a case of one-to-many relationships. In order to establish a relationship between the student table and the department, we need to add a column in the student table to accommodate the department ID from the department table against the student ID row-wise, and this extra column thus establishes the connection between the two tables as shown in Figures 10.8a and 10.8b.

It may be noted that the department ID shown in the student table, which connects the student entity with the concerned department of the student, is, however, non-unique although the same is a unique prime key in the department table. This is because the same department ID can occur more than once (such as in the example department, ID '11' has appeared twice) in the student table though the same is unique in the department table. This is because more than one student belongs to a particular department but not the other way, that is, one student cannot belong to more than one department. A key which is unique in one table and is the prime key in that table may not be unique in another table, but still, it is a key in the table though non-unique. Such a key, which is non-unique in a table, is known as the 'foreign key'. In Figure 10.8b, the department ID, though a unique and 'prime key' in the department table, is the non-unique 'foreign key' in the student table. The foreign key establishes contacts between two tables as shown as Link 1 and Link 2 in Figure 10.8b.

Another feature of the relationship shown in Figure 10.8b is the 'one-to-many' relationship. That is to say, one department has many students, but one student cannot have more than one department. The 'one-to-many' relationship exists in many business situations as shown in Figure 10.9.

10.5.4 Representing Many-to-Many (M:M) Relationships in Relational Database

Unlike one-to-many relationship, we cannot express a many-to-many relationship directly by a foreign key. The relationships in such cases are established between the two tables indirectly by creating a third table for linking through two one-to-many relationships. The method has been explained with an example shown in Figure 10.10. The figure shows a student table and a faculty member table of a college. The relationship between

Figure 10.9 One-to-Many (1:M) Relationships

Faculty Member Table

Faculty Member ID	Faculty Member Name	Tel. No.	Email (ID)	Designation
11	Dr. Santanu Mitra	9431012095	santanum@gmail.com	Professor
12	Dr. Bijon Sarkar	8431122515	sarkarb@...	Associate professor
13	Mr. Subrata Kar	9830132424	skar@...	Assistant professor

1 — M

Faculty Member—Student Table (Linking table)

Faculty Member ID	Student ID
11	103
11	101
12	102
13	103

M — 1

Student Table

Student ID	Student Name	Tel No.	Email ID	Present Class
101	Jayeeta Basak	9830612881	basakj@...	B.Sc 1st year
102		9435712096	arnab@...	B.A. 2nd year
103		9737145111	banerjeep@...	B.Sc 3rd year

Figure 10.10 Many-to-Many Relationships with Linking Table

them is a many-to-many one. Because a student can be taught by many faculty members, at the same time, a faculty member can teach many students. The relationship is established through a linking table, namely the faculty members-student table.

It may be noted that the faculty member table and the student table remain isolated, and the link is established with a faculty member-student table through two one-to-many relationships, as shown in Figure 10.10 and the student ID and faculty member ID relationships (many-to-many) are found in the same linking table. We can go from student ID in the student table to the faculty member-student ID and map the student ID to all faculty member IDs in the same linking table. We can also start with faculty member ID and then map the faculty member ID to all student IDs in the linking table.

10.5.5 Composite Keys

Sometimes, it may so happen that there is no unique column in a table that can identify each row in the table uniquely. In such a situation, though one value does not uniquely identify a row, two values together uniquely identify a row. In that case, we can combine the two column values to make a unique key, which is known as a composite key. Let me illustrate a composite key with an example shown in Table 10.2, which shows a database relation containing records of the office bearers of a club for different years.

Table 10.2 Composite Key Example

Club-Office Bearers				
Post held	*Year*	*Last Name*	*First Name*	*Membership No.*
President	2014	Mehra	Anil	116
Secretary	2014	Baruah	Santosh	201
Treasurer	2014	Saxena	Sanjeev	220
President	2015	Mehra	Anil	116
Secretary	2015	Sarkar	Jayanta	230
Treasurer	2015	Bajaj	Deepak	305

The attributes are the post held, year, last name, first name and membership number of each office bearer of the club during the different years. It may be seen from the following table that no single column has values to identify each row uniquely. The same value can be found in more than one row of each column. Therefore, we are not in a position to find a primary key except by generating a surrogate key uniquely. However, without the same, we can find a combination of the values in the columns post held and year as a unique combination which can uniquely identify each row. In this case, post held and year combined constitute a composite key. For example, president for the year 2014 is a unique value. Composite keys are useful in joining tables together to create multiple relationships.

10.5.6 Transactions and the ACID Test

Data in a database get updated or changed with transactions. A transaction is therefore very important for the operations on databases. If the DBMS does not take care of certain essential features of any transaction, which change the data in a database, there will be an error in the data of the database. For example, a database pertaining to the inventory management system might contain two tables, namely the stock table and the inventory consumption table. There may be other tables also. Now if there is a withdrawal of a certain quantity, say, X units of a particular item of material, the DBMS will first subtract the quantity X from the stock value of the item in the stock table and then will add the same X to the material consumption figure contained in the record of the item in the inventory consumption table.

However, it may so happen that the above transaction (material withdrawal) may update the stock in the stock table but fail to update the inventory consumption table because of any temporary glitch in the system such as power failure. The result will be erroneous data in the inventory consumption table.

Therefore, the DBMS must ensure that in such cases, the data updated in the stock table must be changed back to the original value. This brings the concept of the atomic nature of the transaction, which means that all the changes made to a database by a transaction must be done together. Otherwise, the transaction must not make any of the changes. The other features relating to transactions for database data updating are consistency, isolation and durability and all these features give rise to the acronym 'ACID'.

Consistency implies that any transaction must change the database from one valid state to another valid state based on the rules of the database. Even if a transaction is

End product

End Product ID	Description	Unit of measure	Price (₹)
101	Stop cock	Number	570
102	Plastic tap	Number	50
103	Valve	Number	600

Components

Component ID	Nomenclature	Unit of measure	Price (₹)	End product ID
301	Inner pass	Number	100	101
302	Spindle	Number	150	101
303	Spring washer set	Number	40	103
304	Shower Nozzle	Number	200	110

× Not allowed due to Referential Integrity

Figure 10.11 Referential Integrity and the Relationship Rules

successfully atomic, it cannot still result in a violation of the integrity rules of the database, such as the referential integrity, which means that if B references A, then A must exist. Isolation refers to the data and the transaction being essentially locked during the occurrence of the transaction. Durability refers to the transaction being considered robust, and the change made by it remains guaranteed even in case of any hardware disruption, such as power failure. The majority of DBMS take care of ACID features as explained above.

10.5.7 Relationship Rules and Referential Integrity

Referential integrity basically is a constraint that does not allow any entry in a row of a table if the foreign key for that entry does not exist in the table which has the primary key. Let us illustrate the relationship rules and the referential integrity with an example (Figure 10.11).

Figure 10.11 shows two tables, one being an end-product table and the other the component table. The components are assembled to make up the end products. It may be noted that due to referential integrity, the DBMS does not allow one to create a record with component ID 304 in the component table since the foreign key 110 does not appear in the end-product ID table. Similarly, if one entity (end-product ID 101) needs to be deleted from the end-product table, first the records in the component table pertaining to that particular end-product ID (in this case component ID 301 and 302) need to be deleted, and then the record with end-product ID 101 can be deleted.

10.6 Database Modelling: Normalisation

Normalisation is a process of database modelling where one applies a set of formal criteria and rules known as normalisation in database parlance. Normalisation facilitates optimisation of database design considering data storage, ease of data manipulation, minimum redundancy in data and more reliability to work with the database. The normal forms were developed by Edgar Codd, called the father of the relational database.

Employee ID	First Name	Last Name	E-mail ID	Mobile No.
101	Ashoke	Bose	bashok@........	9431112096
102	Sachin	De	dsachin@........	9832288428
103	Partha	Banerjee	bpartha@........	9433101281

Employee ID	First Name	Last Name	E-mail ID	Mobile Numbers
101	Ashoke	Bose	bashok@..	9431112096, 9831115092
102	Sachin	De	dsachin@..	9832288428, 9731177010
103	Partha	Banerjee	bpartha@..	9433101281, 9432012096

Violates 1NF since more than one value of mobile numbers in a column.

Employee ID	First Name	Last Name	E-mail ID	Mobile No.1	Mobile No.2
101	Ashoke	Bose	boshok@...	9431112096	9831115092
102	Sachin	De	dsachin@...	9832288428	9731177010
103	Partha	Banerjee	bpartha@...	9433101281	9432012096

Repeating group of columns

Violates 1NF since there are repeating groups in mobile numbers data.

Primary Key

Employee ID	First Name	Last Name	E-mail ID
101	Ashoke	Bose	boshok@...
102	Sachin	De	dsachin@...
103	Partha	Banerjee	bpartha@...

One to many relationship
Compliance with 1NF

Foreign Key

Employee ID	Mobile No.
101	9431112096
101	9831115092
102	9832288428
102	9731177010
103	9433101281
103	9432012096

Separate Linking Table

Figure 10.12 First Normal Form

The important normal forms are the first normal form (1NF), second normal form (2NF) and 3NF. However, there are also normal forms higher than 3NF.

10.6.1 First Normal Form (1NF)

The First Normal Form (1NF) stipulates that each column and each table in a database should contain one value and there should not be repeating groups in a table. For example, let us consider an employee table as shown in Figure 10.12 having employee ID (primary key), first name, last name, email ID and mobile number as the columns of the table. Now, it may so happen that any employee can have more than one mobile telephone and we want to store the same in the employee table. One way of doing the same is to store the multiple mobile numbers in the mobile number column separated by delimiters (,) but that violates 1NF as there cannot be more than one value in any field or column. The other way is to create multiple columns for storing more than one mobile number which again violates 1NF as repeating groups are not permitted in 1NF. Hence, in order to comply with 1NF, a separate table has to be created with mobile numbers and employee ID columns. Employee ID in this linking table is a foreign key and the relationship between the employee table and the employee ID—mobile number table is a one-to-many relationship as shown in Figure 10.12.

The solution to the 1NF is through the creation of a new table and the relationship between the two tables though in the above example is one-to-many, it might even require in some cases a many-to-many relationship with a linking table.

10.6.2 Second Normal Form (2NF)

2NF of a relational database is applicable when and only when the following two conditions are satisfied by all the tables of the database.

Condition Number 1: The database has to be in the 1NF. That is, there are no repeating values in any column position for any particular row.

Condition Number 2: Any non-key field should be dependent on the entire primary key.

Now referring to condition number 2, the non-key field means the actual value in a particular non-key column position for a particular row. The Second Normal Form (2NF) may become an issue only when there is a composite primary key and not otherwise. Let me illustrate the above stipulations relating to the 2NF with an example shown in Figure 10.13. The example is about a tour operator operating package tours in various places of tourism in India. The package tour table shown in the upper part of Figure 10.13 is in 1NF since there is no duplicate data or repeating groups in any row.

However, it violates condition number 2 of 2NF since in this case a non-key, namely package tour name does not depend entirely on the composite prime key consisting of two attributes namely tour ID and the start date but it depends on the tour ID only which is a portion of the composite key. Hence, it violates 2NF. However, it can be made to

Package Tour Table

Tour ID	Start date	Package Tour Name	Capacity	Availability	Accommodation
AN 01	10.20.2016	Andaman	40	11	Hotel
KAS 02	07.29.2016	Kashmir	40	18	Hotel
AN 01	12.14.2016	Andaman	50	20	Resort
GOA 03	11.30.2016	Goa	30	15	Guest house
KAS 02	10.31.2016	Kashmir	30	25	Guest house

Composite Primary key

Not in Second Normal Form

Tour ID	Package Tour Name
AN 01	Andaman
KAS 02	Kashmir
GOA 03	Goa

Package Tour Table

Tour ID	Start date	Capacity	Availability	Accommodation
AN 01	10.20.2016	40	11	Hotel
KAS 02	07.29.2016	40	18	Hotel
AN 01	12.14.2016	50	20	Resort
GOA 03	11.30.2016	30	15	Guest house
KAS 02	10.31.2016	30	25	Guest house

Second Normal Form

Figure 10.13 Example of Second Normal From

Tour ID	Package Tour Name
An 01	Andaman
KAS 02	Kashmir
GOA 03	Goa

Package Tour Table

Tour ID	Start date	Capacity	Availability	Accommodation
AN 01	10.20.2016	40	11	Hotel
KAS 02	07.29.2016	40	18	Hotel
AN 01	12.14.2016	50	20	Resort
GOA 03	11.30.2016	30	15	Guest house
KAS 02	10.31.2016	30	25	Guest house

Composite Prime key   Dependence of Capacity on Accommodation Violation of 3NF

Package Tour Table

Tour ID	Start date	Avail-ability	Accommo-dation
AN 01	10.20.2016	11	Hotel
KAS 02	07.29.2016	18	Hotel
AN 01	12.14.2016	20	Resort
GOA 03	11.30.2016	15	Guest house
KAS 02	10.31.2016	25	Guest house

Tour ID	Package Tour Name
AN 01	Andaman
KAS 02	Kashmir
GOA 03	Goa

Accommo-dation	Capacity
Hotel	40
Resort	50
Guest house	30

Third Normal Form (3NF)

Figure 10.14 Example of Third Normal Form (3NF)

comply with 2NF by removing the package-tour name from the original package-tour table and creating a separate linking table with tour ID and the corresponding package-tour name as the attributes. This table then creates a one-to-many relationship with the package-tour table which now does not contain any non-key field dependent entirely on the composite prime key.

10.6.3 Third Normal Form (3NF)

The Third Normal Form (3NF) of a relational database is applicable when and only when the following two conditions are fulfilled by all the tables of the database.

Condition 1: The database has to be in the 2NF. This condition obviously implies that the database is also in 1NF.

Condition 2: Every non-prime attribute of any relation (table) is non-transitively dependent on every prime key (including composite key) of the relation (table).

By transitive dependency, we mean if X is functionally dependent on Y and Y is functionally dependent on Z, then Z is transitively dependent on X via Y. Condition 2 implies that every non-prime attribute of the relation depends on the prime key (including composite key) only and not on any other non-prime key. This means that in the case of 3NF, there cannot be any dependence among the non-prime attributes in any row. Figures 10.14 and 10.15 show two cases of 3NF. Figure 10.14 starts with the same package-tour table in the 2NF shown in Figure 10.13.

The package-tour table in the 2NF contains two non-key attributes, namely capacity and accommodation. However, capacity depends on the accommodation, as can be seen from the table. For example, capacity for hotel accommodation is 40, for resort it is 50 and for guest house it is 30. Hence, the table in 2NF violates the 3NF. However,

Product Table

Product ID	Product Description	UQ	Quantity	Price (₹)	Value (₹)
100	Desktop	No.	50	25,000	1,250,000
101	Laptop	No.	200	35,000	7,000,000
102	Scanner	No.	40	3,000	120,000
103	Laser Printer	No.	50	7,000	350,000

Not in Third Normal Form.
Since Value is depended upon Quantity and Price

↓

Product ID	Product Description	UQ	Quantity	Price (₹)	
100	Desktop	No.	50	25,000	Value =
101	Laptop	No.	200	35,000	Quantity ×
102	Scanner	No.	40	3,000	Price
103	Laser Printer	No.	50	7,000	

Value is not an attribute but can be computed as Quantity × Price

Figure 10.15 Third Normal Form

the package-tour table can be made to comply with the 3NF by removing the capacity attribute and instead making a linking table with accommodation and capacity as the attributes, as shown in Figure 10.14. Now, there is no dependence among the non-key attributes, which are only availability and accommodation. Figure 10.15 shows another relation (table) consisting of product ID, product description, unit of quantity (UQ), quantity, price and value as the attributes for products in a warehouse. It may be noted that in this case, the non-key attribute 'value' is dependent on the other two non-key attributes that are quantity and price and can be derived from those two. Hence, the table is not in 3NF. However, in such cases when a non-key attribute is derived from other non-key attributes, we can remove the same attribute from the table ('value' in this case) and compute its value by the appropriate formula for derivation.

Therefore, we can summarise that the process of normalisation from *1NF* → *2NF* → *3NF* vastly improves the quality of data and also facilitates avoidance of redundant data being stored while maintaining the referential integrity.

10.7 Creating Queries through Structured Query Language (SQL)

SQL, the abbreviated form of Structured Query Language, is not a procedural general-purpose programming language, but it is a small declarative query language focused primarily on working with relational databases and handling queries relating to the data stored in such databases.

SQL is used to select and retrieve or read data from the data tables. It can also create data in the tables, update data tables and delete data from a relational database. All the above operations pertaining to a relational database are known as CRUD, as already mentioned in an earlier paragraph of this chapter.

10.7.1 Creating SQL Queries and the Major SQL Keywords

SELECT: This keyword is used to select and retrieve information from a particular table in the database.

The formats of SELECT query are as follows:

```
SELECT <attribute>
FROM <table>;
SELECT Last name
FROM Employee;
```

The above query will return all the last names of all employees (rows) from the employee table:

```
SELECT last name, first name, Basic pay
FROM Employee;
```

This will return last name, first name and basic pay of all employees from the employee table:

```
SELECT*
FROM Employee;
```

The asterisk (*) after SELECT returns every column from the employee table.

WHERE: This keyword, when applied with the SELECT query, will return values of SELECT columns for those rows when the particular rows fulfil some specified conditions of data in that row. The format of the keyword WHERE is as follows:

```
SELECT Lastname, First name
FROM Employee
WHERE Salary > 30000
```

The above query will return the last name and first name of all the employees from the employee table whose salary exceeds 30,000:

```
SELECT*
FROM Employee
WHERE first name = 'Amar'
```

WHERE clause also allows multiple conditions using AND, OR such as:

```
SELECT*
FROM Employee
WHERE first name = 'Amar' AND Salary > 30000
```

ORDER BY: This will return query results in sorted order (ascending or descending order).

Table 10.3 Employee Table Example

Employee ID	*First Name*	*Last Name*	*Age*	*Salary (₹)*
10	Maya	Mukherjee	56	50,000
11	Ashim	Deb	56	45,000
12	Chitta	Bhadra	32	49,000
13	Ashoke	Basu	32	34,000
14	Soumitra	Dutta	28	25,000

Example: SELECT first name, last name, age, salary

FROM Employee
WHERE Salary > 30,000
ORDER BY Age, last name;

If the employee table is as shown in Table 10.3, the above SQL query will return the following result:

First Name	*Last Name*	*Age*	*Salary*
Ashoke	Basu	32	34000
Chitta	Bhadra	32	49000
Ashim	Deb	56	45000
Maya	Mukherjee	56	50000

The default order is ascending only as in the above example. However, if descending order is desired, then the keyword DESC is to be inserted at the end of the ORDER BY line as follows:

ORDER BY Age, Last Name DESC;

Aggregate Functions: COUNT, MAX, MIN, AVG, SUM and GROUP BY are the keywords used in SQL to get the result of various calculations on a set of data stored in tables. For example, COUNT is an aggregate function that returns a single value which is the aggregation of the number of rows in a table and is used in conjunction with SELECT and/or WHERE;

Example: SELECT COUNT (*)

FROM Employee;

This will return the value 5 since there are 5 employees (rows) in the employee table shown in Table 10.3.

Similarly, the query:

SELECT COUNT (*)
FROM Employee;
WHERE Salary > 34000;

will return the single value 3 since there are three employees (rows) having salary greater than 34,000.

```
SELECT MAX (Salary)
FROM Employee;
```

will return the maximum salary from the employee table, which is 50,000:

```
Similarly SELECT MIN (Salary)
FROM Employee;
```

will return the minimum salary which is 25,000 and

```
SELECT AVG (salary)
FROM Employee;
```

will return the average value of salary of all the rows which in this case is (50,000 + 45,000 + 49,000 + 34,000 + 25,000) / 5 = 40600

```
SELECT SUM (Salary)
FROM Employee;
```

will result in the sum of salaries of all employees (rows) which is (50,000 + 45,000 + 49,000 + 34,000 + 25,000) = 203,000.

Joining Tables: In a relational database, if there are multiple tables, SQL enables us to join columns from two or more different tables. Let us explain with an example shown in Figure 10.16 where there are two tables, namely the employee table and a department table having a one-to-many relationship.

Now, suppose we want to join the two tables such that the columns department name and cost centre code from the Department table are appended to the employee table. The SQL keyword for this is JOIN, and the syntax of the SQL statement is as follows:

```
SELECT First name, Lastname, Age, Salary, Department ID,
Department Name, Cost centre code
FROM Employee JOIN Department ON Employee.
Department ID = Department. Department Id
```

Employee Table

Employee ID	First Name	Last Name	Age	Salary	Depart-ment ID
10	Maya	Mukherjee	56	50000	1
11	Ashim	Deb	56	45000	4
12	Chitta	Bhadra	32	49000	5
13	Ashoke	Basu	32	34000	6
14	Soumitra	Dutta	28	25000	6
15	Subhash	Sen	26	24000	(Null)

Many

Department Table

Depart-ment ID	Department Name	Cost Centre Code
1	Sales	CC01
2	Finance	CC02
3	HR	CC03
4	Purchase	CC04
5	Production	CC05
6	Maintenance	CC06

Figure 10.16 Two Tables Having One-to-Many Relationship

will result in a new table as follows:

Employee ID	*First Name*	*Last Name*	*Age*	*Salary (₹)*	*Department ID*	*Department Name*	*Cost Centre Code*
10	Maya	Mukherjee	56	50,000	1	Sales	CC01
11	Ashim	Deb	56	45,000	4	Purchase	CC04
12	Chitta	Bhadra	32	49,000	5	Production	CC05
13	Ashoke	Basu	32	34,000	6	Maintenance	CC06
14	Soumitra	Dutta	28	25,000	6	Maintenance	CC06

It may be noted that in the above combination of the two tables, only the rows from the two tables having matching Department ID have been joined. For example, in the employee table, the row having Employee ID of 15 has been ignored since it does not have a Department ID value which is (Null). Similarly, from the Department table, the rows pertaining to Department ID 2 (Finance) and 3 (HR) have been ignored since there is no employee in the employee table having Department ID either 2 or 3.

This type of JOIN of two tables is called INNER JOIN, which is the default option of JOIN. However, in the case of joining two tables with all the rows of one of the tables retained after joining, we use the keyword OUTER JOIN. Again, if we want the table name on the left side of the OUTER JOIN to retain all its rows, we use the keyword LEFT OUTER JOIN. Similarly, if we use the keyword RIGHT OUTER JOIN, the joining will retain all the rows of the table name appearing on the right side of the keyword JOIN.

Example:

SELECT First Name, Last Name, Age, Salary, Department ID,
Department Name, cost centre code
FROM Employee LEFT OUTER JOIN Department ON EMPLOYEE.
Department ID = Department. Department ID

will form the following table:

Employee ID	*First Name*	*Last Name*	*Age*	*Salary (₹)*	*Employee Department ID*	*Department Name*	*Cost Centre Code*
10	Maya	Mukherjee	56	50,000	1	Sales	CC01
11	Ashim	Deb	56	45,000	4	Purchase	CC04
12	Chitta	Bhadra	32	49,000	5	Production	CC05
13	Ashoke	Basu	32	34,000	6	Maintenance	CC06
14	Soumitra	Dutta	28	25,000	6	Maintenance	CC06
15	Subhas	Sen	26	24,000	(Null)	(Null)	(Null)

However,

SELECT First name, Lastname, Age, Salary, Department ID,
Department Name, Cost centre code
FROM Employee RIGHT OUTER JOIN Department ON Employee.
Department ID = Department. Department ID

will form the following table:

Employee ID	*First Name*	*Last Name*	*Age*	*Salary (₹)*	*Employee Department ID*	*Department Name*	*Cost Centre Code*
10	Maya	Mukherjee	56	50,000	1	Sales	CC01
(Null)	(Null)	(Null)	(Null)	(Null)	(Null)	Finance	CC02
(Null)	(Null)	(Null)	(Null)	(Null)	(Null)	HR	CC03
11	Ashim	Deb	56	45,000	4	Purchase	CC04
12	Chitta	Bhadra	32	49,000	5	Production	CC05
13	Ashoke	Basu	32	34,000	6	Maintenance	CC06
14	Soumitra	Dutta	28	25,000	6	Maintenance	CC06

INSERT INTO: This keyword creates ('C' of CRUD) new records in a table in a relational database.

Example:

```
INSERT INTO Employee
(Firstname, Lastname, Age, Salary)
VALUES ('Ram', 'Singh', 40, 40000)
```

This will create a new row in the employee table as follows:

Employee ID	*First name*	*Last name*	*Age*	*Salary*
15	Ram	Singh	40	40000

(Auto generated)
UPDATE
SET
WHERE;
updates (changes) a column value for a particular row of a table.

Example:

```
UPDATE Employee
SET Age = 45
WHERE Employee ID = 15
```

Employee ID	*First name*	*Last name*	*Age*	*Salary*
15	Ram	Singh	45	40000

The Age of Employee ID 15 has changed from 40 to 45

DELETE FROM

WHERE:

Deletes an entire row depending upon WHERE Condition.

Example:

DELETE FROM Employee
WHERE EMPLOYEE ID = 15
will delete the entire row pertaining to Employee ID = 15 from the table.

Data Definition Language (DDL): The SQL keywords and the statements explained in the earlier paragraphs such as SELECT, INSERT, UPDATE and DELETE are only examples of data manipulation of an already existing relational database and therefore they form only a part of SQL—data manipulation language known as DML in abbreviated form. DML is not all of SQL as it does not allow us to create a new table or to alter the structure of an existing table. Further, DML does not control the access permissions for the users of a database. Therefore, there are two more languages other than DML known in SQL as data definition language (DDL) and data control language (DCL). DDL has three keywords which are CREATE, ALTER and DROP and these keywords allow us to create a new table or change the structure of a data table or delete a complete table.

Examples:

CREATE Employee
(Employee ID INTEGER PRIMARY KEY,
First name VARCHAR (30) NOT NULL,
Last Name VARCHAR (30) NOT NULL,
Age INTEGER
Salary INTEGER
);

This will create the structure of a table named Employee with Employee ID as an integer and the primary key, First Name and Last Name as the columns of variable characters not exceeding 30 and not null (blank), Age as an integer field or column and Salary as another integer column for the salary of an employee. It may be noted that CREATE only creates the structure of the table named Employee but the table remains blank until data are filled in by the INSERT statement described earlier as DML.

ALTER TABLE Employee
ADD Department VARCHAR (20);

This will add a new column Department which is a data type of variable length character not exceeding 20 characters.

DROP TABLE Employee will delete the entire Employee table.

Data Control Keywords: The two keywords for data control in SQL are GRANT and REVOKE for granting permission and revoking permission to users of the database. However, such keywords are part of the access control of the operating system, which is

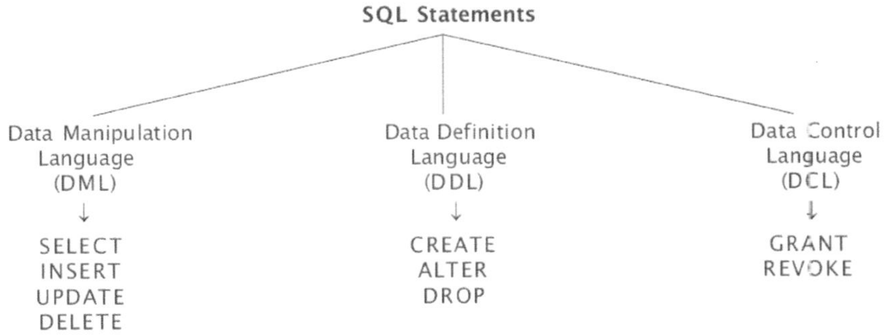

Figure 10.17 SQL Statement Types

a part of the DBMS. The above-mentioned three types of SQL have been schematically shown in Figure 10.17.

10.8 Database and DBMS

A database is the repository of data of an organisation in storage devices. For example, a company may have one integrated database storing all the corporate data, or it may like to have separate databases—one for its customer data, one for all employee data, one for product data and so on. Accordingly, the databases may be named Customer, Employee and Product. Depending upon the type of data and the arrangement of the data elements or items in a database, we can have various types of databases such as hierarchical, network, relational databases, as already described in the earlier paragraphs of this chapter. Besides, there are other types of databases such as HBase, MongoDB and Couchbase, all of which belong to a more recent type of database containing structured, semi-structured and unstructured data, known as NoSQL databases, which have been discussed in a subsequent paragraph.

DBMS, on the other hand, is software that manages the organisational databases. Data definition, data manipulation and data control are all taken care of by the DBMS. One DBMS can manage one or more types of databases. This concept of database and DBMS is shown in Figure 10.18.

A DBMS performs the following tasks relating to a database:

1. Organises the data in a database according to the data definition language.
2. Integrates data in a database to rule out duplication.
3. Filters data according to the needs of the application programmers or users.
4. Controls data storage and retrieval for the application programmers or users.
5. Protects valuable data against unauthorised access, physical damage due to system failure, interruptions and simultaneous updating.

There are various types of DBMS available today, and the popular ones have been shown in Figure 10.19.

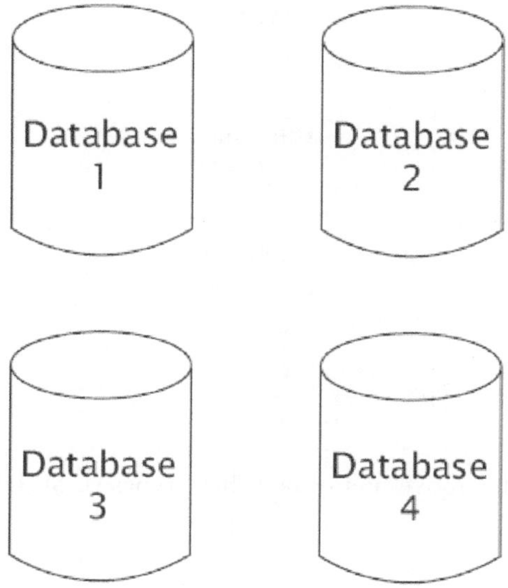

Figure 10.18 DBMS Software for Databases

Hierarchical	Network	Relational	NOSQL
DBMS	DBMS	DBMS Examples: -ORACLE -SQL Server -DB 2 -MYSQL -PostgreSQL -SQLITE -MS ACCESS (with GUI)	DBMS - Cassendra -Couch base -Mongo base -H base

Figure 10.19 Types of DBMS

The selection of a DBMS depends upon multiple factors. The more important ones are as follows:

1. Nature of data—structured, unstructured or semi-structured data: Structured data are those where attributes of the data entities are fixed such as employee data. Unstructured data are those where the attributes of the data change and there may be a variety of data types such as text, integer, image and float in the same field. In other words, in the case of unstructured data, there is no predefined schema as is the case with structured data. Semi-structured data fall within these two extremes, that is, they have a mix of fixed and flexible schema.
2. Ease of updating database.
3. Volume of the database.
4. Data accuracy.
5. Data integrity and privacy.
6. Data redundancy.
7. Data is critical and any business organisation cannot afford to lose any data. By far the relational DBMS is the most common and widely used DBMS because the principles of RDBMS facilitate understanding of the other database systems.

10.9 NoSQL Database Systems

Recently, NoSQL database systems have been developed mostly by big web players, such as Amazon and Google, to cater to the needs of databases for web-scale data which are characterised by volume, variety, velocity—the Vs of big data that have been explained in Chapter 13 of this book. NoSQL databases, unlike the SQL relational databases, deal with voluminous data (magnitude of the order of terabytes or petabytes) of variety, having not only structured data but also semi-structured data consisting of characters, strings, numbers, dates, times and images. Furthermore, they cater to data generated at very high velocity which is known as 'streaming data'. 'NoSQL' stands for 'not only SQL' and they are different from the relational databases which have structured data in the form of tables of rows and columns with fixed schema. NoSQL databases are mostly schema-less and have flexibility in storing a variety of data of semi-structured type such as the log files of users associated with various web applications. Further, most of the NoSQL products belong to the open-source community. Although NoSQL databases can store relational data, they have been designed really for non-relational data with no structure or with semi-structure.

Another important characteristic of NoSQL databases is their high scalability which implies that they can be distributed or partitioned on various physical storages automatically to scale very high volumes of data such as terabytes (10^{12} bytes) or even petabytes (10^{15} bytes). Because of the non-relational and high scalability of the NoSQL database, they lose the transactional consistency of the data stored. In other words, unlike RDBMS, the NoSQL data, because of being scaled, can be in an inconsistent state. Table 10.4 shows a comparison of a SQL and a NoSQL database.

10.10 Categories of NoSQL Databases

There are about 150 categories of NoSQL databases available as of now. However, those can be broadly grouped under five major heads: document store, key-value store (volatile

Table 10.4 A Comparison of SQL And NoSQL Database

SQL Database	*NoSQL Database*
1. Relational database.	1. Non-relational database.
2. Structured data.	2. Usually, semi-structured or unstructured data.
3. Data stored as tables of rows and columns consisting of text, integer, float, currency and date.	3. Data stored as documents (word document or PDF), wide columns, graphs structured with interconnected nodes and the data consist of text, integer, float, currency, date, sensor data and image also.
4. Fixed schema.	4. Flexible schema.
5. Transactional consistency.	5. Inconsistency due to high scalability.
6. No scalability because of volume of data not high.	6. High scalability due to high volume of data.
7. Volume of data is not very high. Usually consists of tables having few thousands or few millions of rows.	7. High volume of data of the order of terabytes or petabytes.
8. Not usually open-source databases.	8. Open-source databases.
9. Availability is high when data volume is not high.	9. High availability with high volume of data.
10. SQL database systems are compatible systems.	10. NoSQL databases are of different types.

or persistent), wide column store, graph store and object databases. The five heads and the subheads within them with popular examples have been shown in Figure 10.20.

10.10.1 Distinctive Features of NoSQL Database Categories

10.10.1.1 Document Store

In this type of NoSQL database, the database integrates documents which are structured typically as JSON objects. The documents have unique IDs and are schema-less. Documents again have fields having field names and values (data as text, numbers, dates and so on). However, pictures (images) can be attached to any field of a document as binary files. Data retrieval specifying search criteria is also possible. Similarly, querying and retrieving of images from documents of the database are possible.

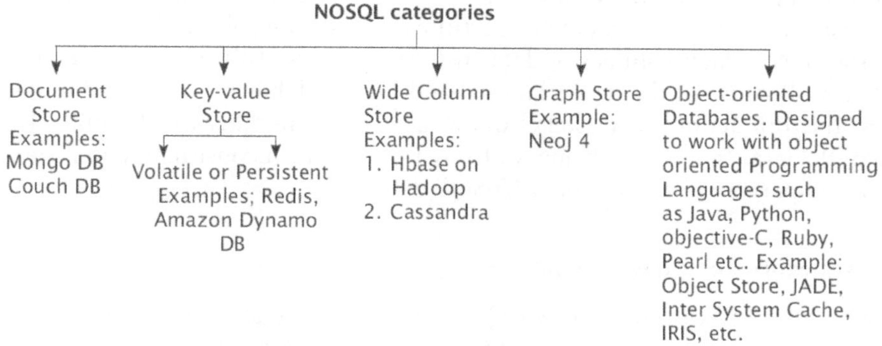

Figure 10.20 Categories of NoSQL Databases

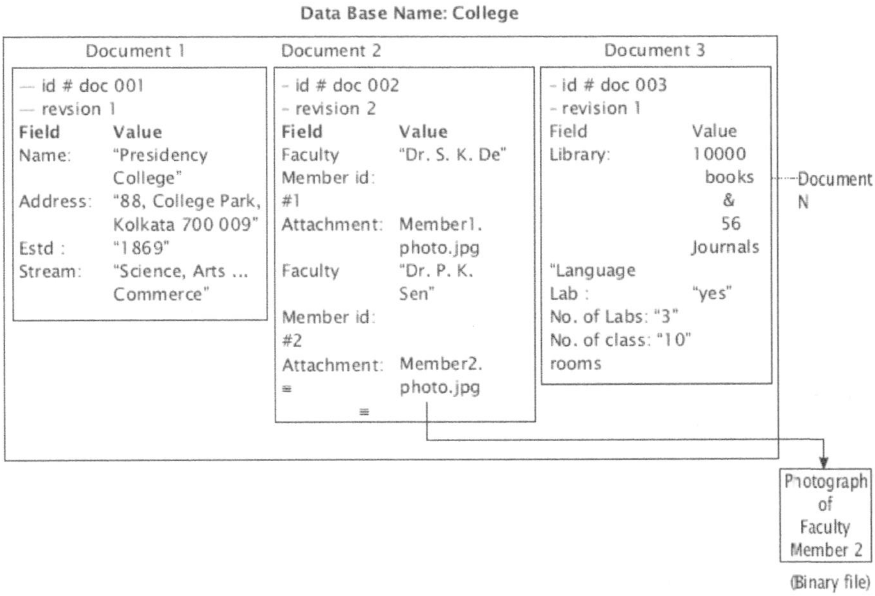

Figure 10.21 Document Database of a College

Figure 10.21 shows a schematic diagram of a document database for a college. The college database as shown in Figure 10.21 is document oriented and has a number of documents. Each document is identified by a document ID which is generated as a hash by the DBMS and has a revision number which shows the number of revisions the particular document has undergone since its creation as a document.

Each document having a structured format such as JSON or XML has fields, each of which has a name and a value as shown in Figure 10.21. Attachments of pictures (images) can be there with any field, and the attachments generally are in the form of binary files. Each document has its unique structure.

MongoDB and CouchDB are two very popular document-store DBMS. It is possible to query a document by its fields.

10.10.1.2 Key-Value Store

Key/value NoSQL databases have keys and corresponding values. They are basically hash tables. Key/value databases accept queries based on the key only. NoSQL databases of this type have just keys and values and are totally schema-less. A key/value database consists of a number of key-value pairs where the key is the name and the value the content of an item of data. Table 10.5 shows an example of a key-value store. Key-value stores can be volatile in memory or persistent on storage.

10.10.1.3 Wide Column Store

A wide column store is another type of NoSQL database which has tables of rows and columns similar to a relational database, but the names and formats of the columns are flexible, unlike a relational database and can vary from row to row in the same table.

Table 10.5 Key/Value Database Consisting of Key/Value. 'Redis' and 'Amazon Dynamo' Are Examples of Key/Value Database

Key	*Value*
Name	John Smith
Age	23
Colour	White
City	Phoenix
Sex	Male

Table 10.6 Wide Column Employee Table Showing Column Families

Row#	*Column Family 1*	*Column Family 2*
101	Name Age Address Shyamal Bose 43 143J. Street	Department Salary ₹ Sales 40000
102	L Name F Name Tel. No. Biswas Ashoke 9433112181	DOB DOJ Salary₹ 30.11.59 01.02.16 30000
103	Name Age email S. Basu 44 sbasu@gmail.com	DOJ Department 03.03.10 Finance

Column spaces may and can vary from row to row in the same table. Column spaces may be empty also, and hence the wide column store is a sparse column set database. Wide column databases are also called 'schema light' as the columns have a flexible schema as explained earlier. Wide column databases are named after Google 'Bigtable' implementation. Only wide column databases have column families having various cells which vary from row to row. Table 10.6 is a schematic representation of a wide column database with column families relating to the employee table. Cassandra and HBase with Hadoop are examples of wide column databases. HBase tables are created through HBase shell running on the Hadoop shell.

10.10.1.4 Graph Store

A graph database is a database which consists of graph-oriented data structures. It consists of data as nodes having names and properties and connected among themselves through relationships with or without properties.

A simple graph model is as follows:

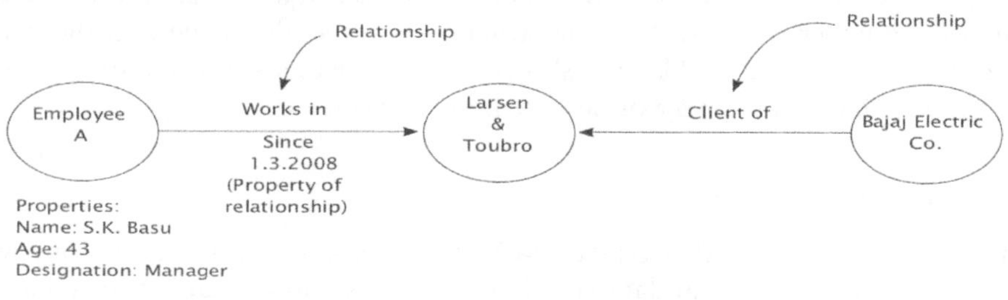

The above is a directed graph as all the relations have a specific direction. There can also be graphs where the edges (relations) do not have specific directions, as shown as follows:

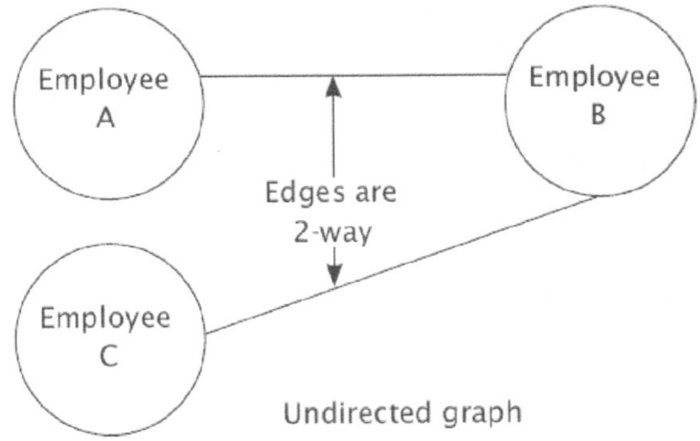

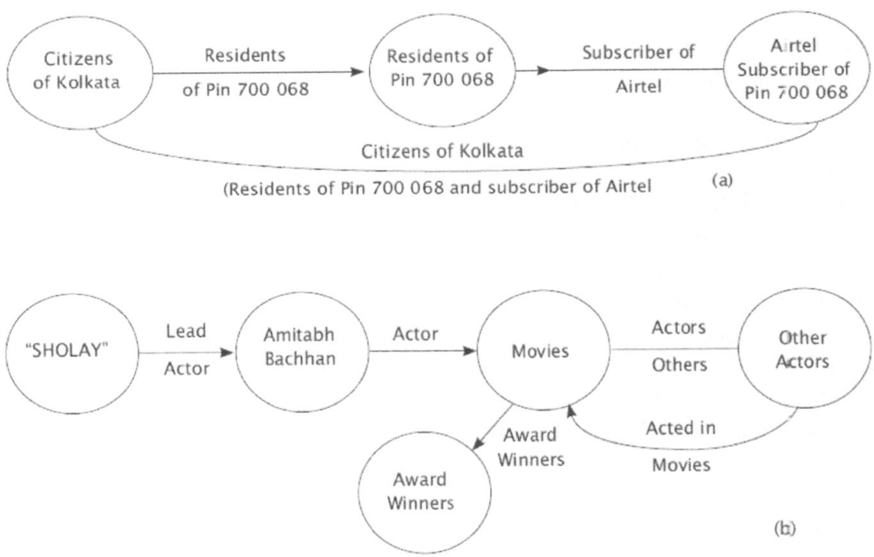

Figure 10.22 Graph Database

The advantage of graph databases over relational databases is the fast retrieval with complex queries and searches involving more than one level of data hierarchy. Moreover, the fast response for queries is facilitated in the case of graph databases by way of recursive searches as shown in Figures 10.22(a) and 10.22(b).

It may be noted that in Figure 10.22(a), a query about the list of citizens of Kolkata who reside in an area having pin 700068 and who are subscribers of Airtel is replied to in a single recursive search which first finds the link from the 'Citizens of Kolkata' node to the 'Residents of Pin 700068' node, which further finds its links to the 'subscribers of Airtel' node and finally through back (recursive) links to the 'Citizens of Kolkata' node.

Similarly, Figure 10.22(b) handles a query, which are the award-winning movies, in which actors other than the lead actor of the film '*Sholay*' acted? The query is replied to through links in the graph database shown in the same figure.

A graph database stores data, where connected data (nodes) are directly linked together without any index or join table with foreign keys, as in the case of a relational database. A typical graph database is Neo4j.

The other advantages of graph databases over relational databases lie in their scalability, schema-less design, efficient storage of semi-structured information, and fast deep traversal instead of slow SQL queries that require many table joins. Moreover, graph databases such as Neo4j support ACID transactions with rollbacks.

It is very easy to represent connected data and relationships through graph databases. The traversal rate for Neo4j is about 4 million nodes per second.

10.11 Case Study: Mongo Data Base

10.11.1 Background

Craigslist Inc. is a popular American classified advertisement website with sections devoted to jobs, housing for sale, items wanted, community and other services. It also serves as a discussion forum in English, French, German, Dutch, Spanish, Italian and Portuguese. Craigslist was established in 1955 and incorporated in 1999 with its headquarters located in San Francisco, USA. The Craig network presently serves 570 cities in 70 countries including India and posts about 1.5 million classified advertisements every day.

Initially, Craigslist stored its data records and information in a MySQL cluster, but with the massive increase of classified advertisements, Craigslist found it extremely difficult to manage billions of records due to a lack of flexibility and data management costs associated with MySQL.

Solution: In order to archive billions of records in many different formats and to query and report on those archives at runtime, Craigslist in the year 2011, transferred more than two billion documents to the MongoDB data store for its scalability and flexible schema. The original Craigslist archive application copied the existing live database data to the archive system. However, using a relational database system not only restricted flexibility but also caused considerable delay because changes in the database schema needed to be incorporated into the system archive. While making amendments to billions of rows in their MySQL cluster, Craigslist could not move data to the archive and consequently archive-ready data used to pile up in the production database. As a result, the performance of the live database deteriorated.

In order to prevent further barriers to the growth of the company and to serve the customers who used to post classified advertisements, Craigslist decided to go for MongoDB. The reason is that MongoDB, because of its sharding capability, provides built-in scalability. Sharding is the process of storing data records across more than one machine in order to cater to the demand of data growth. This is also called horizontal scalability. Each post of advertisement and its metadata can be stored as a single document. Further, as the schema changes on the live database, MongoDB can accommodate these changes without costly schema migrations.

Craigslist used auto-sharding across commodity hardware and deployed the same initially to hold over 5 billion documents of size 2 KB each and the corresponding 10 terabytes (TB) of data. The cluster topology comprises 3-machine replica sets, with each set serving a shard of the Craigslist archive database cluster. The configuration is three replica sets in each collocation centre to handle initial build up.

10.11.2 *Benefits Accrued to Craigslist for Switching Over to MongoDB*

Craigslist can put data into MongoDB faster than getting the same data out of MySQL during the migration. Moreover, MongoDB concepts and features are similar in many respects to relational databases, and the transition to MongoDB was a seamless one.

Review Questions

1. What is a database? What are the typical forms of database models?
2. What is a DBMS? Is MySQL a database?
3. What is a relational database? Explain with examples 'primary keys', 'foreign keys' and 'composite keys'.
4. What are 'schemas' and 'sub-schemas'?
5. What are 'ACID' transactions?
6. What are the different kinds of relationships in a relational database? What do you understand by 'Referential integrity'?
7. What is normalisation? What are the first, second and third normal forms?
8. What are 'data definition language', 'data manipulation language' and 'data control language'?
9. What is SQL? Which of the following is not a valid SQL query?
    a. SELECT * FROM Employee WHERE Salary > 50,000
    b. SELECT * FROM Employee WHERE salary > 40,000
    c. SELECT * FROM Employee WHERE department = 'Finance'
10. What are NoSQL databases? What are their important features? What are the advantages of NoSQL databases?
11. Explain the different types of NoSQL databases.

Bibliography

Date, C. J. *An Introduction to Database Systems*, 8th ed. Beijing: Pearson Education Asia, 2004.

Harrison, G. *Next Generation Databases—NoSQL and Big Data*, 1st ed. New York, NY: Apress, 2015.

Martin, J. *Principles of Database Management Systems*. New Delhi: Prentice Hall of India, 1985.

Perkins, Luc., E. Redmont, and J. R. Wilson. *Seven Databases in Seven Weeks: A Guide to Modern Databases and the NoSQL Movement*, 2nd ed. Raleigh, NC: The Pragmatic Programmers, LLC, 2018.

Vaish, G. *Getting Started with NoSQL*, 1st ed. Birmingham: Packt Publishing, 2013.

11 Computer-Based Management Information Systems

11.1 Introduction

MIS developers have made extensive use of application software to develop various models of MIS in typical Indian organisations. The models can be broadly classified into broad groups, based on the type of software adopted by the developers, as follows:

1. Models based on spreadsheets such as Microsoft Excel various versions;
2. Models based on optimisation techniques such as Operations Research (OR) models developed on computer;
3. Models based on computerised database;
4. Models based on web design and the internet.

In the following paragraphs, a few models of MIS of the above-mentioned types have been discussed.

11.2 Spreadsheet Models

11.2.1 Model 1 (Finished Inventory Analysis System)

Many of the benefits of inventory of finished products analysis software arise from the analysis of finished products in hand, manufacturing cycle time and profit margin of the products. For example, this particular model pertains to M/s ABC, which manufactures and sells a variety of sprockets for various types of customers such as manufacturers of bicycles, power-driven two-wheelers and other power transmission equipment. ABC Company used to maintain the inventory holding of finished sprockets of various nomenclatures on a computer spreadsheet, and the status as on 31 March 2025 is as shown in Table 11.1. However, Mr X, the managing director of the company, felt that information furnished in this form does not facilitate proper decision-making for production planning, since each type of sprocket consumes manufacturing time which was a resource constraint, and further each type of sprocket fetches different profit margins. Mr X, therefore, felt the necessity to redesign the spreadsheet by introducing additional columns which would make the spreadsheet an important MIS and accordingly instructed the MIS department of the company. A new spreadsheet was developed with additional columns as shown in Table 11.2. The formulae for the additional columns of the finished inventory analysis spreadsheet are shown in Table 11.3.

DOI: 10.4324/9781003509714-11

Table 11.1 Inventory Holding as on 31.03.2025 of ABC Manufacturing Co.

ABC Sprocket Manufacturing Co. Pvt Ltd						
Item Code	*Nomenclature*	*Unit Cost (₹)*	*Unit Price (₹)*	*Stock in Hand*	*Units Sold in 2024–25*	*Manufacturing Cycle Time in Minutes*
SP 1001	6 mm bore 21 mm OD 9 teeth	69	94	50	450	8
SP 1002	6 mm bore 23 mm OD 10 teeth	81	101	53	490	9
SP 1003	6 mm bore 32 mm OD 14 teeth	110	139	48	144	13
SP 1004	6 mm bore 40 mm OD 18 teeth	135	174	20	170	17
SP 1005	6 mm bore 50 mm OD 23 teeth	160	226	54	500	19
SP 2001	10 mm bore 60 mm OD 18 teeth	165	215	71	466	20
SP 2002	10 mm bore 78 mm OD 24 teeth	250	310	36	276	28
SP 2003	12 mm bore 84 mm OD 26 teeth	260	349	67	280	30
SP 2004	12 mm bore 87 mm OD 27 teeth	280	371	44	220	32
SP 2005	12 mm bore 90 mm OD 28 teeth	301	379	25	156	35
SP 2006	12 mm bore 96 mm OD 30 teeth	320	425	20	100	37
SP 3001	16 mm bore 72 mm OD 16 teeth	257	342	46	138	31
SP 3002	16 mm bore 73 mm OD 18 teeth	287	383	28	86	35
SP 3003	16 mm bore 74 mm OD 20 teeth	310	413	10	80	36
SP 3004	16 mm bore 76 mm OD 22 teeth	370	490	20	240	43
SP 3005	18 mm bore 78 mm OD 24 teeth	409	536	11	88	49
SP 3006	18 mm bore 80 mm OD 26 teeth	580	779	8	8	67
SP 4001	18 mm bore 82 mm OD 28 teeth	155	200	37	148	18
SP 4002	18 mm bore 83 mm OD 30 teeth	200	263	61	183	23
SP 4003	18 mm bore 84 mm OD 32 teeth	300	344	27	80	35
SP 4004	20 mm bore 88 mm OD 34 teeth	370	486	22	88	43
SP 4005	20 mm bore 89 mm OD 36 teeth	475	641	17	68	55
SP 4006	20 mm bore 90 mm OD 38 teeth	530	720	15	60	60
SP 4007	20 mm bore 91 mm OD 40 teeth	730	985	80	180	80
SP 5001	20 mm bore 93 mm OD 42 teeth	402	550	20	68	46
SP 5002	22 mm bore 94 mm OD 44 teeth	422	562	23	92	48
SP 5003	22 mm bore 95 mm OD 46 teeth	464	619	24	80	53
SP 5004	22 mm bore 96 mm OD 48 teeth	473	631	25	75	55
SP 6001	22 mm bore 97 mm OD 50 teeth	350	463	20	46	40
SP 6002	22 mm bore 98 mm OD 52 teeth	400	528	19	88	45
SP 6003	22 mm bore 99 mm OD 54 teeth	450	598	18	72	51

Finally, for the purpose of decision-making, a spreadsheet was developed by sorting the spreadsheet of Table 11.2 in descending order of gross profit per unit of manufacturing cycle time as the major column and within that stock-in-hand in days of sales as the minor column. The final spreadsheet developed in the above way is shown in Table 11.4.

11.2.2 Model 2 (Financial Feasibility Analysis)

This model pertains to a cost–benefit analysis using the net present value method through spreadsheet. The model was adopted by M/s PQR Forklift Truck Manufacturing

Table 11.2 Additional Columns for Analysis of Stock in Hand as on 31.03.2025 of ABC Manufacturing Co.

ABC Sprocket Manufacturing Co. Pvt Ltd

Item Code	*Nomenclature*	*Annual Sales 2024–25 (₹)*	*Cost of Units Sold 2024–25 (₹)*	*Annual Gross Profit 2024–25 (₹)*	*Cost of Stock in Hand (₹)*	*Gross Margin 2024–25*	*Margin on Cost 2024–25*	*Stock in Hand (Days of Sales)*	*Gross Profit/ Manufacture Cycle Time in Minutes*
SP 1001	6 mm bore 21 mm OD 9 teeth	42,300	31,050	11,250	3,450	0.27	0.36	33.33	3.13
SP 1002	6 mm bore 23 mm OD 10 teeth	49,490	39,690	9,800	4,293	0.20	0.25	32.45	2.22
SP 1003	6 mm bore 32 mm OD 14 teeth	20,016	15,840	4,176	5,280	0.21	0.26	100	2.23
SP 1004	6 mm bore 40 mm OD 18 teeth	29,580	22,950	6,630	2,700	0.22	0.29	35.29	2.29
SP 1005	6 mm bore 50 mm OD 23 teeth	113,000	80,000	33,000	8,640	0.29	0.41	32.40	3.47
SP 2001	10 mm bore 60 mm OD 18 teeth	100,190	76,890	23,300	11,715	0.23	0.30	45.71	2.50
SP 2002	10 mm bore 78 mm OD 24 teeth	85,560	69,000	16,560	9,000	0.19	0.24	39.13	2.14
SP 2003	12 mm bore 84 mm OD 26 teeth	97,720	72,800	24,920	17,420	0.26	0.34	71.79	2.97
SP 2004	12 mm bore 87 mm OD 27 teeth	81,620	61,600	20,020	12,320	0.25	0.33	60.00	2.84
SP 2005	12 mm bore 90 mm OD 28 teeth	59,124	46,956	12,168	7,525	0.21	0.26	48.08	2.23
SP 2006	12 mm bore 96 mm OD 30 teeth	42,500	32,000	10,500	6,400	0.25	0.33	60.00	2.84
SP 3001	16 mm bore 72 mm OD 16 teeth	47,196	35,466	11,730	11,822	0.25	0.33	100.00	2.74
SP 3002	16 mm bore 73 mm OD 18 teeth	32,938	24,682	8,256	8,036	0.25	0.33	97.67	2.74

(Continued)

Table 11.2 (Continued)

ABC Sprocket Manufacturing Co. Pvt Ltd

Item Code	*Nomenclature*	*Annual Sales 2024–25 (₹)*	*Cost of Units Sold 2024–25 (₹)*	*Annual Gross Profit 2024–25 (₹)*	*Cost of Stock in Hand (₹)*	*Gross Margin 2024–25*	*Margin on Cost 2024–25*	*Stock in Hand (Days of Sales)*	*Gross Profit/ Manufacture Cycle Time in Minutes*
SP 3003	16 mm bore 74 mm OD 20 teeth	33,040	24,800	8,240	3,100	0.25	0.33	37.50	2.86
SP 3004	16 mm bore 76 mm OD 22 teeth	117,600	88,800	28,800	7,400	0.24	0.32	25.00	2.79
SP 3005	18 mm bore 78 mm OD 24 teeth	47,168	35,992	11,176	4,499	0.24	0.31	37.50	2.59
SP 3006	18 mm bore 80 mm OD 26 teeth	6,232	4,640	1,592	4,640	0.26	0.34	300.00	2.97
SP 4001	18 mm bore 82 mm OD 28 teeth	29,600	22,940	6,660	5,735	0.23	0.29	75.00	2.50
SP 4002	18 mm bore 83 mm OD 30 teeth	48,129	36,600	11,529	12,200	0.24	0.32	100.00	2.74
SP 4003	18 mm bore 84 mm OD 32 teeth	27,520	24,000	3,520	8,100	0.13	0.15	101.25	1.26
SP 4004	20 mm bore 88 mm OD 34 teeth	42,768	32,560	10,208	8,140	0.24	0.31	75.00	2.70
SP 4005	20 mm bore 89 mm OD 36 teeth	43,588	32,300	11,288	8,075	0.26	0.35	75.00	3.02
SP 4006	20 mm bore 90 mm OD 38 teeth	43,200	31,800	11,400	7,950	0.26	0.36	75.00	3.17
SP 4007	20 mm bore 91 mm OD 40 teeth	177,300	131,400	45,900	58,400	0.26	0.35	133.33	3.19
SP 5001	20 mm bore 93 mm OD 42 teeth	37,400	27,336	10,064	8,040	0.27	0.37	88.24	3.22
SP 5002	22 mm bore 94 mm OD 44 teeth	51,704	38,824	12,880	9.706	0.25	0.33	75.00	2.92
SP 5003	22 mm bore 95 mm OD 46 teeth	49,520	37,120	12,400	11,136	0.25	0.33	90.00	2.92

(*Continued*)

Table 11.2 (Continued)

ABC Sprocket Manufacturing Co. Pvt Ltd									
Item Code	*Nomenclature*	*Annual Sales 2024–25 (₹)*	*Cost of Units Sold 2024–25 (₹)*	*Annual Gross Profit 2024–25 (₹)*	*Cost of Stock in Hand (₹)*	*Gross Margin 2024–25*	*Margin on Cost 2024–25*	*Stock in Hand (Days of Sales)*	*Gross Profit/ Manufacture Cycle Time in Minutes*
SP 5004	22 mm bore 96 mm OD 48 teeth	47,325	35,475	11,850	11,825	0.25	0.33	100.00	2.87
SP 6001	22 mm bore 97 mm OD 50 teeth	21,298	16,100	5,198	7,000	0.24	0.32	130.43	2.83
SP 6002	22 mm bore 98 mm OD 52 teeth	46,464	35,200	11,264	7,600	0.24	0.32	64.77	2.84
SP 6003	22 mm bore 99 mm OD 54 teeth	43,056	32,400	10,656	8,100	0.25	0.33	75.00	2.90

Table 11.3 Finished Inventory Analysis Worksheet Formulae

Column Heading	*Formula Used to Calculate*
Annual gross profit	= (Annual sales) – (Cost of goods sold)
Annual sales	= Unit sales price × units sold in the year
Cost of stock-in-hand	= Unit cost × Stock-in-hand
Gross margin	= (Annual gross profit) / (Annual sales in units)
Margin on cost	= (Unit price – Unit cost) / (Unit cost)
Stock-in-hand in terms of number of days of sales	= (300 × Stock-in-hand) / (Annual sales in units)
Gross profit earned per unit of machining cycle time	= (Annual gross profit) / (Units sold in year × Machining cycle time)

Note: 300 working days in the year have been considered.

Company located in a metro city, manufacturing different capacity forklift trucks for material-handling purposes. The management of the company decided to install a shop floor job-tracking software package since the present manual system of job tracking was considered to be inefficient, time-consuming and costly. Many of the tangible benefits of job tracking software arise from the automation of manufacturing and other allied business processes.

Further, the tracking software has in-built statistical quality control features. However, there are tangible costs associated with such automation apart from the one-time cost of the software package, the necessary hardware required for the same and the recurring maintenance cost of the hardware, as well as the software. Management of the company assessed the tangible benefits recurring annually, as shown in Table 11.5. The one-time costs and the recurring costs assessed are shown in Tables 11.6 and 11.7 respectively. The cost–benefit analysis performed on the spreadsheet is shown in Table 11.8. The recurring costs and benefits have been discounted to their present value. The recurring costs and benefits at various future years have been multiplied by the corresponding present value factor (PVF) given as:

$$(PVF)_N = 1/(1+i)^N \tag{11.1}$$

where i is the discount rate and N is the year.

The net present value of all benefits or costs is obtained by the summation of all benefits or costs of all years, including the current year; accordingly, the formulae have been applied in the worksheet's appropriate cells. The overall net present value is the difference between the net present value of all benefits and the net present value of all costs. In order to make the model flexible with regard to various discount rates, the same has been used as a variable in the formulae of present value of recurring costs and benefits. The discount rate can be changed, and all the formulae referencing this value will automatically recalculate the values for analysis. In Table 11.8, with a discount rate of 0.14, the overall net present value calculates to ₹684.37 lakhs and the break-even point (the point at which the net present value of benefits equals the net present value of costs) appears somewhere in the third year. The internal rate of return (IRR) is the discounting rate at which the net present value of all benefits becomes exactly equal to the net present value

Table 11.4 Items Arranged in Descending Order of Gross Profit Per Unit of Manufacturing Cycle Time

ABC Sprocket Manufacturing Co. Pvt Ltd

Item Code	*Nomenclature*	*Annual Sales 2024–25 (₹)*	*Cost of Units Sold 2024–25 (₹)*	*Annual Gross Profit 2024–25 (₹)*	*Cost of Stock in Hand (₹)*	*Gross Margin 2024–25*	*Margin on Cost 2024–25*	*Stock in Hand (Days of Sales)*	*Gross Profit/ Manufacture Cycle Time in Minutes*
SP 1005	6 mm bore 50 mm OD 23 teeth	113,000	80,000	33,000	8,640	0.29	0.41	32.40	3.47
SP 5001	20 mm bore 93 mm OD 42 teeth	37,400	27,336	10,064	8,040	0.27	0.37	88.24	3.22
SP 4007	20 mm bore 91 mm OD 40 teeth	177,300	131,400	45,900	58,400	0.26	0.35	133.33	3.19
SP 4006	20 mm bore 90 mm OD 38 teeth	43,200	31,800	11,400	7,950	0.26	0.36	75.00	3.17
SP 1001	6mm bore 21 mm OD 9 teeth	42,300	31,050	11,250	3,450	0.27	0.36	33.33	3.13
SP 4005	20 mm bore 89 mm OD 36 teeth	43,588	32,300	11,288	8,075	0.26	0.35	75.00	3.02
SP 3006	18 mm bore 80 mm OD 26 teeth	6,232	4,640	1,592	4,640	0.26	0.34	300.00	2.97
SP 2003	12 mm bore 84 mm OD 26 teeth	97,720	72,800	24,920	17,420	0.26	0.34	71.79	2.97
SP 5003	22 mm bore 95 mm OD 46 teeth	49,520	37,120	12,400	11,136	0.25	0.33	90.00	2.92
SP 5002	22 mm bore 94 mm OD 44 teeth	51,704	38,824	12,880	9.706	0.25	0.33	75.00	2.92
SP 6003	22 mm bore 99 mm OD 54 teeth	43,056	32,400	10,656	8,100	0.25	0.33	75.00	2.90
SP 5004	22 mm bore 96 mm OD 48 teeth	47,325	35,475	11,850	11,825	0.25	0.33	100.00	2.87
SP 3003	16 mm bore 74 mm OD 20 teeth	33,040	24,800	8,240	3,100	0.25	0.33	37.50	2.86

(Continued)

Table 11.3 (Continued)

ABC Sprocket Manufacturing Co. Pvt Ltd									
Item Code	*Nomenclature*	*Annual Sales 2024–25 (₹)*	*Cost of Units Sold 2024–25 (₹)*	*Annual Gross Profit 2024–25 (₹)*	*Cost of Stock in Hand (₹)*	*Gross Margin 2024–25*	*Margin on Cost 2024–25*	*Stock in Hand (Days of Sales)*	*Gross Profit/ Manufacture Cycle Time in Minutes*
SP 6002	22 mm bore 98 mm OD 52 teeth	46,464	35,200	11,264	7,600	0.24	0.32	64.77	2.84
SP 2004	12 mm bore 87 mm OD 27 teeth	81,620	61,600	20,020	12,320	0.25	0.33	60.00	2.84
SP 2006	12 mm bore 96 mm OD 30 teeth	42,500	32,000	10,500	6,400	0.25	0.33	60.00	2.84
SP 6001	22 mm bore 97 mm OD 50 teeth	21,298	16,100	5,198	7,000	0,24	0.32	130.43	2.83
SP 3004	16 mm bore 76 mm OD 22 teeth	117,600	88,800	28,800	7,400	0.24	0.32	25.00	2.79
SP 3004	16 mm bore 76 mm OD 22 teeth	117,600	88,800	28,800	7,400	0.24	0.32	25.00	2.79
SP 3001	16 mm bore 72 mm OD 16 teeth	47,196	35,466	11,730	11,822	0.25	0.33	100.00	2.74
SP 4002	18 mm bore 83 mm OD 30 teeth	48,129	36,600	11,529	12,200	0.24	0.32	100.00	2.74
SP 4004	20 mm bore 88 mm OD 34 teeth	42,768	32,560	10,208	8,140	0.24	0.31	75.00	2.70
SP 3005	18 mm bore 78 mm OD 24 teeth	47,168	35,992	11,176	4,499	0.24	0.31	37.50	2.59
SP 2001	10 mm bore 60 mm OD 18 teeth	100,190	76,890	23,300	11,715	0.23	0.30	45.71	2.50
SP 4001	18 mm bore 82 mm OD 28 teeth	29,600	22,940	6,660	5,735	0.23	0.29	75.00	2.50
SP 1004	6mm bore 40 mm OD 18 teeth	29,580	22,950	6,630	2,700	0.22	0.29	35.29	2.29
SP 1003	6mm bore 32 mm OD 14 teeth	20,016	15,840	4,176	5,280	0.21	0.26	100	2.23

(Continued)

Table 11.3 (Continued)

ABC Sprocket Manufacturing Co. Pvt Ltd

Item Code	*Nomenclature*	*Annual Sales 2024–25 (₹)*	*Cost of Units Sold 2024–25 (₹)*	*Annual Gross Profit 2024–25 (₹)*	*Cost of Stock in Hand (₹)*	*Gross Margin 2024–25*	*Margin on Cost 2024–25*	*Stock in Hand (Days of Sales)*	*Gross Profit/ Manufacture Cycle Time in Minutes*
SP 2005	12 mm bore 90 mm OD 28 teeth	59,124	46,956	12,168	7,525	0.21	0.26	48.08	2.23
SP 1002	6mm bore 23 mm OD 10 teeth	49,490	39,690	9,800	4,293	0.20	0.25	32.45	2.22
SP 2002	10 mm bore 78 mm OD 24 teeth	85,560	69,000	16,560	9,000	0.19	0.24	39.13	2.14
SP 4003	18 mm bore 84 mm OD 32 teeth	27,520	24,000	3,520	8,100	0.13	0.15	101.25	1.26

Table 11.5 Annual Recurring Benefits of Proposed Shop Floor Job Tracking Software

Recurring Benefits Arising Out of	*Approximate Value (₹ Lakhs)*
Increase in productivity	300
Reduction in work-in-process	25
Reduction of scrap and waste	40
Reduced rework	38
Reduction in idle time	30
Better planning and scheduling	100
Reduction in supervisory staff	30
Total	**563**

Table 11.6 One-time Costs for Proposed Shop Floor Job Tracking Software

One-Time Costs	*Approximate Value (₹ Lakhs)*
Cost of software	300
Initial training cost of operating personnel and users	50
Software related hardware purchase	100
Data conversion, database and so on	40
Site preparation including air-conditioning	100
Miscellaneous supplies	40
Total	**630**

Table 11.7 Annual Recurring Costs for the Proposed Shop Floor Job Tracking Software

Recurring Costs	*Approximate Value (₹ Lakhs)*
Software maintenance	50
Hardware maintenance	25
Miscellaneous supplies	50
Salary of IT personnel	60
Cost of electricity, air-conditioning and so on	40
Total	**225**

of all costs over the entire life cycle of the software package. In this model, it works out to approximately 48.60%. Management can apply different discount rates to find the overall net present value of the software package with varying discount rates.

Further, in order to add flexibility to the model to include additional items of benefits and costs, not foreseen in the initial stage, there can be two separate worksheets, one for item-wise costs (one-time and recurring) and the other for benefits with blank rows in each worksheet to allow additional entries in the model. The year-wise totals of the worksheets can then be linked with the appropriate cells of the summary worksheet shown in Table 11.8.

Table 11.8 Cost–Benefit Analysis of a Proposed Job Shop Order Tracking Software

PQR Forklift Truck Manufacturing Co. Pvt Ltd.								
Year (Present year is shown as 0)	*0*	*1*	*2*	*3*	*4*	*5*	*6*	*Totals*
Costs:								
One-time costs ₹	–630							
Recurring costs ₹		–225.00	–225.00	–225.00	–225.00	–225.00	–225.00	
Discounting factor for present value	1	0.877193	0.76946753	0.67497152	0.59208028	0.51936866	0.45558655	
Present value of recurring costs ₹		–197.37	–173.13	–151.87	–133.22	–116.86	–102.51	
Net present value of all costs ₹	–630	–827.37	–1000.50	–1152.37	–1285.59	–1402.44	–1504.95	–1504.95
Benefits:								
Recurring benefits ₹	0	563.00	563.00	563.00	563.00	563.00	563.00	
Discounting factor for present value	1	0.877193	0.76946753	0.67497152	0.59208028	0.51936866	0.45558655	
Present value of recurring benefits net ₹	0	493.86	433.21	380.01	333.34	292.40	256.50	
Present value of all benefits ₹	0	493.86	927.07	1307.08	1640.42	1932.82	2189.32	2189.32
Overall net present value ₹								684.37
Break-even point for discount rate = 0.14				Third year				
Internal rate of return (IRR) = 48.60% approx.								

11.3 Models Based on Optimisation Techniques

11.3.1 Model 3 (Distribution of Electricity in a Metro City at Optimum Cost)

An important operational control decision for a metro city electricity supply corporation that has to be taken very quickly and efficiently is how the transmission and distribution system for electricity will operate. Precisely, it means where the distribution system will receive power (electricity) and distribute the same to which destinations. The sources of power are the generating stations generating electric power and the receiving stations purchasing power from other agencies. The cost per unit of power varies depending on the source. Moreover, the sources of power are located at different distances from the load centres, thereby causing varying transmission losses. Hence, the pattern of distribution of power from the sources to different destinations, technically called the load centres or substations, has an important bearing on the overall economy of the electricity supply corporation. The problem can be formulated as an optimisation model based on operations research techniques as follows:

Mathematical Formulation: Let there be i_{th} number of sources of power, which include the generating stations as well as the receiving stations and j_{th} number of destinations technically known as substations which receive power and distribute the same among the consumers in a particular zone of the metro city wherein

i can be 1, 2, ..., n and
j can be 1, 2, m

B_i: The rated capacity of power supply from the i_{th} source
D_j: The demand for power for the j_{th} substation
C_i The cost per unit of power per second for the i_{th} source
X_{ij}: The quantum of power supplied by the i_{th} source to the j_{th} destination
d_{ij}: The distance between i_{th} source and the j_{th} destination
α: The transmission loss per unit of power transmitted per unit distance

The distribution model is a linear programming model as follows:

$$\text{Minimise cost } \sum_{i=1}^{n}\sum_{j=1}^{m} C_i \, . \, X_{ij}$$

Subject to,

$$\sum_{j=1}^{m} X_{ij} < B_i, \text{ for all } i,$$

$$\sum_{i=1}^{n} X_{ij} . (1 - \alpha . d_{ij}) = D_j \text{ for all } j$$

$$X_{ij} > 0 \text{ for all } i \text{ and } j.$$

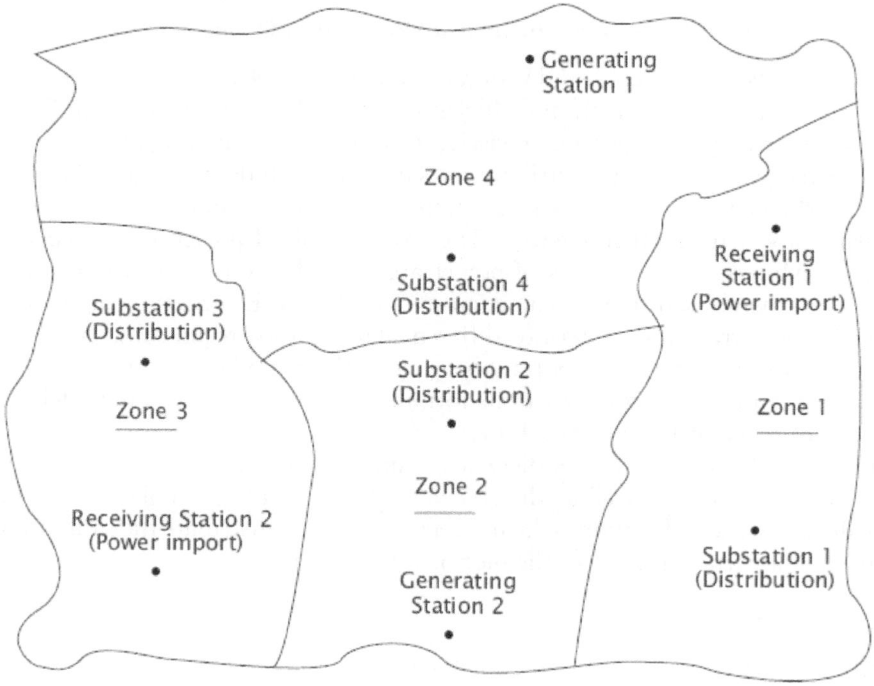

Figure 11.1 City Distribution Zones and Locations of Generating, Receiving and Substations of the Electricity Supply Corporation (Not to scale)

The problem can be converted into a transportation problem with the cost per unit of power transmitted from i_{th} source to j_{th} destination including the cost of transmission losses. In other words, the cost of transmitting one unit of power from i_{th} source to j_{th} destination can be written as:

$$C_{ij} = C_i / (1 - \alpha.\, d_{ij}).$$

The above model was applied in the case of a metro city electric supply corporation. The approximate geographical locations of the generating stations, receiving stations and the substations within the city have been shown in Figure 11.1. Two out of the three generating stations were located at the same place and have been shown as one (generating Station 1). The distances between the generating/receiving stations and the substations for distribution of electricity have been shown in Table 11.9.

The cost per unit of power per second and the rated capacities of the generating/receiving stations are shown in Table 11.10 and 11.11, respectively. The transportation problem as formulated with the help of the distance matrix and cost per unit of electric power at source is shown in Table 11.12. The transmission loss α has been assumed as 0.001 per MW of electricity transmitted per kilometre distance. The optimum solution of the problem is shown in Table 11.13, and the optimum cost is ₹297.69 per second, which is less than the cost at which the system was actually operated by the metro city electric supply corporation on the particular day with the particular load demand pattern

Table 11.9 Distance Matrix in Kilometres (d_{ij})

From i to j	*GS1(i = 1)*	*GS2(i = 2)*	*RS1(i = 3)*	*RS2(i = 4)*
SS1(j = 1)	14	5	4	16
SS2(j = 2)	11	6	10	10
SS3(j = 3)	12	10	18	6
SS4(j = 4)	5	13	9	10

Note: SS: Substation; GS: Generating Station; RS: Receiving Station.

Table 11.10 Cost per Unit of Power per Second (C_i)

i = 1	*i = 2*	*i = 3*	*i = 4*
56	56	63	63

Note: Paisa/megawatt/second

Table 11.11 Rated Capacities (B_i) in Megawatt

i = 1	*i = 2*	*i = 3*	*i = 4*
145	125	175	110

Table 11.12 Power Transportation Problem

Source Destinations	*i = 1*	*i = 2*	*i = 3*	*i = 4*	*Demand (D_j)*
j = 1	56.80	56.28	63.25	64.02	120
j = 2	56.62	56.34	63.64	63.64	110
j = 3	56.68	56.57	64.15	63.38	120
j = 4	56.28	56.74	63.57	63.64	150
Capacities (*B*)	145	125	175	110	

Note: Value in cells in paisa.

Table 11.13 Optimum Solution for Electric Power Distribution

Source Destinations	*i = 1*	*i = 2*	*i = 3*	*i = 4*	*Demand (D_j)*
j = 1	0	5	115	0	120
j = 2	0	110	0	0	110
j = 3	0	10	0	110	120
j = 4	145	0	5	0	150
Capacities (*B*)	145	125	175	110	

Note: Optimum Cost = 29769 paisa = ₹297.69 per second.

shown by ₹2.10 per second. A saving of ₹2.10 in distribution cost per second implies a total saving of approximately ₹662 crores per annum!

Since the load demand as also the availability of power is highly fluctuating in nature, the whole exercise can be computerised, and the computerised results can be used to operate the power supply system at optimum cost. However, such a system has to be online and real time in nature.

11.4 Models Based on Computerised Database

11.4.1 Model 4 (Gold Swimming Club Database)

The model pertains to Gold Swimming Club located in a metro city in India and catering to the swimming practice of various age groups of men and women, including fresh learners. The service of the club is very beneficial for the parents of children who reside in the metro city because of the convenient central location of the club in the metro city. The club is a newly established one and currently has about a hundred members enrolled for learning/practice sessions of 1 hour duration each during 8:00–11:00 am in the morning and 5:00–8:00 pm in the evening for 6 days a week, Monday being a closed day for the club. Because of its international standards, including proper temperature control and purification of the pool water, the club has been registering, on average, five fresh enrolments per week. Presently, the record-keeping system for members' data is a manual one. However, with increasing member strength, the paperwork as also data volume increases significantly. It is found that at times information storage and retrieval for effective and efficient decision-making relating to the allotment of time slots to trainers and for fresh enrolment, resource levelling for the busy and lean slots on various weekdays and other important areas of the club activities take so much time that appropriate decisions are not forthcoming. Therefore, the management of the club decided to develop a computer DBMS for tracking the data of the members (swimmers), available time slots for new enrolments, the trainers' duty roster and other monitoring parameters of the swimming club.

The club management entrusted the job of designing and developing a suitable computer database linked with a GUI to a computer professional, who has proposed the following tables with proper linkages among the tables. The above relational database tables are created and subsequently updated with the addition of records as and when new enrolments are made, deletion when a member discontinues membership or when a trainer leaves his/her job. A basic form design for the creation and addition of records in the data tables as described above is shown in Figures 11.2 and 11.3 respectively.

Information/Reports: The management of Gold Swimming Club requires two routine reports on a weekly basis, which can be generated using the report generation module of the database software. The reports are the trainer schedule and the updated membership list. Since the trainer schedule report requires data both from the member table (Table 11.14) and the trainer table (Table 11.15), it is necessary to build a select query with the two tables linked through the trainer number (TNO) field and thereafter the report can be generated. Figure 11.4 shows a sample trainer schedule report as of a particular date.

The trainer schedule report is generated in the ascending order of the last names of the trainers and within that slot, number-wise in ascending order. The sorting in the same order is performed on the file built up using the select query as mentioned in the earlier paragraph. Further, the trainer schedule report has been prepared for the morning shift first followed by the evening shift by splitting the trainer file built up using the select query.

Gold Swimming Club

Application Form for Membership (Colour: Pink)

Name of member: ____________ ____________

(Last name) (First name)

Sex: Male/female (tick one)

Date of birth DD MM YYYY

Street address:

City: Pin Code:

Phone no: Email address (if any):

Signature of Applicant

(To be filled up by staff after getting from computer)

Membership no.:

Slot no. allotted:

Trainer no.:

Monthly fees:

Date of enrolment:

Figure 11.2 Application Form for Membership

Gold Swimming Club

Trainer Employment Form (Colour: Blue)

Trainer no. (To be filled up by staff after getting from computer)

Name of trainer: Mr/Ms ____________ ____________

Last name First name

Street address:

City: Pin code:

Telephone no:

(To be filled up by staff)

Working shift: Morning/evening (Tick one) Monthly pay (₹):

Email address (if any):

Figure 11.3 Application Form for Employment of Trainer

The sample membership list as on a particular run date is shown in Figure 11.5:

The membership list has been generated in the ascending order of the last name of the club members by performing the required sorting operation on the member table. The computerised database as described in the preceding paragraphs can also provide answers to various queries of club management such as:

1. How many members are trained by each trainer on average?
2. What are the total fees collected as membership fees during a particular month?
3. What are the outstanding dues payable by the members of the club as on a particular date?

Table 11.14 Member Table Structure

Field Name	*Data Type*	*Field Description*	*Field Size*	*Remarks*
M No.	Auto generated number	Is a unique identification for each member	Integer (3 Digits) (001 to 999)	Serves as a primary key
M last name	Text	Last name of a member	25	Required field
M first name	Text	First name of a member	25	Required field
M sex	Text	Sex of member M (Male); F(Female)	1	Required field
M DOB	Date	Date of birth of member	8 (MMDDYYYY)	Required field
M street	Text	Street address of member	25	Required field
M city	Text	City name of member	10	Required field
M pin	Text	Pin of member address	6	Required field
M phone	Text	Telephone number of member	10	Required field
M email	Text	Email address of member	₹XXX.XX	Required field
M fees	Currency	Monthly membership fee of the member	25	Required field
Last payment month	Month/year	Month and year up to which fees paid	MM YYYY	Required field
Slot	Number	Time slot allotted to the member	1 (integer)	Required field
TNo.	Number	Trainer no. of the trainer of member	3 (integers)	Required field
Enrol date	Date	Date of enrolment as member	8 (MMDDYYYY)	Required field
Comments	Memo	Contains any other relevant information		Required field

Note: *Slot: 1 for 8:00–9:00 am; 2 for 9:00–10:00 am; 3 for 10:00–11:00 am; 4 for 5:00–6:00 pm; 5 for 6:00–7:00 pm; 6 for 7:00–8:00 pm.

4. What is the monthly remuneration paid to the trainers for any particular month?
5. Which slot is having the maximum number of members and which slot is having the minimum number of members in any week?

All the above types of queries can be answered using SQL formulations. Further, the answers to queries can be displayed on screen in graphical form by interfacing with the GUI.

11.4.2 Model 5 (Database Model)

This model pertains to the creation of an employee database to facilitate employee training at Precision Tools and Equipment Company Limited. It is a manufacturing company in the eastern part of India, producing a diverse range of precision tools and equipment for

Table 11.15 Trainer Table Structure

Field Name	*Data Type*	*Field Description*	*Field Size*	*Remarks*
T No.	Numeric	Unique identification for the trainer	Integer (3 digits)	Required for linking
T last name	Text	Last name of a trainer	25	Required field
T first name	Text	First name of a trainer	25	Required field
T sex	Text	Sex of trainer M (Male); F(Female)	1	Required field
T DOB	Date	Date of birth of trainer	8 (MMDDYYYY)	Required field
T street	Text	Street address of trainer	25	Required field
T city	Text	City name of trainer	10	Required field
T pin	Text	Pin of trainer address	6	Required field
T phone	Text	Telephone number of trainer	10	Required field
T email	Text	Email address of trainer	20	Required field
T shift	Text	Shift of trainer M(morning); E(evening)	1	Required field
T pay	Currency	Monthly rate of remuneration	₹XXX.XX	Required field
T employ date	Date	Date of appointment	8 (MMDDYYYY)	Required field
Comments	Memo	Contains any other relevant information		

Note: A trainer is appointed for a particular shift only.

Gold Swimming Club

Trainer Schedule

Date: Report Date

Trainer No.	Trainer	Name	Shift	Slot	Members to Be Attended	
015	Biswas	Anil	M	1	Chanda	Mira
					Deb	Paresh
					Samanta	Chandan
			M	2	Adhikary	Pinky
				2	Basu	Gopal
			M	3	Saha	Bimal
					Paul	Joyeeta
					Roy	Samar
011	Chatterjee	Satya	M	1	Mitra	Debabrata
	...			2	Roy	Sudip
	...			3	Poddar	Barun
002	Majumdar	Ranjan	E	4	Sengupta	Arya
	...					
	...					

Figure 11.4 Trainer Schedule Report

Note: **M:** Morning, **E:** Evening, **1:** 8:00–9:00 am; **2:** 9:00–10 am; **3:** 10:00–11:00 am; **4:** 5:00–6:00 pm.

		Gold Swimming Club					Date: Run Date
		Membership List					
Membership No.	Name of Member	Street Address	City	Pin	Telephone No	E-mail	Last Fees Paid for (MM/YYYY)
010	Basu Gopal	531, Gariahat Road	Kolkata	700068	9431166700	—	12/2015
008	Chanda Sumit	F 53 New Alipore Road	Kokata	700053	9830312961	—	03/2016
	...						
	...						

Figure 11.5 Membership List Report

supplying to capital goods industries. Because the very nature of the manufacturing process demands continuous upgrades of technology and necessary training of employees at all levels in the company, the top management of the company is contemplating developing a full-fledged employee training scheme to be operated by the training division of the company. Presently, the training activities are decentralised and the training of employees is being organised departmentally by the heads, and employees are deputed to outside training institutes for attending courses of various durations. Sometimes the departmental heads also arrange for in-house training programmes with the assistance of their own experts as well as by hiring outside experts. The selection of employees working in a particular department for any specific training is done on the basis of the recommendations of their immediate superiors, and the course with the training institute imparting the same course is selected by the departmental heads in consultation with the training division of the company. However, the above system of selection of employees for training has an inherent drawback that no consideration is paid to the past training programmes attended by the concerned employees as well as the company policy for training employees. The present company policy regarding training of all categories of employees is as follows:

- All technical and supervisory persons should attend specialised courses on manufacturing technology and allied areas conducted by reputed technical institutes, including supervisory training institutes, for a duration of not less than 3 weeks every year.
- All skilled and semi-skilled workers should attend skill-development programmes arranged either in-house, conducted by the training division of the company or by deputing the workers to various artisan/industrial training institutes for at least 4 weeks in a year.

Although the company has a laid-down training policy as above, often superiors do not like to spare essential subordinate staff with the apprehension that if employees are sent for training, departmental work may be hampered. As a result, it has been found by the top management of the company that some employees are repeatedly being sent for training to different training institutes, whereas employees who are required to undergo training to develop themselves to contribute much better towards the interests of the company are not spared to undergo training. The above situation has also resulted in under-utilisation of training funds allocated annually in the past.

The top management of the company, therefore, engaged a consultant to develop a database covering the employee data, available training courses offered by the various institutes in India every year and other relevant details. The training division has to update the database for preparing a comprehensive annual training plan for all categories of employees, keeping into consideration the real training needs of the employees, the company's training policy and funds allocated for training for the particular year. The plan should be prepared in advance to be ready in the month of March every year for the next financial year.

The process of preparation of the annual training plan, as proposed in short, is as follows:

During the month of March preceding the plan year, the available training programmes from various institutes for the next financial year and the recommendations of superiors for training their subordinate employees are received by the training division of the company. The available training programme report makes the training division aware of the various training programmes available with the cost per participant as well as the overall fund allocated for each such programme during the plan year. The total training budget for the plan year is also made known to the training division after the company budget has been approved. The departmental heads then meet along with the head of the training division and study the recommendations for each employee for training, the company training policy, the available training programmes and the fund availability for training. After studying the process as described above, the consultant has decided that two database tables are primarily required to be created, which are the available training programmes and the employee data tables. The consultant accordingly designed two tables, which are shown as Tables 11.16 and 11.17 respectively.

Table 11.16 Training Programme Table Structure

Field Name	*Data Type*	*Field Description*	*Field Size*	*Comments*
Progno	Integer	Serves as primary key	3 digits	Required field
Programme name	Text	Specifies the name of the programme	50	Required field
Inhouse	Yes/No (Y/N)	Indicates whether the programme is in-house or conducted by outside institute	Y or N	Required field
Instcode	Integer	Indicates the code number of the institute; for inhouse code is '01'	2 digits	Required field
Instname	Text	Indicates the name of the institute	40	Required for outside programme only
Start date	Date	Indicates course commencement date	8 MMDDYYYY	Required field
Durwks	Numeric	Course duration in weeks	Integer 2 digits	Required field
Fee	Currency	Course fee per participant	₹XXXXXX	Required field
Maxno	Numeric	Maximum number of participants allowed	Integer 2 digits	Required field
Guide	Memo	Provides the eligibility criteria for participants		

Note: A fee is charged notionally for in-house programmes by the training division to defray the expenses such as remuneration to experts hired for the programme.

Table 11.17 Employee Table Structure

Field Name	*Data Type*	*Field Description*	*Field Size*	*Comments*
Empno	Integer	Employee identification number which serves as a primary key	(4 digits)	Primary field and primary key to establish relation with other tables
Lname	Text	Last name of the employee	25	Required field
Fname	Text	First name of the employee	25	Required field
Address	Text	Street address of the employee	25	Required field
City	Text	City of the employee address	10	Required field
Pin	Text	Pin code address of the employee	6	Required field
Telno	Text	Telephone number of the employee	10	Required field
Deptcode	Text	Department code of the employee	2	Required field
Desgn	Text	Current designation of the employee	20	Required field
Category	Text	Employee category 01: Manager 02: Engineer 03: Supervisor 04: Clerical 05: Skilled 06: Unskilled	2	Required field
Policy	Numeric	Training policy for the year in terms of the minimum number of weeks of training for the employee category	2	
DOB	Date	Date of birth of employee	8 MMDDYYYY	Required field
Grosspay	Currency	Present monthly gross pay of the employee	₹ XXXXXX	Required field
Joindt	Date	Joining date of the employee in the service of the company	8 MMDDYYYY	Required field
Recommend	Memo	Recommendation of the superiors regarding training needs		Required field

In the employee table (Table 11.17), there is a recommendation memo field which contains the recommendation submitted by the superiors of the employees through a recommendation form suitably designed as an input to the employee data table. The employee table has several fields which are more or less static in nature such as employee identification, name, contact address, department code, current designation, gross pay, date of birth, date of joining, employee category and training policy.

The third table, which contains the annual training plan of the company, is developed based on the employee table, available training programme table and the past training

Table 11.18 Annual Training Plan

Field Name	*Data Type*	*Field Description*	*Field Size*	*Comments*
EMPNo	Integer	Employee identification number	4 digits	Primary key to establish relation with employee table
Progno	Integer	Programme identification number for the programme for which the employee has been selected	3 digits	Required field for relation with available training programme table
YRSTART	Date	The commencement date of the plan year	8 MMDDYYYY	Required field
REMARKS	Memo	Provides the criteria of selection		Optional but preferred for transparent selection process

records of the employees. The structure of the annual training plan so developed is shown in Table 11.18.

A study of the Table 11.18 reveals that two basic relationships are necessary. First, a relationship between the training programme table and the annual training plan table needs to be established. This is done through the programme identification number. Second, a relationship between the annual training plan and the employee table is necessary. As both the annual plan and the employee tables have the employee number as a field, the same can be used to establish the second relationship. The consultant also decided to enforce referential integrity for each of the above two relationships.

Input Specifications: The creation and subsequent updating of the Training programme table and the employee table require programme and employee forms. The programme form enables the training division to update information about available training programmes and also to add or delete records. The employee form creates and subsequently updates data in two tables, namely the employee table and the past Training Records table, which stores information about the past training programmes attended by the employees. This table shown in Figure 11.17 uses a combination key consisting of programme identification number and employee identification number. Figures 11.6 and 11.7 show the sketches of the programme and employee forms respectively.

Figures 11.8 and 11.9 show the tentative sketches for the main and form switchboards. The query and report switchboards should use a similar format as the main and form switchboards. In order to perform the Exit function, a macro needs to be created and assigned to the Exit to M/s Precision Tools and Equipment Company database button. Several other queries and associated macros are also designed and incorporated in this database model.

Table 11.19 shows the annual training plan printed with the help of the report generator invoked by selecting the Reports button on the main switchboard and using the Annual Training Plan table.

The database model as described above can handle various management queries such as:

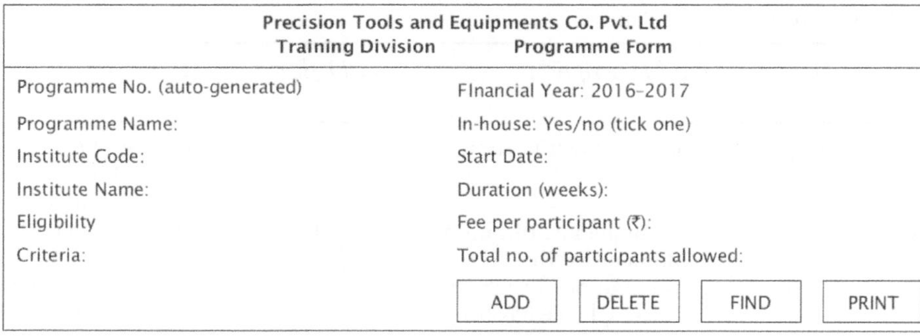

Figure 11.6 Programme Form

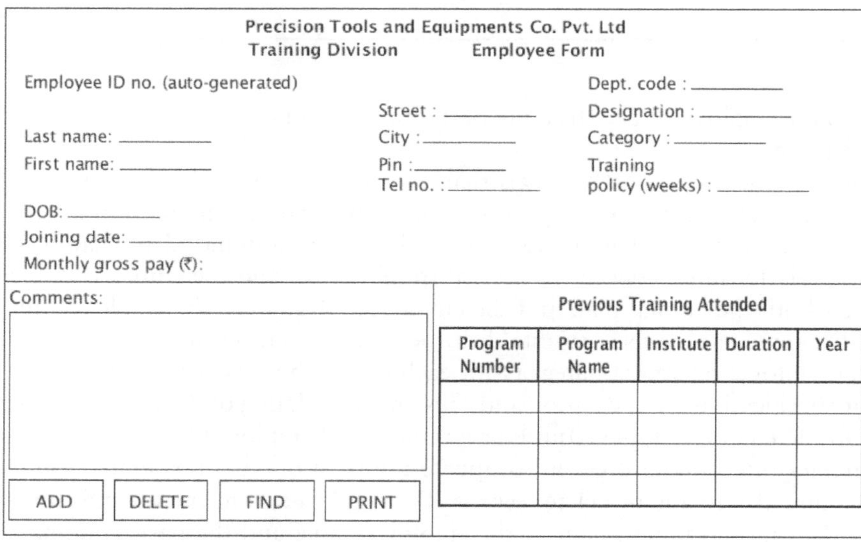

Figure 11.7 Employee Form

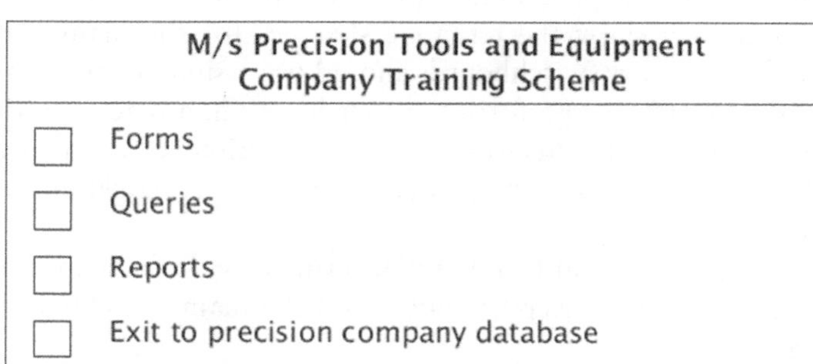

Figure 11.8 Main Switchboard

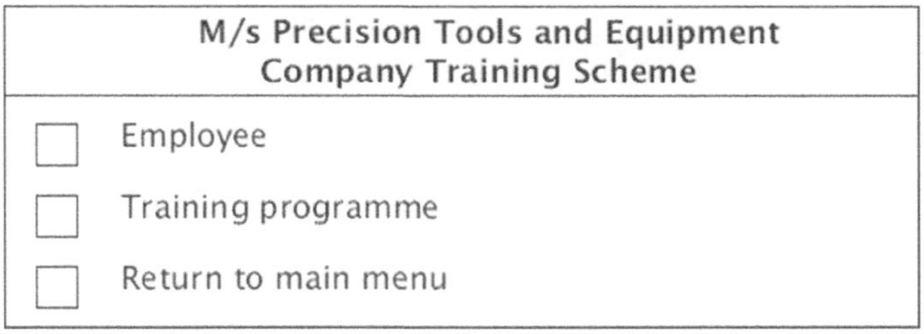

Figure 11.9 Form Switchboard

1. What is the average programme fee per participant?
2. How many participants have been earmarked for training in outside institutes from a particular department?

In order to handle such queries, we can build SQL formulations, and the answers to the queries can be displayed with any GUI.

11.5 Model Based on Web Design

Valuable management information can be provided through pages suitably designed using various web skills, tools and techniques, which facilitate web design and thereafter hosting the designed web pages consisting of a homepage and the detailed pages. Let me illustrate a web-based MIS through the following case pertaining to a metro city beautification-cum-fitness centre named 'Inspire'. 'Inspire' is located in the heart of a metro city providing beautification and fitness services for adult male and female customers who wish to avail themselves of either beautification or fitness services according to their convenient day and time. Ms Lovely Singh, a beautician by profession, owns and operates 'Inspire' with employees consisting of experienced beauticians, dieticians, masseurs, physiotherapists and fitness-cum-slimming experts. 'Inspire' has been in operation for several years and the list of its customers has been increasing rapidly. Since its inception almost ten years ago, the centre has grown from six beautification beds to its present 18 beds and a full-fledged fitness centre. Besides, 'Inspire' sells a variety of cosmetic products of reputed brands to its customers. The centre is open 6 days a week (Monday to Saturday excepting public holidays) from 10:00 am to 8:00 pm. Although walk-ins are appreciated, 'Inspire' Beauty Parlour and Fitness Centre appointments can also be booked in advance over the telephone. The beauty parlour provides herbal beauty treatments, hairstyles, haircuts, facial treatments, waxing, makeup, permanent makeup tattooing, manicures, pedicures, skincare, nail polishing and a host of other services. The fitness centre is a top-class facility equipped with state-of-the-art sports equipment, jacuzzis, steam rooms and saunas, a jogging path, free weights, treadmills, exercise bicycles and so on. When a client joins the fitness centre, a fitness evaluation is done for him/her and he/she is provided with a fitness programme chalked out by a fitness expert. The current price list of 'Inspire' is shown in Table 11.20.

Ms Lovely Singh appreciates the power of the web, and she desires to provide customers, both existing and potential, with information about the parlour, fitness centre and

Table 11.19 Annual Training Plan of Precision Tools and Equipment Company

Precision Tools and Equipment Company
Training Division Annual Training Plan Year: 2022–23

Dept. Code	*Employee Code*	*Employee Name*	*Program Name*	*Duration Weeks*	*Fee (₹)*	*Institute*	*Start Date*
01	1245	Bhattacharyya Rabin	Motivation and leadership	2	80,000	IIM, Bangalore	06/14/2016
	1280	Ghosh Sukumar	Tool and cutter design	1	20,000	CMTI Hyderabad	08/01/2016
20	1341	Adhikary Gautam	TPM and 5S	2	40,000	NPC Chandigarh	11/11/2016

Table 11.20 Current Price List of 'Inspire' Beauty Parlour and Fitness Centre

Beauty Parlour	₹
1 Session	1000.00
4 Sessions	3500.00
8 Sessions	7000.00
10 Sessions	10000.00
One month unlimited	8000.00
Yearly enrolment (new)	90000.00
Old customers (yearly)	80000.00
Fitness Centre	
6-month membership	40000.00
Annual membership	70000.00
Products	
Ponds body lotion 100 ml	65.28
Ponds oil control 350 gm	153.60
Boro plus advance moisturising cream lotion 100 ml	57.60
Moisturising cold cream 100 ml	129.60
Lakme black kajal	165.00
L'oreal Paris excellence	254.00

beautification products through the web. She likes to design a web page for the same and upload it through some hosting company.

11.5.1 Design Specifications

The web page should be informative and at the same time presentable in visual appearance. The main information that Ms Lovely Singh wants to furnish on the web page are the working hours, weekly holiday, the various services and prices for the same. Further, she feels that the web page should be so designed that the visitors can navigate the same quickly and with ease. Figures 11.10–11.15 show the tentative design sketches of the home page and internal web pages of 'Inspire', respectively.

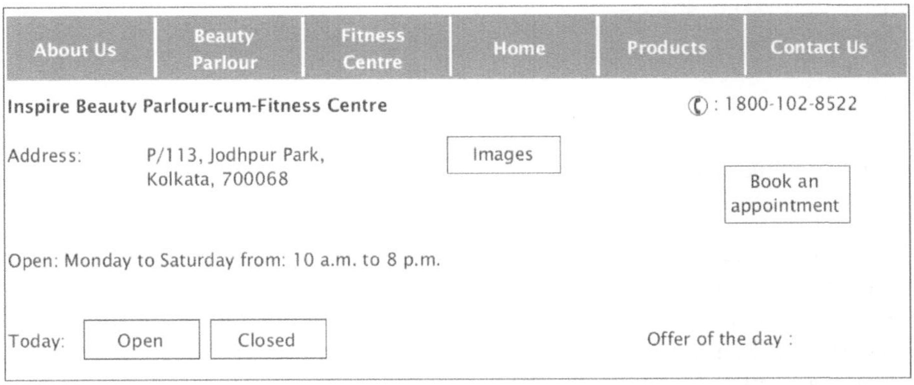

Figure 11.10 Home Page Design of 'Inspire'

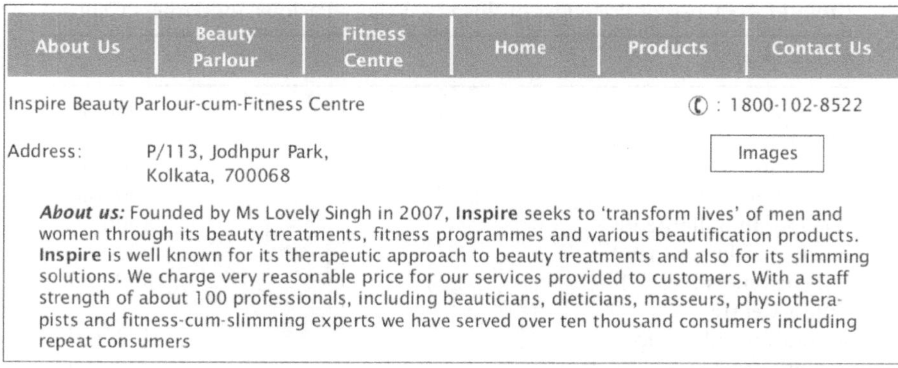

Figure 11.11 Internal Web Page Design of 'Inspire'

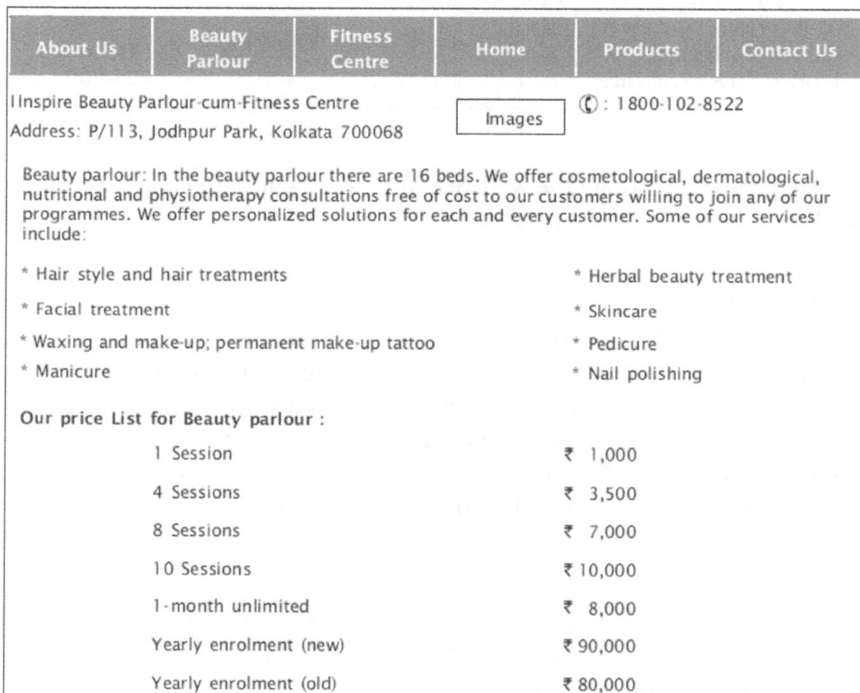

Figure 11.12 Internal Web Page Design of 'Inspire'

The web pages as designed above have been developed using 'Webfix', and examples are shown subsequently (Figures 11.16–11.19).

Web design has evolved and has now become a technology with a blend of different technologies. In the initial stage of development, all that was really needed to design a web page was a little bit of hypertext markup language (HTML) and the creation of a link to place images on the page. However, the scenario now is much more extensive and

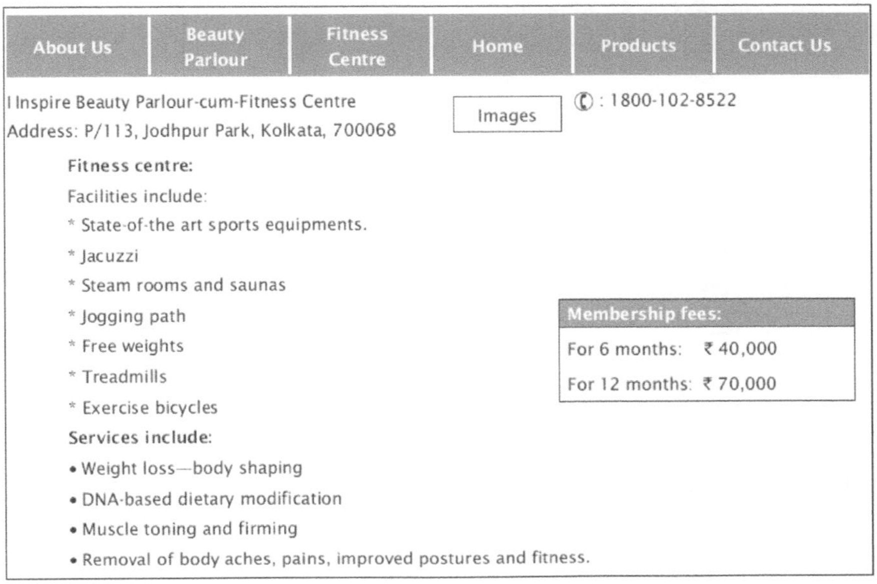

Figure 11.13 Internal Web Page Design of 'Inspire'

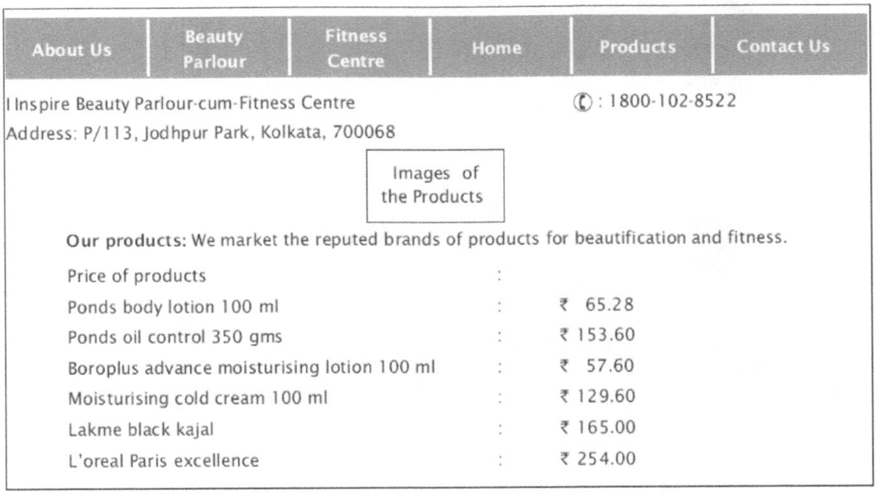

Figure 11.14 Internal Web Page Design of 'Inspire'

different, where so many new technologies and processes exist and web designers specialise in specific technologies of web design. A generalist, however, is a web designer having adequate skill in the core technologies of web design, namely HTML, Cascading Style Sheets (CSS) and Java Scripts (JS). Using the above three core skills, the generalists create websites from scratch through planning, designing, prototyping, testing and developing.

Figure 11.15 Internal Web Page Design of 'Inspire'

Figure 11.16 Example of a Web Page

The other specialised technologies are visual design, user experience (UX), motion graphic designs, content management system (CMS), blog building and so on. Visual designs of sites and interfaces involve colour, layout, typography and graphics.

UX designs focus on user experience, and a true UX designer has to study human behaviour and tendencies in order to facilitate the design of the web. Interactive web designers focus on creating interfaces for seamless interactions between users and websites. They work in close coordination with UX designers but are more focused on

Figure 11.17 Example of a Web Page

behavioural technologies using JS, which allow them to modify static HTML interfaces into interactive experiences. Motion graphic designers are the traditional animators who work on animation required in web design. They mostly use 'Flash' for animation and games on the web.

However, they also make use of JS and HTML5 technologies such as 'Canvas'.

Another area of specialised web design is the CMS, such as Drupal, Joomla and WordPress, which are used to build sites very fast and at the same time with powerful functionality.

Blogs have evolved as powerful tools that can compete with many fully featured sites in terms of capabilities. Many platforms feature free blogs that can be activated for building blogs very fast to get online quickly. It may be incidentally mentioned that front-end web developers focus more on the functionality of sites through client-end scripting. With the help of JS and powerful JS libraries, they facilitate the processing of scripts directly on the browser rather than on the server side. However, for dynamic web pages we can use PHP code or ASP.NET, which are popular server-side programming or scripting languages embedded into the HTML page.

With the help of the above, we can write simple code for web pages to make them dynamic. The output of PHP or ASP.NET is fed to the client-side browser as HTML only. However, PHP or Microsoft ASP.NET processes data obtained from the database,

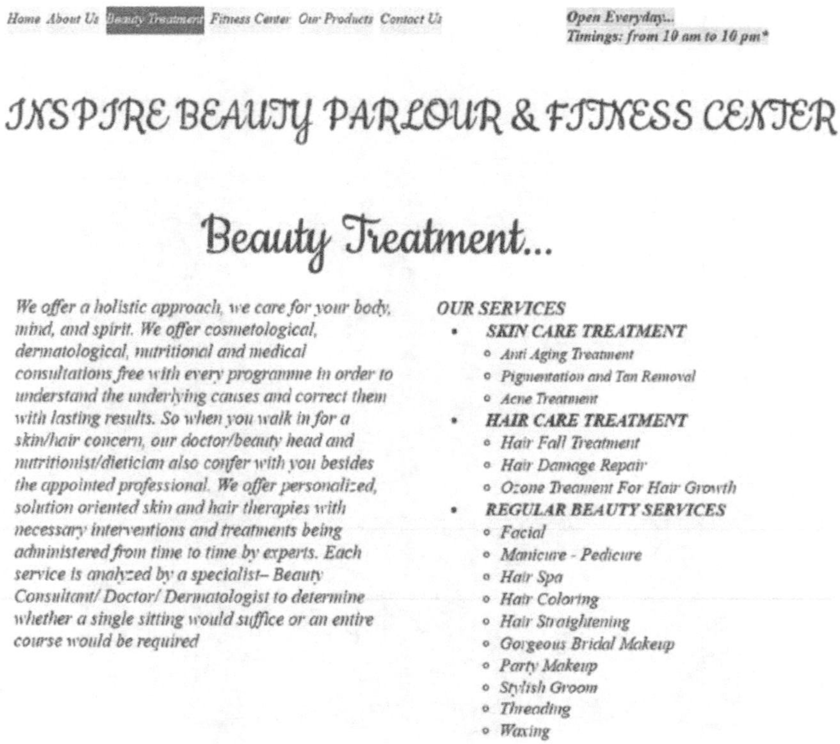

Figure 11.18 Example of a Web Page

Figure 11.19 Example of a Web Page

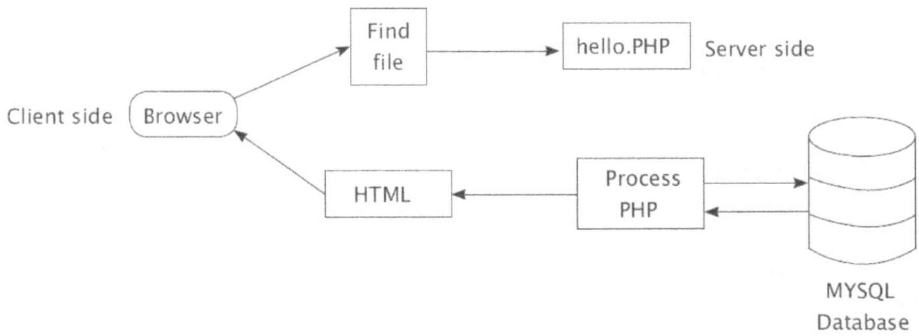

Figure 11.20 Processing of Data from MySQL by .PHP and Feeding the Output as HTML

which is either MySQL or SQL Server. Both MySQL and SQL Server are two leading databases that support front-end applications related to various domains.

Figure 11.20 shows how .PHP processes data from the MySQL database at the back end and feeds the output of the processed data as HTML to the browser at the client side (front end) to make the web pages interactive as well as dynamic (Figure 11.21).

Figure 11.21 Example of a Web Page.

11.5.2 Web Hosting

After designing and developing web pages, we have to choose a web host to upload our web pages. The selection or choice should be guided by the following broad considerations:

1. Price should not be the sole driving factor.
2. The amount of storage (hosting space) required by the site.
3. Data transfer rate.
4. What type of site has been built? Is it a simple blog, e-commerce or does it need server-side scripting?
5. Future changes envisaged for the site so that we can properly select the host who can scale with the site as it changes over the years.

11.6 Case Study: Break-even Analysis of Excess Stock of Slow-moving Items by a Furniture Manufacturing Unit

11.6.1 Background

The case pertains to a furniture manufacturing unit, located in the state of West Bengal, India. The unit was facing a problem of holding excess stock of some items of raw materials. The items were regularly procured based on consumption patterns commensurate with customer demand for the end products. Earlier, the customer demand was very high for the particular end products, and hence the items were fast-moving. However, due to a change in customer preferences for new designs of furniture, the demand for the earlier end products decreased considerably, and as a result, the items procured earlier in large quantities became slow-moving, resulting in excess stock holding.

The management of the unit was in a fix to decide whether to sell the entire stock of the items to reduce inventory-holding costs associated with those items or to hold the items as there was also a risk that if the items were disposed of and in future, customer demand might increase, the same items would have to be purchased at a higher price due to escalation. The manufacturing unit engaged a management consultant to develop a computer-based model to perform break-even analysis of excess stock of such items as mentioned above.

11.6.2 Mathematical Formulation of the Model

The economic ordering quantity of the items based on the present actual consumption pattern of the same items was determined with the holding cost of each of the items per unit per annum, ordering cost per order and the procurement lead time of the items as the parameters. This was followed by the development of the model to determine the break-even quantity of excess stock for each of the items.

The model was developed as follows:

Notations used:

M = Monthly usage of the item in units
i = Rate of interest on capital per annum, %
P = Price of the item, ₹/Unit
C = Inventory carrying cost per month per ₹ stock
E = Excess stock of the item

X = Rate of increase of price of the item per month, %
D = Discount offered while selling excess stock of the item
Q = Economic ordering quantity
B = Ordering cost in ₹ for the item
R = Cost of processing a sale of excess stock in ₹ per unit
If the excess stock E is sold,

Cash return = $D \,.\, P \,.\, E$ (1)

If the excess stock E is sold, then the holding cost saved can be expressed as:

Holding cost saved = P.C. $\sum_{j=0}^{E/m}(E - jM)$ (2) Present worth of gross holding cost saved as shown in (2) above can be expressed as,

$$=\text{P.C.}\sum_{j=0}^{E/m}(E - jM)/(1 + i/12)^{j} \quad (3)$$

Selling cost and repurchase penalty if excess inventory would have been sold may be given as

$$\text{R}+\sum_{j=1}^{E/Q}\left\{B + P.Q(1 + X)^{jQ/M}\right\}/(1 + i/12)^{jQ/M} \quad (4)$$

Combining Equations 1, 2, 3 and 4, net gain, G for holding of excess inventory:

$$\text{G=R}+\sum_{j=1}^{E/Q}\{B + P.Q.(1 + X)^{jQ/M}\}/(1 + i/12)^{jQ/M}\ \text{-D.P.E-P.C.}\sum_{j=0}^{E/M}(E - jM)/(1 + i/12)^{j}\,.\ (5)$$

However, for Break-Even value of $E = E^{*}$, $G = 0$ and from Equation (5);

$$\text{G=0 =R+}\sum_{j=1}^{E^{*}/Q}\left\{B + P.Q.(1 + X)^{jQ/M}\right\}/(1 + i/12)^{jQ/M}\ \text{-D.P.E}^{*}\text{- P.C}\sum_{j=0}^{E^{*}/M}(E^{*} - j.M)/(1 + i12)^{j} \quad (6)$$

From Equation (6) the recommended excess quantity, E^{*} can be found.

11.6.3 Results Obtained

The net gain for holding different quantities of excess inventory was calculated from the parameters shown in the table below for a particular item and plotted in a graph as shown on the following page. It is found from the same graph that break-even quantity E^{*} = 55 kg, which is greater than the EOQ (38 kg).

Further, it can be seen that up to the break-even point (E^*) it is profitable to hold excess stock, and beyond that, holding excess stock is not profitable. The maximum gain can be achieved if excess inventory is kept at 43 kg, as can be seen from the graph.

R	₹3.00 per kg
B	₹4.50 per order
i	15%
C	9.6%
D	70%
X	6%

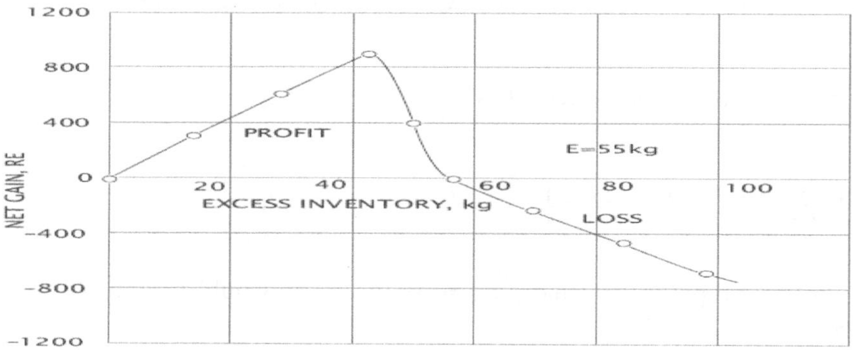

A computer algorithm was developed to solve the equation for net gain and determine the excess stock for maximum gain for all the slow-moving items.

11.7 Conclusion

Similar computer-based mathematical models can be developed to facilitate managerial decisions related to the holding of excess stock of slow-moving items.

Review Questions

1. What are the broad groups of models of computer-based MIS?
2. Mention some common spreadsheet models for facilitating management decisions.
3. Can you think of some limitations of the optimisation models in their application in real-life situations?
4. 'MIS models based on computer database need an efficient DBMS'. Explain with suitable illustrations.
5. Web-based models of MIS have become very popular because of distinct advantages. What are the advantages?
6. What are the various technologies involved in web design?
7. What is CMS? Name some popular CMS.
8. What are the functions of PHP and ASP.NET in web design?
9. What are the criteria for choosing a web host?

Bibliography

Biswas, J. 'A Study and Development of Models of Management Information Systems in Typical Indian Organizations'. PhD thesis, Department of Industrial Management, IISc, Bangalore, India, January 1982.

Miller, L. *MIS Cases: Decision Making with Application Software*, 3rd ed. London: Pearson Education, 2009.

Robbins, J. N. *Learning Web Design: A Beginner's Guide to HTML, CSS, JAVASCRIPT and Web Graphics*, 4th ed. Sebasto pool, MA: O'Reilly Media, 2007.

12 Computer Networking and Communication Technology

12.1 Introduction

During the last two decades, computer networks have grown extensively. Computer networks and the internet have become an important infrastructure for communication and control in every sphere of our activities such as business, education, healthcare, defence and corporate management involving IT. Some of the latest developments such as mobile computing, e-commerce, e-governance, social networks and IoT have been made possible mainly because of this explosive growth in computer networking.

Today, the internet has made it possible to connect millions of people all over the globe. It connects and transmits information across large multinational corporations, schools, colleges and universities, state and central government offices. In addition, it connects private houses and individuals through dial-up telephone systems, cable modulator–demodulator (modems), satellites, digital subscriber lines (DSL) and wireless technologies.

The internet has grown from its early research project to a global communication channel, encompassing about 3,566 million internet users as of June 2016. The rate of growth of internet users all over the world since 2000 AD is fantastic, as shown in Table 12.1.

12.2 Data Transmission Basics

12.2.1 Transmission Media

1. **Copper Wires**: Copper wires are used by conventional computer networks. The data in the form of electric signals is transmitted through insulated copper wires. In order to minimise interference due to emitting electromagnetic waves, there are three basic types of wiring.
   Unshielded twisted pair wiring consists of a pair of wires insulated with insulating material such as plastic and then the pair is twisted together in order to avoid interference with other wires.
   Coaxial cable consists of an inner wire surrounded by insulation and then a metal shield and finally, a layer of outer insulation. The metal shield forms a cylinder around the inner wire such as a cylindrical capacitor and provides a barrier to electromagnetic radiation and higher protection from interference than a twisted pair.
   A *shielded twisted pair*, however, has a metal shield around the twisted pair to reduce interference.

DOI: 10.4324/9781003509714-12

Table 12.1 Growth of World Internet Users since 2000

World Region	*Population 2016 (EST)*	*Population as % of Whole World*	*Internet Users (30.6.2016)*	*Penetration as % of Population*	*Growth 2000–2016(%)*	*Users as % of World*
Africa	1,185,529,578	16.20	333,521,659	28.10	7288.00	9.40
Asia	4,052,652,880	55.20	1,766,289,264	43.60	1445.30	49.50
Europe	832,073,224	11.30	614,974,023	73.90	485.20	17.20
Latin America/ Caribbean	626,054,392	8.50	374,461,854	59.80	1972.40	10.50
Middle East	246,700,900	3.40	129,498,735	52.50	3842.40	3.60
North America	359,492,293	4.90	320,067,193	89.00	196.10	9.00
Oceania/ Australia	37,590,704	0.50	27,508,287	73.20	261.00	0.80
World Total	7,340,093,980	100.00	3,566,321,015	48.60	887.90	100.00

Source: Internet World Stats: www.internetworld stats.com/stats.htm

2. **Optical Fibres**: Optical fibres are made of flexible glass fibres and use light to transmit data in computer networks. Data are transmitted in the form of pulses of light emitted by light emitting diodes (LEDs) or LASERs at one end of a fibre which travel down the optical glass fibre. Optical fibres have many advantages such as a larger distance of transmission of pulses (signals) than copper wires, no electrical interference and a single optical fibre can carry more data than a pair of copper wires needed to form a complete circuit. However, optical fibres require special manufacturing equipment and processes and further, in the case of the breakage of a fibre in a network, it is difficult to repair the same.

12.2.2 Electromagnetic Radiation

Electromagnetic radiation at radio frequency (RF) can be used to transmit computer data without any direct physical connection among the computers in a network such as copper wires or optical fibres. Each computer in the network is attached to an antenna, which can act as a transmitter or receiver of RF.

12.2.3 Microwave

Microwave is electromagnetic radiation beyond the frequency range used for radio and television. It can be used to transmit information as both voice and data over long distances. However, microwaves travel in a single direction unlike low-frequency RF transmission; moreover, they cannot penetrate metal structures. As a result, microwave transmission is possible when a clear path exists between the transmitter and the receiver.

12.2.4 Infrared

Computer networks can also use infrared technology for data communication. Such communication does not require any antenna. However, infrared communication is limited to a small distance, such as a computer in a network within a small room.

12.2.5 Laser

Laser beams can be used to transmit data in a straight line over a long distance. However, because of the fact that it travels in a straight line and cannot penetrate trees and weather conditions such as snowfall and fog, laser transmission for computer networks has limited application.

12.2.6 Satellites

RF technology can be used along with communication satellites to allow transmission over a long distance over the Earth's surface with curvature. Satellites are placed in orbit around the Earth. A satellite consists of transponders which can receive RF transmission signals sent by a ground station antenna, amplify the signal and transmit the amplified signal back to another ground station (receiving station) in a slightly different direction. Figure 12.1 illustrates how a communication satellite in orbit around the Earth can provide a network connection over a mountain range.

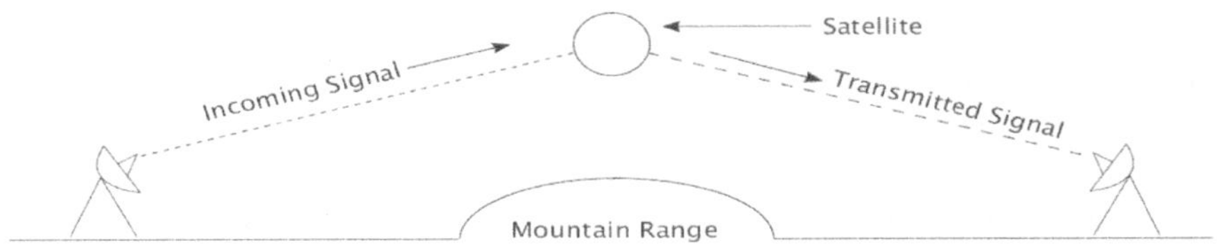

Figure 12.1 A Satellite Used to Provide Communication across a Mountain Range

A single satellite contains multiple transponders. Each transponder operates under a different RF channel, thus making simultaneous communication with multiple users possible. Moreover, by sharing, a single satellite can serve many users connected through a computer network.

Depending upon the height at which they orbit, communication satellites can be categorised as (1) geosynchronous or geostationary earth orbit (GEO) satellites and (2) low earth orbit (LEO) satellites.

A geosynchronous or geostationary satellite is placed in an orbit that is exactly synchronised with the rotation of the Earth. The satellite, when viewed from the ground, appears to remain exactly at the same point in the sky at all times. For example, a geostationary satellite in a circular orbit over the Pacific Ocean can transmit signals between Japan and North America at all times because the satellite remains above the same spot over the ocean. Applying the laws of physics, we can find out that the distance from Earth for the geosynchronous orbit is 35,785 km or 22,236 miles. In order to avoid interference, a minimum distance of separation must be maintained between any two satellites in the geostationary orbit which also depends upon the signal strength of the transmitter. Usually, the angular separation is about 4–8 degrees. Thus, there can only be from 45 (360/8) to 90 (360/4) satellites in the geostationary orbit above the equator.

12.2.7 LEO Satellites

LEO satellites operate in orbit only at a much lesser height from Earth than the geostationary Earth orbit. They usually are 200–400 miles above the Earth's surface. Because the speed of rotation of LEO satellites is faster than the rotation of Earth, they do not appear stationary to an observer on the Earth and appear to be moving across the sky. The obvious disadvantage is that the satellite can only be used to transmit signals during the time it orbits between two ground stations. In order to enable LEO satellites for continuous communication, a set of LEO satellites is launched. In that case, although each individual satellite appears to be moving across the sky, at any point in time, the set of orbiting satellites guarantees that at least one satellite is available to transmit between two ground stations.

Further, in addition to transponders to communicate with ground stations, an array of LEO satellites contains radio equipment used to communicate with each other in the array. This feature facilitates continuous transmission of signals received from one ground station to any intended ground station through the array of satellites.

12.2.8 Local Asynchronous Communication (RS–232)

Computers use binary digits (bits) to represent data. Therefore, the transmission of data is through bits which can be encoded and decoded by the transmitting and receiving end computers. Local asynchronous communication (RS–232) uses electric current to transfer data in digital form (bits) over a short distance such as sending characters from a keyboard to a computer. The term asynchronous implies that the sender and the receiver of data do not need to coordinate or synchronise before every transmission. For example, in case of a keyboard, data are generated and sent to the computer when a user touches a key and no data flows from the keyboard to the computer when the keyboard is idle. This is asynchronous communication only.

The Electronics Industries Association (EIA) standard RS–232C specifies details of physical connection such as the connected distance of less than 50 feet as well as electrical properties, that is, –15 volts to +15 volts to transmit data bits. RS–232 has become a popular standard for serial communication (bit by bit) over short distances of less than 50 feet usually between a computer and an American Standard Code for Information Interchange (ASCII) terminal or a computer and a modem. RS–232 sends each character with seven data bits, serially preceded by a start bit and followed by a stop bit representing an idle period. Each bit is sent in exactly the same period of time.

Figure 12.2 shows how the voltage on a wire fluctuates between –15 volts (representing '1' bit) and +15 volts (representing '0' bit) to send the start bit (0 bit), stop bit (1 bit) and in between the seven bits representing character 'A'. The above sequence is repeated for transmitting the character 'B' from keyboard to a computer using RS–232C. It may be mentioned that the seven bits representing 'A' and 'B' are '1000001' and '1000010' respectively.

Baud rate is the number of bits (0 or 1) transmitted as a signal per second and for RS–232 it is 33,600 bits per second, that is, 33.6 kbps. In case the sending and receiving computers and associated hardware are not configured to use the same baud rate, errors known as 'framing errors' will occur as the receiver's timer will not wait the same length of time as that of the sender for each bit. Therefore, the baud rate for each computer and hardware can be set physically by setting switches on the hardware when it is installed in a computer.

12.2.9 Half- and Full-Duplex Asynchronous Communication

Full-duplex communication takes place when data are transmitted simultaneously in two directions. Half-duplex transmission, also known as simplex transmission, allows data

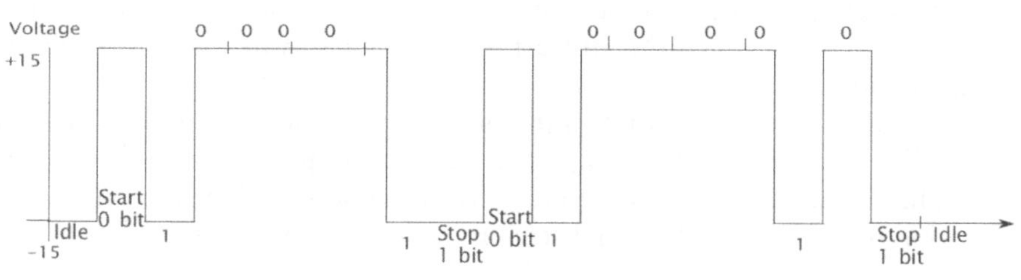

Figure 12.2 Electric Voltage on a Wire as the Two Characters 'A' and 'B' Are Transmitted Using RS–232C

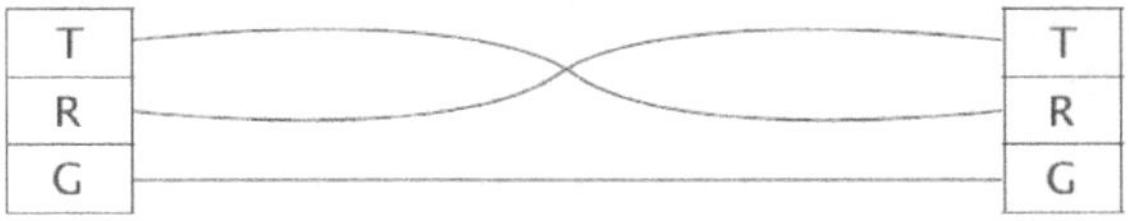

Figure 12.3 Three-Wire Full Duplex Transmission Sharing a Single Ground Wire

transmission in both directions but permits transmission in one direction only at any given time. In other words, simultaneous transmission of data in two directions is not possible in the case of half-duplex or simplex communication.

Full-duplex connection often uses three wires, two for transmitting data in each of two directions simultaneously and a common ground wire for the return path shared by each. Figure 12.3 illustrates a three-wire full-duplex transmission.

12.2.10 Bandwidth and Maximum Data Transmission Rate

Each transmission system has a limited bandwidth, which is the maximum rate of change of signal by the transmission device or hardware. For example, in the case of RS–232, the maximum rate of change of voltage (say, from –15V to +15V) determines its bandwidth. Bandwidth is measured in cycles per second or hertz (Hz). Obviously, the bandwidth of a transmission system has a relation with the maximum data rate, which is the maximum speed of sending bits. Nyquist's theorem provides the relationship between maximum data rate in bits per second (D) and the bandwidth (B) as follows:

$$D = 2B \text{ Log}_2 k$$

where k is possible values of voltage. Applying Nyquist theorem as above to RS–232, where;

k = 2;

and we get

$$D = 2B$$

Nyquist theorem provides the maximum theoretical data rate that is not possible to be achieved in practice because of ground interference, known as noise. Another researcher, Shannon, propounded a theorem known as 'Shannon's theorem', which gives a limit on the maximum data rate in the presence of noise. Shannon's theorem is as follows:

$$C = B \log_2 (1 + S / N)$$

where C is the effective limit on the channel capacity in bits per second, B is the hardware bandwidth, S is the average signal power and N is the average noise power. S / N, which is called the signal-to-noise ratio, is usually expressed as $10 \log_{10} S / N$ and measured in decibels (dB). For example, a ratio of S / N equal to 100 is $10 \times \log_{10} 100 = 10 \times 2 = 20$ dB and similarly, a ratio of 1,000 is 30 dB.

In a voice telephone system, (S / N) is approximately 30 dB and bandwidth approximately 3,000 Hz.

Then, according to Shannon's theorem, the maximum transmission rate in bits per second in a real voice telephone system under noise due to background interference is = 3,000 $\log_2 (1 + 1{,}000)$ or 30,000 bps approximately.

12.3 Long-Distance Communication

A signal in the form of electric current cannot be transmitted over a long distance through copper wire because of transmission loss, which makes the current weaker during propagation. As a result, the signal in the form of electric current cannot be detected by the receiver placed at a long distance. Such loss is due to the resistance to electric current by the copper partially converting electric energy to heat.

Communication scientists, however, studied and discovered that in the case of long-distance transmission, continuous, oscillating signals, usually in the form of a sine wave, propagate farther than any other signal. This continuously oscillating sine-wave signal is known as the carrier, which is, however, subjected to modifications (technically called modulations) by the transmitter. The receiver receives the incoming carrier, detects modulation, reconstructs the original data (signal), and then discards the carrier. A question arises as to how the transmitter modulates the carrier. It is either amplitude modulation (AM)/frequency modulation (FM) or pulse shift modulation (PSM) depending upon the technique adopted by the network technology. Amplitude modulation varies the strength of the carrier wave in proportion to the information being sent; frequency modulation varies the frequency of the underlying carrier in proportion to the information being sent. PSM, which is often adopted by computer networks, changes the timing of the carrier wave abruptly to encode data. Each such change is known as a 'phase shift'. PSM has got an advantage due to its ability to encode more than one-bit value per change. After a 'phase shift', the carrier jumps to a new point in its oscillating cycle. Figures 12.4(a), 12.4(b) and 12.4(c) show examples of AM, FM and PSM respectively.

12.3.1 Modem Hardware

A hardware device that accepts a sequence of data (bits) and modulates a carrier wave to represent the data bits is called a modulator. Likewise, a hardware device that accepts a modulated carrier wave to recreate the sequence of data bits, which was used to modulate the carrier, is called a demodulator.

However, in case of most network systems, the transmission is full duplex, and hence the modulators and demodulators have been combined into a single hardware device known as a 'modem'. One such device is kept at each end of a long-distance connection, as shown in Figure 12.5.

12.3.1.1 Types of Modems

In addition to dedicated wires, modems can be used with optical (glass fibres), radio frequency and conventional telephone connections. In the case of a conventional telephone system, dial-up modems are used to connect computers that are long distances apart, as shown in Figure 12.6.

Dial-up modems appear to be a telephone to the voice telephone system. As the telephone system is designed to carry sound, a dial-up modem contains a circuit to send and receive audio over the telephone line in addition to sending and receiving a carrier.

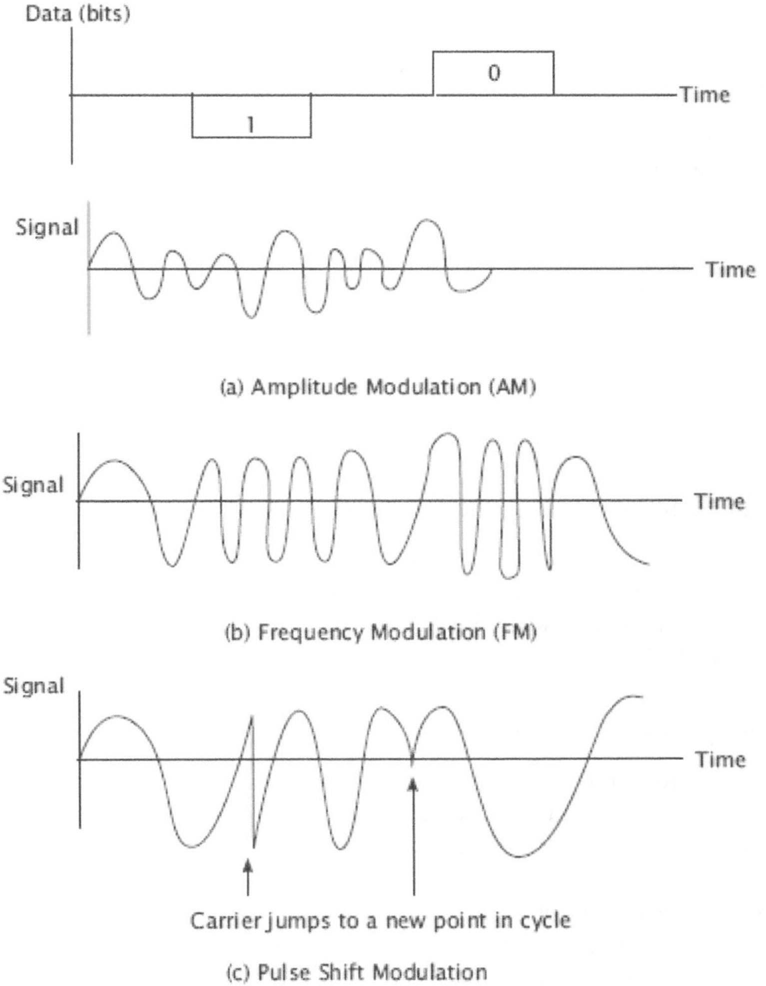

Figure 12.4 A Digital Signal on Top and the Wave Form That Results from Amplitude Modulation, Frequency Modulation and a Pulse Shift Modulation

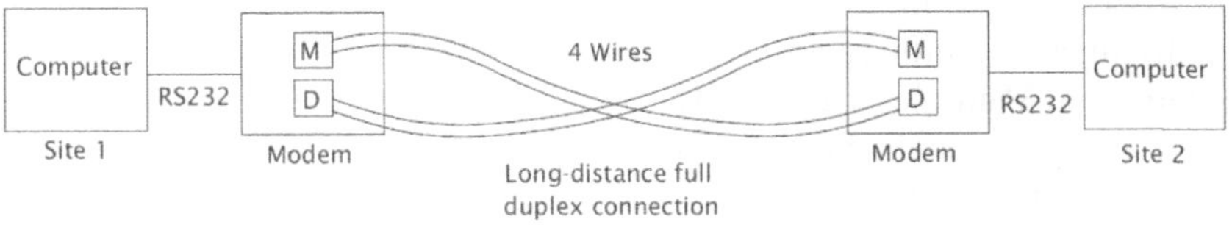

Figure 12.5 Modem for Long-Distance Full-Duplex Connection

12.3.2 *Carrier Frequencies and Multiplexing*

Multiplexing is the principle of sending two or more signals using different carrier frequencies through a single medium simultaneously without interference. Computer networks

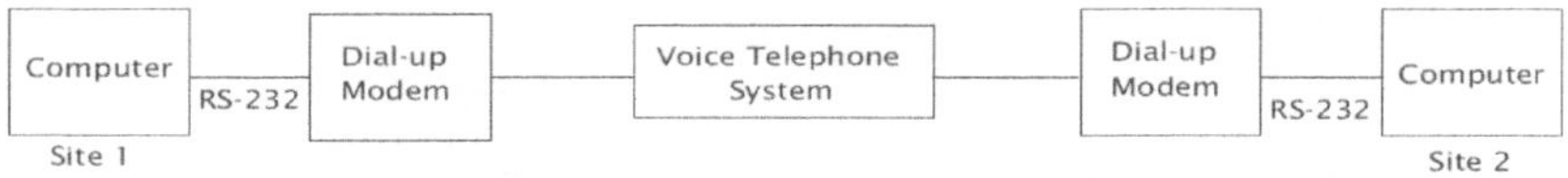

Figure 12.6 Dial-Up Modems Used with Voice Telephone System to Communicate between Two Computers

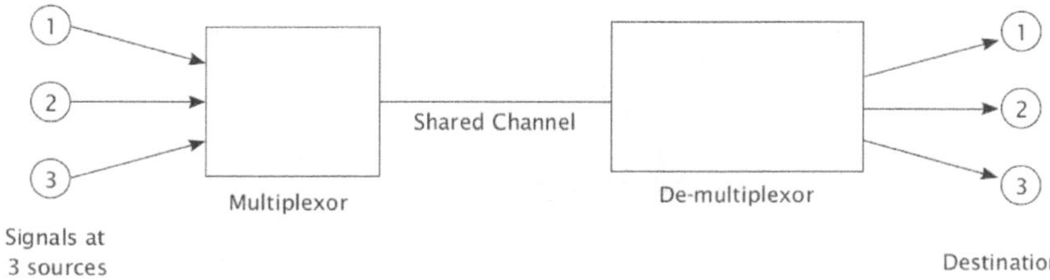

Figure 12.7 Illustration of Frequency Division Multiplexing

use the above principle to permit multiple communications using a single shared physical connection. This is technically known as frequency division multiplexing (FDM) as shown in Figure 12.7.

12.3.2.1 Multiplexing Technologies

The multiplexing technologies are given as follows:

Broadband and Baseband Technologies: In order to achieve higher throughput, the underlying hardware for multiplexing often uses a larger part of the electromagnetic spectrum or, in other words, a larger bandwidth which is called broadband technology. On the contrary, the technology that sends only one signal at a time over a medium using a small electromagnetic spectrum is known as baseband technology.

Wavelength Division Multiplexing: Wavelength division multiplexing is applicable in the case of optical FDM. It operates multiple lights of different wavelengths through a single optical fibre. At the receiving end, an optical prism is used to separate the light waves with different wavelengths and therefore different frequencies.

Spread Spectrum: Spread spectrum uses a transmitter to send the same signal on a set of carrier frequencies to improve the reliability of transmission. The receiver checks for all carrier frequencies in the spectrum and selects the desired one.

Time Division Multiplexing (TDM): It is basically a time-sharing multiplexing in which sources share a single medium according to turn.

TDM can be either synchronous, in which case sources take turns in a round-robin fashion with time slices allotted to each source, or statistical multiplexing, in which case, if a given source does not have data, the same will be ignored.

12.4 Packet Networks

Packets are small blocks of data, which a network system sends individually. Packet networks, also known as packet switching networks, send data in packets, and the technology is known as packet technology. The use of packets facilitates two things.

First, it ensures proper coordination of sender and receiver to see that data in packets arrive correctly at the receiver from the sender. Second, communication circuits and the associated modems being expensive, multiple computers often share underlying connections and hardware. The network permits one computer to send a packet at a time and then waits for other computers to send packets according to their turn before being allowed to send a second packet. This sending of packets in a sharing mode by each computer is taken care of by the network system using packet switching technology. This is illustrated in Figure 12.8.

Dividing data into small packets facilitates TDM as all data sources (computer 1, 2, ..., *N*) get an equal share of time for transmitting one packet each at a time.

Packets are associated with frame which defines a packet used with any specific type of network. A frame consists of a block of data preceded by an unprintable ASCII character known as start of header (SOH) and followed by another unprintable ASCII character to mark the end of transmission (EOT) of the frame. An example of a frame is shown as follows:

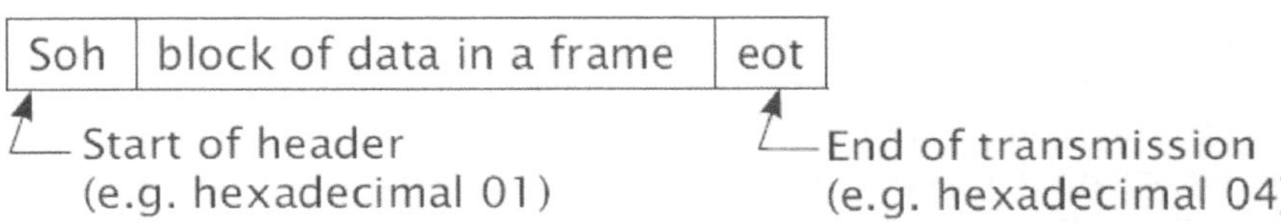

The main advantage of sending data in a frame with a character at the beginning and end of a frame arises when there is a large delay in the transmission of data due to crashing of a computer system. Rebooting using two characters to delimit a frame takes care of such eventualities. However, there is an obvious disadvantage of extra overhead associated with extra bits between blocks of data (one EOT and one SOH between two successive blocks).

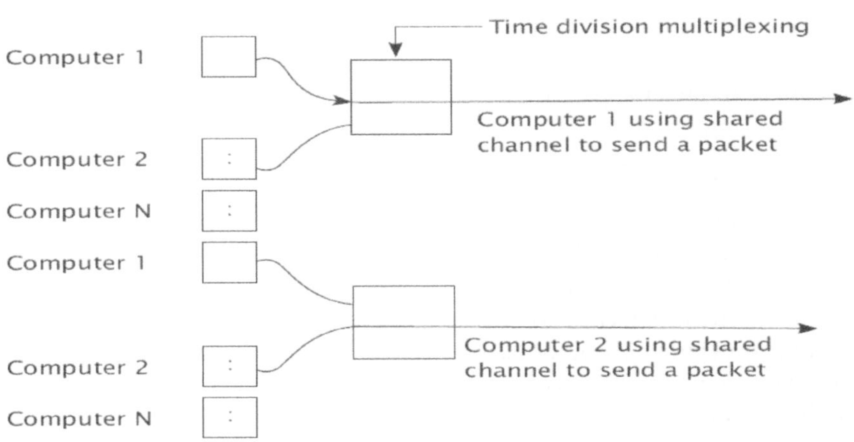

Figure 12.8 Illustration of Time Division Multiplexing with Packets

In order to permit a frame to carry arbitrary data, the same must be modified before transmission and restored after reception. Techniques used for modification are referred to as data or byte stuffing because the modification involves inserting extra bits or bytes.

12.4.1 *Transmission Errors, Parity Bits and Checks*

Data transmission through electronic circuits or copper wires is susceptible to error due to interference caused by lightning, power surges and other forms of electromagnetic interference. Such interference changes the electrical signal representing data causing the receiver to misinterpret one or more bits of data.

This gives rise to transmission errors. Networks are therefore designed to enable hardware and software mechanisms with checks to detect such errors and rectify those. RS–232 circuits, in addition to declaring an error, in case a fixed voltage does not remain during the expected duration of each bit or if the stop bit does not occur at an appropriate time, use a second mechanism to ensure that each character arrives intact.

This mechanism is technically known as a 'parity check', which requires the sender to compute an additional bit, known as a 'parity bit', and attach it to each character before transmitting. The receiver receives all bits of a character and then removes the parity bit and does the same computation as done by the sender and checks that the computation results in the same value as per the parity bit. If there is any loss of bit during transmission, the computation done by the receiver will not tally with the parity bit and the receiver will send an error message to the sender. Parity checks may be even or odd as shown below:

Transmission Character	*Parity Check for '1' Bits*	*Parity Bit*
0100101	Even	1
0101101	Even	0
0100101	Odd	0
0101101	Odd	1

Parity bit has been selected so as to make the total number of '1' bits even or odd depending upon the even or odd parity check.

However, it may be noted that in case of any transmission error involving the loss of an even number of bits, the parity check will fail to detect the same.

12.4.2 *Checksum as Error-Detecting Mechanism*

Often computer networks make use of a checksum as a mechanism for the detection of errors. The sender computes the checksum as the sum of a sequence of binary integers which represent the data transmitted. This is illustrated in Figure 12.9.

Checksum mechanism has advantages such as smaller transmission overhead as checksum technique uses either 16-bit or 32-bit checksum and hence a single checksum is computed for an entire packet. Moreover, the computation of checksum is much easy being simple addition of binary integers. However, checksum can not detect all common errors as shown in the example in Figure 12.10.

Data Item in Binary	Checksum Value
00010	2
00001	1
00100	4
00010	2
Total	9

Figure 12.9 Illustration of a Checksum Value

Data Item in Binary	Checksum Value		Data Item in Binary	Checksum Value
00010	2	Transmission	00011	3
00001	1	Error converts	00000	0
00100	4	Data item in	00000	0
00010	2	binary as	00110	6
Total	9			9

Figure 12.10 Example of a Checksum Failing to Detect Transmission Errors

12.4.3 Error Detection with Cyclic Redundancy Checks (CRC)

CRC techniques can detect more errors in a computer network system than checksums. CRC employs two simple hardware components, namely an exclusive or (XOR) unit and a shift register. Figure 12.11 shows an XOR unit and the output table corresponding to four combinations of two inputs to the XOR unit. The output will be true (1) when two inputs differ; otherwise, it is false (0).

The other device used to compute a CRC is a shift register. A shift register has an output that gives the value of the leftmost bit. The shift register further reads an input on its right side only when a shift operation occurs. For example, Figures 12.12(a) and 12.12(b) show that although the input is ‘0’, the rightmost bit in the shift register remains ‘1’ until the instant the shift takes place.

The CRC method is based on the division of a polynomial of degree m (where m + 1 represents the bits of the message sent from receiver to sender) by another polynomial whose degree n determines the length of the CRC shift register. The second polynomial

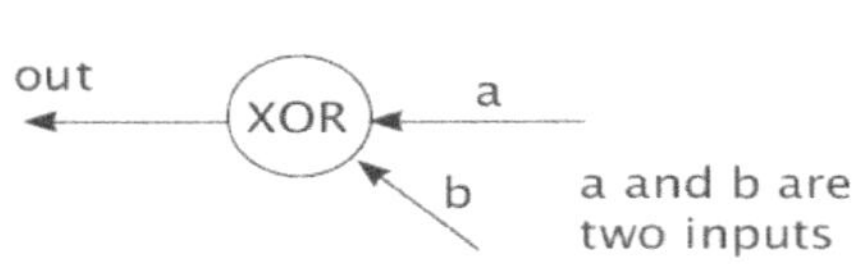

a	b	output
0	0	0
0	1	1
1	0	1
1	1	0

Figure 12.11 Exclusive OR Unit with Output Value Corresponding to Different Input Values

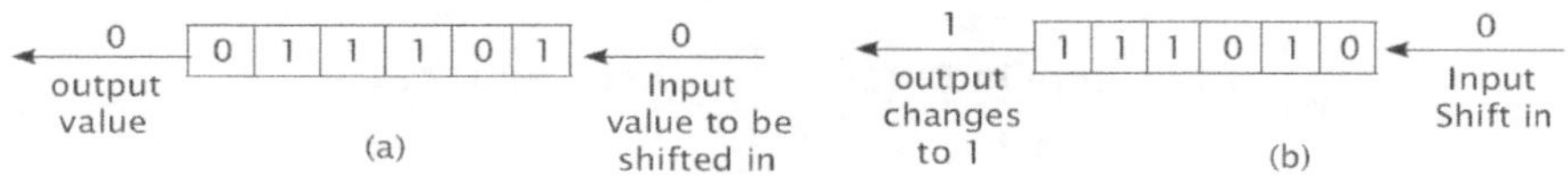

Figure 12.12 A Shift Register (a) before and (b) after a Shift Operation

of degree n is called the generator (G) which is known to both the receiver and the sender of the message of length (m + 1). The following example shows how the CRC works to detect errors.

Let the message represented by the polynomial M be:

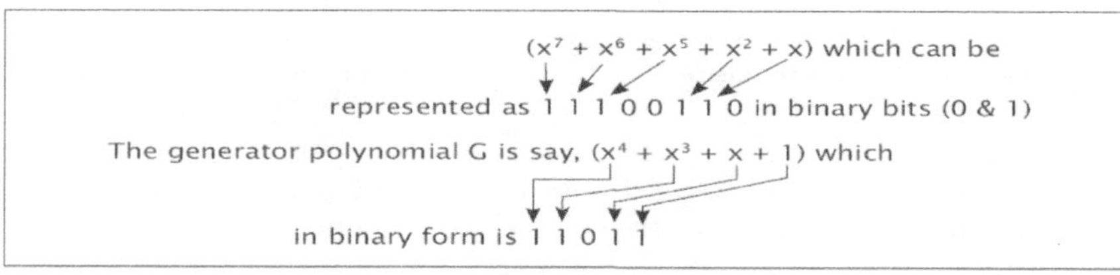

Therefore, the CRC shift register will be of length (5 – 1), that is, 4 which is the degree of the G polynomial.

The division of M by G is taken care of by the hardware components performing X or (represented as +) and the CRC shift register in the following steps, separately shown for the sender and receiver.

Sender:

Step 1: Initialise the shift register with all 0's and append an equal number of 0's to M

CRC Shift Register

0	0	0	0

M with appendix

1	1	1	0	0	1	1	0	0	0	0	0

Step 2: If the order bit (leftmost) of the shift register is '0'; shift the leftmost bit of CRC and the leftmost available bit of M together; otherwise, if the leftmost bit of CRC is '1'; shift CRC by one leftmost bit and M by the leftmost available bit and perform XOR on CRC by n low order bits of generator G of degree n. Since in this case the leftmost bit in CRC is 0, we shift both shift registers with the leftmost bit of message M, giving rise to:

CRC

0	0	0	1

(M – 1)

	1	1	0	0	1	1	0	0	0	0	0

Again, since leftmost bit of CRC is 0, we perform same shift operations giving rise to

CRC

0	0	1	1

(M – 2)

		1	0	0	1	1	0	0	0	0	0

Again, since leftmost bit of CRC is 0, we perform same shift giving rise to

CRC

0	1	1	1

(M – 3)

			0	0	1	1	0	0	0	0	0

CRC (M - 4)

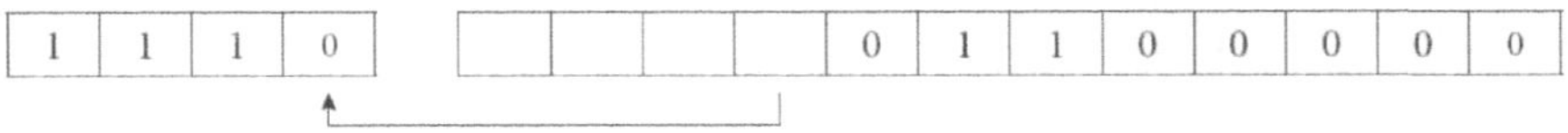

Now, leftmost bit of CRC is '1', we perform shift first and then X or with four (degree of generator) low order bits of G which is 1011, resulting in as follows:

(M - 5)

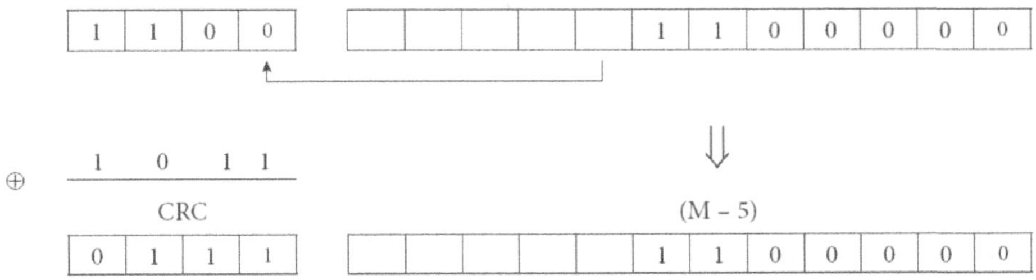

Now, the leftmost bit of CRC is '0', so we perform only shift operation giving rise to:

CRC. (M-6)

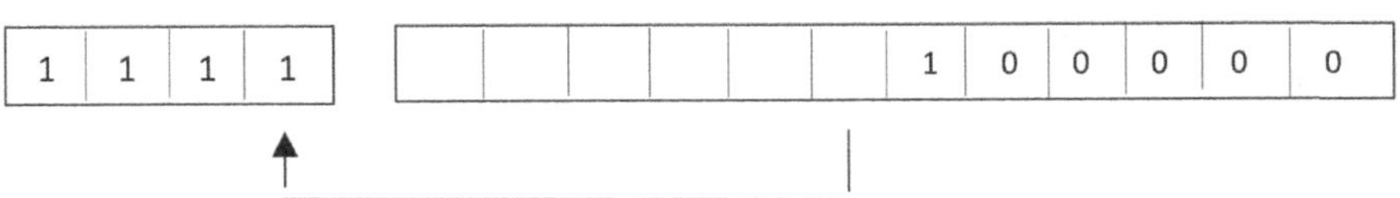

Since the leftmost bit of CRC is '1', we perform the shift operation first and then XOR as before with 1011 giving rise to:

CRC. (M-7)

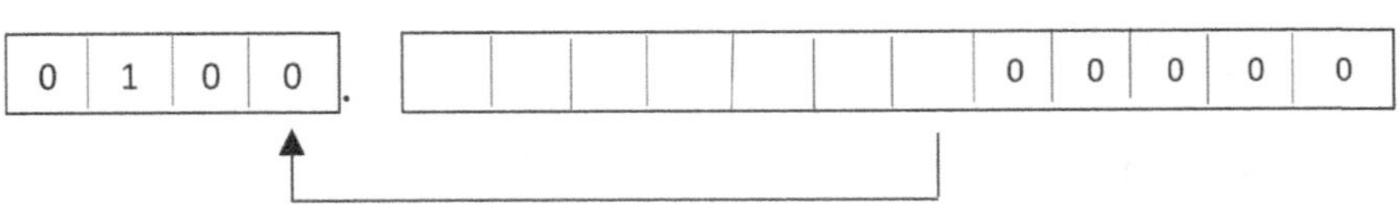

Now leftmost bit of CRC is '0', so we perform only shift operation giving rise to:

CRC. (M-8)

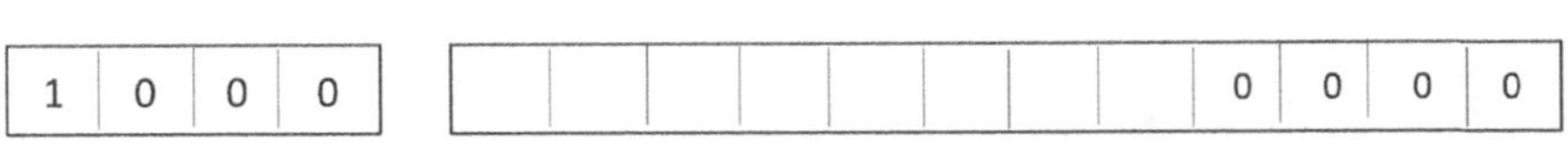

Now leftmost bit of CRC is '1'; hence we perform the shift first and then XOR as before with 1011 giving rise to:

CRC. (M-9)

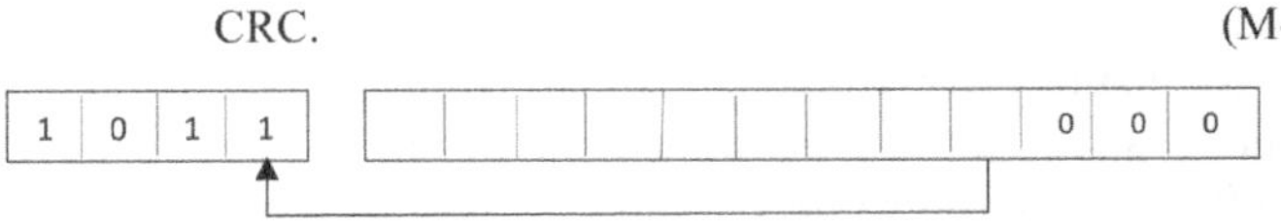

Now leftmost bit of CRC is ‘1’; hence we proceed with shift first and then XOR as before with 1011 giving rise to:

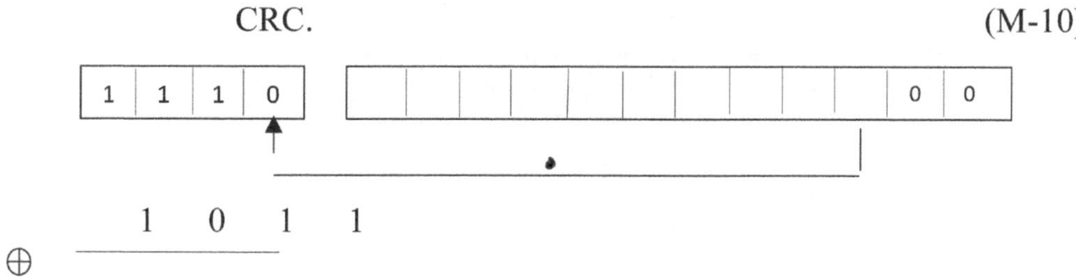

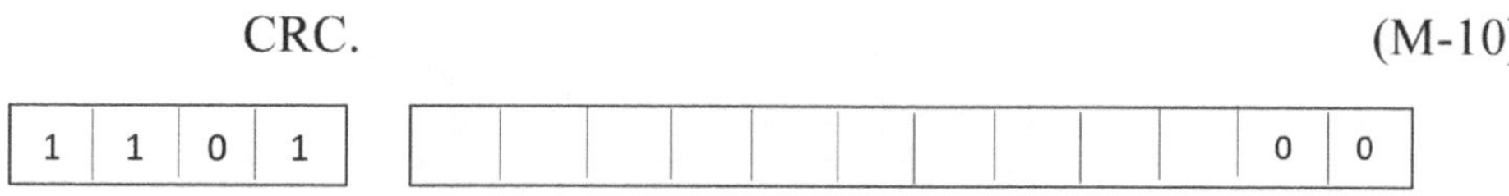

Now leftmost bit of CRC is ‘1’; hence we proceed with shift first and then XOR as before with 1011 giving rise to:

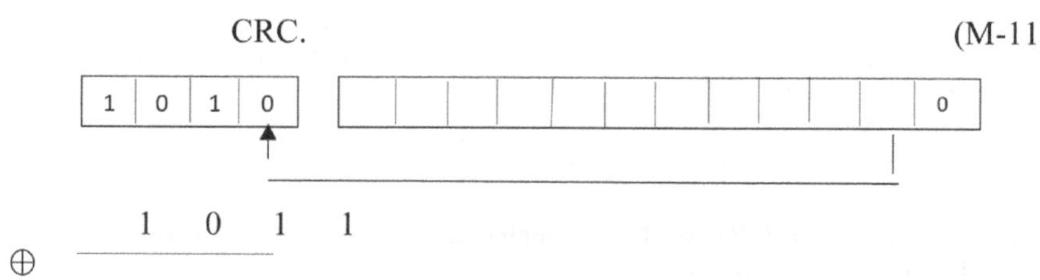

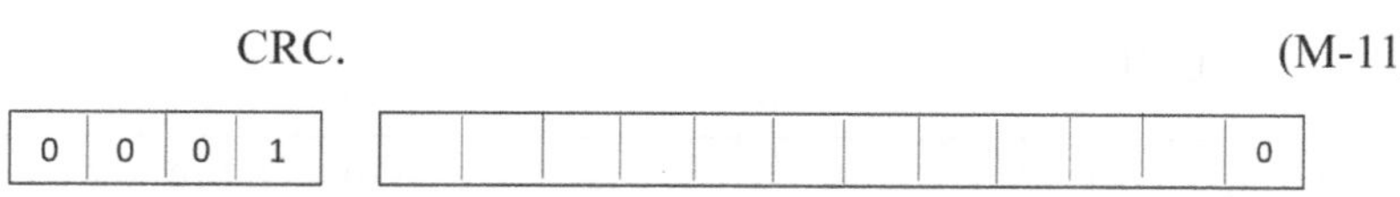

Now, leftmost bit of the CRC is ‘0’ hence we proceed with the same shift giving rise to: We are left with the message as blank.

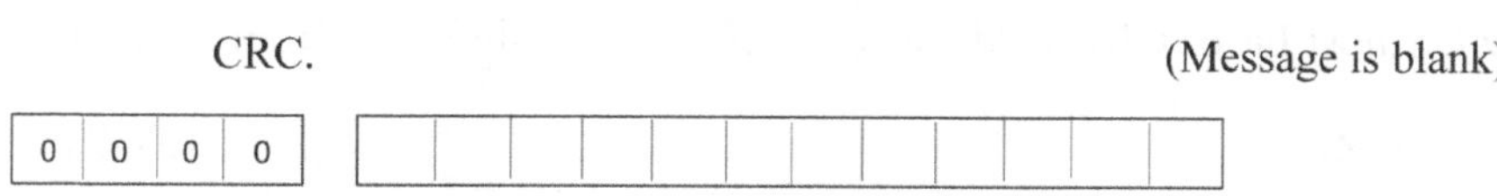

Since no bit is left in the appended message, the CRC content ‘0000’ is the remainder which the sender will append with the message and transmit to receiver as follows:

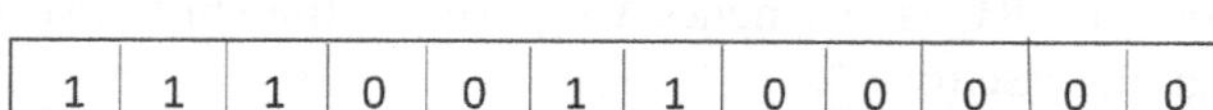

Now in order to ensure error-free transmission, the receiver will either perform the same steps as done by sender on the main message by eliminating the last four low order bits appended and arrive at the same remainder ‘0000’ or perform the steps with the received message as it is and arrive as ‘0000’ remainder. If the result of either operation as mentioned above is different, the receiver will report transmission error to sender. Let us perform the second alternative in steps as performed by receiver.

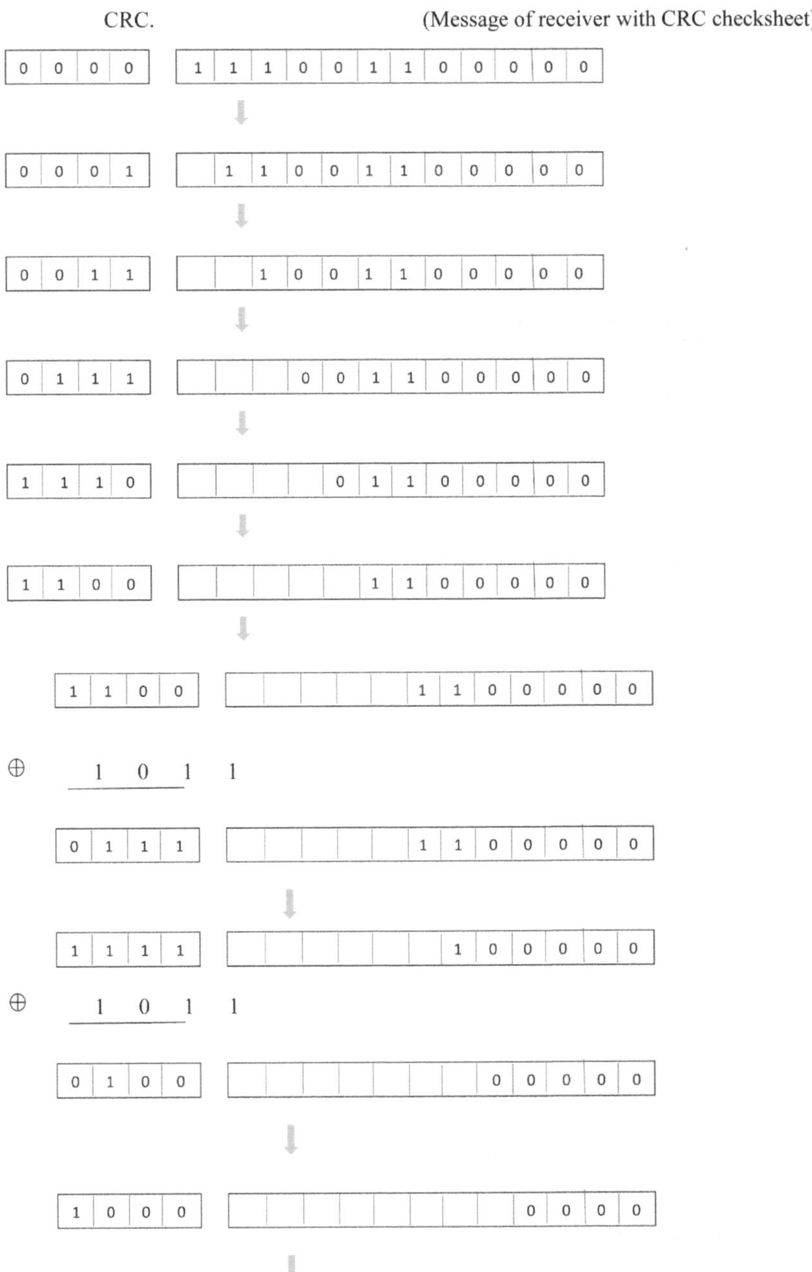

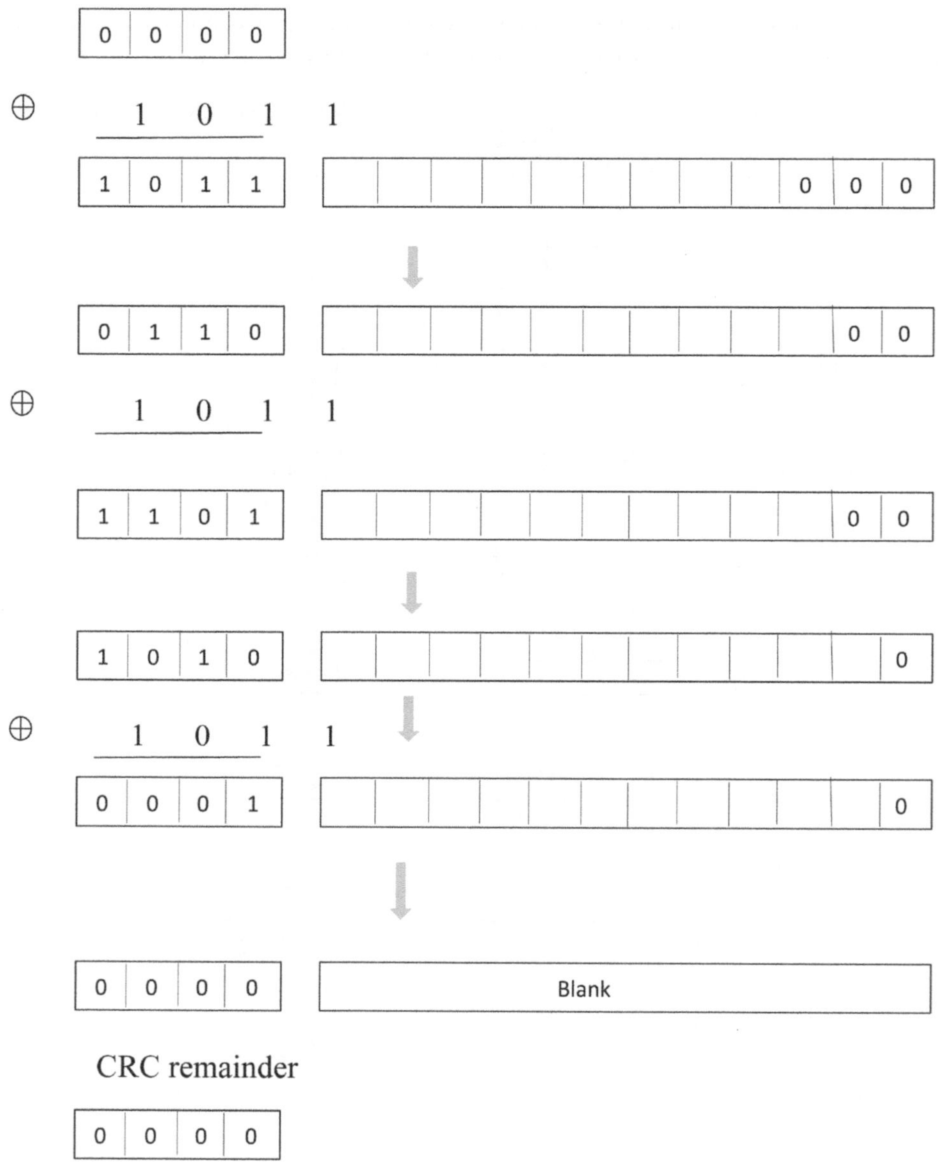

The remainder is ‘0000’, which shows that there is no transmission error.

12.5 LAN Technology and Network Topology

Direct point-to-point connection requires a dedicated connection for each pair of computers in the network, which is obviously disadvantageous since there will be many dedicated connections for the computers belonging to two locations. Therefore, the technology adopted for LAN is designed for sharing the communication line instead of separate modems and cables for each pair.

12.5.1 LAN Topologies

Networks are classified into different categories known as topologies such as star, ring and bus. They are described as follows:

Each computer (C1, C2, C3, ...C8) is attached to a central hub. For example, asynchronous transfer mode (ATM) is an electronic switch developed by telephone companies. ATM is connected to multiple computers, each one being connected to the switch through a pair of optical fibres; each fibre transmits data in one direction only at a speed of 155 Mbps or faster.

Computers (C1, C2, C3, C4) are connected to one another in a ring.

12.5.2 Token Passing

Computers attached in a ring topology network use a token, which is a short message to coordinate error-free transmission of data. The bit pattern of the token is different from the data frame bits. The token rotates around the ring and allows one computer at a time to transmit exactly one frame and then passes the data frame to all other computers and then reaches back to the sender computer to return the same frame. The sender computer compares the frame transmitted with the frame received from the token and if both are found the same, error-free transmission is ensured. During the cycle of rotation of the token with a frame of data, when the token reaches the destination computer (recipient of the frame), the same makes a copy of the frame and allows the token to pass to the next computer. The token allows the computers to send one frame at a time each in rotation and if no computer has data to transmit, the token cycles round the ring (known as 'token ring') at a very high speed. Figure 12.13 shows a 'token ring' with the flow of bits of a frame in it.

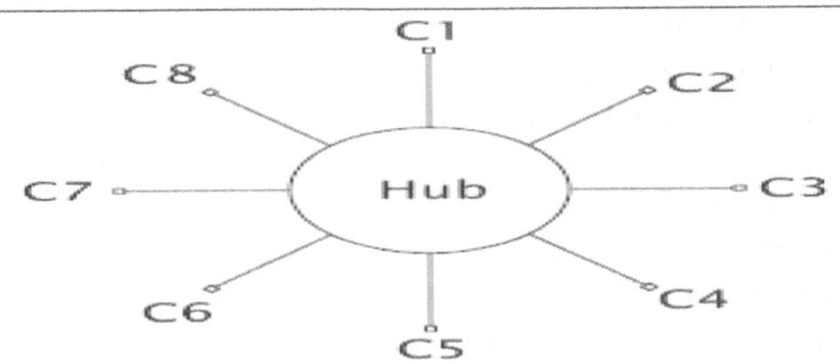

Star topology

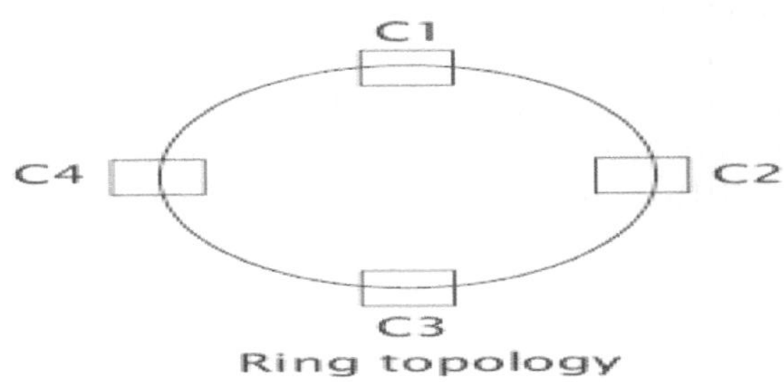

Ring topology

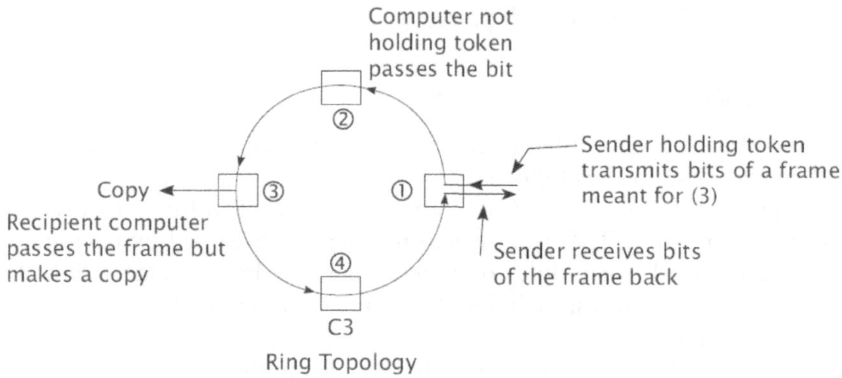

Figure 12.13 Token Ring with Flow of a Frame

12.5.3 Self-healing Token Ring

In case of a normal token ring, any failure of a single computer attached to the ring will make the complete token ring inoperative since each computer attached to the ring must pass the frame to the next one in the cycle. Hence, self-healing token rings have been designed to take care of failure of any computer by bypassing the same one and completing the cycle with the other computers through another inner ring (cable). Necessarily, therefore, self-healing token rings have two concentric rings connecting the computers. The outer ring is used for normal transmission of data and the inner ring is unused for data transmission except in the case of any failure, and the inner ring facilitates completing the path by looping back by the computer adjacent to the failed computer as shown in Figure 12.14.

In bus topology, a single long cable known as a bus is used to which computers are attached. Any computer attached to a bus can send a signal when all other attached computers receive the signal. However, the transmission is coordinated in such a way that one computer is allowed to send a signal at any time. Popular Ethernet is a bus network first developed at Xerox Corporation's Palo Alto Research Centre in the early 1970s. It consists of a single coaxial cable (bus) to which multiple computers are connected. Ethernet has a limitation of 500 metres in length and a minimum separation distance of 3 metres between each pair of computers connected to Ethernet. The original Ethernet of the 1970s had a speed of 10 Mbps; however, the speed was enhanced subsequently to 100 Mbps or even 1 Gbps (Gigabytes per second) in the case of gigabit Ethernet. Ethernets use Manchester encoding in which case bits (0 or 1) are represented by changes in voltage rather than fixed voltage as in the case of RS–232.

A change from positive to zero voltage represents a '0' bit, and a change from zero to positive voltage represents a '1' bit. This is because researchers observed that a hardware device detects a change in voltage more promptly than a fixed voltage value. A comparison of the encoding according to RS–232 with the Manchester encoding used by Ethernet for the same message '101011' transmitted is shown in Figure 12.15.

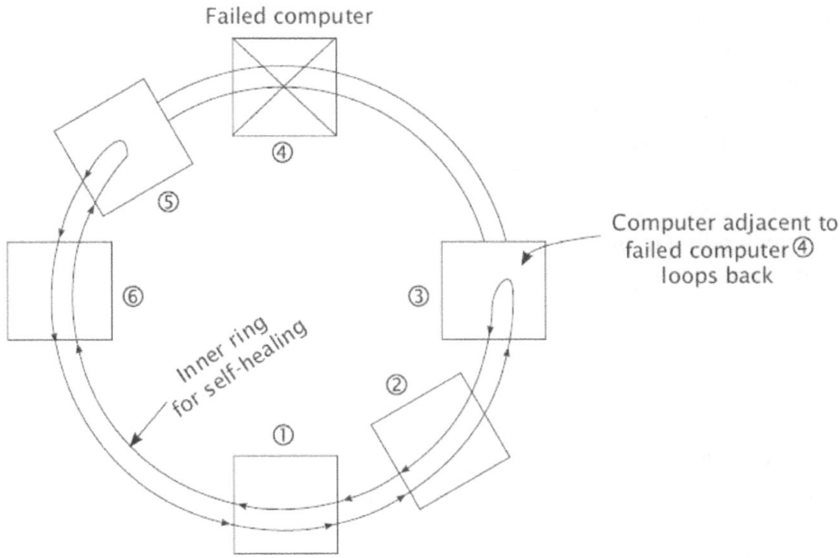

Figure 12.14 Self-healing Token Ring

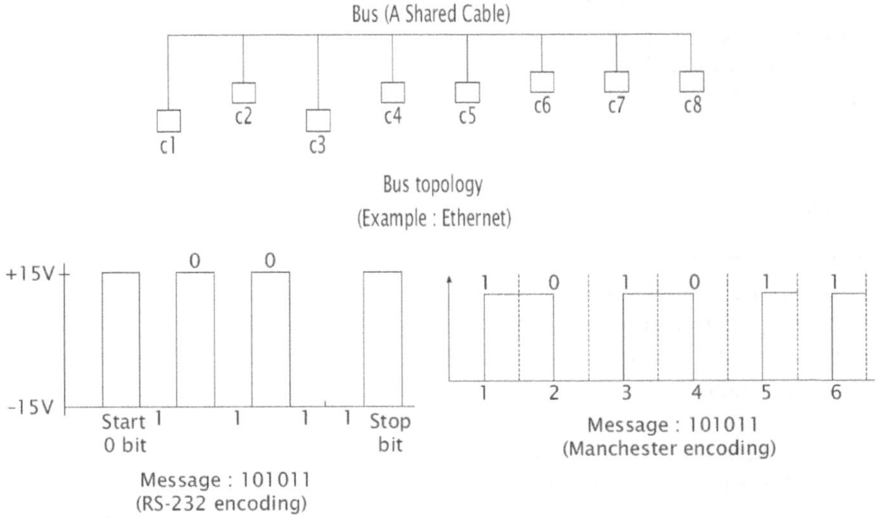

Figure 12.15 Comparison between RS–232 and Manchester Encoding

Ethernet allows any one computer to transmit a frame at a time and all other computers wait until the transmission is over. The frame bits pass one by one across the cable to all computers connected, and the destination computer receives a copy of each bit. The bus technology is adopted by a multi-access shared network in order to detect by any computer at any time whether the cable is engaged with any electrical signal (technically called carrier) before transmitting any signal. The network is known as carrier sense multiple access (CSMA) network. In order to ensure that no two computers transmit simultaneously, causing a collision, the sending station monitors signals on the cable and if it finds that the signal on the cable is different from the one it is sending, it will realise that a collision has occurred, and immediately it will stop transmission. Technically, the process of detecting any collision during transmission through a 'cable carrier sensing' is known as the CSMA with collision detection (CSMA/CD) mechanism. Although the Ethernet is very popular bus technology LAN, other technologies such as 'Local Talk' invented by Apple Computer Corporation (through 230.4 kbps) use bus topology for connecting Macintosh computers. It is a low-cost network.

12.5.4 Collision Avoidance through Carrier Sensing in Case of Wireless LANs

Wireless LAN adopts a modified form of CSMA/CD, known as CSMA with collision avoidance (CSMA/CA). The sender sends first a control message to the receiver before transmitting the frame. The receiver responds by sending another control message indicating that it is free to receive a frame.

After the sender receives the same control message as a response from the receiver, it starts transmitting a frame. Since control messages are generally much shorter than a frame, the collision of control messages, if it occurs, can be handled at first instance only by back off by the sending stations, and the chance of a second collision is almost ruled out, and eventually one of the two control messages arrives as it is to the receiving computer, and the same then transmits a response. The Institute of Electrical and Electronics Engineers (IEEE) standard 802.11b, known as 'Wi-Fi', operates at 11 Mbps and 2.4 GHz frequency range. A standard known as 'Bluetooth', which specifies a short distance wireless LAN technology, employs the CSMA/CA method.

12.6 Hardware Addressing and Frame Type Identification

The hardware of a computer attached to a network consists of two main components. The first component is the Network Interface Hardware (NIH), which basically transmits and receives frames on the LAN. The second component is the processor and the memory unit, which handles incoming data, processes the data and generates outgoing data. This component constantly interacts with the NIH. Figure 12.16 shows schematically the organisation of the LAN hardware and the CPU and memory.

Hardware addressing is very important for direct communication among the network computers. The frame transmitted by any computer in a shared network (LAN) essentially contains the address of the sender, the source address and the intended recipient, the destination address. Therefore, each computer on the LAN is assigned a unique numeric address, called its physical address. Different LAN technologies employ different formats or types of physical addresses of the hardware, which are of three main categories, namely:

1. Static physical address which is assigned by the hardware manufacturer and is fixed for a particular hardware.

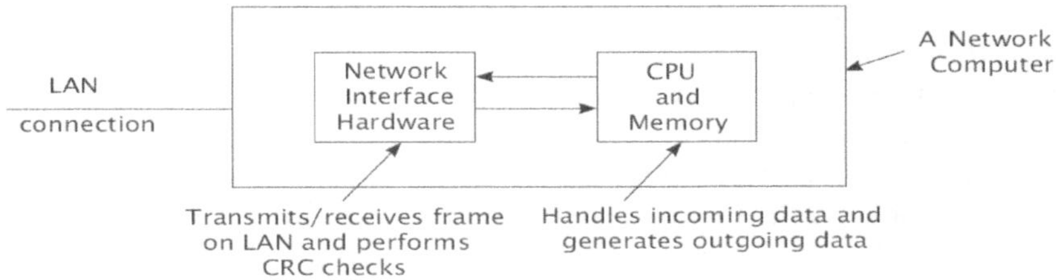

Figure 12.16 Hardware Organisation of a Network Computer

2. Configurable physical address which is set by the customer (user) when the hardware is first installed in a LAN.
3. Dynamic physical address which is automatically assigned to a computer when the computer in the network first boots. Dynamic addressing is facilitated by some randomising algorithm to ensure that assigned address is not already being used by any other computer in the network.

(i) **Addressing Mechanism for Broadcasting and Multi-casting**: Broadcasting makes a copy of the transmitted data available to all computers on the network so that the particular computer for which the message is applicable would respond. Multi-casting is a restricted form of broadcasting introduced to take advantage of broadcasting without wasting CPU resources of all other computers on a shared network.(ii) **Frame Format**: A frame consists of two parts, namely a frame header which contains mainly the addresses of the source and destination and the frame type as the first part followed by the second part known as the payload which is the data part being sent and much larger than the first part. A format of the frame as defined by Ethernet is shown in Figure 12.17.

The 64-bit preamble contains alternating 1s and 0s and is used to synchronise the receiver hardware with the incoming frame. Ethernet uses static addressing with 48 bits. The 16-bit frame type contains a unique value for each possible use of the network. The receiver examines the frame type field to determine the mode of handling the frame.

12.7 LAN Extension

LAN technology as such is best suited in case of computers located in a single building or office at a distance limited to a few hundred metres. However, there are mechanisms for LAN extension using fibre modems, repeaters, bridges or switches. Fibre modems in

Preamble	Destination Address	Source Address	Frame Type	Data in Frame	CRC
8	6	6	2	46–1500	4
	Header			Pay load	

Figure 12.17 Frame Format Used with Ethernet

Note: The number in each field gives the field size in 8-bit octets; for example, preamble is of 8x8 that is 64 bits.

a pair with optical fibres are used to connect a computer to a distant network hub. Since the fibre has low transmission time and high bandwidth, it allows longer distance (several kilometres) transmission than the typical cable LAN.

A repeater is an analogue electronic device which joins together two LAN segments by monitoring the electrical signals in either of the two and transmits the signal with amplification to the other. A pair of computers on the extended LAN can communicate with each other without knowing that there is a repeater separating them. The Ethernet standard, however, specifies that because of the limitation on transmission delay, the extension network will not function properly if more than four repeaters are used to separate any pair of stations. Repeaters, however, have several disadvantages. The most important disadvantage is that repeaters cannot understand complete frames. Therefore, in addition to propagating copies of valid signals from one Ethernet segment to another, a repeater also transmits other electrical signals such as collisions or electrical interference from one segment to another. Bridges are also electronic devices that connect two LAN segments. However, unlike repeaters, bridges are digital devices having the same network interface as a computer and thus can handle frames. Bridges are more advantageous than repeaters because, unlike repeaters, bridges will not propagate any electrical interference caused by lightning and other reasons from one segment of Ethernet to another segment. Bridges will simply discard an incorrectly formed frame in much the same way as a network computer discards a frame with an error. Similarly, a bridge will not forward a collision from one segment to another. A bridge using a leased satellite channel can connect two LAN segments at two sites across a long distance as shown in Figure 12.18.

Switching is another mechanism of connecting one or more computers with an electronic device known as a switch. A switched LAN consists of a single switch that transmits frames among many computers.

A switch consists of processors and interconnects such as an electronic crossbar. The processor, being an intelligent device, is capable of finding the destination address of an incoming frame from a computer connected to one of its ports and then uses the interconnect to transfer the frame to the correct output port. Figure 12.19 shows the concept of a switched LAN.

A switch differs from a network hub in that the hub connects computers with no understanding of the frames it transfers. It simply receives a frame of data and transfers (broadcasts) the same to all other connected devices irrespective of which device responds

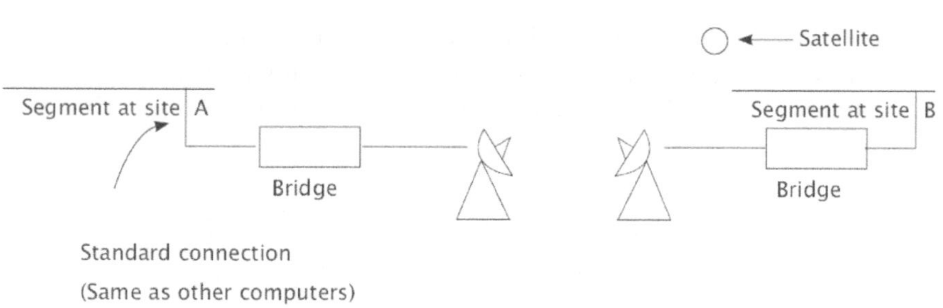

Figure 12.18 A Bridge Using a Leased Satellite Channel Connects Two LAN Segments at Two Sites

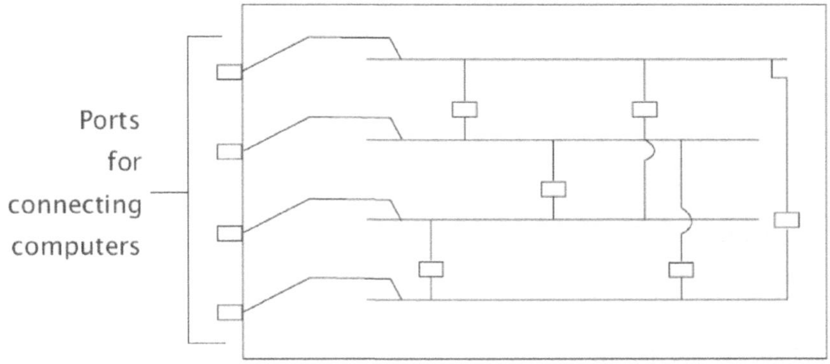

Figure 12.19 Concept of a Switched LAN

as the final destination. The network bandwidth is split among all the connected devices or computers, which naturally implies slower transmission speed. On the other hand, a switch receives a frame of data from a computer and determines which computer or device the frame is intended for and sends it to that computer or device only.

Obviously, the network bandwidth is not shared by all connected devices as in the case of a hub and makes the speed of transmission much faster and the network efficient. Hence, switches are preferred over hubs.

Router is another piece of hardware which connects two heterogeneous networks. A computer network can be connected to the internet through a router. A router contains a processor and memory and a separate network I/O interface for each network it connects. The basic difference between a switch or hub and a router is that, unlike a switch or hub, which transmits data packets among local computers, a router routes frames of data to other networks. Routers have more logic built into them and can determine the best path or route for transmitting the data packets.

12.8 Long-Distance and Local-Loop Digital Technologies

The two main limitations of the LAN are its inability to connect any arbitrary number of computers and to connect computers located at sites large distances apart. In order to overcome the above two limitations, the following two developments were made.

12.8.1 Digital Telephony Circuits

Digital telephone circuits developed by telephone companies were adopted for the purpose of long-distance connections in a large network. Digital telephone circuits designed to carry voice traffic in a digital form through analogue to digital form and vice versa through appropriate converters (analogue to digital and digital to analogue) have been used for data traffic also. The digital circuits leased from telephone companies form the fundamental components for long-distance computer networks. However, a special

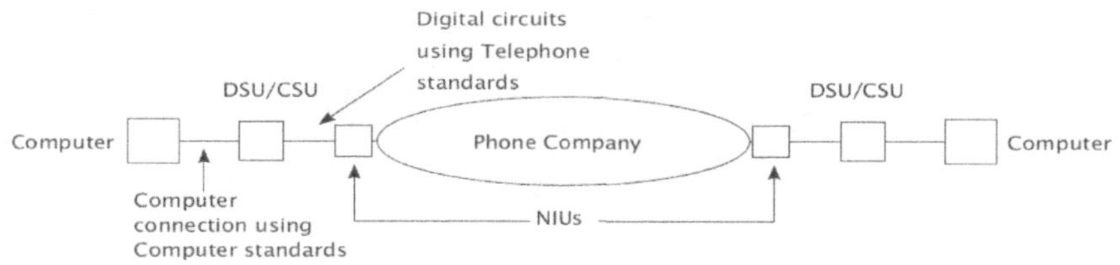

Figure 12.20 Illustration of a Digital Circuit with a DSU/CSU at Each End
Source: Comer (2004, 180).

hardware device is needed to interface a computer in a network to a digital circuit developed by a telephone company. This hardware device contains two functional parts known as data service unit (DSU) and channel service unit (CSU). The need for the hardware device DSU/CSU arose because of the different standards developed by telephone companies for their digital circuits and the same developed by the computer industry. A DSU/CSU is required at the end of a leased digital circuit as shown in Figure 12.20.

The DSU of the device handles the data, whereas the CSU handles line termination, diagnostics and a loop-back test facility to send a copy of all data that arrive at the circuit back to the sender without further processing. The network interface unit (NIU) shown in Figure 12.20, is an equipment provided by the telephone company and is an interface between the facilities of the phone company and those of the subscriber.

Digital signal (DS) level multiplexing facilitates multiple phone calls onto a single carrier system connection. For example, DS1 denotes multiplexing of 24 phone calls onto a single circuit. The other important standards that classify the digital circuits of the carrier system are the T-standards, which define the underlying carrier systems based on their data rates in Mbps and the number of voice circuits such as 24 and 96. Some of the popular T-standards are as follows:

Name of T-Standard Line	*Bit Rate (Mbps)*	*Voice Circuit Channels*
T1	1.544	24
T1C	3.152	48
T2	6.312	96 (4 × 24)
T3	44.736	672 (28 × 24)
T4	274.176	4032
T5	400.352	5760

It may be noted that the T3 circuit can multiplex 28 numbers of T1 circuits.

TDM technology is used to further subdivide T1 circuits, and one of the such popular fractional T1 capacities is 64 kbps leased by the telephone companies, who do not need T1 capacity.

A DS1 telephone circuit is made up of 24 8-bit channels and is a full-duplex circuit. The bandwidth is achieved by pulse code modulation (PCM) of 8 kHz (8,000 frames per second) for each of the 24 channels. The calculation is as follows:

(8 bits per channel × 24 channels × 8,000 frames/sec)
= 1,544,000 bits per second
= 1.544 Mbps

In the late 20th century, parts of the network created primarily to transmit voices were upgraded with large-scale digital services to subscribers under the name of integrated services digital network (ISDN) and DSL to handle traffic of digital data. In the telecommunication arena, DSL is now widely understood as the asymmetric digital subscriber line (ADSL).

ISDN handles data and voice in a digitised form for subscribers over conventional local loop wiring with twisted copper wires. It provides three separate digital channels to subscribers. The three are B, B and D usually denoted as 2B + D. The 'B' channels are for carrying digitised voice or compressed video and operate at a speed of 64 kbps. The 'D' channel which operates at 16 kbps is basically a control channel. Subscribers use the 'D' channel to request services (data, fax or voice), which are then supplied through the 'B' channels. The subscriber also uses the 'D' channel to manage a session in progress or to terminate the same. However, with the development of dial-up modems and other technologies such as the internet providing higher data transfer rates across the local loop wiring at lower cost, ISDN now has limited application.

ADSL is one of the most important DSL technologies and is a local loop technology that accommodates users who receive much more information (a higher bit rate downstream) than they send (a lower bit rate upstream). Hence, the name of the DSL is prefixed with the word 'asymmetric'. In the case of a typical ADSL, the maximum downstream rate can be as high as 6.144 Mbps; whereas the upstream rate is a mere 640 kbps. Because the mandatory network control channel requires 64 kbps, the effective upstream rate is (640 – 64) = 576 kbps only. In order to achieve high bit rates downstream over conventional twisted-pair wiring, ADSL uses an adaptive technology in which a pair of modems (one providing a digital connection to the local loop network and the other to the service provider) probe many frequencies on the line connecting them and select frequencies and modulation techniques best suited to the line condition.

12.8.2 Wireless Networks

Technologies such as DSL and ADSL have limitations, particularly in remote areas. Further, copper wiring for ADSL networks needs sufficient gauge; otherwise, the digital signals will be attenuated. In order to overcome such limitations of wired networks, wireless networks have been developed. WiMAX, developed by IEEE, is a high-speed wireless network used in metropolitan areas with a throughput of up to 155 Mbps. WiMAX is capable of spanning larger distances than a LAN, but obviously less than a wide area network (WAN). WiMAX can either replace a local loop technology or link an internet service provider with a neighbourhood in a city, providing high-speed access. Another wireless alternative for digital communication is through broadcast satellite systems. However, in order to devise a low-cost local loop system through satellites, two developments were made. First, instead of treating satellites as a point-to-point communication system, a broadcasting system was devised. Second, for low-cost solution instead of a large ground station, an alternative uplink transmission path was made. The first development enabled the satellite to broadcast each packet, a copy of which can be received by all stations tuned to the satellite. Each station is assigned a unique address; the station filters incoming packets, and a packet is accepted by a station only when the address of the packet is the same as the address of the station. Other packets are discarded by the station.

The uplink transmission path was taken care of by adopting the concept of asymmetric delivery by the broadcast satellite technology. In such situations, the broadcast satellite is used for downstream traffic only and upstream traffic travels over a low-capacity network such as a conventional dial-up telephone connection.

Synchronous optical networking (SONET) and synchronous digital hierarchy (SDH) are standardised protocols that transfer multiple digital bit streams synchronously over optical fibre using lasers or light from LEDs. SONET specifications include framing of data, multiplexing circuit capacity enhancement and synchronising clock information along with data.

12.9 WAN Technologies

Unlike LAN and MAN (metropolitan area networks such as WiMAX), WAN can connect sites located in multiple cities, countries and continents. The other distinguishing feature of WAN is its scalability to connect many sites with many computers in each site. Because of its scalability, a WAN can connect computers located in offices or business units of a multinational company with large geographical dispersions. In spite of large scalability, WAN is capable of connecting large numbers of computers without any trade-off in its performance of speed and efficient communication.

WAN is made up of many switches to which individual computers are connected. The switches are known as packet switches because they move complete packets of data from one connection to another. The digital connection may be from one switch to another or may be from a computer to the switch as shown in Figure 12.21.

A packet switch is conceptually a small computer having its processor, memory and I/O devices for sending and receiving packets. The I/O connectors which connect a packet switch to a digital circuit leading to another packet switch operate at high speed, whereas the I/O connectors which connect individual computers to the switch operate at lower speed. The digital connections in a WAN can include leased data circuits, optical fibres, microwaves and satellite channels depending upon the particular WAN design. The interconnections among switches and their capacities are chosen according to the traffic

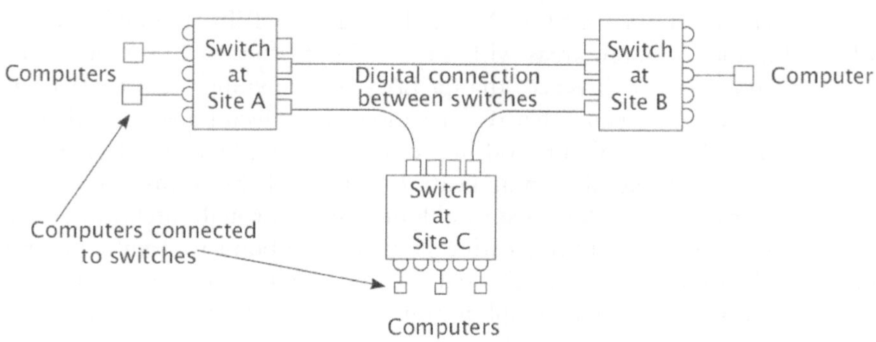

Figure 12.21 WAN Formed with Packet Switches and Computers

expected and additional redundancy to take care of contingencies such as failures. In that sense, a WAN need not be symmetric.

12.9.1 Store and Forward

WAN permits many computers to send packets simultaneously by the Store and Forward technique. The technique allows a packet switch to store in buffer a short burst of packets that arrive at a time to the switch. The store operation, which occurs first, stores a copy of the packets received by the I/O hardware of the packet switch into its memory. Next, the forward operation takes place. If the device is not already busy, the processor of the packet switch checks each packet for its destination, determines the interface over which it should be sent and starts the output hardware device over which it should be sent, or else the processor places the outgoing packets in a queue associated with the output device. As soon as the device finishes sending a packet, it extracts and begins sending the next packet in the queue on a first-come-first-serve basis.

12.9.2 Physical Addressing Method in a WAN

Each address in a WAN consists of two parts: the first part identifies the particular packet switch and the second part identifies the computer connected to the switch. Figure 12.22 illustrates the addressing method in a WAN.

The two-part addressing in a WAN, as shown in Figure 12.22 is also known as the hierarchical address of a WAN. In actual practice, the address is represented as a single binary value, with some bits of the value representing the first part of the address and the remaining bits representing the second part. Because each address in a WAN is represented as a single binary value, users and application programmers treat the address as an integer and need not know that addresses are hierarchically assigned.

A packet switch in a WAN works on the principles of 'source independence' and 'next-hop forwarding', which means that a packet switch has to keep the information about the next place (technically known as 'next hop') to forward the packet so as to eventually reach its destination, without any dependence on either the original source of the packet or the path already traversed by the packet before arriving at the particular switch. This mechanism of 'next-hop' forwarding with 'source independence' in a WAN makes the computer network compact and improves its performance.

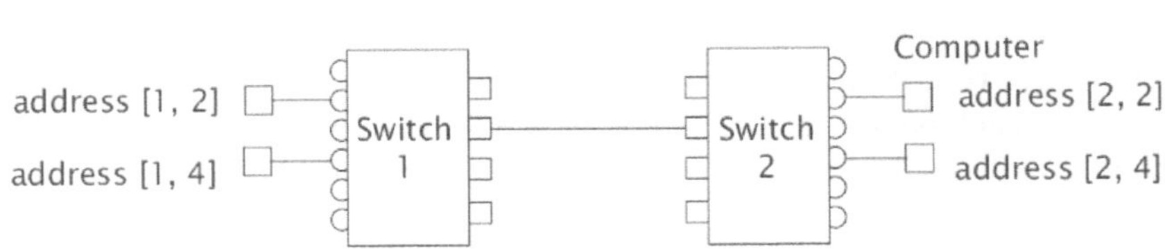

Figure 12.22 Addressing Method in a WAN

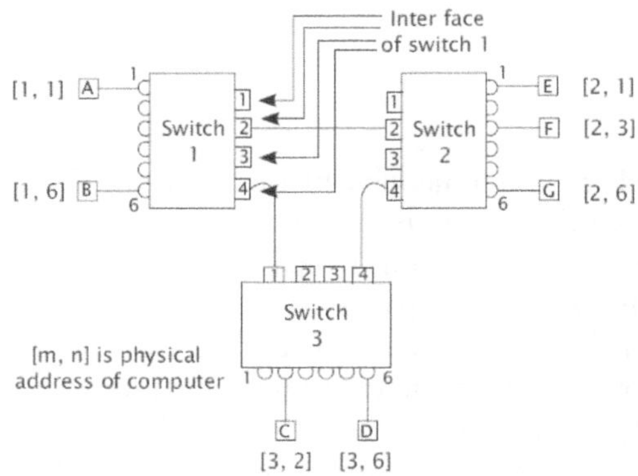

Destination	NEXT HOPS		
	Switch 1	Switch 2	Switch 3
[1, 1]	Computer A	Interface 2	Interface 1
[1, 6]	Computer B	Interface 2	Interface 1
[2, 1]	Interface 2	Computer E	Interface 4
[2, 3]	Interface 2	Computer F	Interface 4
[2, 6]	Interface 2	Computer G	Interface 4
[3, 2]	Interface 4	Interface 4	Computer C
[3, 6]	Interface 4	Interface 4	Computer D

Figure 12.23 Illustration of Routing Table

Note: Routing table for each switch is stored in the same switch.

12.9.3 Routing Table in a WAN

Routing table is a table used by a WAN to store next-hop information of its packet switches. Figure 12.23 illustrates a routing table. (The routing table for each switch is stored in the same switch.)

12.9.4 Interior and Exterior Switches in a WAN

Interior packet switches in a WAN are those that do not have any computers attached. Such switches are only to handle traffic (load). Exterior switches have computers attached to them.

For any WAN to function correctly and optimally, both interior and exterior packet switches must have a routing table for each, and both types must forward packets through the 'next-hop forwarding' mechanism. Moreover, the routing table for each packet switch must have values to fulfil the following criteria:

1. **Universal Routing**: It means the routing table in each switch must have a next-hop route for each possible destination.
2. **Optimal Routes**: In a packet switch, the next hop value in the routing table for a given destination must point to the shortest path to the destination.

Based on the above criteria, computer-based algorithms are used to compute routing table entries for each packet switch in a large WAN. The computation follows two basic approaches as explained below:

1. **Static Routing**: A computer program computes the routes when a packet switch boots. The routes once computed do not change with the changes in the network conditions such as traffic.
2. **Dynamic Routing**: In this case, the program develops an initial routing table when a packet switch boots, but the table is subsequently altered as and when the condition of the network changes.

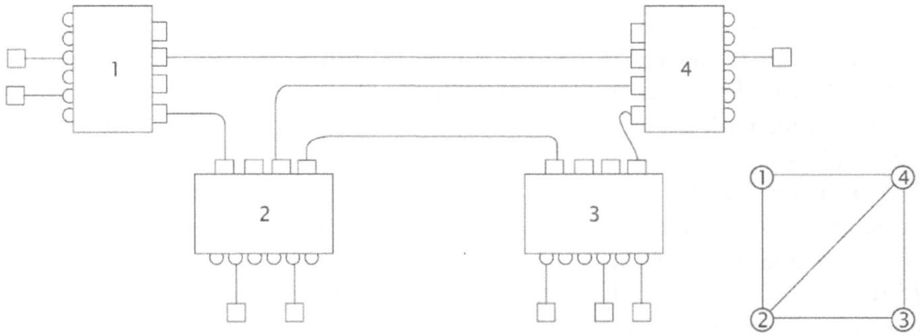

Figure 12.24 WAN and the Corresponding Graph

Although static routing is simple and has less network overhead, it is inflexible. Therefore, many networks follow dynamic routing because of its obvious advantages such as handling dynamic network traffic and, in case of failure of network hardware, its capability to modify the routes to take care of the failure.

The software for computation of entries for a routing table is based on the shortest path from a particular source to each of the destinations adopting the famous Dijkstra's algorithm. In order to facilitate the application of the same algorithm, a WAN is treated as a graph with the nodes of the graph corresponding to the packet switches and with each edge of the graph connecting two nodes to represent a digital connection between the corresponding packet switches as shown in Figure 12.24. The routing table corresponding to each node of the graph is shown in Table 12.2.

The Dijkstra's algorithm finds the distance along the shortest path from a single source node to each of the other nodes (destination) in the graph, and accordingly, the next-hop routing table is constructed during the shortest path determination. The distance of each edge is the weight assigned to the edge during the computation of the shortest path. Thus, a path with the least number of edges may not be the path with the least weight. For example, in the graph shown in Figure 12.24, the path from node 1 to node 3 could have been either (1, 2) → (2–3) or (1–4) → (4, 3). However, the next hop has been shown as (1, 2) as the former path (1, 2) → (2–3) might have been less in weight compared to (1–4) → (4, 3).

Table 12.2 Routing Table for Each Node of the Graph Shown in Figure 12.24

Node 1		*Node 2*		*Node 3*		*Node 4*	
Destination	*Next Hop*	*Destination*	*Next Hop*	*Destination*	*Next Hop*	*Destination*	*Next Hop*
1	-	1	(2,1)	1	(3,2)	1	(4,1)
2	(1,2)	2	-	2	(3,2)	2	(4,2)
3	(1,2)	3	(2,3)	3	-	3	(4,3)
4	(1,4)	4	(2,4)	4	(3,4)	4	-

12.9.5 Popular WAN Technologies

Few of the popular WANs are the Advanced Research Projects Agency Network (ARPANET), X.25, Frame Relay, switched multi-megabit data service (SMDS) and ATM.

ARPANET was developed by the US Defence Department in the late 1960s and is a legacy WAN technology with leased data lines connecting packet switches at a slow speed of 56 kbps.

X.25 was a standard for WAN technology developed by the Consultative Committee for International Telephone and Telegraph (CCITT) using two or more X.25 packet switches connected by leased lines.

X.25 operates at a speed of a maximum of 100 kbps.

Frame relay is a high-speed WAN used by many phone companies to provide high-speed WAN service up to 1.5 Mbps. Frame relay service is designed to accept and deliver blocks of data, each block containing up to 8K octets of data. Frame relay can bridge two LAN segments located in two different distant geographic locations, such as two cities. In order to connect two LAN segments, a frame relay can be designed to operate at a high speed of 4 Mbps or more. However, in practice, frame relay subscribers choose to operate at either 1.5 Mbps or a lower 56 kbps. SMDS is also a high-speed (1.544–44.736 Mbps) WAN data service offered by long-distance carriers. SMDS is designed to carry data instead of voice traffic to achieve the highest speed of 44.736 Mbps over DS Level 3 (DS–3) transmission. ATM also provides WAN technology developed by the telecommunications industry to handle both conventional telephone voice traffic and data traffic. ATM was also designed to serve as both LAN and WAN technologies.

12.10 Network Characteristics

Apart from the underlying technologies, which classify networks into various categories such as MAN, LAN and WAN, there are additional characteristics such as ownership, service paradigm and performance of the network in terms of its transmission delay and throughput.

Ownership of a network can be either private or public, and accordingly there can be private networks or public networks. A network is called a private network if its use is limited to a single individual or a company.

A public network, on the other hand, is owned and operated by a service provider such as a common carrier, such as a telephone company. Any subscriber can avail themselves of the service of a public network to communicate with any other subscriber to the service. A virtual private network (VPN) is one having the advantages of both private and public networks because it allows an individual company with multiple sites to have the feel of a completely private network, although using a public network to carry the traffic between the sites, because the VPN system restricts incoming and outgoing packets at each site so that no packet can enter the site of a company unless it arrived from one of the other sites of the same company. Likewise, no outgoing packet can leave the site of a company unless its destination is another one of the same company's sites. Moreover, VPN systems use encryption to assure absolute privacy of the packets sent by a company. Even if anyone who is not connected with the company obtains a copy of a packet, the same person will be unable to decipher the contents of the packet.

12.10.1 Service Paradigm

For the sake of explaining the variety of services by a network to the computers attached to it, networks can be broadly categorised as connection-oriented (CO) service or connectionless (CL) service.

A connection-oriented service requires a connection to be established between two computers before any data can be transferred from one to the other, and when the transfer of data is complete, the connection is terminated. This is similar in concept to telephonic communication.

A connectionless service requires a computer to arrange the data to be transmitted in the appropriate frame and to attach the address of the computer to which the data have to be delivered and then pass the frame to the network for delivery. The connectionless network system then transports the frame to the destination computer and delivers the same. The connectionless network system is analogous to the postal mail system where the sender writes his message (data) and places the same in an envelope on which the address of the receiver is written and then the envelope is mailed for delivery. Both connection-oriented and connectionless networks have their own service paradigms. For example, connection-oriented network technologies have design features to provide variations in service such as continuous traffic at a uniform rate to handle voice or video or burst traffic which is typical of computer communication. The other variations are simplex (one-way traffic flow) or full duplex (two-way traffic flow in one connection), permanent or switched connection that can be established or terminated fast automatically, service guarantee in terms of throughput rate and maximum packet-loss rate, stream data or message data interface depending upon whether the data interface accepts continuous data even though the sender generated the data in blocks or accepts the same data in the same block size as the sender transmitted. Likewise, connectionless network technologies differ in terms of addressing scheme (length of address and method of assigning the same), maximum frame size and minimum packet size.

It may be worthwhile to mention that a network may have different mixed-service paradigms—one for interior and another for exterior. For example, ARPANET provides connectionless service to attached local computers while its internal services are all connection oriented. Table 12.3 shows the service paradigms offered by a few popular network technologies.

In a connectionless network, each packet contains the address of remote destinations, whereas in the case of connection-oriented networks, the destination address is required only when establishing a new connection; thereafter, the packet flowing through

Table 12.3 Paradigms Offered by Few Popular Network Technologies. The Technologies Suitable for WAN Are Used in Public Networks

Technology	*Connection Oriented*	*Connection Less*	*Used for LAN*	*Used for WAN*
Ethernet		✓	✓	
Token ring		✓	✓	
FDDI		✓	✓	
Frame relay	✓			✓
SMDS		✓		✓
ATM	✓			✓
Local talk		✓	✓	

the connection contains only a connection identifier which is much smaller than a full address.

12.10.2 Performance Characteristics of a Network

Performance characteristics of a network mainly include delay, throughput and jitter. Delay and throughput together provide a quantitative measure relating to the network capacity. Delay specifies the time taken by a data bit to travel through the network from one computer to another, measured in seconds or fractions of a second (milliseconds). The total delay comprises propagation delay, switching delay, access delay and queuing delay. Propagation delay is the time taken by a signal to travel across a wire or optical fibre and depends upon the distance of travel. It is a significant part of total delay being of the order of milliseconds. Switching delay is much smaller than propagation delay and is the small amount of time taken by bridges or packet switches to choose and send a received packet to the next hop. Access delay is also significant and is the time a LAN has to wait before a shared medium is available to a particular computer in the shared LAN. Queuing delay occurs in the case of packet switched WANs only when an incoming packet to a switch may have to wait in a queue when the CPU forwards the packets which arrived earlier. This delay is associated with the store-and-forward process of a packet switch. Propagation delay is the major delay associated with network performance.

Throughput is the second performance parameter of a network, and it is the rate at which data can be transmitted through the network. It is usually expressed in bits per second (bps) or million bits per second (Mbps). Another way of specifying throughput is the bandwidth, which is the upper limit of throughput of a network. This is because a frame contains a header, which is an overhead and reduces the effective throughput obtained with a particular bandwidth. However, throughput is a measure of the network capacity.

It may be emphasised that throughput and delay are not independent of each other. As the utilisation of network capacity increases (the throughput increases), network delay also increases because of increased traffic congestion. The relationship can be expressed as

$$D = D_0 / (1 - U)$$

where D is the delay associated with utilisation U, and D_0 is the delay when the network is idle ($U = 0$). U can have values between 0 and 1. When $U = 1$, that is, 100% utilisation, delay (D) becomes very large. Therefore, network designers prefer to keep the utilisation of network capacity below 90%.

Transit volume of data in a network is the total number of data bits in transit in the network at any point in time and is obtained by multiplying delay (D) with throughput (T).

The third performance characteristic of a network is jitter. Jitter is the measure of variance in delay in a network. It is a very important parameter for networks that handle voice and video traffic as any variation in the network delay may cause flawed output. If the jitter is zero, the audio/video output will exactly synchronise with the input and the output will be flawless. Networks with zero or very little jitter are known as isochronous networks in which case the separate paths transmitting digitised voice/video data have all the same delay. However, asynchronous networks for which the delay in the separate paths transmitting packets varies require additional protocol support (protocol has been explained in subsequent paragraphs of this chapter) to offset the jitter when audio and video are transmitted across such network.

12.11 Protocols and Layering in Network Communication

Similar to a diplomatic protocol, a term used by diplomats as an agreed set of rules followed while communicating with each other for exchanging messages, a set of rules that specify the format of messages and the actions associated with each such message is known as a network protocol or communication protocol in computer or internetwork parlance. The software that implements such a protocol is called protocol software. Protocol software, similar to a high-level language, provides an interface between the application programmes that make use of a network and the network hardware. An application programme interacts with the protocol software, which follows the rules of any given protocol to communicate with the network hardware.

12.11.1 Protocol Suites and Layering

Instead of having a single large protocol to specify all rules of the protocol for all possible variations in the forms of communication, protocol designers preferred to divide the communication protocols into pieces according to the various problems associated with the communication. This facilitates ease of design, analysis, testing and implementation of each protocol.

The pieces which together describe the complete protocol suite are known as layers, and the tool that describes the layers is known as the protocol layering model. The layering of a protocol suite, however, must ensure the following aspects:

1. The entire suite is designed to make the communication system efficient and effective.
2. Each layer of the protocol suite handles part of the communication problem not handled by the other protocols.
3. Layers of protocol should be designed so that they can share structures of data and information.
4. The combination of all protocol layers should handle all possible communication problems, including failures and other exceptional conditions.

A historic seven-layer OSI reference model and the five-layer internetwork TCP/IP reference model (described in subsequent paragraphs) are shown in Figure 12.25.

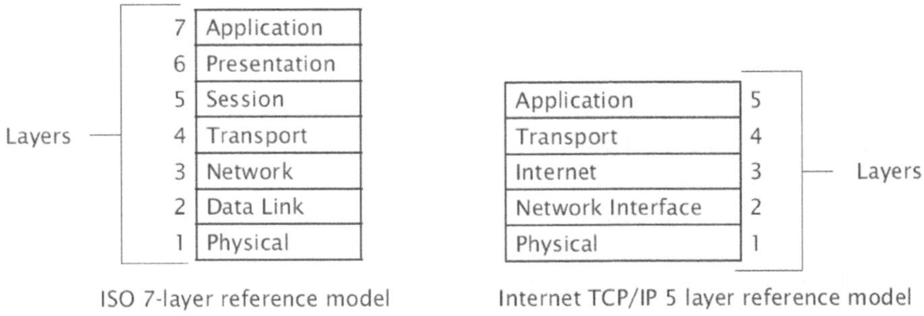

Figure 12.25 ISO Seven-Layer and Internet TCP/IP Five-Layer Model

In the ISO model as well as the internet model, the first layer (physical layer) relates to the network hardware and the other higher layers (2–7) relate to the software that uses the hardware, the highest seventh layer being the application layer.

Data link protocols (second layer) contain rules for organising data into frames and mechanisms of transmission of frames through a network. Frame format, byte stuffing, checksum and CRC computation as explained in Section 12.4 are included in layer 2.

Layer 3 (network) relates to the addressing system for the packet switches and computers and the method of routing the packets from the source at one end to the destination at the other end of the network.

Layer 4 (transport) protocols specify the details of reliable transfer of packets in a network. Transport protocols make use of a number of tools to tackle complicated communication problems such as out-of-order delivery of packets and their proper sequencing, duplicate packets and their elimination, lost packets and their retransmission, replay caused by excessive delay and flow control through suitable rate control mechanisms that monitor the rate of production of packets and reduce the same when congestion occurs until the congestion is overcome.

The out-of-order deliveries of packets are taken care of by transport protocols through sequencing of the packets. The sending side attaches a sequence number to each packet it transmits and the receiving side stores the sequence number of the last packet received and separately the list of packets arrived out-of-order.

If the next packet received has a sequence number higher than the sequence number of the last packet, the protocol software delivers the packet to the next higher layer protocol and then checks the list of out-of-order packets to see whether additional packets can be delivered out of the same. Sequencing also helps in eliminating the problem of duplicate packets. Packet loss is a basic problem in computer networks and arises mainly due to two reasons: first, because of transmission errors making bits corrupted resulting in an invalid frame and second, due to congestion in the network traffic. Transport protocols use two different methods to take care of the above two causes for ensuring reliable transmission without any packet loss. The first method is to send an acknowledgement (ACK) which is a small message sent by the receiving transport protocol when it receives a frame intact. The sender starts a timer for a small time duration when it sends a packet successfully and waits for the acknowledgement. If the same is received before the timer expires, the sender protocol software cancels the timer. However, if the timer expires before the acknowledgement arrives, the sender protocol software sends another copy of the packet and sets the timer to start again. The second copy is called a retransmission. However, retransmission will fail in case there is crashing of the receiving computer or the network gets disconnected due to hardware failure. Therefore, transport protocols usually have a bound on the maximum number of retransmissions and beyond that, it stops retransmitting.

Replay caused by excessive delay happens when there is heavy delay on a route, and consequently the protocol software changes the route and retransmits the delayed packet and the subsequent packets. However, this replay may affect the later communication because the delayed packet from the earlier (old) conversation might be accepted by the receiving computer and the correct packet discarded as a duplicate. In order to avoid replay, protocol software marks each session of communication with a unique session ID such as the time of commencement of the session, and the session ID is incorporated in each packet transmitted during the session. In order to avoid replay, the protocol software discards any packet at the receiving end that contains an inconsistent session ID.

Flow-control mechanism handles data overrun and consequent network congestion. Data overrun occurs when the sending computer transmits data through the network at a faster rate than the capacity of the receiving computer to receive data. Obviously, such a situation gives rise to network congestion which may eventually result in data loss. One of the flow-control techniques used by protocols is known as 'sliding window' which efficiently prevents data overrun while maintaining high throughput rates consistent with network capacity. In the case of a sliding window, the sender and receiver agree as per protocol to use a fixed amount of data in terms of number of packets (window size) that can be sent by the sending side before receiving an acknowledgement from the receiving side for the window-size packets. Figure 12.26 illustrates the 'sliding window' mechanism with a window size of three packets, and a total of nine packets are transmitted.

The advantage so far as throughput is concerned is obvious from Figure 12.26. It can be seen that through a window size of 3 packets, 9 packets have been transmitted in 3 × (2σ) time, where σ is the transmission delay for a packet to reach from sending computer

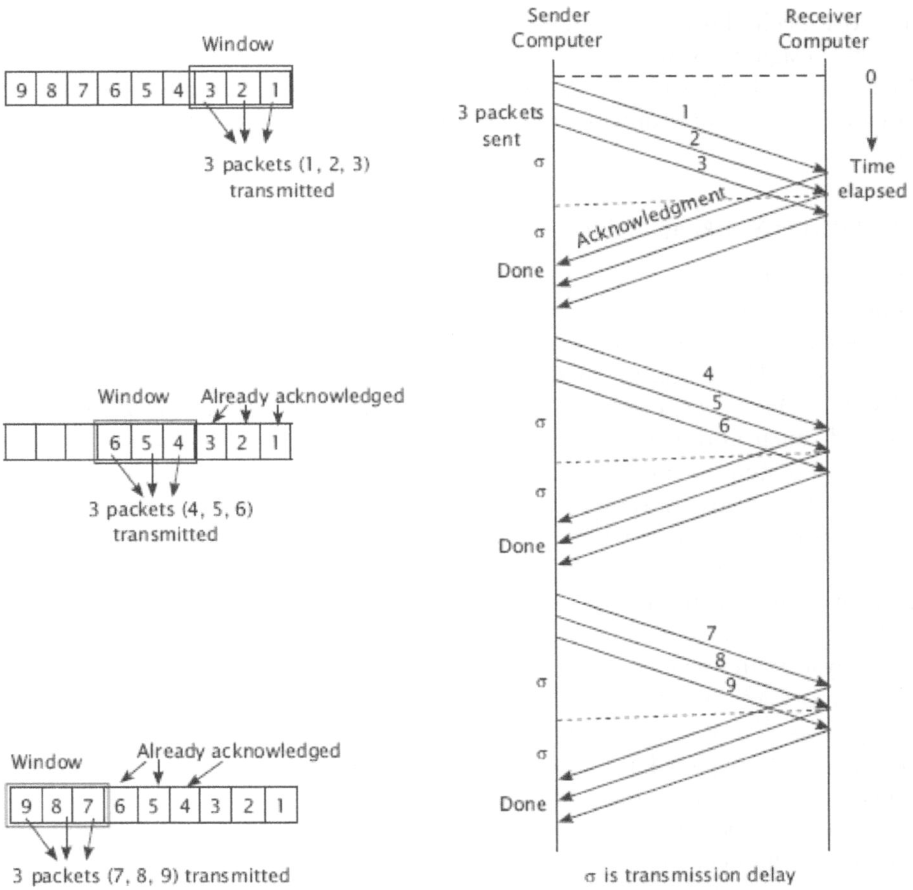

Figure 12.26 A Three-Packet Window Sliding through Outgoing Data of Nine Packets

to receiving computer. If, otherwise without a sliding window, the packets would have been sent one at a time at an interval of 2σ, the time delay between sending one packet and waiting till the acknowledgement is received by the sending computer; total time would have been 9 × (2σ), which is 18σ, three times more. Hence, the throughput with a window size (W), Tw can be written as:

$T_w = W \times T_0$

Here, T_0 is the throughput without a sliding window.

By increasing the window size, the throughput can be increased, but a large window size may give rise to data overrun; hence, an optimum size of the sliding window is decided to commensurate with the underlying hardware capacity (bandwidth).

Congestion in network results in packet loss. Retransmission can recover lost packets, but retransmission reduces effective throughput. Hence, protocols try to avoid congestion by arranging packet switches to send a special message to the source of packets to control the rate of transmission of packets when congestion occurs. Further, protocols adopt the quantum of packet loss as an estimate of congestion in the network for remedial measures.

Layer 5 protocols specify the method of starting a communication session with a remote system.

Layer 6 protocols specify how data are represented in various computers, and Layer 7 protocols specify how any particular application uses a network.

Finally, designing protocols is very important for eliminating the problems associated with network transmission as mentioned earlier. A systematic and detailed study is essential for the sake of protocol design as protocols can interact adversely in unexpected ways.

12.12 Internet Working Technology

We have seen in earlier sections of this chapter that the network technology varies depending upon the user needs. For example, LAN is a technology suited to high-speed communication across short distances, whereas WAN is designed to communicate across large distances. Therefore, no single network design is best for all-purpose use or universal service. However, need was greatly felt to have a communication system which will provide such universal service by connecting the heterogeneous networks so that any pair of computers connected to arbitrary network technologies can communicate with each other. Network designers and researchers finally devised a scheme known as internetwork or the internet which provides such universal service among heterogeneous networks. Internet uses both additional hardware and software on attached computers which provide universal service.

Additional hardware includes a basic component known as 'router' to interconnect a set of physical and heterogeneous networks. A router such as a bridge has got a processor, memory and a separate I/O interface for each network to which it connects. A network treats a router as a computer. Figure 12.27 shows a router connecting two physical networks depicted as clouds since the network may be using different technologies, media, frame formats and addressing schemes.

An internet can be formed by using more than one router to connect a set of physical networks. The number and type of networks and the interconnection topology decide the number of routers. Figure 12.28 shows an internet to connect five physical networks having different technologies.

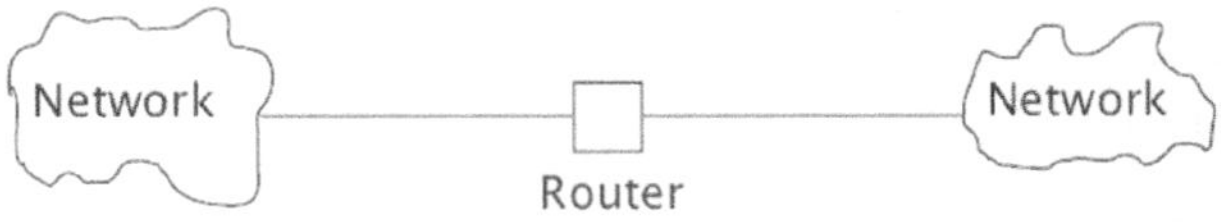

Figure 12.27 Two Physical Networks Connected through a Router

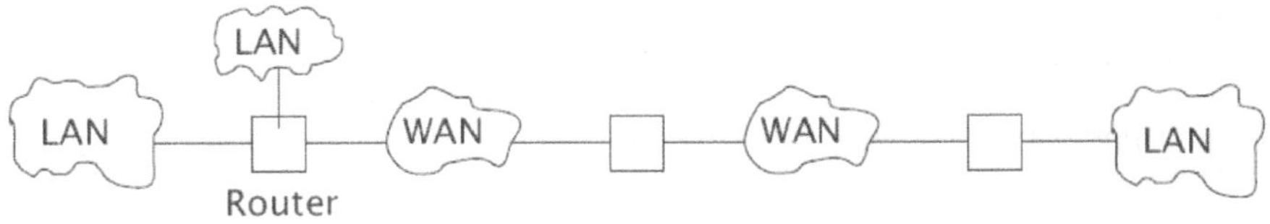

Figure 12.28 Three Routers Connecting Five Networks (Three LANs and Two WANs)

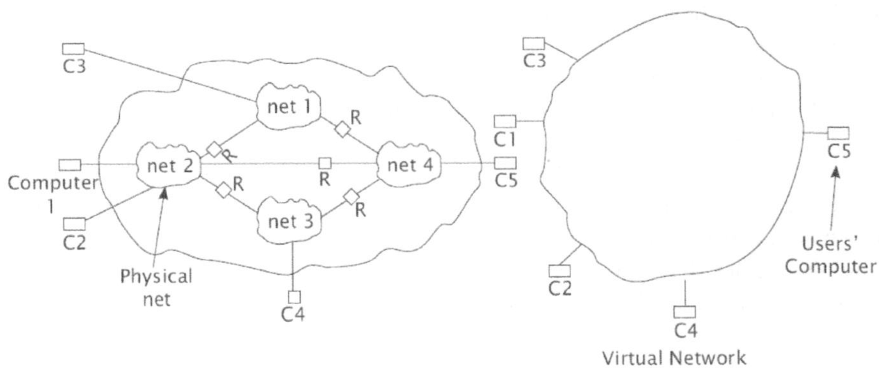

Figure 12.29 The Illusion of a Single Network (Virtual Network) That TCP/IP Software Provides to Users/Applications

12.12.1 Internet: A Virtual Network

Internet is not restricted in size. It can contain hundreds of networks and each network can connect hundreds of computers. However, the internet protocol software (known as transmission control protocol/internet protocol, abbreviated as TCP/IP) provides the illusion to the computers attached to a single seamless communication network known as a virtual network system. The name virtual network for an internet arises because the system is an abstraction. Figure 12.29 illustrates the abstraction concept of a virtual network and the corresponding physical networks.

12.12.1.1 Layers of TCP/IP Protocols

TCP/IP protocols are organised into five layers: physical, network interface, the internet, transport and application. These layers of the TCP/IP layering model, also known as the internet layering model, are shown in Figure 12.26 along with the ISO seven-layer model.

Table 12.4 Layers of TCP/IP Reference Model and Corresponding ISO Model Layers

Layers of TCP/IP Model	*Corresponding Layers of the ISO Model*
Layer 1: Physical layer relates to basic network hardware.	Layer 1: Physical
Layer 2: Network interface specifies organisation of data into frames and transmission of frames across the network.	Layer 2: Data link
Layer 3: Internet specifies format of packets sent across internet and method of forwarding packets from source to destination through routers.	No corresponding layer
Layer 4: Transport specifies how to ensure reliable transmission of data in the form of packets.	Layer 4: Transport
Layer 5: Application specifies how an application makes use of internet.	Layer 6: Presentation and Layer 7: Application

Four of the layers (physical, network interface, transport and application) of the TCP/IP model correspond to one or more layers of the ISO model. However, the ISO model has no internet. Likewise, the TCP/IP model has no session layer.

Table 12.4 shows the purpose of each of the five layers of TCP/IP reference model and the corresponding layers of the ISO seven-layer model.

Layering principle stipulates that a particular layer, say, the Nth layer at the destination, applies the inverse of the transformations applied in the same Nth layer at the source. The collection of the modules is known as a protocol stack. Therefore, the layering principle implies that outgoing data pass down through the layers of the stack on the sending side and pass up the stack on the receiving side as shown in Figure 12.30.

12.12.1.2 Protocols for Routers

Unlike host computers, TCP/IP protocol software for routers usually does not contain Layer 5 (Application) because routers generally do not run applications as do host computers.

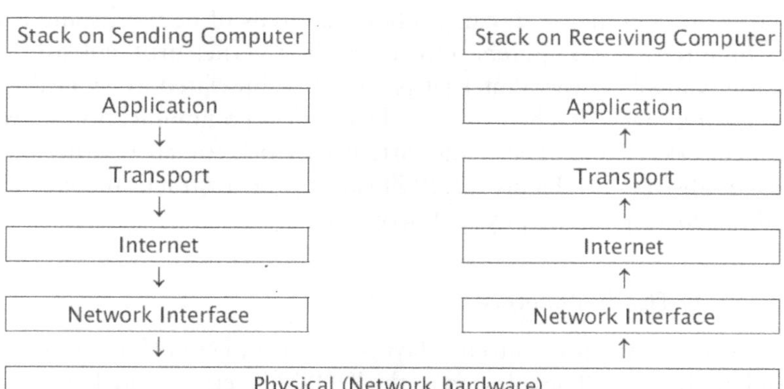

Figure 12.30 The Conceptual Path of Data from an Application on Computer Sending Data to

12.13 IP Addressing

In TCP/IP, the internet protocol specifies the addressing scheme. IP divides the internet address for each computer attached to a two-level hierarchy.

The two levels are the prefix of an address, which identifies the network to which the computer is attached, and the suffix, which identifies the particular computer on the network. In order to ensure unique addresses throughout the internet, a central authority assigns network prefixes in the address hierarchy. Once a prefix has been assigned, a local network administrator (such as the internet service provider) can assign a unique suffix to each host on the network. For example, if an internet contains four networks, the four can be assigned prefixes as 1, 2, 3 and 4. If four computers are assigned to network 1, those can be assigned suffixes 1, 2, 3 and 4, while four computers attached to network 2 can also be assigned suffixes 1, 2, 3 and 4. However, the four computers attached to network 1 will have different prefixes (being 1) from those of network 2 (being 2), and thus all computers attached will have unique addresses. User application programmes and other higher layers of protocol software use the abstract IP addresses as explained in order to communicate. The IP address is a unique 32-bit binary number assigned to a host for communicating with the host. The address bits are numbered from left to right, and the first (left most) bit is numbered 0 and the right most bit 31.

The 32-bit address is divided into three parts. The first four bits determine the class of the address; the next part represents the prefix and the last part the suffix of the IP address. There are five classes of IP address, of which three (classes A, B and C) are primary classes used to denote host addresses. The fourth class (class D) is used for multicast addresses, where a set of host computers share the multicast address and a copy of any packet sent to the same address will be received by each host belonging to the set. Class E, the fifth class, has been reserved for future use only. Class A addresses have '0' as the first bit, and the boundary between prefix and suffix is at the end of the first octet. Class B has '1' and '0' as the first two bits and places the boundary between prefix and suffix after the second octet. Class C has '1', '1' and '0' as the first three bits and places the same boundary after the third octet. The five classes of IP addresses are shown in Figure 12.31.

12.13.1 Dotted Decimal Notation for IP Addresses

Although IP addresses are 32-bit binary numbers, the software uses a notation known as 'dotted decimal notation' for the IP addresses for interacting with users for their convenience.

The 'dotted decimal notation' consists of four decimal values separated by periods (.), and the values correspond to the four octets of binary digits in the 32-bit IP address of the three primary classes A, B and C. Table 12.5 shows examples of 32-bit binary addresses and the equivalent dotted decimal addresses.

Dotted decimal addresses can range from 0.0.0.0 to 255.255.255.255, equivalent to binary octets of 00000000 and 11111111 respectively. All the addresses mentioned above are examples of classful addresses. It may be mentioned that increasing the number of bits in the prefix will enable a greater number of networks to be accommodated and a smaller number of bits in the suffix, which results in a smaller number of hosts per network. Accordingly, the maximum number of networks and hosts per network have been calculated for the three primary address classes A, B and C as shown in Table 12.6. It can be noted that the size of a network determines the address class.

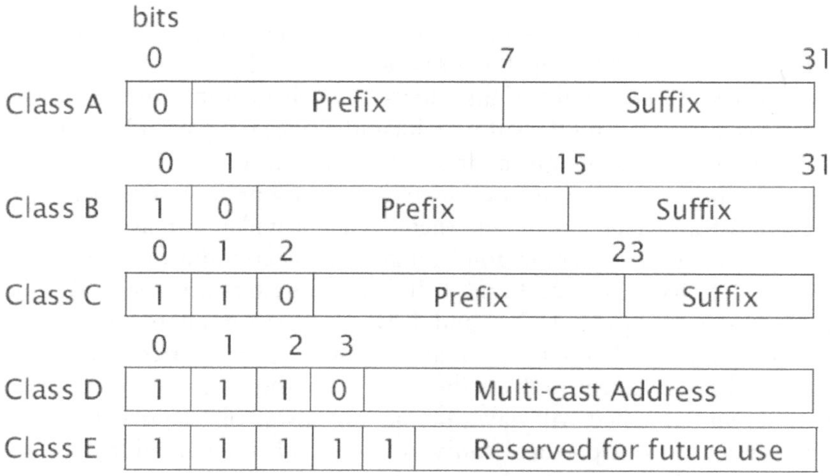

Figure 12.31 The Five Classes of IP Address

Table 12.5 Examples of 32-Bit Binary Addresses and Their Equivalent Dotted Decimal Addresses

32-Bit Binary Address				*Equivalent Dotted Decimal Address*			
00001111	00000100	00000000	00100101	15.	4.	0.	37
10111111	00011100	00000111	00000011	191.	28.	7.	3
11011111	01110000	11111111	01010101	223.	112.	225.	85
10101111	10000111	11001011	00000000	175.	135.	203.	0

Table 12.6 The Maximum Number of Networks and Hosts per Network for Each of the Three Primary Address

Class of Address	*Bits in Prefix*	*Maximum Number of Networks*	*Bits in Suffix*	*Maximum Number of Hosts per Network*
A	7 (8 – 1)	128	24	16777216
B	14 (8 – 2 + 8)	16384	16	65536
C	21 (8 – 3 + 8 + 8)	2097152	8	256

12.14 Classless Addressing, Address Masks and Classless Inter-Domain Routing (CIDR) Notation

One serious limitation of the classful addressing scheme is the non-utilised address spaces. Suppose a network has only 10 hosts; obviously, a class C address, which has the minimum number of hosts possible (256), will be chosen. However, for 10 hosts only, four bits of suffix will be needed and therefore the remaining four bits will be non-utilised. In order to overcome the above limitation, a classless addressing scheme was invented in which the division between prefix and suffix in the 32-bit address can occur at any arbitrary bit boundary. In the above example of a network with 10 hosts, the protocol for classless addressing will assign a prefix 28 bits long so that the suffix with four bits can accommodate up to 15 hosts.

The classless addressing scheme divides an IP address range using a combination of the IP address and the associated 'address mask' or 'subnet mask' which specifies the boundary between the network prefix and suffix. The address mask is also stored along with the 32-bit IP address as a 32-bit binary value wherein '1' bits mark the network prefix and '0' bits mark the suffix or the host portion. For example, in the previous example of a network with 10 hosts only and a prefix of 28 bits, the address mask will be:

11111111 11111111 11111111 11110000 which is 255.255.255.240 in dotted decimal notation.

CIDR notation, which stands for classless inter-domain routing, specifies the address mask associated with an IP address by appending to the IP address in dotted decimal a slash (/) followed by the size of the mask (for '1' bits).

Examples of CIDR address block:

1. 128.211.0.16/28 represents
   10000000 | 11010011 | 00000000 | 00001 0000
   Prefix → Suffix

2. 128.211.0.32/28 represents
   10000000 | 11010011 | 00000000 | 0010 0000
   → Suffix

Prefix is different from the same in Example 1.
3.192.168.12.0/23 = 192.168.12.0/24 + 192.168.13.0/24

It means 192.168.12.0/23 is a combination of two class C subnets 192.168.12.0/24 and 192.168.13.0/24

12.14.1 Special IP Address

IP reserves host address (suffix) as all zeroes to denote a network with the assigned prefix. Thus, the address 128.211.0.16/28 denotes a network with prefix as:

10000000 11010011 00000000 0001 and suffix 0000.

Similarly, a network suffix with all ones identifies a directed broadcast address as follows:

128.211.0.15/28 which in binary form is:

10000000 11010011 00000000 0000 | 1111
← prefix → | ←→ suffix

In case of directed broadcast, transmission of a packet will reach all host computers on the network.

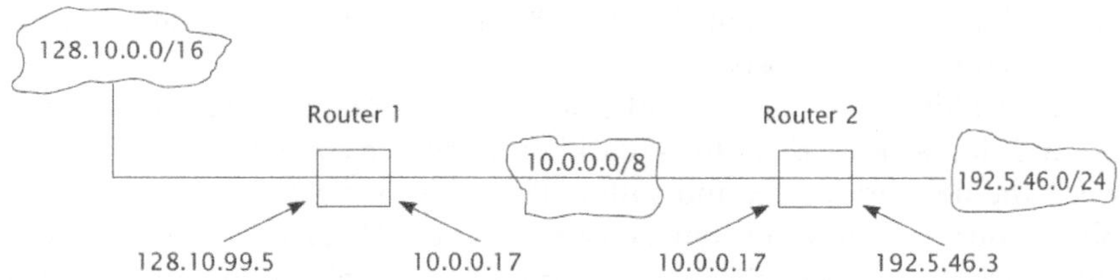

Figure 12.32 Illustration of Addresses Assigned to Two Routers—Each Interface of the Routers Is Assigned an Address Containing the Prefix of the Network to Which the Interface Connects

12.14.2 *IP Addressing for Routers*

Routers which connect more than one physical network have more than one IP address. Each such IP address for a router has a prefix, which specifies one physical network. Figure 12.32 illustrates the concept of multiple IP addresses assigned to two routers. IP does not require that the same suffix be attached to all interfaces of a router.

12.14.2.1 Address Resolution

The protocol addresses described in the earlier paragraphs are only IP addresses maintained by the protocol software and those addresses are not understood by the networks or host computer hardware. Therefore, a packet transmitted across a physical network pre-requires that the IP address of the receiver computer must be translated into its equivalent hardware address. The process or technique of translating a computer's protocol address into the equivalent hardware address is called 'address resolution'. There are three basic techniques of address resolution. They are (1) table lookup meant primarily for WAN hardware, (2) closed-form computation where the algorithm for address resolution can translate the protocol address of a computer into the hardware address of the hardware using Boolean and arithmetic and (3) message exchange

used with LANs having static addressing. In this case, one computer sends a message requesting an address translation and another computer sends the requested information. The three basic techniques have been illustrated below as examples. Table lookup contains a table having two columns, the IP address and the corresponding hardware address as shown in Table 12.7. Each entry (row) of the table corresponds to one computer of the network.

This table contains the IP address and the corresponding hardware address of the four host computers attached to the physical network prefix 128.211.0.0/16 which is a

Table 12.7 Example of Address Binding Table

IP Address	*Hardware Address*
128.211.5.1	0A—07—4B—12—82—36
128.211.5.2	9C—AD—97—84—6A—8D
128.211.5.3	A0—14—52—44—F2—91
128.211.5.4	0A—04—BC—00—03—28

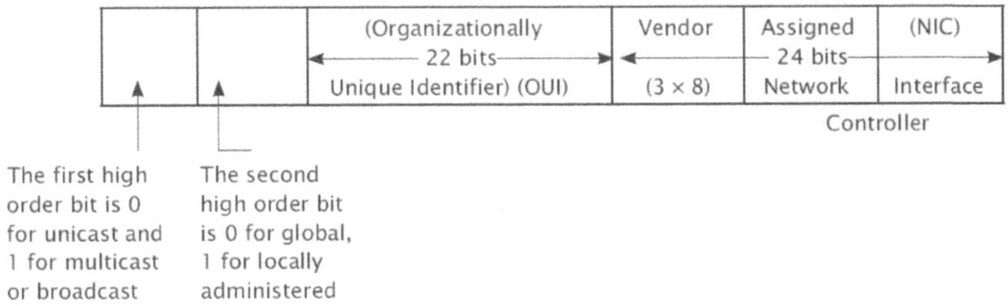

Figure 12.33 Structure of Physical Address of a Hardware

B-class network. A separate address binding table is needed for each physical network of the internet. The hardware address is also known as its physical or media access control (MAC) address, which can be found for a host computer with Windows operating system invoking the command prompt and then typing the command:

C: > ipconfig/all

The physical address of the hardware of the computer is a 48-bit unique address consisting of 6 bytes (6 × 8) having hexadecimal values. The structure of the address is as shown in Figure 12.33.

Address Resolution with Closed-Form Computation:

Unlike a static physical address, as described in the case of table lookup, closed-form computation for address resolution adopts configurable addressing of the network interface hardware by a suitable mathematical function that maps an IP address to a hardware address. For example, the IP address suffix representing a host can be matched to be the hardware address of the host.

Thus, a network 128.211.0.0/16 can have the first host computer IP address as 128.211.5.1 with a matching hardware address as 1 and so on.

Address Resolution with Message Exchange:

Message exchange is used with LANs having static addressing. In this case, a computer attached to a network that requires an address resolution sends a message as a request with an IP address and receives a reply with the corresponding hardware address. The protocol for address resolution with message exchange can be of two types or designs. In the first case, dedicated servers are earmarked in the network to answer all address resolution requests. In the second case, no special address resolution servers are used; instead, each computer in a network participates in address resolution by agreeing to reply to any request for its address. Any computer in the network, in order to resolve an address, broadcasts the request to all other computers in the network. All computers receive the request and examine the requested address, and if it matches with a computer's address, the same will respond. The TCP/IP suite contains a standard address resolution protocol (ARP). The ARP standard defines two basic message types—a request and a response. A request message contains the IP address, whereas a reply (response) contains both the IP address and the hardware address requested for. Finally, although the ARP message format for both the request and the response is sufficiently general to allow arbitrary

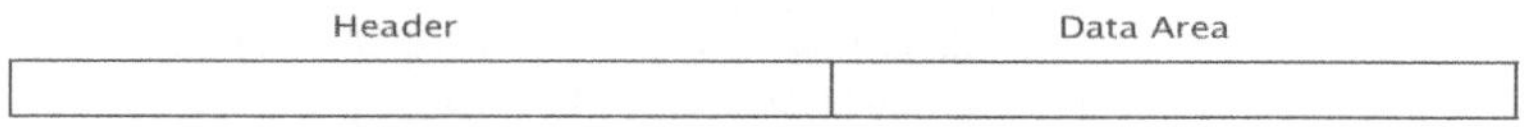

Figure 12.34 General Form of an IP Datagram

protocol and hardware addresses, ARP almost always resolves a 32-bit IP address into a 48-bit (6 bytes of 8 bits each) Ethernet address.

12.15 IP Datagrams and Forwarding Datagrams

The internet protocol defines an internet packet format that is independent of the heterogeneous networks and their hardware.

This packet, which is universal and virtual, is known as an IP datagram and is the basic unit of transfer of data across a TCP/IP internet. The format of an IP datagram is similar to a hardware frame, as it begins with a header followed by a data area which contains the data to be transferred across the internet. Figure 12.34 is a general format of an IP datagram.

The header contains IP addresses of the source and destination of the datagram and other information as fields. The fields of the header of a datagram along with size in bits are shown in Table 12.8. The amount of data carried in the data area of a datagram is variable and depends upon the type of application. IPV4 (Internet Protocol Version 4), which is the current IP version, permits a datagram size from one octet of data up to a

Table 12.8 Fields in the IP Datagram Header

Header Fields	*Size in Bits*
First 32 bits	
Version number of protocol (4 for current version)	4 (0 to 3)
Header length (in number of 32 bits)	4 (4 to 7)
Service type (a value to specify minimum delay or maximum throughput for a datagram	16 (8 to 15)
Total length in 16-bit integer to denote the total no. of octets in the datagram (both the header and data)	16 (16 to 31)
Second 32 bits	
Identification: Unique identification number for each outgoing datagram	16 (0 to 15)
Flags (to specify a fragmented datagram)	3 (16 to 18)
Fragment offset (to indicate the position of a fragment in the original datagram)	13 (19 to 31)
Third 32 bits	
Time to live (a positive integer value between 1 and 255 specifying a time to prevent a datagram traveling indefinitely around a path containing a loop due to error in configuring the root)	8 (0 to 7)
Type (datagram data: audio, video or key stroke and so on)	8 (8 to 15)
Header checksum (to ensure that bits of datagram header are not changed in transit)	16 (16 to 31)
Source IP address	32 (fourth 32 bits)
Destination IP address	32 (fifth 32 bits)

maximum of 64K octets inclusive of the header. However, the header is usually much smaller in size as compared to the data area because the header is an overhead associated with the cost of transmitting data.

12.15.1 Mechanism of Forwarding an IP Datagram

Datagrams travel across an internet from the initial source to the final destination. In this travel path, datagrams pass through one or more heterogeneous networks connected by routers. Each router plays a vital role in receiving a datagram, extracting its destination address and forwarding the datagram according to its destination address either to a next-hop router or to the final destination network. In order to facilitate the same, each IP router keeps a routing table which contains a set of entries for each destination and the corresponding next hop used to reach the same. Figure 12.35 illustrates a routing table for a router in an internet with five networks. The destination addresses shown in the routing table are the network prefix of the network, and hence the second field in the table contains the address mask to specify the bits of the destination corresponding to the network prefix. Each router has got two or more interface IP addresses depending upon the networks it connects. It may be noted that each destination in a routing table is a network and not an individual host. The purpose is to keep the size of the routing table small. The destination network receiving a datagram can deliver the same locally to the particular host (suffix of IP address).

It may be stated that once a router forwards a datagram to another router or network, the destination address contained in the header of the datagram remains as it is and always refers to the ultimate destination and the next hop address never appears in the datagram header. It may further be stated that IP does not guarantee handling the problems of datagram duplication, delayed/out-of-order delivery of datagrams, datagram corruption and loss in order to ensure best-effort delivery of datagrams. Higher layers of protocol software that use IP take care of such errors for best effort delivery to take place.

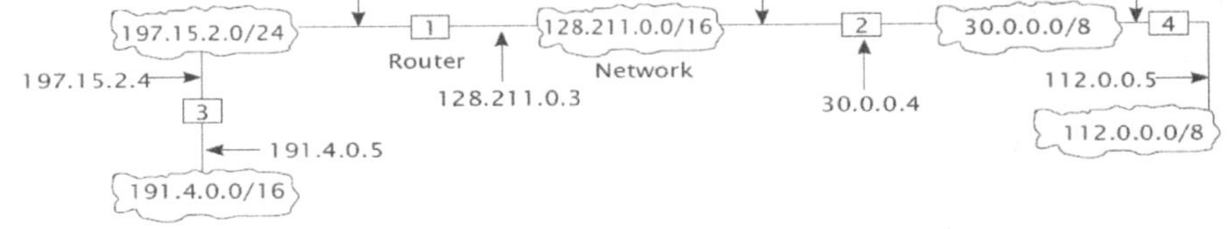

Routing Table for Router 2

Destination	Mask	Next HOP
128.211.0.0	255.255.0.0	Direct delivery
197.15.2.0	255.255.225.0	128.211.0.3
191.4.0.0	255.255.0.0	128.211.0.3
30.0.0.0	255.0.0.0	Direct delivery
112.0.0.0	255.0.0.0	30.0.0.5

Figure 12.35 An Internet of Five Networks and Four Routers with Routing Table for Router 2

12.16 IP Encapsulation, Fragmentation and Reassembly

12.16.1 Encapsulation

In the previous paragraph, we have seen that an IP datagram, in the course of its traverse from a source (host or router) to the destination through one or more next hops, passes through one or more heterogeneous networks, whose hardware do not understand datagram format. This is because each heterogeneous network hardware understands its own frame format which may differ among the networks, through which the IP datagram has to pass in its traverse across the internet from source to destination. The technique adopted to transmit a datagram across a network that does not understand its format is known as 'encapsulation'. Encapsulation is the method of placing the entire datagram in the data area of the frame of the network through which the datagram has to pass. The network hardware treats a frame containing a datagram exactly similar to any other frame except that the frame-type field of the frame contains a special and agreed value for all networks to identify a frame with a datagram.

The destination address of the frame containing a datagram is the address of the next hop to which the datagram should be sent, and the same address is obtained by translating the IP address of the next hop to an equivalent hardware address using address binding as described in earlier paragraphs. Figure 12.36 illustrates how a datagram is encapsulated and unencapsulated as it travels from a source host to a destination host through four networks and three routers.

It may be seen that hosts and routers store a datagram in memory with no additional header. Further, when a datagram is encapsulated during its traverse through a physical network as a frame, the header of the frame such as Header 1, Header 2, ... as shown in Figure 12.37 depends on the particular network. For example, the header can be an Ethernet header. Every time the datagram reaches a network or the final destination, it is extracted and the frame that carried the datagram is discarded.

12.16.2 Fragmentation

Every network hardware technology has a limit on the maximum amount of data that a frame can carry through the network. This limit is known as 'maximum transmission unit' or MTU of the network. In the case of an internet consisting of heterogeneous networks, the MTU may be different for the networks through which the datagram has to traverse. This implies that the datagram travelling across the internet has to be smaller than or equal to the MTU of each physical network; otherwise, it cannot be encapsulated.

Obviously, this creates a problem as the router, which connects two networks with different MTU values, may receive a datagram from the network with a higher MTU but cannot send the same through the network with a lower MTU if the datagram size is equal to the higher MTU. An IP router uses a 'fragmentation' technique to take care of such problems of heterogeneous MTUs. If a router has to send a datagram through a network whose MTU is less than the size of the datagram, the router fragments the datagram into pieces and sends each piece or fragment separately through the network. Each fragment has the IP datagram format but carries only part of the data of the original datagram. A bit in the flag field of the IP header (please refer Figure 12.37) indicates whether a datagram is a fragment or a complete one, and the fragment offset field of the header of a fragment indicates the position of the fragment in the original datagram. Figure 12.37 illustrates the 'fragmentation' process.

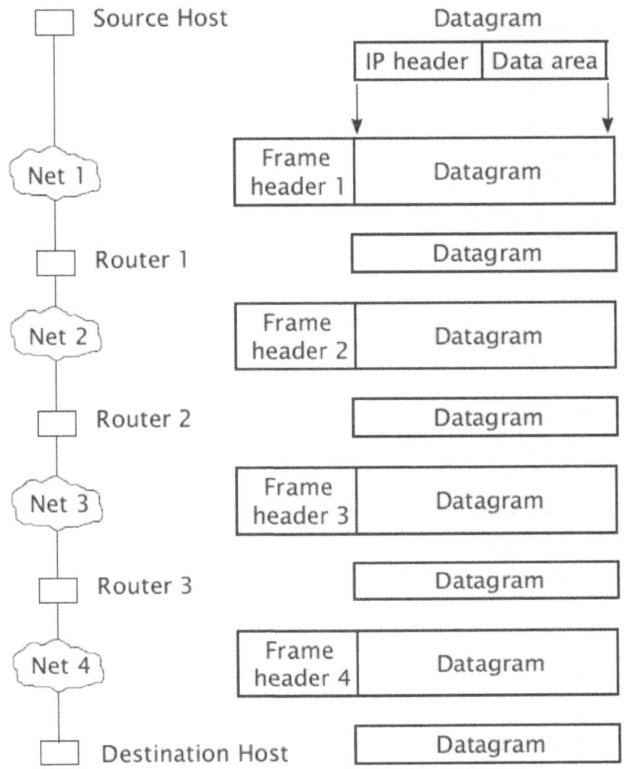

Figure 12.36 A Datagram As It Travels across the Internet

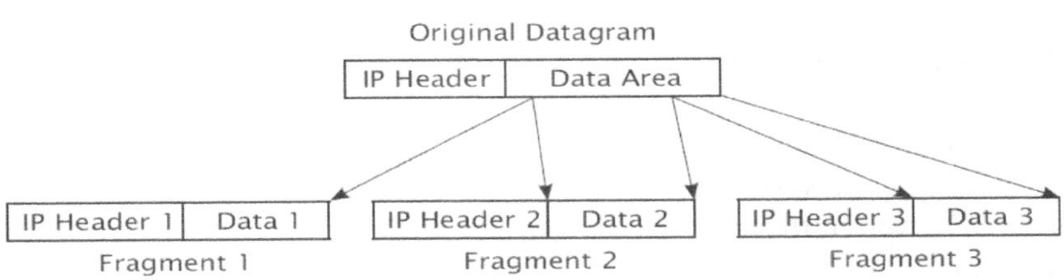

Figure 12.37 An IP Datagram Divided into Three Fragments, IP Headers of the Three Are Similar to the Original Datagram IP Header

12.16.3 Reassembly

Reassembly of the fragments to create a copy of the original datagram is done at the destination, which is the same for all the fragments as well as the original datagram. The destination receiver host performing the reassembly ensures the arrival of all fragments through the offset field of the fragments and also an additional bit to indicate the final fragment.

12.17 IPV6 (Future IP)

IPV4, the current version of IP, has been successful for the internet to handle data transmission through heterogeneous networks while also taking care of large scalability. However, with the exponential growth of the internet worldwide, a need was felt, first, to increase the address space to accommodate the growth.

Second, need was also felt for changes in IP to take care of newer internet applications, such as audio and video conferencing in a real-time delivery environment. Therefore, researchers started developing a new version of IP for the future—IPv6.

2.17.1 Features of IPV6

The distinctive features of IPV6 include the following:

1. **128-bit Address**: A 128-bit address (unlike 32 bits for IPv4) to accommodate the future growth of the internet worldwide. Further, unlike the dotted decimal notation as in the case of IPv4, IPv6 uses a more compact form of address in colon hexadecimal notation in which each group of 16 bits is written in hexadecimal with a colon (:) as the separator between two successive groups and there are eight groups ($8 \times 16 = 128$ bits) as shown below:

   FFFF: 8 COA: B1: 1280: 0: 0: 0: C1

   Moreover, in order to further reduce the address size, the zeroes are replaced with successive

   colons ':' as follows:

   0: 0: 0: 0: 0: 0: B1: F F F F

   Replaced with: B1: F F F F

2. **Header Format**: Unlike IPv4, which has a single header format for all datagrams, IPv6 has a compulsory header followed by one or more optional extension headers. A datagram in the case of IPv6 consists of the base header followed by zero or more extension headers and then followed by the data area. The length of a datagram (payload length), unlike IPv4, specifies only the size of the data area and the size of the header is excluded. The general form of an IPv6 datagram is shown in Figure 12.38. The reasons for having extension headers are economy and extensibility. It is economical because it saves space by having a small subset out of many features of the IPv6 protocol. Extensibility allows IPv6 to add any new feature to a protocol, which is not possible in the case of IPv4 without a complete change in the design of its fixed header.

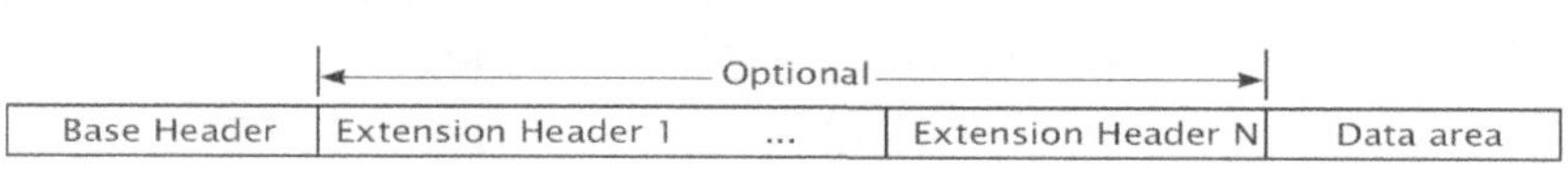

Figure 12.38 Format of an IPV6 Datagram

Table 12.9 Base Header Format (IPV6)

Header Fields	*Size in Bits*
First 32 bits	
Version (IPV6)	4 (0 to 3)
Traffic class (such as keystrokes, real-time audio, video and so on)	8 (4 to 11)
Flow label (specifies the path through the network depending upon traffic class)	20 (12 to 31)
Second 32 bits	
Pay-load length	16 (0 to 15)
Next header (to specify the extension header or the type of data in data area if there is no extension header)	8 (16 to 23)
Hop limit: Time-to-live for a datagram before it reaches the destination	8 (24 to 31)
Source address	128 (next four 32 bits)
Destination address	128 (next four 32 bits)

The base-header format is as shown in Table 12.9.

3. **Support for Audio and Video Traffic**: IPV6 allows a sender and receiver to establish a high-quality or a low-cost path through the internetwork in order to associate use of audio and video applications in one hand and other datagrams on the other hand through the low-cost path. Further, IPV6 addresses are of three types basically—unicast, multicast and anycast. A unicast address corresponds to a single host computer and a datagram meant for any unicast address is routed to that host computer address through the shortest path. When a datagram is sent to a multicast address, IPV6 delivers a copy of the same to each member of a set of computers belonging to the same multicast address. An anycast address corresponds to a set of computers that share a common address prefix such as a single local network. A datagram destined for an 'anycast' address is routed and delivered to any one of the computers nearest to the sender through the shortest path.
4. **Fragmentation, Reassembly and Path MTU**: Unlike IPV4, in the case of IPV6, the base header does not include fragmentation information fields and instead places such information in a separate fragment extension header for each fragment as illustrated in Figure 12.39.

Further, unlike IPv4 wherein fragmentation is done by the routers, the fragmentation in case of IPv6 is done by the host computer sending a datagram. In order to facilitate the same, the sending host in the case of IPv6 contains the MTU data for each network, which the datagram has to traverse along its path to the destination, and chooses a fragment size to fit the smallest MTU. The minimum MTU in a path from source to destination is known as the 'Path MTU' which is determined by the sending host following an iterative procedure in the case of IPV6.

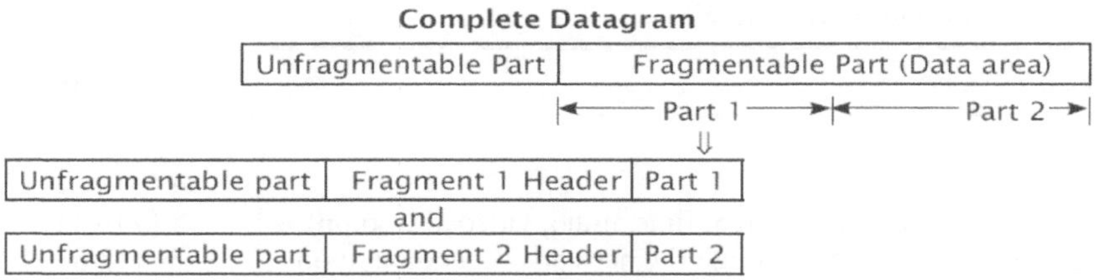

Figure 12.39 Illustration of Fragmentation in Case of IPV6

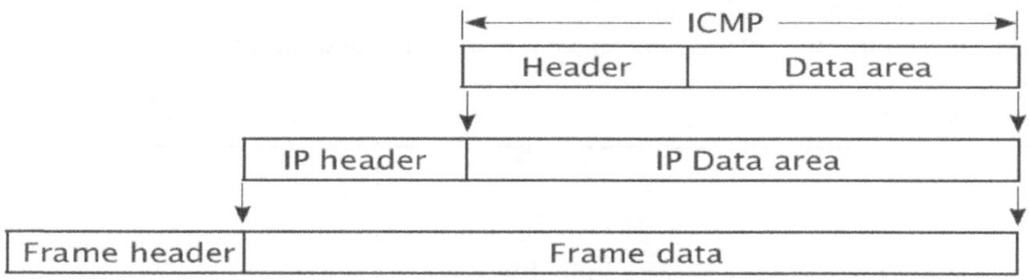

Figure 12.40 Two Levels of Encapsulation for Sending ICMP Message

5. **Error Reporting Mechanism**: In spite of best-effort delivery by IP, it attempts to avoid errors and therefore has an error detection and reporting mechanism included in the TCP/IP suite. The mechanism is known as the 'Internet Control Message Protocol' abbreviated as ICMP.

IP and ICMP are codependent. IP uses ICMP to send an error message, and ICMP uses IP to transport a message identified by an 8-bit type of message field. Figure 12.40 illustrates how a router sends an ICMP message through an IP datagram using two levels of encapsulation: the first level encapsulates the ICMP header and data area together inside an IP data area and the second level encapsulates the complete IP inside a frame data area. It may be mentioned that ICMP messages can be both error and informational messages. For example, source quench is a type of ICMP error message which a router sends to the source host to reduce its rate of transmission because the router has to discard an incoming datagram as its buffer space is full. The echo request and reply messages of ICMP are used by a host computer to determine whether a destination is reachable. ICMP messages can also be used by a host to determine path MTU for a given destination. Routers send ICMP error messages to the original source of a datagram that causes any error.

12.18 User Datagram Protocol (UDP)

UDP takes care of the need for end-to-end transport protocols. We have seen from the previous paragraphs that IP provides a service through which a datagram can pass from a sending computer to a receiving computer traversing across one or more physical networks. However, IP lacks its ability to support multiple applications running simultaneously on the same computer. This is because the datagram headers that IP supports contain information about the source and destination addresses for the host computers only, but not about the application programmes on those hosts. A protocol which allows an individual application programme to serve as the end point of communication is known as the 'end-to-end transport protocol' or simply a 'transport protocol'. The transport protocol has been designed as layer 4 of TCP/IP protocols. Further, this layer 4 of the TCP/IP suite contains two protocols for transport, namely the UDP and the TCP.

12.18.1 Protocol Port Numbers for Endpoint Identification

UDP defines an abstract set of identifiers known as protocol port numbers for different application programmes run on each computer independent of its operating system (OS). This is because heterogeneous computers can run applications on different operating systems such as Windows, Mac and Linux (Ubuntu or Red Hat). Some OSs use daemon or process identifiers; others may use job names or task numbers to identify individual application programs.

Port numbers in the range from 0 to 1023 are the well-known system ports. For example, port number 50 is for 'remote mail checking protocol', 118 for 'SQL services' and so on. All computers with UDP can recognise the standard protocol port numbers independent of the underlying OS. Thus, when a UDP message arrives at a computer for port 118, the software protocol for UDP must identify which programme on the computer implements the SQL services and then forwards the message to that program.

12.18.2 UDP Datagram

Each UDP message makes a user datagram which consists of a header of 64 bits (8 octets) followed by the payload that carries the UDP data. The total size of the UDP message is measured in octets. The format of the UDP user datagram header is as follows:

Header Fields	*Size in Bits*
First 32 bits	
UDP source port (contains port number of sending application)	16 (0 to 15)
UDP destination port (port number of the application to which message is sent)	16 (16 to 31)
Second 32 bits	
UDP message length (message length in number of octets)	16 (0 to 15)
UDP checksum (optional if it is not there all bits will be zero)	16 (16 to 31)

It may be noted that the user datagram header has no field for either source IP address or destination IP address. Those addresses are contained in the IP datagram that carries the UDP message consisting of the UDP header and the UDP data. Similar to ICMP, UDP is also encapsulated with two levels of encapsulation, as shown in Figure 12.41.

UDP offers the same best-effort delivery to the applications as in the case of an IP, which means a UDP message can be lost, duplicated or delivered out of order. However, applications such as audio or video can sustain packet delivery errors, but for other applications, such errors can have serious consequences.

Finally, UDP allows arbitrary interaction involving one-to-one (one application exchanges messages with only one other application), one-to-many (one application sends a message to multiple recipient applications), many-to-one (one application receives

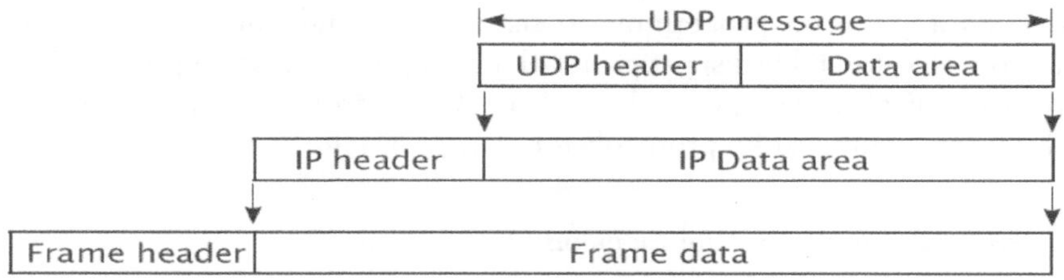

Figure 12.41 Two-Level Encapsulation of UDP Message

messages from multiple sender applications) and many-to-many (applications exchange messages with one another).

12.19 TCP for Reliable Transport

TCP is the main transport protocol in the TCP/IP suite and ensures reliable delivery of packets. It ensures connection-oriented, full duplex, stream transport service (an application can send a continuous sequence of octets without the concept of records and similarly data can be delivered in a stream of octets), end-to-end service with complete reliability. TCP guarantees data transmission with zero missing or out-of-order delivery. Further, the TCP connection is started reliably in which case two applications create a new connection with no duplicate packet from any previous connection allowed. Similarly, the connection is shut down with all data delivered before the connection is terminated.

TCP uses IP to carry messages known as 'segments'. Each TCP segment is encapsulated in an IP datagram and sent across the internet. When the datagram reaches the destination host, IP passes the segment to TCP. IP never reads or interprets the TCP segments. It only acts as a communication system between two hosts at two end points of a connection.

Some of the distinctive features or techniques adopted by TCP for achieving reliability are (1) adaptive retransmission, (2) flow control through window advertisement, (3) three-way handshake to ensure start-up and termination of connections reliably and (4) mechanism to control congestion in the internet by measuring packet loss and responding to congestion by reducing temporarily window size to reduce data transmission rate.

Through the adaptive retransmission for packet loss, TCP measures the current round trip delay (the time delay between the sending of a TCP segment by a sending host and the receipt of the acknowledgement from the receiving host) for each connection and then estimates statistically time out for each connection to set the retransmission timer for the same.

In order to control the flow of data, TCP uses a window advertisement technique. Whenever TCP establishes a connection, each end of the connection earmarks a buffer to hold incoming data and sends information about the size of the buffer to the other end. As data arrives, the receiver sends an acknowledgement, which also specifies the remaining buffer size, known as 'window' through a notification known as 'window advertisement' in TCP parlance. A receiver sends a window advertisement with each acknowledgement. If the sender transmits faster than the receiver can consume in its application, the window size will gradually reduce and at one time becomes zero, thereby causing the receiver to

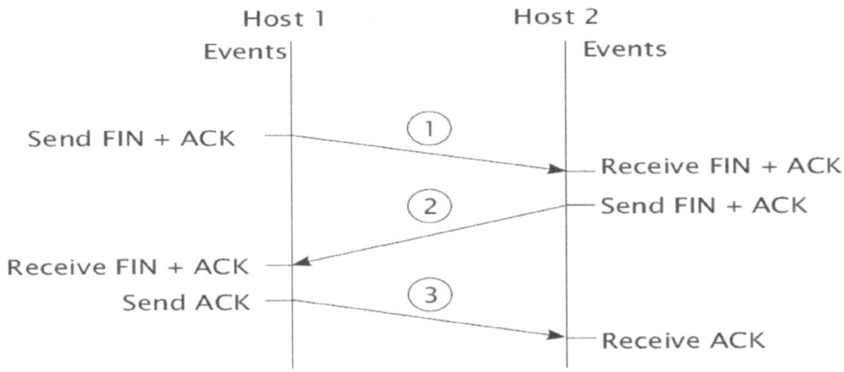

Figure 12.42 Three-Way Handshake Used by TCP to Close a Connection

advertise a 'zero window'. The sender, on receiving a 'zero window' advertisement, has to stop transmission till the receiver again advertises a positive window along with an acknowledgement of the last data octet received.

The three-way handshake guarantees reliable start-up or termination of a connection by the exchange of three messages between the two hosts located at the two ends of the connection. TCP uses the term 'SYN' segment (synchronisation segment) to establish a connection and the term 'FIN' segment (Finish segment) to describe messages in a three-way handshake to terminate a connection. Figure 12.42 illustrates the three-way handshake used to terminate a connection.

12.20 Private IP Addressing and Network Address Translation (NAT) Private IP Addressing

In an attempt to conserve address spaces, in addition to subnet and classless addressing schemes described in earlier paragraphs, the private addressing scheme was invented and introduced. A private network is a network with computers attached to it; however, the network administrator assigns a locally unique address to each computer connected to the private network known as its private address or non-routable address, which are not valid on the global internet. The private network will have a single globally valid IP address. Routers at the site with private addresses are configured to forward datagrams containing sources with private addresses. However, before allowing a datagram with a private source address to the internet, a device known as NAT translates the private IP source address into a global IP address recognised by the internet. Similarly, in the case of an incoming datagram from a computer in the global internetwork to a private address, NAT translates the global IP address of the private network to a private address used at the site. The conservation of address spaces arises because, in the case of a site with private addresses, all the individual nodes or computers will not have separate globally valid IP addresses, but the whole set of computers within the private network will have one globally valid IP address assigned to the private network site.

The private IPV4 address space specified in request for comment 1918 (RFC 1918) is defined by the following address blocks:

1. 10.0.0.0/8, which is a single class A network with an IP address range from 10.0.0.0 to 10.255.255.255. The host ID size is 24 bits and can accommodate 16,777,216 number of addresses.
2. 172.16.0.0/12, which is 16 contiguous class B networks with an IP address range from 172.16.0.0 to 172.31.255.255. The host ID size is 20 bits and can accommodate 1,048,576 number of addresses.
3. 192.168.0.0/16, which is 256 contiguous class C networks with an IP address range from 192.168.0.0 to 192.168.255.255. The host ID size is 16 bits and can accommodate 65,536 number of addresses.

12.20.1 NAT Technology

NAT basically provides two views:

1. From the internet perspective, the private site appears to have a single host computer with a single global IP address assigned to it. Datagrams appear to have originated from the same IP address and responses are sent to the same IP address.
2. From the perspective of any one computer in the site, the internet appears to accept and route private addresses.

In order to provide the above views or illusion, the NAT device processes each incoming datagram to a private site and each outgoing datagram from a private site. The process is rewriting of IP addresses in the datagram as illustrated in Figure 12.43.

12.20.1.1 Network Address and Port Translation (NAPT) and Translation Table

NAPT is the abbreviation of 'network address and port translation' and is a more popular form of NAT. NAPT takes care of two limitations of NAT. First, if more than one computer at a site with private addresses communicates with the same destination D, basic NAT will fail because there will be more than one private address corresponding to the same destination address D. Therefore, it will not be possible for NAT to identify the particular source of the private site from which an incoming datagram arrives for D.

Second, if more than one application running on a particular computer at the private site communicates with different destinations on the internet, NAT cannot manage the situation since its translation does not involve the port number for any particular application running on a computer.

NAPT allows a private site to have more than one application running on one or more computers to communicate with one or more destinations on the global internet. In order to facilitate the above feature, NAPT translates both IP addresses and protocol

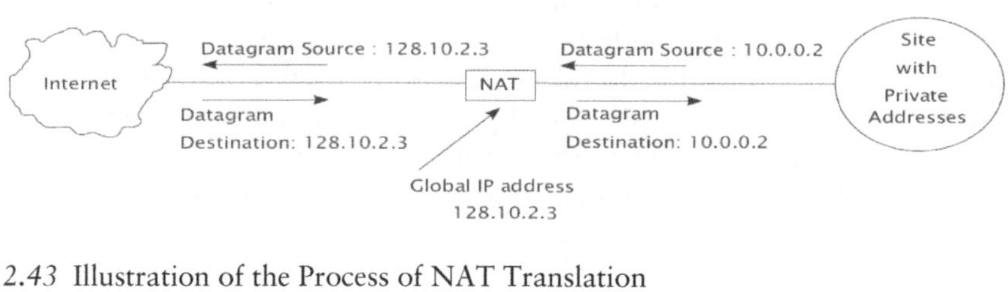

Figure 12.43 Illustration of the Process of NAT Translation

Table 12.10 An Illustration of NAPT Translation Table for TCP Connections

Direction	*Fields*	*Old Value*	*New Value*
Outgoing	IP source: TCP source	10.0.0.207.7000	128 .10 .2. 3: 7101
Outgoing	IP source: TCP source	10.0.0.208.7000	128 .10 .2. 3: 7102
Incoming	IP destination: TCP destination	128.10.2.3:7101	10. 0. 0. 207: 7000
Incoming	IP destination: TCP destination	128.10.2.3:7102	10. 0. 0. 208: 7000

port numbers, unlike NAT which only translates IP addresses. NAPT uses a translation table, which contains both old value and new value of IP addresses and protocol port numbers. However, in case two computers in a private site send datagrams using the same local port number (similar application) and both form a TCP connection to a web server at a particular port number through a NAPT device, to avoid such conflicting situations, NAPT assigns different TCP source port numbers to the two computers running similar applications. This is illustrated schematically with a NAPT translation table in Table 12.10.

Private addresses with NAT find common use in residential networks, since most 'Internet service providers' (ISPs) only allocate a single routable public IP address to a residential customer, but many homes have more than one computer or other internet-connected devices, such as smartphones. In such cases, a NAT gateway is used to provide internet connectivity to multiple hosts. Private addresses are also often used by corporate networks because of security reasons. Such networks are not connected directly to the internet. Private addresses thus enhance network security for the internal network, since it is difficult for an internet host (external host) to connect directly to an internal network. Finally, NAT can be implemented in software on a conventional PC (software defined NAT) or as a dedicated hardware device.

12.21 Internet Routing Protocols

We have seen from the previous paragraphs that IP uses routing tables contained in both hosts and routers to facilitate the forwarding of datagrams. IP routing deals with the propagation of routing information for creating and updating routing tables. There are several routing protocols for the global internet. Certain concepts such as static routing and dynamic routing related to IP routing need elaboration. Static routing relates to routes, which do not change unless an error in the network is detected. Dynamic routing, on the contrary, changes routes and updates the routing tables of the routers to learn about optimal routes for each location to ensure datagrams follow the same routes. Static routing is simple, easy to specify but inflexible. It is mostly used by hosts, particularly in cases where the host has one network connection, as in the case of Ethernet, and the network is connected to the rest of the internet by a single router. The routing table in the case of static routing for a host has only two entries, one for the network to which it is attached and the other for a default route meant for all other destinations, as shown in Figures 12.44(a) and 12.44(b). Static routing is limited to simple configuration as shown in Figure 12.44. However, when there is more than one router, each connected to separate ISPs, and the ISPs also connect with each other through a network, the routers have

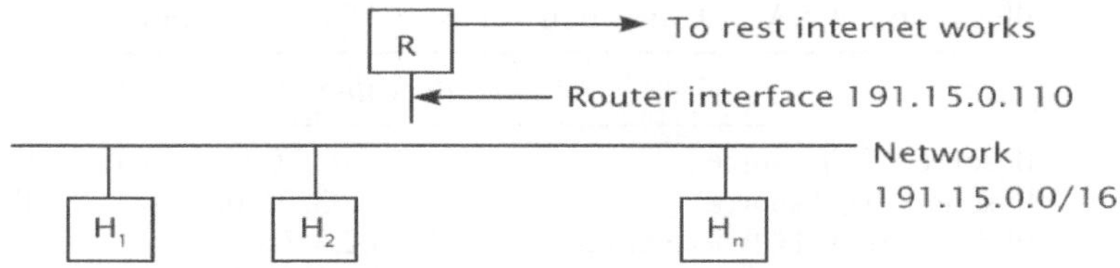

(a) Static Routing

Network	Mask	Next hop
191.15.0.0	255.255.0.0	Direct
Default	0.0.0.0	191.15.0.110

(b) Routing Table for a host

Figure 12.44 (a) Static Routing (b) Routing Table Used by a Host

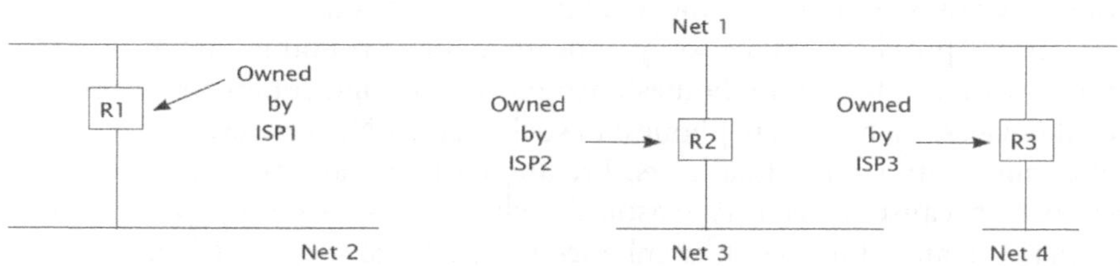

Figure 12.45 Four Networks Connected by Three Routers Belonging to Three ISPs Leading to Dynamic Routing to Propagate Routing Information

to exchange routing information and update the individual routing table dynamically. The architecture for a dynamic routing situation has been illustrated in Figure 12.45.

12.22 Autonomous System (AS) Concept

Basically, a route propagation protocol allows each router to exchange routing information with another router. However, in the case of the global internet, if each router exchanges routing information with another router, the total routing information traffic will become enormous and will not be scalable by the internet works. In order to limit the routing traffic, routers and networks are divided and grouped into 'Autonomous systems' numbered as AS1, AS2, ... ASn such that routers within a particular AS exchange routing information among themselves. Then, at least one or more routers in each AS summarise the routing information within the autonomous group before passing it to the other AS. An AS is a contiguous set of networks and routers under the control of one administrative authority such as an ISP, one small corporation or a large corporation with a number of sites in a metro city.

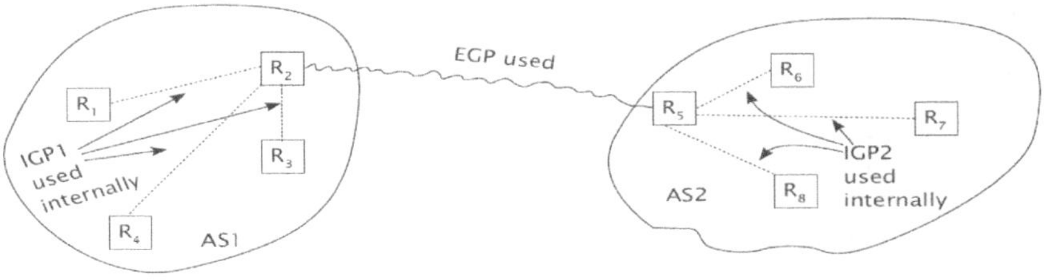

Figure 12.46 The Internet Routing Architecture with IGP and EGP

Internet routing protocols within an autonomous system are collectively known as Interior Gateway Protocol (IGP), which governs the exchange of routing information among the routers within the system.

A router in one AS uses an Exterior Gateway Protocol (EGP) to exchange routing information with a router in another AS. In order to save traffic, an EGP passes only summarised routing information from one AS to another AS. Figure 12.46 illustrates the IGP and EGP routing architecture of the internet.

In the figure, AS1 uses IGP1 to use internally the exchange of routing information among the routers R_1, R_2, R_3 and R_4. Similarly, AS2 uses IGP2 internally. R_2 summarises routing information for AS1 and R_5 does the same for AS2. R_2 and R_5 use EGP to communicate the summarised routing information between AS1 and AS2. Additionally, R_2 and R_5 accept the summary from each other and propagate the same to their routers in AS1 and AS2 respectively. Some of the important internet routing protocols belonging to IGP and EGP are shown in Table 12.11.

12.22.1 Optimal Routes, Routing Metrics and Administrative Distance

In principle, internet routing protocols find all possible paths from a router to each destination and then choose a path that is optimal for each destination and updates the routing table accordingly. However, there is no universally agreed criterion of optimality of a path. The optimal path selection is based on a number of parameters such as type of application, associated delay, throughput and jitter. Routing protocol designers refer to a term known as 'routing metric' as a measure for selecting an optimal path. Although it is possible to use parameters as mentioned above such as throughput, delay or jitter as a routing metric, in practice, internet routing is often based on two metrics, namely hop

Table 12.11 The Internet Routing Protocols for IGP and EGP

IGPs (Interior Gateway Protocols)	*EGPs (Exterior Gateway Protocols)*
RIP (routing information protocol)	EGP
OSPF (open shortest path first)	BGP (Border Gateway Protocol) version 4
IGRP (interior gateway routing protocol)	EBGP
EIGRP (enhanced interior or gateway routing protocol)	
IS—IS (intermediate system to intermediate system)	

Table 12.12 Administrative Distance for Various Routing Protocols Used on CISCO Routers

Routing Protocol	*Administrative Distance (Arbitrary Units Based on Reliability)*
Directly connected interface	0
Static route out at interface	1
Static route to next-hop address	1
Dynamic mobile network routing	3
EIGRP summary route	5
External BGP	20
Internal EIGRP	90
IGRP	100
OSPF	110
IS-IS	115
RIP	120
Exterior gateway protocol (EGP)	140
On-demand routing (ODR)	160
External EIGRP	170
Internal BGP	200
Next-hop resolution protocol (NHRP)	250
Floating static route (Ex. DHCP)	254
Unknown others	255

count (the number of intermediate routers or networks on the path to destination) and administrative cost assigned manually as per corporate policy to control the traffic flow along different paths. Moreover, the decision as regards choosing a particular internet routing protocol is based on its reliability for selecting the optimal routing. A number of arbitrary units known as 'administrative distance' are assigned to dynamic routes, static routes and directly connected routes. The value of administrative distance is used to rank routes from most preferred (with low administrative distance value) to least preferred (with high administrative distance value).

Administrative distance assigned to internet routing protocol bears an inverse relationship with its reliability for optimal routing. The lower the administrative distance value, the higher the reliability.

The default administrative distance for various routing protocols used on Cisco routers is shown in Table 12.12.

An administrative distance of 255 will cause the router to remove the route from the routing table and not use it because of very poor reliability for optimal routing. It may be noted that within an AS, IGP software uses a routing metric to determine the optimal path to each destination. However, EGP finds only the path to each destination but cannot determine an optimal path as it cannot compare the routing metrics from more than one AS, which may vary for the various AS. In the case of IGP, the routers mainly exchange routing information and update the individual routing tables, and the hosts listen passively to the routing information to update their individual routing tables.

The internet routing protocols for IGP can be broadly categorised into two groups. One group consists of distance-vector-based protocols and the other link-state-based protocols. Typical examples of the distance-vector-based IGP protocols are: routing information protocol (RIP), interior gateway routing protocol (IGRP) and enhanced interior gateway routing protocol (EIGRP), whereas open shortest path first (OSPF) and intermediate system to intermediate system (IS–IS) are examples of link-state-based protocols.

Distance-vector protocols are based on calculating the direction and distance to any link in a network within an administrative system. 'Direction' here means the next-hop address together with the exit interface. 'Distance' here is a measure of the cost to reach a certain node. The minimum cost route between any two nodes is the route with minimum distance. Each node (router or host) maintains a vector (array or table) of minimum distance to every node. The cost of reaching a destination is calculated using various route metrics. RIP uses the hop count as a measure of distance to destination, where each network between the source and destination counts as a single hop. It also uses origin as one counting, meaning that a directly connected network is one hop away and not zero. IGRP, however, takes into account other information such as node delay and available bandwidth for considering distance.

A router informs its neighbours of topology changes periodically so that updates are performed by the neighbours, and these are configured to use the same distance-vector routing protocol. Distance vector routing protocols use various algorithms to calculate paths such as Bellman-Ford, Ford-Fulkerson or dual finite state machine (FSM).

The basic concept of link-state routing is that every switching node (router) constructs a graph of the connectivity to the network; the edges of the graph show which nodes are connected to which other nodes. This is illustrated in Figure 12.47. Each node then determines the next best path from it to every possible destination in the network.

The consolidation of the best path for a particular node will be its routing table. The difference between distance vector routing protocols and link state routing protocols lies in that in case of the former, each node shares its routing table with neighbours, whereas in the case of the latter, the information exchanged among the nodes is connectivity oriented.

RIP was among the first routing protocols based on the distance–vector approach. It is simple and requires little configuration. It has important features such as hop count metric, use of UDP for all message transmission, broadcast or multicast delivery, support for default route propagation and passive version for hosts, as explained earlier. OSPF is an interior gateway protocol that uses a link-status algorithm to propagate routing information. It supports multi-access networks also. Each router participating in OSPF

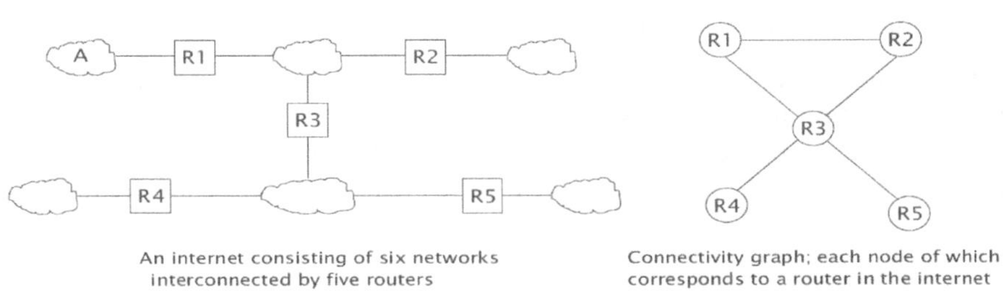

Figure 12.47 Illustration of Link State Graph Corresponding to an Internet Consisting of Six Networks Interconnected by Five Routers

periodically broadcasts link status to adjacent routers, which use Dijkstra's shortest path first algorithm to compute the shortest path. The following table shows important differences between RIP and OSPF, as discussed earlier also.

RIP	*OSPF*
It is a distance vector protocol.	It is a link-state protocol.
The metric used in RIP is hop count.	The metrics used in OSPF are bandwidth and delay.
RIP uses distance vector algorithms such as Bellman Ford, Ford-Fulkerson or Dual FSM to determine the best path.	OSPF uses Dijkstra's SPF algorithm to determine the best path.
In RIP, networks are not divided in areas or tables.	OSPF allows partitioning of the routes and networks in an autonomous system into multiple areas, subareas and backbone areas. OSPF can handle a large number of routers than RIP.
Maximum hop count is 15.	No hop count.
Periodic routing updates every 30 seconds and convergence time is high.	Much less convergence time.
RIP routes have an administrative distance value of 120.	OSPF routes have an administrative distance value of 110.
Routing is both classful and classless for different versions of RIP.	Classless.
RIP uses UDP.	OSPF uses IP.

Note: A convergence time is a measure of how fast a group of routers attains the state of convergence (a state of a set of routers that have the same topological information about the internet in which they operate).

12.22.1.1 *Border Gateway Protocol (BGP)*

BGP version 4, the current version, is the most important EGP and is used to exchange routing information among AS in the global internet. BGP version 4, abbreviated as BGP–4, ensures correct transmission of a datagram from an arbitrary source host to any arbitrary destination through consistent global routing information propagation. BGP–4 has important features such as provision for policies enforced by the sender and receiver (regarding routes, security restrictions and advertisements), transit routing and reliable transport using TCP. The TCP ensures that data arrive in the correct order without any loss.

12.22.1.2 *Multicast Routing Protocol*

Since internet multicast allows dynamic grouping and further because an arbitrary source can send information to a multicast group without being a member of the group, multicast route propagation is a very complex and difficult situation. Even though there are several multicast routing protocols, global internet-wide multicast protocol technology exists.

12.23 Client–Server Paradigm of Interaction

Network application software provides high-level services available on the internet. Further, application programs that communicate with each other on a network or on the internet use the client–server paradigm of interaction. In this paradigm, two applications are involved in the communication process: client and server applications. A server program or application waits passively for contact or to be invoked, while a client application initiates communication actively. A client application software is an arbitrary program invoked directly by a user and runs locally on the user's computer to actively initiate contact with a server program. The client application software can access multiple server programs running on a single-server computer or on more than one server computer. It can actively contact one remote server at a time. Generally, client applications do not require any sophisticated hardware or operating system.

Server software, on the contrary, is a single dedicated service-oriented privileged program which can serve multiple remote clients at a time. In other words, it waits passively for contact from one or more arbitrary remote clients to whom it offers a single service. The server software gets invoked when the server system boots and continues to execute through many sessions. The server software runs on a shared computer with powerful hardware and a sophisticated multi-user operating system such as UNIX.

Information flow between a client and a server can be in either one or both directions. In general, a client sends a request for a service to a server and the server returns a response to the client. In some cases, however, a client sends multiple requests such as queries, and the server sends more than one response. For example, a database client may seek from an overseas employment database server all openings for civil engineering graduates, and the server sends responses for more than one opening at a time. Bi-directional information flows also involve a case of a file server receiving a copy of files from a client for storage and sending a particular file to the client on request. A client or server application interacts with the transport layer of the TCP/IP suite to establish communication. The transport layer, in turn, uses lower-layer protocols to send and receive individual packets. Thus, both the computers for a client and a server need the complete stack of protocols.

A server-class computer can offer more than one service at the same time. The computer in that case must have large memory, a fast processor and an operating system such as UNIX or Windows which can run multiple application programs concurrently. The computer offers more than one service and waits passively for client active communication for the offered services. Likewise, more than one remote client may like to avail themselves of the same service from a server-class computer at the same time. This is facilitated due to a feature known as 'support concurrency' which allows multiple copies of a server offering a single service. The application program having more than one thread of control or execution is known as a concurrent program. Concurrent execution is essential to the client–server model of interaction as a concurrent server offers the same service to multiple clients simultaneously without any client waiting for any other previous client to finish availing themselves of the service. In a concurrent server, the main server thread creates a new service thread to handle each client. The service thread entertains one particular client request and then terminates, but the main thread keeps the server alive for another one or more requests to arrive. Thus, if N number of clients are using a service on a single computer, there will be (N + 1) threads providing the service. N threads will be providing service to N clients, and the main thread waits passively for additional requests. Figure 12.48 illustrates the arrangement of multiple services with multiple copies of a single service on a computer accessed by remote clients through the internet.

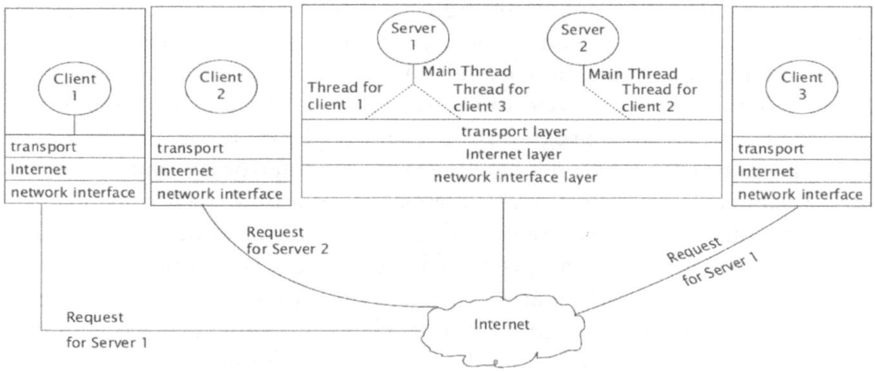

Figure 12.48 Two Servers on a Single Computer Accessed by Three Clients on Three Other Computers with Concurrent Support by Server 1

A question arises as to how to identify a particular service being offered by a server (such as a web server or file server) and how a client will specify unambiguously the service it requests. For this, the client–server interaction paradigm assigns a unique identifier for each service, and the same identifier will be used by both the server, which offers the same service, and the client, which actively communicates for the service. Protocol software uses the identifier to direct each incoming request to the correct application server. As an example of a service identifier, TCP uses 16-bit integer values known as TCP port numbers to identify services and assigns a unique port number to each service. TCP software on the server-side computer uses the protocol port number in an incoming request from a client to determine the server that should handle the request. In the case of multiple copies of a server to handle multiple clients requesting the same service, the transport protocols, in practice, assign each client a unique identifier and require the particular client to include its identifier while making a request. Transport protocol software on the server computer uses both the client and server identifiers to seek the copy of the server created for the client. In the case of TCP, each client selects a local protocol port number, which is not assigned to any service, and specifies the same in the source port field and the protocol port number of the server in the destination port field of the TCP segment, which the remote client sends. TCP on the server's machine uses the combination of client and server port numbers to choose the correct copy of a concurrent server.

Finally, clients and servers can use either a connection-oriented interface (as in the case of TCP) or a connectionless interface (as is the case of UDP).

In case of connection-oriented transport, a client first forms a connection to a specific server and then sends requests and receives responses until it finishes using the service and closes the connection. In contrast, connectionless protocols allow clients and servers to exchange individual messages.

For example, a client can send each request and the server can return each response as a single message.

12.24 Application Programming Interface (API)

The interface between an application programme and the transport protocols for communication is known as API. Most APIs define a set of procedures (one for each logical function) such as one procedure to establish communication and another procedure to transmit data. In addition, API specifies the arguments associated with each procedure and the data type.

The standard API available with various operating systems such as Microsoft's Windows and also UNIX systems is the socket API often abbreviated as 'socket'. Vendors of various operating systems created a 'socket library', which provides applications with a socket API on a computer system which has no native sockets. When an application calls for one of the socket procedures, control passes to a routine in the socket library to implement the socket procedure. Sockets were originally developed as a part of the Berkeley Software Distribution (BSD) UNIX operating system.

Before an application can use protocols to communicate, the application must request the operating system to create a socket that will be used for communication. The operating system returns a small integer descriptor, which will be used by the application to reference the socket. The socket procedure which creates a socket for an application and returns a descriptor is as follows:

Descriptor = Socket (proto-family, type, protocol)

These three arguments are:

1. **Proto-family**: Proto-family specifies the protocol family to be associated with the socket. For example, proto-family PF_INET indicates the TCP/IP protocol suite.
2. **Type**: Type specifies the type of communication the socket will use; the typical values are SOCK_STREAM for connection-oriented type and SOCK_DGRAM for a connectionless message-oriented transfer.
3. **Protocol**: Protocol permits a single protocol suit to include two or more protocols to provide the same service.

The other common procedures with their formats are as follows:

1. **Close (Socket)**: Here, socket is the integer descriptor for the socket being closed. It immediately terminates use of the socket, and the descriptor is released, preventing the application from sending or receiving any further data.
2. **Bind (Socket, Localaddr, Addrlen)**: It allows a server to supply the protocol address at which the server will wait passively for contact. The argument 'socket' is the descriptor of the socket created but not bound, 'localaddr' specifies the local address assigned to the socket, and 'addrlen' is an integer specifying the length of the local address.
3. **Listen (Socket, Queuesize)**: This is for a socket for a server computer to be in passive mode awaiting contact from clients. It has two arguments, namely 'socket', which is the descriptor of a socket that has been created and bound to a local address by the 'bind' procedure and the 'queuesize', which specifies the length of queue for the socket's requests. If the queue is full, no further request will be accepted by the socket.

4. **New Sock = Accept (Socket, Caddress, Caddresslen)**: It is associated with the call for the procedure 'accept' in the case of connection-oriented transport to accept a new connection request from a client.

The argument 'socket' is the descriptor of a socket that the server has created and bound to a specific protocol port. The 'accept' procedure fills in the argument 'caddress' with the address of the client that formed the connection and sets 'caddresslen' as the length of the same address.

The 'accept' procedure creates a new socket for the new connection request from a client and returns the descriptor of 'newsock' to the caller (client). The server uses the new socket to communicate with the client and closes the socket 'newsock' when finished. However, the original socket remains as it is and is used by the server to accept the next connection from any client.

The procedure Connect (socket, saddress, saddresslen) is used to establish a connection by a client with a specific server where 'socket' is the descriptor of a socket on the client computer for the connection, 'saddress' specifies the end point address of the server (a combination of server address and the protocol port number), 'saddresslen' specifies the length of server address in octets:

send (socket, data, length, flags)
send to (socket, data, length, flags, destaddress, addresslen)
sendmsg (socket, msgstruct, flags)

The 'send', 'send to' and 'sendmsg' procedures are used to send data/information by both clients and servers.

The 'send' procedure is used to send data when the socket has been created and connected, whereas both 'Send to' and 'sendmsg' are procedures used by either a client or a server to send a message using unconnected sockets. It has four arguments, namely 'socket', 'data', which is the address in the memory of the client or server computer where the data to be sent exists, 'length', an integer which specifies the number of octets of data, and 'flags', which contains bits for special option requests such as debugging of the system.

The 'send to' procedure contains two additional arguments, namely 'dest address' and 'addresslen' to specify the address of the destination and the length of the destination address.

The 'send msg' procedure performs the same procedure as 'send to' but has only three arguments.

The arguments 'socket' and 'flags' are similar to the 'send to' procedure. However, 'msgstruct' is a structure that contains information about the destination address, the length of the same, the message to be sent and the length of the message:

recv (socket, buffer, length, flags)
recv from (socket, buffer, length, flags, sndaddress, saddrlen)
recvmsg (socket, msgstruct, flags)

The procedures 'recv', 'recvfrom' and 'recvmsg' are used by a client or a server to receive data/information sent by the other. They are very similar in form to the three Send procedures as explained earlier except that the argument 'buffer' specifies the address in memory where the incoming message (data or information) should be placed and the

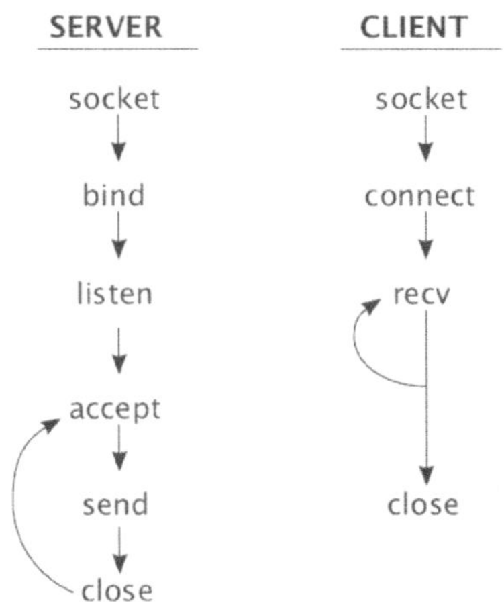

Figure 12.49 The Sequence of Socket Procedures for a Client and Server Calls

argument 'length' specifies the buffer size. The 'recv' procedure is for connected sockets, whereas 'recvfrom' and 'recvmsg' are for sockets not connected.

The arguments 'sndaddress' and 'saddrlen' are the pointers to a socket address structure to denote the sender's address and the length of the same. The argument 'msgstruct' gives the address of a structure that holds the address for an incoming message and the location for the sender's IP address.

Sequence of 'Socket' Procedure Calls: Figure 12.49 illustrates the sequence of socket procedures for a client and server calls. It may be noted from the figure that the server must call 'listen' before a client calls 'connect'.

12.25 Domain Name System (DNS)

Internet users do not always require remembering IP addresses of the destination computers. Instead, they can remember with much more ease symbolic names assigned to such computers. For example, in case of a client–server interaction, the client can send a message to a recipient server and use a string specifying the name of the server computer. Likewise, a computer name can be specified as a string by a user to reach a particular site on the World Wide Web.

A question arises as to how the computers will understand symbolic names. In other words, although application software permits users to enter symbolic names, the internet protocol requires equivalent IP addresses, and therefore an application program must convert every symbolic name into its equivalent IP address before transmitting the message. In order to facilitate the conversion of symbolic names into equivalent IP addresses, a structure of symbolic computer names, known as the 'Domain Name System' (DNS), has been designed. Further, the database of computer names resides on a number of computers located at different sites across the internet. The servers which handle the naming information are known as the DNS servers. An application program converts the computer symbolic names into the equivalent IP addresses with the help of DNS servers through client–server interaction, which has been explained in subsequent paragraphs of this chapter.

Top-Level Domain Name (TLDs)		Assigned to
com	...	Commercial organization
edu	...	Educational institution
org	...	Non-commercial organizations
gov	...	US Government
aero	...	Air transport industry
arpa	...	Infrastructure domain
museum	...	Museums
net	...	Major network support centre
biz	...	Businesses
country code (such as uk, in, etc.)	...	A country

Figure 12.50 Some Typical Values for Top-Level Domain Names

12.25.1 Structure of DNS

Domain names are hierarchical and consist of alphanumeric parts separated by periods. The hierarchy order follows that the most significant part of the name is on the extreme right and the other parts on the left, one before the other in order of significance.

The left-most part indicates the name of a computer.

For example, the domain name 'apple.econ.jadavpur.edu' symbolically indicates a computer named 'apple' in the economics department of 'Jadavpur University', an educational institution. Similarly, a domain name 'macintosh.cognizant.com' symbolically indicates a computer named 'macintosh' at 'cognizant' a company.

The Domain Name System neither puts any stipulation on the number of parts or segments in each name, nor does it specify what those segments represent. However, DNS specifies the values for the most significant part (rightmost part) of a domain name, which is known as TLD (top-level domain). TLDs are assigned and controlled by the 'Internet Corporation for Assigned Names and Numbers' (ICANN), and some typical values of TLDs are shown in Figure 12.50. It may be stated that DNS does not differentiate between names in upper or lowercase characters.

In order to obtain a domain, an organisation has to register with an approved registrar and a unique domain suffix is assigned to each organisation from among the list of TLDs. DNS allows an organisation to use a suffix to denote geographic location (country, state and city). For example, 'incometax.gov.in' is the domain registered by the income tax department of the Government of India.

Likewise, UK universities register under the domain 'ac.uk', where 'ac' stands for academic and 'uk' for United Kingdom.

DNS also permits hierarchical order of names within an organisation. Even individual groups or departments within an organisation can have an appropriate hierarchical structure of the names. Each name in the hierarchy has a corresponding segment in a domain name, and there is no universal standard for the names in the hierarchy. Similarly, there is no restriction regarding the levels of the naming hierarchy in DNS. The naming hierarchy facilitates achieving autonomy by allowing an organisation to control all names with a particular suffix.

For example, Figure 12.51 shows graphically the DNS hierarchy of a company named Zenith which has two broad divisions—pump and motor—and pump has two subdivisions, namely centrifugal and submersible. The motor division has three subdivisions, namely synchronous, induction and series.

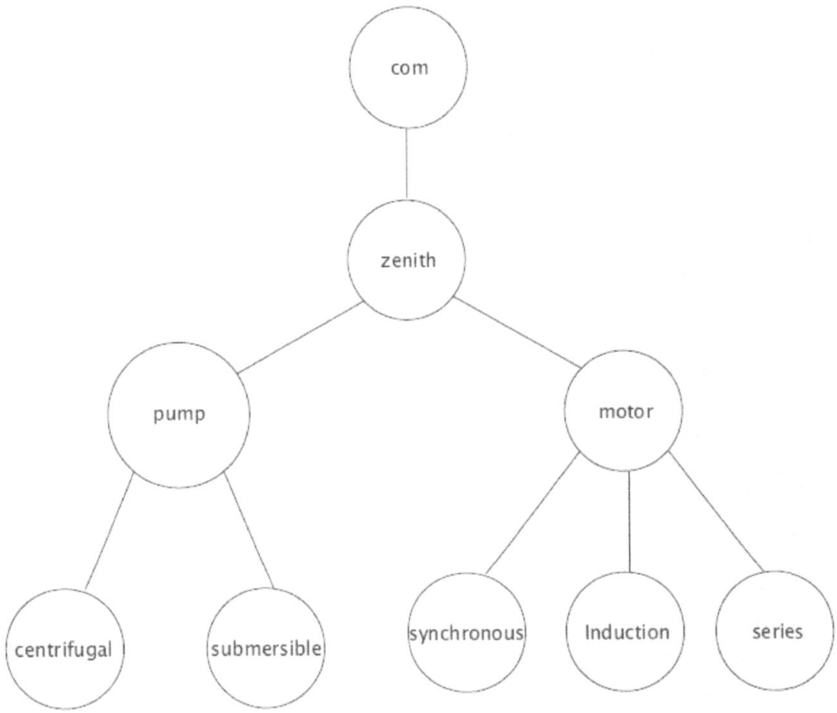

Figure 12.51 A Graphical Representation Showing How a DNS Hierarchy Can Be Structured in an Organisation

Individual computer names within the sub-divisions can be the domain names as follows:

computer.centrifugal.pump.zenith.com
computer.submersible.pump.zenith.com
computer.synchronous.motor.zenith.com
computer.induction.motor.zenith.com
computer.series.motor.zenith.com

Although in the names shown above, the first name is the name of a computer, the same first label can be used for denoting a service that a computer provides. For example, the first label www indicates the name of a computer which runs the web server. However, this is merely a naming convention for helping users to remember the service that a first name provides.

DNS uses a client–server interaction model, wherein the entire naming system (the domain names along with the equivalent IP addresses) operates as a large and distributed database. Each organisation with internet connection runs a domain name server which is linked with other domain name servers and the integrated set of DNS Servers functions as the database of domain names. A user application becomes a client of the DNS server when it needs to translate a name into an IP address. The client sends a DNS request message with a particular domain name to be translated to a DNS server. The server extracts the name from the message, translates the name to an equivalent IP address and returns the same to the client as a reply message.

The translation of a domain name into an equivalent IP address is called 'name resolution', and the software which performs the 'name resolution' is called 'name resolver' or simply 'resolver' software. Operating systems in general have the name 'resolver' software as an in-built library routine, which an application program can invoke. For example, in the case of UNIX operating system, the library routine to resolve a name is called 'gethostbyname'. The argument of 'gethostbyname' is the domain name as a character string. If the domain name can be successfully resolved 'gethostbyname' returns a list of one or more IP addresses corresponding to the argument. However, if the name in the argument cannot be resolved a 'NULL' is returned instead of any IP address. In order to understand how the resolver works to resolve a name with the help of the DNS servers, let us look into the hierarchy and architecture of the DNS servers.

DNS servers are arranged in a hierarchy, which matches with the naming hierarchy with each one server corresponding to a part of the naming hierarchy. The root server sitting on the top of the hierarchy is meant for the top-level domains (such as .edu) as mentioned in Figure 12.50. The root server contains information about other servers to fetch all possible domain names. It may be mentioned that although the hierarchy of DNS servers matches the naming hierarchy, the structure or the architecture is not identical and the same is designed or chosen by every organisation depending upon how it divides names among one or more servers. For example, Figures 12.52a and 12.52b illustrate two different architectures for the DNS servers for the same name hierarchy shown in Figure 12.51.

The resolver software in a host goes by a recursive resolution to find the equivalent IP address for a name. Each resolver is configured with the address of a local DNS server. The resolver becomes the client of the same DNS server and sends a DNS request message to the local server and waits for a reply. If the local server is an authority for the name specified in the request message from the resolver, the server directly replies after searching for the name in its local database. However, if the name with the request is beyond the authority of the local server (that is, the name with the request is not available in the

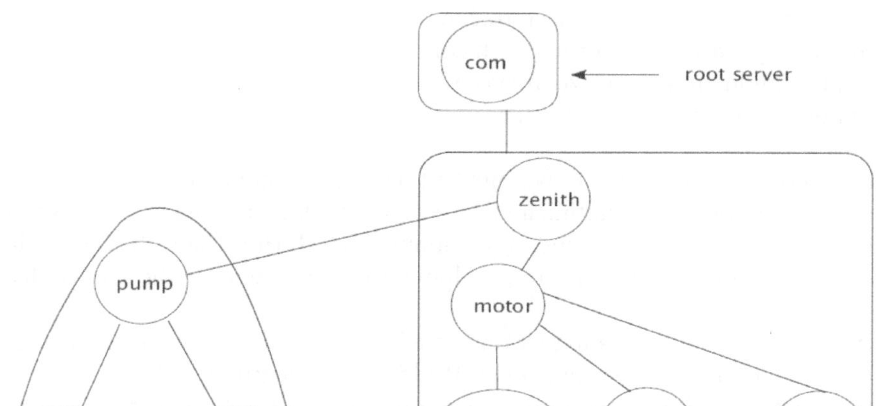

Figure 12.52a Architecture of DNS Servers for the Name Hierarchy of Figure 12.51

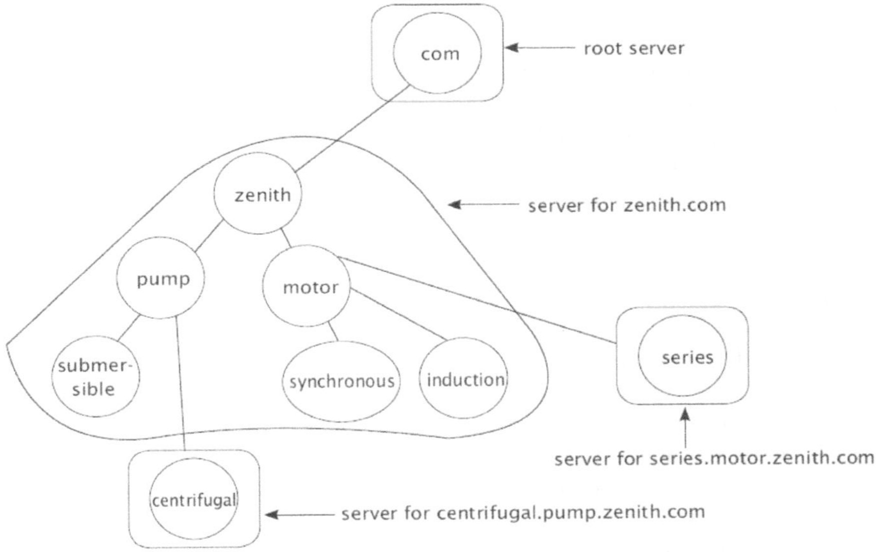

Figure 12.52b Architecture of DNS Servers for the Name Hierarchy of Figure 12.51

local database), the local server for the time being becomes a client for another name server and further client–server interaction takes place. When the other server returns and answers, the original server sends a copy of the answer back to the resolver who sent the request. This type of iterative search begins with the root server whose address is known to each other DNS server. Further, the iterative search for resolution proceeds through the server hierarchy beginning with the root server one level at a time.

12.25.2 DNS Entry Types

The DNS database records have three elements, namely domain name, record type and a value for the equivalent IP address. The record type indicates how the value is to be interpreted. For example, type 'A' addresses are for computer names for applications such as file transfer protocol, internet browser and many other programmes, whereas type MX is for mail exchanger, which maps computer names found in an email address into the equivalent IP address.

Whenever a resolver looks up a name, the resolver has to specify the type that is desired in order to enable a DNS server to return only entries that match the specified type.

12.25.3 Optimisation Techniques for Performance of DNS Servers

Two optimisation techniques, namely replication and caching, are adopted by DNS servers to improve performance in terms of response. Replication is carried out by creating multiple copies of the root server around the world in order to reduce the load on any particular server.

The local DNS servers pertaining to any site are configured with the list of all the root servers. The local server for a site uses a root server that is most responsive at a given time.

DNS caching is more important because of the principle of locality, that is a tendency for a user to look up the same name repeatedly. Each server maintains a cache of names with already resolved bindings. When an application looks up a name for the first time, the local DNS server places a copy of the resolved binding into its cache. The server can then entertain subsequent requests by checking first its cache instead of contacting the authoritative server again.

12.26 Electronic Mail (Email) Transfer

Email is a type of client–server interaction involving the basic mail transport, mail forwarding and access to mailbox. An email is a message that consists of a header followed by the body, which is the text of the message. The header specifies the sender of the message, one or more recipients, a subject and date the message was sent.

The address of either the sender or the recipients of an email is a string divided into two parts by the '@' (at sign) character. The first part (left part) is a mailbox identifier, and the second part denotes the name of the computer on which the mailbox resides. The mailbox is a storage area assigned to a participant of email (a sender and each recipient) into which messages (emails) can be stored. The email box is a private mailbox with permission to allow the email software to place or store incoming mails into it but denies permission to anyone except the owner of the mailbox to read the messages or remove them. A few examples of email addresses are as follows:

jaytilak.biswas@yahoo.com
12345.6789@zenith.com
ibmnce@cal3.vsnl.net.in

The first example indicates the mailbox of the user with the first name 'jaytilak' and the last name 'biswas' residing on the computer of Yahoo commercial organisation. The second example indicates the user's login ID '12345.6789' as his/her mailbox identifier, which is resident on a computer of Zenith Corporation.

Figure 12.53 illustrates an email message. The header lines begin with a keyword and colon. The typical keywords are From, To, Date, Subject, CC (carbon copy) and BCC

```
From : ray_debansu@yahoo.co.in
To: jaytilak@yahoo.com
Date: Fri, 11 Nov at 9.30 PM
Subject: Examination schedule
CC: rita_nce@yahoo.com

Sir,
Please confirm through return e-mail whether you have received
the Examination Schedule for 1st semester 2016.

Debansu Ray
```

Figure 12.53 An Example of Email Message

(blind carbon copy). The email uses the keyword 'CC' to denote a carbon copy similar to the conventional office memos. The message (email) will be received by all recipients whose email addresses are specified against the keyword 'CC'.

The keyword 'BCC' stands for blind carbon copy, and the recipients whose email addresses are specified against the 'BCC' keyword will also receive a copy of the message, similar to CC, but the difference is that neither the BCC field itself nor the email addresses in it will appear in any of the copies, even to the original recipient whose address appears after the keyword 'To'. The 'BCC' line will appear blank to all recipients. A blank line separates the header from the body.

After composing an email message and specifying the recipients, when a user submits the same by pressing the 'send' button, the email software transfers a copy of the message to each recipient. The email software basically performs two functions: first, it allows a user to interact with the email interface program to compose messages or read messages. Second, the software handles an email transfer program for sending a copy of a message to a remote computer. The mail transfer program on the sender's computer becomes a client of the remote mail server, and the same uses the second part of the email address of the recipient to select the destination.

The mail transfer program receives composed messages, places the messages in a queue and then transfers a copy of each message to each recipient. The message is appended in the mailbox of each recipient. Figure 12.54 illustrates the path of an email message from user (sender) to the mailbox of a recipient.

The simple mail transfer protocol (SMTP) is used to transfer email between the sender computer and the recipient computer. The connection is first formed as a TCP connection and through the same connection, both the client and server identify themselves. It may be mentioned that SMTP uses ASCII text for all communication. After a message is transferred, the sender (client) sends a QUIT command to terminate the connection and the server of the recipient computer replies to end the connection. Each side then closes the TCP connection.

Mail transfer programs are capable of handling multiple recipients on a given remote computer. For example, if a user on computer zenith.com sends an email to three separate recipients at computer nexus.com, the mail transfer programme on zenith.com does not establish three separate connections at nexus.com, but it establishes a single connection to the server on nexus.com and multiple RCPT TO commands to specify all three

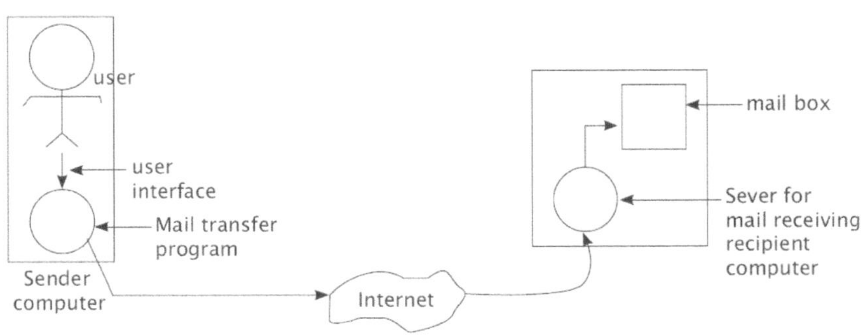

Figure 12.54 The Path of an Email Message

Table 12.13 Example of Mail Exploder Database

List	*Email Addresses of Members*
Students	anita@zenith.com, smita@jadavpur.edu, benoy@stxaviers.edu, rita@wbu.edu
Teachers	asit@cu.edu, bimal-mitra@tcs.com, palash@nexus.com

recipients before sending the body of the message. The server accepts the message and delivers it to each of the three recipients.

A mail exploder program uses a database of a group mail participants with a common group mail name. When a message is sent to the group mail name, the mail exploder programme forwards a copy of the message to each member of the group. Table 12.13 is an example of a mail exploder database. Each shown in Table 12.13 has got two mailing lists.

12.26.1 *Mail Gateways*

In case the mail lists of the mail exploder database become large enough, it occupies considerable storage space and also processing time on conventional computers. In such a situation, organisations select a dedicated set of computers to store the mail exploder database and run exploders to forward emails. Such dedicated computers for processing emails are called mail gateways or email gateways. However, the mailing lists maintained on mail gateways are public, which means that any user can join the list or any user can send a message to the list. Figure 12.55 illustrates how the mail transfer programme interacts with the exploder when any user sends a message to a mailing list on a mail gateway computer.

12.26.2 *Mailbox Access*

Usually, a mailbox is a storage location, and it is accessed by a mail server program that receives incoming email and stores the same in the appropriate mailbox. In the case of a powerful computer system, the mail server program operating in the background allows more than one client to send emails simultaneously. However, a mailbox cannot be placed in a computer without running a mail server continuously. Such a computer system needs to have enough memory, high processor capacity and an operating system

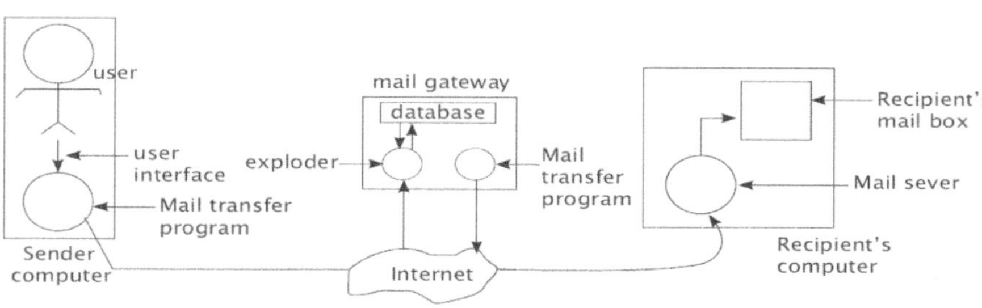

Figure 12.55 The Path of a Message as It Passes from Sender to Recipient through Mail Gateway

that permits mail server programmes to run in the background with other application programmes and, most importantly, cannot be disconnected from the internet at any point in time. Therefore, a personal computer or any computer that has to be switched off or disconnected from the internet beyond working hours,

will not suffice as an email receiver and hence cannot accommodate a mailbox. TCP/IP, therefore, includes a protocol known as the 'Post Office Protocol' (POP) and a user runs a 'POP' client to access the mailbox kept on another computer, which runs the mail server round the clock and an additional POP server. The separate computer, which contains the mailbox, runs two servers: a mail server which receives emails and stores them in the correct mailbox and a POP server which allows a user on a remote machine to access the mailbox. However, the former uses SMTP, while the latter uses POP. Unlike SMTP, POP allows a user to access the mailbox after proper authentication such as a password.

Further, a POP server also provides the user with information about the emails contained in the mailbox.

12.27 File Transfer Protocol (FTP)

FTP is a standard internet protocol for providing file transfer services between computers using TCP/IP connections. FTP is a general-purpose client–server protocol, which can be used by a client to upload, download, delete, rename, move and copy files from a server. FTP permits the transfer of files with arbitrary data. It also transfers a copy of files between any arbitrary pair of computers. A very important feature of FTP is that it has a feature that allows ownership of files and access restrictions to files.

12.27.1 FTP Prompt and Commands

A user invokes FTP either through a program or interactively. When a user invokes FTP interactively, the interactions are command-driven ones. In order to enable a user to enter a command, FTP issues a prompt (ftp>) and the user enters one of the FTP commands which is executed, and then another prompt is issued by FTP for the next command.

For example, FTP commands to connect to the FTP server it.ju.edu are:

ftp> open ftp.it.ju.edu

It may be stated that by default, the 'open' command uses the TCP port 21 to make the control connection.

Similarly, in order to get file or files from the server to the user's computer, the 'get or mget' commands are used. Of course, before the same, the username and password prompt will appear, and the user has to enter those to complete the authentication. However, some FTP servers allow 'anonymous' login using 'guest' or an email address as a password.

ftp> get coursefile.htm (to get coursefile.htm)
ftp> mget *.htm (to get all files that end with .htm)

FTP allows file transfer in either direction. After a user establishes a control connection to a remote computer, he or she can either obtain a copy of a remote file or transfer a copy of a local file to the remote computer subject to access permissions. The transfer of files either way is completed through a data connection separately from the control connection, which has been explained in a subsequent paragraph of this chapter.

FTP is not an encrypted transmission, which means data sent through it, including the authentication username and password, can be accessed by others. In order to ensure secure file transfer, another version of FTP known as SFTP (Secure File Transfer Protocol) is used to encrypt the contents. FTP is often also secured with secure shell (SSH) FTP, which has a technology different from the same for the usual FTP.

12.27.2 File Types and Transfer Modes

Even though files can be represented differently by two different computers, FTP does not handle all different possible file representations and instead defines two basic transfer modes for files: textual used for text files and binary for non-text files. However, in the case of binary mode, the transmitted copy may be meaningless as FTP does not convert values to the local representation.

12.27.3 Control and Data Connections

FTP is built on a client–server interaction model which uses separate control and data connections between the client and the server. The control connection is meant for sending commands and receiving responses, whereas the data connection is for file transfer. After sending one file either way (client to server or server to client), the data connection is closed. If the user requests another file transfer, a new data connection is established. However, the control connection remains open. In order to avoid conflict between the control and data connections, separate protocol port numbers are used for each of the above connections.

FTP sessions may run in either active or passive mode depending upon how the data connection is established. In both cases, the client creates the TCP control connection from an arbitrary port to the FTP server command port 21. In the active mode of the FTP session, after the client initiates a session through the command channel request, the server initiates a data connection back to the client and begins data transfer. However, in the passive mode, the server instead uses the command channel to send to the client the information needed by the client to open a data channel. As the passive mode has the client initiating all connections, it works well across firewalls and NAT gateways. The main difference between the two modes is that in the case of active mode, the client initiates the control connection and the server initiates the data connection, whereas in the case of passive mode (PASV is the command for passive mode), the client initiates both the connections. Both modes of FTP have been illustrated in Figure 12.56(a) and (b) respectively.

12.27.4 Trivial File Transfer Protocol (TFTP)

TFTP is a second internet protocol for file transfer service using UDP instead of TCP. It only supports file transfer and does not support interaction that allows users to list the contents of a directory, file name translation and setting file transfer mode for textual and binary files. As such, TFTP is simpler with a small set of commands, and it does not have provision for authorisation with login name and password.

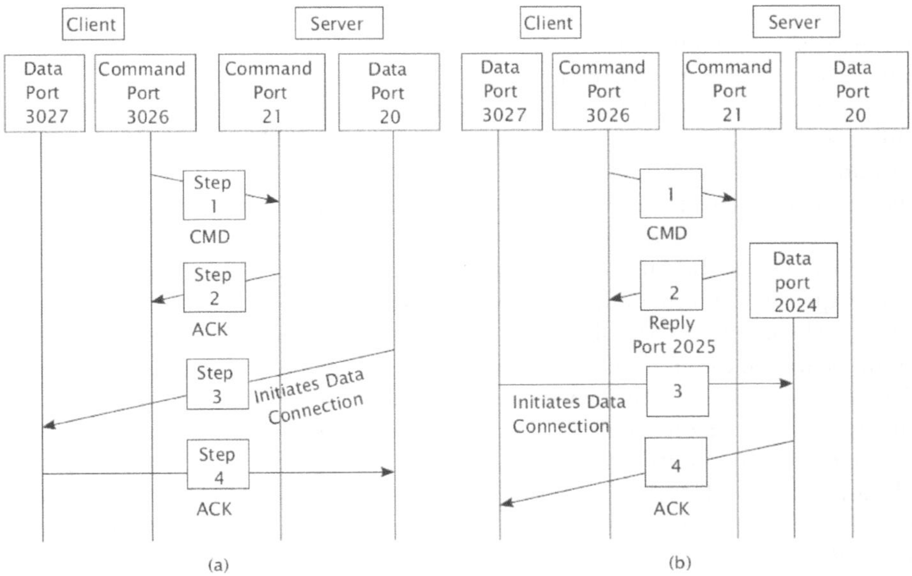

Figure 12.56 Illustration of (a) Active Mode and (b) Passive Mode of FTP

Also, the code for TFTP requires less memory compared to the same for FTP, thereby making TFTP useful for bootstrapping a hardware device with a small read-only memory (ROM) in which TFTP, UDP and IP can be put.

12.27.5 Network File System (NFS)

NFS provides a file access service used with TCP/IP which allows an application to read or modify parts of a remote file without copying an entire file. It also allows file sharing in which more than one client can access a file over a server. Unlike FTP, NFS is integrated into a computer's file system. Whenever an application performs a file operation on a file kept on a remote computer, NFS client software communicates with the remote computer to perform the desired operation. NFS provides for the conventional file operations such as 'open', 'read' and 'write'.

12.28 Configuration

Configuration refers to the initialisation of the variables and the steps needed to be taken before a protocol software gets ready for use. Configuration or initialisation is, in fact, one of the application programmes that use client–server. A protocol software contains parameters. The parameters correspond to internal values such as the address that corresponds to the host computer or externally to the default router. Values of parameters are required to be supplied before protocol software can be used, and the process of supplying values to parameters of the protocol software is known as 'protocol configuration'. There are two methods of reading configuration information: some operating systems read configuration information from a file on permanent storage, whereas in the other case, the operating systems use a network through which the information is obtained. In the second method, layers of protocol software are configured in order from lowest to highest, making it possible for each layer to use layers beneath it in order to communicate with the network to obtain configuration information.

The items of information that TCP/IP protocol software needs to configure consist of IP addresses, default IP router address, address mask(s), DNS server address and printer server address.

The protocol software converts values supplied during configuration to a form used internally (such as value in ASCII text to binary) and stores the same as an appropriate variable in memory. Because computers require protocol configuration information to change frequently, automatic updates become necessary using automated protocol configuration. Thus, with a portable laptop needing to be connected to different networks at different locations, the configuration information relating to each new environment must be changed before using it in the new environment.

The use of separate protocols to obtain each item of configuration information results in a sequence of configuration steps. For example, a computer can use the Reverse Address Resolution Protocol (RARP) to find out its IP address and use a separate protocol, ICMP, to find the subnet mask of the default router. Although using a separate protocol to obtain each individual piece of configuration information has flexibility, it suffers from a serious disadvantage of network traffic and results in delay. In order to overcome the above-mentioned disadvantage, two more protocols, namely the 'Bootstrap Protocol' (BOOTP) and 'Dynamic Host Configuration Protocol' (DHCP), were invented by TCP/IP designers.

The BOOTP is a computer networking protocol used in 'Internet protocol' networks to automatically assign IP addresses to network devices from a configuration server. BOOTP software broadcasts a BOOTP 'request message' to obtain configuration information. When the BOOTP configuration server receives the request message, it finds out multiple pieces of configuration information for the computer that sent the request and places all such information in a single BOOTP 'response message' and sends the message to the requesting computer. Thus, in a single step, a computer can obtain multiple pieces of configuration information like the IP address of the computer, the IP address of the server and the IP address of a default router. The BOOTP configuration server assigns IP addresses based on the request from a pool of addresses configured by an administrator. The BOOTP message (request) from a computer gets invoked when the computer connected to the network is powered up and the same boots into the operating system. BOOTP uses the UDP as the transport protocol, the BOOTP server uses port 67 to receive requests, and port 68 is used by the client to receive server responses. BOOTP operates only on IPV4 networks.

The DHCP is also a standard network protocol used by IP networks. It extends beyond BOOTP in the sense that, unlike the BOOTP server, wherein a network administrator manually enters the configuration information for computers that enter the network into the server's database, the DHCP server dynamically assigns network configuration parameters such as IP addresses into its database.

DHCP permits completely automated address assignment. This implies that DHCP permits a computer to join a new network and obtain a valid IP address for use in configuration without any administrator needing to enter the information about the computer in the server's database.

Another important feature of DHCP is that its server never assigns an address permanently. It specifies a lease during which the address can be used, and a computer has to either extend the lease or stop using the address when the lease period is over.

12.29 Network Security Aspects

Network security is not absolute in the sense that each organisation defines the level of access to its network that is permitted or denied, such as read only, read and amend data and read and execute operations on data.

There are important aspects based on which organisations define their computer network security policy. Those are generally data integrity, data availability without disruption, data confidentiality and data privacy.

Data integrity refers to protection of data from change or accidental damage. It is ensured through various mechanisms such as parity bits, checksums and CRCs, which have already been described. However, such mechanisms fail to support data integrity in the case of compensating alteration of the data and the value of the checksum, in which case the alteration of the data remains unnoticed. Therefore, there are other methods to ensure data integrity, such as the encoding of transmitted data with a Message Authentication Code (MAC), which makes it impossible for unauthorised persons to break or forge the data. Data availability refers to protection against disruption of data transmission. Data confidentiality refers to safeguards against unauthorised data access and is facilitated through access control or a password assigned to each user. Whenever a user needs to access a protected resource, the user is asked to enter the assigned password. Data confidentiality is also ensured through encryption and decryption using two keys (public key and private key). Encryption basically scrambles the message bits in a form that only the receiver and no one else can unscramble (decryption). In many encryption schemes, the key for encryption must remain secret to anyone else other than the sender and the receiver of the encrypted message to avoid compromising data security. However, in the case of encryption using the two keys, the encryption function has the mathematical property that a message encrypted with the public key cannot be easily decrypted except with the private key. Similarly, a message encrypted with the private key cannot be decrypted except with the public key. The keys are basically long random numbers generated by a key generator algorithm using randomising routines (an example is 'PuTTY' key generator).

An example of a public key is as follows:

3 4 0 1 0 1 4 3 0 0 C 9 1 8 F A C F 8 D E B 2 D E F D 5
B A F A 3 6 2 F 9 2 2 B F 0 1 B 2 F 4 0 C 7 4 4 2 6 5 4 C O D

The public key, as its name suggests, is made available to everyone through a public repository or directory, whereas the private key remains confidential except with its respective owner.

Privacy refers to the ability of the sender of a message to remain anonymous. An encryption mechanism can be used to authenticate the sender. The mechanism is known as a 'digital signature'. In order to digitally sign a message, the sender encrypts the message using a key known to the sender only. The recipient uses the inverse function to decrypt the message. The recipient knows who sent the message because only the sender can perform the same encryption using the key which the sender has. Moreover, the

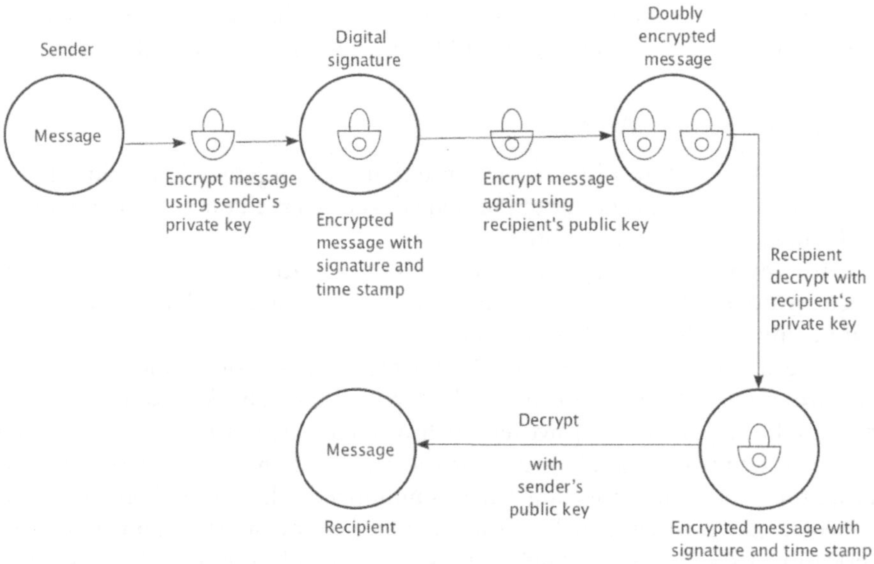

Figure 12.57 Double Encryption and Decryption of Message with Signature to Guarantee Authentication

encryption of the message with a digital signature has the time stamp of the signature which uniquely identifies the time of the signature. In order to ensure authentication and confidentiality, a message can be encrypted doubly; first, the message is signed using the sender's private key to encrypt it, and then the encrypted message is again encrypted using the recipient's public key. At the recipient end, the decryption processes are just the reverse of the two encryption processes. The encryption and decryption processes have been illustrated in Figure 12.57.

12.29.1 Internet Firewall

Internet firewall is another technology to protect an organisation's computers and networks from undesirable internet traffic. A firewall as shown in Figure 12.58 is placed between an organisation's network and the rest of the internet. Obviously, if an organisation has more than one internet connection, a firewall has to be placed at each such connection.

The basic mechanism adopted to build a firewall consists of packet filters in routers as well as in the secure host that runs application gateways. A packet filter consists of software configured by the network administrator or manager to check the header of each packet to determine the packets which are to be allowed to pass through the router and the packets which are to be discarded. For example, in order to allow a computer with IP address 192.5.48.37 on a network to communicate with any computer on another network, a manager specifies that the filter in the router connecting the two networks should allow all IP packets with source address 192.5.48.37 to pass on to the other network. Similarly, to allow a computer in a network with IP address 128.10.0.20 to receive

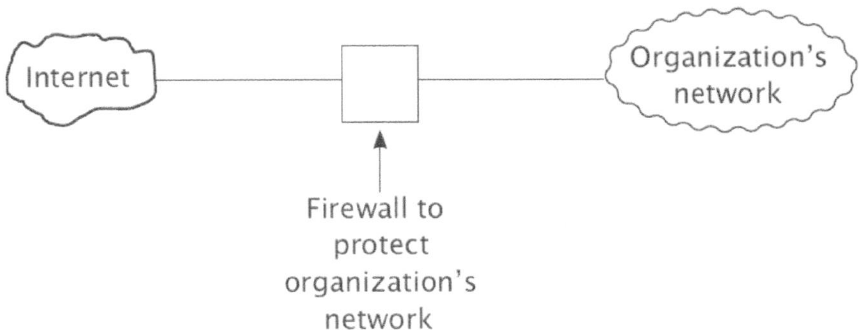

Figure 12.58 Illustration of a Firewall

any packet from another network, the filter in the router connecting the two networks should allow all IP packets with destination address 128.10.0.20. A packet filter software permits complex boolean combinations of source, destination address and service type.

12.29.2 Security Technologies

In order to detect unwanted attacks, an organisation uses various security technologies with the internet. Some of them are listed as follows:

1. Intrusion Detection System (IDS);
2. Pretty Good Privacy (PGP);
3. SSH based on encrypting data before transmission;
4. Secure Sockets Layer (SSL) based on encryption;
5. IP security (IPSec) using cryptographic techniques;
6. Remote Authentication Dial-in User Service (RADIUS);
7. Wired Equivalent Privacy (WEP).

12.30 Software-Defined Networking (SDN)

SDN is a networking architecture that separates the network control from the forwarding functions. This facilitates the network control to be directly programmable and the underlying infrastructure to be abstracted for application and network services. The SDN is based on the OpenFlow protocol, which makes it an extremely dynamic, manageable, cost-effective and adaptable architecture that gives network administrators a high degree of programmability, automation and control. The OpenFlow standard protocol advocated by the Open Networking Foundation (ONF) enables remote programming of the forwarding plane. The architecture of software-defined networking is shown in Figure 12.59. It has been modelled as a set of client–server interactions with the SDN controller at the core of the control plane. The service client manages and controls network services through the SDN controller. Thus, clients/applications interact directly with network control. Clients also send/receive data using network resources.

Network resources service provider maps client service intent onto resources which include forward processing and storage domains. The service provider recursively maps

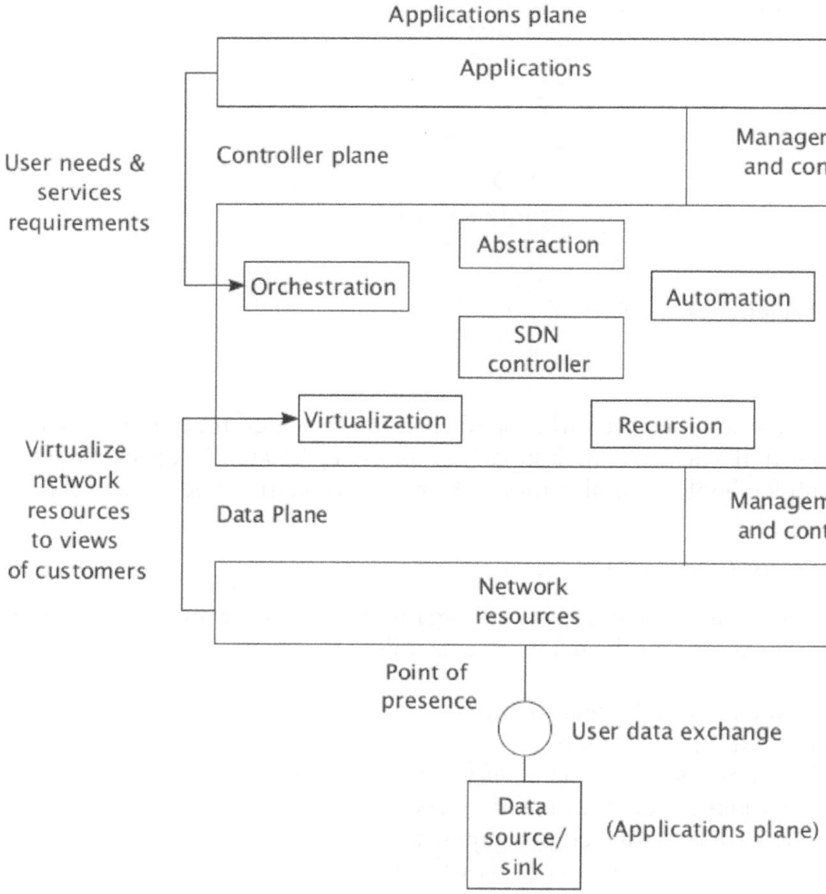

Figure 12.59 Architecture of Software-Defined Networking

services and resources to scale to multiple administrative domains to take care of large-scale parallel processing algorithms associated with mega data sets known as 'Big data' across an entire computing pool. 'Orchestration' shown in the architecture is to orchestrate resources to meet client service needs.

The SDN architecture facilitates network control as directly programmable by decoupling it from forwarding functions. The other features are its agility to adjust network-wide traffic flow to changing needs, centralised control of network intelligence, automatic configuration and, most importantly, open standard based, which makes it independent of vendor specific devices and protocols.

The purpose of SDN is to reduce costs and improve user experience by automating the full range of network services from end user to network elements.

12.31 Case Study: SHI International Implements Software-Defined Networking for a Global Packaging Company for Improved Performance, Manageability and Saving in Networking Cost

12.31.1 Customer Profile and the Background

A global leader in consumer packaging and dispensing systems employing more than 13,000 employees spread across 40 locations all over the world was experiencing frequent network delays in their main data centre, adversely affecting their manufacturing operations in various geographical locations. An inspection of its existing network equipment revealed that the data centre switches and network-interface hardware were very old and lacked flexibility and were also not dynamic with respect to network traffic.

The packaging company decided to go for a replacement of its age-old Cisco Nexus 5,600 series infrastructure. The company needed a robust solution that could be managed easily and was financially feasible at the same time. They got an offer from a vendor, but the same was overpriced. The company thereafter approached Software House International (SHI) for a feasible alternative solution for their primary data centre networking.

It is worth mentioning that SHI is a 10 billion USD global provider of IT products and services. SHI offers custom IT solutions for its customers such as software and hardware procurement, deployment planning, configuration, data centre optimisation, IT asset management and cloud computing.

12.31.2 Solution

During an initial 'whiteboard' session, SHI solution architects familiarised themselves with the offer on the table and predicted the performance of the same in the customer's desired environment. Subsequently, SHI recommended several alternate Cisco solutions designed to improve the networking performance within the budgetary constraints of the company.

After evaluating the alternative solutions as recommended by SHI, both from technical and programme angles, the packaging company decided to replace the existing Nexus 5600 series infrastructure with four 93180 and two 93108 Nexus switches. The company also purchased and installed Cisco's application centric infrastructure (ACI) which is an SDN and controls all other network devices from a single location. The company also purchased two Nexus 9K ACI spines and ACI mentored implementation services from SHI. The whole project took only 5 months.

12.31.3 Benefits and Results

The above-mentioned replacements and the new solution made it possible for the company's IT team to manage and monitor all the devices from one place. Further, with easy access, the server team could make changes and create configurations without engaging the networking team, thus reducing the number of touch points. The new solution also offered scalable growth options and the choice to utilise copper cable or fibre optic connections.

Finally, the network performance improved significantly and the packaging company saved 30% expenditure compared to the originally offered solution.

Review Questions

1. Draw the waveform diagram that results when the word 'CAB' is sent in ASCII across an RS–232 connection (use: 7-bit ASCII character code table from the internet).
2. Suppose you want to send 5,000, 7-bit characters across an RS–232 connection. How much time does the transmission require?
3. What happens if an RS–232 transmitter and receiver are programmed to send and receive at different baud rates?
4. If amplitude modulation with a sine wave operates at a frequency of 500 Hz, how many bits per second can be encoded and why?
5. FDM can improve throughput if it replaces a multiplexer with TDM. Do you agree? If so, why?
6. What is half- and full-duplex asynchronous communication?
7. What is the difference between a packet and a frame? What do you understand by the term 'packet switching'?
8. Suppose malfunctioning hardware in a character-oriented transmission system sets all bits transferred to zero. Does a parity bit catch the problem? Why or why not?
9. What is CRC? What are the hardware components required for CRC computation?
10. Classify the topology of computer networks in a particular site. What is CSMA/CD?
11. What data values in an Ethernet packet result in the maximum number of voltage transmissions when the packet is transmitted using Manchester encoding?
12. Illustrate the general frame format used with Ethernet.
13. What are the functions of repeaters, bridges, switches and routers?
14. Consider a packet sent across a bridged LAN to a non-existent address. How far will bridges forward the packet?
15. Can a bridge connect a Wi-Fi network to an Ethernet? Why or why not?
16. Explain the terms 'store and forward', 'next-hop forwarding' and 'universal routing'.
17. What are 'ARPANET' and 'frame relay'?
18. What is a 'VPN'?
19. Explain the terms 'delay', 'throughput', 'bandwidth' and 'jitter' with respect to network performance.
20. State the names with a brief explanation of the TCP/IP layers based on the following:
    (i) I am responsible for the routing of information and managing the logical addressing. What layer am I?
    (ii) I am responsible for the initial request for network communication. What layer am I?
    (iii) I am responsible for ensuring packets are assembled in the correct order and ensuring that the information has been delivered. What layer am I?
    (iv) I am responsible for the physical addressing and conversion of packets to electrical signals. What layer am I?
    (v) I am responsible for placing the electrical signals on wires. What layer am I?
    (vi) I am responsible for establishing and managing the session. What layer am I?
21. Draw a TCP/IP internet that consists of two networks connected by a router. Show a computer attached to each network. Show the protocol stack used on the computers and the stack used on the router.

22. What are the five classes of IP addresses in classful scheme? Explain with examples 'dotted decimal notation'.
23. What are 'address masks'? What is the chief advantage of CIDR over the original classful addressing scheme?
24. Explain why a router is assigned two or more IP addresses.
25. How does a computer know whether an arriving frame contains an IP datagram or an ARP message?
26. What is an IP datagram? What is its general form?
27. If a datagram contains one 8-bit option and one 8-bit data value, what values will be found in header fields HLEN and total length?
28. Why is fragmentation needed on the internet but not on a typical WAN?
29. Why is encapsulation needed for transmitting a datagram?
30. What are 'MTU' and 'path MTU'?
31. Suppose a datagram passes through N routers on a trip across an internet. How many times is the datagram encapsulated?
32. What are the features of IPv6 which are not there with IPv4?
33. How many octets does the smallest possible IPv6 datagram contain? The largest?
34. What do you understand by UDP? What is the size of the largest possible UDP message?
35. What is NAT? What is the difference between NAT and NAPT?
36. What is dynamic routing? Explain the terms 'EGP', 'IGP', 'BGP', 'RIP' and 'OSPF'.
37. What is 'concurrency' with reference to the client–server paradigm?
38. What do you understand by 'socket API'?
39. Many companies prefer to use the organisational structure for domain names instead of the geographical structure. What is the main advantage of the same?
40. What is DNS server hierarchy? Does limiting the number of levels in a DNS hierarchy result in faster name resolution? Explain your answer.
41. What is an email gateway? What is 'Post Office Protocol' (POP)?
42. Explain with a suitable illustration the difference between active and passive modes of FTP.
43. What is DHCP? Explain.
44. What is the difference between a 'private key' and a 'public key'?
45. Explain the advantages of SDN. What is the OpenFlow protocol? Show the SDN architecture.

Bibliography

Comer, D. E. *Computer Network and Internet: With Internet Applications*, 4th ed. London: Pearson Education, 2004.

Gorranson, P., C. Black, and T. Culver. *Software Defined Networks: A Comprehensive Approach*, 2nd ed. Waltham, MA: Morgan Kaufmann, 2016.

Patil, S., and M. S. Subhedar. 'Analysing MPLS Performance by SDN'. *Proceedings of IEMIS* 3 (2018): 589–598.

Sybex. *Networking Complete*, 3rd ed. New Delhi: BPB Publications, 2002.

13 Big Data Analytics and Cloud Computing

13.1 Introduction

Data in an organisation that cannot be processed using traditional data management techniques and technologies can be broadly categorised as 'Big data'. Big data is characterised by important dimensions known as the V's of 'Big data'. IBM data scientists defined four such dimensions as the four V's, namely volume, variety, velocity and veracity. *Volume* implies the large scale of data generated worldwide every day, expressed in zettabytes (1 zettabyte = 1 million petabytes and 1 petabyte = 10^{15}bytes. *Variety* implies the different forms of data such as numbers, text, strings, images and networked graph data generated through different sources such as social networks, stock exchanges, logistics, health care, the hospitality sector, security devices and sensors such as CCTV and surveillance cameras and weather and aviation data generated by radars, defence, infrastructure sectors, banking, insurance and many others. For example, during 2011, about 30 billion pieces of content were shared on Facebook every month. During 2014, about 400 million tweets were sent per day by about 200 million monthly active users, 4 billion hours of video were watched on YouTube every month and about 421 million wearable and wireless health monitors were in use. The traditional data or small data that were created in the past were structured data which could be stored in columns and rows as relational databases. However, big data generated by organisations today is not only structured or semi-structured but also unstructured in nature because of the wide variety of the data. Big data, therefore, requires a different approach and techniques of storage and analysis. *Velocity* refers to huge rates of influx and analysis of data. For example, about 1 terabyte of trade information is generated by the New York Stock Exchange during each trading session. About 18.9 billion network connections globally in 2016 transmitted data at high speed. *Veracity* implies the uncertainty of the data because of inaccuracy and poor quality, which make it less credible. Therefore, organisations need to ensure that both the data and analysis are correct and trustworthy.

13.1.1 Three Additional V's

Apart from the four V's as described above, three additional V's, namely variability, visualisation and value are worth mentioning as those are also important for organisations to consider while developing their big data strategy. Variability is not the same as variety. Variability can be explained with a simple example of a bread shop which sells breads of different brands. Variety, in this case, implies the different brands. However, if the taste of the bread of a particular brand differs every day, the same is due to variability of the

DOI: 10.4324/9781003509714-13

same brand. The same concept is true for data; if the same data carry different meanings under different situations or contexts, it will have a great impact on data homogenisation. Variability of data is an important factor to be considered in sentiment analysis. In order to perform such analysis properly, algorithms need to be developed to understand the context and accordingly decipher the exact meaning of data (words) in that context, which is a complex task. Data visualisation is very important to facilitate proper decision-making. For example, using graphical representation of large amounts of complex data is much more effective in conveying the meaning of the data than spreadsheets and allied reports full of numeric figures and formulae. Huge amounts of raw data remain useless without proper comprehension.

13.1.2 Value

Big data, if analysed properly and utilised, facilitates the creation of value for organisations, society at large and consumers. Of course, data in itself are not valuable at all. Proper analysis of the data and transformation of the data into information and knowledge to turn organisations into information-centric companies create value for those companies. According to McKinsey, the potential value of big data to the US healthcare industry is about 300 billion USD annually, which is a lot of value.

Besides the volume, variety, velocity, veracity, variability, visualisation and value, there are a number of practical issues that can make things more complex with big data than with small data. Let us elaborate on those issues. The first is the goal. Unlike small data, which is gathered for a specific goal, big data may serve multiple goals such as providing valuable information for the use of consumers, predictive marketing strategy and fraud detection. Second, the location of the data is usually a single one, typically a single computer file for small data. However, for big data, it may be distributed in multiple files on different computers located in various geographic locations. Third, data preparation and analysis for small data are done by the end users for their own purposes, but with big data, the same is often prepared by one group, analysed by a second group for ultimate use by a third group. The fourth difference is in the retention period or longevity of the data. Small data is preserved for small and specific time durations, whereas big data, as it is associated with high costs of storage and analysis and often gets converted into other forms of data, has to be retained for a very long time. The fifth difference is in the measurement protocols. Small data are usually measured with a single set of units under a single protocol, whereas big data, being located in different locations involving different computers, organisations and people, is often measured using different protocols. The sixth difference is in reproducibility. Small data can be reproduced in their entirety if something goes wrong with it. Big data, being stored in different computers located at different places, may not be reproduced totally if some problem crops up with the data. The seventh difference is in the stakes. In the case of small data, the cost of corruption or loss is limited, but in the case of big data, such loss of data can cost an enormous amount of time and money. Finally, the analysis of small data is usually done in a single procedure from a single computer file. However, with big data, because data are so enormous and spread across different files and servers, analysis is carried out using multiple procedures such as extraction, reduction, normalisation, transformation and other steps. Moreover, big data analysis deals with part of the data at a time to make it more manageable and then summarises the results.

We can summarise the major differentiators of big data as follows:

- No *finite* structure.
- High *volume.*
- *Ambiguous* in metadata. Metadata is data about the nature, location, time stamp of actual data.
- *Loosely* connected in structure.
- If data are linguistically oriented, processing will be heavily *contextual.*
- If data are numerically oriented, processing needs more granular data or more
- *Number crunching.*
- If semi-structured data, it needs more expansion and can have a *mixed workload.*

13.1.3 Various Sources of Big Data

The sources of big data can broadly be divided into two categories: one is generated by human beings and the other generated by machines, including mobile apps and sensors.

Big data generated by human sources can be again classified into the following groups:

1. **Social Media**: Twitter, LinkedIn, Facebook, Blog, SlideShare, YouTube, Google+, Instagram, Pinterest, Vimeo, WordPress, Chatter and many such sources of data.
2. **Public Web Services**: Government, weather, traffic, regulatory compliance, health care, economic, census, public finance, stock market, World Bank, Reserve Bank of India, other nationalised banks, Wikipedia and similar web services.
3. **Business Operations and Functions**: Project management, marketing functions, logistics and supply chains, production and productivity, CRM, ERP systems, human resources, human skill management, financial management, Google documents, intranets, web portals and so on.
4. **Documents and Files**: Excel spreadsheet (XLS), portable document format (PDF), comma separated values (CSV), email, Word, PPT, hypertext markup language (HTML), plain text, XML and JSON (XML and JSON stand for extensible markup language and JavaScript object notation respectively). XML and JSON represent mainly semi-structured data as explained in a subsequent paragraph.
5. **Media**: Images, videos, audio, flash, live streams and so on.
6. **Database and Data Storage**: SQL, NoSQL, Hadoop Distributed File System (HDFS), document repository, various other file systems.
7. **Archives**: Archives of scanned documents, newspapers, rare collections of literary works, trade and industry journals, bulletins, medical records, contracts, customer correspondence, feedback forms and such other archives.

Machine- and sensor-generated big data is as follows:

1. **Machine Log Data**: Event logs, server logs, application logs, business process logs, audit trails, call records, mobile location and app usage data, click stream data, data generated by IoT and machine-to-machine data generated by a machine for communicating with another machine. The concept of IoT has been explained in a subsequent paragraph of this chapter.
2. **Sensor Data**: Medical devices such as electrocardiogram data, smart utility metre readings, car sensor data, surveillance camera images, satellite data, traffic recording device data, weather radar data, video device images, household appliances

Table 13.1 Illustration of Structured Data Table

Games	*Teams*
Football	East Bengal
Football	Mohun Bagan
Cricket	Mumbai Indians
Cricket	Kolkata Knight Riders

data, radio frequency identification device (RFID) data, assembly lines, smart buildings, cell towers, jet engines, thermostats and cut-off relays for refrigerators and air conditioners, and proximity devices for entry and exit control.

The above lists are only illustrative and not exhaustive. However, they only show the broad categories of big data sources.

13.2 Structure of Big Data

Big data can be structured, unstructured or semi-structured. Data are said to be structured when they are placed in a file with fixed fields of variables. A simple example of structured data is the spreadsheet, where every column is a variable and every row is a particular case or observation. A large amount of structured data is stored in rows and columns as relational databases. For example, Table 13.1 is a structured data table having two columns indicating different games in the first column and the team names associated with the games in the second column. Each team will have one row.

However, if we write the above data in a different way as a natural language (text), the same becomes: two football teams are 'East Bengal' and 'Mohun Bagan' and two Indian Premier League (IPL) teams are 'Mumbai Indians' and 'Kolkata Knight Riders'.

While the above data are very easy to understand by a person knowing English, it is much more difficult for a machine to understand the same. This is because the above data cannot be easily sorted, rearranged or appended to other data and counting the number of teams is not easy; hence, it is unstructured in nature. We have to adopt techniques of text mining or semantic analysis (as explained later) to analyse such types of unstructured data. Incidentally, it may be stated that the majority of big data relating to business environment is unstructured data in the form of text, images, presentations and so on. A third type of data is semi-structured data, which are not in fixed fields such as the rows and columns of a spreadsheet, but the fields and the data thereof are identifiable. Two very common formats for semi-structured data are XML and the JSON. The same game data as above can be represented in the XML format as follows:

```
<games>
<football>
<team>East Bengal</team>
<team>Mohun Bagan</team>
</football>
<cricket>
```

```
<team>Mumbai Indians</team>
<team>Kolkata Knight Riders</team>
</cricket>
</games>
```

The above XML format is good for nested data or hierarchical structures, though it is a little wordy. A more recent format is JSON, which is similar to XML but there is not much text and the brackets will be there as curly brackets. The above game data expressed in JSON will be as follows:

```
{
'games': {
'football': {
'team': {
'East Bengal',
'Mohun Bagan',
}
},
'cricket': {
'team': {
'Mumbai Indians',
'Kolkata Knight Riders'
}
}
}
}
```

13.3 Big Data Applications

The major applications of big data can be broadly grouped as consumer applications, business applications, research applications and IoT applications. Consumers use big data for a variety of applications. The first one is that through an Apple iPhone or iPad and using Siri (a computer program which acts as an intelligent personal assistant and knowledge navigator) for big data analysis, consumers can find out the available sources of goods or services they want to avail themselves of. For example, one can search for restaurants of a particular type such as Thai, Mexican or Chinese in one's convenient location and also get a recommendation for the same based on many reviews from those who had been to those restaurants earlier. Also, recommendation engines are capable of making specific suggestions based on big data analysis techniques such as data mining or text analytics. For example, when we search for a book for a particular subject or title, Amazon.com makes recommendations for the books of our requirement.

Another important consumer application for big data is through the use of photos taken by powerful cameras, Google Maps, satellites and so on and analysis of the generated big data. Valuable information can be provided thereby regarding traffic conditions or weather forecasts to the interested persons.

Big data have revolutionised the business world by changing the way people do commerce. There are a number of applications of big data in business. The first application pertains to the search for anything of interest through search engines such as Google. Besides getting the search results, people also receive, through big data analysis, a number of advertisements based on what a person searches for, as well as suiting his/her likes or dislikes as known to the search engines during all previous searches. Google or any other search engine analyses all the things that the user searched for on all earlier occasions along with any other pertinent information about the users available with Google and attempts to place advertisements that the users will most likely select. The next important area of business application is what is known as predictive marketing. Predictive marketing means making decisions by predicting which marketing actions are more likely to succeed and which are more likely to fail. It has profound implications throughout the marketing process.

Big data are used to identify the target consumers while launching new products or services. This is based on a study of major life events. Major life events such as getting a good job, marriage or childbirth are associated with a whole series of commercial transactions. Similarly, companies going for predictive marketing look at consumer behaviour. Consumer behaviour study is linked with customer sentiment analysis, which is a popular technique of big data analytics. Just to illustrate sentiment analysis, the following statements representing customer sentiments for particular types of health drinks, such as 'Horlicks' and 'Frooti', are reproduced below:

'I personally like the **taste** of Horlicks and while the **price** is much higher than I would like to pay, I would pick up Horlicks at Frank Ross in the **evening**.'

'I occasionally pick up a **Frooti Juice** in the **morning** but this is a little **cheaper** and packs more **calories** and gives **nutrition**.'

'Of course at ₹10 a pack, I will stick to my Sumit Power Juicer and make my own.'

The sentiment analysis based on the above statements yields the following:

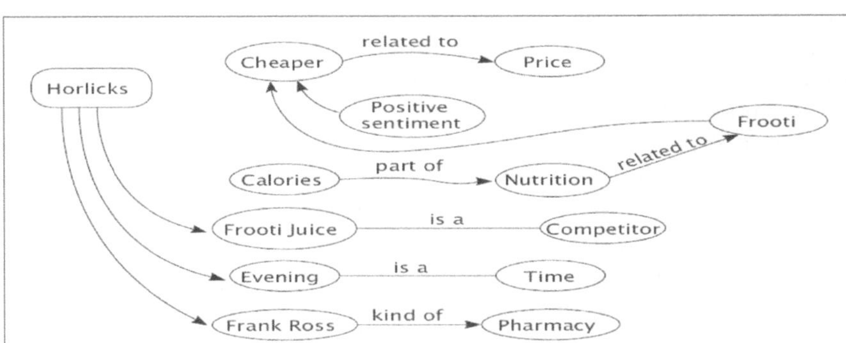

A number of technologies for semantic analysis of textual contents include:

- Clustering algorithms for obtaining semantic word clusters.
- Algorithms for extracting salient phrases and ranking them using context.
- Random tree algorithms.
- Bayesian models and associated algorithms.

A study of consumer behaviour also calls for consumer habits such as how often one logs into different websites and looks for particular items. A lot of data regarding consumer habits can be made available through websites' browsing history.

Similarly, demographic information such as age, marital status, family size, salary, home address and the credit cards one holds are of importance for predictive marketing. Another important use of big data relating to business and commerce is in the area of trend prediction. For example, big data analysis has its use to predict fashion trends. It means telling retailers in advance what the most popular colours, styles and brands are going to be and when those are going to be popular. Obviously, such information relating to the future trend of different products will be of paramount importance to the companies who will be selling those products in future. A very important use of big data in commerce is for fraud detection. Fraud detection has become a major issue in the case of online business transactions. The gravity of this issue can be visualised by the fact that in the USA alone online retailers lose about 3.5 billion USD every year due to online fraud. Fraud detection is based on analysis of data concerning point of sale (POS), the website being used for online transactions, physical location of the persons making online transactions, the IP addresses of the computers, log in time of usual transactions for a particular computer and a lot of other data. Biometric data also help detection of fraud. For example, the way people move their mouse, the response time to online queries or the time between two successive pressing of keys on the computer keyboard are distinctive measures of individuals. All this data comprise big data sets which enable analysts to determine whether the genuine persons are making online transactions and which in turn facilitate detection of anomalies leading to potential fraud.

Finally, big data facilitate risk management. Technologies relating to big data can help risk managers gain more accurate risk intelligence, drawn from a variety of data sources for structured as well as unstructured data in almost real time. It can improve the predictive capability of various risk models involving credit risk, money laundering risk, market risk, operational risk, compliance risk and churn analysis.

Credit risk models derive better predictive power from the real-time big data drawn from data lakes of new data sources such as social media and marketing databases. Financial institutions have thorough knowledge of their clients and can harness big data to develop more robust predictive indicators (such as credit score) in the credit risk domain. Besides traditional data such as income, profession and property details of the customers, big data sources can reveal vital information such as a costly divorce, an expensive purchase, or a gambling habit for any customer, which will go a long way towards credit risk prediction. Credit firms can take full advantage of big data technologies to detect early warning signals by observing customer behaviour in real time and acting in time.

So far as money laundering risk is concerned, big data can provide real-time actionable insights to risk managers. The recent money laundering scandals of some non-banking financial institutions and terrorist financing prompted banks, financial and credit guarantee institutions to look for innovative ways to address the limitations of the traditional approaches to anti-money laundering. Traditional approaches are again based on structured data, and the analysis thereof is rule-based. Obviously, such approaches suffer limitations of laborious manual searches of keywords through the reports. For example, a financial institution in its payment advice specifies State Bank of India (SBI) only. The SBI branch can be in New Delhi, Kolkata or Chennai. So operational staff responsible for anti-money laundering to whom the transactions were routed have to manually review the transactions for the particular branch of SBI, which is a time-consuming and error-prone task. Big data analytics, however, allow both advanced statistical analysis of structured data and statistical analysis such as 'text mining' ('text mining' has been explained in a subsequent paragraph) of unstructured data to facilitate proper visualisation of hidden links between transactions and accounts leading to the detection of suspicious transaction patterns.

Advanced analytics can generate real-time actionable insights, preventing potential money laundering and at the same time allowing fund transfers for genuine cases.

In case of market risks involving market price/volatility, new client trades and counterparty credit risk management, volume and velocity of data are the prime factors. Counterparty credit risk assessment has now become more complex and involves: (1) debt valuation adjustments (DVA), (2) credit valuation adjustments (CVA) and (3) funding valuation adjustments (FVA), all in sets with different pricing data for getting 'risk neutral' CVA. The above exercise needs to be repeated at different frequencies for reporting monthly, weekly or daily. The calculation involved in finding the above risk components is highly data-intensive, and processing has to be done speedily. For example, to fully simulate all the potential scenarios of all path-dependent derivatives as structured portfolios, banks need to run about 100,000 Monte Carlo scenarios. Traditional data analysis techniques are not capable of processing such high volumes of data at high speed. Big data analytics technologies such as Hadoop and its ecosystems (described in subsequent paragraphs of this chapter) can provide enormous help in this type of increasingly data-heavy market risk assessment by bringing out accurate and incremental 'what-if' statistics. In other words, banks with increased Monte Carlo abilities will be able to price 'path dependent' derivatives at better levels than their competitors.

According to Andy Smith—Managing Director, operational risk management—Bank of New York Mellon, in operational risk the power of big data lies in the ability to integrate vast information from legacy platforms into a single highly flexible solution. For example, we can leverage big data solutions to gain superior insights for access control management across the various platforms in which our clients interact with us, helping us to ensure the safety, security and confidentiality of client transactions at all times.

13.3.1 Compliance Risk

Compliance risk is the threat posed to an organisation's financial, organisational or reputational standing resulting from violations of laws, regulations, codes of conduct or organisational standards of practice. Big data analysis enables continuous compliance risk assessment and automated operational risk management that can be used by various stakeholders including senior management, audit and risk committees and even external regulatory and audit organisations.

13.3.2 Churn Analysis

Churn analysis is another analytic application, also called churn prediction. Churn means a customer who discontinues getting service from any service provider or products from any company or who switches from one company to another company for any service or product. Churn analysis aims at retaining existing customers and keeping them satisfied instead of inducting new customers into the customer base of a company or service provider such as the telecom companies. The reason behind this is that inducting new customers costs high, especially in saturated markets, whereas retaining existing customers results in lower costs and also augments loyalty benefits. Therefore, companies should make dedicated efforts to retain their existing customers. Churn analysis helps identify the determinants of churn so that improvements can be made in those areas to retain customers. The analysis is based on big data mining to arrive at a good churn prediction model. The objectives of the model are to correlate churn and customer attributes, predict future churn based on past churn and target a retention campaign towards high-risk customers who are most likely to churn or leave. Churn prediction models are based on logistic regression, decision trees, support vector machines, neural networks, survival (time-to-churn) analysis and relational classifiers (customer social network analysis). Social network analysis also often leads to additional customer attributes, which are relevant for the analysis. Churn analysis input data sources may be more than one. For example, to understand the churn behaviour of customers of a mobile telephone operator, the input data are collected from the following data tables.

1. Customer table, which contains basic customer information such as customer identification (say, mobile number, customer account number), address, age, gender, education and monthly income.
2. CDR table contains details of all call data records in transactional form. Each record provides the duration of specific types of calls such as local, STD and international calls on a daily basis aggregated over a month.
3. Billing data table which contains monthly usage, monthly billing, average billing, payment, number of delayed payments, mode of payment of bills and so on. Customer service data table, which contains basic information concerning service subscribed to by the customer such as handset model/class, length of service in months, tariff plan and type, number of complaints in the past made to customer care executives and the churn state (active or de-active). Apart from the above sources of data, social networks also form a vital input data source for churn analysis. The churn prediction process can be described by a flow diagram depicting the steps as shown in Figure 13.1.

IoT is a very recent development for connecting various objects through the Internet. It makes great use of big data analysis of the data generated by sensors or machines. It has been described in subsequent paragraphs of this chapter.

13.4 Data Mining

Big data analysis involves a popular technique known as 'data mining'. The technique facilitates the process of extraction of knowledge from huge amounts of data stored in databases. Knowledge extraction or discovery process is also known as 'KDD' (Knowledge

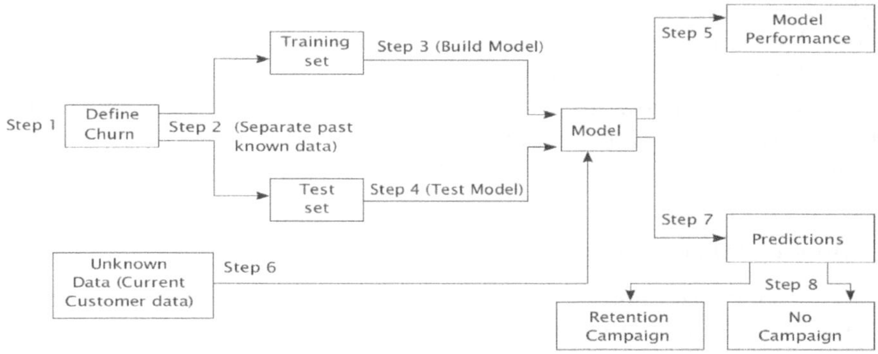

Figure 13.1 Churn-Prediction Process

Discovery in Databases) process. Data mining is one of the steps in the same (KDD) process and can be compared with gold mining from rock or sand. The knowledge discovery process involves data cleaning, data integration, data selection, data transformation, data mining, pattern generation, pattern evaluation/presentation and finally knowledge discovery as 'knowledge nuggets' such as the gold nuggets produced out of rock and sand. The KDD process along with the sequence of the above-mentioned steps is shown in Figure 13.2.

Data cleaning refers to the removal of noise, inconsistent or irrelevant data to achieve data quality. The next step is the integration of data from multiple sources, both formal and informal. Careful integration of data avoids redundancies and thus enhances the speed of data mining. Data selection picks data that are relevant for analysis.

Data transformation converts the selected data into a format to suit the analysis and to speed up the data mining process. For example, daily sales figures may be aggregated to generate month-wise sales figures or item-wise total monthly sales figures. Data mining

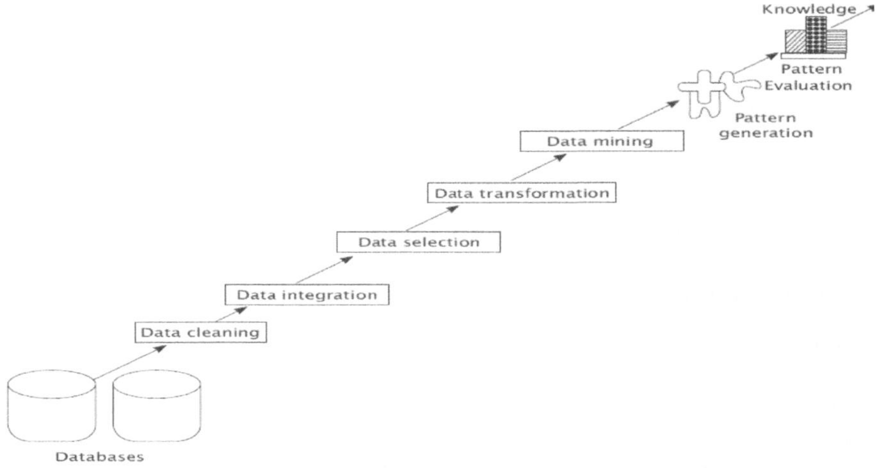

Figure 13.2 Knowledge Discovery in Databases

refers to the application of various algorithms to generate data patterns. It adopts various techniques such as association rule, clustering and classification of data. It generates interesting data patterns that are evaluated to obtain useful patterns and present the same to users to draw some inference on the data.

The last step is the knowledge discovery, which presents the knowledge to the users. The three important techniques of data mining have been described as follows with suitable examples.

13.4.1 Association Rule of Data Mining

Association rule of data mining is a method of finding useful relations or associations among the variables in a large database. Association rules help prediction of customer behaviour while marketing various products.

Example 1: Bread ⇒ jelly, which means that when a customer buys bread from a shop, he/she is quite likely to buy jelly also. Hence, the sale of bread is associated with the sale of jelly also.

Example 2: Buys (salt, chilli powder) ⇒ buys (pepper), which means a customer buying salt and chilli powder is also very likely to purchase pepper.

Association rules are expressed in the form of if-then statements and are useful in the case of market-based analysis for product marketing and pricing. Two parameters are associated with association rules known as 'support' and 'confidence'. Support is a measure of the probability of buying both bread and jelly by a customer in the case of Example 1 above, whereas confidence is a measure of the probability that a transaction involving bread also contains jelly. Here, bread is an antecedent and jelly is a consequence.

Suppose in the case of Example 1, the support is 60% and confidence is 80%, the association rule can be expressed as bread ⇒ jelly (60%, 80%) and which is knowledge discovered by data mining. Let me illustrate how to calculate support and confidence with an example involving 5 items in 10 transactions as shown below:

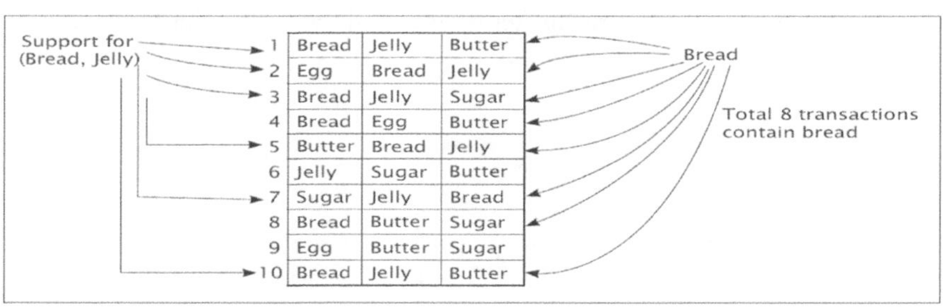

In the case of above 10 transactions involving 10 customers:

Support for (Bread, Jelly) = 6/10 = 0.6, that is, 60%

Confidence for Bread ⇒Jelly = 6/8 = 0.75, that is, 75%

Out of eight transactions with bread as one of the items, six times, bread was purchased with jelly.

Therefore, we can say with 75% confidence that if a customer buys bread, he/she will also buy jelly. Association rule mining makes use of a very important algorithm known as the 'Apriori' algorithm to find frequent item sets. The 'Apriori' algorithm can be stated as follows:

'For a given minimum support S as the interesting criterion, all item sets of interest having i elements are a subset of all item sets of interest having $(i + 1)$ elements', which means that to find the interesting association of i items having required minimum support, we do not need to search all the associations of all items, but only to search the interesting association of $(i - 1)$ items having support of the required minimum and to join $(i - 1)$ item sets within themselves and then prune the subsets of i item sets, which are not of interest (do not have the minimum support). Let me explain the Apriori algorithm with the previous example of 5 items (bread, jelly, butter, egg and sugar) with 10 customer transactions of buying.

Let the minimum support be 0.3, that is, 3 out of 10.

1. **Interesting (1-Element) Item Sets**: That is, one item set with three or more transactions is (bread), (butter), (jelly), (egg), (sugar)
2. **Interesting (2-Element) Item Sets**: That is two item sets with three or more transactions

   (bread, butter), (bread, jelly), (bread, egg)

   (bread, sugar), (butter, jelly), (butter, egg)

   (butter, sugar), (jelly, egg), (jelly, sugar)

3. **Interesting (3-element) Item Sets**: We have to search from 3-element possible combinations out of 2-element sets. There is only one set of three items having the required minimum support: (bread, butter, jelly). Furthermore, the subsets of (bread, butter, jelly), that is, (bread, butter), (bread, jelly) and (butter, jelly) all have the minimum support of 0.3.

The above shows that in order to find the interesting set with a particular number of items, we do not have to search the entire data sets but only to search the previous iteration of interesting sets with one number fewer of items.

13.4.2 Data Classification

Data classification is another important technique of data mining. Classification consists of predicting outcomes based on certain input parameters. It follows a systematic approach and uses a number of algorithms such as decision tree, random forest, rule-based induction, neural networks and Bayesian network.

The application of classification techniques in data mining finds use in fraud detection, credit risk assessment, weather prediction and many other big data applications. The classification process consists of a learning phase based on training data, followed by the classification model development phase with the help of classification algorithms such as decision trees to predict unknown values. Let me illustrate the data classification process with a simple example as shown in Figure 13.3.

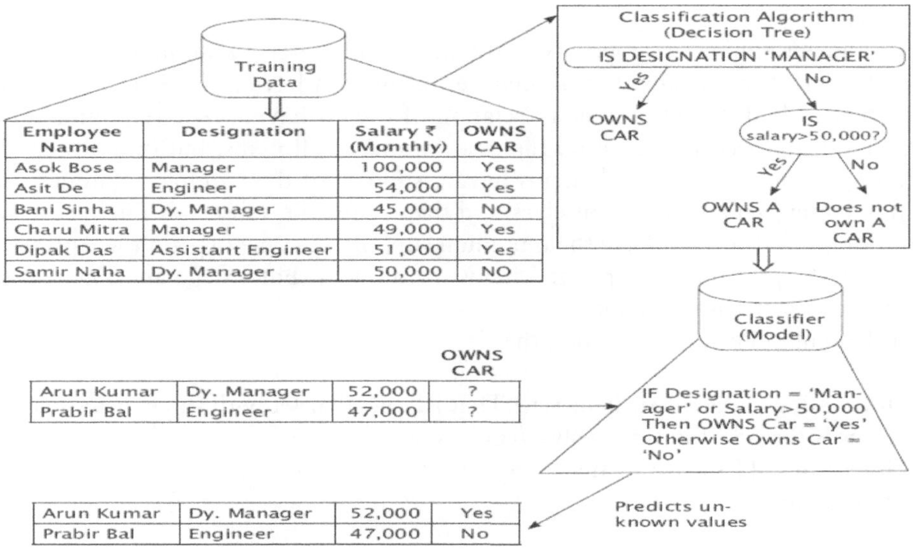

Figure 13.3 Data Mining with Classification

13.4.2.1 Clustering

Clustering in data mining is the grouping of objects based on the similarity of their characteristics. Cluster analysis is one of the main and most important tasks of the data mining process. Clustering can be performed using various methods based on algorithms. Clustering methods basically partition the data based on similarity into clusters such that there exists similarity among the data points within a cluster, but no similarity exists between the data points of two different clusters. For example, if we collect the data relating to monthly income and expenditure of people of a locality and cluster the data into three different clusters, the clusters may be represented as shown in Figure 13.4.

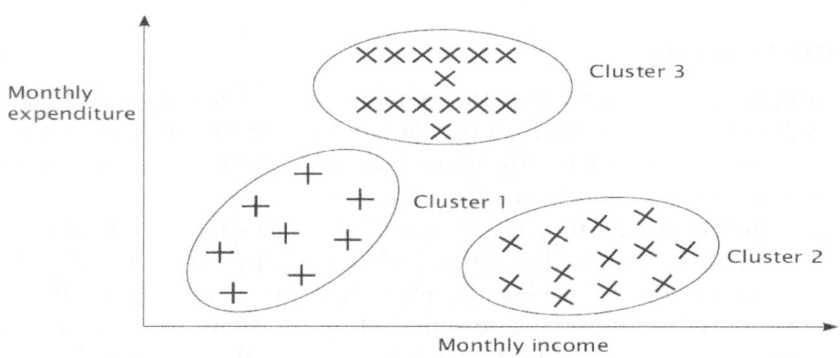

Figure 13.4 Representation of Clusters

Clustering of data has important applications in various fields such as:

- Market research, market segmentation and target market
- Pattern recognition
- Image processing
- Social network analysis
- The World Wide Web and search engines
- Genetics

For example, if we search the web through the Google search engine to find books on 'Environmental ecology', it will retrieve the cluster of all relevant books belonging to the Environmental ecology subject.

Similarly, in the case of social network analysis, clustering helps find communities among a large number of people. In the case of marketing, clustering helps marketing managers of companies in fast-moving consumer goods to cluster the customers according to their income and apply different pricing policies for customers belonging to different income groups and who buy the company's products.

Clustering in data mining of big data has its distinctive advantages such as:

1. **High Scalability**: Clustering algorithms are capable of handling large amounts of data.
2. **High Dimensionality**: Clustering algorithms can handle multidimensional data. For example, they can cluster consumers based on income, expenditure, credit ranking and many similar dimensions.
3. **Comprehensibility**: The results of clustering can be easily interpreted, understood and used in practise.
4. **Interoperability**: Clustering algorithms are simple and can be operated on databases stored on different platforms.

Clustering adopts various approaches such as partitioning, model, hierarchy, density and constraint-based approaches.

There are a number of clustering algorithms such as:

1. K-means
2. Fuzzy C-means
3. Hierarchical clustering
4. Mixture of Gaussian

The most popular and widely applied clustering algorithm is the K-means clustering. K stands for the number of clusters, and the K clusters are based on least aggregate distance of the data points of clusters from the mean or centroid of the same cluster.

Let us illustrate the K-means clustering algorithm with an example of one-dimensional data, say the annual income of a few people in lakhs of ₹ as follows:

3 5 7 8 11 12 15 18 29 32

Let us take K = 3 (3 clusters), that is, let us group the above data into 3 clusters.

Step 1: Select cluster centres (three) from the above data points such that the centres are farthest apart from each other.

(3)	5	7	8	11	(12)	15	18	29	(32)
C1					C2				C3

Step 2: Now check all other data points as regards to their nearness to the cluster centres C1, C2 and C3 and assign the label of any centre which is nearest. The result will be as follows:

(3)	5	7	8	11	(12)	15	18	29	(32)
C1	C1	C1	C2	C2	C2	C2	C2	C3	C3

Step 3: Recalculate the cluster centres by finding the mean of the data points belonging to the same cluster formed with data points labelled as in Step 2.

(3)	5	7	8	11	(12)	15	18	29	(32)
↓	↓	↓	↓	↓	↓	↓	↓	↓	↓
C1	C1	C1	C2	C2	C2	C2	C2	C3	C3
mean of C1 is 5			mean of C2 is 12.80					mean of C3 is 30.50	

Step 4: Now repeat Steps 2 and 3 till convergence is reached when data points do not move between clusters and cluster centres stabilize and do not shift. The iteration is as follows:

3	5	7	8	11	12	15	18	29	32
↓	↓	↓	↓	↓	↓	↓	↓	↓	↓
C1	C1	C1	C2	C2	C2	C2	C2	C3	C3
mean = 5.75				mean = 14				mean = 30.5	

The result finally has been obtained as above and all the data points within a cluster are nearer to the cluster centre than the cluster centres of the other clusters. Hence, the algorithm K mean clustering has formed the three clusters as follows:

Cluster 1	Cluster 2	Cluster 3
3 5 7 8	11 12 15 18	29 32

It may be noted that the K-means clustering, as illustrated above, is suitable for data mining of numeric data and not suitable for text data mining. Text mining, also known as 'text analytics', is typically achieved through the devising of patterns and trends of association and frequency of occurrences through techniques of statistical pattern learning. However, in almost all text mining applications, we need to assess the quality of text retrieval, which is denoted by the relevance of such retrieval of text data or generation of patterns on the basis of the usefulness of the patterns to the users. Usually, there are three primary metrics for assessing the quality of text data mining. They are (1) precision, (2) recall and (3) F-score.

Precision is denoted by the fraction of retrieved text data that is relevant to the user. Recall is the fraction of text data that is relevant to the user and is actually retrieved. The above measures can be expressed as follows:

Precision = [{Relevant} n {Retrieved}]/[{Retrieved}]

Recall = [{Relevant}n{Retrieved}]/[{Relevant}]

F-score is a measure of trade-off between precision or otherwise and is defined as the harmonic mean of recall or precision and expressed as follows:

F-score = (recall × precision) / (recall + precision) / 2

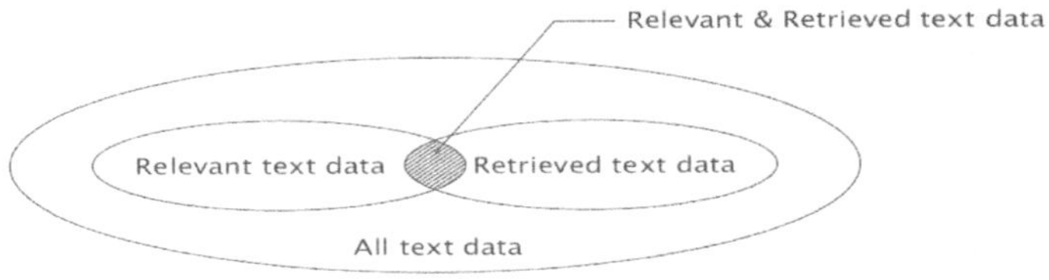

Figure 13.5 Measure of Quality Text Data Mining

The above measures can be visualised by a diagram as shown in Figure 13.5.

Text mining can help an organisation derive potentially valuable business insights from text documents such as word documents, emails and postings on social media streams such as Facebook, Twitter and LinkedIn. Text data mining is often challenging because natural language text is often ambiguous due to inconsistent syntax or semantics. Text analytics software, however, can help by transposing words or phrases in unstructured data into numerical values, which can then be linked with structured data in a database so that traditional data mining techniques can be applied.

Example of R-codes for clustering of cricket players of IPL:

R-codes for cluster analysis of cricket players of the Indian Premier League (IPL): The following is the R script for cluster analysis which was done for 22 players based on 13 parameters of past performance in various matches. The parameters are like number of wickets taken, maiden overs bowled, number of matches played, number of boundaries, over boundaries, ducks and many more. The purpose of the script is to form a dendrogram which is a diagrammatic representation of the clusters. Four clusters were formed and the cluster having the maximum values of the descriptive statistics was considered as the best cluster consisting of efficient players.

```
ipl <- read.csv('D:\\BISWAS 19.03.17\\E Drive Backup\\R\\R CSV\\
Cluster_ipl.csv',header = T)
view(ipl)
iplstandard<-scale(ipl[,2:14])
```

Remarks: The first code imports the IPL file. Next, we are viewing the file with 22 players and their 13 performance parameters from column 2 to 14. The first column contains the names of the players:

```
distmat<-dist(x=iplstandard,method = 'euclidean')
```

Remarks: The above code finds the Euclidean distance:

```
summary(distmat)
```

Remarks: The descriptive statistics of the calculated Euclidean distance are found out:

```
Cluster_result<-hclust(d=distmat^2,method ='ward.D')
```

Remarks: The above code finds the Euclidean distance and squares the same to avoid negative values and stores the same in cluster result. Here, we are using the Ward's minimum variance method:

```
plot.new()
plot(cluster_result)
```

Remarks: First, we are creating the new plotting window and in the next line of code plotting cluster_ result. This is the diagrammatic representation of clusters known as a dendrogram and the same shows the cluster information.

```
View(iplstandard)
clus1<-ipl[clusterNum= =1,]
clus2<-ipl[clusterNum= =2,]
clus3<-ipl[clusterNum= =3,]
clus4<-ipl[clusterNum= =4,]
```

The above codes are forming subsets. When clusterNum=1, the data will be stored in clus1 and so on for the other 3 clusters:

```
summary(clus1)
summary(clus2)
summary(clus3)
summary(clus4)
```

Remarks: The above codes calculate the descriptive statistics of each cluster. The values of the descriptive statistics were found to be maximum for Cluster 4 in the above case:

```
View(clus4)
```

Remarks: We are viewing the best or most efficient cluster 4 consisting of efficient players of the IPL.

13.5 Machine Learning

In Chapter 5, we have seen the various methods through which machines learn, such as supervised, unsupervised, reinforced learning, analytic learning and also deep learning. Let us elaborate a little more on machine learning in the following paragraphs in the context of data mining.

Human beings learn by experience; machines also learn through data. According to Ron Bekkerman, 'Machine learning develops algorithms for making predictions from data'. In that sense, machine learning is quite similar to data mining because data mining also uses techniques to generate patterns and make predictions of values of unknown data. However, data mining generates data sets as patterns which give rise to knowledge, whereas machine learning also uses training data and test data for a particular purpose or task and accordingly makes a classifier model to derive a data set B similar in properties to the original data set A. In fact, machine learning applies statistical methods to real-world tasks and thereby predicts outcomes related to the tasks.

Data for the sake of machine learning consist of data instances (similar to the rows of a relational database), and the data instances are represented as feature vectors (similar to the data attributes or columns of a relational database). Features are chosen in machine learning based on the specific tasks.

For example, if the task is to select basketball players, the features such as height and weight are relevant, whereas if the task is to select candidates who can teach machine learning, such features are of no use. Hence, feature vectors of data instances for machine learning are task-specific.

Machine learning is all about making sense of existing data and then making predictions about new data instances. For example, if we group people according to their annual income into high-, medium- and low-income groups, then if a person with a particular income becomes a new data instance, we can say 'this person belongs to the high-income group' if his income matches the income of our existing classification for the high-income group.

Machine-learning processes can be either supervised or unsupervised. Supervised learning takes place when there is pre-defined knowledge about the data items as to their structure or the target associated with each input data, whereas unsupervised learning takes place when the structure of the data is not known and the learning process tries to find the similarities of the data items based on certain distinctive features. For example, clustering is a process of unsupervised learning since the grouping of items or objects is done based on certain features or attributes such as colour, shape or size. Classification is, however, a supervised-learning process since the classification of data items or objects is made based on pre-defined knowledge and training about the rules of classification. Both the above types of learning have been illustrated with some practical examples.

Example 1: A basket of fruits and vegetables can be left with a child. The child can segregate the items in the baskets in the following ways depending on whether the child has been taught (supervised learning) what are vegetables and fruits or not taught (unsupervised learning).

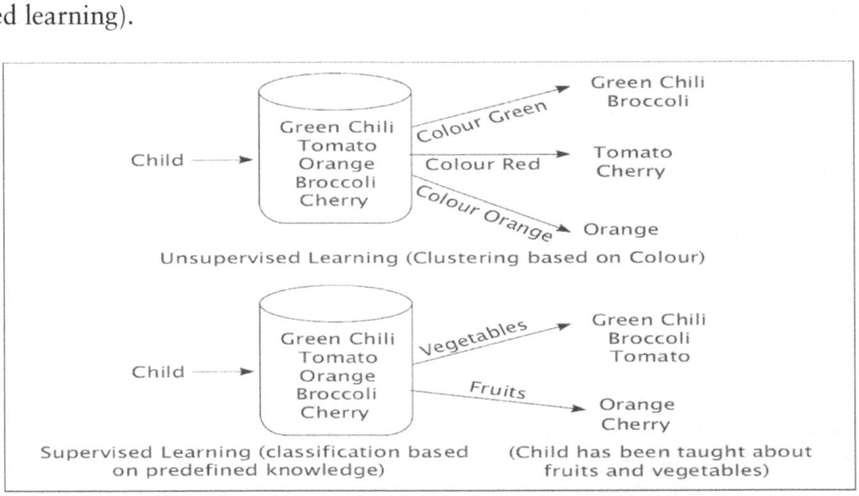

Example 2: Arrival time of flights at a particular airport depending on weather conditions.

The historical data regarding the arrival of flights on time, ahead of time or late, and the corresponding weather conditions can be our training data sets for supervised learning, based on which we can predict the arrival time of flights given a particular weather condition. However, in the case of unsupervised learning, we can only group the flights depending upon their arrival pattern and cannot make any predictions. This is explained as follows:

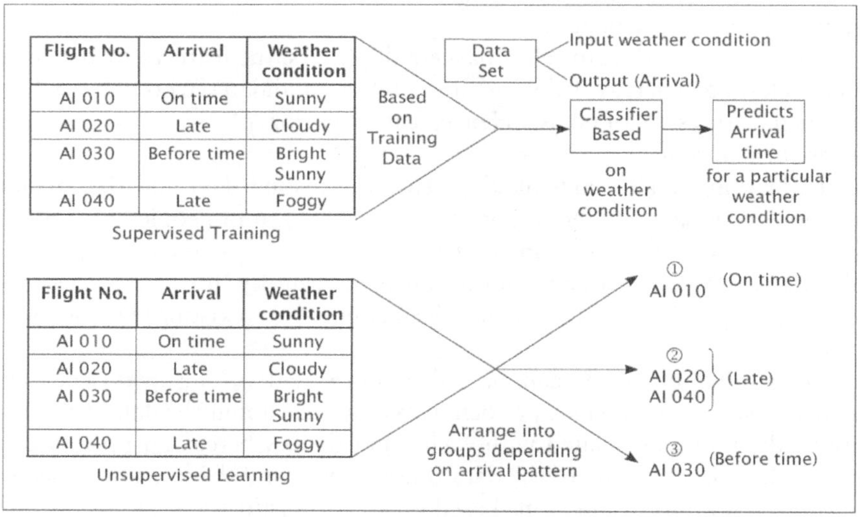

Machine-learning tasks use techniques of data mining, namely classification, clustering and association. However, machine learning also uses both linear and logistic data regression. Some interesting machine learning examples are the classification of incoming emails into spam and non-spam groups based on some classifier algorithm and also handwritten digits recognition based on classifier features. Figure 13.6 illustrates the machine learning process for handwriting recognition using classifier features and a decision tree.

Out of the techniques adopted by machine-learning tasks, classification, clustering and association of data have been explained in earlier paragraphs on data mining. The remaining technique of data regression, which is also widely used by machine-learning tasks, can be either linear or logistic regression.

Regression is basically a relation of the value of one variable (output), which is called the dependent variable, with the corresponding values of one or more independent variables. For example, there may be a relation between the university grade point average (GPA) of a person and his/her school GPA. Here, university GPA is the dependent variable and depends on the school GPA, which is the independent variable. In the case of linear regression, the relationship can be expressed as a linear equation of the form:

$$Y = \beta 0 + \beta 1 * X$$

where Y is the dependent variable and X is the independent variable. In this case, the output or dependent variable (say Y) can be a continuous variable, that is, it can have many possible values such as age, income and height expressed as numerical values. Linear regression consists of finding the best fitting straight line through the actual data points.

In case of logistic regression, however, the output or dependent variable is a categorical variable such as gender (male or female), city or 'Yes or No', which has a finite number of values (usually binary) or outcomes. Just to illustrate binary outcomes, the following are the examples:

- Is a bank transaction fraudulent?

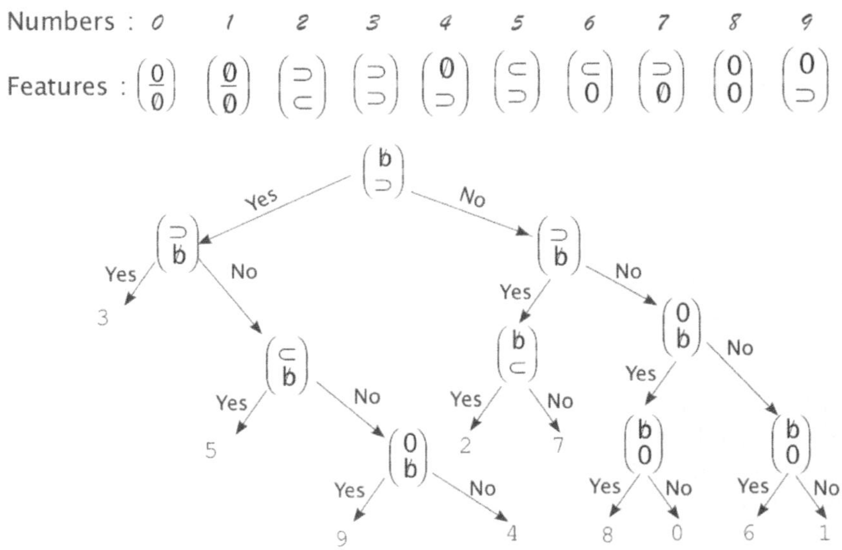

Figure 13.6 Illustration of Handwritten Number Recognition

- Is a customer likely to buy a new product?
- Is a tumour benign or malignant?

The outcome can be either 0 or 1, 0 if 'No' and 1 if 'Yes'. Here, the outcome is represented by a dummy (zero-one) variable. Figure 13.7 shows a linear regression model and a logistic regression model with Y, the dependent variable and X, the independent variable.

Now, if we convert the binary outcome of a logistic regression model into a probability, we can get a continuous value of p (Y), where p (Y) is the probability of the outcome of the binary variable Y and the value of p (Y) can be represented as $0 < p(Y) < 1$. Hence, the logistic regression model of Figure 13.7 can be represented as shown in Figure 13.8.

13.6 Metadata

Metadata is another example of big data. For example, email metadata, cell phone metadata consisting of time and location of calls, photograph exchangeable image file (EXIF)

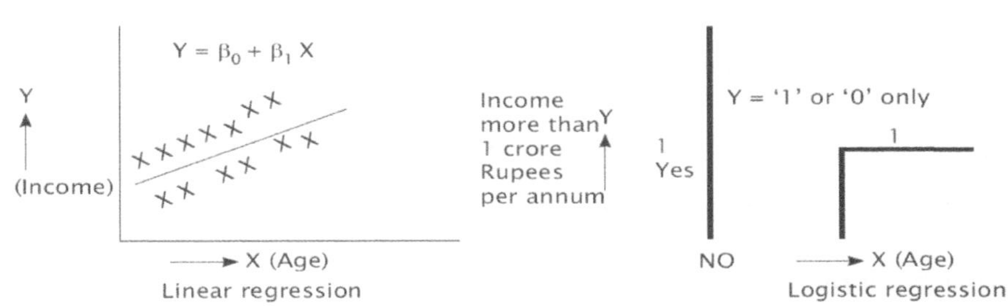

Figure 13.7 Linear Regression Versus Logistic Regression

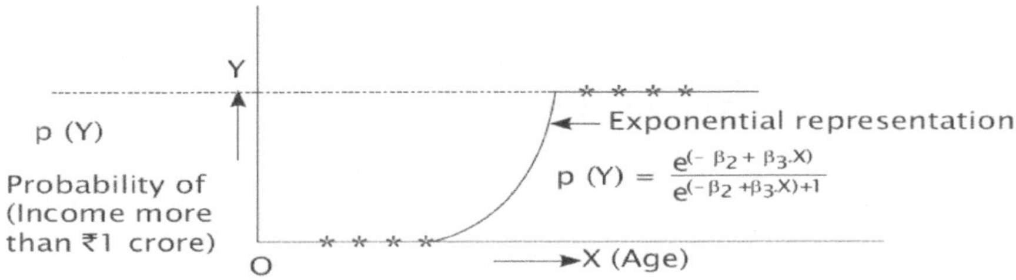

Figure 13.8 Logistic Regression Model

metadata and metadata related to social networks, such as Twitter form a considerable chunk of big data which can be analysed to furnish information for predictive marketing, market research and e-commerce. The following is a simple example of the volume of data generated by the log file of a particular Gmail account. Each email (incoming or outgoing) will have one usual entry as follows:

Date time From/To Subject/Body Attachments

Assuming about 100 kB of storage space will be required for each mail and on average 10 such mails for semi-structured data are received per day, in a month the total data volume generated for the log file will be 10 × 100 × 30 ~ 30 MB, which is a high volume indeed. The log file has no finite or fixed structure as some of the fields can have different types of contents.

13.7 Attributes of Highly Effective Big Data Environment

Big data environment has got certain distinct attributes as we have seen in the preceding paragraphs of this chapter. Those can be listed as follows:

1. **Seamless Integration**: Seamless integration of data through mixing, combining and contrasting of data sets. Forrester Research has mentioned that 80% of the value of big data comes through integration.
2. **Flexibility with Low Cost:** Low cost and low complexity with sufficient flexibility to scale the feed needs is the target.
3. **Stability**: Users need to easily access and interact with data and in this sense, infrastructure performance with stability is a key to boosting business performance through big data.

Big data thus pose some challenges as shown in Figure 13.9.

13.8 Big Data—Infrastructure Requirements

Infrastructure for storage, processing and retrieval of big data has the following requirements:

- Scalable platform.
- Scalable and reliable storage.
- Database independent.

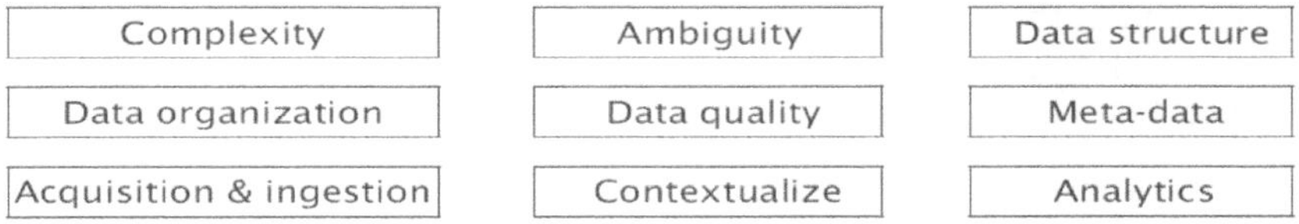

Figure 13.9 Big Data Challenges

- Supported by standard toolset.
- Fault tolerant.
- Data centre ready.
- Low cost of acquisition.
- Capable of processing dynamic and unstructured data.
- Capable to perform complex operations within reasonable response time.

13.9 Hadoop Story Line

Google was the first to conceive the idea of developing a distributed file system to process big data and published a paper in 2004 that described the architecture of Google's distributed file system known as GFS.

In the same year, Google also published a paper on the MapReduce (MapR) framework explaining a system that they used to scale their own search system. Doug Cutting immediately saw the suitability of the Global Forecast System (GFS) and MapR technologies for Nutch, which is an open-source web search engine and a part of the Lucene project widely used in text search library. Later on, in late 2005, Nutch was rewritten by Doug Cutting and his team to use MapR to boost Nutch's scalability. In 2006, Hadoop was born out of Nutch and Yahoo hired Doug Cutting in 2006 itself to work with a dedicated team on improving Hadoop as an open-source project. In 2007, 'Times Machine' came as a backup software application, which creates incremental backups of files that can be restored at a later date. 'Times Machine' was based on the concept of distributed file system. In 2008, Hadoop became a top-level Apache project. Later on, at the end of 2008, Hadoop achieved the Terra Sort benchmark (209 seconds!) and Yahoo announced that Hadoop running on a 10,000+ core Linux clusters was in a production system for indexing the web (http://developer.yahoo. net/blogs/hadoop/2008/02/yahoo-worlds-largest-production-hadoop.html).

The name Hadoop was adopted by Doug Cutting as the name used by his son as a toddler for a yellow-stuffed elephant toy.

13.10 Apache Hadoop

Apache Hadoop is a platform for data storage and processing which is scalable, fault tolerant and open source. It has two core components, namely HDFS and MapR / Yet Another Resource Negotiator (YARN).

The two core components have been described in the subsequent paragraphs. However, some of the features of Hadoop are listed as follows:

- Consolidates mixed type of data.
- Complex and relational data into a single repository.
- Inexpensive storage because of use of commodity hardware (daily usable hardware).

- Keeps raw data available at all times.
- Processes data at the source.
- Eliminates ETL bottlenecks.
- Mines data first, governs later.

13.11 Hadoop Distributed File System

HDFS is a specially designed file system to store huge data files in a cluster of commodity hardware. Here, by commodity hardware, we mean daily usable hardware built on inexpensive servers.

A data file may be stored in more than one storage device, hence the name Distributed File System. Hadoop is based on the concept of distributed storage coupled with distributed processing of the data in a file. This means storage and processing need to be tightly coupled in a high-volume data-based distributed environment.

13.11.1 HDFS Building Blocks

On a fully configured cluster of Hadoop, daemons or services run. These daemons which are basically resident processes have specific roles and some exist only on one server, while some of them may exist across multiple servers. Further, the daemons follow a master–slave architecture. Master daemons activate the slaves and at the same time, master services can talk to each other and similarly the slave daemons can also communicate among themselves. The daemons are grouped accordingly and shown in Figure 13.10. Each daemon and its role in Hadoop have been described as follows:

NameNode: It is the most important daemon of the Hadoop daemons and is the master of HDFS that directs the slave DataNode daemons to perform the low-level tasks. NameNode is the metadata of HDFS and keeps track of how the files are split into various blocks and stored in DataNodes. NameNode also monitors the health of the DataNodes and the entire distributed file system. The NameNode server is a single one and does not store any user data or perform any computation process. However, NameNode can be a single point of failure of the entire Hadoop cluster if it does not function.

DataNode: Each slave storage device hosts a DataNode daemon to perform the read and write operations of the actual file on HDFS. A file is broken into blocks of data of typical size 64 MB and stored in one or more DataNodes. NameNode keeps account of the individual blocks and the DataNodes on which they reside.

HDFS sits on top of local and traditional file systems and supports write-once-read-many-times with read at streaming speed. The typical block size of 64 MB on the DataNodes can be increased to blocks of 128 MB also. Further, a DataNode may

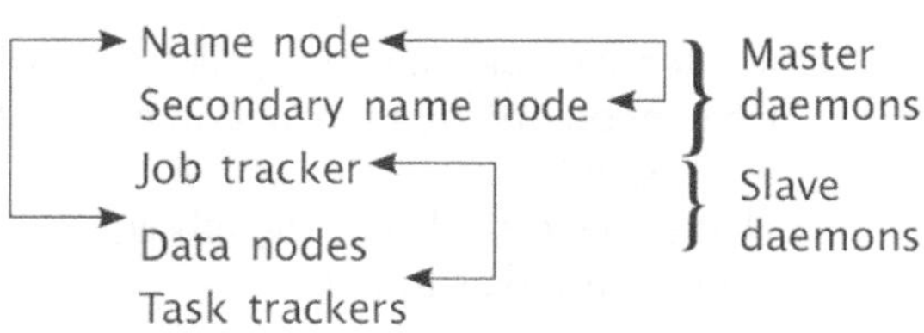

Figure 13.10 Master and Slave Daemons in Hadoop

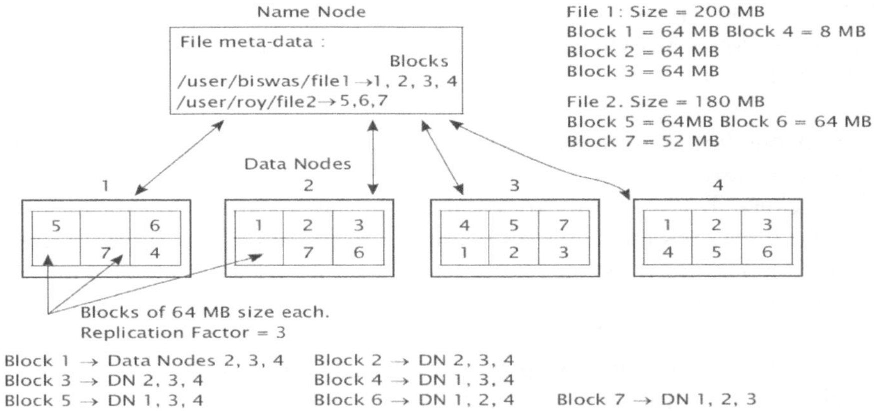

Figure 13.11 NameNode/DataNodes Interaction in HDFS

communicate with other DataNodes to replicate its data blocks for redundancy. The default replication factor is 3. Figure 13.11 illustrates the way files are stored among DataNodes with three replicas and the role of NameNode as a metadata for the data files in the DataNodes.

Each DataNode constantly informs the NameNode about the blocks in which it is storing data and also receives instructions to create, move or delete blocks from the local disk. The NameNode monitors continuously the health of DataNodes by sending heartbeat signal for 10 seconds. In case it does not receive a response within 10 seconds, it sends the second heartbeat for another 10 seconds and finally a third heartbeat signal for 10 seconds. If the DataNode does not send a response within 30 seconds, the NameNode declares the DataNode as problematic and informs the other DataNodes having the replica of the affected DataNode blocks accordingly.

Secondary NameNode (SNN): The SNN is an assistant daemon which acts as a backup node for the NameNode. Like the NameNode, each HDFS cluster has one SNN which typically resides on its own machine (server) and no other DataNode or task tracker daemon runs on the same server. The SNN does not record HDFS metadata on a real-time basis but it only communicates with the NameNode to take snapshots of the HDFS metadata as available on the NameNode at intervals as defined by the HDFS cluster configuration. In the case of Hadoop 1.0, the interval is 1 hour.

Job Tracker: The Job Tracker daemon acts as a liaison between individual client applications and Hadoop. The Job Tracker determines the schedule of execution of tasks involved with the client application and assigns the tasks to Task Trackers of different nodes. The Job Tracker performs the following services:

1. It communicates with the NameNodes to determine the location of data (file splits).
2. Job Tracker communicates with Task Trackers to locate available slots.
3. Job Tracker submits the tasks to the chosen Task Trackers.
4. After submission of tasks, the Job Tracker monitors all the Task Trackers by the use of heartbeat signals. If no response is received up to a predefined limit of attempts, the Job Tracker will automatically reschedule the task to a different Task Tracker.

5. Job Tracker decides whether to declare a Task Tracker as unreliable.
6. When the client job is finished, the Job Tracker updates its status to signal back to the NameNode. Any client application can pool the Job Tracker for output or for information logs.

There is only one Job Tracker per Hadoop cluster. It typically runs on a server as a master node of the cluster.

Task Trackers: Task Trackers are computing daemons and slaves to the master Job Tracker, which oversees the overall execution of MapReduce jobs. Task Trackers manage the execution of individual tasks allotted to each slave DataNode. It is interesting to note that although there is a single Task Tracker per DataNode, each Task Tracker can create multiple Java Virtual Machines (JVMs) to handle many parallel MapReduce tasks. Map and Reduce are basically Java programs. Figure 13.12 shows the interaction among client applications, the Job Tracker and the Task Trackers.

The architecture of a typical Hadoop cluster is shown in Figure 13.13.

As already stated in earlier paragraphs, Hadoop consists of HDFS, the distributed file system and MapR, the distributed processing associated with each distributed DataNode. MapR is the data processing or analysis function which again comprises ETL and analytics using various statistical and simple analytic techniques.

13.12 MapReduce

Before we discuss the MapR framework consisting of Input Split, Record Reader, mapper, intermediate grouping, shuffling and reducer, the MapR function has been explained with a simple word count example. Let us consider a text file as follows:

hi how are you
how is your job
how is your bro
how is your sis
how is your spouse
how is your family
what is your hobby

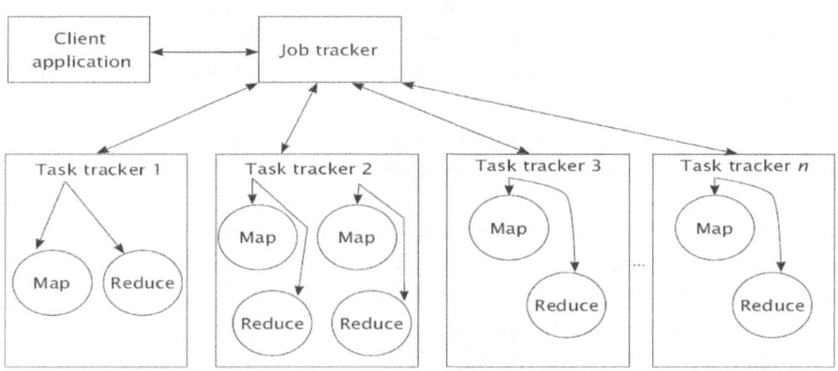

Figure 13.12 Interaction among Client Application, Job Tracker and Task Trackers

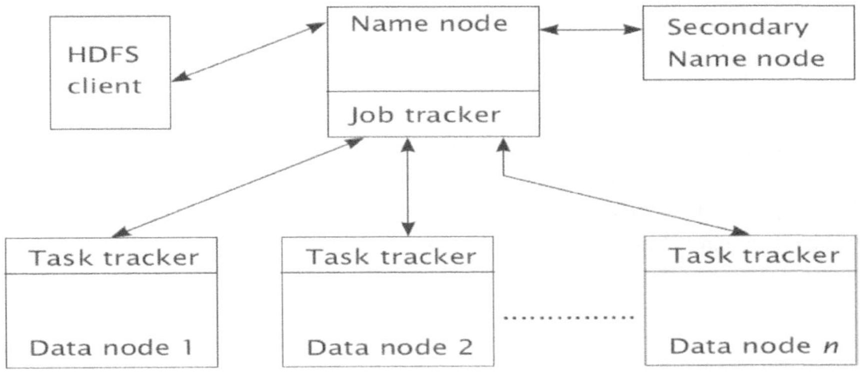

Figure 13.13 Architecture of a Typical Hadoop Cluster

Suppose we want to count the number of each word in the above file. Let us assume that the size of the file is 200 MB. For the purpose of the word count, we split the input into four blocks of 64 MB each as follows and then proceed to find the word count for each Input Split separately. The Map function has been explained below:

Input split 1 (64 MB)	Input split 2 (64 MB)	Input split 3 (64 MB)	Input split 4 (8 MB)
hi how are you	how is your bro	how is your spouse	what is your hobby
how is your job	how is your sis	how is your family	
(hi, 1)(how, 1)(are, 1)	(how, 1)(is, 1)(your, 1)	(how, 1)(is, 1)(your, 1.)	(what, 1)(is, 1)
(you, 1)(how, 1)(is, 1)	(bro, 1)(how, 1)(is, 1)	(spouse, 1)(how, 1).	(your, 1)(hobby, 1)
(your, 1)(job, 1).	(your, 1)(sis, 1).	(is, 1)(your, 1) (family, 1)	

Next, the intermediate output of the Map function, as explained, is shuffled and grouped word-wise, which is the key, as shown below. Each time a word appears, we put a count 1.

hi, (1) how, (1, 1, 1, 1, 1, 1) are, (1) you, (1)

is, (1, 1, 1, 1, 1, 1) your, (1, 1, 1, 1, 1, 1) job, (1) bro, (1)

sis, (1) spouse, (1) family, (1) what, (1)

hobby (1)

After shuffling as above, the Reduce function reduces the individual counts of each word into a total count, and the output of the Reduce function will be as follows:

hi, (1) how, (6) are (1) you, (1) is, (6)

your, (6) job (1) bro, (1) sis, (1)

spouse, (1) family, (1) what, (1) hobby (1)

The output is the word count and is in the key-value format.

MapR framework is shown in Figure 13.14.

Both Mapper and Reducer are small programmes. Mapper does computation on Input Split line by line each line being read by the reader as byte offset entire line, as shown below:

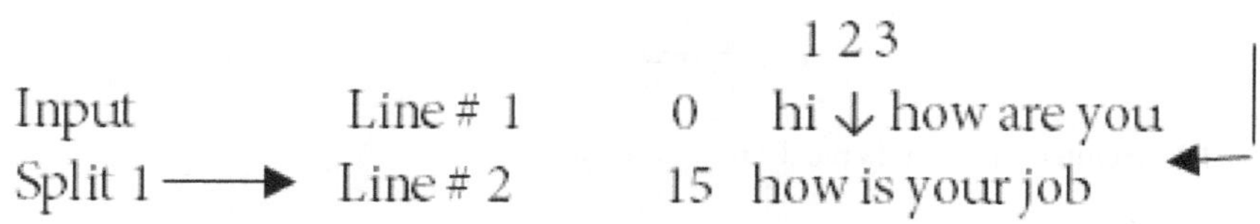

The byte offset is the number of characters that exist from the beginning of a line. In the above case, the byte offset for line 1 is 0 and the same for line 2 is 15. The byte offset is used as a key by Hadoop while mapping (key-value).

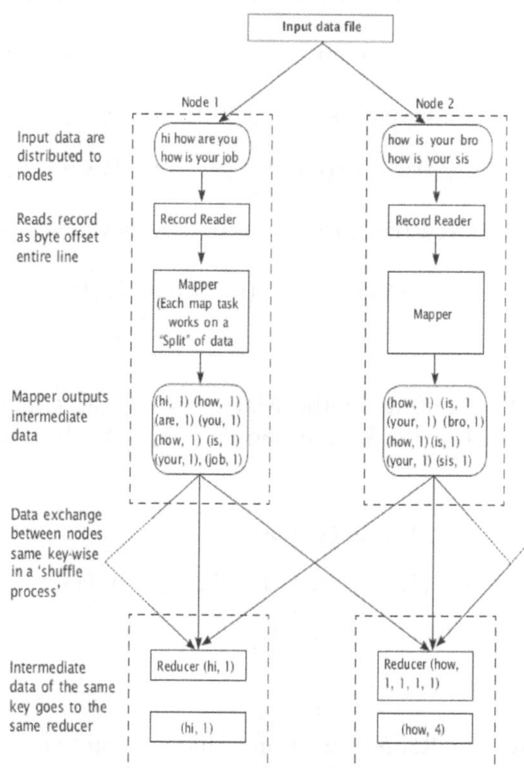

Figure 13.14 MapReduce Framework

The anatomy of a MapR programme, as obtained by manipulating (key-value) pairs in the general form is as follows:

Map: (K1, V1) → list (K2, V2)
Reduce: (K2, list (V2)) → list (K3, V3)

Here Map (K1, V1) is input to Mapper and refers to key K1 as byte offset and V1 as the value. For example, for Line 1 of Input Split 1, the entire line read by the reader relates to (K1 = 0) and the same line is 'hi how are you'. Similarly, for Line 2 (K1 = 15), the line is 'how is your job'.

The Map program converts the same to a list (K2, V2), where K2 is the keyword such as 'hi' and 'how' and V2 is its value as integer 1:

list (K2, V2) = (hi, 1) (how, 1) (are, 1) (you, 1)
(how, 1) (is, 1) (your, 1) (job, 1)

which is the intermediate output of Mapper.

After shuffling, list (K2, V2) results in (K2 list (V2)) which is as follows:

(K2 list (V2)) = (hi, 1) (how, (1, 1)) ...

(K2, list (V2)) is fed to Reducer and the output is list (K3, V3) where K3 is the keyword and V3 is the total count for the same. For our example:

list (K3, V3) = (hi, 1) (how, 2) ...

A listing of a partial view of the word count programme in Java is as follows:

```
Public class- word count extends configured implements Tool {public static Class
Map class extends MapR Base implements, Mapper < Long Writable, Text, Text, Int
writable> {private Text word = new
Text ();

public void map (Long Writable key. Text value, output
collector < Text, Int writable > output, Reporter reporter) throws
IO Exception {
String line = value. to string ();
String Tokenizer itr = new string Tokenizer (line); while (itr.
Has More Tokens ()) {
word.set (itr.next Token ()); output. collect (word, one);
}
}
}
public static class Reduce extends MapReduce Base implements
Reducer < Text, Intwritable, Text, Intwritable > {public void reduce
(Text key, Iterator
< Intwritable > values, output collector < Text,
```

```
Intwritable > output, Reporter reporter) throws IO Exception {
int sum = 0;
while (values.has Next ()) {sum + = values.next () .get ();
}
output.collect (key, new Intwritable (sum));
}
}...
```

For the word count example with multiple reducers shown in Figure 13.14, shuffling is done with a default behaviour to hash the key (word such as hi, how...) and depending on the same, the reducer is determined. For example, all 'hi' in one reducer, all 'how' in another reducer and so on. However, in case of sorting of the output of the mapper or any other type of analysis, we have to customise the partitioner for directing the mapper output for the particular application to different reducers through shuffling. Such type of hash partitioning with multiple reducers facilitates parallel computation. Combiners are optional, and they perform local reduce for the intermediate output of the mappers before we distribute the mapper results through shuffling. Each mapper has its own combiner. Combiners increase the speed and efficiency of intermediate storage as well as shuffling of mapper output.

For example, in the case of word count, if a document for the job contains the word 'how', say 200 times, it is much more efficient to store and shuffle the pair ('how', 200) once instead of the pair ('how', 1) 200 times. This processing step of local reduce is known as 'combining'.

13.12.1 Data Flow in a MapR Program in Hadoop

Figure 13.15 illustrates the data flow in a MapR programme in Hadoop. Before we go into details of components of Hadoop 2.0, let us get into the architecture of both Hadoop 1.0 vis-a-vis Hadoop 2.0 as shown in Figure 13.16. APP Master stands for application master. There is one APP Master for every application instance.

Basically, it manages the application life cycle and task scheduling. APP Master gets MapReduce status from each container and also sends a request for resource allocation to the resource manager.

A container is a pool of resources in terms of memory and processor. The entire resource of a DataNode is divided into a number of containers. For example, if the total

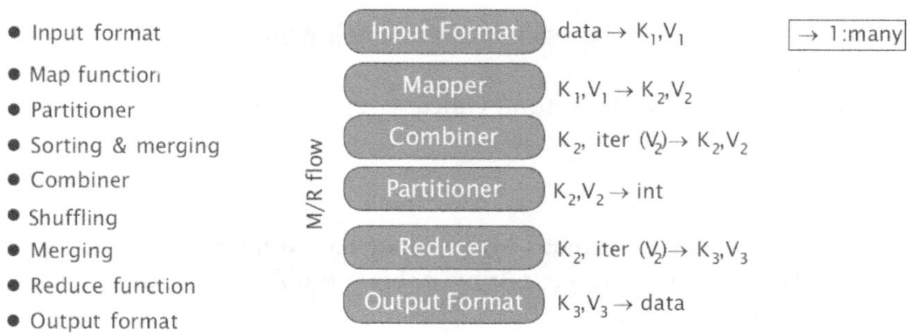

Figure 13.15 Data Flow in a MapReduce Programme

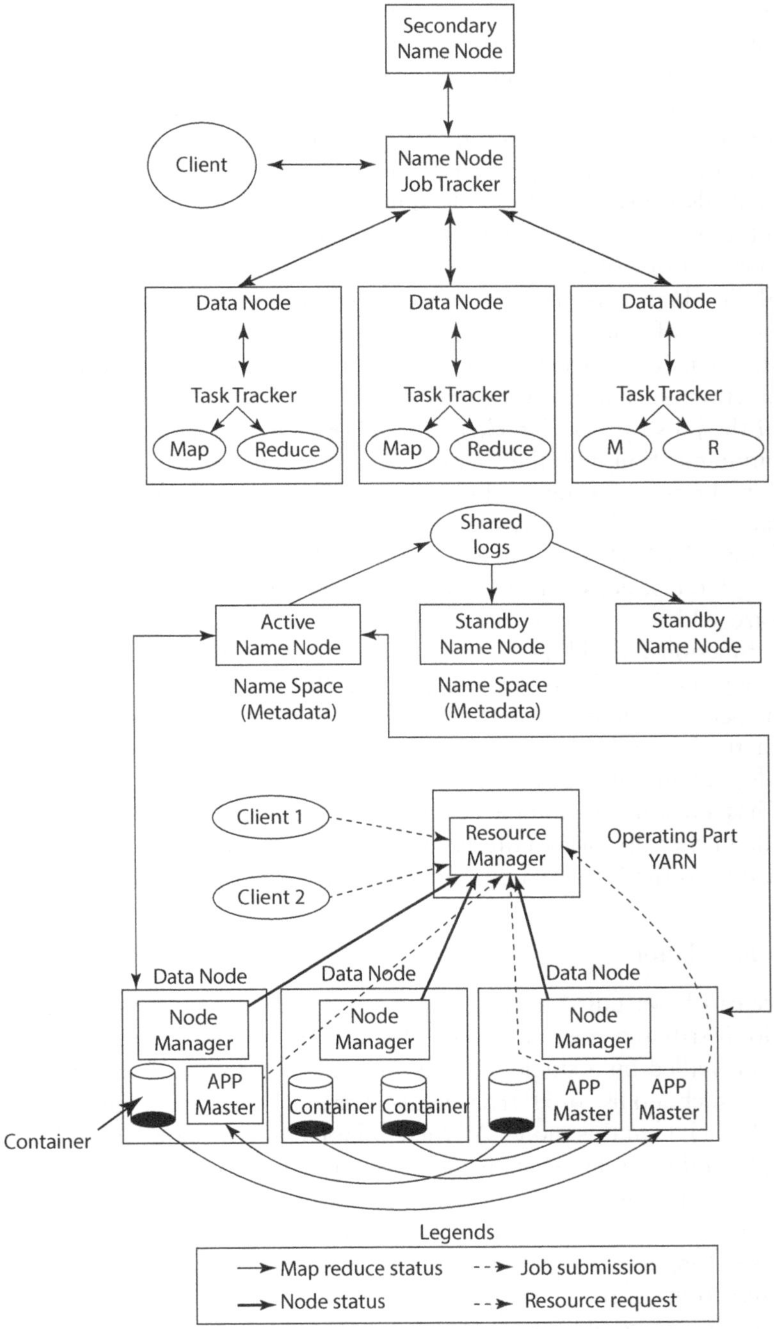

Figure 13.16 Architecture of Hadoop 1.0 vis-à-vis Hadoop 2.0

memory of a node is 100 GB, it may be sliced into 25 containers of 4 GB each and say one core of processor. The resource manager allocates resources to each APP Master in terms of containers. For a MapR application, the total number of containers is equal to the sum total of number of Mappers and the number of Reducers. Containers hold a predefined quantity of memory and processor. For instance, in the above example, if an application requires a memory of 5 GB, it will be allotted 2 containers of 4 GB each.

Node manager administers resources of a node, and there is one node manager for each DataNode. It also furnishes the node status to the resource manager. Resource manager is a central agent (similar to Job Tracker), and it manages and allocates cluster resources. Hadoop 2.0 obviously has several advantages over Hadoop 1.0 such as its horizontal scalability, higher availability of resource manager as compared to the same for Job Tracker in case of Hadoop 1.0.

It may be stated that Job Tracker is overburdened in the case of Hadoop 1.0 because of its multiple functions such as the assignment of jobs to Task Trackers, the submission of the outputs of the jobs by Task Trackers to Job Tracker, the monitoring of the Task Trackers and communication with the clients (users) of Hadoop 1.0.

Hadoop 1.0, the first-generation Hadoop, is made up of HDFS, MapR, NameNode, SNN, Job Tracker, DataNode and Task Tracker. However, in the case of the second-generation Hadoop 2.X, YARN is a new component known as 'MRV2' which is now characterised as a large-scale, distributed operating system for big data applications. YARN is software which separates resource allocation and scheduling of tasks from data processing functions, enabling Hadoop 2.0 to handle more varied applications and their processing. Besides, in the case of Hadoop 2.0 and above, there are multiple NameNodes, one being the active NameNode and the others the SNN. Each SNN shares the logs of the active NameNode continuously and the Namespace (metadata) of the active NameNode is maintained on a real-time basis by all the standby NameNodes as a federation. This has a distinct advantage of immediate recovery of the Namespace of the active NameNode in the case of its failure, unlike in the case of Hadoop 1.0, in which case the SNN maintains the Namespace at hourly intervals only.

13.13 Hadoop Installation

Hadoop software can be installed in three modes of operation, namely (1) stand-alone mode, (2) pseudo-distributed mode and (3) fully-distributed mode. In the stand-alone mode, Hadoop is installed on a single node and there is no need to communicate with other nodes, and as such, no use of HDFS is made in stand-alone mode. Further, Hadoop daemons are not launched in this mode. All the Hadoop configuration files (XML extension) remain empty in this mode, which is the default mode of Hadoop. This software in the stand-alone mode runs as a single monolithic Java process. This mode of operation of Hadoop is primarily used for developing and debugging the logic of MapR program on small data sets before actually executing the same with big data and with additional complexity of interactions of the Hadoop daemons.

The pseudo-distributed mode runs Hadoop on a single-node cluster with various daemons of Hadoop running as separate Java processes on the same node or machine. In this mode, NameNode, DataNode, SNN, Job Tracker and Task Tracker run on the same machine. This mode of operation of Hadoop also facilitates debugging of MapR code with memory usage, HDFS issues and with interaction among the daemons. Before beginning the installation steps of Apache Hadoop (Apache Hadoop is open-source software), which is a Java framework and can be installed with ease on Linux operating systems such as Ubuntu (various versions), it is therefore recommended to install Apache Hadoop on Ubuntu, and some knowledge of basic Linux commands will be helpful in normal operation connected with the installation task. The prerequisites for the installation are Java Development Kit (JDK) 1.6 and onward versions and SSH. The listing for installation of Hadoop 2.6 on Ubuntu is as follows:

```
# Installation of Java #
: ~ $ Sudo apt-get install openjdk–7-jdk
: ~ $ java-version # # To check whether, Java downloaded # #
java version '1.7.0.79'
# Creating a Hadoop user for accessing #
# HDFS and MapReduce #
# We will create hadoop as system group #
# hduser as system user #
: ~ $ Sudo addgroup hadoop
: ~ $ Sudo adduser hduser
# installing SSH #
# SSH is a protocol for securely accessing one machine from another #
: Sudo apt-get install open SSH-server
# configuring SSH #
# To do this we need to copy generated RSA Key #
# (id-rsa.pub) pairs to authorized_keys folder of SSH #
: ~$ Sudo Su hduser
# Generate SSh key for hduser account
hduser@ubuntu: ~ $ ssh-keygen-t rsa-p' '
# Copy id_rsa.pub to authorized keys from hduser
# Disabling IPV6 since Hadoop does not work on IPV6
# Need to update/etc/sysctl.conf by adding following lines
hduser@ubuntu: ~$sudo vi/etc/sysctl.conf
# Add following lines after the end of the file
net.ipv6.conf.all.disable_ipv6 = 1
net.ipv6.conf.default.disable_ipv6 = 1
net.ipv6.conf.IO.disable_ipv6 = 1
# Hadoop installation from Apache Hadoop 2.6.0
# Source from Apache download Mirrors
# Location for installation is/usr/local/hadoop
hduser@ubuntu: ~ $ cd/usr/local/
## Extract Hadoop Source from hadoop–2.6.0.tar.gz
hduser@ubuntu: ~$sudo tar-XZvf hadoop–2.6.0.tar.gz
## Move hadoop–2.6.0 to hadoop folder
: ~$ Sudo mv hadoop–2.6.0/usr/local/hadoop
## Assign ownership of this folder to Hadoop user
: ~$ Sudo chown hduser: hadoop-R/usr/local/hadoop
: ~$ ssh local host
## Create Hadoop temp directories for NameNode and DataNode
: ~$ sudo mkdir-p/usr/local/hadoop_tmp/hdfs/namenode
: ~$ sudo mkdir-p/usr/local/hadoop_tmp/hdfs/datanode
```

```
## Again assign ownership of this hadoop temp folders to Hadoop user.
: ~$ sudo chown hduser: hadoop —R/usr/local/hadoop_temp
## update hduser configuration files by appending the
## following environment variable at the end of
##. bashrc file.
: ~$ sudo gedit. bashrc
# - - HADOOP ENVIRONMENT VARIABLES START--#
export JAVA_HOME = /usr/lib/jvm/jdk 1.7.0_79
export HADOOP_HOME = /usr/local/Hadoop
export PATH = $PATH: $ HADOOP_HOME/bin
export PATH = $ PATH: HADOOP_HOME/sbin
export HADOOP_MAPRED_HOME = $ HADOOP_HOME
export HADOOP_COMMON_HOME = $ HADOOP_HOME
export HADOOP_HDFS_HOME = $ HADOOP_HOME
export YARN_HOME = $ HADOOP_HOME
export HADOOP_COMMON_LIB_NATIVE_DIR = $ HADOOP_HOME/lib/
native
export HADOOP_OPTS = '—Djava.library.path = $HADOOP_HOME/lib'
# — — HADOOP ENVIRONMENT VARIABLES END — — #
# Configuration file: hadoop.env.sh
# To edit the file, the following command to be executed
hduser@ubuntu : /usr/local/hadoop/etc/hadoop $ sudo gedit hadoop-env.sh
# update JAVA_HOME variable
export JAVA_HOME=/usr/lib/jvm/jdk 1.7.0_79
## configure file: core—site.Xml
hduser@ubuntu:/usr/local/hadoop/etc/hodoop $ sudo gedit core-site-Xml
# Paste these lies into<configmation>tag
<property>
<name>fs.default.name</name>
<value>hdfs://local host: 9000</value>
</property>
## configure file : hdfs—site.Xml
hduser@ubuntu : /usr/local/hadoop/etc/hadoop $sudo gedit hdfs-site.Xml
# Paste these lines into<configuration>tag
<property>
<name>dfs. replication</name>
<value>1</value>
</property>
<property>
<name>dfs.namenode.name.dir</name>
<value>file: /usr/local/hadoop_tmp/hdfs/namenode</value>
</property>
<property>
<name>dfs. datanode. data. dir</name>
<value>file : /usr/local/hadoop_tmp/hdfs/datanode</value>
</property>
# configure file :yarn—site.Xml
hduser@ubuntu :/usr/local/hadoop/etc/hadoop $sudo gedit yarn-site.Xml
# Paste these lines into<configuration>tag
```

```
<property>
<name>yarn.nodemanager.aux-services</name>
<value>mapreduce_shuffle</value>
</property>
<property>
<name>yarn.node manager.aux-services.mapreduce.shuffle-class</name>
<value. org.apache.hadoop.mapred.shuffle Handler</value>
</property>
# configure file : mapred-site.Xml
# copy template of mapred-site.Xml.template file
cp/usr/local/hadoop/etc/hadoop/mapred-site.Xml.template/usr/local/
hadoop/etc/hadoop/mapred—site.Xml
# To edit the file
hduser@ubuntu: /usr/local/hadoop/etc/hadoop $ Sudo gedit mapred-Sie.Xml
# Paste these lines into<configuration>tag
<property>
<name>mapreduce. framework.name</name>
<value>yarn</value>
</property>
cd..
cd..
hduser@ubuntu: /~$ Sudo chmod—R 777/usr/local/hadoop
# Format namenode
hduser@ubuntu: /~$ hdfs namenode—format
# Start hdfs daemons
hduser@ubuntu: /usr/local/hadoop $ start-dfs.sh
# start MapReduce daemons
hduser @ ubuntu: /usr/local/hadoop $ start-yarn.sh
```

Instead of the two above commands, we can also use start_all.sh, but that is now deprecated and so is not recommended to be used for better Hadoop operations.

```
# verify Hadoop daemons

hduser@ubuntu :jps
```

13.13.1 Hadoop 2.6.0 Installation in Fully Distributed Mode

Let us now install Hadoop 2.6.0 on Ubuntu in a cluster of three nodes: one master (NameNode) and two slave nodes (DataNodes).

The steps and listing are as follows:

1.0: Installing Oracle Java version 1.7.0_45 on all three machines (nodes):

```
: ~ $ Sudo apt-get update
$ Sudo add-apt-repository ppa: webupd8team/java
$ Sudo apt-get update
$ Sudo apt-get install oracle-jdk 7-installer # To check Java
version #
$ java-version
java version '1.7.0_45'
```

2.0: Add all host names to /etc/hosts directory in all three machines (master and two slaves):

```
: ~ $ Sudo getdit/etc/hosts
# Add following host names and their IP addresses
Big Data Analytics and Cloud Computing 447
# host table
192.168.2.10 Hadoop Master
192.168.2.11 Hadoop Slave 1
192.168.2.12 Hadoop Slave 2
```

3.0: Creating a Hadoop user for accessing HDFS and MapR:

```
# we shall Create hadoop as system group and
# hduser as system user in all the three nodes
: ~ $ Sudo addgroup hadoop
: ~ $ Sudo add user ——ingroup hadoop hduser
: ~ $ Sudo usermod—a—G
: ~ $ Sudo hduser
```

4.0: Download Hadoop. Let us download Hadoop 2.6.0 from apache mirror.gtcomm .net/hadoop/common/hadoop—2.6.0/hadoop–2.6.0 tar.gz

```
# issue wget command from shell hduser@Hadoop Master: ~$ Wget
http: //apache.mirror.gt comm.net/hadoop/common/hadoop—2.6.0/
hadoop—2.6.0. tar.gz
# unzip the file
: ~ $ Sudo tar —XZVf hadoop—2.6.0 tar.gz
# For ease of operation and maintenance let
# us rename the 'hadoop—2.6.0' directory to 'hadoop'
: ~ $ mv hadoop—2.6.0 hadoop
```

Repeat Step 4.0 for slave 1 and slave 2 also.

5.0: Verify SSH installation. If not, open SSH in the same way as we did for the single node Hadoop installation for the master and the two slave nodes.

6.0: Configuring password-less key-based logins on servers. After setting up SSH on every node, we have to use ssh-keygen on the master of the Hadoop Master node to generate the Rivest, Shamir, Adleman (RSA) key pair in order to enable the Hadoop Master node to communicate with the other nodes without any prompted password.

```
hd user @ Hadoop Master: ~$ Sudo hduser

hd user @ Hadoop Master: ~$ ssh-keygen -t rsa

# Generating public/private RSA key pair
```

Enter the file in which to save the key: (/home/hduser/.ssh/id_rsa)

Enter passphrase (empty for no passphrase):

Enter the same passphrase again:

```
#/home/hduser/.ssh/id_rsa
#/home/hduser/.ssh/id_rsa.pub (public key)
# Distribute public key and validate logins
```

Copy the public key to every slave node as well as the master node by secure copy (SCP)

```
hduser@Hadoop Master: $ scp ~/hduser/.ssh/id_rsa.pub
hduser@Hadoop Master: ~/hduser/master-key
hduser@Hadoop Master: ~ $ mkdir ~/hduser/.ssh
hduser@Hadoop Master: ~ $ chmod 700 ~/hduser/.ssh
hduser@Hadoop Master: ~ $ mv ~/hduser/master-key ~/hduser/-ssh/
authorized keys hduser@Hadoop Master: ~ $ chmod 600 ~/hduser/.ssh/
authorized-keys
# Secure copy public key to master key in slaves
hduser@Hadoop Master: ~ $ scp ~/hduser/.ssh/id_rsa.pub
hduser@Hadoop Slave 1
: ~/hduser/master-key
hduser@Hadoop Master: ~ $ scp ~/hduser/.ssh/id_rsa.pub
hduser@Hadoop slave 2: ~/hduser/master-key
```

Next, manually log in to slave nodes and set the master key as an authorised key and change the mode to 600 for the authorised key as done above in the case of Hadoop Master.

7.0: Setting up environment variable for hduser. Update the .bashrc file to add important Hadoop paths and directories.

Navigate to home directory hduser @ Hadoop Master: $ cd

```
# open.bashrc file in Vi editor
: ~ $ Vi. bashrc
# Add following at the end of file
export HADOOP_CONF=/home/hduser/hadoop/conf
export HADOOP_PREFIX=/home/hduser/hadoop
# set JAVA_HOME
export JAVA_HOME=/usr/lib/jvm/java–7-oracle
export PATH=$PATH: $ JAVA_HOME/bin
# Add Hadoop bin/directory to path
export PATH=$ PATH: $ HADOOP_PREFIX/bin export
PATH=$ PATH: $ HADOOP_PREFIX/S bin
```

Save and exit. Repeat 7.0 for the two slave machines (nodes).

8.0: Hadoop cluster configuration:

We have to configure the following:

- hadoop-env.sh (for JAVA_HOME)
- core-site.xml (key property fs.default.name for NameNode configuration)
- hdfs-site.Xml (key property-dfs.replication-by default it is 3)
- mapred-site.xml (for MapR framework which is YARN)
- yarn-site.Xml (for node manager and resource manager)

We will first start with the master (NameNode) and then copy the above XML changes to the two slave nodes.

```
# hadoop-env.sh
: $ vi $ HADOOP_CONF/hadoop-env.sh
export JAVA_HOME=/usr/lib/jvm/java–7-oracle
# Core-site. Xml
: $ Vi $ HADOOP_CONF/core-site Xml
```

We are going to add two properties:

1. fs. default.name will point to the NameNode URL and port (9000 usually)
2. hadoop.temp.dir—A base for other temporary directories. It is important to note that every node needs the hadoop.tmp directory. We shall create a new directory 'hdfstmp' as below in all three nodes.

```
: ~ cd
: ~ $ mkdir hdfs.tmp
<configuration>
<property>
<name>fs.default.name</name>
<value>hdfs://Hadoop Master: 9000</value>
</property>
<property>
<name>hadoop.temp.dir</name>
<value>/home/hduser/hdfstmp</value>
</property>
</configuration>
# hdfs-site.Xml on master
```

We are going to add the following properties:

1. dfs.permissions.enabled with value 'false'. If 'true' it means permission checking is enabled.
2. dfs.replication. The default value is 3 since we have two slave nodes; we will set the same to 2.
3. namenode.name directory and datanode.data directory.

```
<configuration>
<property>
<name>dfs. replication</name>
<value>2</value>
</property>
<property>
<name>dfs.permissions</name>
<value>false</value>
</property>
<property>
<name>dfs.namenode.name.dir</name>
```

```
<value>/home/hduser/hdfs_tmp/hdfs/namenode</value>
</property>
<property>
<name>dfs.datanode.data.dir</name>
<value>/home/hduser/hdfs_tmp/hdfs/datanode</value>
</property>
</configuration>
```

Open mapred-site.xml and replace configuration as follows:

```
<configuration>
<property>
<name>mapreduce.framework.name</name>
<value>yarn</value>
</property>
</configuration>
```

Next open and configure yarn-site.xml on Hadoop Master:

```
<configuration>
<property>
<name>yarn.node manager.aux-services</name>
<value>mapreduce_shuffle</value>
</property>
<property>
<name>yarn.node manager.aux-services.mapreduce_shuffle.class</name>
<value>org.apache.hadoop.mapred.shuffle Handler</value>
</property>
<property>
<name>yarn.resource manager.resource-tracker.address (/name)
<value>Hadoop Master: 8025</value>
</property>
<property>
<name>yarn.resourcemanager.scheduler.address</name>
<value>Hadoop Master :8030</value>
</property>
<property>
<name>yarn. resource manager.address</name>
<value>Hadoop Master :8033</value>
</property>
</configuration>
```

9.0: Move configuration files to slaves using scp. Start with Slave1 from Hadoop Master shell:

```
hduser@Hadoop Master :~/hd user/hadoop/conf$scp
hadoop-env.sh core-site.Xml hdfs-site.Xml mapred-site.Xml
yarn-site.Xml hduser@Hadoop Slave1 :/~hduser/hadoop/conf
```

Repeat the above SCP for slave 2 also.

10.0: Configure master and slaves. Every Hadoop distribution comes with master and slave files. By default, it contains one entry for the same files, and we have to edit these two files on both 'masters' (Hadoop Master) and 'slaves' (Hadoop slave 1 and Hadoop slave 2) machines as follows:

Edit/modify masters file on the master machine

$ Vi $HADOOP_CONF/masters

□ *masters*
Hadoop Master

Next edit/modify the slaves file in the master machine.

$ Vi $ HADOOP_CONF/Slaves

□ *Slaves*
Hadoop Master Hadoop Slave 1 Hadoop Slave 2

Next, configure the master and slaves on the 'slaves' node since we are configuring slaves (Hadoop Slave 1 and Hadoop Slave 2) and the masters file on the slave machine is going to be empty. We edit the 'slaves' file on slave server (Hadoop Slave 1).

$ Vi $ HADOOP_CONF/masters

$ Vi $ HADOOP_CONF/Slaves

□ *slaves x*
Hadoop Slave 1

Similarly update masters and slaves for Hadoop Slave 2.

11.0: Hadoop daemon setup. The first step for starting up the Hadoop installation is formatting the Hadoop file system, which runs on top of the local file system of our cluster. We need to do it the first time we set up a Hadoop installation. However, we must format a running Hadoop file system, which will cause all our data to be erased. We have to format the NameNode (only on the master machine). To format the NameNode, the command is as follows:

$ hadoop namenode-format

Let us now start all Hadoop daemons from the Hadoop NameNode:

$ cd $ HADOOP_CONF

$ start-all.sh

Next, we can check all the daemons running on both master and slave machines with the command: jps.

hduser@Hadoop Master: ~/hadoop/conf$ jps 16833 Node Manager 16116 Name Node 16582 Resource Manager 20784 jps 16431 Secondary Name Node 16255 Data Node hduser@Hadoop Master: ~/hadoop/conf$	**On master**
hduser@Hadoop Slave 1:~S jps 11816 jps 12211 Date Note 11977 Data Manager hduster@Hadoop Slave 1:~S jps	**On slave 1**
hduser@Hadoop Slave 2:~S jps 10815 Data Node 11210 jps 10976 Node Manager	**On Slave 2**

13.14 Ecosystems of Hadoop

Hadoop ecosystems run on HDFS and YARN. Each member of the ecosystems is in particular application-oriented. For example, 'Mahout' is one of the ecosystems of Hadoop and pertains to machine-learning applications based on HDFS and the Hadoop daemons. Figure 13.17 shows the major ecosystems of Hadoop.

We are already familiar with HDFS, YARN and MapR. Pig, often referred to as Pig Latin, has no revision or version. It is a scripting language having two major components.

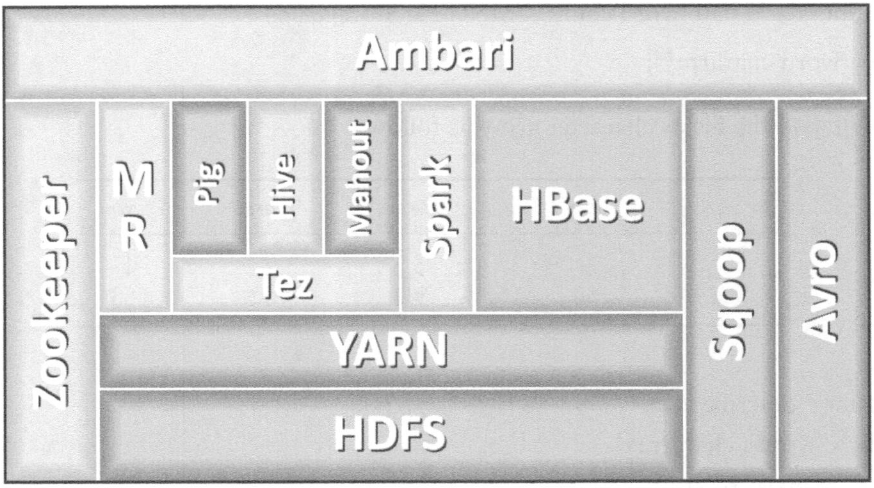

Figure 13.17 Major Ecosystems of Hadoop

One is a high-level data processing language and the other is a compiler that compiles and runs Pig Latin scripts in a choice of evaluation mechanism. Pig uses ETL tools and facilitates rapid development because of the ease of programming. It is considered a data-flow language. It should be used for structured or semi-structured data such as web logs, click streams and search platforms involving large data sets, time-sensitive data analysis such as weather data. However, Pig is generally not used for audio/video and human-readable text data. It can be run in two modes: (1) local mode and (2) Hadoop (MapR) mode. In order to run Pig in local mode, we need access to a single machine, and in order to run it on the Hadoop (MapR) mode, we need access to a Hadoop cluster and HDFS installation. The corresponding commands are:

1. Local mode:

   ```
   $>Pig-X local
   grunt>
   ```

2. Hadoop (MapR) mode on HDFS:

   ```
   $>Pig
   grunt>
   ```

Pig shell is the 'grunt' interactive shell. Pig-script files are saved with '.pig' extension. Pig scripts can be embedded into other scripts also. Pig Latin scripts usually consist of loading a file, identifying the fields in the tuple and the data types of the fields, then filtering or grouping the tuples based on given criteria and finally generating counts for the groups. In addition, it has two more functions, namely 'DUMP' and 'DESCRIBE'; the former prints the entire file or the computational output, while the latter describes the data types of the fields or computed fields. It may be mentioned that Pig assumes the default data type as byte array. The 'STORE' function is similar to 'DUMP' except that it dumps the file tuples as a separate file storage.

Example 1: Let 'word count' be a file containing—hi how are you.
Then,

```
grunt>abc=Load 'word count' USING Pig Storage (' ')
As (word chararray);
```

This will load the file as character array as follows:

abc ⇒	*hi,*	*how,*	*are,*	*you*
	↓ \$0	↓ \$1	↓ \$2	↓ \$3

```
grunt > describe abc;
abc : {word : chararray}
grunt > DUMP abc;
```

hi, how, are, you

grunt>STORE ABC INTO 'output',

grunt>DUMP 'output';

output, hi, how, are, you

In Pig, we have data models as follows:

Atom (is a single piece field or a datum)

Map

[Key # value]

Field = (Atom 1, Atom 2 ......)

↓

Tuple = (Field 1, Field 2 ......)

↓

Bag (Data bag represents a combination of tuples)

Atom is the basic datum for the Map function.
Example 2: Let us consider the following car data set as an example:

Id, car_name

01, Santro

02, Swift

03, Alto

A field is a piece of data such as car_name consisting of atoms which are Santro, Swift and Alto. A tuple is a set of fields such as (01, Santro). In the above example, there are three tuples. A bag is a collection of tuples. In the above example, Bag is {(01, Santro), (02, Swift), (03, Alto)}. A map is a set of key/value pairs. A key must be unique and be a string (chararray). The value can be of any type.

13.14.1 Pig Architecture

Pig Latin consists of the basic Pig script for which no Java codes are required. However, the core architecture of Pig is Java in the form of pig.jar class files. Finally, the execution plan consists of map, filter, reduce and count. Figure 13.18 shows the Pig architecture.

Figure 13.18 Pig Architecture

13.14.1.1 Sample Pig Scripts

It may be stated that Pig supports schemas in processing structured data, yet it is flexible enough to work with unstructured text or semi-structured XML data. Two sample Pig scripts with and without schema are illustrated as follows:

Without Schema	***With Schema***
grunt > A = load 'passwd' using Pig Storage (' : ');	grunt > A = LOAD 'student_data' AS (name:chararray,age:int,gpa:float);
> B = foreach A generate $ 0 as id;	> B = FOR EACH A GENERATE myudfs. UPPER (name);
> store B into 'id.out';	

Word count using Pig Latin script:

```
grunt > a = Load '/user/file path';
> b = foreach a generate flatten (TOKENIZE (chararry)
($0)) as word;
> c = group b by $0;
> d = foreach c generate count (b), group;
> dump d
```

The function flatten (TOKENIZE ((char array) $0)) as word, arranges hi how are you
as (hi)
(how) hi, {hi.}
⇒ how, {how…} as data bags
(are) are, {are.}
(you) you, {you.}
↓
$0
d: (hi, 1)
(how, 1)
(are, 1)
(you, 1)

Table 13.2 Atomic Data Types in Pig Latin

Int	signed 32-bit integer
Long	signed 64-bit integer
Float	32-bit floating point
Double	64-bit floating point
Charray	character array (string)
bytearray	Byte array (binary object)

Pig atomic data can be of various types as shown in Table 13.2 above. Pig allows use of expressions and functions to data fields to compute various values. It has two types of functions—built-in and UDF. Built-in functions are 'AVG' for calculating average, 'MAX', 'MIN', 'SUM' for finding the maximum, minimum value in a single column bag of numeric or array type and sum of numeric values in a single column bag and many similar built-in functions.

The UDF are always written in Java and packaged in jar files. In order to use a particular UDF's class file, Pig supports two main categories of UDFs: eval and load/store. We use load/store functions only in LOAD and STORE statements to help Pig read and write special formats. Most UDFs are eval functions that take one field value and return another field value. In order to create an eval UDF, we make a Java class that extends the abstract Eval Func <T> class. It has only one abstract method that we need to implement, for example, abstract public T exec (tuple input) throws IOException. This method is called on each tuple in a relation, where each tuple is represented by a tuple object. The exec() method processes the tuple and returns a type T corresponding to a valid Pig Latin type. T can be any one of the Java classes listed in Table 13.3, some of which are native Java classes, and some are Pig extensions.

13.14.1.2 Relational Operators

The most salient characteristic of Pig Latin is its relational operators which make Pig Latin a data processing language. Some of the common relational operators are 'UNION', 'SPLIT', 'FILTER', 'FOREACH', 'JOIN', 'GROUP', 'ORDER' and so on. A few illustrative examples of use of relational operators in Pig are as follows:

Table 13.3 Pig Latin Types and Their Equivalent Java Class

Pig Latin Type	*Java Class*
bytearray	Data byte array
charray	string
Int	Integer
Long	Long
Float	Float
double	Double
tuple	Tuple
bag	Data bag
map	Map < object, object >

```
grunt>x=load 'A' using Pig Storage (', ') as (x1 : int,
x2 :int, x3 :int); grunt>y=load 'B' using Pig storage
(', ') as (y1 : int, y2 int, y3 :int), grunt>DUMP x;
(1, 2, 3)
(4, 5, 6)
grunt > DUMP y;
(7, 8, 9)
(1, 3, 5)
grunt>C=UNION x, y;
grunt>DUMP C;
(1, 2, 3)
(4, 5, 6)
(7, 8, 9)
(1, 3, 5)
grunt>SPLIT C INTO d IF $0==4, e IF $0==1;
grunt>DUMP d;
(4, 5, 6)
grunt>DUMP e;
(1, 2, 3)
(1, 3, 5)
```

One important application of Pig Latin is in the analysis of stock data relating to stock exchange trading of listed shares of various companies. The data volume is huge and streaming in nature. Figure 13.19 shows a (.CSV) file containing data related to daily opening, maximum, minimum, closing price and the total number of shares traded for various groups of companies in the National Stock Exchange.

The file was analysed to find the annual average opening price of the companies, namely ABB, HCL, NTTM, ABCSE, GARTNER and HOST.GTR using Pig Latin script

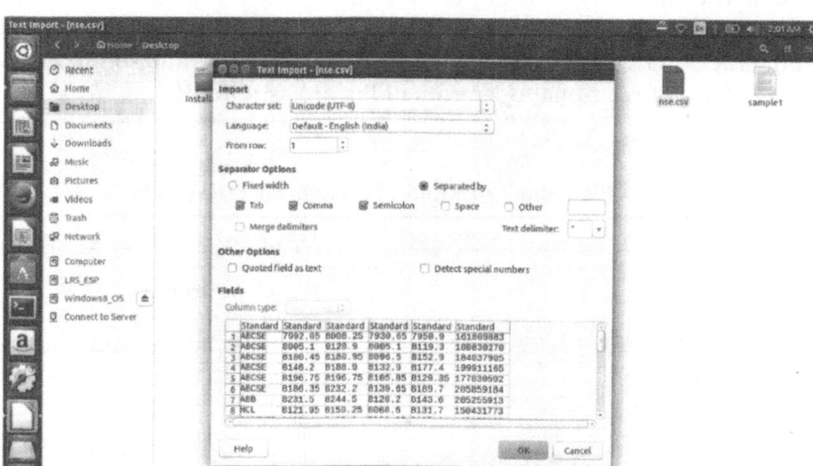

Figure 13.19 Company-wise Daily Share Transaction Values Traded in National Stock

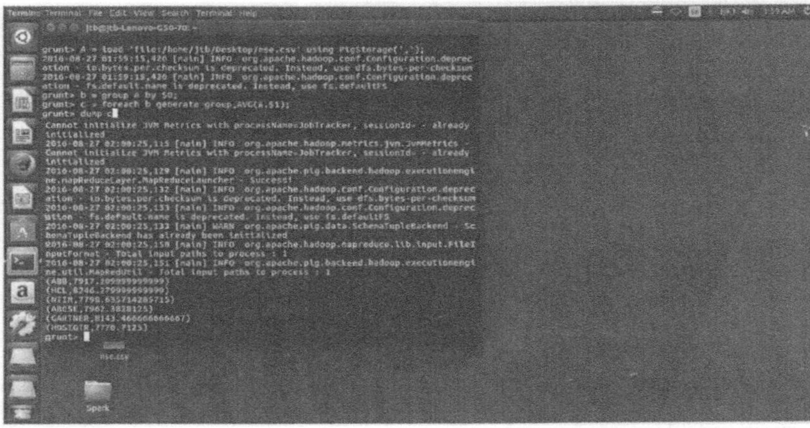

Figure 13.20 Pig Latin Script for Generating Average Value of Opening Stock Price and the Result Dumped on Terminal

as shown in Figure 13.20. The result has been dumped on the terminal shown in the same figure such as (ABB, 7917.2099) and (H CL, 8426.27999...).

13.14.2 Hive

Hive is a SQL-like data warehouse infrastructure tool that is built on Hadoop to process structured data. It was developed by Facebook to suit non-Java programmers and its query language, known as Hive QL or HQL, facilitates querying and analysis with big data. The target users of Hive are data analysts who are comfortable with SQL. We interact with Hive by issuing

queries in a SQL-like language, the HQL. For example, a query to get all active users from a user table looks as follows:

```
INSERT OVERWRITE TABLE user_active
SELECT user.*
FROM user
WHERE user.active=1;
```

Hive also uses familiar concepts from RDBMS such as rows, columns, tables and schema to facilitate learning Hive. Further, in order to improve upon query performance, Hive can use directory structures. Another important feature of Hive is its 'meta-store' which stores schema information. The meta-store resides in a relational database. The architecture of Hive on Hadoop is shown in Figure 13.21.

We can interact with Hive using several methods as shown in Figure 13.21 such as Web, GUI, Java database connectivity (JDBC) and command line interface (CLI). However, major interactions take place over a CLI. Hive stores metadata in a standard relational database, which in case of a multi-user environment uses a shared SQL database such as MySQL, Postgre SQL and Oracle, although any JDBC compliant database will also do.

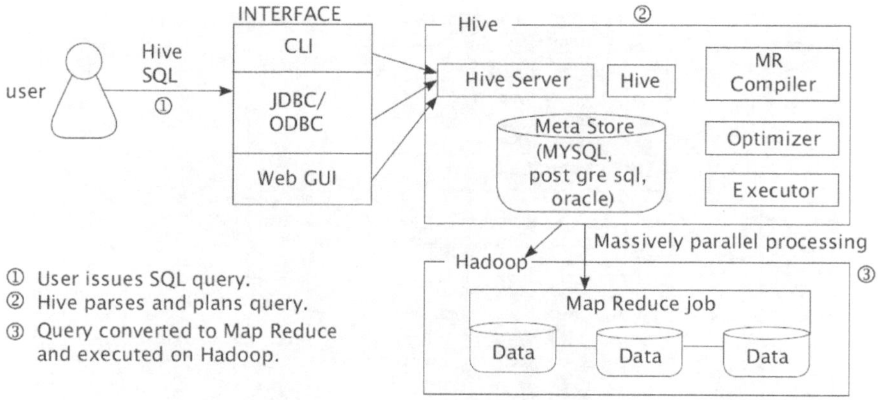

Figure 13.21 Hive Architecture

13.14.2.1 Hive Data Types

Hive supports the following simple data types:

TINYINT: 1-byte signed integer, for example, 100

SMALLINT: 2-byte signed integer, for example, 100, 100

INT: 4-byte signed integer, for example, 100, 1000, 5000

BIGINT: 8-byte signed integer, for example 100, 1000, 10^{10}

FLOAT: 4-byte single-precision floating point, for example, 1500.00

DOUBLE: 8-byte double-precision floating point, for example, 750000.00

DECIMAL: 17-bytes precision up to 38 digits, for example, DECIMAL (5, 2)

STRING: Sequence of characters, for example, 'Welcome to Hive'

VARCHAR: Maximum length allowed is 65355 bytes. Similar to SQL's

VARCHAR, for example, 'Welcome to Hive'

CHAR: Similar to SQL's CHAR with fixed length. Value shorter than fixed length (of 255 bytes) is padded with spaces, for example, 'Welcome to Hive'

DATE: Values are represented in YYYY-MM-DD format, for example, '2017–04–08'

TIMESTAMP: yyyy-mm-dd hh:mm:ss

In addition to the above data types, Hive also supports complex or collection data types, which, unlike the simple data types, are not available in many relational DBMS. Complex types are built up from simple types and other composite types. Hive currently supports four complex data types, namely array, map, struct and union.

Array is an ordered sequence of similar type elements which are indexable using zero-based integers. For example, array ('Ram', 'Lakshman', 'Sita'). The second element can be accessed with array {1}.

MAP is a collection of key-value pairs. Fields are accessed using array notation of keys.

Example: 'first'→'Ram', 'last'→'Sita' is represented as map ('first', 'Ram', 'last', 'sita'). Now 'Sita' can be accessed with map {'last'}.

Struct is similar to STRUCT in C language. It is a record type which encapsulates a set of named fields of simple data type. Elements in STRUCT type are accessed using the dot (.) notation.

Example: For a column C of type STRUCT {a INT; b INT}, the 'a' field is accessed by the expression 'c . a'

Union Type is similar to unions in C. At any point in time, a union type can hold any one data type from its specified data types.

Example:

CREATE TABLE test (Col 1 UNIONTYPE<INT, DOUBLE, ARRAY<VARCHAR>,

STRUCT<a: INT, b. CHAR>>);

Then retrieving results from Column 1 of test table can be any one of the following:

SELECT col 1 FROM test;

{0: 1}//Matching INT types

{1: 10.0}//Matching DOUBLE types

{2: {'MY' 'SQL'}}//Matching ARRAY with VARCHAR type

The difference between traditional relational databases and Hive lies in the feature that in the case of the former, insert, delete and update of data in a table take place one at a time, whereas in the case of the latter (Hive), bulk insert, delete and update are possible. For example, we can drop a whole table at a time using Hive.

13.14.2.2 Hive Tables

Hive deals with two types of data tables, namely the managed or internal tables and the external tables.

In case of an internal table, the schema (table metadata) as well as the data of the table both reside inside the warehouse directory of Hive. If the table is dropped, then the table metadata as well as the data will be deleted. In case of an external table, the data of the table reside on HDFS or the local file system and the metadata is only stored in the Hive meta-store. If the external table is dropped, then only the metadata is deleted in Hive, whereas the table data remain intact on HDFS or the local File system. Figure 13.22 shows the difference between an internal and external employee table in case of Hive.

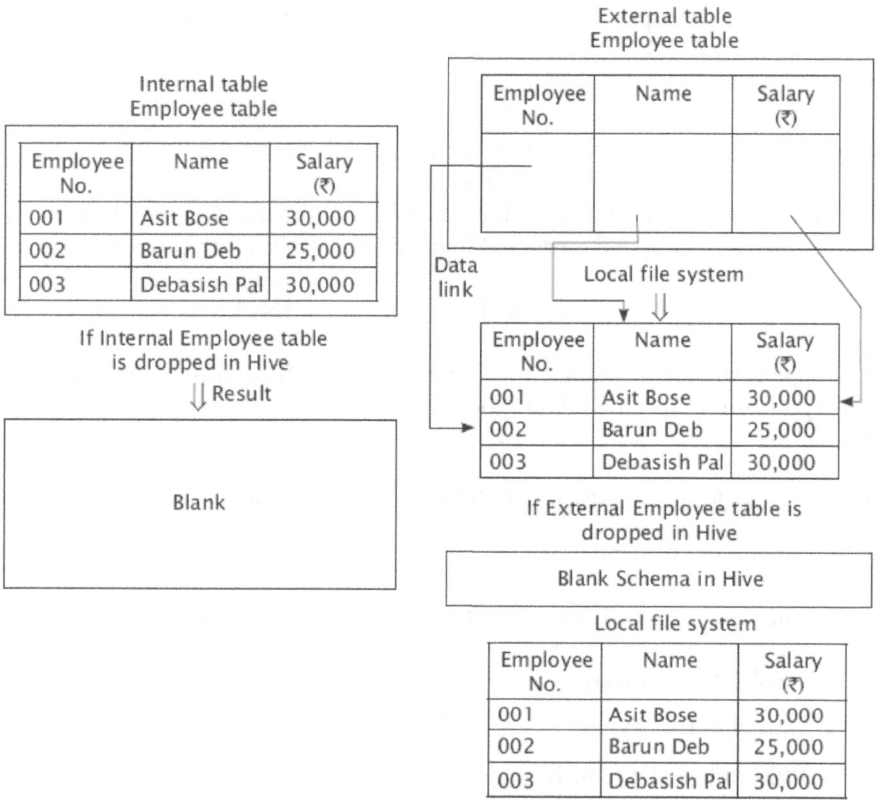

Figure 13.22 Difference between Hive Internal and Hive External Tables

13.14.2.3 Partitioning and Bucketing in Hive

A Hive table can be partitioned to slice the data in the table horizontally using one or more columns either for the entire range or a smaller range of values. It may be mentioned that Hive physically stores tables as directories under the path /user/Hive/warehouse. For example, if we create a student table for a 3-year degree college for year (1st, 2nd and 3rd), stream (Science, Arts and Commerce) and name of the students as the three columns, the data will be stored under the /user/Hive/warehouse/students directory. If we partition the same student table on two columns year and stream, the table will have each partition as a directory and the structure of the table will be as follows:

/user/Hive/warehouse/students/year=1ST/stream=Science
/user/Hive/warehouse/students/year=1ST/stream=Arts
/user/Hive/warehouse/students/year=1ST/stream=Commerce
——

/user/Hive/warehouse/students/year=2ND/stream=Science
/user/Hive/warehouse/students/year=2ND/stream=Arts
/user/Hive/warehouse/students/year=2ND/stream=Commerce

——

/user/Hive/warehouse/students/year=3RD/stream=Science
/user/Hive/warehouse/students/year=3RD/stream=Arts
/user/Hive/warehouse/students/year=3RD/stream=Commerce

All student names for the science stream of the 1st year will reside in one directory and similarly, data for other partitions will reside in other directories. There will be $3 \times 3 = 9$ directories corresponding to 9 partitions.

It may be stated that partitioning reduces query time since, depending upon a query, Hive has to search a particular partition and not the entire data table of students. In addition to partitioning, Hive data tables adopt a concept of buckets, which provide efficient query handling in a random sample of data.

Bucketing divides data into a specified number of files based on a hash algorithm of the bucket column.

For example, in the above students table, if we specify four buckets based on student names, the student names appearing in each partition under a directory will be stored in four buckets (each bucket being a file) depending on the hash algorithm, like all student names beginning with, say, letters A–F in one bucket, G–M in the second bucket and so on. In order to search for a particular student name beginning with, say, the letter C in the 1st year Science stream, Hive has to search the first bucket in the partition directory of the 1st year Science stream and not search the other buckets, improving query handling efficiency greatly. The full directory and file structure of the student table will look as follows:

Partition Directory→/user/Hive/warehouse/students/year=1ST/stream = Science

Name	*Type*	*Size*	*Replication*	*Block Size*	*Permission*	*Owner*	*Group*
000000–0	file	0.02 KB	1	64 MB	rw-r--r-	root	Super Group
000001–0	file	0.03 KB	1	64 MB	rw-r--r-	root	Super Group
000002–0	file	0.04 KB	1	64 MB	rw-r--r-	root	Super Group
000003–0	file	0.03 KB	1	64 MB	rw-r--r-	root	Super Group

The above partition contains 4 buckets (files)

Partition Directory→/user/Hive/warehouse/students/year=1ST/stream = Arts

Name	*Type*	*Size*	*Replication*	*Block Size*	*Permission*	*Owner*	*Group*
000000–0	file	0.03 KB	1	64 MB	rw-r--r-	root	Super Group
000001–0	file	0.04 KB	1	64 MB	rw-r--r-	root	Super Group
000002–0	file	0.02 KB	1	64 MB	rw-r--r-	root	Super Group
000003–0	file	0.02 KB	1	64 MB	rw-r--r-	root	Super Group

Each file representing a bucket contains the names of students as per hash.

As we know, the number of reduce tasks determines the number of output files. So, in the above example, we have defined the table as four buckets and accordingly, the number of reduce tasks is four, as highlighted above.

Examples of Hive queries:

Let us see a few Hive queries from CLI. We assume we have the employee data Emp.t xt on our local machine and it is a comma-separated data set of employees. In Hive, we first define a table that will store the data:

```
Hive > Create Table Emp (id INT, name STRING, sal FLOAT)
> Row format delimited
> fields terminated by ','
> stored as text file;
OK
Time taken: 0.246 second
```

It may be noted that HQL statements are terminated by semicolons. If we want to see the tables available with Hive, the command is:

```
Hive > show tables;
OK
Emp
Time taken: 0.053 second
Hive > describe Emp;
OK
id int
name string
sal float
Time taken: 0.13 second
Let us now load the employee data from Emp.txt into the Emp table on Hive.
Hive > Load data local inpath 'Emp.txt'
> overwrite into table Emp;
copying data from file: /root/Emp.txt
Loading data to table Emp
OK
Time taken: 9.52 seconds
```

The above command tells Hive to load data from a file called Emp.txt in the local file system into the Emp table. Underneath the hood, the local machine uploads this data into HDFS under some directory managed by Hive under /user/Hive/warehouse.

The command, if we transfer data from HDFS to the Hive table, will be, however, as follows:

```
Hive > Load data inpath 'Emp.txt'
> Overwrite into table Emp;
```

It may be stated that while loading data, Hive will not load any data into a table that violates its schema. In place of such data, Hive will substitute a null. For example, if we have the column names in the Emp.txt as the first line and then we use the SELECT command to list data from the Emp table, the result will be as follows:

Hive > SELECT * from Emp limit 5;

OK

Null	*Name*	*Null*
001	A. K. Bose	50000
002	C. Prasad	25000
003	J. K. Lahiri	30000
004	S. K. Singh	40000

The lines after the CREATE TABLE command instruct Hive how the data are stored as a text file and how the data should be parsed; that is, each line of data is stored in a row and the fields are separated by commas.

A table can be deleted or dropped by the DROP TABLE command:

```
Hive > DROP TABLE Emp;
OK
Time taken: 0.34 second
```

To terminate the Hive session, we use the exit command.

Some more Hive commands:

```
Hive > create database if not exists emp_table;
OK
Hive > create Schema emp_table;
Hive > Drop database if exists emp_table;
Hive > drop schema emp_table;
Hive > create table if not exists Emp_table (id int, name string,
Sal float)
> row format delimited
> lines terminated by ' n'
> fields terminated by ' t'
> Stored as text file;
```

13.14.2.4 Commands in Hive for Managing Tables

Complicated tables can be created part by part using commands such as page_view followed by partitioning and bucketing as described earlier.

```
Hive > Create Table page_view (Empid int,
Name string, Sex string, Sal float)
Comment 'This is the page-view Table' partitioned by (joinyr
string, Dept string
Clustered by (Empid) into 32 Buckets Row Format Delimited
```

Fields terminated by ' t'

Lines terminated by ' n'

Stored as Sequence File;

The first part of the above commands specifies the name of the table (page_view) and its schema, which includes the name of the columns as well as their types.

The next part of the CREATE TABLE statement specifies the partition columns: joinyr and Dept, which are both string types. The partition columns are distinct from the data columns of Empid, Name, Sex and Sal. The value of a partition column for a particular row is not explicitly stored with the row; it is implied from the directory path. The last part: clustered by (Empid) into 32 buckets specifies the number of buckets based on the column (Empid) from which random samples will be taken and the number of buckets which depend upon (1) the size of data under each partition and (2) the size of the sample we intend to use.

13.14.2.5 Word Count Using Hive Command

Figure 13.23 shows the Hive command for word count.

Hive > SELECT word, COUNT(*) FROM doc LATERAL VIEW explode (split

(text, ' ')) ltable as word GROUP By word;

which was run to count words from table doc which was created and loaded from a local file system abc shown in Figure 13.24 using following Hive commands:

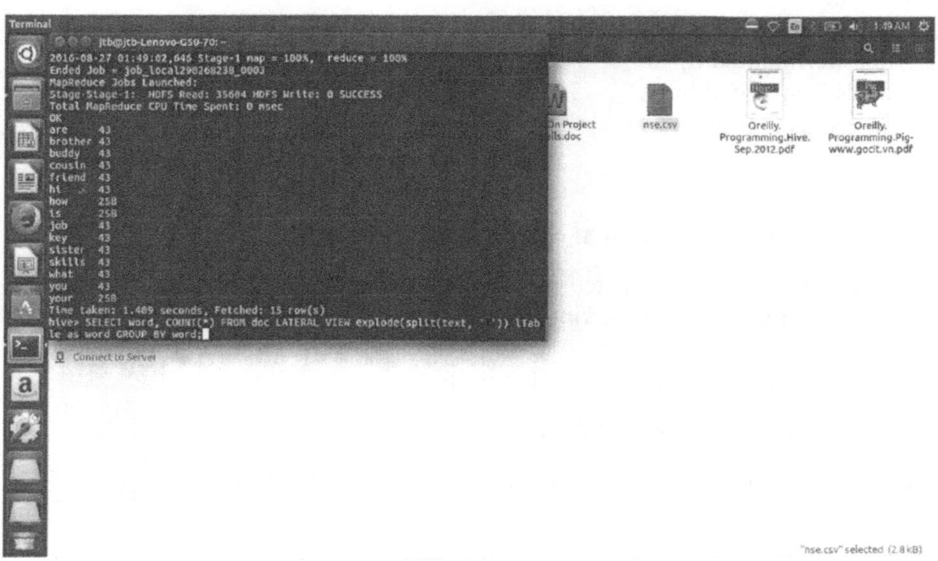

Figure 13.23 Hive Command for Word Count from Table Doc

Figure 13.24 Local File 'abc' Created for Word Count with Hive Command

Hive > CREATE TABLE doc (text string) row format delimited fields

terminated by ' n' stored as text file;

OK

Hive > Load data local inpath '/home/jtb/Desktop/word count/abc'

overwrite into Table doc;

Ok

13.14.3 Sqoop

Sqoop is a tool designed for seamless import or export of bulk data between Hadoop or HDFS or related Hadoop ecosystem (Hive, HBase and so on) and external data stores such as relational databases or enterprise data warehouses. Sqoop (SQL + Hadoop) works with relational databases such as MySQL, PostgreSQL, Oracle and Teradata.

We can import/export all the tables in a database or part of a table or part of a database using Sqoop. It may be stated that Sqoop uses MapR framework to import or export the data, which provides a parallel mechanism as well as fault tolerance. Sqoop allows CLI for developers who just have to provide information regarding source, destination and database authentication details in the Sqoop commands and Sqoop takes care of other details. Sqoop commands of the end users are parsed by Sqoop, which launches Hadoop map task to import or export data. Figure 13.25 shows the architecture of Sqoop on Hadoop.

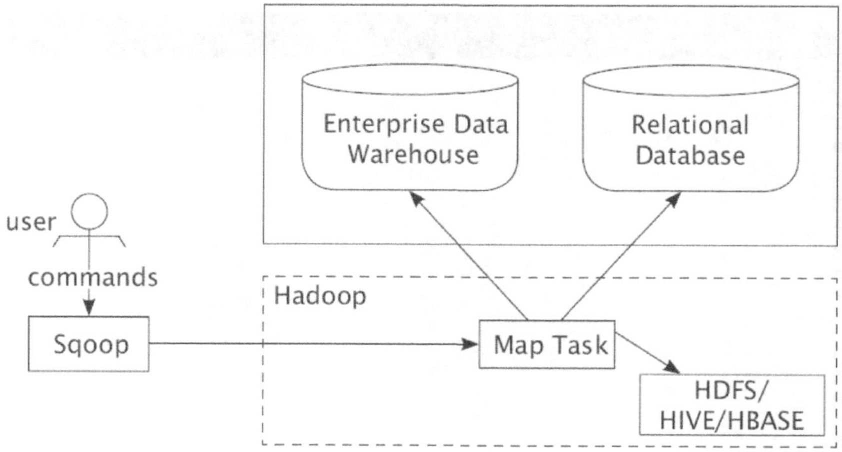

Figure 13.25 Sqoop Architecture

13.14.3.1 Basic Sqoop Commands and Syntax

1. Importing a table into HDFS.

Syntax:

> $ Sqoop import—connect jdbc: mysql: //<host name>: port No./
> — table<table name>—username<username>
> — password<password>— fields terminated by ' t'—target-dir<target
> directory> ↵

The above Sqoop command takes JDBC URL and connects to the database.

Database host should not be used as 'local host' as Sqoop launches mappers on multiple datanodes and the mapper will not be able to connect to the DB host. '—target-dir' is the specified directory to which data is imported. The default port number is usually 80.

2. Importing part of a table.

Syntax:

> $ Sqoop import—connect jdbc: my sql//<host name>.port No./
> — table<table name>—username—password
> — fields-terminated by 't'—columns 'id,
> name, salary'—where 'salary>15000' ↵

Here, '—columns' selects subset columns and '—where' retrieves the data, which satisfies the condition (in the above case salary > 15000). '—password' parameter is insecure as anyone can read it from the command line. '-p' option can be used in lieu, which prompts for password in console.

3. Importing all tables in an RDBMS database to HDFS: In this case, data from each table is stored in a separate directory in HDFS syntax:

```
$ Sqoop-import-all-tables—connect jdbc: my sql: //<host name>port
No./<database
name>— username<username>
— password<password>
— fields terminated by ' t' ↵
```

In order to use 'Sqoop-import-all-tables' command, the following conditions need to be fulfilled:

   (i) Each table should have a single column primary key.
   (ii) All columns of each table have to be imported.
   (iii) No splitting of any column or any check condition using 'where' clause is allowed.

4. Exporting data from HDFS directory back to RDBMS table: The target table should already exist in the database.

Syntax:

```
$ Sqoop-export
$>—connect jdbc: mySql://<host name>: port No./<database name>—username
<username>
— password<password>
$>—table<table name>—input-fields-terminated-by '/t'
$>—export-dir<HDFS directory path> ↵
```

The Sqoop-export command prepares INSERT statements with sets of input data, then hits the database. If the table has unique value constant with primary key, export fails as the insert statement fails. Thus, it is for exporting new records only.

5. Listing all databases available on RDBMS server:

Syntax:

```
$>Sqoop list-databases—connect jdbc: my sql: //<host name>port no/
— username<username>
—password<password> ↵
```

6. Listing all tables in a specified database:

Syntax:

```
$ Sqoop list-tables
— connect jdbc: my sql: //<host name>: port no./database name/$
— username<username>—password<password> ↵
```

If the above command is executed successfully, then it will display the list of tables in the specified database.

13.14.4 HBase and Zookeeper

In Chapter 10, we have seen HBase as a column-oriented NoSQL database capable of handling and processing a large volume of tables having millions of rows and columns speedily. We also know about the HBase data model consisting of rows, columns, column families and row keys as the primary keys.

In the subsequent paragraphs of this chapter, let us see how the HBase architecture falls in line with its data model and makes it capable of large storage of data together with high processing speed. HBase has got a master–slave architecture consisting of H Master, HBase region servers (slaves), Zookeeper and the combination runs on Hadoop. Before we go through the details of the above components of HBase including their functions, the total HBase architecture is shown in Figure 13.26.

H Master is responsible for the following actions:

1. Coordinating with the region servers for assigning regions (portion of the whole HBase table) at the start and thereafter reassigning regions for recovery or load balancing.
2. Interfacing with regions for creating, deleting and updating tables.

In short, Region assignment and DDL (create, delete tables) operations are the main functions handled by H Master.

Region servers serve data mainly for reads and writes. Clients communicate with HBase region servers directly for accessing data. Region servers consist of regions which are obtained by partitioning the HBase tables horizontally according to row key range. For example, an HBase table having 10,000 rows can be divided into five regions having rows from 1–2000 | 2001–4000 | 4001–6000 | 6001–8000 | 8001–10000 |. Each region is identified by the starting row key and the end key as shown below.

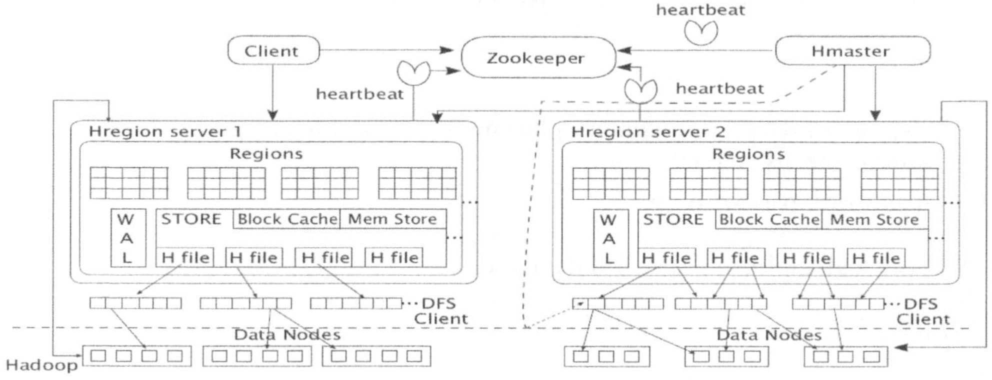

Figure 13.26 H Base Architecture

	Key	*Column A*	*Column B*
Start key →	XXX	Value	Value
	XXX	Value	Value
End key →	XXX	Value	Value

REGION

A region server can serve up to about 1,000 regions and runs on an HDFS DataNode which stores the data managed by the region server. Partitioning the HBase table into regions and putting the data of the regions into region servers enables handling huge data at a fast speed. Region servers perform write, read and other HBase operations with the help of their components as follows:

1. **Write Ahead Log (WAL)**: It is a file on the HDFS and is used to store new data before putting the same into permanent storage. It is basically used for data recovery in case of failure of a region server.
2. **Block Cache**: Block cache is the read cache. It stores frequently read data in memory. Least Recently Used (LRU) data are evicted when the block cache gets full.
3. **Mem Store**: This is the write cache which stores new data which has not been written to disk. It is sorted row key-wise, and there is one Mem Store per column family per region. The Mem Store stores updates in memory as sorted key value per column family with the version (time stamp) of each particular update. When the Mem Store accumulates enough data, the entire sorted set is written to a new H File in HDFS and the Mem Store is flushed. HBase uses multiple H Files per column family which contain the actual cells or key value instances. When the Mem Store is flushed into H File, the last written sequence number is also saved in H File metadata so that the system knows what persisted till the time the flushing took place. The Mem Store writes the sorted set of key-values into a new block of H Files on HDFS sequentially and very quickly.
4. **H Files**: H Files store the rows as sorted key values on disk.

Zookeeper provides the coordination service in HBase. HBase uses Zookeeper, which maintains server state in the cluster. Zookeeper maintains the state of servers (H Master as well as region servers) as alive and available and provides server failure notification. The Zookeeper maintains ephemeral nodes for active sessions through heartbeats as shown in Figure 13.26. Zookeeper also has another important function of holding the location of a meta table, which in turn, contains the location of regions in the cluster of region servers.

13.14.4.1 Functioning of the HBase Components Together

Region servers and the active H Master connect themselves in a session to Zookeeper. Each Region server creates an ephemeral node and the H Master monitors these nodes to find out the available region servers. H Master also monitors the failed server nodes. H Masters also create ephemeral nodes and

Zookeeper finds the first one and uses the same to make sure that only one master is active at a time. If at any time, either the active H Master or any region server fails to send a heartbeat, the session is terminated and the corresponding ephemeral node is deleted.

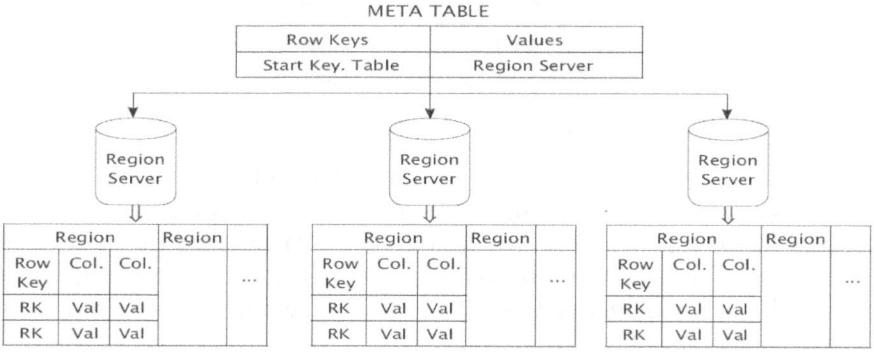

Figure 13.27 Meta Table in H Base

13.14.4.2 HBase Search Mechanism

In order to facilitate the search of a particular row key and the corresponding region, HBase has a special catalogue table, the meta table. It maintains the list of start keys of the regions with its ID and the corresponding region server value, which is the path of the same region server. The meta table is shown in Figure 13.27.

For a first-time read or write operation, the client gets the region server that hosts the meta table from the zookeeper. Next, the client finds from the meta table server the particular region server corresponding to the row key the client wishes to access. The client caches this information along with the meta table location. Then the client gets the desired row from the corresponding region server and the region.

13.14.4.3 HBase Write Mechanism

The client willing to write data on HBase first writes it to the WAL. Once the data have been written on WAL, the same is copied from WAL to Mem Store. After the data have been fully copied to Mem Store, WAL sends an ACK to the client. The Mem Store always updates the data stored in it sequentially as sorted key values for each column family. When the Mem Store becomes full or reaches its threshold, it dumps all the data in a new H File in a sorted manner and saves the data on HDFS. Figure 13.28 shows the write mechanism as explained above.

13.14.4.4 HBase Read Mechanism

A H File has got a multi-layered index which allows HBase to seek and read the desired data without reading the whole file. The index is loaded when the HFile is opened and kept in memory in order to facilitate look ups to be performed with a single seek.

We can see that the key value cells corresponding to a row can be in multiple locations such as H Files for saved row cells, Mem Store for recently written (updated) cells and block cache. Therefore, HBase reads data and merges the same in the following steps:

1. First, it looks for the row key-value cells in the block cache.
2. Next, it looks for the row cells in the Mem Store.

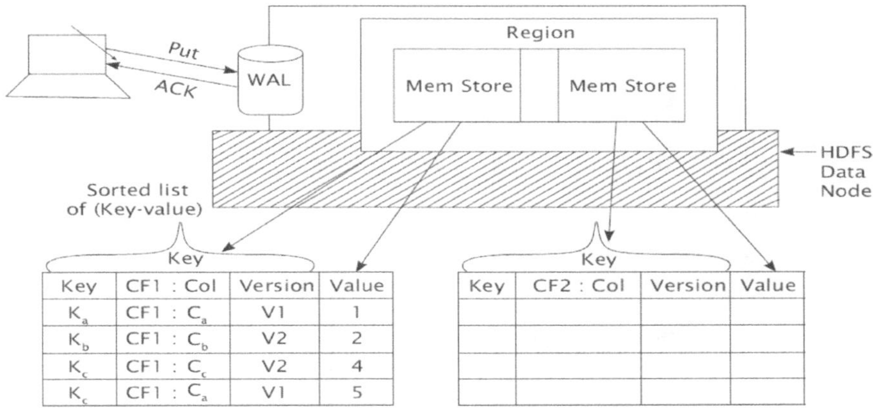

Figure 13.28 Write Mechanism in H Base

3. If all row cells are not found in Mem Store or block cache, HBase read-merge operation will look for row cells in H Files. However, as discussed earlier, there may be many H Files per Mem Store which implies for a read, multiple H Files may be required to be looked into which is known as read amplification in HBase.

Besides the above, HBase performs other operations such as major and minor compaction, region split, read-load balancing, data replication and crash recovery. We have already become familiar with several ecosystems of Hadoop such as MapR, Zookeeper, Pig, Hive, HBase, Sqoop, Yarn and HDFS. However, there are some more ecosystems of Hadoop such as Mahout, Tez, Avro and Ambari as shown in Figure 13.18. A brief introduction for each of these ecosystems of Hadoop has been given below.

Mahout: It is an open-source project mainly used for developing scalable machine-learning algorithms. Mahout runs on top of Hadoop.

Tez: It acts as an interface between applications such as Pig (scripting) and Hive (SQL) and Yarn to reduce operations and complexity of backend processing. Tez reduces or saves on MapR or hard-disk operations. It provides a 'service' which always attempts to decrease start times of jobs. Tez also allows caching of data in memory.

Avro: It is a serialisation framework developed within Apache's Hadoop. Its primary use is in providing a serialisation format for persistent data. Avro facilitates conversion of unstructured and semi-structured data into structured way using schemas.

Spark: It is a separate and fast MapR such as engine for very fast iterative queries. Spark is up to 40 times faster than Hadoop. Spark can also read from/write to any Hadoop supported system such as HDFS, HBase and sequential files.

13.15 Cloud Computing

The practice of using a network of remote servers hosted on the Internet to store, manage, process and retrieve data, rather than a single local server or a personal computer, is known as cloud computing. It is a model for enabling ubiquitous and on-demand access

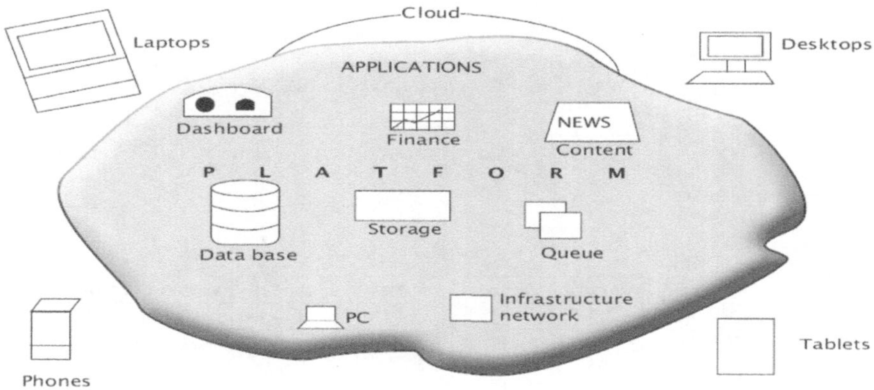

Figure 13.29 Cloud Computing

to a shared pool of configurable computing resources such as computer networks, servers, storage devices, applications and services, which can be provisioned and released with least management effort. The term cloud computing is a metaphor because to a user of cloud computing, the elements providing the computing services remain invisible or obscured like a cloud as shown in Figure 13.29.

Cloud computing has an inherent advantage of resource sharing to achieve coherence and economy of scale. It enables companies to lay emphasis on their core business instead of developing in-house elaborate IT infrastructure. Moreover, cloud marketers allow users to pay according to their requirements for computational facilities.

13.15.1 History of Development of Cloud Computing

Cloud computing came into existence in 2000. In August 2006, Amazon introduced the Elastic Computing Cloud (ECC). In early 2008, NASA introduced 'open Nebula', the first open-source software deploying private and hybrid clouds. Simultaneously, efforts were made to provide quality service to cloud-based infrastructures to facilitate real-time interactive applications. In July 2010, Rackspace Hosting and NASA jointly launched an open-source cloud software known as 'OpenStack'. The project was intended for organisations offering cloud computing services running on standard hardware.

Thereafter in March 2011, IBM announced its 'SmartCloud' framework to support cloud computing. On 7 June 2012, Oracle announced the 'Oracle Cloud', which is supposed to be the first to provide users access to an integrated set of IT solutions under the cloud layers of applications—software, platform and infrastructure. In May 2012, Google released 'Google Compute Engine' in preview before being rolled out into full-fledged general availability in December 2013.

13.15.2 Service Models of Cloud Computing

Cloud-computing service providers offer their services according to different models. Three such standard models, as per the National Institute of Standards and Technology

(NIST) of the USA, are (1) software as a service (SaaS), (2) platform as a service (PaaS) and (3) infrastructure as a service (IaaS).

NIST defined the above service models as follows:

Software as a Service (SaaS): The service provider's applications are accessible to the users through a client interface such as a web browser or a program interface. The user does not manage or control the underlying cloud infrastructure such as network, servers, storage devices and even the individual application capabilities. SaaS is sometimes referred to as 'on-demand software' and usually priced on a pay-per-use basis or a subscription fee per user per month or year.

Platform as a Service (PaaS): The service provided to the user is to deploy onto the cloud infrastructure user-created or acquired applications developed using programming languages, libraries, services and tools supported by the cloud-service provider. The user has control over the deployed applications, including possibly configuration settings for the application-hosting environment only. However, the user does not have any control over the cloud infrastructure including network servers, operating system or storage. PaaS vendors offer application developers a development environment.

Infrastructure as a Service (IaaS): The capability provided to the user is to provide processing, storage, networks and other fundamental computing resources using which the user can deploy or run arbitrary software such as OS and applications. In the IaaS model, the user does not control the underlying cloud infrastructure except for limited control over some networking components such as host firewalls. IaaS is the most basic cloud service model providing computing infrastructure such as virtual machines and other resources. Pools of hypervisors run the virtual machines with an ability to scale services up and down according to users' varying requirements. The cloud-computing service models are shown in Figure 13.30 as layers in a stack, but they are not related.

Besides the above three types of service models, there is a mobile 'backend' as a service (MBaaS), also known as backend as a service (BasS). In this service model, web application and mobile application developers link their applications to cloud storage and cloud computing services with APIs pertaining to their applications and software development

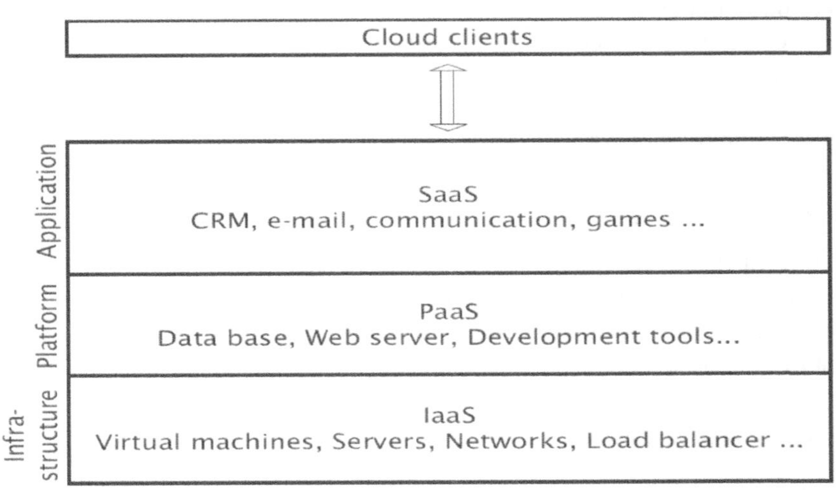

Figure 13.30 Cloud Computing Service Models

kits. BaaS includes many services such as client management and integration with social networking services. BaaS start-ups date back to 2011 and onwards, and these services are gaining significant mainstream traction with enterprise consumers.

13.15.2.1 Serverless Computing

Serverless computing is a cloud computing code execution model in which the cloud provider fully manages starting and stopping virtual machines to serve user requests, and the billing is done based on the resources actually utilised to satisfy the request, instead of per virtual machine (VMs) per hour rate. However, serverless computing is really not executing code without servers. It only signifies the fact that the service provider does not have to purchase, rent or provision servers or VMs for the backend code to run on.

13.15.2.2 Cloud Deployment Models

Cloud deployment models include mainly private, public and hybrid clouds. Private cloud is cloud infrastructure operated solely for a single entity or organisation, managed either internally or by a third party and hosted either internally or externally. Private cloud for an organisation is generally resource intensive because of space, hardware, software and the necessary environmental controls. Moreover, security issues need to be addressed properly to rule out severe vulnerability. However, private cloud if properly managed can improve business decisions and performance.

Public cloud provides services over a network which is open to the public for use. Public cloud service providers, such as Amazon Web Services (AWS), Microsoft and Google, own and operate the infrastructure at their data centres and access to the public is through the Internet. Community cloud is a particular type of cloud similar to public cloud, wherein the cloud infrastructure is shared by a few organisations belonging to a specific community with common concerns for security, areas of operation, compliance and so on. The cost for operation is shared by the few users unlike a public cloud.

Hybrid cloud, as the name signifies, is a cloud composed of two or more clouds (public, private or community) that remain distinct entities but are tied together and offer the benefits of more than one deployment model. Gartner Inc. defined a hybrid-cloud service as a cloud computing service that is composed of some combination of private, public and community cloud services provided by different service providers. Besides the above deployment models, there are other types of cloud deployment such as distributed cloud, intercloud and multi-cloud also.

13.15.3 Cloud Architecture

Architecture of the cloud software system for the delivery of cloud-computing services typically involves multiple cloud components such as cloud platform, cloud infrastructure and cloud storage communicating with each other over a loose coupling mechanism such as a messaging queue.

13.15.4 Limitations and Disadvantages

Cloud computing has some limitations and disadvantages also. First of all, cloud computing has a limited scope of customisation for users. Moreover, the control of the backend infrastructure is limited to the cloud vendors only, and cloud users have little control over their applications, data and services. Privacy and confidentiality are big concerns for cloud users because the service provider can access the data that is in the cloud at any time. Many cloud providers can share information with third parties if necessary for the purpose of law and order even without prior permission or notice. This is permitted in their privacy policies which cloud users have to agree to as a precondition for using cloud services.

According to the Global Cloud Security Market Professional Survey Report 2016, the top three threats in the cloud are insecure interfaces and APIs, data loss and leakage and hardware failure, which accounted for 29%, 25% and 10% of all cloud-security outages respectively. Together, the above security concerns form shared technology vulnerabilities.

13.15.5 Popular Cloud Services

Three popular cloud-computing services are Microsoft Azure, IBM Bluemix and AWS. The Microsoft Azure cloud-computing service was created by Microsoft for developing, deploying and managing applications and services through Microsoft managed data centres all over the world connected through a global network. Azure provides SaaS, PaaS and IaaS, besides supporting many programming languages, tools and frameworks developed by Microsoft and third parties. Microsoft Azure came into existence in March 2014 when Microsoft renamed Windows Azure as Microsoft Azure. There are about 600 Azure services available today, such as VMs, compute services, mobile services and storage services.

IBM Bluemix is a cloud platform as a service developed by IBM. It supports several programming languages such as Java, Node.js, Python, PHP, Ruby and Swift. IBM Bluemix also provides integrated software development and IT operation services to build, run and deploy applications on the cloud. The initial release of Bluemix was made by IBM in June 2014.

AWS are, by far, the most popular and widely deployed cloud services. One can hire computing and storage services on demand from AWS as per the scale of requirement for the same. Because of its flexibility and cost-effectiveness, running Hadoop on AWS cloud has become a popular setup. AWS offers its Elastic Compute Cloud (EC2) and Simple Storage Service (S3) as the two core services. The EC2 service provides compute capacity for running Hadoop nodes. We can think of EC2 as a large collection of VMs. An EC2 instance is, in AWS terminology, a virtual compute unit, and each Hadoop node will take up an EC2 instance. One can rent as many EC2 instances matching the requirement as long as one needs and pays on an hourly basis. Whenever the requirement scales down, one can terminate the instances not required and need not pay rental. It is because of the above feature that the name is Elastic Compute Cloud.

The Amazon S3 service is a cloud storage service provided for storing all data pertaining to an EC2 instance, which is deleted when the instance is terminated by a user and the user may use the data in future.

Each EC2 instance functions like a commodity Intel hardware which one can access and control over the Internet. We can boot up an instance using an Amazon Machine Image (AMI). Some images are only basic OSs. EC2 supports more than six variants of Linux, Windows Server and Open Solaris. It is worth mentioning that AWS offers preconfigured images of Hadoop running on Linux and Hadoop in turn has inbuilt support for working with both EC2 and S3.

13.16 Internet of Things (IoT)

IoT was first used in 1999 by British technology pioneer Kevin Ashton to describe a system in which objects in the physical world could be connected to the Internet by sensors. There is, however, no single universal definition for IoT. The term 'internet of things' refers to a scenario wherein network connectivity and computing extend to objects, sensors (also referred to as 'smart devices') and everyday items not normally considered as computers such as vehicles, garage doors and buildings. IoT allows these devices to generate, exchange and consume data without human intervention.

13.16.1 IoT Connectivity Models

There are four common connectivity models used by IoT. They are (1) device-to-device (2) device-to-cloud (3) device-to-gateway and (4) backend data sharing.

Device-to-device communication involves two or more devices that directly connect and communicate among themselves through various types of networks such as IP networks of the Internet and Bluetooth. This model is very common for home automation systems to transfer small data packets of information between devices such as thermostats, light bulbs, light switches, door locks and timers.

Device-to-device communication is also popular among wearable IoT devices used for healthcare, such as a heart monitor connected to a valve controlling the flow of saline (electrolyte) into the patient's body.

Device-to-cloud communication enables an IoT device to connect directly to an Internet cloud service provider to exchange data and control message traffic. Figure 13.31 shows an example of the device-to-cloud communication model where two devices with temperature and carbon monoxide sensors communicate with a cloud application service provider.

Device-to-gateway is similar to a device-to-cloud model except that in this case, IoT devices basically connect to an intermediary device, usually a local gateway device such as a smartphone or a hub, to access a cloud-service provider. The intermediate gateway provides security and other functionalities such as data or protocol translation.

Backend data sharing essentially is a single device-to-cloud communication model extended to more than one application service provider, as shown in Figure 13.32.

13.16.2 IoT Applications

According to Gartner Inc., there will be 30 plus billion permanent devices on the IoT by 2030. The former British Chancellor of the Exchequer, George Osborne, posited that the IoT is the next stage of the information revolution and mentioned the interconnectivity of everything from urban transport to medical devices and household appliances. It is obvious that the growth of IoT to connect a very large number of devices through the Internet over the years is tremendous. IoT finds applications in nearly every field, starting with media to environmental monitoring, infrastructure management, manufacturing, energy management, healthcare management, building and home automation, transportation, management of urban facilities, consumer applications and many other similar fields.

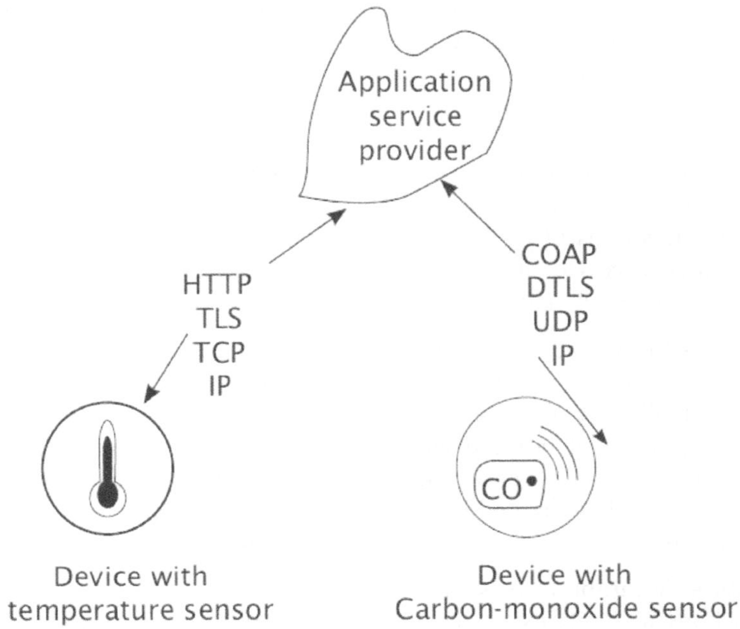

Figure 13.31 Example of Device-to-Cloud IoT Model
Source: TSchofenig, Arkko and Thaler (2015).

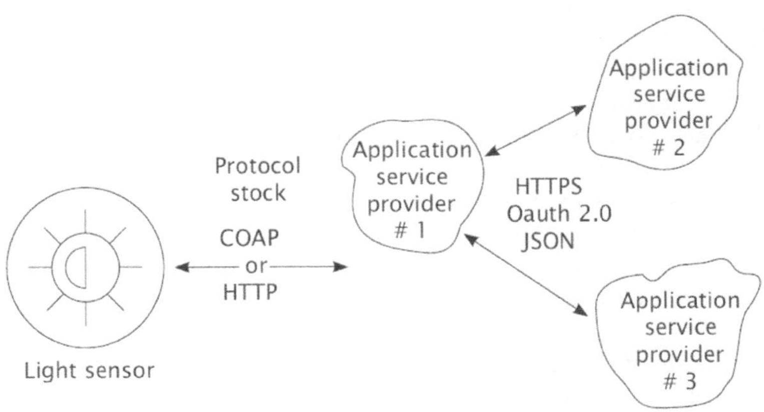

Figure 13.32 Backend Data Sharing IoT Model
Source: Tschofenig, Arkko and Thaler (2015).

Not all connected devices contribute to big data, but connected devices are a large and visible portion of what makes up the IoT and are the source of a variety of new data inputs and data considerations. IoT goes hand in hand with big data and advanced analytics due to the variety of data it produces. There are numerous connected home appliances in the field, from security systems and thermostats to keyless entry, refrigerators and garage doors. Today, about 56% of big data and advanced analytics developers work on projects for which connected devices are client devices, which, besides personal computers, include home devices or appliances, wearable devices, industrial sensors, automotive devices and so on.

An overview of some of the major application areas of IoT is provided as follows:

1. **Smart Home**: There are many smart home products that are connected as IoT to facilitate home automation. Some activities such as setting up a light to turn on or off at the whims of occupants are simple and relatively inexpensive, whereas sophisticated access control and modern surveillance cameras require a greater investment of money. However, a smart home has the following major features:
   - (i) IoT-driven efficient building energy management system.
   - (ii) Real-time monitoring of energy consumption and occupant behaviour for controlling energy consumption.
   - (iii) Integration of home devices for control of operations relating to garage door, door lock security and access control, surveillance, watering of plants in the garden, fire and noxious gas detectors and alarms and so on.
   - (iv) Temperature and humidity control for comfort.
2. **Wearables**: Wearables are smart electronic devices which can be worn on the human body as implants or accessories. Examples include smart watches, fitness trackers and sport trackers. Such devices belong to the IoT that enable objects to exchange data through the Internet with a manufacturer, operator, or other connected devices without human intervention.
3. **Manufacturing**: Process control, production scheduling and control, dynamic response to product demands and real-time optimisation of manufacturing and supply-chain networks bring IoT within the realm of smart manufacturing applications. It also extends itself to asset management through predictive maintenance and statistical evaluation to maximise reliability.
4. **Retail Smart Store**: A smart store is a retail store which uses smart technologies such as smart shelves, smart cards and smart trolleys. Smart stores generally deliver retail services to customers through the Internet, smartphone apps and augmented reality applications in real stores. Such technologies enhance the productivity of store space and inventory. For example, RFID technology allows for the use of kiosks and self-checkout terminals for keeping track of all incoming and outgoing goods.
5. **Transportation and Automotive**: The IoT can facilitate dynamic communication and control among the components of various transportation systems such as the vehicle, infrastructure, driver or user. Some of the features of such dynamic communication are intra-vehicular communication, smart traffic control, smart parking bays, toll collection, fleet management, vehicle movement control including speed limits, safety and road assistance.
6. **Environmental Monitoring**: Environmental monitoring applications of the IoT typically monitor the quality of the biophysical environment such as air, water and soil, as well as environmental stress of various types involving even movements of wildlife and habitats. The purpose is to protect the environment. Further, early warning systems for disaster management involving earthquakes and tsunamis, with devices connected to the Internet, form another important application area. IoT devices for

environmental monitoring typically span a large geographical area and can also be mobile.

7. **Healthcare**: Connected devices are essential for healthcare IoT. They collect data, communicate with each other and integrate with larger systems through high-speed data networks, cloud computing and mobile technology. Such devices create new possibilities in healthcare and patient care too. A few examples are location monitors, defibrillators, telehealth, and temperature and humidity sensors.

   Another healthcare application area is the stationary medical device. These devices are used for prevention, diagnosis and treatment of diseases. For example, hospital telemetry monitors, imaging machines, intravenous infusion equipment, ventilators and similar other life-sustaining equipment work over Wi-Fi or cellular 'Medical Body Area Networks' (MBANs). The devices can be linked together through different enterprise platforms for data transfer among healthcare systems.

   A very recent development is the internally embedded medical devices such as insulin pumps, pacemakers, drug dispensers, nerve simulators and artificial body implants. These often use proprietary and secured wireless protocols or Bluetooth to connect themselves with larger systems. A good example is a pacemaker which continually transmits data to cardiologists over Wi-Fi and an artificial pancreas having a continuous glucose monitor connected through Wi-Fi to an insulin pump. Another example is chip-based orthopaedic implants which can communicate information about wear and tear, alerting a patient when an artificial joint needs replacement. Ingestibles and adhesives are pill-like devices (also known as e-pills) that monitor internal physiological data such as temperature, activity level, flow rate and reaction to a particular medication. For example, healthcare equipment companies have developed ingestible pill-like sensors, which can reach a patient's stomach and through a miniature Bluetooth antenna can send vital data of the stomach to smartphones accessible to healthcare providers including physicians.

   Many health-related things such as drug inventory, pill bottles, medical insurance cards, hospital wristbands and sleep monitors can be made 'smart' by equipping them with radio frequency identification tags or other sensors that can work with near-field communication (NFC), Wi-Fi, cellular data or Bluetooth. A sleep monitor attached as a wristband can work on mobile phone technology to furnish data relating to hours of sound sleep, number of tosses in bed, hours of no sleep and so on pertaining to a continuous night the patient spent. Similarly, Adhere Tech's pill bottles track and improve medication adherence. The bottles, which again work on mobile phone technology, light up and sound an alert when patients forget to take their medicine in the prescribed time.

8. **Sports/fitness**: Devices and apps used by consumers to track health, fitness and wellness are gaining a lot of importance of late. Examples are Jawbone, Fitbit, smartphone apps for tracking calories and menstrual cycles. Other advanced examples include smart toothbrushes, wireless elementary monitors for blood pressure, blood sugar and smart clothing. Apple Inc. is working with large healthcare systems to integrate its health app data into electronic medical records (EMRs).

   The IoT is revolutionising the sports world. The richness and the speed at which data are captured during a sporting event with IoT devices are certainly innovative. Smart sportswear allows us to transcribe body data into training advice and all kinds of sports equipment are increasingly capable of measuring our performance and reporting the same to our smartphones.

9. **Infrastructure Management**: Monitoring and controlling operations of urban and rural infrastructures such as tunnels, bridges, highways, railway tracks and on- and off-shore wind farms are key applications of IoT relating to infrastructure management. Scheduling and control of repair and maintenance activities in an efficient manner for infrastructures can be undertaken by communication and coordination of tasks among different service providers and users of the facilities.
10. **Smart Cities**: IoT has brought about the smart city concept. A 'smart city' is an urban region that is highly advanced in terms of overall infrastructure, sustainable real estate, communication and market. It is a city where IT is the principal infrastructure and forms the basis for providing essential hi-tech services to residents. There are identified indicative areas that make a smart city. Some of those areas are listed as follows:
    - (i) Water supply
    - (ii) Air quality
    - (iii) Healthcare
    - (iv) Education
    - (v) Intelligent transport system
    - (vi) Waste management
    - (vii) Safety and security
    - (viii) IT/Wi-Fi connectivity
    - (ix) Intelligent government service
    - (x) Online shopping mall
    - (xi) Walkability, which is an important concept in sustainable urban design.

13.17 Case Study: *The New York Times* Converted 11 Million Articles as Images into PDF Version

In the year 2007, *The New York Times* decided to make all the public domain articles from 1851 to 1922 available on their website free of charge. These articles were in the form of images scanned from the original papers. Each article actually comprised numerous smaller tag image file format (TIFF) images that needed to be scaled and combined together coherently. Doing this required a scalable image conversion system.

Previously, the Times had generated all PDFs dynamically. Although the same approach worked reasonably well, it might not scale up to handle the significant possibility of traffic increases due to the free availability of the articles. Pre-generating all these articles as PDF files and statically serving them would be a challenging option because of the massive archive of 11 million articles consisting of 4 TB of data.

Derek Gottfrid, a software programmer at *The New York Times*, got the idea of using Amazon's S3 service for storage and retrieval of the 4 TB of TIFF images and also the converted PDF version of the articles. He also thought of writing some code that would run on multiple instances of EC2 under the Hadoop framework to generate the PDF.

Derek copied the 4 TB TIFF images into S3. Next, he 'started writing code to pull all the parts that make up an article out of S3, generate a PDF back in S3. This was easy enough using the JetS3t–open-source Java toolkit for S3, iText PDF library and installing the Java advanced image extension'. After tweaking and bug fixing, Derek deployed

Hadoop and his code running on 100 EC2 instances (nodes). The job took only 24 hours to churn through 11 million articles and generated another 1.5 TB of data to store in S3.

Assuming an EC2 reserved instance's price of about \$0.05 per hour in all, the above conversion was completed with a cost of only \$120 (100 instances × 24 hours × 0.05)! This is amazing.

Review Questions

1. What are the characteristics and sources of big data? Illustrate with suitable examples.
2. Mention some major applications of big data.
3. What is 'churn analysis'? What is its scope and applicability?
4. What is the KDD process? What are the major techniques of data mining?
5. What are the measures of quality of text mining?
6. What is machine learning? What is the basic difference between supervised and unsupervised learning?
7. What are the master and slave daemons of Hadoop? What is the default replication factor of Hadoop?
8. What is the function of the combiner in Hadoop? What is shuffling in MapR?
9. What are the differences between Hadoop 1.0 and Hadoop 2.0? What does 'rsa' stand for?
10. What are the major ecosystems of Hadoop? What are their basic functions?
11. Which ecosystem of Hadoop has 'grunt' shell?
12. What are the functions of 'WAL' and 'Zookeeper'?
13. What is a 'time stamp'? How does it facilitate the analysis of streaming data?
14. What is cloud computing? Explain the three service models of cloud.
15. What is elastic cloud? What are its advantages? Mention the name of any popular elastic cloud computing service provider.
16. What is IoT? Illustrate with examples.
17. What is the importance of wearable technologies in overall healthcare?
18. How do you think IoT can provide a business with a competitive advantage?
19. What is collaborative technology? Explain.

Bibliography

Bughin, J. 'Big Data: Getting a Better Read on Performance'. *McKinsey Quarterly* (February 2016). Available at: https://www.mckinsey.com/industries/technology-media-and-telecommunications/our-insights/big-data-getting-a-better-read-on-performance (accessed on 29 March 2020).

Dasgupta, N. *Practical Big Data Analytics*. Birmingham: Packt Publishing, 2018.

Dean, J. *Big Data, Data Mining and Machine Learning: Value Creation for Business Leaders and Practitioners*. Hoboken, NJ: Wiley, 2014.

Evans, J. *Business Analytics, Methods, Models and Decisions*, 2nd ed. London: Pearson, 2017.

Harrison, G. *Next Generation Databases: NoSQL and Big Data*, 1st ed. New York, NY: Apress, 2015.

Inmon, W. H., and K. Krishnan. *Building the Unstructured Data Warehouse*. Bradley Beach, NJ: Technics Publications, 2011.

Karen, R., D. E. Scott, and C. Lyman. 'The Internet of Things (IoT): An Overview—Understanding the Issues and Challenges of a More Connected World'. Internet Society, October, 2015.

Krishnan, K. *Data Warehousing in the Age of Big Data*. Waltham, MA: Morgan Kaufmann, Elsevier, 2013.

Krishnan, K., and S. Rogers. *Social Data Analytics: Collaboration for the Enterprise*. Waltham, MA: Morgan Kaufmann, Elsevier, 2015.
Shmueli, G., P. C. Bruce, I. Yahav, N. R. Patel, and Kenneth C. Lichtendahl Jr. *Data Mining for Business Analytics*. Hoboken: NJ: John Wiley & Sons, 2018.
TSchofenig, H., J. Arkko, and D. Thaler. 'Architectural Considerations in Smart Object Networking'. Internet Architecture Board RFC 7452, March 2015.

14 Business Process Re-engineering

14.1 Introduction

BPR is the *fundamental rethinking* and *radical redesign* of *core business processes* to achieve *dramatic improvements* in critical, contemporary measures of performance such as *quality, cost and cycle time*.

The words in *italics* are very important. Fundamental rethinking implies that re-engineering of business processes has to start from scratch, considering the ground reality and without any bias towards the existing processes or systems. Michael Hammer, the founder of the BPR concept, published the article 'Reengineering Work: Do not Automate, Obliterate' in the *Harvard Business Review (HBR)* in 1990. In this article, what Hammer wanted to mean is that re-engineering is neither simply automating the existing systems, including the legacy systems, nor is it for obliterating those systems. Radical redesign involves the transformation of business processes and every aspect of the organisation to avail of the full benefits of the BPR exercise. Dramatic improvements imply a quantum jump and not continuous incremental business improvements. Quality, cost and cycle time are key performance indicators, which lead to customer satisfaction.

Re-engineering focuses on rethinking for more efficient ways of working and eliminating unproductive work or processes that do not add value to the customers. Companies reduce organisational layers and eliminate unproductive work in two significant areas. First, they change functional departmentalisation into cross-functional teams, and second, they employ information, communication and other state-of-the-art technologies to facilitate data and information dissemination for effective and efficient decision-making and resource management.

A business process is a collection of activities which together produce something of value to the customers. According to Thomas Davenport, 'A process is simply a structured, measured set of activities designed to produce a specific output for a particular customer or market'. A business process is characterised by its (a) specific sequence of work activities across time and space; (b) a beginning and an end; (c) clearly defined inputs and outputs; (d) customer focus; (e) work procedure; (f) process ownership and (g) measurable performance indicators of quality, cost, cycle time and overall customer value addition.

Let us illustrate business processes with some real-life examples:

- Customer-order processing is a business process consisting of the activities of customer-order acceptance, resource utilisation, local purchase of input materials, input material receipt and delivery of goods and services to the customer.

DOI: 10.4324/9781003509714-14

- Student admission in a business school is a business process consisting of receiving application forms for admission, scrutiny of the forms, written test, group discussion, personal interview, selection, publication of admission list, collection of fees from the students selected for admission and registration of the students.
- Accounts receivable process in a manufacturing organisation consists of customer order, preparation of invoice, dispatch of invoice and dispatch of finished products, receipt of cash/cheque/bank draft or real-time gross settlement (RTGS) or National Electronic Funds Transfer (NEFT) from the customers and preparation of accounts receivable statement.

BPR also includes the innovation of new products and services. It may be stated that BPR changes business processes and not functions, activities, tasks or departments. Some proponents of BPR consider the same as a business management strategy because it focuses on the analysis, design and workflow of business processes within an organisation in order to improve customer service, cut operational costs and to become a world-class competitor.

BPR is exercised through the six R's of re-engineering, namely *realisation* for change, *requirement, rethinking, redesign, retooling* and last but not least important *re-evaluation.* It is an all-pervasive organisational development exercise to improve existing business processes by way of changing organisational structure, improving systems and procedures, introducing better work culture, replacing old business practices with new ones and diversifying the products and services to suit customer needs. The success of BPR largely depends upon the correct assessment of the shortcomings in the existing organisational systems and the measures to eliminate the same. However, proper risk analysis of the changes with technical and operational feasibility studies is an essential pre-requirement.

BPR needs effective planning for the changes to be introduced in the business processes with priorities for each individual change and the modalities for effecting the changes. Obviously, it involves a lot of trial-and-error exercises. Also, the right kind of analysis of causes of failures, if any, is needed during the re-engineering exercise to avoid mistakes and achieve ultimate success.

Transformation of employees, particularly their behaviour and attitude towards change, is of paramount importance as the success of BPR largely depends upon the extent of cooperation and involvement of the employees of an organisation.

14.2 BPR Methodology

BPR involves the following methodology broadly:

1. **Process Identification through Business Process Mapping (BPM)**: The steps of BPM have been listed in a subsequent paragraph.
2. **Process Rationalisation through Value-chain Analysis**: In this phase, the value addition of each process is critically examined in order to eliminate non-value-adding or non-essential processes.
3. **Process Simplification through Redesign**: The processes retained after the 2 above are redesigned to make them work more efficiently.

4. **Process Integration**: The reengineered processes after the 3 above are integrated in proper sequence and implemented, resulting in effective and efficient performance of the whole organisation.

14.3 Steps of Business Process Mapping (BPM)

BPM consists of the following steps:

1. Identification of each distinct process and the start and end activities of each process.
2. Collection of relevant information about tasks from different people associated with the process. The different categories of the processes such as reactive processes that create bottlenecks in daily activities, strategic processes and customer-oriented processes must be prioritised.
3. Correct sequencing of all activities between the start and end of the process.
4. Matching of all activities with proper symbols.
5. Preparation of the process flow chart depicting workflow mapping.

The purpose of the workflow mapping process is to analyse the existing processes in an organisation and to understand if the process workflow is in keeping with the business objectives and strategic plan formulated by the top management of the organisation.

14.4 Steps Involved with BPR

BPR is carried out in an organisation in the following sequential steps. Each step consists of one or more tasks as mentioned under each step:

1. Initiate organisational changes. The tasks involved with this step are:
   (i) Assessment of the current state of the organisation.
   (ii) Understand the existing processes through process overview, mission, scope and boundaries of each process.
   (iii) Understanding customers' expectations from the process.

2. Develop and communicate a vision for improved processes:
   (i) Communicate with all employees to make them aware of the vision of the future.
   (ii) Demonstrate to employees the necessity of BPR.
   (iii) Clearly identify opportunities for improvement such as quality improvement, cost and time reduction and value addition.
   (iv) Resolve inconsistencies among processes, if any, and make predictions for the consequences of the changes.
   (v) Remove any fear among employees regarding job security.

3. Identify action plans for BPR:
   (i) Evaluate the existing business policies and customer requirements.
   (ii) Identify new business opportunities and develop an improvement plan which should include a diversification plan for products and services.
   (iii) Select the core processes that need to be re-engineered.
   (iv) Identify the process owners.
   (v) Identify potential barriers to implementation.
   (vi) Simplify processes to reduce process time and cost.

(vii) Remove no value-added activities.
(viii) Formulate new process-performance strategies.

4. Changes in work culture:
   (i) Brainstorm the BPR principles through questionnaires, meetings and focus groups.
   (ii) Make customer delight the focal point.
   (iii) Explain the new value system and culture to the employees.
   (iv) Set up re-engineering team, executive improvement team and cross-functional groups. The re-engineering team has to include the BPR leader.
   (v) Allow the workers to participate in decision-making.
   (vi) Consultants may be engaged for quick implementation of BPR. However, adequate consultation with all employees is needed to ensure initiative on the part of all employees.

5. Establish new business system:
   (i) Draw a new workflow diagram.
   (ii) Document the new organisation structure.
   (iii) Standardise processes and automation, if feasible, that have to be adopted.
   (iv) Upgrade equipment and describe new technologies if adopted.
   (v) Redesign the information requirement.

6. Execute the transformation process:
   (i) Develop a correct change strategy.
   (ii) Plan and schedule the changes.
   (iii) Map the new skill requirements.
   (iv) Train the employees to take care of the new processes.
   (v) Reallocate work among the workforce.
   (vi) Design performance metrics for the new processes.
   (vii) Design and establish a feedback system.
   (viii) Benchmark the processes and transform the organisation.

14.5 Process Re-engineering Life Cycle

Aphrodite Tsalgatidou introduced the concept of 'process life cycle' based on her comparative study of four popular BPR methodologies, namely Hammer and Champy (1993), Davenport and Short (1990), Process Analysis and Design Methodology (PADM) developed by the Informatics Process Group of Manchester University, UK in 1994 and the object-oriented BPR by Jacobson and others (1994).

Hammer and Champy's definition of BPR has already been mentioned in an earlier paragraph of this chapter. They mentioned 'fundamental rethinking and radical change'. According to them, any BPR effort changes every organisational aspect such as the business processes, employees, jobs and structures, management and measurement systems, values and beliefs as all these aspects are related to the business processes. The 'business system diamond', a term coined by them, represents the above-mentioned aspects as the four corner points of the diamond, as shown in Figure 14.1. According to Hammer and Champy, IT plays a crucial role in BPR.

Davenport and Short (1990) placed IT at the heart of BPR. Their strategy for BPR is more modest and tempered with the approach of continuous process improvement. They also recommended selecting the critical processes, analysing and redesigning them iteratively.

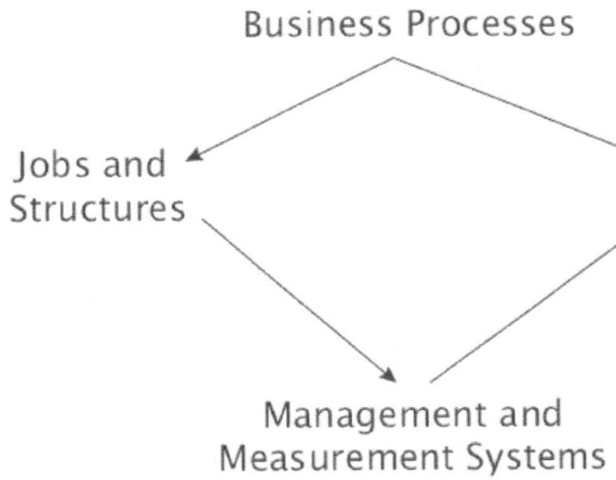

Figure 14.1 The Business System Diamond

Source: Hammer and Champy (1993).

PADM emanated out-of-process modelling techniques which describe two phases of the technique, namely representation and refinement phases. Both phases incorporate continuous and iterative process improvement as key to BPR. PADM, however, recognises the relationship between IT and processes as reciprocal, which implies that changes in IT may require process changes and similarly, the changes in process may require changes in IT.

The object-oriented BPR as advocated by Jackobson and others defines an object as an occurrence containing information and behaviour that is meaningful to the business organisation and hence needs to be described in the organisational environment. For example, supplier, customer, supply order and invoice are objects. The behaviour of the object and related information can be used by other objects also. Work tasks in an organisation can be modelled as objects. The processes are modelled with the objects for clarifying the inner workings of an organisation.

Re-engineering work is performed within the framework of BPR in two steps, namely *reverse engineering* the existing organisation, where an abstract model of the business and the processes under study is constructed as it is, and *forward engineering*, where the reverse-engineered business is redesigned with new processes.

Aphrodite Tsalgatidou recommended, as an outcome of her study, five phases for a BPR project cycle.

The phases are as follows:

1. Learning the processes.
2. Creating the business vision.
3. Model and analyse the current (as-is) processes.
4. Model and analyse the future (to-be) processes.
5. Transition to a continuous improvement effort.

The phases form the BPR cycle of continuous process improvement.

14.6 BPR and Its Linkage with IT and ISs

ISs encompass IT and the systems relating to the management and the organisation. BPR and IT/IS are closely related to each other. A successful BPR project owes its success to IT/IS. In BPR, an effective IT facilitates sharing of databases, development of expert systems, development of communication networks, use of decision-making tools, effective interaction with customers, retrieval of appropriate information and computation at a high level of aggregation.

On the other hand, BPR projects can be directed towards IT/IS revamping by way of upgrading the client–server technology, mobile computing, data storage and retrieval, BPM, workflow management, ERP, CRM, SCM, DSS, data mining, BI and also web-enabled services. ERP is an integrated suite of business management software which helps in managing business needs. Experts believe that BPR makes ERP implementation in an organisation faster, less expensive and easier due to acceptability on the part of the employees.

14.7 Some Important Concepts about BPR

1. BPR changes processes and not functions, activities, departments, geographies or tasks.
2. Re-engineering is not only reorganising. Reorganising is redesigning an organisation's structure to support re-engineered business processes.
3. Re-engineering is not downsizing or reduction of workforce to achieve short-term cost savings. Re-engineering, on the contrary, emphasises rethinking from the point of view of ground reality for more efficient ways of working, including the elimination of unnecessary work.
4. Re-engineering is not automation of ineffective and obsolete processes.

14.8 Factors Leading to the Success of BPR

The important factors, which lead to the success of BPR in an organisation, are listed as follows:

1. Proven and tested methods should be adopted.
2. Employees should be convinced about the need for BPR.
3. Drive for innovation should come from the employees.
4. Prior analysis of business needs should consider the strategy and long-term objectives of the organisation.
5. BPR team should effectively manage the changes within the prescribed time frame and with the least impact on the business.
6. Adequate IT infrastructure is one of the factors which facilitates implementation of the re-engineered processes.
7. Customer needs and customer-centric processes should direct business practices.
8. Ultimate results should be the main focus. The processes should go beyond the traditional tasks and functional boundaries to achieve the attainment of the objectives of the organisation.
9. Work simplification is to be carried out to eliminate unnecessary complexities.

In the above context, it may be stated that the objectives of BPR are mainly customer delight, effectiveness and efficiency of business processes in terms of cost, quality, time and effort.

14.9 BPR Success Stories in the Real World

Example 1: Ford Motor Company—Accounts payable process.

Ford's accounts payable process was slow and cumbersome, and 500 clerks were engaged mainly for reconciling mismatches among purchase orders, goods receipt documents and invoices before releasing payment to vendors. The process (as-is) shown in Figure 14.2 was slow, awkward and had frequent mismatches due to mistakes. After re-engineering the procurement process, there was a reduction in headcount in the accounts payable process by 75%. Invoices were eliminated, and matching was computerised resulting in improved accuracy, a faster and more efficient process. Ford's procurement process (to-be) after re-engineering are shown in Figure 14.3.

Example 2: New life insurance policy application process at Mutual Benefits Life before re-engineering had 30 steps, 5 departments and 19 persons. The issuance application processing cycle time used to vary from a minimum of 24 hours to an average of 22 days, even though the actual processing time of an application was only 17 minutes. The workflow process of Mutual Benefits Life before re-engineering are shown in Figure 14.4.

After re-engineering one mainframe computer, one PC workstation and a LAN server were used to take care of the whole processing. The case manager could handle the same volume of policy applications with a processing cycle time of a minimum of 4 hours and an average of 2–5 days. Moreover, the application handling capacity increased by two times compared to before re-engineering. The life insurance company could also cut 100 positions in the field office. The new life insurance policy application processing method after re-engineering are shown in Figure 14.5.

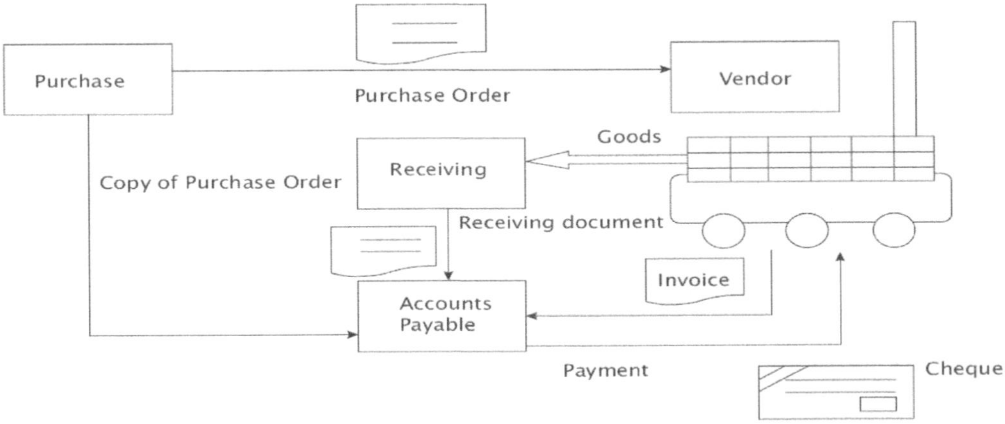

Figure 14.2 Ford's Accounts Payable Process (As-is) before Re-engineering

Source: Hammer and Champy (1993).

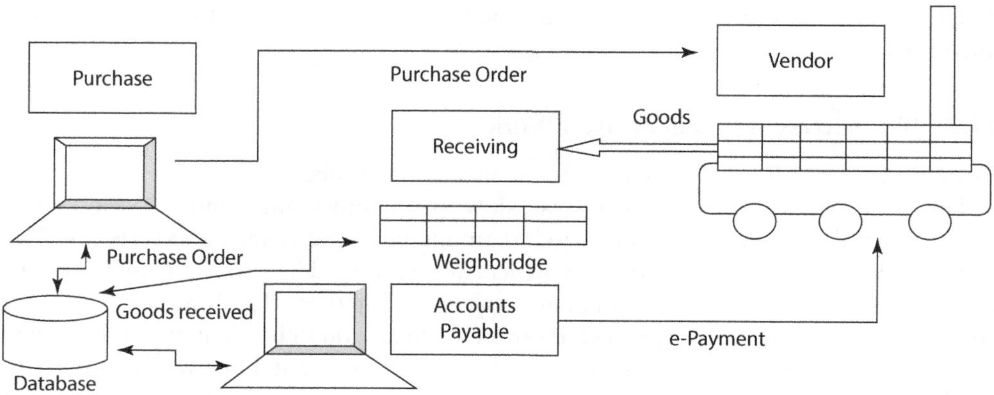

Figure 14.3 Ford's Accounts Payable Process after Re-engineering
Source: Hammer and Champy (1993).

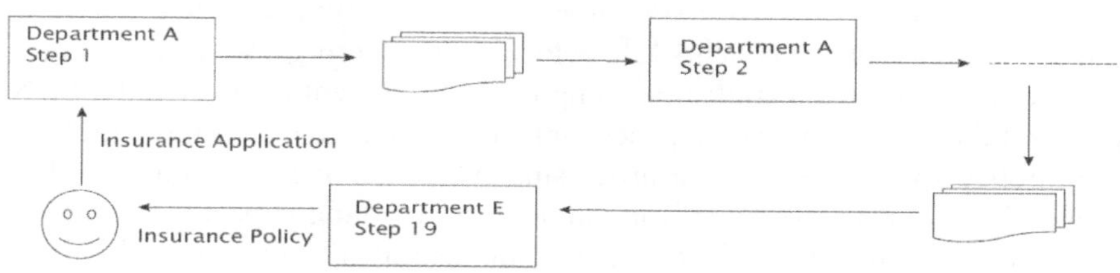

Figure 14.4 Mutual Benefits Life (As-is) before Re-engineering
Source: Eccles (1991).

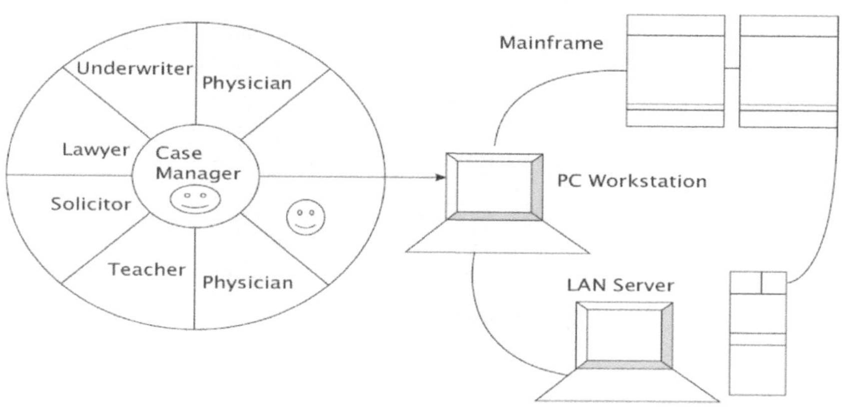

Figure 14.5 New Life Insurance Policy Application Process after Re-engineering

14.10 BPR Case Studies in Indian Corporate Sector

14.10.1 Case 1: BPR in ICICI Bank

ICICI Bank (earlier known as Industrial Credit and Investment Corporation of India) is a large Indian MNC banking entity with a market capitalisation of about ₹2,562,055.3 million as on 2 April 2019. The bank has 4,867 branches and 14,367 ATMs in India and also has overseas branches in 16 countries, including the USA, China, Singapore and many more countries. ICICI Bank offers a wide range of banking and financial services to corporate as well as retail customers, such as investment banking, life and non-life insurance, venture capital and asset management. BPR was carried out in ICICI Bank in the year 2000 and onwards when anytime and anywhere banking facilities were introduced in India.

14.10.1.1 Background and Justification of BPR

The traditional legacy systems at ICICI Bank were very much branch-centric. ICICI Bank authorities decided to change the branch-centric model in order to make its services available all over India. In order to facilitate the above, it was necessary for ICICI Bank to centralise its banking applications and also to have a centralised data repository.

14.10.1.2 Teams Involved with the BPR for Appropriate Technology Transfer

Infosys was the main technology partner that provided the required assistance to ICICI Bank to implement Finacle for handling all the banking activities such as:

- Bill Desk for online payment
- Sybase, an SAP company
- SAS for business analytics software and services.

ICICI Infotech, which is a company promoted by ICICI, designed the initial network for the ICICI group in 1999. The initial design was a hub-and-spoke architecture.

ICICI had to modify the initial design, because it was not able to cater to the need for centralisation of data available with the stand-alone legacy systems of the branches. The data from one branch was not available to the other branches. The above-mentioned problem led the ICICI Bank to design a new hub-and-spoke architecture.

Supporting Tools and Techniques: The following tools and techniques were used by ICICI Bank:

1. Finacle: The core banking and universal banking solution developed by Infosys. Finacle was needed to seamlessly integrate multiple applications such as credit cards, mutual funds, brokerage, data warehouses and call centres.
2. The network follows a hub-and-spoke architecture consisting of a mix of very-small-aperture terminals (VSATs), leased lines, ISDN and radio links. The network has around 800 leased lines, about 600 VSATs, approximately 800 ISDN lines and multiple 34 Mbps lines.

There is a primary site from where the spokes emanate and reach the regional branches and other offices. The secondary site has the disaster recovery facility in ICICI Bank.

Hardware at each site varies from low-end new technology (NT) servers to the high-end Sun Enterprise 10k (Sun E10k) along with 12 terabytes of data storage at each end connected through a storage area network. Unix is the operating system for the major part of the hardware, while the databases mainly use Oracle and a few use Sybase and MS SQL. High-end Cisco routers and switches have been deployed to establish connectivity. The network is monitored using HP OpenView and CiscoWorks.

More than 30 portals are being operated using highly secured state-of-the-art security features such as firewalls, IDS, antivirus and other security tools. The network architecture was designed to establish a good relationship among the technology consultants (network integrators), the vendors and the clients.

14.10.1.3 Results Achieved

ICICI Bank adopting the scalable and open systems-based architecture with Finacle has been able to manage successfully an increased transaction level from 0.4 million in the year 2000 to roughly 2.1 million in 2005, nearly five and a half times. There has been a quantum jump in all other areas of performance of ICICI Bank also. On the whole, ICICI Bank after BPR has grown significantly, resulting in a present net worth of about ₹1,083,680 million as on 31 March 2019.

14.10.2 Case 2: BPR in Mahindra and Mahindra (M & M) Company

The company was started in the year 1945 by two brothers, namely J. C. Mahindra and K. C. Mahindra to manufacture general-purpose utility vehicles. In October 1947, the first batch of 75 jeeps was produced by the company. In the course of time, the company diversified its business into other segments such as hotels, financial services, auto components and IT. In 1994, a major restructuring exercise was initiated as part of a BPR programme, and the company was regrouped into six distinct autonomous strategic business units (SBUs) with empowered presidents for the SBUs.

14.10.2.1 Background and Justification for BPR

Before the implementation of BPR in M & M, there were certain factors present which led to manufacturing inefficiencies, resulting in low productivity. Moreover, the production cycle time was long due to poor scheduling, frequent imbalance in the assembly lines and idle time of workers due to unorganised processes. The work culture was unhealthy, and corruption among employees was widespread.

The top management, therefore, decided to focus on productivity increase, delivery of world-class quality products at competitive cost with the strategic intent of becoming the largest tractor manufacturer in the world. In short, the three C's (customers, competition and change) led M & M to implement BPR.

14.10.2.2 Major Changes Pursuant to BPR Exercise

Business of the company was restructured into core and non-core business units as shown in detail in Table 14.1.

Project 'Vishwajeet': A major programme conceptualised by McKinsey, was undertaken by M & M to make it the largest global manufacturer of tractors by the year 2005.

Table 14.1 Restructuring M & M into Core and Non-core Business Units Details

Core Business Units:	
Automotive	MUVs and SUVs
Farm equipment	Tractors and other farm equipment
Non-core Business Units:	
Trade and financial service	Imports, exports, lease financing, hire purchase, domestic trading and marketing
Infrastructure development	Real estate

The project envisaged division of farm equipment business into five distinct departments, namely marketing and customer relations, manufacturing and supply chain, product development and R&D, performance management and internal operations.

Project 'Blue Chip': Due to depressed revenue, high costs and reduced profit margins in 2002 resulting in share price fall from ₹322 in 2000 to ₹114 in 2002 and return on capital employed (ROCE) sliding down from 17.09 to 8.92 during the same period, M & M set up a corporate turnaround programme office and articulated the need for a sharper focus on financial returns. Consequently, a restructuring exercise called 'blue chip' was undertaken by M & M to raise the level of performance. The major actions on the part of 'blue chip' for financial revival were as follows:

1. ROCE replaced the benchmarks such as market share, sales and profit.
2. A policy was formulated that business units would have to compete among themselves for capital based on the returns made by them.
3. M & M overhauled operations for cost cutting and streamlining the manufacturing facility. HR management also underwent crucial changes.

14.10.2.3 Results Achieved

Due to BPR, the tractor division brought down the break-even point from 54,000 to 35,000 units due to cost-cutting.

Net sales and operating profit increased by 28% and 34% respectively for the first half of the financial year 2004–2005.

M & M stock touched ₹390 as against ₹112 only a year before the BPR exercise.

14.10.3 Case 3: BPR in Indian Railways Catering and Tourism Corporation (IRCTC)

IRCTC is a subsidiary of Indian Railways set up by the Ministry of Railways, Government of India. IRCTC started its operations on 27 September 1999. Its corporate office is located in New Delhi. IRCTC is headed by its managing director, who is assisted by the director (catering services), director (tourism and marketing), director (finance), chief vigilance officer, company secretary and 17 group general managers reporting to him directly. Approximately 2 million tickets are sold per day through the website of IRCTC.

14.10.3.1 Background and Justification of BPR

The ticket booking system prior to the introduction of BPR was an offline manual system wherein there were many counters, each of which was meant for booking and reservation of a particular train or a few numbers of trains. As a result, passenger rush and waiting time were heavy. In order to avoid this rush in the railway booking-cum-reservation offices, the ticket booking and seat reservation process was re-engineered and, with the assistance of M/s Computer Maintenance Corporation (CMC), Indian Railways developed the online booking and seat reservation system using the Customer Information Control System (CICS). It was mainly for customer (passenger) satisfaction and a comfortable journey that BPR was implemented in Indian Railways and IRCTC became operational. Also, prompt delivery of passenger services and eliminating inefficient operations for increased revenue were the other prime considerations leading to the BPR exercise.

14.10.3.2 Present Scenario of Ticket Booking and Passenger Services

Today, IRCTC is offering various re-engineered services to the railway passengers through online systems, some of which are as follows:

1. Passenger information and enquiry.
2. Railway reservation and ticket-booking services which include Internet and mobile ticketing, booking history, ticket printing and cancellation.
3. Catering and vending services.
4. Railway claims and refunds.
5. Booking of retiring rooms at railway stations.

The above services are provided by intelligent use of IT through:

- Freight Operations Information System (FOIS).
- Passenger Reservation System (PRS).
- Unreserved Ticketing System (UTS).
- Interactive voice response system which is a passenger feedback system.
- E-ticketing system.
- Rail net, also known as the Corporate Wide Information System (CWIS), connects the Railway Board with all zonal, divisional, sub-divisional headquarters, production units, research development and standardisation organisation (RDSO) and all other units.
- Radio-frequency identification device (RFID) for wagon and consignment tracking system.

14.10.3.3 Results Achieved

IRCTC led to phenomenal improvement in performance in Indian Railways after BPR. Some of those worth mentioning achievements are as follows:

1. Total earnings increased by about 17.3% in one year after BPR due to a quantum jump in ticket sales through internet ticketing.
2. Tourism activities through Indian Railways have considerably increased.

3. Indian Railways became unit-cost-focused rather than tariff-focused.
4. The earlier thinking of restructuring and right-sizing changed towards competitiveness.

Review Questions

1. What is BPR? How is it different from TQM?
2. What are the steps in BPR?
3. What are the roles of ISs and IT in BPR?
4. Why is BPR at all needed in an organisation?
5. Why is BPR required for the successful implementation of ERP? Which of the two needs to be carried out first?
6. What are the factors leading to the success of a BPR exercise?
7. What is the relationship between BPM and BPR?
8. Which of the following actions on the part of a company are within the scope of BPR?

    (i) Outsourcing of components needed for the end products.
    (ii) Opening a new retail outlet in a remote location.
    (iii) Cutting the strength of the office by offering a voluntary retirement scheme as a cost-reduction measure.

Bibliography

Davenport, T. H. *Process Innovation: Reengineering Work through Information Technology*. Boston, MA: Harvard Business School Press, 1992.

Davenport, T. H., and J. E. Short. 'The New Industrial Engineering: Information Technology and Business Process Redesign'. *Sloan Management Review* 31 (1990): 11–27.

Eccles, Robert G. 'Rethinking the Corporate Workplace: Case Manager at Mutual Benefits Life'. Harvard Business School, Case 9 492–015, 1991.

Grover, V., S. R. Jeong, W. J. Kettinger, and J. T. Teng. 'The Implementation of Business Process Reengineering'. *Journal of Management Information Systems* 12, no. 1 (1995): 109–144.

Hammer, Michael. 'Reengineering Work: Don't Automate, Obliterate'. *Harvard Business Review* 68, no. 4 (1990): 104–112.

Hammer, Michael, and James Champy. *Reengineering the Corporation: A Manifesto for Business Revolution*. New York, NY: HarperCollins Publishers, 1993.

Jacobson, I., Ericsson, M., and Jacobson, A. *The Object Advantage: Business Process Reengineering with Object Technology*, 1st ed. Boston, MA: Addisson-Wesley, September 1994.

Tsalgatidou, Aphrodite. 'Methodologies for Business Process Modelling and Reengineering'. Department of Information and Telecommunication, University of Athens, Greece, 2014.

15 Generative Artificial Intelligence

15.1 Introduction

Generative Artificial Intelligence (GenAI) is a type of artificial intelligence which creates or generates new content like text, images, audio, video or codes for a programme based on existing data. Generative AI is not a new concept and as early as in 2006 we had Google Translate, Siri and Amazon Alexa which all had the features of Generative AI. For example, when we compose a text or an email on our computer or phone, very often the computer or phone attempts to auto-complete the sentences we type.

15.2 The Chronology of Development of Generative AI

During the period 2000 to 2014, Recurrent Neural Networks (RNNs) and Long Short-Term Memory (LSTMs) were adopted by deep learning models mainly for prediction based on sequential data. Those models were, however, not suitable for sequence-to-sequence data transfer like the machine translation task (language translation) because of their inherent difficulty in handling variable input and output sentence lengths. For example, if the task is the translation of an English sentence to a German sentence, the number of words in the English sentence may not be the same as in the translated German sentence.

In order to overcome the above-mentioned difficulty, in late 2014, the Encoder–Decoder architecture was first introduced by Ilya Sutskever et al. (2014) to solve the sequence-to-sequence problems. The encoder accepts the input sentence token by token each token may be assumed as one word of the sentence. The encoder then creates a context vector which represents the summary of the whole sentence to be translated into another language. The context vector, which is a set of numbers, is then fed to the decoder which, in turn, understands the context vector and then translates it token by token and finally prints the translated sentence. The Encoder–Decoder architecture was trained through the back propagation process. It was, however, observed that the architecture, as mentioned above, had a limitation of scalability since it lacked parallel processing capability.

Therefore, in 2017, the concept of 'Attention' mechanism was introduced by Ashish Vaswani et al. of Google Brain, which led to the development of transformers. Subsequently, in 2018, transformer learning was introduced employing BERT (Bi-directional Encoder Representation from Transformers), which is a model for natural language processing developed by Google. During this period, GPT (short form of Generative Pre-trained

DOI: 10.4324/9781003509714-15

Transformers) was also developed by OpenAI, an artificial intelligence research laboratory located in California, USA.

During the years 2018 to 2020, the vision transformers came into existence for image classification employing transformer architecture to convert an image into a sequence of patches. During this period of time also AlphaFold 2 was introduced by Google DeepMind, incorporating transformer architecture to predict a protein's 3-D structure based on its primary amino acid sequence. During 2021 and onwards, Generative AI came in a big way, and OpenAI/ChatGPT introduced GPT-3.5 and GPT-4, both of which are Large Language Models (LLMs) capable of generating coherent and contextually relevant texts. GPT-3.5 was trained on 175 billion parameters, while GPT-4 had about 1 trillion parameters. The training process needed massive data obtained from multiple sources like Wikipedia, books, articles, scientific journals, computer codes and other licensed data from third parties. Simultaneously, Generative AI for image data, text-to-image conversion, audio and video generation also evolved. For example, Stable Diffusion, introduced in 2022, can produce unique photo-realistic images from text. OpenAI also introduced DALL-E 2 and DALL-E 3, which were capable of generating images from text captions in natural languages.

15.3 Basic Concepts Underlying Generative AI

15.3.1 Language Modelling

Generative AI models like GPT and their variants work on the principle of language modelling. A language model accepts a sequence of words that form the context so far present and, based on the same, predicts what follows. For example, if the context is as follows:

'I want a glass of …'

then, the continuation can be either 'water' or 'milk'.

A language model is trained to understand and predict the next word (in the case of the above example 'water' or 'milk') in a sequence based on the preceding words. The model is, however, a probabilistic one because it assigns probabilities to predict the likelihood of the next sequence of words, as shown in the following examples.

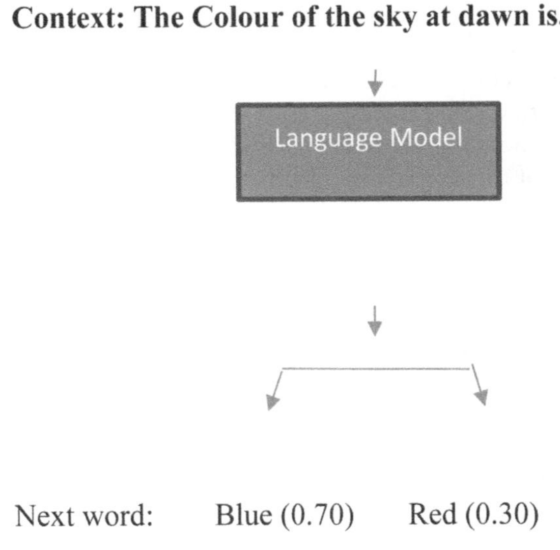

The values within parentheses indicate the probabilities of the next word in the sequence based on the context.

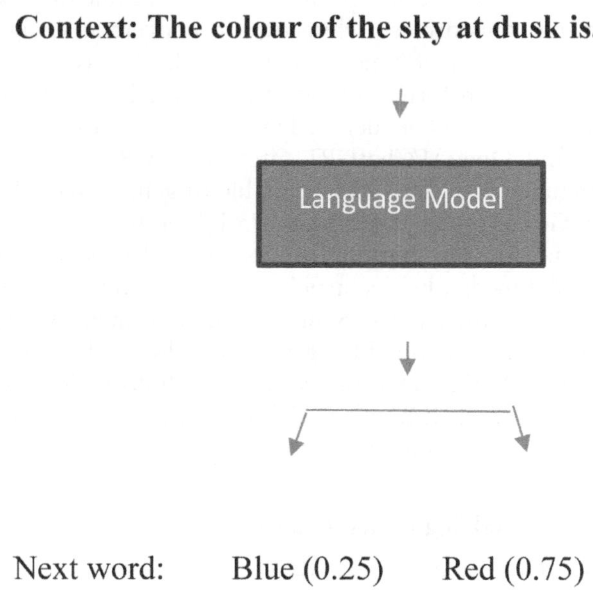

Language models are basically neural networks, which learn things through a self-supervised training process with a huge corpus of data from Wikipedia, books, the internet, Quora, social media, news items, and many other sources. The training process takes a considerable time from a few months to even years. The neural network starts from scratch and predicts the next word in a sequence randomly, and after each prediction adjusts its parameters through feedback (back propagation) to finally match the ground truth. An example of a very simple neural network language model may be as shown in Figure 15.1.

The simple neural network language model, as shown in Figure 15.1 has got three input nodes (represented by three small circles), two output nodes and one hidden (middle) layer having four nodes. The inputs and outputs of all the layers are actually vectors, and each vector is a set of numbers. Each vector consists of a set of numbers. There may be one or more hidden layers that generalise the inputs and visualise patterns in the inputs that are not apparently present. The size of the neural network depends upon the number of parameters that are trained.

The parameters are actually the weights and biases of the connections among the modes and in the case of the simple neural network shown in Figure 15.1 it is 26.

15.3.2 Large Language Models (LLMs)

In case of the tiny neural network shown in Figure 15.1, there are only 26 parameters. However, in the case of Large Language Models, there can be neural networks made of millions or even billions of parameters that govern the behaviour of the models and which are pre-trained with a massive corpus of data. Popular among the LLMs are the GPT-4 of OpenAI, Llama of Metal AI (Facebook) and PALM of Google and many such LLMs. While GPT-4 has got 1 trillion parameters, Llama models are available in various

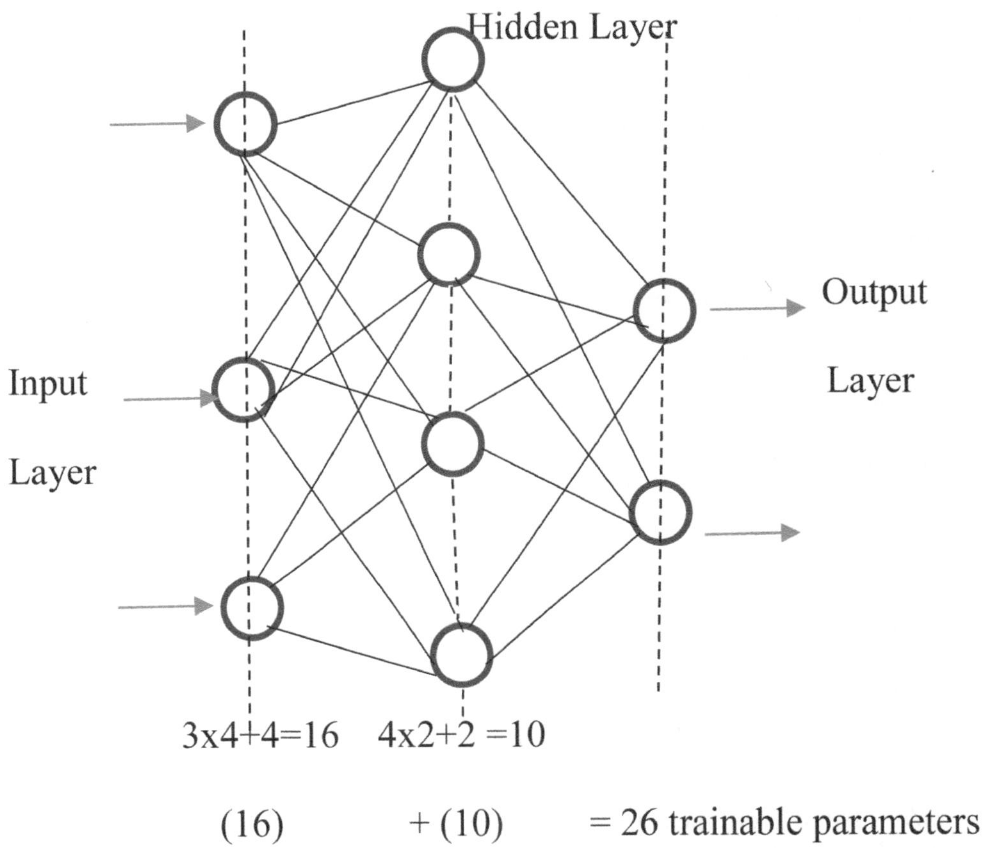

Figure 15.1 A Very Simple Neural Network Language Model

sizes ranging from 7 billion to 65 billion parameters. LLMs are mainly used to model and process human languages.

In reality the LLMs like GPT-4 are made up of blocks which consist of a large number of neural networks. The blocks are connected one after another. The architecture of a transformer has been shown in subsequent paragraphs of this chapter.

Further the cost of training a LLM like GPT-4 is enormous. GPT-3 was trained with 45 terabytes of data gathered from books, websites, the internet and many other sources. The hardware requirement for the training of a transformer is also highly expensive. GPT-3 training, for example, required a cluster of 1000 GPUs of Nvidia company. GPU is the short form of Graphical Processing Unit. Additionally, the cost of energy consumption, like electricity costs for the training of a LLM, is also very high, and this in turn gives rise to sustainability concern.

15.3.3 Reinforced Learning from Human Feedback (RLHF)

Besides self-supervised training with labelled data and statistical predictions, LLMs use another approach called Reinforced Learning from Human Feedback (RLHF). For

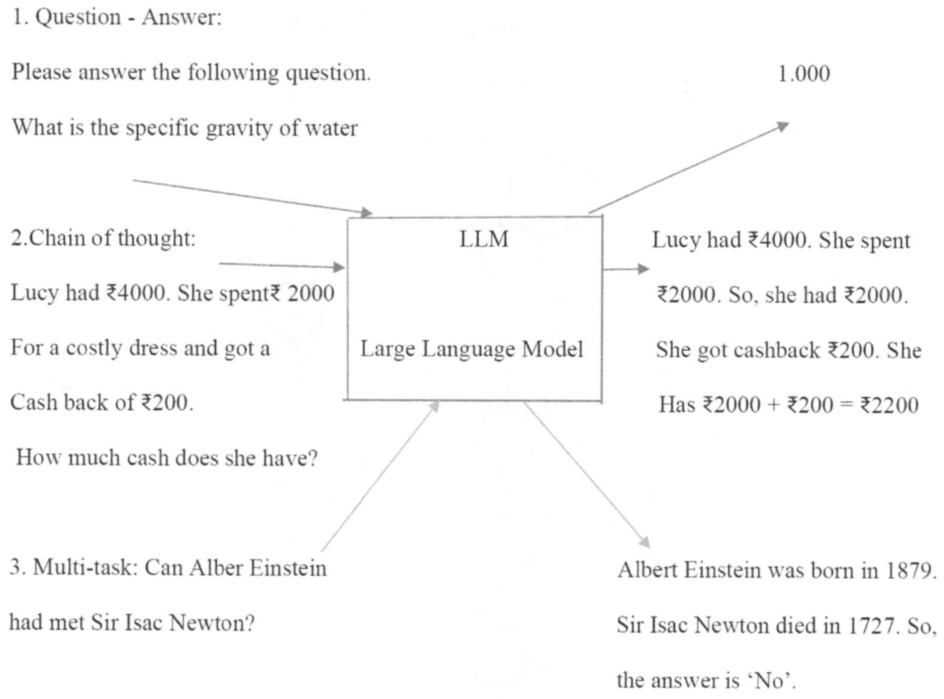

Figure 15.2 Finetuning of a LLM for Varied Functions

example, ChatGPT of OpenAI which is an application of Generative AI using GPT-3, adopts RLHF. The responses generated by ChatGPT against any query are ranked by humans, and the same rankings are provided to ChatGPT as feedback for reinforcement learning.

15.3.4 Foundation Models

A foundation model is a machine learning or deep learning model that is trained on vast data sets, and the model can be finetuned and applied on domain-specific use cases. An LLM is an example of foundation models, which can be finetuned for variety of uses. The foundation models made it possible for AI adoption in various domains such as health care, education, legal and many other areas.

Because the foundation models are able to perform multiple tasks involving different functions, they undergo unsupervised training with unstructured or unlabelled data. Figure 15.2 is an example of finetuning of an LLM as a foundation model for different functions.

Fine tuning is very important because it allows foundation models to perform specialised tasks as illustrated in Figure 15.3.

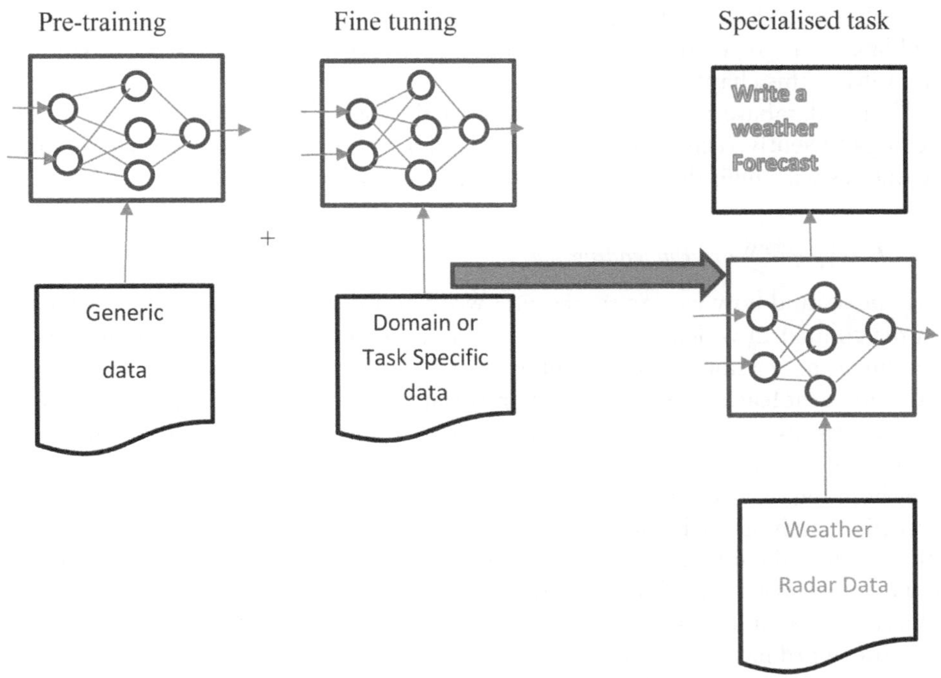

Figure 15.3 Finetuning Pre-trained Models for Special Task

Let us summarise the principles behind foundation models as follows:

1. Foundation models adopt deep learning techniques
2. Foundation models practise unsupervised learning with massive unstructured and unlabelled data
3. Foundation models adopt the principle of attention mechanism. The attention mechanism has been described in subsequent paragraphs of this chapter
4. Foundation models are pretrained on a huge corpus of data
5. Foundation models are designed to be scalable for efficient training with huge data sets with the advantage of parallel processing.

The various types of foundation models are listed as follows:

1. Language models such as OpenAI/GPT series
2. Vision models such as DALL-E, OpenAI/CLIP
3. Multi-modal models like Image Captioning
4. Domain-specific models such as Healthcare, Legal, Chemistry, Molecular biology, Climate change and Code generation.

15.4 Embedding and Vector Database

Embedding is a numeric representation of a word in a text, as a vector based on the semantics and relationship with other words in the text. The embeddings of words are generated by training a machine learning model on a large amount of text data. There are mainly two types of embeddings, namely, the static embedding and the contextual embedding. Both types of embeddings have been explained elaborately in subsequent paragraphs of this chapter.

A Vector database is a specialised type of database that is capable of storing and retrieving efficiently vector data. A vector database is optimised for managing and handling queries with high-dimensional vector representations.

15.4.1 Example of Word Embedding

Let us understand how we can represent a word as a numeric representation of a vector, given the context in which the word is used in a sentence. Word embedding or sentence embedding is only a numeric representation of a text. The dimensions of the vector represent the different features of the word. For example, if we search the location of 'Amazon' in Google, it shows two nouns as Amazon; the first one is a river in South America while the second one is a company providing web services like elastic cloud computing and also online shopping facilities. Google uses a technique called 'semantic search' which means not exactly matching the keyword of the user query in the search process but understanding the intent and context of the query to perform the search. Google does all the above search through word embeddings. Figures 15.4, 15.5 and 15.6 show the word Amazon in a numeric representation given the particular context. Some of the properties or features of the same word have been considered for the various contexts to assign numeric values for those features and the values together form multi-dimensional vectors.

Amazon (Context: Customers of Amazon):
However, if we consider Amazon in the context of a river, the embedding might look something different as shown in Figure 15.5 below.

Amazon (Context: Length of Amazon):
Let us now put the embedding of Hudson by the side of the two embeddings of Amazon as shown in Figure 15.6 below. Looking at the embeddings, it can be observed that there are similarities between the second Amazon and Hudson, whereas Hudson is not similar to the first Amazon.

Further the word embeddings make it possible to perform complex mathematics with words or texts such as *King – man + woman = Queen*, which is a popular equation in

Amazon (Context: Customers of Amazon)

related_to_web services		1	
related_to_online shopping		1	
Active Customers		3	Number of Customers is 3 billion.
Length	0		
is river	0	Vector [1 1 3 0 0 0]	
has basin.	0		

Figure 15.4 Vector Representation of Amazon Company

related_to_Online shopping	0	
Active customers	0	
Length of Amaron	6400	Length of river Amazon is 6400 Kms
is-river	1	
has basin	1	Vector [0 0 0 6400 1 1]

Figure 15.5 Vector Representation of River Amazon

Amazon 1 Context: Customer	Amazon 2 Context: Length	Hudson Context: Length
1	0	0
1	0	0
3	0	0
0	6400	504
0	1	1
0	1	1

Figure 15.6 Embeddings of Two Amazons and Hudson

the NLP domain. The embeddings of the words King, man, woman and Queen based on the features assumed in this example and the equation as mentioned earlier are shown in Figure 15.7.

15.5 Types of Generative AI

The following is a broad list of the types of Generative AI. The list is, however, not exhaustive and is subject to on-going research in this field. Moreover, there are variations within each type in so far as the neural network architectures as developed by various companies like Google, Meta of Facebook, OpenAI and others, are concerned.

1. Transformers
2. Generative Adversarial Networks (GANs)
3. Variational Auto Encoders (VAEs)
4. Diffusion models for image-based Generative AI applications.

Let us look into the features of the above-mentioned types of Generative AI.

Vectors

Features	King	Man	Woman	Queen
power	1	0.3	0.3	1
gender	1	1	–1	–1
rich	1	0.2	0.2	1
has horse?	1	0	0	1
has long hair?	0	0	1	1

Vectors

King	-	man	+	Woman	=	Queen
1		0.3		0.3		1
1		1		-1		-1
1		0.2		0.2		1
1		0		0		1
0		0		1		1

Figure 15.7 Complex Mathematical Equation with Embeddings

15.5.1 Transformers

Transformers are a type of neural network which transforms or translates an input sequence of data (text or image) into an output sequence. Transformers perform the above-mentioned sequence-to-sequence task by learning the context and tracking relationships among the sequence components which may be words, texts or images. For example, sequence-to-sequence tasks include machine translation (say, from English to Spanish), Question-answering, text summarisation and such other tasks. Before we look into the architecture of neural networks and how they operate in a transformer, let me explain some of the key mechanisms or principles behind the functioning of the transformer.

15.5.1.1 Attention Mechanism

Sequence-to-sequence learning like machine translation from one language to another was performed using Encoder–Decoder architecture adopting neural networks comprising of LSTMs or RNNs up to the year 2014. The architecture was similar to what is shown in Figure 15.8 below.

Figure 15.8 shows a short sentence 'Gold is precious' as the input sentence, which is to be translated into Spanish 'oro es preciosa'. The input is fed sequentially (word by word) in hidden time steps into the neural network of the encoder, and the summary of the whole sentence as a context vector output of the encoder is fed into the decoder. The decoder translates word by word into Spanish the sentence as its output, which is compared with the Spanish translation of the sentence, and the result of the comparison is back propagated for the learning of the neural network of the decoder.

The above-mentioned Encoder–Decoder architecture works well so long as the input sentence is small in length (up to 30 words or so). However, in the case of a long sentence or large text, the quality of translation deteriorates. The reason is due to the limitation of the context vector which is only a set of numbers in the case of the above-mentioned architecture and which represents the whole sentence fed to the encoder as input. Obviously, when the sentence is a large one, the context vector fails to retain or represent the context of the long sentence correctly, and as such, the translation quality deteriorates. In order to overcome the above-mentioned problem, the 'attention mechanism' was introduced for the first time by Bahlanau Dzmitry et al. in May 2016. The attention mechanism allows a transformer model to automatically search for parts of an input (source) sentence instead of the whole sentence based on their importance and relevance for predicting a target translated word. The attention mechanism facilitates the creation of a context vector corresponding to each word by the encoder and to forward the same to the decoder in parallel for the training and learning of the neural network, which in turn improves the quality of translation by the decoder. Very large sentences or texts can be processed sequence to sequence adopting the 'attention' principle. For example, let us consider the following sentences:

'John had gone to a furniture shop and purchased a table made of wood. He also purchased an electric fan and returned back to his home'.

In the above sentences, each word needs attention with a few other words. For example, the word 'table' needs the attention of the words 'furniture' and 'wood' and needs very little or no attention of the words 'electric' and 'fan'.

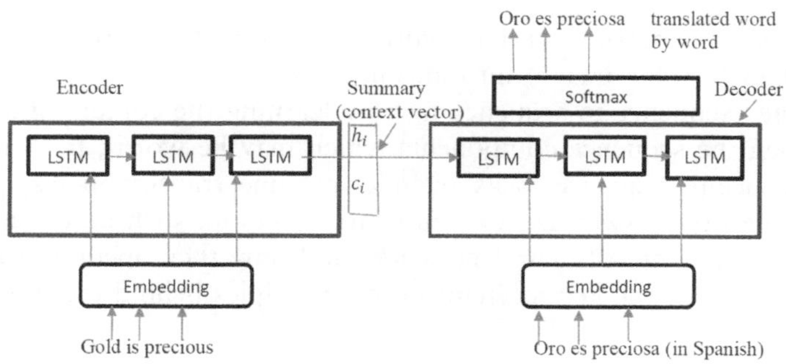

Figure 15.8 Encoder–Decoder Architecture (Sequence-to-Sequence Learning)

Note: In Figure 15.8 softmax is an activation function for the decoder and has been explained in subsequent paragraphs of this chapter.

Let us express the words 'Table' and 'Fan' as 2-dimensional vectors, the dimensions being Furniture and Electricity as follows:

Table = 0.8 * Furniture + 0.2 * Electricity
Fan = 0.1 * Furniture + 0.9 * Electricity

In 2-dimensional space, the vectors for Table and Fan will appear as shown in Figure 15.9 below.

The relative values of the dimensions of each word are known as attention weights or scores. Now that we have an idea of attention, let us see how the attention concept can overcome the problem of Encoder–Decoder architecture for machine translation. Unlike a context vector representing a whole sentence, we can think of creating a context vector for each word in a sentence in parallel with proper attention weights for other words in the sentence, which has been explained in Figure 15.10 below for the same sentence 'Gold is precious'.

Because of attention with parallel processing, the quality of translation improves when the lengths of sentences increase. However, the inherent drawback was that the process was basically sequential in nature as the words in the input sentence had to be fed to the encoder one after another, which creates a problem of training the architecture with massive data sets requiring excessive time. In order to overcome this drawback, the concept of 'self-attention' was introduced by Ashish Vaswani et al. in 2017 in a famous paper titled 'Attention Is All You Need'. The architecture of a transformer was also designed in the same paper. Further, LSTM was replaced by 'self-attention'.

15.5.1.2 Self-attention

In order to comprehend the concept of 'Self-attention' let us begin with static embedding and derive contextual embedding. We consider the word 'chest' in two different contexts namely, chest medicine department and bank currency chest. The static embedding for the word 'chest' is assumed as shown below:

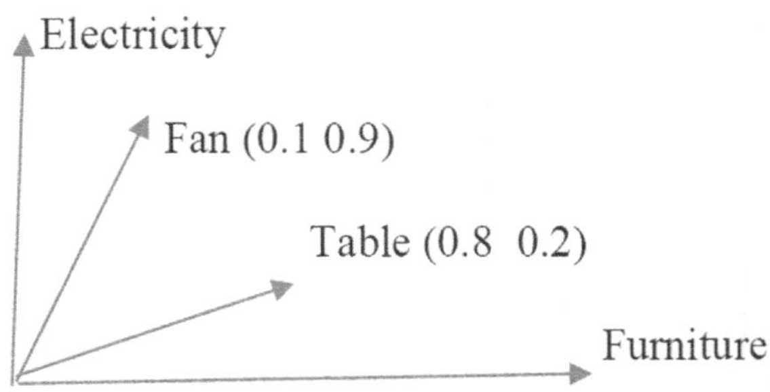

Figure 15.9 Fan and Table as 2-dimensional Vectors

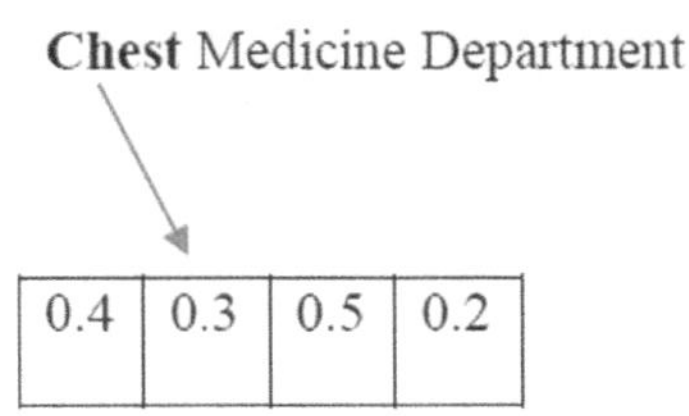

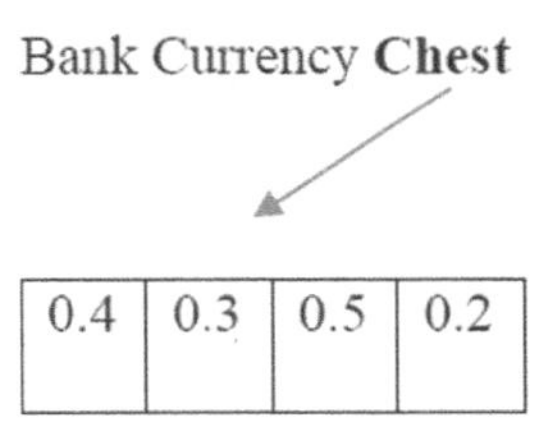

It may be observed that though the static embedding of the word 'Chest' is the same in both the above sentences, the meaning of the word is different in the two sentences. In the case of the first sentence, the meaning of 'Chest' is a part of the human body, whereas in the second one 'Chest' is a box for the safe custody of bank currency notes (cash). In order to overcome the above problem with the static embedding of a word, a dynamic and contextual embedding is required depending upon the context in which the same word is used in a sentence. Self-attention actually performs the task of converting the static embeddings into dynamic contextual embeddings. The self-attention mechanism has been explained in the subsequent paragraphs using the two sentences as mentioned above.

Chest Medicine Department
Chest Med Dept

Bank Currency Chest
Bank Curr chest

We can write the words of each sentence in the proper context assumed as follows:

Chest (New) = 0.6 chest + 0.3 Med + 0.2 Dept

Med (New) = 0.3 chest + 0.5 Med + 0.2 Dept

Bank (New) = 0.7 Bank + 0.2 Curr + 0.1 chest

Curr (New) = 0.3 Bank + 0.6 Curr + 0.1 chest

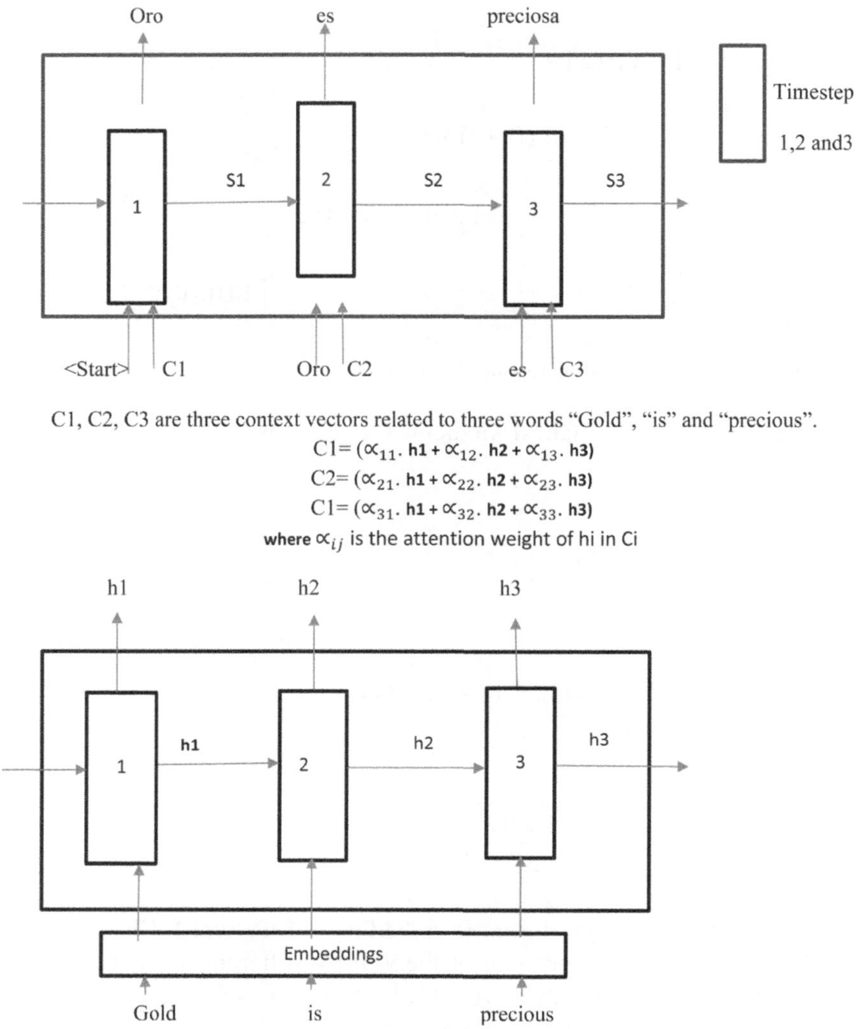

Figure 15.10 Machine Translation Adopting Attention

Dept (New) = 0.2 chest + 0.6 Dept + 0.2 Med

Chest (New) = 0.2 Bank + 0.4 Curr + 0.5 chest

It can be seen from the above that the contextual embeddings of the word 'chest' in the two sentences have become different. We can represent the words in the above equations with their static embeddings Z and the new embedding Z′ as follows for sentence 1.

$$Z'_{chest} = 0.6\ Z_{chest} + 0.3\ Z_{Med} + 0.2\ Z_{Dept}$$
$$Z'_{Med} = 0.3\ Z_{chest} + 0.5\ Z_{Med} + 0.2\ Z_{Dept}$$
$$Z'_{Dept} = 0.2\ Z_{chest} + 0.2\ Z_{Med} + 0.6\ Z_{Dept}$$

It may be mentioned that in the above equations, the fractional coefficients represent the similarities between the new contextual embedding and the static original embeddings of the respective words in the sentence. For example, in the equation for Z'_{chest}, 0.6 is the similarity of Z_{chest} with Z'_{chest}. Likewise, 0.3 is the similarity of Z_{Med} with Z'_{chest} and 0.2 is the similarity of Z_{Dept} with Z'_{chest}.

Now, all these word embeddings are actually vectors in high-dimensional spaces. Hence the similarity between two vectors can be represented as a dot product of the two vectors. Let me clarify the above statement with an example.

Let us consider three vectors (1 4), (3 2) and (5 1) in 2-dimensional space as follows:

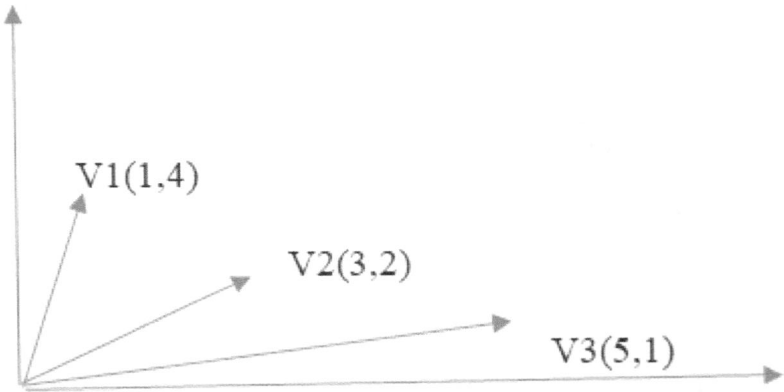

Dot product of V1 and V2 is a scalar which is = $1 \times 3 + 2 \times 4 = 11$; Dot product of V1 and V3 = $1 \times 5 + 4 \times 1 = 9$.

Because the dot product of V1 and V2 is higher than the dot product of V1 and V3, V1 is more similar (close) to V2 rather than to V3. Hence, the three equations representing the new embeddings of the words, as shown above, can be rewritten as follows:

$$Z'_{chest} = [Z_{chest} \cdot Z^T_{chest}]\, Z_{chest} + [Z_{chest} \cdot Z^T_{Med}]\, Z_{Med} + [Z_{chest} \cdot Z^T_{Dept}]\, Z_{Dept}$$
$$Z'_{Med} = [Z_{Med} \cdot Z^T_{chest}]\, Z_{chest} + [Z_{Med} \cdot Z^T_{Med}]\, Z_{Med} + [Z_{Med} \cdot Z^T_{Dept}]\, Z_{Dept}$$
$$Z'_{Dept} = [Z_{Dept} \cdot Z^T_{chest}]\, Z_{chest} + [Z_{chest} \cdot Z^T_{Med}]\, Z_{Med} + [Z_{chest} \cdot Z^T_{Dept}]\, Z_{Dept}$$

where T is for the transpose of the matrix representing the vector.

The dot products within the parentheses are the attention scores and let us represent them as S_{11}, S_{12} and S_{13} respectively for the equation for Z'_{chest}. Similarly, the attention scores of Z'_{Med} and Z'_{Dept} are represented by S_{21}, S_{22} and S_{23} and S_{31}, S_{32} and S_{33} respectively. The attention scores of each word are then passed through the softmax function for normalisation of the scores and we obtain as output the attention weights for each word. Let us represent the attention weights of the word chest as w_{11}, w_{12} and w_{13}. Similarly, the attention weights for the word med are represented as w_{21}, w_{22} and w_{23} and the same for the word dept are represented as w_{31}, w_{32} and w_{33} respectively.

The attention weights for the word chest are calculated by the softmax function as follows:

$$w_{11} = e^{s11} \,/\, (e^{s11} + e^{s12} + e^{s13})$$
$$w_{12} = e^{s12} \,/\, (e^{s11} + e^{s12} + e^{s13})$$
$$w_{13} = e^{s13} \,/\, (e^{s11} + e^{s12} + e^{s13})$$

Similarly, the attention weights are calculated using the same formula as above for the words namely med and dept respectively. The attention weights for a word embedding will add up to 1. Finally, for each word in the sentence, we multiply the attention weights with the original embeddings of each word and add them up to obtain the new embedding of each word. The whole process is shown in Figure 15.11.

It can be observed from Figure 15.11 that the operations for generating the contextual embeddings for the words are performed in parallel and independent of each other. Hence Figure 15.11 can be represented in matrix form as shown below:

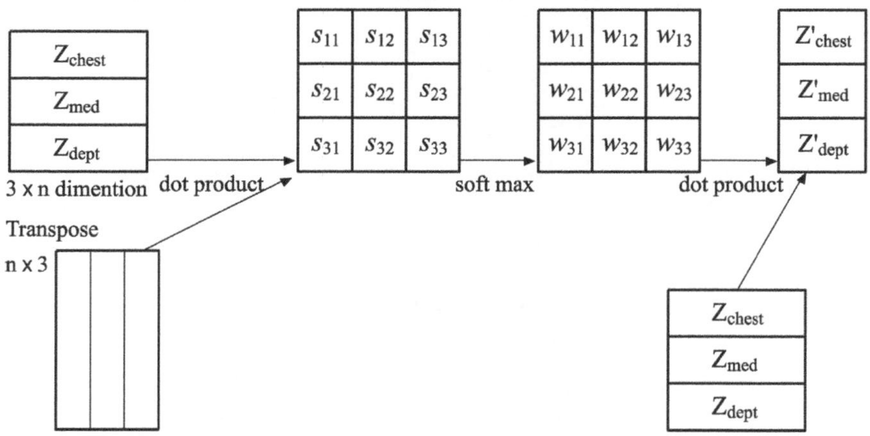

Although the operations are parallel, one drawback of the above model is that there are no learning parameters in the operations and hence the model cannot be trained with actual data through back propagation. This implies that the new embeddings are general contextual embeddings only and not oriented with any specific semantics of the sentence. For example, let us consider the following sentences: 'There was silence. He broke the ice and started talking'. The general contextual meaning of 'broke the ice' is breaking a piece of ice. But in the above sentences the meaning is something else which is 'breaking the silence'. Further, it may be observed that the original embedding of each word in Figure 15.11 appears in three different roles. First as a query which is about its similarity with other word embeddings, second as a key to the query and finally as a value in the equations of the new contextual embeddings of the words. Hence, we create three vectors out of each original static embedding of each word and these vectors are the Query, Key and Value vectors. The three vectors are created by applying the principle of linear transformation of a vector by multiplying it with a matrix of weights. The weights are the learning parameters and their initial values will be assumed randomly and subsequently through the training and back propagation process the optimum values of the weights will be determined based on actual data. In fact, there will be three matrices of weights, one for Query (q), one for Key (k) and one for Value (v). However, the same matrices with the same initial random numbers will be used for all the words of the sentence. The operations will be performed in parallel for the words of the sentence as shown in Figure 15.12.

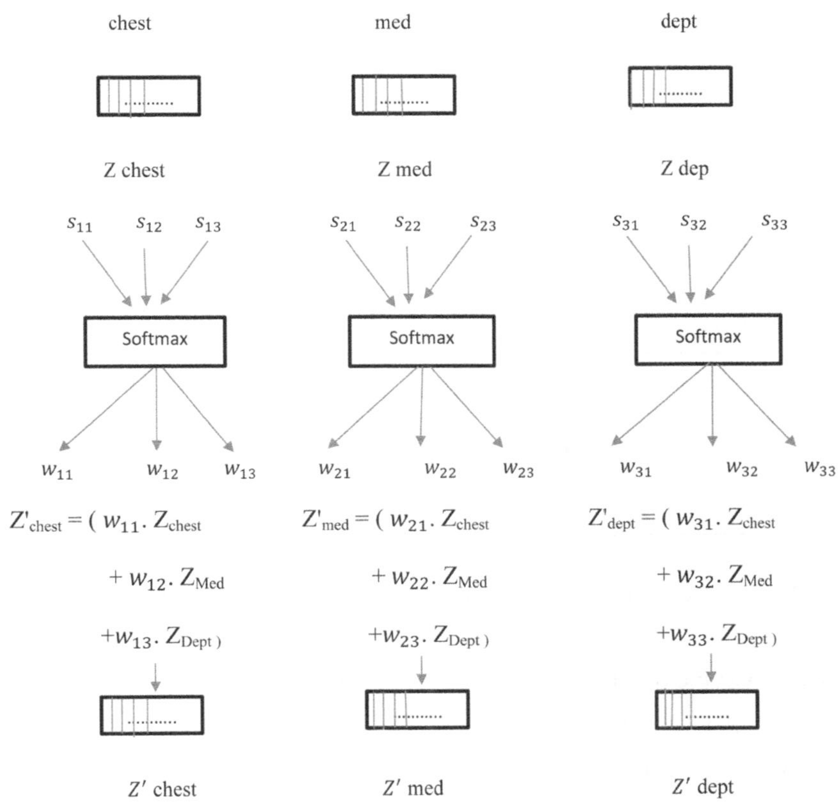

Figure 15.11 Conversion of Static Embedding into Contextual Embedding

The attention scores are divided by the square root of the dimension of the key vector to obtain the scaled attention, which passes through the softmax function to alter the weights of scaled attention. The value vector is multiplied with the scaled attention weights as a dot product to obtain the contextual embeddings of the words. The scaling of the attention scores is necessary to eliminate the gradient problem and to keep the variance under control when the weights are optimised. The above-mentioned process of computing the matrix of output has been described by Ashish Vaswani et al. by the equation Attention (q, k, v) = Softmax $(q \cdot k^T / \sqrt{d_k})v$

Example: Let us consider the sentence 'Chest Medicine Department' once again and assume the original static embeddings of the words as follows:

Chest [1 1 0 1]
Medicine [2 0 1 1]
Department [1 0 0 1]

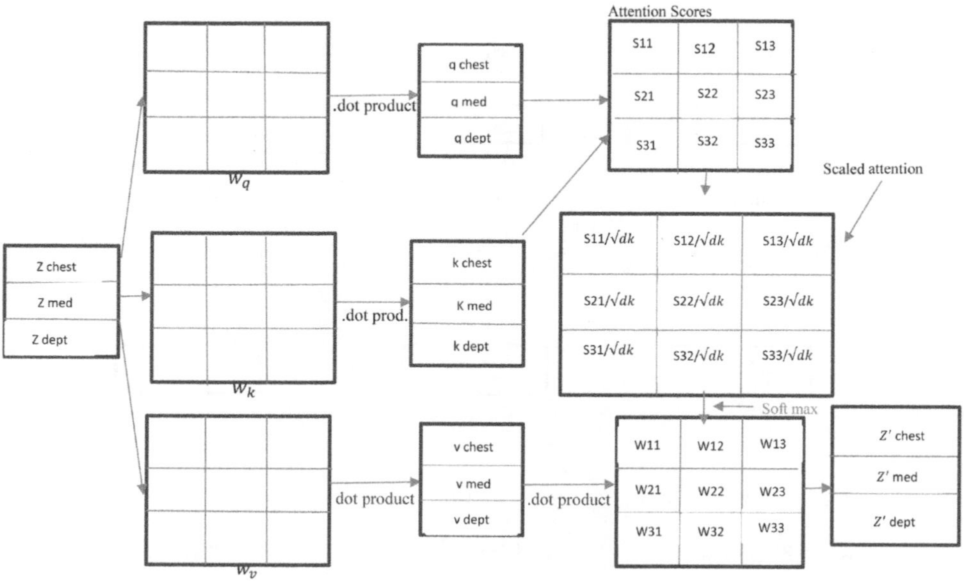

Figure 15.12 Query, Key and Value Vectors Generate Contextual Embeddings

Let us also assume the initial values of the set of weights as follows:

$$w_q = \begin{bmatrix} 0.4 & 0.1 & 0.3 \\ 0.1 & 0.2 & 0.2 \\ 0.2 & 0.3 & 0.54 \end{bmatrix}$$

0.3 0.4 0.2

$$w_k = \begin{bmatrix} 0.3 & 0.2 & 0.3 \\ 0.1 & 0.4 & 0.2 \\ 0.2 & 0.1 & 0.5 \\ 0.3 & 0.3 & 0.1 \end{bmatrix}$$

$$w_v = \begin{bmatrix} 0.2 & 0.4 & 0.2 \\ 0.1 & 0.3 & 0.4 \\ 0.2 & 0.1 & 0.1 \\ 0.4 & 0.2 & 0.2 \end{bmatrix}$$

$q_{chest} = 1 \times 0.4 + 1 \times 0.1 + 0 \times 0.2 + 1 \times 0.3 = 0.8$
$q_{med} = 2 \times 0.1 + 0 \times 0.2 + 1 \times 0.3 + 1 \times 0.4 = 0.9$
$q_{dept} = 1 \times 0.3 + 0 \times 0.2 + 0 \times 0.4 + 1 \times 0.2 = 0.5$
$k_{chest} = 1 \times 0.3 + 1 \times 0.1 + 0 \times 0.2 + 1 \times 0.3 = 0.7$

$k_{med} = 2 \times 0.2 + 0 \times 0.4 + 1 \times 0.1 + 1 \times 0.3 = 0.8$
$k_{dept} = 1 \times 0.3 + 0 \times 0.2 + 0 \times 0.5 + 1 \times 0.1 = 0.4$
$v_{chest} = 1 \times 0.2 + 1 \times 0.1 + 0 \times 0.2 + 1 \times 0.4 = 0.7$
$v_{med} = 2 \times 0.4 + 0 \times 0.3 + 1 \times 0.1 + 1 \times 0.2 = 1.1$
$v_{dept} = 1 \times 0.2 + 0 \times 0.4 + 0 \times 0.1 + 1 \times 0.2 = 0.4$

Hence, the attention scores are calculated as follows:

$S_{11} = q_{chest} \times k_{chest} = 0.8 \times 0.7 = 0.56$
$S_{12} = q_{chest} \times k_{med} = 0.8 \times 0.8 = 0.64$
$S_{13} = q_{chest} \times k_{dept} = 0.8 \times 0.4 = 0.32$

The dimension of the key vector $d_k = 4$ in this case. Hence, = 2. We divide the attention scores as above by 2 and obtain the scaled attention as: 0.28, 0.32 and 0.16.

Next, we apply softmax to the scaled attention values and obtain attention weights as,

Softmax (0.28, 0.32, 0.16) → 0.34, 0.36, 0.30
Therefore $w_{11} = 0.34$; $w_{12} = 0.36$ and $w_{13} = 0.30$
Weighted Sum for Chest = 0.34 chest + 0.36 med + 0.30 dept
Similarly, we can calculate the weighted sum for Medicine and Department as,
Weighted Sum for Medicine = 0.37 chest + 0.42 med + 0.21 dept
Weighted Sum for Department = 0.34 chest + 0.35 med + 0.31 dept

15.5.1.3 Multi-head Attention

Self-attention has a problem which is that, in the case of a sentence having an ambiguous meaning, self-attention will capture only one meaning.

For example, we write a sentence as follows:

'John saw his wife while driving'.

The above sentence can have dual meanings like

1. John saw his wife while he was driving.
2. John saw his wife while she was driving.

In the above situation, the problem is that self-attention will lead to one perspective only. Hence, the concept of multi-head attention was developed in the transformer architecture. Multi-head attention is basically multiple self-attention only, wherein the contextual embeddings are concatenated one after another and the resultant vector is multiplied (dot product) with an output weight matrix, having the weights whose values are obtained as learning parameters through the training process. The final output matrix obtained after training is a balanced mixture of the different perspectives of the sentence. The process of multi-head attention for the two words 'Currency' and 'Chest' is shown in Figure 15.13 for two heads only.

15.5.1.4 Masked Self-attention

Masked Self-attention is used during training the decoder of a transformer model in auto-regressive mode to ensure that the model of the decoder does not consider the tokens in the input sequence which come in future after the current token in order to prevent data 'leakage'. Auto-regression implies that in the case of a sequence-to-sequence task like machine translation of a sentence from one language to another, the current token (word) is translated based on the previous tokens (words) only and not considering the tokens (words) which will come subsequent to the current token (word) as otherwise that would involve information from the future which constitutes data leakage (or cheating). Let me clarify the above statement with a simple machine translation example of the English sentence,

'I know swimming' to French as 'Je sais nager'

While generating the word 'Sais' (English 'know') it is required to mask the word 'nager' to prevent the model from learning from the same word and at the same time ensuring that the generation of the word 'Sais' (English 'know') is conditioned only on 'Je' (English

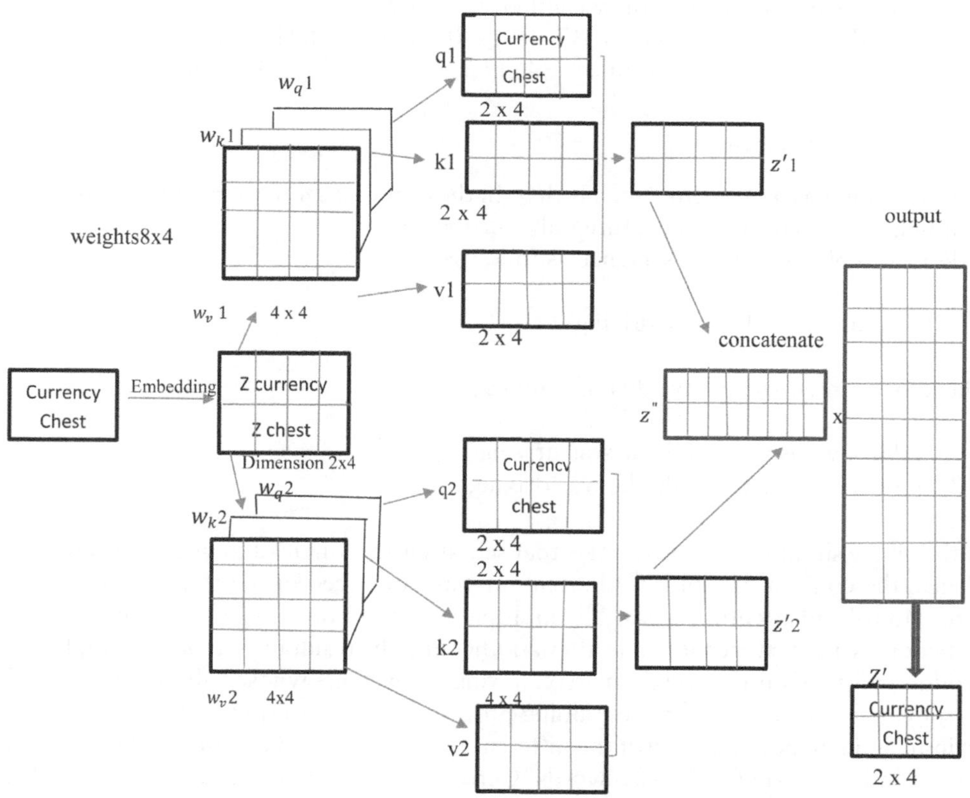

Figure 15.13 Mult-head Attention (2-Heads)

'I') the previous token (word). Masked self-attention is performed by masking the future tokens by substituting their weights with (-) inf (infinity) before the softmax normalisation operation. This causes these tokens to attain zero weights after the softmax operation and as a result, the model pays attention only to tokens previous to the current token in the sequence as illustrated in Figure 15.14 below.

15.5.1.5 Cross Attention in Transformers

Self-attention computes the attention among the different tokens of an input sequence such as the words in an English sentence. Cross attention, however, computes the attention among the tokens of two different input sequences, as in the case of sequence-to-sequence tasks like machine translation or summarisation, image to text or text to image and the like.

Cross attention is important in the case of the decoder. Whenever a new token (word) is generated, say, in the case of a machine translation task, the decoder considers not only the previous tokens (words) generated but also the words of the input sentence and their relationship with the output sentence words or tokens. The mechanism of cross attention has been illustrated with the example of the machine translation of the English sentence 'I know swimming' to French as 'Je sais nager' as shown below:

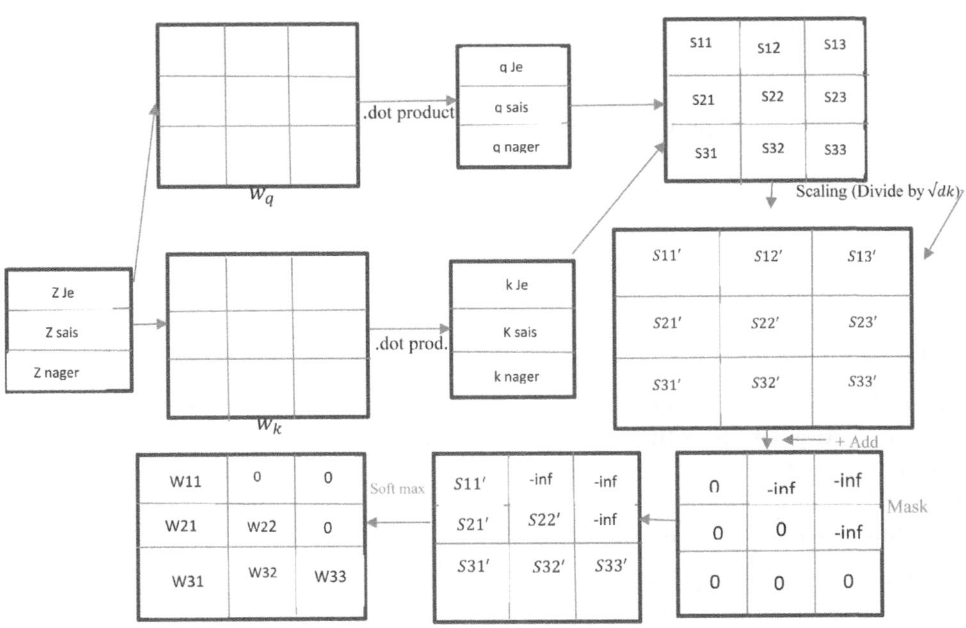

Figure 15.14 Masked Self-attention

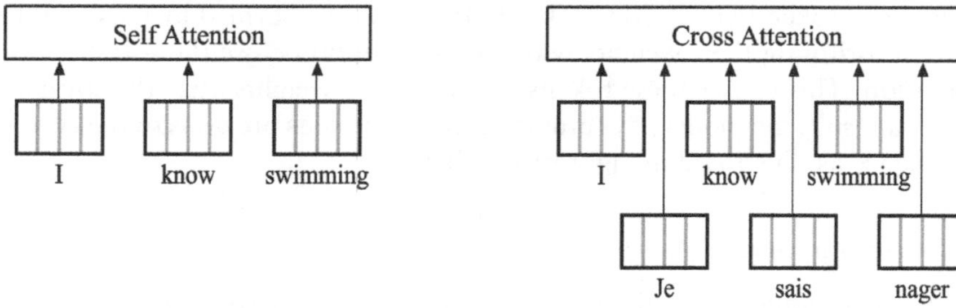

Unlike self-attention which has one input sequence of embeddings of tokens, cross attention has two input sequences, which are embeddings/contextual embeddings of the words of the English sentence and the other the embeddings/contextual embeddings of the words of the translated French sentence.

In case of the Encoder–Decoder architecture of the transformer, cross attention is obtained by taking the query vector from the output of the previous layer of the decoder and the corresponding Key and Value vectors from the encoder output. The detailed process of cross attention is shown in Figure 15.15 for the translation of the English sentence 'I know swimming' into French 'Je sais nager'.

The attention weights are the similarities between each word of the translated sentence (French) with each word of the input sentence in English, as shown in the matrix below:

Input Sequence

Output Sequence	I	know	swimming
Je	w_{11}	w_{12}	w_{13}
sais	w_{21}	w_{22}	w_{23}
nager	w_{31}	w_{32}	w_{33}

15.5.1.6 Positional Encoding in Transformers

Positional encoding represents the location or position of a token in a sequence of tokens, such that each position in the sequence is uniquely represented. In NLP-based applications, the position of a word in a sentence matters a lot in conveying the meaning of the sentence. For example, the following two sentences with the same words have two different meanings with the change of respective positions of the words.

Sentence 1: John outperformed Jack.
Sentence 2: Jack outperformed John.

However, the self-attention mechanism will convey the same meaning for both the sentences. Hence, the necessity arises for incorporating the positional encoding in the self-attention mechanism.

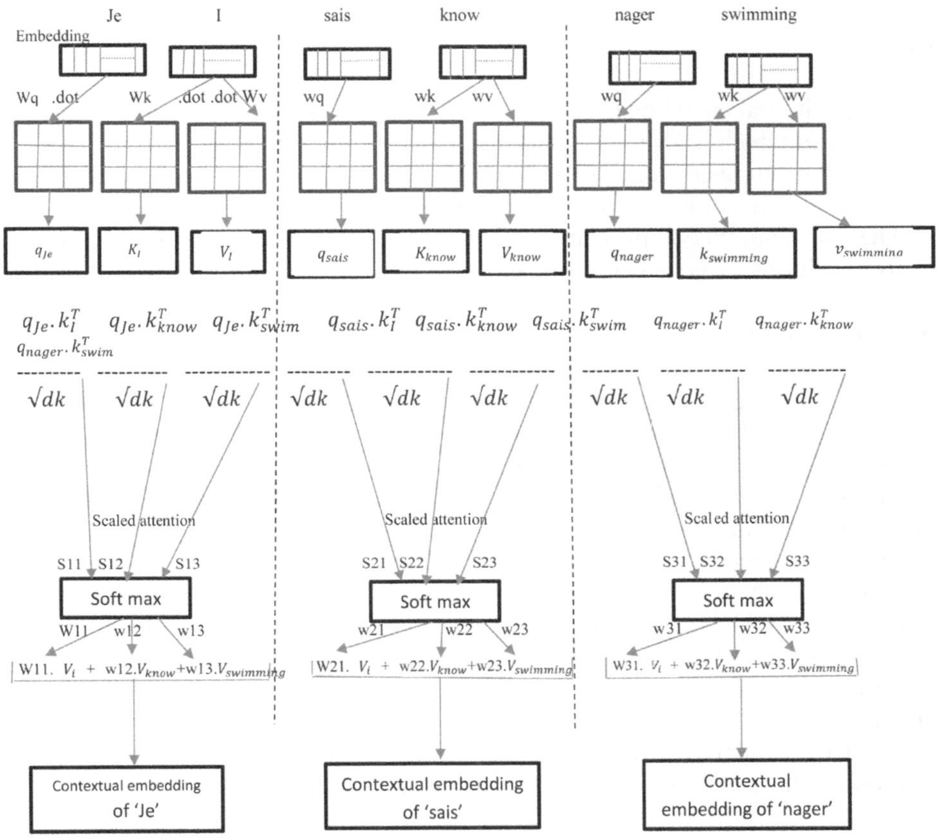

Figure 15.15 Cross Attention Process (Input-Process-Output)

The simple method of positional encoding is to count each word in the sentence and number them as 1, 2, 3 … . The numbers can be fed into the self-attention block along with the respective embedding of the words by adding an extra dimension, as illustrated below:

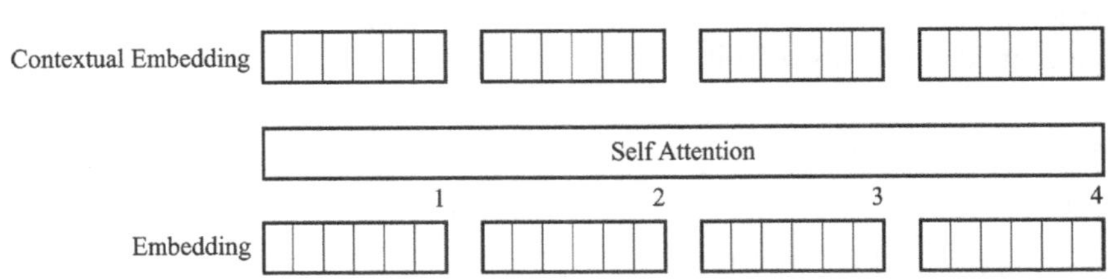

The above method of positional encoding has practical drawbacks and, as such, cannot be applied for positional encoding in a transformer. The drawbacks are mentioned below:

1. The positional encoding is unbounded as there is no upper limit for the count (1, 2, 3 …) and which leads to gradient instability during training.
2. The count numbers are discrete numbers like 1, 2, 3 and, as such, cause hindrance to the smooth training of neural networks.
3. The count numbers represent the absolute positions of the words and not the relative positions, which create problems for transformers.

In order to avoid the above drawbacks, the proponent of the transformer architecture proposed multiple trigonometric functions like sine and cosine functions with different frequencies for the purpose of positional encoding of words in a sentence. They further proposed positional encoding of a word or token as a vector with dimension equal to the dimension of the embedding Vector of the same word. The dimension of the positional encoding vector is obtained as pairs, each pair being the function values of a sine and the corresponding cosine function.

The positional encoding vector of a word obtained as above is added to the embedding Vector of the same word by vector addition instead of concatenation in order to reduce the parameters of the input to the self-attention block, which in turn reduces the training time of the neural network of the transformer. The positional encoding vectors added to the embedding vectors of the words in a sentence are submitted to the self-attention mechanism.

The exact formulae for calculating the positional encodings mentioned in the paper 'Attention Is All You Need' by Ashish Vaswani et al. in 2017 are as follows:

$$\text{PE (pos, } 2i) = \text{Sin (pos} / 10000^{\frac{2i}{d_{model}}})$$

$$\text{PE (pos, } 2i+1) = \text{Cos (pos} / 10000^{\frac{2i}{d_{model}}})$$

where, pos is the position of the word/token, i is the dimension and d_{model} is the dimension of the positional encoding vector. The formulae as above return the values of consecutive pairs of dimensions like (0, 1) (2, 3) (4, 5) and so on. Let me illustrate how to calculate the positional encoding vector using the above formulae for a sentence with two words 'chest' and 'medicine' only as follows:

pos = 0   pos = 1 $d_{model} = 6$

chest   medicine

Embedding   [ ]   [ ]

i = 0 1 2 3 4 5   0 1 2 3 4 5

$i = 0; i = 0;$

PE (0, 0) = Sin ($0 / 10000^0$) = 0   PE (1, 0) = Sin ($1 / 10000^0$) = .01

PE (0, 1) = Cos ($0 / 10000^0$) = 1   PE (1, 1) = Cos ($1 / 10000^0$) = .99

$i = 1; i = 1;$

PE (0, 2) = Sin $(0 / 10000^{\frac{2}{6}})$ = 0   PE (1, 2) = Sin $(1 / 10000^{\frac{2}{6}})$ = .04

PE (0, 3) = Cos $(0 / 10000^{\frac{2}{6}})$ = 1   PE (1, 3) = Cos $(1 / 10000^{\frac{2}{6}})$ = .99

$i = 2; i = 2;$

PE (0, 4) = Sin $(0 / 10000^{\frac{4}{6}})$ = 0   PE (1, 4) = Sin $(1 / 10000^{\frac{4}{6}})$ = .00

PE (0, 5) = Cos $(0 / 10000^{\frac{4}{6}})$ = 1   PE (1, 5) = Cos $(1 / 10000^{\frac{4}{6}})$ = .99

PE of chest [0 1 0 1 0 1]   PE of medicine [.01 .99 .04 .99 .00 .99]

15.5.1.7 Layer Normalisation in Transformers

Normalisation in the case of deep learning is a process of scaling input data or output of any hidden layer to controllable or reasonable limits, thereby reducing the exploding gradient problem. In other words, normalisation facilitates stable optimisation and reduced training time by controlling the variation of gradients during the back propagation process.

The process transforms data to achieve a mean of (zero) and a variation of 1.

Let me illustrate normalisation with the following example.

Data set $[x_i]$ i = 1, 2, 3, 416, 22, 42, 60
Mean, $\mu = (16 + 22 + 42 + 60) / 4 = 35$
Variance $s^2 = [(16 - 35)^2 + (22 - 35)^2 + (42 - 35)^2 + (60 - 35)^2] / (4 - 1)$
$= [361 + 169 + 49 + 625] / 3$
= 401.33 say 400

Hence standard deviation s = 20

The normalised values of the above data set will be (Xi – 4) / s and are as follows:

(16 – 35) / 20 (22 – 35) / 20 (42 – 35) / 20 (60 – 35) / 20

which are –0.95 –0.65 0.35 1.25

It can be observed that the range of the input data set before normalisation was (60–16) = 34; whereas the same after normalisation has become 1.25 – (–0.95) = 2.20 only.

There can be two types of normalisation, namely, Layer normalisation and Batch normalisation. However, transformers follow Layer normalisation only because batch normalisation does not perform well with sequential data and hence is not adopted for the self-attention mechanism. Let me explain both the above-mentioned types of normalisation and why batch normalisation is not applied for self-attention with the following example.

Let us consider a batch of two sentences as parallel inputs to a self-attention block. The sentences are

1. Good morning James and
2. Are you going to the office?

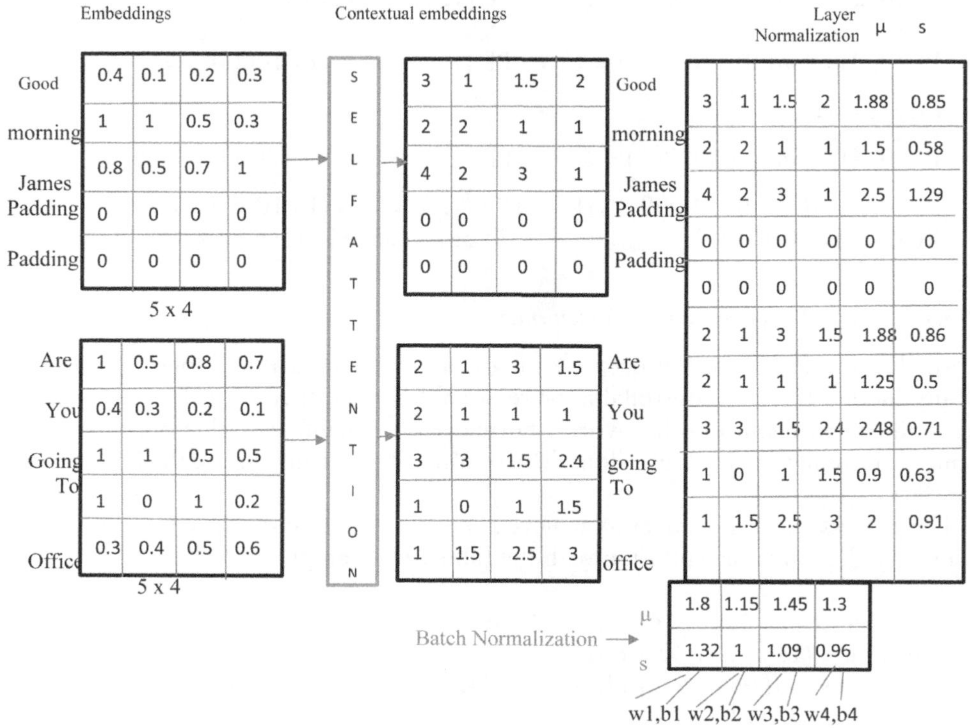

Figure 15.16 Batch Normalisation and Layer Normalisation

Note: The embeddings/contextual embeddings have been assumed as examples only. (w1, b1); (w2, b2); (w3, b3); (w4, b4) are the pairs of weights and biases of the dimensions 1, 2, 3 and 4 of the contextual embedding vectors which are learnable parameters.

Let us also assume that each word of the sentences has a word embedding vector of fourdimensions. Since the two sentences have unequal words and are submitted in parallel to the self-attention block, the sentence with a lesser number of words is required to be padded with tokens of zero value in order to make both the sentences equal in length (number of tokens) as shown in Figure 15.16.

It can be observed from Figure 15.16 that in case of batch normalisation the mean and standard deviation are not the true mean and standard deviation of the data in each dimension (column) because of the padding zero vectors. Because of the above reason, batch normalisation is not applied in the case of self-attention. Instead, layer normalisation is applied in which case the mean and standard deviation of contextual embeddings are calculated layerwise across the dimensions of each word, as shown in Figure 15.16.

The normalised value of each embedding figure is calculated as follows:

For the first word 'Good' and its first dimension, the contextual embedding is 3 and its normalised value = $[(3 - 1.88) / 0.85] \times w_1 + b_1$.

Similarly, for the word 'morning' and its second dimension, the contextual embedding is 2 and its normalised value = $[(2 - 1.5) / 0.58] \times w_2 + b_2$.

15.6 Transformer Architecture

The important concepts underlying the functioning of a transformer like self-attention, multi-head attention, masked-multi-head attention, cross attention, positional encoding and layer normalisation have already been explained in the earlier paragraphs of this chapter. So, let us now look into the details of the exact architecture of a transformer which was developed incorporating these concepts. The typical transformer architecture, which consists of mainly two parts, namely an encoder and a decoder, is shown in Figure 15.17.

In Figure 15.17 the encoder portion bounded by blue lines has been shown on the left side of the diagram with inputs (sequence 1) and the decoder portion bounded by red lines has been shown on the right side of the diagram with output (shifted right) as its one input (sequence 2). In the Figure 15.17, Nx represents the number of encoder blocks, which is 6 in the case of the particular paper, and each block is exactly similar in architecture, but the parameters (weights and biases) are different for different blocks. The encoder architecture with the input, the blocks arranged one after another and the

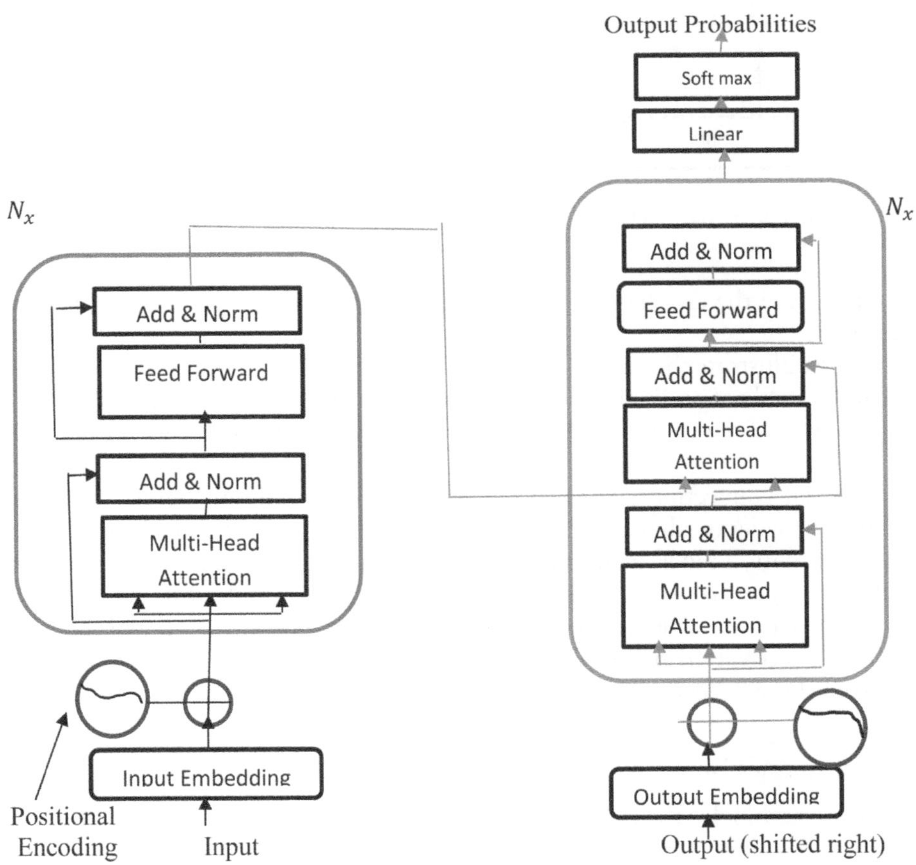

Figure 15.17 Transformer Architecture

Source: 'Attention Is All You Need' by Ashish Vaswani etal., 2017.

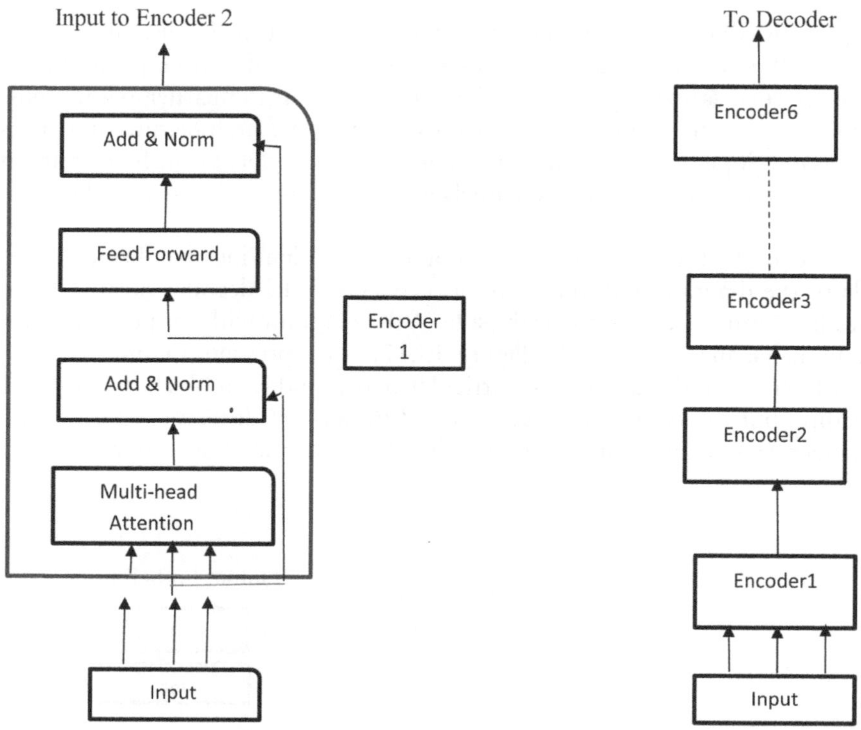

Figure 15.18 Encoder Architecture in a Transformer

final output from the last encoder block, which is the input to the decoder, is shown in Figure 15.18.

Let me first illustrate the various functions of one encoder and the flow of data through it with the example of an English sentence 'God is great' which will be translated into the French sentence 'Dieu est grand' by the decoder of the transformer as shown in Figure 15.19.

The residual connections, as shown in Figure 15.19 facilitate stable training of the model and provide an alternate path to bypass the transformation block, such as the multi-head attention block or feed forward neural network block, in case the particular block does not perform satisfactorily in training. Further, the feed forward neural network, which is a 2-layer neural network, introduces non-linearity in the process because of the 'ReLU' activation function of the neurons in the first layer of the network. The output from the sixth encoder block will be the input to the decoder of the transformer.

15.7 Transformer Decoder Architecture

Like the encoder blocks, the transformer again consists of multiple decoder blocks having exactly similar architecture, but the different blocks have different parameters (weights and biases). In the case of the transformer architecture shown in Figure 15.17 there are six decoder blocks arranged in sequence (1, 2, ... 6) and each block receives data as input in the form of embeddings/contextual embeddings from the encoder output (sequence

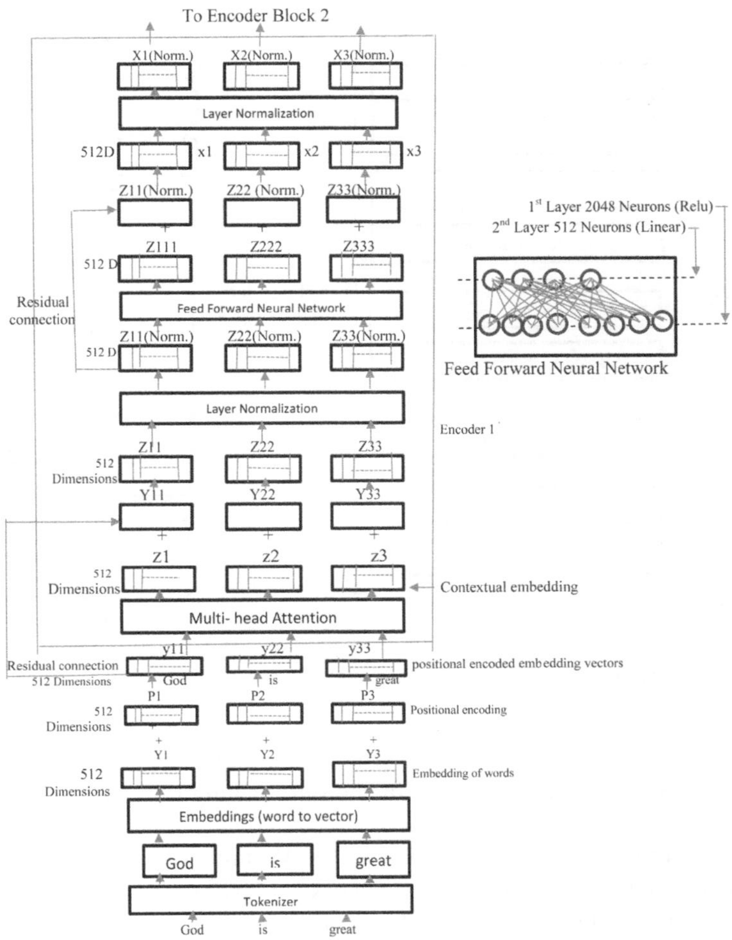

Figure 15.19 Flow of Data through Encoder Block 1

1) and the output of the previous decoder block for blocks (2 to 6) and for block 1, the position encoded embeddings of the tokens of the output sentence (French translation) shifted one position right (sequence 2). The decoder architecture of the transformer is shown in Figure 15.20.

The behaviour of the decoder during training is non-autoregressive while the same during prediction/inference time is autoregressive. The functioning of the decoder with the flow of data through different sequential operations inside during training time, for the machine translation of the English sentence mentioned earlier into French is shown in Figures 15.21 and 15.22 respectively.

Figure 15.21 Shows the flow of data through the decoder block 1 and the output of the same is fed to the decoder block 2. Figure 15.22 shows the flow of data through the decoder blocks 2 to 6 in sequence. However, for each block, the key and value vectors are obtained from the encoder value vectors for the purpose of cross attention. Finally, the output of the last decoder block 6 passes through a single layer linear neural network

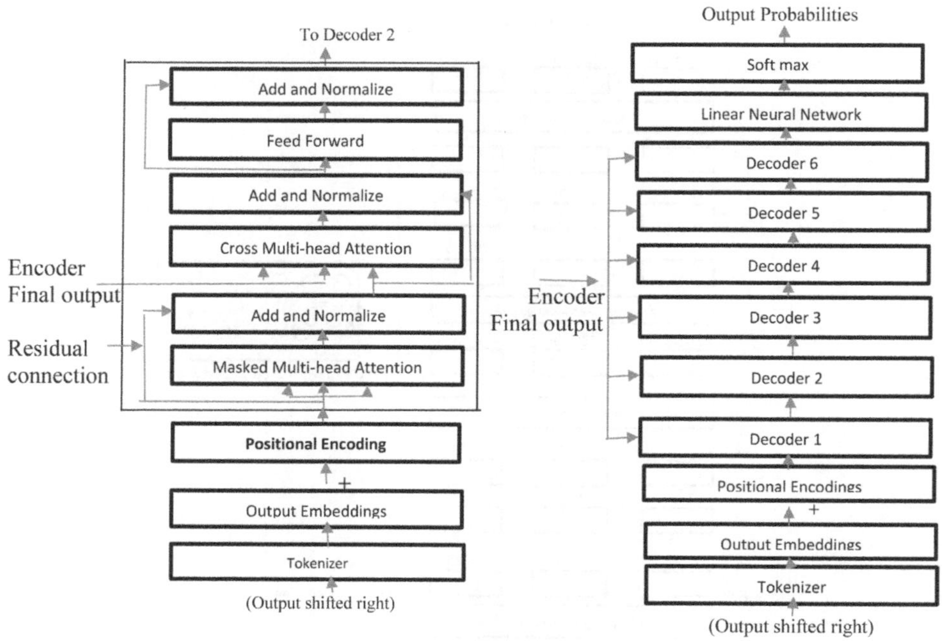

Figure 15.20 Decoder Architecture in a Transformer

having a number of neurons (V) equal to the total number of unique words in the sentences for the machine translation task in the output language, which is French in our example.

The output of the linear neural network will be V number of scalar values corresponding to V neurons obtained by multiplying each token of 512 dimensions with the V number of weights and then adding V number of biases. The values so obtained are fed through softmax to obtain the output probabilities associated with each of the V number of words (or tokens). The word with the highest probability value will be the output word. For example, as shown in Figure 15.22, the next word corresponding to <start> is the word 'Dieu' with the highest probability value of 0.5. Likewise, the next word corresponding to 'Dieu' is 'est', and corresponding to 'est' the next word is 'grand'. It may be stated that during training all the contextual embeddings of the words are fed in parallel and the outputs are obtained through the softmax operation, and the parameters (weights and biases) are adjusted through back propagation process. Hence, the process is non-autoregressive.

During inference/prediction stage, however, the output tokens are fed one after another in the time steps of the decoder, and the contextual embedding obtained for a token is only fed to obtain the immediate next token generated, which in turn is again fed to the input of decoder block 1. This is why the inference/prediction is basically auto-regressive in nature. It may be stated that there are 'Decoder-only' transformers like GPT4 of OpenAI which have been pre-trained for generation of texts and images mainly but those are capable of machine translation tasks also. Such transformers take care of the role of encoder through decoder blocks only and obviously have more layers of decoder blocks compared with transformers having both encoders and decoders. For example, GPT4 has

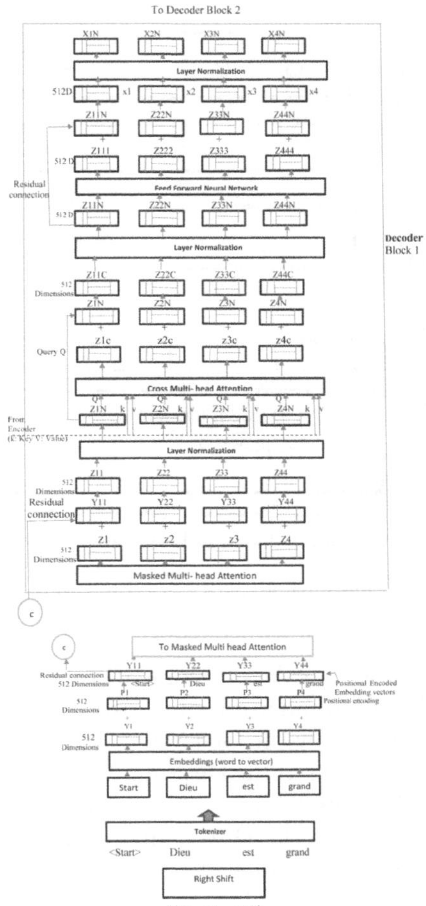

Figure 15.21 Flow of Data through Decoder Block 1

twelve decoder blocks. Similarly, there are 'Encoder-only' transformers like BERT developed by Google. BERT, which stands for 'Bi-directional Encoder Representations from Transformers' is a language model introduced in 2018. The details of such transformers are however beyond the scope of the present text. Interested readers may refer to the available literature on such types of transformers.

15.8 Generative Adversarial Networks (GANs)

Generative Adversarial Network (GAN) consists of two deep neural networks known as the Generator and the Discriminator. The two networks again consist of many layers of convolution, batch normalisation and ReLU and Sigmoid activation functions. The Generator generates fake images, music, sound and voice from noise following unsupervised training whereas the Discriminator undergoes supervised training with real data of images, voice, music and so on. The Generator produces fake data to fool the

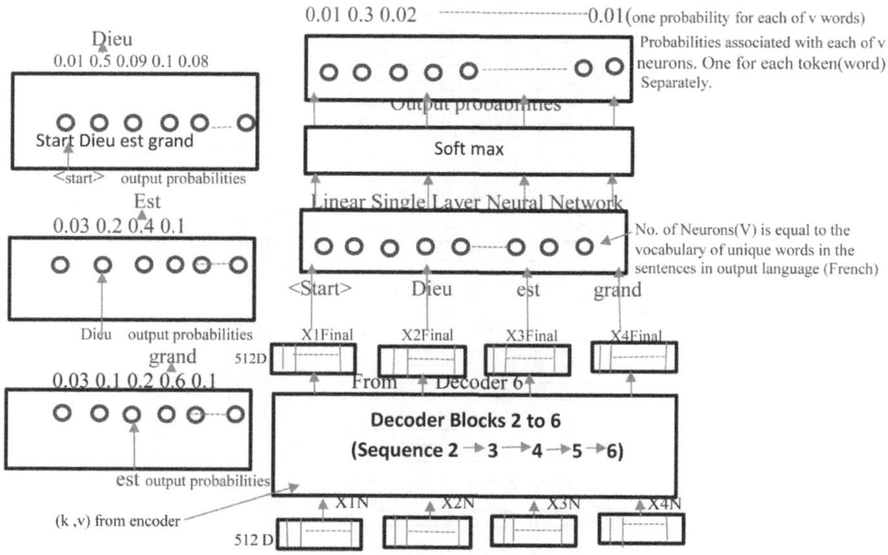

Figure 15.22 Flow of Data from Decodes Block 6 to Output Probabilities

Discriminator, which detects the fake data by comparison with the real data with which it is trained. The output of the Discriminator is obviously either 'True' or 'False' depending upon whether the data submitted by the Generator are real or fake. The Discriminator acts in the role of police. The output of the Discriminator is fed to the Generator through backpropagation, which will improve upon and produce new data (image, voice, music etc.) and again submit the same to the Discriminator. The Discriminator also receives feedback through backpropagation and will become more and more stringent in discriminating between the fake and the real data very minutely.

For example, if the Generator produces the image of a fake currency note of a particular denomination, the Discriminator will be able to detect the same as fake because it has been trained and has access to the images of real currency notes.

The Generator will generate fake images again and again and every time, based on the back propagation, will improve the images to be more and more like the real image to befool the Discriminator. The Discriminator will also improve upon its ability to detect the minute differences between the fake image submitted by the Generator and the real image. Once the Generator produces an image almost like a real one and the Discriminator fails to detect any difference between them, the training or purpose of the GAN model is achieved. This way, GAN can produce images of flowers, animals, birds, art, music and even voices of famous people, handwritten texts and many more things, which are the real applications of GANs. The components of the GAN, as explained above, and its functions are shown in Figure 15.23.

15.8.1 The Steps Involved in the Training of a GAN Model

The steps involved in the training of a GAN model as shown in Figure 15.23 are as follows:

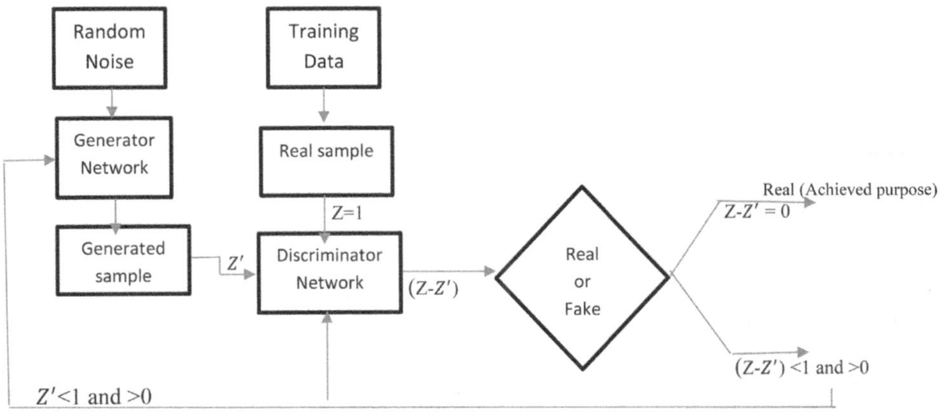

Figure 15.23 GAN Components and Functions

- Step 1: Define the task like create an image
- Step 2: Decide on the network architecture of the Generator and the Discriminator such as the hidden layers, the neurons in each layer and the activation functions like ReLU/Leaky, ReLU/ Sigmoid
- Step 3: Train the Discriminator on real data
- Step 4: Generate fake inputs for the Generator from random noise
- Step 5: Train Discriminator on fake data provided by the Generator
- Step 6: Generator is trained with the output of Discriminator.

15.8.2 Major Applications of GAN

1. Creating new images
2. Image-to-Image translation
3. Text-to-Image generation (object GAN)
4. Semantic-Image-Photo translation
5. Photograph editing
6. Generating music by using some cloned voice (cloning voice)
7. Animation production
8. Image super resolution (low to high resolution)
9. Interactive image generation
10. Generate new human poses and many more applications.

15.8.3 Types of GANS

There are three major types of GANs:

1. Unsupervised GANs—In this type, the generator network takes random noise as input and produces finally a photo-realistic image very close to the images of the training data set. Examples of this type of GANs are GAN of original version, DC-GAN etc.

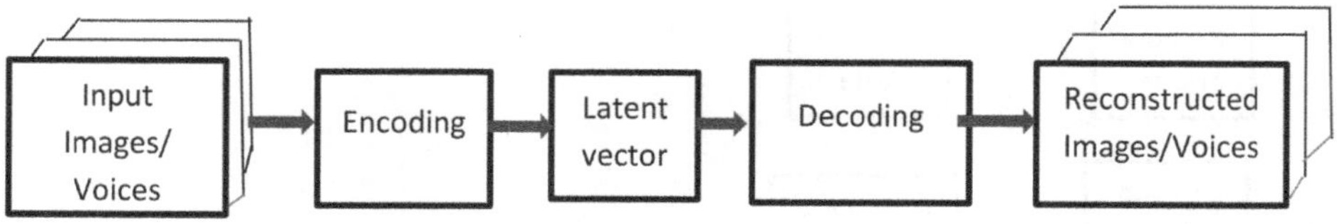

Figure 15.24 Auto Encoder Architecture

2. Style-transfer GANs which translate images from one category to another like from horse to zebra, from sketch to images etc. Examples of this type are cycle GAN and pix-to-pix.
3. Conditional GANs which jointly learn on features and images to generate images subject to conditional features. For example, images of birds can be passed to the GAN network with the actual labels such as parrot, pigeon, robin, etc. Examples include Big GAN which is a state-of-the-art conditional GAN from DeepMind of Google.

15.8.4 Variational Auto Encoders (VAEs):

VAEs are powerful generative models having varied applications such as generating pure synthetic music, fake human faces, or adding sunglasses to the face of Monalisa and so on. The architecture of an auto encoder is shown in Figure 15.24.

The input data (image/voice/music) is encoded into a smaller space, the latent vector and then decoded back into the reconstructed original data. The application of the auto encoder is two-fold. Firstly, it can encode noisy images or data into low-dimensional latent vector representation, which the decoder can convert to noiseless images/data, and the decoder can be trained accordingly. Secondly, it can reduce reconstruction loss or error due to anomalous data.

VAES are generative because, for an input image, it can generate output images with variations. The Variational Auto Encoder's primary role is to let us know how to identify appropriate latent vectors for data like an image or a voice. The Variational Auto Encoder (VAE) constrains the latent vector values for the data/images to a specific continuous region. Further, VAEs map the latent variable vectors for the data/images to a normal distribution and use the mean (□) and standard deviation (□) to describe the distribution. The distance between the learnt distribution and the standard normal distribution, as mentioned above, is expressed as a loss function using Kullback–Leibler (KL) divergence. KL divergence is a method of measuring the difference between two probability distributions over the same variable. Hence, while training the VAEs, the objective is to force the distribution close to the standard normal distribution by using KL as the loss function in addition to the reconstruction loss due to anomalous data, as mentioned in an earlier paragraph of this chapter. The architecture of a Variational Auto Encoder (VAE) is as shown in Figure 15.25.

Referring to Figure 15.25; Z = μ+ ɕ . € where μ and ɕ are the learnt parameters during back propagation of the VAE whereas, €~N(0, I) is the standard normal distribution and is not learnt during back propagation and denotes the random sample in the fixed space.

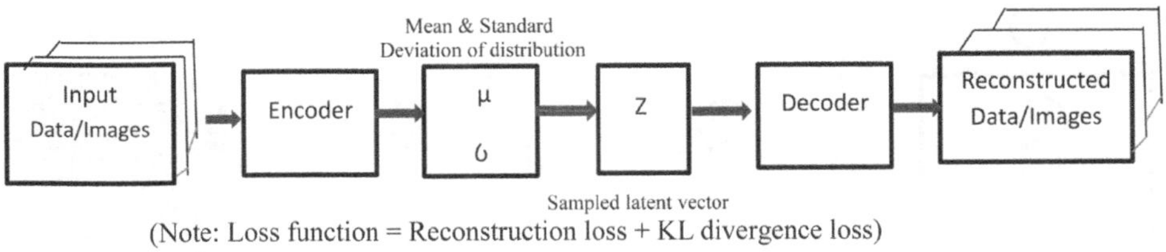

Figure 15.25 Variational Auto Encoder (VAE) Architecture

15.8.5 Diffusion Models

Diffusion models are also a class of generative models which are used for various applications like high quality image generation, audio generation and similar applications. For example, Dall-E 2 of OpenAI can create realistic images and art from a text description such as 'an astronaut riding a horse'. Diffusion models are powerful tools for artists, designers and content writers. More complex diffusion models are 'Glide' a text guided model, 'Midjourney' a Generative AI program (mainly text-to-image AI) hosted by San Francisco based research Laboratory Midjourney and 'Sora' of OpenAI. Sora creates video from text.

Diffusion models were inspired by the principle of non-equilibrium thermodynamics according to which a system in a non-equilibrium state tends to undergo transition to an equilibrium state by diffusion of matter/particles from high concentration zone to low concentration zone for achieving homogeneity. For example, if we pour milk into a glass of clear and transparent water, the milk spreads in the water and the water becomes turbid. Following the above-mentioned principle of thermodynamics, Diffusion models start with clear image data and gradually add random (Gaussian) noise (pixel values) into it step-by-step, introducing a little bit of noise in each step and finally completely destroying the image (data) into full noise. This sequence of steps comprises the forward process of the Diffusion model. Later the model learns how to reverse and remove the noise following the same steps backward and restore the clear image with some variations as conditioned by the training process.

The sequence of steps for the restoration of clear images from full noise with some variations comprises the reverse process of the Diffusion model. The model learns through training how noise was added in each step of the forward process and in the same way how to remove the noise in each step of the reverse process. The transition of the clear image into complete noise in a sequence of steps in between, follows a Markov chain, which implies that the transition process of adding noise at any stage depends upon the immediate, preceding stage of the image in the forward process as shown in Figure 15.26. This sequence of transition as a Markov chain facilitates the restoration of the image from noise, stage by stage, in the reverse process of removing noise.

The Gaussian noise introduced in the forward process is a noise having the Gaussian or normal probability distribution with different means and variances. The location of the noise also changes accordingly. Introducing Gaussian noise into an image will change the values of the pixels of the image slightly in the area of the distribution. Reversing or removing the noise means recovering the pixel values of the image so that the recovered image looks like the original image. In order to perform the reverse process from full

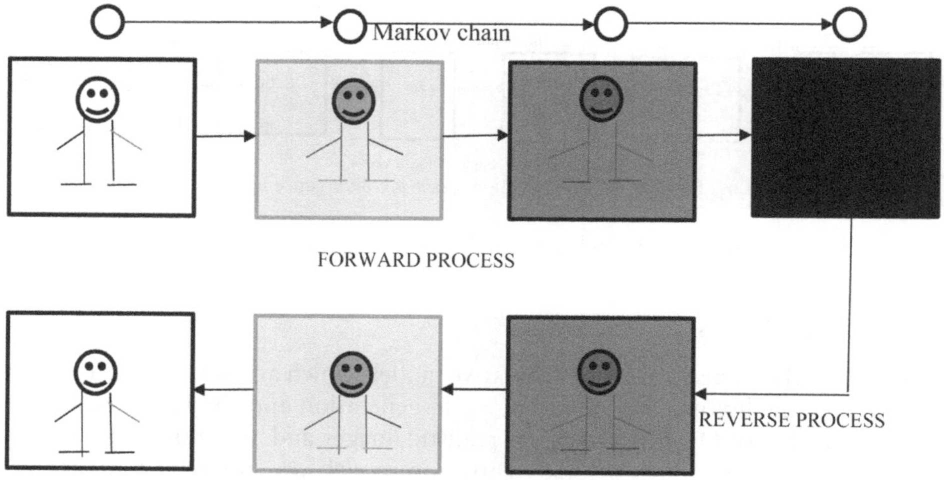

Figure 15.26 Forward Process and Reverse Process of Diffusion Model

noise, we feed the full-noise image as input to a Convolutional Neural Network (CNN), and the CNN converts the image at any step to its previous step, removing a little bit of noise and the process continues step by step through a series of convolutions known as 'U-Net' because of its shape like 'U'. The image is first made to a small representation through convolution, which is the base diffusion model, and which is then up-scaled to the original dimensions of the input image.

15.8.5.1 Stable Diffusion with Latent Diffusion model

Stable Diffusion was developed by Patrick Esser and Robin Rombach at Stable AI, a start-up company based in London (UK) and California (USA). Stable diffusion adopts the latent diffusion model architecture. Figure 15.27 shows the Stable Diffusion process with latent diffusion model.

The Latent Diffusion Model shown in Figure 15.27 Consists of three parts, namely a Variational Auto Encoder (VAE), a modified U-Net comprising a Residual Net with Skip Connection along with a cross-attention mechanism and a text encoder.

The encoder (VAE) compresses the image from pixel space to a smaller dimensional latent space with the more fundamental semantic meaning of the image to reduce significantly the cost of training. Subsequently, Gaussian noise is iteratively applied to the compressed latent representation during the forward diffusion process. The U-Net block comprising a Residual Net backbone with skip connections denoises the output of forward diffusion (Z_T) backward to obtain a latent representation (Z) which is converted to the final image by the VAE decoder back into the pixel space. The denoising step can be conditioned with a text, an image or any other modality. In order to facilitate conditioning on text, a clip text encoder (ViT-L/14) is used to transform text prompts to an embedding space. The encoded conditioned data is fed to the denoising U-Net through a cross-attention mechanism for the training of both ${}_{\theta}$ and τ_θ jointly.

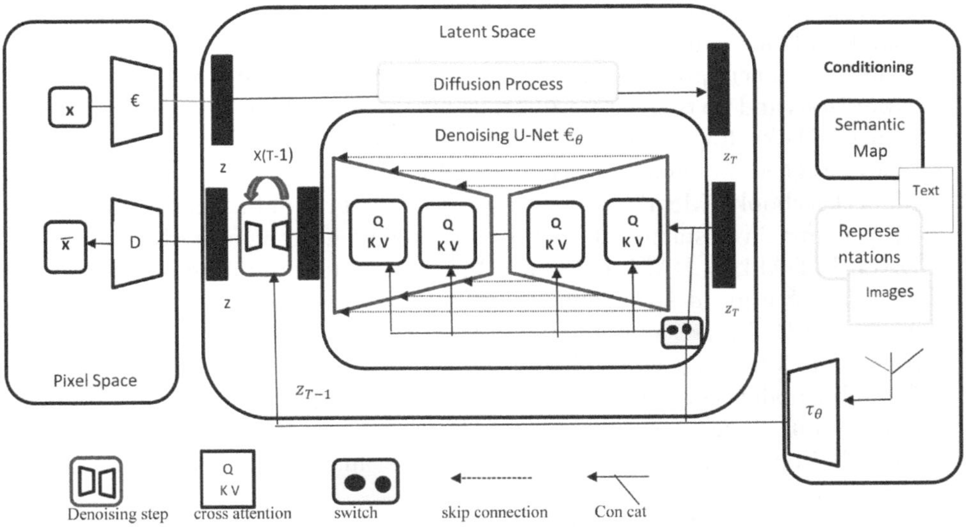

Figure 15.27 Stable Diffusion with Latent Diffusion Model

Source: Rombach Robin et al. 'High Resolution Image Synthesis with Latent Diffusion Models' in *CVPR*, pp. 10689–10695, 2022.

15.9 Generative AI Tools

Generative AI tools facilitate the ease of development of user-friendly applications for generating texts, videos, codes and images according to user needs. For example, the conversational Generative AI chatbots can prepare a proposal, a business report, a PowerPoint presentation, a Python code or emails to shareholders of a company forwarding the meeting notice with agenda and also can perform a vast number of similar tasks rapidly. Once upon a time, human beings like programmers, managers or other professionals used to perform such tasks spending considerable time and effort. We can adopt our favourite AI chatbot and write a short prompt for a particular task, and a trained and disembodied AI performs the task to our satisfaction. 'Prompt' depicts the context, query or specific instruction through which users interact with the AI system to obtain the desired outcome.

Generative AI tools include a variety of chatbots, Python composable frameworks for formulation of prompts, libraries of foundation models and the like. The following is a list of important Generative AI tools being used extensively.

1. **ChatGPT**: ChatGPT is OpenAI's powerful chatbot through which users can get their queries answered with the intelligence of Large Language Models (LLMs) like GPT-3 and the later GPT-4.
2. **Gemini**: Gemini is a Generative AI chatbot developed by Google. Gemini is based on the Gemini Large Language Model of Google and was launched in 2023 as a competitor to OpenAI's ChatGPT. It is a chatbot for content generation. In 2023, Google announced the state-of-the-art language model PALM 2 powering Gemini.

3. **Claude**: Claude is a chatbot by Anthropic, an AI Safety and Research Company. The chatbot is built on a family of Large Language Models (LLMs) also named Claude. Claude can be used to do varied tasks like idea generation, creation of images, document processing, etc. Claude can accept as input—tables, lists, numeric expressions and texts. The latest Claude family of LLMs consists of three modules, namely, Haiku for speed, Sonnet for balanced capabilities and performance and Opus designed for complex reasoning tasks.
4. **Meta (Facebook)**: Meta's AI chatbot is operating behind Instagram and Facebook. Meta Llama 3 is a state-of-the-art open-source Large Language Model.
5. **DALL-E**: DALL-E, DALL-E 2 and DALL-E 3 are text-to-image models developed by OpenAI using deep learning methodologies to generate digital images from 'prompts'. DALL-E 2 and DALL-E 3, the latest ones, use a diffusion model conditioned on CLIP image embeddings.
6. **GitHub Copilot**: GitHub Copilot is an AI tool for code completion assistance and also an automatic programming tool developed by GitHub and OpenAI jointly. GitHub Copilot can generate suggestions for autocomplete style that assist the users who write code.
7. **Microsoft Copilot**: Microsoft Copilot is a conversational chatbot that allows users to search for specific information, chat about any topic of interest and get answers to questions. Besides, Microsoft Copilot (formerly known as Bing Chat) can generate images and also helps users with vacation planning, fitness training and cooking recipe generation.
8. **Jasper Chat**: Jasper formerly known as Jarvis, is an AI-powered chatbot for content writing that enhances marketing efforts, thus helping enterprise marketers. Jasper Art is a Generative AI tool for authors, commercial designers and generative and social media managers as well.
9. **Chat Sonic**: It was developed by Write Sonic as a chatbot. It can write articles, blog posts and a variety of documents. It can also copy, edit and summarise large documents. Chat Sonic has a special feature that it can read and understand the news and update the content to make it current.
10. **Lang Chain**: Lang chain is an open-source Python and JavaScript development framework which provides tools and flexible abstractions for developers who build applications on LLMs. Lang chain simplifies the process of building such applications.

    For example, developers can use Lang chain components to build new prompt chains or customise existing templates (Frameworks). Let us summarise the major functionalities of Lang chain as follows:

    (i) Combines LLMs with external data like various company documents, databases, etc.
    (ii) Transforms data into vector representation for efficient searching and retrieval
    (iii) Actions on retrieved data—Lang chain allows us to perform various actions on the retrieved data such as generating PDFs, sending emails, etc.
    (iv) Applications developed with Lang chain provide great utility for various use cases such as question-answering, text generation tasks and more complex solutions using LLM as a 'reasoning engine'.

    Some of the use cases of Lang chain are as follows:

- Data analysis
- Flight reservation
- Educational tools
- Code analysis for debugging
- Personal AI agents
- Connecting various APIs.

11. **OpenAI Codex**: Codex is an AI developer tool for code generation in many different programming languages like Python script, JavaScript, Perl, Ruby, Swift, etc.
12. **Streamlit**: Streamlit, an open-source Python framework, is a tool for easy and rapid development of interactive applications on Generative AI foundation models. Streamlit facilitates the app creation process.
    The following is a list of major Streamlit apps:
    - Streamlit templates
    - NLP
    - Engineering and science
    - Computer vision and images
    - Business and finance
    - Management of educational systems
    - Data visualisation
    - Society
    - Geography and many other apps.
13. **Amazon Bedrock (AWS Bedrock)**: Amazon Bedrock on AWS is a fully managed service that offers a number of Generative AI foundation models from leading companies of artificial intelligence such as Anthropic, Cohere, Meta, Mistral, AI 21 Labs, Stability AI and many others with complete security and privacy. Some of them are listed as follows:
    (i) Claude Versions 1.2, 1.3 and 2 from Anthropic
    (ii) Stable Diffusion
    (iii) Jurassic 2-Mild and Jurassic 2-Ultra from AI 21 Labs.
    (iv) Llama 2 from Meta
    (v) Command from Coherie
    Users with the help of Amazon Bedrock can customise the top foundation models for individual use cases through Finetuning and Retrieval Augmented Generation (RAG) techniques.
14. **Hugging Face**: Hugging Face is a platform for artificial intelligence (AI) and machine learning community similar to GitHub for open-source software development community. It is designed to be more accessible, collaborative and open to everyone in the AI community. Originally founded in 2016 as a company by French entrepreneurs Clement Delangue, Jullien Chaumond and Thomas Wolf in New York City, USA for developing chatbot apps for teenagers, today it has become a US $4.5 billion company with a repository of open-source LLMs, PyTorch Hub, TensorFlow Hub, pretrained transformer library, datasets of various categories and spaces (free tier), where developers can host their own demo applications for encouraging open-source development. Hugging Face has got in its repository about 900,000 models, 200,000 datasets and 300,000 demos. Many organisations like Google, Meta, Amazon Web Services, Microsoft and Grammarly are using Hugging Face. The repositories of Hugging Face can be listed by browsing through GitHub.

15. **PyTorch**: PyTorch is a Python framework used for developing deep learning models pertaining to applications such as image recognition and natural language processing. Machine learning developers find it easy to learn and apply PyTorch because of its simple features. The Python framework consists of efficient and flexible backend libraries of Torch with an intuitive Python frontend PyTorch which facilitates rapid prototyping, readable code and development of wide varieties of deep learning models. PyTorch was released to open source in 2017.
16. **TensorFlow**: TensorFlow is also an open-source machine learning framework in Python. TensorFlow can be used for a variety of tasks, but its main use involves training and inference of deep neural networks. A tensor is basically a multidimensional array with multiple indices, which describes a multi-linear relationship between sets of algebraic objects related to a vector space. Both PyTorch and TensorFlow use graphs and tensors and process those through GPUs (Graphical Processing Units) and TPUs (Tensor Processing Units).
17. **Keras**: Keras is a high-level API for deep learning neural networks developed by Google. Keras is in Python and makes it easy for human developers to implement neural networks. Keras offers a friendly interface for quick experimentation and prototyping.

15.10 Important Case Studies of Application of Generative AI Models Like ChatGPT in Various Areas

1. **Healthcare**: Patient care and medical assistance—a healthcare service provider in the USA used ChatGPT to provide detailed post-treatment care guidance.

2. **Education and Learning**: Self-study—students use ChatGPT for problem solving and clarifications on complex topics of study. For example, a teacher in India leveraged ChatGPT to explain science, technology, engineering and mathematics concepts in local schools for deeper comprehension among students. Generative AI platforms create customised lesson plans, quizzes and interactive content customised to individual learning styles.
3. **Business and Marketing**: ChatGPT is adopted to create blogs, product specifications, email templates and social media posts. For example, a start-up in Europe automated 80% of its blog creation using AI tools.
4. **Programming and Software Development**: Debugging and code generation in various programming languages like R, Python and Java are very common applications of ChatGPT. The following is the Python code (screenshot) for finding the factorial of a digit (n) generated using ChatGPT.

   A simple Python code to calculate the *factorial* of a number:

Using a loop:

```
python
Copy Edit
def factorial(n):
if n < 0:
return 'Factorial is not defined for negative numbers'
result = 1
```

```
for i in range (1, n + 1):
result *= i
return result
# Example usage
Print (factorial (5)) # Output: 120
```

Using recursion:

```
python
Copy Edit
def factorial _recursive(n):
if n < 0:
return 'Factorial is not defined for negative numbers'
if n == 0 or n == 1:
return 1
return n * factorial_ recursive (n – 1)

# Example usage

Print (factorial_recursive (5)) # Output: 120
```

A game development company saved 15% of production time by using ChatGPT for optimising non-critical backend logic.

5. **Customer Support**: ChatGPT works like a virtual assistant to answer customer queries and resolve common complaints round the clock (24/7). For example, a telecommunications company used ChatGPT for online customer support to reduce problem resolution time by 30%.
6. **Legal Assistance**: Drafting legal documents such as contracts, agreements and assurances can be done using ChatGPT. For example, a law firm in Australia adopted ChatGPT to draft legal documents, saving significant time for lawyers.
7. **Creative Writing and Entertainment**: Script and story writing—script writers use ChatGPT to brainstorm ideas, generate dialogues and create story plots. For example, an Indian story writer used ChatGPT to make character dialogues, making them more entertaining.
8. **Art and Design**: AI tools like Runway Machine Learning and Adobe Firefly enable artists to generate high-quality visuals with minimal effort. Fashion brands use Generative AI to design custom apparel.
9. **Finance**: Streamlining of financial operations and financial fraud detection has been adopted with considerable success adopting Generative AI. For example, financial analysts use Generative AI for generating reports and summaries of financial operations of an enterprise. Chatbots provide investment advice for customers, and fraudulent transaction patterns are identified using AI-generated datasets.
10. **Sustainability Initiatives**: AI-generated climate models simulate environmental impact and predict weather patterns. Likewise, AI-generated synthetic data facilitate analysis of natural resource management.
11. **Research and Scientific Analysis**:
    (i) Data analysis and summarisation—a research team in Japan relied on ChatGPT to generate summaries of journals for their systematic review project.

(ii) Application of Generative AI on life science advances—Arc Institute, which is an independent research institute with faculty members from Stanford and Berkeley universities in the USA, has made extensive use of Generative AI in life sciences. Similar to ChatGPT of OpenAI and Gemini of Google, which are Large Language Models, Evo is a biological foundation model developed by researchers of Arc Institute, as reported by Eric Nguyen et al. in a paper in February 2024. Evo is a long-context model (length 131 kilobases at single nucleotide byte resolution) that can be used for the prediction of tasks and generative tasks from molecules to genome scale. The genome is a sequence that completely encodes the DNA, RNA and proteins that orchestrate the function of the whole organism. It is trained on a massive dataset of whole prokaryotic genomes. Evo is scaled to 7 billion parameters. Prokaryotes are organisms whose cells lack a nucleus and other organelles. Prokaryotes can be either bacteria or archaea, which bioscientists believe have unique evolutionary lineages. Evo can predict the function of genes and also generate new CRISPR systems. CRISPR (short form of 'Clustered Regularly Interspaced Short Palindromic Repeats') is a technology that researchers use to selectively modify the DNA of living organisms. CRISPR was adopted by genome editing systems found in bacteria.

Evo is the first model able to design CRISPR systems at the whole genome scale. In future, Evo can be applied to accelerate discoveries in biology, chemistry and materials science.

15.11 Key Benefits of Generative AI

The key benefits of Generative AI are as follows:

1. Increased productivity is achieved due to the automation of repetitive and time-consuming tasks like content creation, coding, data analysis and so on. For example, software developers save time by using tools like GitHub Copilot to generate boilerplate code.
2. Enhanced creativity on the part of artists who use Generative AI tools like DALL-E or Mid Journey to create unique designs of visual art, music or stories in minutes only.
3. Personalisation—Generative AI creates customised outputs tailored to user preferences and behaviours. For example, many e-commerce platforms use Generative AI to generate customised product recommendations.
4. Cost efficiency is achieved due to the reduction of operational costs by automating workflows and minimising the need for human intervention in repetitive tasks. Many organisations deploy AI chatbots to handle customer inquiries for service, thereby cutting staffing costs. ChatGPT can be used to provide improved customer support and enhance customer satisfaction.
5. Scalability is obtained through handling large-scale tasks efficiently, like generating a huge number of unique outputs or analysing vast datasets. For example, Generative AI can generate advertising materials for marketing campaigns targeting diverse demographics across multiple geographic regions.
6. Improved decision-making is achieved by way of generating insights, forecasts and simulations which facilitate strategic planning decisions.

7. Accessibility to expertise is by way of offering advanced technical know-how to users who require such know-how. For example, non-programmers can use Generative AI to write scripts.
8. Faster innovation—for example, AI models like AlphaFold accelerate protein structure prediction, which speeds up drug discovery.
9. Data generation—Generative AI often generates synthetic data for training models or for testing various scenarios without depending upon real-world data sets.
10. Bridging language barrier—Generative AI facilitates multi-lingual communication by generating translations and summarising content across languages.
11. Environmental benefits—Generative AI can simulate and predict environmental changes, which facilitate resource management and sustainability. AI models help optimise energy consumption or predict climate change impacts.
12. Democratisation of technology—Generative AI provides powerful tools to individuals and small business enterprises that were previously available only to large public sector enterprises and private organisations only.

15.12 Demerits of Generative AI

Generative AI has many merits, such as speed, creativity, a large knowledge base, scalability and improved customer support, which have made a significant impact on many domains. However, Generative AI has its demerits as well, such as vulnerability to bias, ethical issues like job displacement, accuracy, data privacy, limited contextual understanding, limited emotional intelligence and environmental concerns relating to excessive energy consumption, all of which need to be addressed properly to fully harness the advantages of Generative AI and make it ethical and responsible to society.

15.13 Impacts of Generative AI on Economy and Society at Large

1. Positive impacts are as follows:
    - (i) Economic growth through increased productivity by automating repetitive tasks, innovation and new business models. For example, AI-generated marketing strategies, product designs and process designs help small enterprises and startups compete with larger business units
    - (ii) Improved customer satisfaction by providing round-the-clock customer support
    - (iii) Enhanced creativity—tools like DALL-E empower artists to produce stunning creations of art, music and storytelling
    - (iv) Improved education by way of self-learning experience enhances access to information, knowledge base especially for underserved communities
    - (v) Improved healthcare—ChatGPT can be used in the healthcare industry to provide patients with immediate access to medical information and answer questions relating to their health conditions.
2. Negative impacts are as follows:
    - (i) Job Displacement—as more businesses adopt Generative AI technology, some jobs, especially in repetitive and creative roles, may become redundant.

For example, content writers and graphic designers face competition from AI-generated outputs

(ii) Ethical concerns—the ethical concerns raise questions about bias, accuracy, data privacy and security. For example, Generative AI systems trained on large datasets may inadvertently expose sensitive data or private data without proper safeguards

(iii) Misinformation and deepfakes—deepfake videos spread false narratives, undermining trust in media and institutions

(iv) Reduced analytical thinking and problem-solving skills in individuals—for example, students using Generative AI for home tasks may bypass the learning practice, which may adversely impact intellectual growth

(v) Resource Consumption—large scale Generative Pretrained Transformers (GPTs) consume huge quantities of electric power, raising carbon footprint significantly.

15.14 Strategies to Address the Various Negative Impacts of Generative AI

Strategies to address the various negative impacts of Generative AI above are as follows:

1. Ethical issues can be to a large extent eliminated by instilling transparency, adopting diverse and inclusive datasets for training and framing ethical guidelines for developers and users of Generative AI.
2. Proper regulation and governance by way of specific legislation and regulations for Generative AI usage.
3. Misinformation and proliferation of deep fakes by developing appropriate AI tools to detect and label AI-generated content. For example, Adobe is implementing content credentials to verify the origin of digital assets.
4. The job displacement problem can be properly solved through reskilling and upskilling programmes for employees in Generative AI affected areas of activities.
5. Energy efficiency and sustainability concerns can be tackled to a large extent by switching to renewable energy for training of transformers, reducing the computational needs by designing efficient models and developing regulatory frameworks to monitor and control the environmental impact of large-scale Generative AI models.
6. Over-reliance on Generative AI may diminish critical thinking and creativity of human beings. It is recommended that AI should be adopted as a supporting tool to enhance human capabilities rather than replacing them.
7. Public awareness and education levels can be raised by conducting public awareness programmes to educate users on responsible use of AI.

The key stakeholders for implementing the above-mentioned strategies are the governments, corporations, academic institutions, non-profit organisations and NGOs.

15.15 Future Role of Generative AI in Management Information Systems

1. The whole process of MIS activity flow beginning with source data collection and ending with decision implementation can be automated end-to-end by adopting Generative AI

2. Generative AI will in future optimise the decision support systems based on past performance
3. Management Information systems will adopt Generative AI tools with IoT, blockchain and AR/VR for enhancing their capabilities through interdisciplinary integration
4. Stringent guidelines on Generative AI's role in managerial decision-making will ensure accountability and transparency.

Bibliogarphy

Bandhanu, Dzmitry, Kyung Hyun Cho, and Yoshua Bengio. "Neural Machine Translation by Jointly Learning to Align and Translate." *arXiv* preprint arXiv:1409.0473v7 [cs.CL], May 2016.

Gozalo-Brizuela, R., and Eduardo C. Garrido-Merchán. "A Survey of Generative AI Applications." *arXiv* preprint arXiv:2306.02781v2 [cs.LG], 2023.

Lund, B. D., and Ting Wang. "Chatting about Chat GPT: How May AI and GPT Impact Academia and Libraries." *Library Hi Tech News* 40, no. 3 (January 2023): 26–29.

Nguyen, Eric, Michael Poli, et al. "Sequence Modelling and Design from Molecular to Genome Scale with Evo." *Science* 386, no. 6723 (November 2024).

Ning, Yilin, Salinelat Teixayavong, et al. "Generative AI and Ethical Considerations in Health Care: A Scoping Review and Ethics Checklist." *The Lancet Digital Health* 6, no. 11 (November 2024): e848–e856.

Rombach, Robin, Andreas Blattmann, Dominik Lorenz, Patrick Esser, and Björn Ommer. "High Resolution Image Synthesis with Latent Diffusion Models." *arXiv* preprint arXiv:2112.10752 [cs.CV], December 2021.

Sengar, S. S., Affan Bin Hasan, Sanjay Kumar, and Fiona Carroll. "Generative Artificial Intelligence: A Systematic Review and Applications." *arXiv* preprint arXiv:2405.11029v1 [cs.LG], May 2024.

Sohl-Dickstein, Jascha, Eric A. Weiss, Niru Maheshwaranathan, and Surya Ganguli. "Deep Unsupervised Learning Using Nonequilibrium Thermodynamics." *arXiv* preprint arXiv:1503.03585v8 [cs.LG], November 2015.

Sutskever, Ilya, Oriol Vinyals, and Quoc V. Le. "Sequence to Sequence Learning with Neural Networks." *arXiv* preprint arXiv:1409.3215v3 [cs.CL], December 2014.

Vaswani, Ashish, Noam Shazeer, Niki Parmar, et al. "Attention Is All You Need." *arXiv* preprint arXiv:1706.03762v7 [cs.CL], June 2017.

16 Information Systems for Managerial Decisions: The Future

16.1 The Future: An Overview

Many managers, particularly those in the IT industry, expect that big data analytics and cloud marketing will be the largest employer of IT professionals in the near future. Besides being large in volume or physical output, new data types such as big data, social media data, corporate data and image data all emanating out of smarter consumers, global competition and digitally connected devices, will have a larger influence on the world.

Today the world is rapidly changing both socially and technologically. According to Professor Warren G. Bennis (1968), the managerial skills needed for effectiveness in such a changing environment include a knowledge of complex systems and 'an ability to develop and use all types of information systems, including high-speed electronic computers. The job of the leader will be to collect, organize and transmit information'.

Many visionaries and leaders deem digital intelligence derived out of new types of data, analytics and computer-based ISs, a prerequisite for survival and growth in the forthcoming decades. The existence of an information-oriented management system is one of the conditions for the success of business organisations.

Notwithstanding its importance in managing the business enterprises, it is in other areas that information and communication technology may have its greatest impact in the years to come. More important perhaps is the area of social applications such as healthcare, education, transportation, welfare and urban development. Information and communication, coupled with computer technology, have made tremendous changes in educational methodology. Today, we have smart classrooms where entire lecture sessions can be recorded and also students, with the help of the internet, can attend the class sitting at home. The next decade will see the impact of computers and IT on common people.

Computer terminals and mobile phones (Android, iOS or BlackBerry) are finding their places in homes, business offices or classrooms in schools.

Current data management and processing platforms mostly do not cater to incessant data growth, elastic scalability, sustained 'Google-like' performance, new types of requirements for new data types, new analytics, heavy workload and new metadata.

Next-generation data warehouse will evolve to be a dynamic decision support and analytics platform that needs to be scalable, real-time, flexible and also will support hundreds of users whether on-site or on cloud.

Hadoop and distributed data processing in general are fast becoming an important skill set for many IT managers. Today, an effective IT manager must have knowledge of

DOI: 10.4324/9781003509714-16

relational databases, networking and data/information security, all of which were considered optional skills about 15–20 years back.

Similarly, a basic understanding of distributed data processing will become an essential part of every programmer's skill set in the near future. None of these developments will look unusual to the managers of the future. It will be natural for them to face the exponential growth of big data and the analytics thereof in dealing with customers, vendors, government agencies and other stakeholders of the company. The managers will realise that distributed file systems, digitisation of data, NoSQL databases, mobile and cloud computing will become important parts of their social and business life as time passes. Rather than being confused by the above-mentioned developments, they will welcome the changes. The future managers will understand IT and will become involved in the design of ISs affecting their jobs.

16.2 Future Trends in ISs for Managerial Decisions

It is very difficult to forecast the future of ISs for managerial decisions in totality. However, by reviewing the literature, observing the developments and by listening to the experts in the field, we find several trends are emerging that may reflect on the design and development of ISs for managers in the future years to come. We shall discuss those trends under the following headings:

1. The changing nature of managerial decision-making process
2. Real-time systems
3. Big data and analytics
4. The internet and web technology
5. IoT
6. Cloud computing
7. Social media
8. Mobile technology and wearables
9. Data security and privacy aspects
10. Impact of ISs on management echelon.

16.3 The Changing Nature of Managerial Decision-making Process

Managerial decision-making process has undergone significant changes over the last two decades. Today, decisions are taken not only based on intuition and judgement but also on evidence generated by data and business analytics. Decision-making in future, particularly at the strategic and tactical levels, will become more streamlined due to a consistent structure for addressing ill-structured or unstructured problems based on facts and not on intuition. Rapid evolution in information and communication technology helped the managers in making decisions more on the 'Prescriptive model' rather than on the 'Descriptive model' in the terminology of Herbert A. Simon (1955). Decisions are taken with more rationality, unlike in the past.

Development of the internet and other communication devices has given rise to continuous globalisation. Table 16.1 shows the growth of internet users during the period from 2005 to 2023.

Globalisation of business operations led to managerial decisions more as an outcome of computational thinking—a perfect blend of critical thinking and IT. Beginning with

Table 16.1 Global Growth of Internet Users, 2005–2023

Worldwide Internet Users (In % of Population)				
Region/Worldwide	*2005*	*2010*	*2017*	*2023*
Africa	2	10	21.8	37
Americas	36	49	65.9	87
Arab States	8	26	43.7	69
Asia and the Pacific	9	23	43.9	66
Commonwealth of Independent States	10	34	67.7	89
Europe	46	67	79.6	91
Developing World	8	21	41.3	60
Developed World	51	67	81	93
Worldwide	16	30	48	67
Worldwide Population (Billion)	6.5	6.9	7.4	8.0
Worldwide Internet Users (Billion)				5.3

Sources: 1. International Telecommunication Union Stats. 2. Internet World Stats. 3. The US Census Bureau Stats.

the traditional electronic data processing of clerical applications, there had been an evolution of ISs and ITs. Today, business managers in the globalisation perspective are applying technology to understand and predict human behaviour.

Big data and predictive analytics will guide managerial decision-making by predicting, forecasting and optimising through statistical analysis using 'SPSS or R'.

Globalisation further enables the sharing of data by managers, which leads to collaborative decision-making and the development of GDSSs.

Many of the operational controls and some of the management controls, which earlier used to be taken by managers, have now been automated through sensor-driven decision analysis.

The IoT also can support long range and more complex human planning systems that generate a variety of graphical displays for analysing data. Further, automated variance analysis to reveal root causes, 'what-if' analysis and sensitivity analysis led to improved strategic and tactical decisions. Big data analytics and the associated technologies will enable managers to move more towards the upper levels of knowledge and wisdom of the Haeckel's (1993) information hierarchy as shown in Figure 16.1.

The above-mentioned movements in turn facilitate conversion of tacit knowledge (subjective) gained from experience and practice into explicit knowledge based on more theory and rationality as a continuous process. In future, when decision-makers address problems, particularly unstructured and ill-structured ones, they will more often convert knowledge from one form to the other. The future decision-makers will enhance their base of explicit knowledge in extent and function through the above-mentioned conversion process. However, the internet will play a key role in the sharing of tacit knowledge. The outcome will obviously be streamlined strategic and tactical planning, increased business insight, improved and faster strategic decision-making.

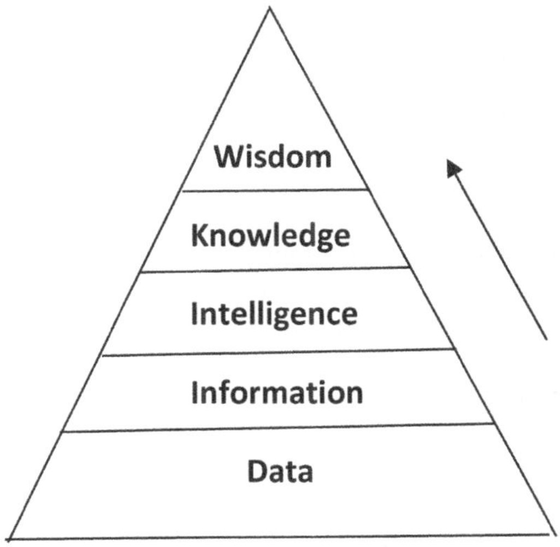

Figure 16.1 Haeckel's Information Hierarchy

16.4 Growth of Real-Time ISs

Real-time information processing, which had its beginning with passenger seat reservation at airline ticket counters or railway berth reservation in trains and even with the inter-state bus seat booking counters, has grown over the years in various operational control and even management control areas to facilitate monitoring and control because of its speed of response. Today, real-time systems are operational in job progress control in manufacturing, inventory ordering, cash flow analysis and forecasting. Because of its speed of response, real-time systems find great use in the aviation sector for flight control, traffic control on highways and even in automation of process control in manufacturing, such as chemical plants.

Compared with batch processing, the real-time applications, though fewer in number, are highly advocated because of their exciting nature and great potential for the future.

Real-time systems have three distinctive features: (1) data are maintained online, (2) data are updated as and when events occur unlike batch processing in which case all master data are updated at periodic intervals and (3) the computer database can be interrogated from remote terminals or other devices by multiple users. Some managers often raise a doubt as to whether they really need the above-mentioned capabilities of real-time systems in more than a small fraction of their daily information needs. However, the fact remains that many current real-time applications are little more than online versions of previous systems and are primarily single application-oriented with little integration between the various functional subsystems. The development in real-time processing coupled with the design of common database systems will provide real-time IS where all information required to run a company will be within the reach of the management of the company. Such an IS will be of immense help for intense monitoring and control on a real-time basis as in the case of a project command and control centre known as a 'dashboard'.

Model building will become easier as system designers and managers familiarise themselves with real-time systems for problem solving. The remote terminals, the integrated data bank, the real-time processing and the library of retrievable programs and mathematical models will provide a business experimentation laboratory in which managers can test the results of their decisions before implementing them.

16.5 Big Data and Analytics

Since the dawn of time up to 2003, mankind has created 2 exabytes of data, but today at least that much data is created each and every day! New technologies are changing the way we design and build data warehouses.

The new technologies are evolving to effectively link unstructured and semi-structured data with traditional relational data to support our information requirements to meet the business needs and organisational goals. We have already become aware of 'big data'—its sources, characteristics, storage, processing and analysis of the same. We have also become familiar with Hadoop and its ecosystems. The storage of big data emanating from the business environment, corporate world, social media and sensors in the form of structured as well as unstructured or ill-structured data, scientific data, streaming data and the analysis of such huge data are subjects of continuous research. Furthermore, many new ecosystems of information storage and retrieval for managerial decision-making will emerge in the future. Because of advancements in big data analytics using statistical techniques, decision-making at the strategic level will become more rational and streamlined, and uncertainties in the decision-making process will be considerably reduced, if not totally eliminated.

Future ISs for managerial decision will be addressing more and more ill-structured or unstructured data and will have more flexibility, scalability, speed and predictability to evolve a dynamic decision support and analytics platform. Big data and predictive analytics will make prediction models based on patterns of behaviour of performance variables, and the patterns will become institutional knowledge for managers. The future trend of ISs will be integrated DSSs providing BI. Figure 16.2 shows the paradigm shift with big data from the traditional structured data.

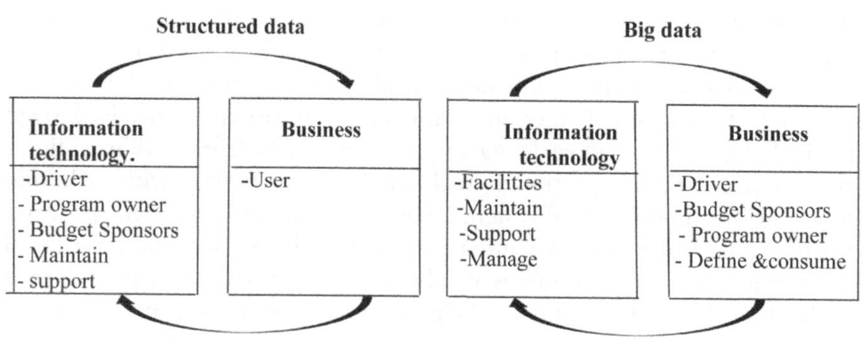

Figure 16.2 Paradigm Shift with Big Data from the Traditional Structured Data
Source: Krishnan (2015).

16.6 Internet and Web Technology

As stated earlier in this chapter, the internet accelerated globalisation through the sharing of knowledge and information across the world. Rapid development of the internet made information and knowledge available online to grow exponentially. This had a profound effect on organisation structure and its functioning. As information is available to the managers who need it and when they need it, lines of control and influence become distinct and departments often self-organise in new and more effective ways. The result is not only the flattening of organisation structure but also the changing of skill set of employees.

The internet has made it possible to establish direct contact between buyers and sellers, thus eliminating the middle layer in distribution channels besides significantly reducing inventory costs. Since the advent of the internet, retail marketing has been largely transformed. CRM by companies using the internet has become dynamic with the changing nature of customer needs.

The internet's capabilities to empower consumers, to facilitate dynamic information exchange among organisations and to flatten organisation echelons, promise to result in new operational strategies, business models, service delivery models and above all improved organisational decision-making.

Business applications are now web-based to increase flexibility with accessing systems and upgrades. Today organisations have adopted web 2.0 applications such as Facebook, Google Plus, email, blogs, Wiki and many others to interact online with clients and customers. Web technology switches from a keyword-based search to semantic technologies in which search is conducted by context analysis and word meanings. The semantic web is not only more accurate in search but also extracts information from multiple sources and their comparison permits a variety of services such as e-commerce and e-health services. It is important to mention that e-commerce encompasses business processes to include the entire value chain comprising purchasing, marketing, sales, customer service and business relationships.

16.7 Internet of Things

The 'IoT' as we have seen in Chapter 13, refers to the idea of physical objects being connected to the internet. Developments in the field of wireless technologies and sensors allow physical objects to transmit and also receive data about themselves. Many applications involving IoT are already available today.

McKinsey & Company in a report in 2010 broadly identified six such application areas of IoT. Those are as follows:

1. **Tracking Behaviour**: When products are embedded with sensors, companies can track the movements of the products and also monitor their interactions. Business models can be developed to make use of such behavioural data. For example, some insurance companies install location sensors in their customers' cars to enable the companies to formulate the base price of policies on how a car is driven as well as the running pattern of the car.
2. **Enhanced Sensor-Driven Decision Analysis**: As already stated in an earlier paragraph of this chapter, sensor-driven DSS can support long range and more complex

human planning systems that generate a variety of graphical displays for data analysis.

3. **Enhanced Security and Surveillance**: Data from a large number of sensors deployed at sensitive locations, including the entrance and exit of buildings and roads and analysis of the same data serve to detect security lapses, including unauthorised persons entering restricted areas. Similarly, reports on environmental conditions, including soil moisture, ocean currents and weather, can make decision-makers aware of early warnings for disaster management.
4. **Process Optimisation**: Process industries, such as chemical plants, are controlling the process parameters with the aid of legions of sensors installed along the process flow line. These sensors feed data to computers, which in turn analyse the data and then send signals to actuators that adjust processes by modifying ingredient mixtures, temperature or pressure.
5. **Optimum Resource Consumption**: Sensors connected to automated feedback mechanisms can change usage patterns for scarce resources such as water, energy and fuel. This can also be accomplished by controlling the price of these scarce resources to regulate demand.
6. **Complex Autonomous Systems**: A very important application of the IoT involves the sensing of unpredictable conditions and instantaneous responses on a real-time basis guided by autonomous systems. This type of real-time decision-making resembles human reactions, but at a very high level of performance. For example, the automobile industry is adopting systems that can detect imminent adverse conditions and take remedial measures.

16.8 Cloud Computing

Cloud computing has become a new model for fulfilling corporate IT needs. Flexible and elastic cloud services deliver resources as required, such as infrastructure, platform and software to corporates similar to other utilities such as water, fuel or electricity. This has resulted in cost-saving by organisations as they do not need to create permanent or fixed IT resources. IT departments often face serious problems due to outdated infrastructures, underutilised capacity and rigid architecture, particularly with changing technological, economic and other environmental conditions. As businesses nowadays have to survive harsh economic fluctuations, ISs of the future have to be agile to save on budget and to face unexpected sudden changes such as enhanced competition and changing customer preferences. Cloud computing and similar latest technologies promise to turn the IT department that had always been viewed as a cost centre into a source of saving money and instilling flexibility and agility to the IS. Flexibility is the adaptability to changing markets. Agile methods were used in software development for complex systems that require frequent changes, quick responses and short release times. Research has witnessed that IS agility is one of the most vital factors in sustaining strategic alignment of a company. An agile enterprise builds an agile IS.

However, in order to leverage the full benefit—both present and potential—as promised by cloud services (software as a service [SaaS], platform as a service [PaaS] and infrastructure as a service [IaaS]), numerous challenges such as specific requirements of existing and legacy applications are to be addressed. The agility, which can be driven into IS of any particular organisation, has to be judged within the context of the same organisation. Imache, Izza and Nacer in 2012 proposed a five-element framework known as process, organisation, information, resource and environment (POIRE) to assess an enterprise IS agility. Sawas and Watfa in 2015 conducted an extensive study and research on the impact of cloud computing services on IS agility, and their finding is that there is an association between using IaaS as a cloud service model and improving the technical infrastructure agility or the IT process agility of the IS. However, there is no evident association between IaaS and other agility categories. They further found that there is an association between using PaaS as a cloud service model and improving the human characteristics or the business aspects of the IS. No other association was found by them between PaaS and other agility categories.

There exists no association between SaaS and any agility category. This finding was quite interesting as it appears that SaaS would normally imply less IT staff and lower running costs of IT, which in turn normally would mean more business agility.

16.9 Social Media

Social media, an evolving phenomenon, has got the highest impact on continuous communication of an organisation with the customers and the public at large. They consist of social networks such as Facebook, Twitter, Instagram, YouTube, Flickr, corporate blogs, multimedia sites, company-sponsored websites and collaborative websites. Facebook helps us to share ideas with people in our lives. WhatsApp is a simple, secure and reliable messaging and calling medium. Twitter shows happenings. Instagram allows users to sign up and see photos and videos from friends. Social media today play an ever-increasing marketing platform for a company's products and services. They are also recognised as a powerful medium in the business environment and have grown from a local niche phenomenon to mass adoption.

Social media form a vital source of information for managerial decisions. Du and Jiang (2015) observed that the performance of firms improves due to the use of Facebook and Twitter. The present trend of growth of social media indicates that the future opportunities that may be forthcoming will be for the creation of new technologies for the integration of existing social media into accounting ISs as well as analytical systems for BI.

Perdana et al. (2015) considered social media from the perspective of a vehicle for community learning, information dissemination and for the institutionalisation of knowledge. There are many areas in which accounting plays an important role and where social media are particularly influential, such as behavioural finance. Moreover, exploration of social media trends would appear to provide powerful insights into organisations that auditors could leverage for engagement planning and risk management.

16.10 Mobile Technology and Wearables

Mobile technology is perhaps the most significant digital innovation in the last decade, starting with the simple cell phones in the 1990s, the development of smartphones and finally the tablets of today. The fantastic growth of mobile technology can be witnessed from the following facts:

- In 2011, smartphone sales exceeded the sales of personal computers in monetary terms.
- The number of smartphone subscribers grew by 31% in 2013.
- In May 2013, mobile accounted for 15% of all internet traffic.

- Facebook reported that 68% of its active users used their mobile platforms to access the social network.
- Tablet sales now outpace sales of notebook PCs and desktop PCs.

16.11 Wearables

On average, a smartphone user looks at his/her smartphone 150 times a day for functions such as messaging, phone calls, social media and listening to music. In order to facilitate the above functions, the technology can be worn on or physically integrated into human bodies and the same is known as 'Wearables'. Wearables such as hearing aids and Bluetooth earpieces are some of the examples of wearable technology. Now we have seen many new innovative wearable technologies such as the 'Google Glass', which one wears over the eyes such as a pair of eyeglasses. 'Google Glass' can project images into one's field of vision based on context and voice commands. Wearables are also very common in the case of healthcare such as Jawbone, which monitors sleep.

As technology continues to evolve in the future, there will be many more mobile computational devices and wearables which will generate a variety of graphical displays for analysing data. Moreover, with more and more use of smartphones and wearables, storage and analysis of data will be within the reach of many persons, and they will be sharing the data and analysis thereof with each other for mutual benefit and group decision support. Some of this data sharing can be done passively, such as disclosing one's location in order to update traffic statistics on a real-time basis. However, data can also be reported actively, such as uploading customer ratings of a restaurant to review sites. Mobile and wearable technologies will have a significant effect on healthcare and traffic ISs.

Further, traditional marketing ISs based on market research will be significantly changed by way of compilation of customer ratings for products and services such as restaurants and shopping malls and then allowing consumers back to search through the ratings via their website or mobile phone app, which is giving rise to the digital marketing concept of today.

16.12 Data Security and Privacy

In case of all computer systems that maintain and process valuable information or provide services to multiple users concurrently, it is necessary to provide security against unauthorised access, use or modification of any data file. Computer systems must also be protected against disruption of operations and physical damage. The exponential growth of big data and the increasing number of computer applications involving valuable information resulted in a huge amount of data transmission through networks and shared computing, including cloud services. This increased data transmission and shared computing underscore the need for finding effective solutions to computer security problems. In future, data privacy and data security will have to become an integral part in planning and designing computer systems, applications and business models adopting new technologies and services.

Data privacy is an issue that concerns the computer community, maintaining personal information of individuals in computerised record-keeping systems. Privacy deals with the right of individuals regarding the collection of information in a record-keeping system about their personal data and the processing, dissemination, storage and use of such data in making determinations about them.

Turn and Ware (1976) mentioned about five basic principles relating to personal information recordkeeping systems in both the private sector and government, which are as follows:

1. There must be no personal data record-keeping system whose very existence is secret.
2. There must be a way for an individual to find out what information about him/her is on record and how it is used.
3. There must be a way for an individual to correct or amend a record of identifiable information about him/her.
4. There must be a way for an individual to prevent his/her personal information that was obtained for one purpose from being used for other purposes without his/her consent.
5. Any organisation creating, maintaining, using or disseminating records of identifiable personal data must guarantee the reliability of the data for their intended use and must take precautions to prevent misuse of the data.

Maintaining privacy is challenging today with the World Wide Web. Even diligently removing cookies, super cookies and browsing history cannot guarantee that they are entirely invisible. Further, long-term durability of data is a growing concern since the current memory technologies have a data lifetime expectancy of a few decades only. The nanotechnology being researched to solve this problem is simply amazing and promising durability of a billion years and a density of one trillion bits per square inch.

Data security includes the procedural and technical measures required:

1. To prevent unauthorised access, modification, use and dissemination of data stored or processed in a computer system;
2. To prevent any deliberate refusal of data service;
3. To protect the data and computer system from physical harm.

Security safeguards include physical safeguards such as locks, fire and water protection, computer hardware safeguards such as memory protection, software safeguards such as file access control schemes, security permissions such as read, write, execute, communication safeguards to ensure the secrecy of information in transit over communication channels and personnel safeguards such as background checks and biometric checks. Security safeguards also include all aspects of administrative and management controls such as inspections, tests and security audits. A variety of equipment and techniques exist for providing physical security such as fire controllers and digital locks for controlling physical access. Currently, techniques for the protection of programs and data within the computer system include positive identification of all users and authentication, isolation of users and their processes from each other and system supervisory programs, concealment of information on removable storage media and in communication channels by encryption techniques. Commonly used identification techniques include a username, personal number or account number. Authentication techniques commonly used include passwords, combinations of locks or some facts about a person's background.

Cryptographic techniques can be used in communication links between computers and terminals to protect information against interception by wiretapping or capture and modification at illicit terminals or computers secretly inserted in the system. Popular algorithms such as RSA and PuTTY generate unique keys (public and private) to encrypt and decrypt data and information. Integrity and auditing of security safeguards must be a continuous process of monitoring to be effective.

Pitkanen et al. (2011) mentioned about future information security trends. Some of their observations in this regard can be stated as follows:

1. Information security issues become more international.
2. The interdependency between societal processes and ISs increases rapidly.
3. Increasing data gathering and data combination from different sources do occur.
4. The correctness of information becomes increasingly important.
5. Automation/autonomous systems are increasingly employed to effect security.
6. Traceability of persons and goods increases.
7. Malicious action against ISs increases.
8. Commercial interests drive actors to restrict access to proprietary information resources.
9. Governance of access to information resources in organisations becomes more difficult.

Some of the future trends in security techniques are worth mentioning. For example, cloud context will provide a wealth of challenges, such as autonomous checking of cloud security configurations, setting up of security systems known as 'honey pots' to lure intruders and to collect incriminating evidence about them for seeing or overseeing insecure end devices with more sophistication.

The development of new software will also lead to new tools and techniques to cope with information security requirements in a better way.

Future demand for traceability for counterfeit prevention and surveillance of life-saving drugs manufacture will open up possibilities of economic security solutions. Hardware-assisted security of end-user platforms as well as the software run on such platforms will improve because of increasing industry investment in these areas. For example, Trusted Platform Modules (TPM), processor memory area protection and many other such security functions are likely to come up in future.

Lately, attacks targeting service disruptions, technically known as distributed denial-of-service (DDoS), have gained attention after cyberattacks on Estonia and other places. In future, networks will evolve to provide some automatic response to such cyberattacks, but this needs an overhaul of the underlying networks.

Internet and cloud computing technologies will share common ground with the evolution of information networks in the future. Both are more likely to prefer true names over IP addresses while discussing with each other. The result will be more complicated networks and a more simplified client side, and thereby the security issues will be shifting more towards the network. From the end user's point of view, there will be no border or gateway within clouds to oversee traffic or to see it at all. This implies that user visibility will be limited to the application level, with more emphasis on application-level security tools for data loss prevention, identity management, IDS and intrusion prevention system (IPS).

From the cloud service providers' viewpoint, they will need to deploy tools to deter attacks, to detect suspicious user activity and to collect forensic data. Public law enforcement agencies are in the process of engaging 'net traffic police' to ensure fast network traffic response.

16.13 Impact of ISs on Management Echelon

Traditional approaches to decision support and analysis require several management layers, usually the three tiers, namely strategic planning at the top of the hierarchy, management control in the middle and operational control at the bottom. However, with the advances in IT and innovative DSS, many of the decisions taken by managers at the operational control and the management control levels have been automated. Further, the role of the management control level, which was earlier translating the strategy formulated by the strategic planning level of managers into operating plans for the operational control level of managers, has diminished with the advent of communication technology such as the internet and knowledge-based systems, giving rise to computational thinking. It is likely that in future the management control level will split up into two parts, one part consisting of managers who are experts in systems approach, big data analytics and the like, will merge with the strategic planning level to create knowledge and wisdom for strategic and tactical decision-making. The other part will join with the operational control level to monitor and control the operations and implement the decisions of the higher echelon of managers.

The future management echelon will consist of two levels only, the top and the bottom levels. The top level will consist of managers who will be concerned with organisational goals and will be understanding the need to bring the diverse elements of the organisation together in a system. The bottom level will be having managers who will be in the implementing role for the decisions of the top level, and they will also look after the operations and maintenance of the advanced technology of hardware, software and communication devices. Figure 16.3 shows the future trend of management echelon with the advancement of IT.

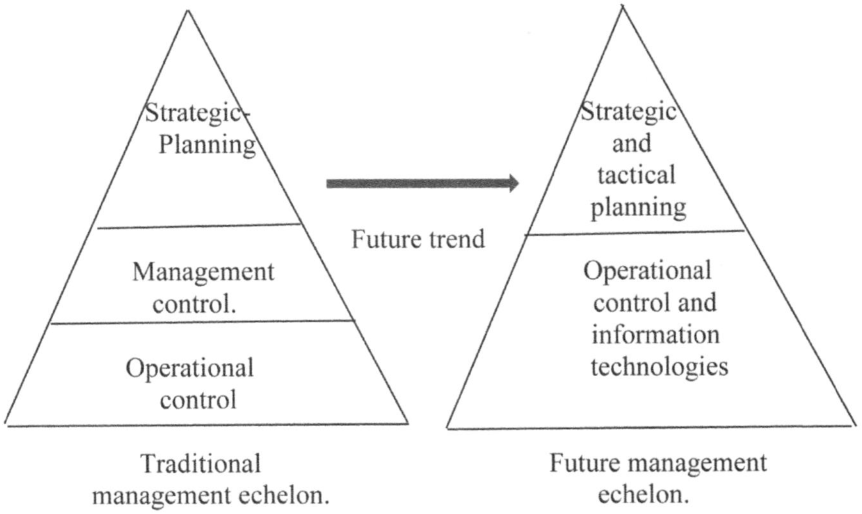

Figure 16.3 Future Management Echelon

Bibliography

Bennis, Warren G. 'New Patterns of Leadership for Tomorrow's Organizations'. *Technology Review,* April 1968, p. 37.

Chui, Michael, Loffler, Markus, and Roberts, Roger. 'The Internet of Things'. *McKinsey Quarterly*, March 2010.

Du, H., and W. Jiang. 'Do Social Media Matter? Initial Empirical Evidence'. *Journal of Information Systems* 29, no. 2 (Summer 2015): 1–4.

Haeckel, S. H., and R. L. Nolan. 'The Role of Technology in an Information Age: Transforming Symbols into Action'. In *The Knowledge Economy: The Nature of Information in the 21st Century*, 1–24. Queenstown, MD: The Aspen Institute, 1993.

Imache, Rabba, Izza, Said, and Nacer, Mohammad Ahmed. 'An Enterprise Information System Agility Assessment Model'. *Computer Science and Information Systems* 9, no. 1 (January 2012): 107–133.

Krishnan, Krish. 'Big Data: Architecting for Business Intelligence and Data Warehousing in Your Organization'. Data Management Forum Seminar on the Big Data, Hotel Pennsylvania, New York City, September 2015.

Perdana, A., A. Robb, and F. Rhode. 'XBRL Diffusion in Social Media: Discourses and Community Learning'. *Journal of Information Systems* 29, no. 2 (2015): 71–106.

Pitkanen, Olli, Risto Sarvas, A. Lehmuskallio, et al. 'Future Information Security Trends'. In *Research Publication*. Helsinki: Aalto University, 2011.

Sawas, M. S., and M. K. Watfa. 'The Impact of Cloud Computing on Information Systems Agility'. *Australasian Journal of Information Systems* 19 (2015): 97–112.

Simon, H. A. 'A Behavioural Model of Rational Choice'. *The Quarterly Journal of Oxford University Press* 69, no. 1 (February 1955): 99–118.

Turn, R., and W. H. Ware. 'Privacy and Security issues in Information Systems'. *IEEE Transactions on Computers* C-25 (1976): 1353–1361.

Index

Note: Page numbers in **bold** indicate tables, and page numbers in *italics* indicate figures.

For Product Safety Concerns and Information please contact our EU representative GPSR@taylorandfrancis.com Taylor & Francis Verlag GmbH, Kaufingerstraße 24, 80331 München, Germany